Linux Apache Web Server Administration

Second Edition

Charles Aulds

SYBEX

San Francisco   London

Associate Publisher: Neil Edde
Acquisitions and Developmental Editor: Maureen Adams
Editor: Donna Crossman
Production Editor: Dennis Fitzgerald
Technical Editor: Sean Schluntz
Book Designer: Bill Gibson
Graphic Illustrator: Eric Houts, epic
Electronic Publishing Specialist: Jeff Wilson, Happenstance Type-O-Rama
Proofreaders: Emily Hsuan, Dave Nash, Lori Newman, Laurie O'Connell, Nancy Riddiough
Indexer: Nancy Guenther
Cover Designer: Ingalls & Associates
Cover Illustrator/Photographer: Ingalls & Associates

Library of Congress Card Number: 2002108074

ISBN: 0-7821-4137-4

Foreword

Linux and open-source software are synonymous in the minds of most people. Many corporations fear Linux and reject it for mission-critical applications because it is open source. They mistakenly believe that it will be less secure or less reliable because the code is openly available and the system has been developed by a diverse collection of groups and individuals from around the world. Yet those same organizations depend on open-source systems every day, often without being aware of it.

The Internet is a system built on open-source software. From the very beginning, when the U.S. government placed the source code of the Internet Protocol in the public domain, open-source software has led the way in the development of the Internet. To this day, the Internet and the applications that run on it depend on open-source software.

One of the greatest success stories of the Internet is the World Wide Web—the Internet's killer application. The leading Web server software is Apache, an open-source product. No library of Linux system administration books could be complete without a book on Apache configuration and administration, and Charles Aulds has written a great one! I have learned more about Apache by reviewing *Linux Apache Web Server Administration* than I ever knew.

But don't take my word for it; others have also been impressed by the quality and completeness of this book. Jeff Durham, in his May 2002 article "Apache Roundup" for UnixReview, compared the five top-selling Apache books and picked the first edition of *Linux Apache Web Server Administration* as the best of the bunch. The second edition of *Linux Apache Web Server Administration* is even better, with expanded coverage and new material on Apache 2.0.

Linux and Apache are a natural combination—two reliable, powerful, open-source products that combine to create a great Web server! This book gives you all of the information you need to build that server.

Craig Hunt
July 2002

Acknowledgments

If I ever believed that a technical book was the work of a single author, I no longer hold that belief. In this short section, I would like to personally acknowledge a few of the many people who participated in writing this book. A lot of credit goes to the Sybex production and editing team, most of whom I didn't work with directly and will never know.

Craig Hunt, editor of this series, read all of the material and helped organize the book, giving it a continuity and structure that brings together all of the many pieces of the Apache puzzle. Before I met Craig, however, I knew Maureen Adams, the acquisitions editor who recommended me for this book. Her confidence in my ability to accomplish this gave me the resolve to go further than simply saying, "I believe that some day I might write a book." Associate Publisher Neil Edde's can-do attitude and problem-solving skills also helped the project over a few bumps in the road.

Also part of the Sybex team, Production Editor Dennis Fitzgerald kept the project on schedule. Many times, prioritizing a long list of things that needed to be done is the first step toward their accomplishment. I also thank Donna Crossman for her valuable editing contributions. Sean J. Schluntz was the technical editor for the second edition book, and his conscientious testing and obvious knowledge of the material filled in more than a few gaps in my own store of knowledge. Electronic Publishing Specialist Jeff Wilson handled the typesetting and layout promptly and skillfully, as usual.

I greatly appreciate the time my keen engineering friend, Carl Sewell, spent reviewing all of the material I wrote for both editions. I would also like to thank another colleague for the knowledge he shared: Robert Schaap, whose comments on the use of the mod_rewrite module proved quite valuable.

Last, but certainly most of all, I want to thank my dear wife, Andrea, for her unwavering support during the writing of both editions of this book. My biggest challenge was finding the time to do it, and much of that time was her gift to me, for which I'm deeply grateful. Without her support, it would have been quite impossible for me to complete this project. In addition to doing a multitude of farm chores, many of which had been my responsibility, she homeschools our daughter, Brittany.

Contents at a Glance

Contents

Introduction

The first Internet Web servers were experimental implementations of the concepts, protocols, and standards that underlie the World Wide Web. Originally a performance-oriented alternative to these early Web servers, Apache has been under active development by a large cadre of programmers around the world. Apache is the most widely used Web server for commercial Web sites and it is considered by many Webmasters to be superior to commercial Web server software.

Like Linux, Apache owes much of its incredible success to the fact that it has always been distributed as open-source software. Apache is freely available under a nonrestrictive license (which I'll discuss in Chapter 1) and distributed in the form of source code, which can be examined or modified. There's nothing up the developers' sleeves. While the sharing of intellectual property has always appealed to those who program computers primarily for the sheer love of it, until quite recently the motivations of the open-source community were lost on the business world, which understood only the bottom line on the balance sheet.

Today, however, the situation is much different from what it was when Apache and Linux were first introduced, and many companies now see open source in terms of cost savings or as a way of leveraging technology without having to develop it from scratch. The open-source software model seems to be with us to stay, and many companies have been structured to profit from it, by offering solutions and services based on computer programs they didn't create. While recent security and performance enhancements to its commercial rivals have left Apache's technical superiority in question, there is no doubt that Apache is a robust product in the same class as commercial Web engines costing far more. Apache is free, which enables anyone willing to make a moderate investment in inexpensive computing equipment to host Web services with all the features of a world-class site.

This second edition brings the book up-to-date with the current state of Apache, version 2.0. This new version of Apache is the first major rewrite of the Apache code base since Apache 1.3.0 was released in June 1998, and it introduces many long-awaited features. These features are discussed in Chapter 2 of this book, but the main promise of Apache 2.0 is an open-code base with an easy-to-use programmer's interface (API) that will allow talented, creative programmers to leverage the strengths of Apache and the support community that has grown up around it. No proprietary Web server can make the same claim.

Apache 2.0 was used for the testing and research that went into this book, and the few places where Apache 2.0 versions were unavailable for testing are clearly indicated.

Prerelease copies of several modules obtained from the authors were used in some of the testing, but every effort was made to ensure that the information provided was consistent with the final release versions.

While Apache on Linux/Unix servers is the predominant Web server platform on the Internet today, most Web client computers are PCs running one of the Microsoft Windows operating systems, though the use of Linux as a workstation operating system is on the rise. Microsoft's own Internet Explorer Web browser is, by far, the most widely used, and it is unlikely that there is any reader of this book who is not familiar with Microsoft IE. For this reason, many of the screenshots in this book were made with the Internet Explorer browser, though you will also find screenshots from Netscape, Opera, Mozilla, and Konqueror, all excellent alternatives to IE and all of which are available for Linux.

Who Should Read This Book?

This book is intended for the owner or administrator of one or more Linux workstations or servers who is interested in using the open-source Apache Web server software. A familiarity with Linux is assumed, and the book is ideal for the Linux administrator who needs to learn about Apache. The typical reader has access to a Linux system (and may have personally installed Linux on that system) and is anxious to know how to make use of the Apache software that came with the Linux distribution. This book will provide a valuable companion reference for anyone administering a Web server for a small to medium-sized company. While the book is not a professional programmer's reference, it provides an introduction to all aspects of programming for the Web, with useful examples of Web-based programs and server-side Web page parsing.

Linux is an excellent platform upon which to run a Web server. A review of Web server engines by *Network Computing* magazine made the point that, while some commercial applications now (surprisingly) exhibit performance superior to that of Apache, the underlying operating system plays a critical role in determining the overall reliability, security, and availability of a Web server. This is particularly true in e-commerce applications. Apache was given high marks when coupled with the robustness provided by the Linux operating system. While Apache is now available for non-Unix/Linux platforms, the real value of Apache is realized on Unix-like operating systems. To an increasing number of businesses today that means using Linux, with its unparalleled ability to compete on a price/performance basis.

Whenever Linux is used to provide commercial-quality Web services, Apache is the first and best choice of Web server software. The intended reader of this book is someone who is using both Apache and Linux for the same reasons: quality, reliability, features, and price.

How This Book Is Organized

The chapters of this book are grouped into four parts: How Things Work, Essential Configuration, Advanced Configuration Options, and Maintaining a Healthy Server.

You can read this book either as a whole, from beginning to end, or by using the index and table of contents to find the topics you currently need to learn about. We start with foundation material that explains the basics of the World Wide Web and the architecture of Apache. The book then describes installation and basic configuration of the Apache software. The next group of chapters describes the advanced features used to create a dynamic, interactive server. The book concludes with a section that describes the day-to-day tasks of a Web administrator. A reader who understands the fundamentals of the Web and the Apache architecture can jump to the Essential Configuration section. An experienced administrator who understands all of the basics of Apache configuration can jump to the Advanced Configuration Options part of the book. However, most Web administrators will benefit from reading the entire text.

Many of the topics involved in Apache administration are closely related to each other; for example, you can't adequately discuss request redirection without assuming some familiarity with virtual hosting. Throughout the book, I've used cross-references to help you trace these relationships without wading through too much repetition.

Part 1: How Things Work

Part 1 provides the introductory information the reader will need to understand what the Apache Web server does, how it is designed, and how it compares to alternative software that performs the same tasks.

Chapter 1: An Overview of the World Wide Web

Chapter 1 provides a brief history of the World Wide Web, how it came to exist, and why. The chapter describes how the Web works, with a discussion of the network mechanisms and protocols used (IP, HTTP, HTML, etc).

Chapter 2: Apache and Other Web Servers

Chapter 2 provides an overview of the features and architecture of an Apache server, explaining the process swarm and other fundamentals of the Apache design. This chapter also surveys the various Web servers that compete with Apache, both free and commercial. As you'll see, Apache compares quite favorably to most of them.

Part 2: Essential Configuration

Part 2 details the compilation, installation, and configuration of a working Apache server. The chapters here cover the basics to get your server up and running.

Chapter 3: Installing Apache

To install Apache, you can either download and compile it yourself or use a precompiled binary distribution. This chapter first helps you decide between these options and then demonstrates each method, step by step.

Chapter 4: A Basic Apache Server

Directives are the administrator's primary tools for configuring Apache and controlling its operation. Chapter 4 discusses the basic concepts underlying the use of directives, including the essential topic of directive scope, and then summarizes the most important directives.

Chapter 5: Apache Modules

All of Apache's directives are grouped into modules. Chapter 5 discusses the Apache core module and the most important add-on modules.

Chapter 6: Virtual Hosting

Chapter 6 describes how to use virtual hosting to make your server function as if it were actually several different servers. Virtual hosting is used extensively by Web hosting services and ISPs to give clients their own (virtual) Web server, often hosting a number of these virtual sites on a single Web server.

Part 3: Advanced Configuration Options

The chapters in Part 3 discuss configuration options that are eventually required by a professional Webmaster. These options extend beyond the requirements of a basic Web server that provides only static documents.

Chapter 7: Server-Side Includes

Server-Side Includes (SSI), also known as server-parsed HTML, offers the simplest way to add dynamic content to a Web page. This technique embeds commands to the server directly in HTML content. Chapter 7 shows how to configure Apache to work with SSI and presents the most important SSI commands, known as *tags*.

Chapter 8: Scripting/Programming for Apache

Today, interactivity is a requirement for any commercial Web site. The ability to script or program a Web server greatly extends its value. This chapter covers the most widely used Web-programming methods, with an emphasis on preparing Apache to support these. Programming examples are provided to show the basics of user input (Web form), database query (using a MySQL database), and returning data to the user.

Chapter 9: Aliasing and Redirection

Nearly every Apache administrator needs to know how to implement the *aliasing* and *redirection* of client requests for resources that may not always be located where the server expects to find them. Chapter 9 first describes the capabilities provided by the standard mod_alias module and then provides a path through the complexities of the powerful third-party URL rewriting tool mod_rewrite.

Chapter 10: Controlling Apache

Chapter 10 is a quick look at starting and stopping the server both manually and programmatically, along with Apache's built-in monitoring tools and some third-party GUI configuration tools.

Part 4: Maintaining a Healthy Server

Part 4 is an administrator's handbook that covers the day-to-day activities of managing an Apache server, updating the information that is available from it, and ensuring that the server and the information that reside on it are secure.

Chapter 11: Apache Logging

The Apache logfiles provide the information you need to understand who is using your server and how they are using it. This chapter discusses the basics of logging, including the standard log formats. It describes how logs can be customized using the mod_log_config Apache module. This chapter discusses techniques for interpreting the Apache logs, finding information in them, and rotating logs, and it also discusses the programs available for summarizing logs.

Chapter 12: Proxying and Performance Tuning

Once you have a working Apache Web server, you will want to tune the server to optimize its performance—minimizing the delay experienced by users in retrieving resources from your server and maximizing the number of requests you can respond to in a given time. Apache is already highly optimized and offers the administrator only a few performance directives. Chapter 12 discusses these directives and then examines one of the most important tools you can use to minimize document retrieval times on a local area network, Web caching using Apache as a proxy server.

Chapter 13: Basic Security for Your Web Server

Security is an essential topic for administrators of both Internet-connected and intranet servers. Web servers are particularly attractive targets for purveyors of mayhem on the Internet and crackers who want to compromise system security and steal information such as credit card numbers. The first of two chapters on security, Chapter 13 shows how to implement basic access control through authorization and authentication.

Chapter 14: Secure Sockets Layer

For sites that need to go beyond the basic security techniques discussed in Chapter 13, this chapter shows how to implement Netscape's Secure Sockets Layer technology and explains how it works.

Chapter 15: Metainformation and Content Negotiation

In order to do its job and deliver the optimum content acceptable to each client, Apache needs to know as much as possible about each resource that it serves. Metainformation not only tells the server how to process the data, it also instructs the client browser how to handle the data, determining which application to pass the data to if the browser is incapable of dealing with it directly. Chapter 15 shows how to work with metainformation in Apache.

Appendices

Four appendices present essential reference information about various aspects of Apache administration.

Appendix A: Apache Directives

Appendix A is a table listing all the directives included in the standard Apache distribution, summarizing each directive's context, overrides, module, and any default value.

Appendix B: Online References

Apache and Web services are complex topics. The Web itself is a great source of information to shed light on these topics. This appendix provides an extensive list of pointers to online information that can help you learn more about Apache and the Web.

Appendix C: Transferring Files to Apache

Appendix C shows how files are uploaded and placed on the Apache server. The discussion covers tools specifically designed for this purpose, like the PUT handlers used to accept uploads from products like Netscape Composer and Apache modules like the one for Microsoft FrontPage Extensions. This appendix also covers the use of FTP, the most common means of updating files on a Linux Apache Web server, and WebDAV, which may well make all the other techniques obsolete.

Appendix D: Using Apache Documentation Effectively

Perhaps the most important reference information about Apache is provided by its own documentation. This appendix is a quick guide to getting the most out of the help system.

Conventions

This book uses the following typographical conventions:

`Program Font` is used to identify the Linux and Apache commands and directives, filenames and pathnames, and URLs that occur within the body of the text and in listings and examples.

Bold is used to indicate something that must be typed in as shown, such as command-line input in listings.

Italic is used in directive or command syntax to indicate a variable for which you must provide a value. For example,

`UserDir enabled` *`usernames`* means that in entering the `UserDir` directive with the `enabled` option, you would need to supply real usernames.

`[ ]` in a directive's syntax enclose an item that is optional.

`|` is a vertical bar that means you should choose one keyword or another in a directive's syntax.

Help Us Help You

Things change. In the world of computers, things change rapidly. Information presented in this book, although it's current now, will become invalid over time. When that happens, we need your help locating the necessary changes. In addition, a 600-page book is bound to have typographical errors. Let us know when you spot one. Send your improvements, fixes, and other corrections to `support@sybex.com`.

Part 1

How Things Work

Featuring

- A brief history of the World Wide Web and Apache

- How the HyperText Transfer Protocol (HTTP) works

- HTTP/1.1 response codes and other headers

- Apache's importance in the marketplace

- Other Web servers: free and commercial alternatives to Apache

- Major features of Apache

- New features in Apache version 2.0

1

An Overview of the World Wide Web

No book written about Apache, the most widely used Web server software on the Internet today, would be complete without a discussion of the World Wide Web (WWW) itself—how it came into existence and how it works. A key part of mastering any complex software application is understanding the technology underlying that system, and the technology that underlies Apache is the World Wide Web. This chapter is an introductory overview of a vast topic. The chapter begins with a history of the World Wide Web, introducing the Apache Web server, and then moves through an explanation of how the Web works, with a short introductory tour of the inner workings of the HyperText Markup Language (HTML) and the HyperText Transfer Protocol (HTTP). We'll look at the important features of the HTTP/1.1 version of the protocol, and use three common tools to observe the protocols in action.

A Brief History of the Web

The World Wide Web (referred to throughout this book simply as *the Web*) is the result of years of evolutionary change. No one person or group can be credited with its creation. Indeed, it is unlikely that the original designers of the Web had notions as grand as the eventual reality of their accomplishment. Although based on the concept of embedded links between documents, called *hypertext* links, which has its beginnings in the mid-1940s, the Web is generally considered the idea of one man, Tim Berners-Lee.

In 1989, Berners-Lee submitted a proposal for a research project to CERN (*Conseil Européen pour la Recherche Nucléaire*) in Geneva, Switzerland. Berners-Lee's proposal outlined a hypertext-based system that we would all recognize as today's Web, but it didn't discuss the technical foundation of that system, and didn't address the need to develop network protocols to support the system. The paper basically proposed extending the HyperCard system that was available for the Apple Macintosh computer to a local area network–based system. The Web actually had a very humble beginning; the proposal did not, for example, foresee the expansion of the proposed system to global proportions.

The following year, 1990, a NeXT Cube workstation was purchased by CERN, and work began on the first graphical hypertext delivery system—the first Web *browser*. The CERN labs also distributed technical details that allowed developers to create their own Web servers. The first Web sites were initially set up as experimental, or "proof of principle" sites, mostly by academic and research institutions with the resources to develop them. Most of these were very simple servers, consisting of a few hundred lines of C code, based on source code obtained from CERN. In November 1992, the CERN list of "reasonably reliable servers" consisted of only 26 servers, at sites around the world.

All that changed in 1993. CERN was making available its own "reasonably reliable" server, with instructions on how to port and compile it to different types of hardware. In the United States, the National Center for Supercomputing Applications (NCSA), located at the University of Illinois at Urbana-Champaign, released NCSA Mosaic. The development and free distribution of the Mosaic browser was the catalyst that caused a sudden and sustained increase in the proliferation of Web servers on the Internet. NCSA also offered its own version of a Web server that was freely downloadable and relatively easy to install. The NCSA server was more widely adopted than the CERN server and led the way with the addition of new features.

By 1994, the most widely used Web server software in the world was NCSA `httpd`. NCSA also had the lead in the development of the HTTP client software with its Mosaic browser. The Web looked like it belonged to NCSA—a *nonprofit* organization, something that is almost inconceivable from our viewpoint a mere eight years later. Progress on the NCSA server project stalled when its developer, Rob McCool, left NCSA in mid-1994. Since the source code for the NCSA server was widely available, many developers were already working on improvements and bug fixes. This trend toward decentralized, uncoordinated development continued into 1995, the year in which the Apache server was born.

The Apache server was assembled and released in early 1995 as a set of patches to the NCSA `httpd` 1.3 Web server. The name Apache is derived directly from this beginning as *a patchy server*. Get it? Numerous individual programmers, loosely bound into a consortium initially called the Apache Group, contributed the original source code patches that made up the first Apache server. In the true spirit and style of what is best about the Internet and open-source development, they collaborated by sharing ideas, criticism, encouragement, and camaraderie via e-mail and Usenet newsgroups.

Less than a year after the Apache group was formed, the Apache server replaced NCSA `httpd` as the most-used Web server. There are several reasons why Apache was so rapidly accepted and widely installed so soon after its initial availability. First and foremost, Apache was functionally identical to, and administered exactly like, NCSA `httpd`. With virtually no alterations to the filesystem or configuration files, Apache could be used as a drop-in replacement for NCSA. And there were good reasons to do so: Apache was faster, it was more reliable, it enjoyed wide support—and it was cool. Apache administrators immediately became part of a development effort that was on the leading edge of a new technology that was changing every facet of computing. Later developments only increased the superiority of Apache over the noncommercial, freely distributed servers available at the time. The most significant change was probably its support for add-on modules; this was achieved by exposing the internal workings of the server engine to third-party programs through a set of Application Programming Interfaces (APIs). This allowed anyone, anywhere, to customize Apache to meet their own specific needs, but more important, it led to the development of modules that can be freely obtained and added to the server to extend its capabilities. Many of these modules have been adopted for inclusion as part of the Apache distribution, though the use of most is optional.

With the decline in use of the two most prominent HTTP servers of the mid-1990s (new development for both CERN and NCSA HTTP servers was completely abandoned), Apache grew to become the most widely used Web server software on the Internet. As shown on the timeline in Figure 1.1, it achieved this status in April 1996, according to the Netcraft Web Survey (www.netcraft.com), and has held this position continuously since.

Figure 1.1   A timeline of the Web and Apache

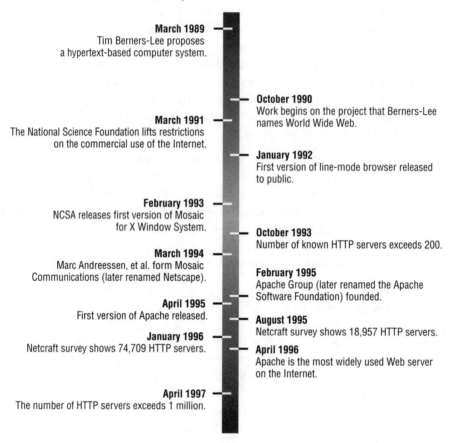

March 1989
Tim Berners-Lee proposes
a hypertext-based computer system.

October 1990
Work begins on the project that Berners-Lee
names World Wide Web.

March 1991
The National Science Foundation lifts restrictions
on the commercial use of the Internet.

January 1992
First version of line-mode browser released
to public.

February 1993
NCSA releases first version of Mosaic
for X Window System.

October 1993
Number of known HTTP servers exceeds 200.

March 1994
Marc Andreessen, et al. form Mosaic
Communications (later renamed Netscape).

February 1995
Apache Group (later renamed the Apache
Software Foundation) founded.

April 1995
First version of Apache released.

August 1995
Netcraft survey shows 18,957 HTTP servers.

January 1996
Netcraft survey shows 74,709 HTTP servers.

April 1996
Apache is the most widely used Web server
on the Internet.

April 1997
The number of HTTP servers exceeds 1 million.

Today most competing servers are commercially developed and supported, predominately those from Netscape and Microsoft. The growth of commercial servers doesn't reflect superiority over Apache as much as it points to the increasing use of the Web for commercial purposes. Many large companies, integrating their Web commerce engines with legacy databases and enterprise resource planning (ERP) systems, insist on using only commercial software. Traditionally, noncommercial software has been seen as experimental and not production-ready, incapable of performance and reliability equal to software developed for commercial resale. It's also possible to sue a commercial software vendor, even if it is difficult to win such a lawsuit.

Apache and software servers like Apache that use Linux have slowly overcome corporate prejudice to make major inroads in changing industry perception of noncommercial open-source software. In September 2001, Apache received a tremendous vote of confidence from the Gartner Research Group when it released a report urging corporations to abandon the use of the most prevalent commercial Web server in favor of Apache, which it considered far more securable. As PCs did in the early 1980s, Apache and Linux continue to filter steadily into Fortune 1000 firms.

The Apache License

What does it mean to describe Apache as open-source software? Open-source software is often associated with the GNU Public License (GPL), mainly because the GPL is the licensing agreement used by Linux and many applications written for Linux. Apache, however, does not use the GPL and has a special license of its own. The Apache license, which can be retrieved from `http://httpd.apache.org/docs-2.0/LICENSE`, doesn't specifically prohibit any use of Apache and, unlike the GPL, does not require that modifications to Apache be made public. The Apache license exists mainly to limit the liability of the Apache Software Foundation (formerly known as the Apache Group) for damages or loss resulting from the use of Apache software. It also requires that the Foundation is properly credited in any commercial use of Apache or products based on the Apache server.

The essential thing to remember about the Apache license is that it expresses a copyright held by the Foundation for the Apache source code. Apache is not in the public domain. Control of the Apache source code remains ultimately in the hands of the Apache Software Foundation. Although it is possible that the Foundation could suddenly decide to pull the rug out from under hundreds of thousands of site administrators by requiring licensing or even prohibiting use of the software for commercial purposes, the likelihood of that happening is extremely remote. You'll find more precedents of commercial software vendors suddenly deciding to change their corporate practices or policies to the detriment of their clients, deciding, for example, that it is no longer economically feasible to support particular software. How many times has a software support technician told you, "You need to buy an upgrade to fix that problem"? Using open-source software can often protect your company from the vagaries of software vendors in a ruthless marketplace.

How the Web Works

The rapid adoption of the Web can be largely attributed to the accessibility of its technology. From the very first, Web browsers have been freely distributed, and it is highly unlikely that use of the Web would have exploded in the mid-1990s had the situation been any different. The Web provides an interface to information that is simple and intuitive, providing links to millions of sites around the world. We now have access to vast repositories of information, and much of it is free for the taking.

Was it our relentless search for intellectual self-improvement that enticed most of us into downloading our first Web browser onto our PCs, or an insatiable need for information to help us do our jobs more efficiently? Hardly. The truth is that the character of the early Web sites had a lot to do with the Web's instant popularity. What Web user wasn't first attracted by the interesting new combinations of text and color graphics (not to mention the fact that the personal computer gave a sense of security that the boss didn't know what we were *really* doing with our computers on company time)?

We were checking out something cool and always looking for something even cooler. It's not surprising that time spent using the new information-distribution system became known by a simple nontechnical term: "browsing" the Web. The system of hyperlinks that allows one page to reference others, each of which leads to other (hopefully related) pages is what opened the Web to a vast, mostly nontechnical audience. The Web was an astounding success because, even on a 14-inch monitor with a pixel resolution that is a joke by today's standards, nearly everyone said the same thing when they saw their first Web page: "Cool!" No competing scheme for exchanging information that ignored the "cool" factor stood a chance against the Web.

At the heart of the design of the Web is the concept of the hyperlink. The clickable links on a Web page can point to resources located anywhere in the world. The designers of the first hypertext information system started with this concept. For this concept to work on a major scale, three pieces of the Web had to be invented. First, there had to be a universally accepted method of uniquely defining each Web resource. This naming scheme is the Uniform Resource Locator (URL), described in the accompanying sidebar. The second piece was a scheme for formatting Web-delivered documents so that a named resource could become a clickable link in another document. This formatting scheme is the HyperText Markup Language (HTML). The third piece of the Web is some means to bring everything together into one huge information system. That piece of the puzzle is the network communication protocol that links any client workstation to any of millions of Web servers: the HyperText Transfer Protocol (HTTP).

A hyperlink embedded in an HTML-formatted page is only one way to use a URL, but it is the hyperlink that gave rise to the Web. If we had to resort to exchanging URLs by writing them on napkins, there would be no Web. Most of us think of the Web in terms of visiting Web sites, but the mechanism is not one of going somewhere, it is one of retrieving a resource (usually a Web page) across a network using the unique identifier for the resource: its URL.

URLs can also be manually entered into a text box provided for that purpose in a Web browser or saved as a bookmark for later point-and-click retrieval. Most e-mail programs today allow URLs to be included in the message body so that the recipient can simply click them to retrieve the named resource. Some e-mail packages allow you to embed images in the message body using URLs. When the message is read, the image is retrieved separately; it could reside on any Internet server, not necessarily the sender's machine.

What Is a URL?

A Uniform Resource Locator (or URL) is a means of identifying a resource that is accessible through the Internet. Although the distinction is academic, a URL is a special case of a Uniform Resource Identifier (URI) that is understood by Web servers. A URI is any string that uniquely identifies an Internet resource.

Each URL is composed of three parts: a mechanism (or *protocol*) for retrieving the resource, the hostname of a server that can provide the resource, and a name for the resource. The resource name is usually a filename preceded by a partial path, which in Apache is relative to the path defined as the DocumentRoot. Here's an example of a URL:

```
http://www.apache.org/docs/misc/FAQ.html
```

This URL identifies a resource on a server whose Internet name is www.apache.org. The resource has the filename FAQ.html and probably resides in a directory named misc, which is a subdirectory of docs (a subdirectory of the directory the server knows as DocumentRoot) although as we'll see later, there are ways to redirect requests to other parts of the filesystem. The URL also identifies HTTP as the protocol to be used to retrieve the files. The http:// protocol is so widely used that it is the default if nothing is entered for the mechanism. The only other common retrieval method you're likely to see in a URL is ftp://, although your particular browser probably supports a few others, including news:// and gopher://.

A URL can also invoke a program such as a CGI script written in Perl, which might look like this:

```
http://jackal.hiwaay.net/cgi-bin/comments.cgi
```

It was the Web browser, with its ability to render attractive screens from HTML-formatted documents, that initially caught the eye of the public. Beneath the pretty graphical interface of the browser, however, the Web is an information-delivery system consisting of client and server software components that communicate over a network. These components communicate using HTTP. The following sections describe this client/server relationship and the HTTP protocol used to move Web data around the world. This provides an introduction to the subject of the book, Apache, which is the foremost implementation of the HTTP server component.

What Is a Web Server?

Essentially, a Web server is a software application that listens for client connections on a specific network port. When a connection is made, the Web server then waits for a request from the client application. The client is usually a Web browser, but it could also be a Web site indexing utility or perhaps an interactive telnet session. The resource request, usually a request to send the contents of a file stored on the server, is always phrased in some version of HTTP.

Although the Web server's primary purpose is to distribute information from a central computer, modern Web servers perform other tasks as well. Before the file transfer, most modern Web servers send descriptive information about the requested resource, instructing the client how to interpret or format the resource. Many Web servers perform user authentication and data encryption to permit applications like online credit-card purchasing. Another common feature of Web servers is that they provide database access on behalf of the client, eliminating the need for the client to use a full-featured database client application. Apache provides all of these features.

The HyperText Transfer Protocol (HTTP)

The Web consists of all the Web servers on the Internet and the millions of client systems that are capable of establishing temporary connections to them. The essential glue that holds the Web together is the set of interoperability standards that permit these clients and servers to exchange information across the Internet. These well-defined standard methods of communicating across a network are called *protocols*. To understand the Web, it is important to understand the protocols that establish and define it.

What is a protocol? Traditionally, the word refers to the rules of social behavior followed by dignitaries and heads of states. In computer networking, the term also refers to rules of behavior—those that apply to the two sides of a network connection. In this sense, the HTTP protocol defines the behavior expected of the client (browser) and server components of an HTTP connection. A browser can be written only if it knows what to expect from the servers it connects to, and that behavior is defined by the protocol specification (HTTP).

Generally, when an HTTP/1.1 server like Apache receives a request from a client browser, it will perform one of two actions. It will either respond to the request by sending a document (either static or dynamically generated by a program) or refuse to respond to the request, sending instead a numeric status code indicating why. If the numeric status code is in the range 300–399, it indicates to the browser that the server is redirecting the request to an alternate location.

A Web server cannot *force* a browser to retrieve a resource from an alternate location. It sends a status code showing that the server couldn't respond to the browser's request, along with a Location: directive indicating an alternate location for the resource. The browser is politely asked to redirect its request to this location. The important thing to keep in mind is that the server does not control the browser's behavior, but simply suggests or requests a certain action. That's the essence of a protocol, which is simply a codification of the acceptable (proper) and expected behavior of the components of a system.

The one protocol that all Web servers and browsers must support is HTTP. HTTP is actually not very complex as protocols go. The first version of HTTP (now referred to as version 0.9, or HTTP/0.9, although at the time there was no official versioning of the protocol) was extremely simple, designed only to transfer raw data across the Internet. The early Web servers that implemented this now-obsolete version of HTTP responded to simple requests like:

```
GET /welcome.html
```

Upon receiving this request, a server responded by sending a document stored in the file welcome.html, if it existed in the server's defined DocumentRoot directory, or an error response if it did not.

Today's Web servers still respond to HTTP/0.9 requests, but only the very oldest browsers in existence still form their requests in that manner. HTTP/0.9 was officially laid to rest in May 1996 with the release of Request for Comments (RFC) 1945 ("Hypertext Transfer Protocol—HTTP/1.0"), which formally defined HTTP version 1.0. The most important addition to the HTTP protocol in version 1.0 was the use of *headers* that describe the data being transferred. It is these headers that instruct the browser how to treat the data. The most common header used on the Web is certainly this one:

```
Content-Type: text/html
```

This header instructs the browser to treat the data that follows it as text formatted using HTML. HTML formatting codes embedded in the text describe how the browser will render the page. Most people think of HTML when they think of the Web. We're all familiar with how an HTML document appears in a browser, with its tables, images, clickable buttons, and, most importantly, clickable links to other locations. The use of HTML is not limited to applications written for the Web. All of the most popular electronic mail clients in use today support the formatting of message bodies in HTML.

The important thing to remember is that the Web's most commonly used formatting specification (HTML) and the network transfer protocol used by all Web servers and browsers (HTTP) are independent. Neither relies exclusively on the other or insists on its use. Of the two, HTTP is the specification most tightly associated with the Web and needs to be part of all World Wide Web server and browser software.

NOTE   The operation of the Web is standardized by a number of documents called Requests for Comments (RFCs). While many of these are considered "informational" documents and have no status as standards or specifications, those that have been accepted by the Internet Engineering Task Force (IETF) are the accepted specifications that are used in the development of network applications. While RFCs are available from a number of sites, probably the best source is www.rfc-editor.org, which is funded by the Internet Society.

New Features in HTTP/1.1

The current version of HTTP is version 1.1, which is described and defined by RFC 2616 ("Hypertext Transfer Protocol—HTTP/1.1"). The official date of this document is June 1999, but work on the specification has been ongoing for years, and features embodied in the specification slowly found their way into mainstream servers and clients during that time. Version 1.1 includes several important new features that have been requested for years. You can expect HTTP/1.1 to be fully supported in all versions of Apache starting with version 1.3.4.

Most of the changes to HTTP in version 1.1 were made to the way HTTP client and server programs communicate, and are designed primarily to enhance performance, especially using caching proxies (Chapter 12, "Proxying and Performance Tuning"). Most features of HTTP/1.1 operate almost unchanged from HTTP/1.0, but some of the changes are quite visible and important to the Web site administrator.

One of the features of HTTP/1.1, hostname identification, is a way for the server to determine which of several virtual hosts should receive the request. In Chapter 6, "Virtual Hosting," we'll see how this eliminates the need for Web site hosting services to reserve unique IP addresses for each virtual Web site on a single host server. Hostname identification was one of the most requested changes in HTTP/1.1.

HTTP/1.1 supports a feature called *content negotiation*, in which an exchange of new HTTP/1.1 headers allows the browser and server to negotiate a common set of settings. This is useful, for example, in cases where a Web server provides resources in several versions (called *representations* or *variants*). The content negotiation feature of HTTP/1.1 allows the browser to automatically indicate a preferred language for the requested resource, or perhaps an alternate format for a document like PDF or PostScript. Content negotiation is covered in Chapter 15, "Metainformation and Content Negotiation."

Four new request methods, described in detail in the next section, were added to HTTP/1.1: OPTIONS, TRACE, DELETE, and PUT (Table 1.1). Ever encounter a Web site that lets you upload a file from your Web browser? Probably not. That feature isn't seen more often because it requires that both server and browser support the PUT request method introduced in HTTP/1.1. (Actually, it is possible to upload files to a Web server using the POST method and CGI in earlier versions of HTTP, but HTTP/1.1 is the first to support two-way file transfers.) Few Web site administrators are willing to rely on a new feature that would exclude a significant number of potential customers who are using outdated browsers. Soon, most browsers in use on the Internet will support HTTP/1.1. Increased server support for HTTP/1.1 has been introduced in each new release of Apache since work began on the specification several years ago.

Regardless of the browser you choose, ensuring compatibility with the very latest release has become almost essential. Although I had to have my fingers pried from Netscape Navigator 3.04, which I used for several years, I will never again use a Web browser even a few revisions old, in order to have the latest features of most modern browsers. On computers running Microsoft Windows operating systems, the choice of Web browser has been narrowed to Microsoft's own Internet Explorer (IE), by far the most popular browser; no competitor comes close to the popularity it enjoys. In fact, many of the Web browser screenshots in this book were made from the IE browser. The real threat to the dominance of the Internet Explorer browser is from the increasing number of people using Linux as a desktop operating system. IE isn't available for Linux and probably never will be, but open-source browsers like Konqueror (popular with users of the KDE desktop) and Mozilla (more commonly used with the Gnome desktop) are excellent.

HTTP Request Methods

All HTTP requests begin with a header that specifies the request *method*. The most common method is the one used to request a resource from the server. This is the GET method. It is used to retrieve a resource from a Web server whenever you type a URL in the text box of your browser. The GET method is also used to invoke scripts, and it has provision for parameters to be appended to the method to allow data to be sent to the server. The primary use of the GET method, therefore, is resource retrieval.

Table 1.1 shows the eight methods supported by HTTP/1.1. With the exception of the first three, GET, HEAD, and POST, all of these methods were added in HTTP/1.1 and were not part of HTTP/1.0 and earlier. Not all of these are retrieval methods; the PUT and POST methods are used to send data from the client to the server.

Table 1.1   HTTP/1.1 Methods

Method	Purpose
GET	Retrieves the resource identified in the request URL.
HEAD	Identical to GET except that the server does not return a message body to the client. Essentially, this returns only the HTTP header information.
POST	Instructs the server to receive information from the client; used most often to receive information entered into fields of a Web form.
PUT	Allows the client to send the resource identified in the request URL to the server. The server, if it will accept the PUT, opens a file into which it saves the information it receives from the client.
OPTIONS	Used to request information about the communication options provided by the server. This allows the client to negotiate a suitable set of communication parameters with the server.
TRACE	Initiates a loopback of the request message for testing purposes, allowing the client to see exactly what is being seen by the server.
DELETE	Requests that the server delete the resource identified in the request URL.
CONNECT	Instructs a Web proxy to tunnel a connection from the client to the server, rather than proxying the request.

Observing the HTTP Protocol in Action

The quickest path to understanding how a basic HTTP retrieval works is to connect directly to a Web server and enter the HTTP request manually. Observing the protocol interactions between a client and server or manually requesting a resource and observing the server's response to your request shows the full range of HTTP protocol interactions. You can do this with a few different tools:

telnet   A terminal emulation protocol that is commonly used in TCP/IP-based networks and on the Internet. It is normally used to log onto a remote computer and run a terminal session remotely, but it can also be used to connect to any TCP (Transmission Control Protocol) socket on a remote server to manually control the connection. Since **telnet** is considered an inherent part of the TCP/IP communications protocol, any computer that supports TCP/IP network communications should supply a reasonably useful **telnet** client utility.

lwp-request   A Perl tool that allows you to control an HTTP connection manually.

HttpSniffer.pl   A Perl tool you can use to observe the HTTP connection between a client and server.

Using *telnet*

You can connect directly to a Web server and enter the HTTP request manually with the Linux **telnet** command, which allows you to connect to a specific TCP port on the remote system. Not only will this allow you to see the complete exchange of messages between the client and server, it also gives you complete control of the session and provides a valuable tool for troubleshooting your Web server.

Enter the following **telnet** command at the shell prompt, replacing *somehost.com* with the name of any server accessible from your workstation and known to be running a Web server:

```
telnet somehost.com 80
```

This command instructs **telnet** to connect to TCP port 80, which is the well-known port reserved for HTTP connections. You should receive some confirmation of a successful connection, but you will not receive data immediately from the remote server. If the process listening on port 80 of the remote system is an HTTP server (as it should be), it sends nothing upon receiving a connection, because it is waiting for a request from the client. This behavior is defined by the HTTP specification.

The examples that follow are actual traces from my Linux server, which hosts a fully operational Apache server. I **telnet** to *localhost*, which is a special reserved hostname for the local system. You can do the same, if the system on which you are executing **telnet** also hosts an HTTP server. (If you stay with me through Chapter 5, "Apache Modules," you'll have a working system on which to test these commands.) Until then, you can connect to any Web server on the Internet to perform these tests.

```
$ telnet localhost 80
Trying 127.0.0.1...
Connected to localhost.
Escape character is '^]'.
```

At this point, telnet has an open connection to the remote HTTP server, which is waiting for a valid HTTP request. The simplest request you can enter is

GET /

This requests the default Web page for the directory defined as the server root. A properly configured HTTP server should respond with a valid page. Our request, which makes no mention of the HTTP version we wish to use, will cause the server to assume we are using HTTP/0.9. This shouldn't cause problems with any server, but it is considered an obsolete form. All requests in HTTP/1.0 and subsequent versions should contain the HTTP version of the requester (or browser software):

```
$ telnet localhost 80
Trying 127.0.0.1...
Connected to localhost.
Escape character is '^]'.
GET /
<HTML>
<HEAD>
<TITLE> Simple Test Page </TITLE>
</HEAD>
<BODY>
<H1> Simple Test Page </H1>
</BODY>
</HTML>
```

The server, which assumes you are a client that understands only HTTP/0.9, simply sends the requested resource (in this case, the default page for my Web site). In Listing 1.1, I've issued the same request, but this time my GET line specifies HTTP/1.0 as the version of HTTP I'm using. Notice this time that the server will not respond as soon you type the request and press Enter. It waits for additional information (this is normal HTTP/1.0 behavior). Two carriage-return/line-feed character pairs are required to indicate the end of an HTTP/1.0 request.

Listing 1.1   Testing Apache with telnet

```
$ telnet localhost 80
Trying 127.0.0.1...
Connected to localhost.
Escape character is '^]'.
GET / HTTP/1.0
```

```
HTTP/1.1 200 OK
Date: Wed, 20 Feb 2002 18:14:05 GMT
Server: Apache/2.0.32 (Unix) DAV/2
Last-Modified: Wed, 20 Feb 2002 18:05:13 GMT
ETag: "53c25-7d-6e514840"
Accept-Ranges: bytes
Content-Length: 125
Connection: close
Content-Type: text/html; charset=ISO-8859-1

<HTML>
<HEAD>
<TITLE> Simple Test Page </TITLE>
<H1> Simple Test Page  </H1>
</HEAD>
</HTML>
```

Using *lwp-request*

If you've installed the collection of Perl modules and utility scripts collectively known as libwww-perl, you can use the lwp-request script that comes with that package to test HTTP connections. With this script, you can specify different request methods and display options. The following example illustrates the use of the -e argument to display response headers (more on headers shortly) with the -d argument to suppress the content in the response:

```
$ lwp-request -e -d http://localhost/
Connection: close
Date: Wed, 20 Feb 2002 18:18:48 GMT
Accept-Ranges: bytes
ETag: "53c25-7d-6e514840"
Server: Apache/2.0.32 (Unix) DAV/2
Content-Length: 125
Content-Type: text/html; charset=ISO-8859-1
Last-Modified: Wed, 20 Feb 2002 18:05:13 GMT
Client-Date: Wed, 20 Feb 2002 18:18:48 GMT
Client-Response-Num: 1
Title: Simple Test Page
```

Be sure to explore the other options available for lwp-request. For example, you can use the -H option to specify arbitrary request headers. This can be especially useful when experimenting with HTTP. For example, you can add Referer: and Host: headers to your request with this command:

```
lwp-request -H 'Referer: http://another.url.com/'  \
    -H 'Host: vhost1.hiwaay.net' http://jackal.hiwaay.net/
```

libwww-perl consists of several scripts, supported by the following standard Perl modules (available separately, although most easily installed as part of the libwww-perl bundle):

URI   Support for Uniform Resource Identifiers

Net::FTP   Support for the FTP protocol

MIME::Base64   Required for authentication headers

Digest::MD5   Required for digest authentication

HTML::HeadParser   Support for HTML headers

Even though you may not actually use the functionality of all of these modules, they must be properly installed on your machine to use the utility scripts provided with lib-www-perl. Use the following commands to install everything at once on a Linux system on which you have the CPAN.pm module:

```
# perl -MCPAN -e shell;
cpan> install Bundle::LWP
```

Among the utilities provided with libwww-perl, the most important (and the one most useful for examining the exchange of headers in an HTTP transaction) is lwp-request. Another that I find very useful, however, is lwp-download, which can be used to retrieve a resource from a remote server. Note that besides the HTTP shown in this example, you can also use FTP, which gives you a simple, interesting way to automate FTP downloads:

```
# lwp-download http://jackal.hiwaay.net
Saving to 'index.html'...
3.85 KB received
```

CPAN

The best way to maintain the latest versions of all Perl modules is to use the CPAN.pm module. This powerful module is designed to ensure that you have the latest available versions of Perl modules registered with the *Comprehensive Perl Archive Network*, or *CPAN* (http://cpan.org). CPAN archives virtually everything that has to do with Perl, including software as source code and binary ports, along with documentation, code samples, and newsgroup postings. The CPAN site is mirrored at over 100 sites around the world, for speed and reliability. You generally choose the one nearest you geographically.

The CPAN.pm Perl module completely automates the processes of comparing your installed modules against the latest available in the CPAN archives, downloading modules, building modules (using the enclosed makefiles), and installing them.

> **CPAN (*continued*)**
>
> The module is intelligent enough to connect to any one of the CPAN mirror sites, and (using FTP) can download lists of the latest modules for comparison against your local system to see whether you have modules installed that need upgrading. Once you install it, CPAN.pm even updates itself! Not only does the module automate the process of updating and installing modules, it makes the process almost bulletproof. I have never experienced problems with the module.

Another powerful Perl tool for observing the HTTP protocol is HttpSniffer.pl. Although not as convenient as lwp-request because it does require setup and a separate client component (usually a Web browser), HttpSniffer.pl allows you to "snoop" on a real-world HTTP exchange. As you'll read next, it is more useful when you need to examine header exchanges with a browser (during content negotiation, for example).

Using *HttpSniffer.pl*

HttpSniffer.pl acts as an HTTP tunnel, connecting directly to a remote server, forwarding connections from client browsers, and displaying the headers (or writing them to a log file) exchanged between the client and server.

Download HttpSniffer.pl directly from its author's Web site at www.schmerg.com. You can run the program on any platform running Perl 5.004 (or later). Figure 1.2 shows a typical session. The command window in the foreground shows how I invoked HttpSniffer.pl, pointing it at my Web server, jackal.hiwaay.net, with the -r argument. HttpSniffer.pl, by default, receives connections on TCP port 8080 and forwards them to the specified remote host. The browser in the background (running on the same computer as HttpSniffer.pl) is pointed at the URL http://localhost:8080. It appears to receive a page directly from jackal.hiwaay.net, but the connection is actually made by HttpSniffer.pl, which displays both the client request HTTP headers and the server response HTTP headers. The pages retrieved from jackal.hiwaay.net by HttpSniffer.pl are returned to the requesting browser.

HttpSniffer.pl is not only an invaluable debugging tool, it is also the best way to learn the purpose of HTTP headers by watching the actual headers that are part of an HTTP exchange. If you have access to a proxy server, on a remote server or through Apache's mod_proxy (discussed in Chapter 12), you can point HttpSniffer.pl at the proxy, and then configure your client browser to connect to HttpSniffer.pl as an HTTP proxy server. That way, you can use your browser to connect to any remote host as you normally would, and all requests will be redirected (or *proxied*) by HttpSniffer.pl. Be prepared for lots of output, though. Generally, you should invoke HttpSniffer.pl with a line like the following (the -l argument causes all of the output from the command to be written into the text file specified):

```
# HttpSniffer.pl -r jackal.hiwaay.net -l /tmp/httpheaders.txt
```

Figure 1.2   HttpSniffer.pl at work

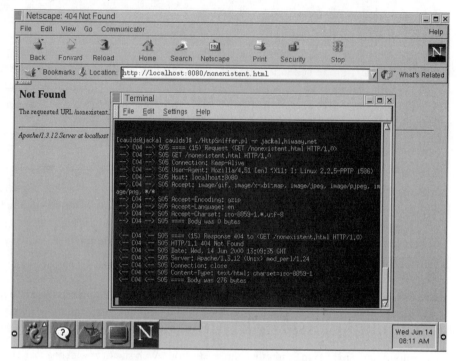

The only problem with HttpSniffer.pl and lwp-request is that they are not available on every Linux system. But telnet is. For that reason, I use telnet in the examples in this chapter; every Linux administrator has access to it and can duplicate these examples. However, if you have HttpSniffer.pl or lwp-request, I encourage you to use them for testing.

The Response Code Header

In Listing 1.1, notice that HTTP sends a group of headers before sending the requested resource. The first header identifies the version of HTTP supported by the server and sends a request response code. The response code is in two parts, a number and a comment: 200 is the response code for a fully successful request, the OK is the comment provided as a convenience for human viewers only.

In Listing 1.1, the server replies with the response code 200, indicating that everything went well. Of course, that is not always the case. HTTP response codes fall into five categories, with a range of codes for each category:

Code Range	Response Category
100–199	Informational

Code Range	Response Category
200–299	Client request successful
300–399	Client request redirected
400–499	Client request incomplete
500–599	Server errors

The response categories contain more than 40 individual response codes. Each is accompanied by a short comment that is intended to make the code understandable to the user. To see a full list of these codes, go to the HTML Writers Guild at `www.hwg.org/lists/hwg-servers/response_codes.html`.

When using `telnet` to test an HTTP connection, it is best to replace the GET request method with HEAD. This prevents the server from actually sending the requested resource; it sends only the headers in reply. For `telnet` tests, the headers are what you're interested in. The resource is best viewed with a real browser.

The request shown in Listing 1.2, specifying HTTP/1.1, has a very different result from the first test.

Listing 1.2   The Headers in a Failed Test

```
$ telnet localhost 80
Trying 127.0.0.1...
Connected to localhost.
Escape character is '^]'.
GET / HTTP/1.1

HTTP/1.1 400 Bad Request
Date: Wed, 20 Feb 2002 19:06:18 GMT
Server: Apache/2.0.32 (Unix) DAV/2
Content-Length: 370
Connection: close
Content-Type: text/html; charset=iso-8859-1

<!DOCTYPE HTML PUBLIC "-//IETF//DTD HTML 2.0//EN">
<html><head>
<title>400 Bad Request</title>
</head><body>
<h1>Bad Request</h1>
<p>Your browser sent a request that this server could not understand.<br />
client sent HTTP/1.1 request without hostname (see RFC2616 section 14.23):
/</p>
```

```
<hr />
<address>Apache/2.0.32 Server at 127.0.0.1 Port 80</address>
</body></html>
Connection closed by foreign host.
```

The response code header clearly indicates that our request failed. This is because HTTP/1.1 requires the client browser to furnish a hostname if it chooses to use HTTP/1.1. Note that the choice of HTTP version is always the client's. This hostname will usually be the same as the hostname of the Web server. (Chapter 6 discusses *virtual hosting*, in which a single Web server answers requests for multiple hostnames.)

In addition to warning the client about a failed request, the server makes note of all request failures in its own log file. The failed request in Listing 1.2 causes the following error to be logged by the server:

```
[Wed Feb 20 13:06:19 2002] [error] [client 127.0.0.1] client sent
HTTP/1.1 request without hostname (see RFC2616 section 14.23): /
```

> **NOTE**   Logging is an important topic that is covered extensively later in this book. Chapter 11, "Apache Logging," is a complete discussion of connection and error logging in Apache. The path and filename of the log are defined in the Apache configuration, as we'll see in Chapter 4, "The Apache Core Directives."

Request redirection is an essential technique for many Web servers as resources are moved or retired. (Chapter 9 shows how to use Apache's tools for aliasing and redirection.) Listing 1.3 illustrates a redirected request.

Listing 1.3   A Redirected Request

```
# telnet localhost 80
Trying 127.0.0.1...
Connected to localhost.
Escape character is '^]'.
GET /manual HTTP/1.0

HTTP/1.1 301 Moved Permanently
Date: Wed, 20 Feb 2002 19:12:36 GMT
Server: Apache/2.0.32 (Unix) DAV/2
Location: http://jackal.hiwaay.net/manual/
Content-Length: 316
Connection: close
Content-Type: text/html; charset=iso-8859-1
```

```
<!DOCTYPE HTML PUBLIC "-//IETF//DTD HTML 2.0//EN">
<html><head>
<title>301 Moved Permanently</title>
</head><body>
<h1>Moved Permanently</h1>
<p>The document has moved <a
href="http://jackal.hiwaay.net/manual/">here</a>.</p>
<hr />
<address>Apache/2.0.32 Server at jackal.hiwaay.net Port 80</address>
</body></html>
Connection closed by foreign host.
```

If the browser specifies HTTP/1.1 in the request line, the very next line *must* identify a hostname for the request, as in Listing 1.4.

Listing 1.4   Using the HTTP/1.1 Host Command

```
# telnet localhost 80
Trying 127.0.0.1...
Connected to localhost.
Escape character is '^]'.
GET / HTTP/1.1
Host: www.jackal.hiwaay.net

HTTP/1.1 200 OK
Date: Wed, 20 Feb 2002 19:13:38 GMT
Server: Apache/2.0.32 (Unix) DAV/2
Last-Modified: Wed, 20 Feb 2002 18:05:13 GMT
ETag: "53c25-7d-6e514840"
Accept-Ranges: bytes
Content-Length: 125
Content-Type: text/html; charset=ISO-8859-1

<HTML>
<HEAD>
<TITLE> Simple Test Page </TITLE>
</HEAD>
<BODY>
<H1> Simple Test Page </H1>
</BODY>
</HTML>

Connection closed by foreign host.
```

If our server answers requests for several virtual hosts, the Host: header of the request would identify the virtual host that should respond to the request. Better support for virtual site hosting is one of the major enhancements to the HTTP protocol in version 1.1.

The Other Headers

The response code header is always the first header sent by the server, and is usually followed by a number of other headers that convey additional information about the HTTP message or the resource it contains (usually referred to as the *message body*). For example, the test shown in Listing 1.4 produced seven additional headers after the response code header: Date, Server, Last Modified, ETag, Accept-Ranges, Content-Length, and Content-Type. The following sections briefly outline these and other HTTP headers.

General Headers

Headers that carry information about the messages being transmitted between client and server are lumped into the category of general headers. These headers do not provide information about the content of the messages being transmitted between the client and server. Instead, they carry information that applies to the entire session and to both client request and server response portions of the transaction. They include:

Cache-Control   Specifies directives to proxy servers (Chapter 12).

Connection   Allows the sender to specify options for this network connection.

Date   Standard representation of the date and time the message was sent.

Pragma   Used to convey non-HTTP information to any recipient that understands the contents of the header. The contents are not part of HTTP.

Trailer   Indicates a set of header fields that can be found in the trailer of a multiple-part message.

Transfer-Encoding   Indicates any transformations that have been applied to the message body in order to correctly transfer it.

Upgrade   Used by the client to specify additional communication protocols it supports and would like to use if the server permits.

Via   Tacked onto the message by proxies or gateways to show that they handled the message.

Warning   Specifies additional information about the status or transformation of a message, which might not be reflected in the message itself.

Request Headers

Request headers are used to pass information from HTTP client to server; these headers always follow the one mandatory line in a request, which contains the URI of the request itself. Request headers act as modifiers for the actual request, allowing the client to include additional information that qualifies the request, usually specifying what constitutes an acceptable response:

Accept   Lists all MIME media types the client is capable of accepting.

Accept-Charset   Lists all character sets the client is capable of accepting.

Accept-Encoding   Lists all encodings (particularly compression schemes) the client is capable of accepting.

Accept-Language   Lists all languages the client is willing to accept.

Authorization   Provides the user's credentials to access the requested resource (usually a username/password pair).

Expect   Indicates server behaviors that are required by the client.

From   An Internet e-mail address for the person controlling the requesting user agent (browser).

Host   Indicates an Internet hostname and port number for the resource being requested. Used by HTTP/1.1 clients to specify a single virtual host among many on a server.

If-Match   A client that has one or more resources previously obtained from the server can verify that one of those resources is current by including a list of their associated tags in this header.

If-Modified-Since   Specifies a date found in a previously received entity to check it for currency.

If-None-Match   Similar to the If-Match: header, but used to verify that none of the previously received resources is current.

If-Range   When a client has a partial copy of a resource in its cache, it can use this header to retrieve the rest of the resource if it hasn't been modified.

If-Unmodified-Since   Used by caching engines to specify that the resource should be sent only if not modified since a specified date.

Max-Forwards   Specifies the number of times this client request can be forwarded by proxies and gateways.

Proxy-Authorization   Supplies the credentials that the client must supply to use a proxy server.

Range   Specifies the retrieval of a portion of a resource, usually specified as a range of bytes.

Refererer   Specifies the URI of the resource from which the request URI was obtained (usually from a hyperlink in another Web page).

TE Indicates what transfer encodings the client is willing to accept and whether it will accept headers in trailer fields in chunked transfer-coding.

User-Agent Contains information about the user agent (browser) originating the request.

Response Headers

The server uses response headers to pass information in addition to the request response to the requesting client. Response headers usually provide information about the response message itself, and not necessarily about the resource being sent to satisfy a client request. Increasingly, response headers serve to provide information used by caching gateways or proxy server engines. The response headers will be an important part of the discussion on proxy caching (Chapter 12). They include:

Accept-Ranges Specifies units (usually bytes) in which the server will accept range requests.

Age The server's estimated time (in seconds) required to fulfill this request.

Etag Contains the current value of the requested entity tag.

Location Contains a URI to which the client request should be redirected.

Proxy-Authenticate Indicates the authentication schema and parameters applicable to the proxy for this request.

Retry-After Used by the server to indicate how long a URI is expected to be unavailable.

Server Contains information about the software used by the origin server to handle the request. Apache identifies itself using this header.

Vary Indicates that the resource has multiple sources that may vary according to the supplied list of request headers.

WWW-Authenticate Used with a 401-Unauthorized response code to indicate that the requested URI needs authentication, and specifies the authorization scheme required (usually a username/password pair) and the name of the authorization realm.

Entity Headers

Entity headers contain information directly related to the resource being provided to the client in fulfillment of the request—in other words, the response message content or body. This information is used by the client to determine how to render the resource or which application to invoke to handle it (for example, Adobe Acrobat Reader). Entity headers contain *metainformation* (or information about information, the subject of Chapter 15):

Allow Informs the client of valid methods associated with the resource.

Content-Encoding   Indicates the encoding (usually compression) scheme applied to the contents.

Content-Language   Indicates the natural language of the contents.

Content-Length   Contains the size of the body of the HTTP message.

Content-Location   Supplies the resource location for the resource in the message body, usually used when the resource should be requested using another URI.

Content-MD5   Contains the MD5 digest of the message body, used to verify the integrity of the resource.

Content-Range   Sent with a partial body to specify where in the complete resource this portion fits.

Content-Type   Describes the MIME media type of the contents.

Expires   Specifies a date and time after which the resource should be considered obsolete.

Last-Modified   Specifies the date and time at which the original document or resource was last modified.

NOTE   More details about these and other headers are available in the HTTP specification, RFC 2616 (see www.rfc-editor.org).

In Sum

This chapter looked at the World Wide Web, its origins and history, and described briefly how it functions. An essential part of the design of the Web is the standard set of protocols that allow applications to interoperate with any of the millions of other systems that make up the Web. The protocol that enables the Web to exist is the HyperText Transfer Protocol (HTTP), which defines how data is communicated between Web clients and servers. This chapter demonstrated a couple of ways to view HTTP headers and listed those headers that are defined by the HTTP specification (or RFC). The chapter concluded with a discussion of the important enhancements to the HTTP protocol that were added in its current version, HTTP/1.1. This information provides the foundation for understanding what Apache does and how it does it.

Although Apache is quite well established as the leading Web server on the Internet, it is by no means the only Web server to compete for that status. The next chapter provides a brief look at the most important of its competitors, in order to place Apache in its proper context as it stands out as the best of the breed, even among champion contenders. I'll also discuss the important changes that have been made to Apache 2.0, the latest major upgrade to the Apache Web server. These changes will ensure that Apache maintains its dominance of the Internet Web server market.

2

Apache and Other Web Servers

Chapter 1 presented a brief historical overview of the World Wide Web and the technologies that make it possible. Fast-forward to the present, and there are a number of good servers for the Web. This chapter provides a very brief description of the best of these and compares their architecture to that of Apache.

I generally don't like one-size-fits-all systems, and I try to avoid products that are marketed as the best solution for everyone's needs. Apache is an exception to this rule, largely because it is easily customized by design. While Apache runs well on commercial Unix platforms and Microsoft Windows NT/2000/XP, it truly shines on the open-source Unix variants. Apache is the number one choice for a Web server for both Linux and FreeBSD, and in this chapter, I'll tell you why.

The first part of this chapter takes a look at the major Web servers in use on the Internet. The chapter continues with a look at the present state of Apache, including its current feature set, and ends with a discussion of why Apache is an excellent and exciting choice to run an Internet Web site.

Who Are the Major Players?

Since a Web server can be any software used to implement HTTP, there are far too many different types of Web servers in use for me to describe them all. Some are completely homegrown solutions unique to their developers, but most are recognizable and identifiable by a specific name and version. Despite the large number of different HTTP server engines available, a small field of competitors handles the majority of HTTP traffic on the Internet.

In determining what Web servers are currently in use on the Internet, and in what relative numbers, I first turned to two respected surveys from the consulting firms Netcraft (www.netcraft.com) and SecuritySpace.com (www.securityspace.com). These surveys are widely accepted as accurate, objective, and credible; and they don't seem to be controlled by commercial interests. The companies publish these surveys as a free service to augment their consulting services, and neither profits directly from its market share survey.

I also ran my own survey, using an HTTP/1.1 HEAD request (see the previous chapter) incorporated into a simple Perl script that I ran on my Web bookmarks list, which consists of 564 sites, mostly of a technical orientation. The results of my informal survey are summarized below, along with the February 2002 survey results from Netcraft and SecuritySpace:

Server	Aulds Survey	Netcraft	SecuritySpace
Apache	63.9%	58.4%	65.8%
Microsoft	23.5%	29.1%	24.9%
iPlanet	5.7%	2.9%	2.0%
Zeus	0.2%	2.2%	1.1%
Other	6.7%	7.4%	6.2%
Total	100.0%	100.0%	100.0%

My own personal survey of Internet Web sites, while not very scientific, does back up the more widely-accepted surveys and (at least for me) tends to add a measure of credibility to both. And from the results, I think it's very safe to say that Apache continues to hold the lion's share of the Web server market, and the vast majority of these Apache servers are certainly being run on Linux platforms. You're in good company.

Alternatives to Apache

While the surveys say that Apache leads the pack, it is not the only Web server in widespread use. This section examines the features and architectures of several other Web servers. None is clearly superior to Apache when judged on its feature set and configurability, and certainly none can beat Apache's price tag since it is distributed free of charge. The two areas in which these servers are legitimate contenders with Apache for market share are where the raw speed of delivering static Web pages is critical and when the most expensive multiprocessor hardware is used. We'll see that it is in the former area (raw speed) where the free Apache alternatives dominate, and in the latter area (high-end hardware) where a commercial server may still be the better (if more costly) choice.

The Free Servers

Some of the best Web server software available is free software. Apache itself is free, open-source software. The roots of the Web—its protocols, browsers, and servers— spring from a free and open academic environment. The free CERN and NCSA servers started the Web revolution, and while neither is currently a viable choice, several choices of server software maintain that free tradition to this day.

thttpd

One of the most interesting free HTTP servers is a product called simply thttpd. The thttpd server is the work of one man, Jef Poskanzer, a Berkeley, California-area consultant, who distributes freeware through a nonprofit site called ACME Laboratories (www.acme.com).

Thttpd is one of two HTTP servers I'll mention that are designed to be extremely fast, have small memory footprints, are simple to install and manage, are highly secure—and are almost feature-free. In most environments, thttpd performs comparably to any other Web server. Under extreme loads, however, thttpd runs away from the pack.

It is unlikely that your Internet server has a data pipe large enough to flood a single Web server with such a large number of requests that a server like thttpd is needed. If your company has an internal server attached to the network with a Gigabit Ethernet link, you might find you need a super-fast server; the problem is that on an intranet server, you'll almost certainly need features that aren't found in thttpd. High-performance servers like thttpd are a little like Formula One race cars: our highways aren't built for them, and they aren't designed to carry payload.

Mathopd

Minimization is taken to the extreme with Mathopd (available from its author at www.mathopd.org). The number of options and features in Mathopd is deliberately small. The server is made available for Unix and Linux operating systems only.

Why would anyone want to run Mathopd? The code is designed to handle a very large number of simultaneous connections. Like the thttpd server, Mathopd uses the `select()` system call in Unix, rather than spawning a number of processes or threads to handle multiple client connections. The result is a very fast Web server, designed to handle the basic functions required by HTTP/1.1 and occupying a very small memory footprint on a Unix machine.

A cinch to install and configure, and optimized for the maximum possible speed in serving static documents to a large number of connecting clients, Mathopd at first seemed a very attractive alternative to Apache. However, Mathopd offers no user authentication, secure connections, or support for programming. Upon reflection, I realized that the server was too limiting for most administrators, without the ability to add functionality, and almost no one has data pipes sufficiently large to require the speed of Mathopd. What it does, though, it does better than anyone.

Boa

The last server I'll mention in the free software category is Boa (`www.boa.org`), a respectable alternative to Apache for those administrators who are looking for greater speed and system security and are willing to sacrifice some functionality to get it. Boa is another of the nonforking, single-process servers that use the `select()` system call to multitask I/O.

Boa turns in very good numbers for CGI scripts, probably some of the best numbers (measured in transactions handled per second) that you'll get on a Linux Web server. The performance gain apparently comes from the fact that output from CGI scripts spawned by Boa is sent directly to the client. This is unlike most Web servers, which receive data output from CGI programs and then send it to the Web client (browser).

The Commercial Variety

Commercial Web servers are in demand by a certain type of organization. Some organizations have a difficult time accepting that open-source software can have better quality and support than commercial software. These organizations demand commercial software, and several companies have responded to this demand by creating commercial Web server software. Here are several of the best commercial products.

Stronghold (from Red Hat)

For those sites that require strong security based on the Secure Sockets Layer (SSL), using a commercial server often seems an attractive alternative to open-source Apache. There are good reasons for these e-commerce Web sites to use commercial software. Probably the best reason to choose a commercial solution is for the support offered by the vendor. If you go the commercial route, you should take full advantage of that product support. You are paying not so much for the product as for that company's expertise in setting up an SSL Web site. You should expect all the handholding necessary from these companies in getting your site up and running.

Many commercial Web products are derived from open-source software, and Stronghold (sold by Red Hat) is no exception. Stronghold is Apache server software, specially modified to include strong SSL support and sold as a ready-to-install product supported by the vendor. There's absolutely nothing wrong with this, and the value added to open-source Apache may be exactly what you need. What you're buying, however, is essentially what you can put together through lots of sweat, trial and error, and time spent in books like this one. You may well decide that the effort required to "roll your own" pays off rich dividends in education and familiarity with your system. If so, Chapter 14 is all about SSL. And since Stronghold is Apache, nearly everything in this book is directly relevant to a Stronghold server.

With Apache 2.0, SSL support became a standard part of Apache, which really lessened the need for a commercial SSL version of the Apache server. Chapter 14 of this book should provide enough information about setting up the mod_ssl module that is part of the standard Apache distribution. The process can appear dauntingly complex, but followed logically, step-by-step, it's really not as difficult or time-consuming as it may first appear. Consider using the SSL support in standard Apache if you need a secure server. Consider Stronghold if support from Red Hat and its consulting arm is important to you. If you just want to save time in setting up Apache, or don't want to bother reading the rest of this book, you will probably be best served by the Covalent Enterprise Server, discussed later in this chapter. (As you will read later, Covalent's tight relationship with the Apache development team is a major point in its favor.)

For additional information on Stronghold, visit Red Hat's Apache Solutions site at `www.redhat.com/software/apache/stronghold`.

iPlanet (Formerly Netscape Enterprise)

Probably the best commercial server available for high-end multiprocessing hardware is iPlanet Web Server (`www.iplanet.com`) from Sun Microsystems, Inc. iPlanet was known for years as Netscape Enterprise Server, but renamed when America Online (which owns Netscape Communications) and Sun created the Sun-Netscape Alliance. In March 2002, the Sun-Netscape Alliance officially concluded, and iPlanet became a division of Sun. iPlanet Web Server is now the Web server component of Sun's Open Net Environment (ONE).

The industrial-strength iPlanet Web Server can still be purchased as a stand-alone product and is available for a wide variety of operating systems including Linux. iPlanet for Linux version 6.0 bears a price tag of $1500 per CPU. This price climbs steeply (to $20,000/cpu) for the complete iPlanet Application Server, Sun's Java Web services application-development platform. Most of the sites that use iPlanet in the future will be those who have chosen to run Sun's application server software on Sun hardware.

These will be large sites whose development staffs program almost exclusively in Java. As a stand-alone server, iPlanet has few advantages over Apache, except on Sun's multi-processor Solaris Unix servers.

Many IT managers in the past chose iPlanet (or its predecessor, Netscape Enterprise Server) because it was fully backed by Sun or Netscape Communications. Such support can be quite valuable. In my opinion, however, the odds of finding documentation that addresses your problem, a savvy tech who's willing to offer truly useful advice, or better still, someone who has overcome the same problem in the past, are much better with an open-source application like Apache. Online resources (like those listed in Appendix B) are often every bit as valuable as technical support for commercial software. As attractive as these commercial servers are, if you are using Linux, Apache should be the first Web server you evaluate.

Roxen

Roxen is not actually a single Web server product; the name is used to refer to a line of Internet server products offered by Idonex AB of Linkoping, Sweden (`www.roxen.com`). Roxen Challenger is the Web server and is available for free download. Roxen Challenger, however, is part of a larger set of integrated Web site development tools called Roxen Platform. Roxen SiteBuilder is a workgroup environment that lets a group of Web site developers collaborate in designing a Web site. Like most modern development systems, SiteBuilder concentrates on separating site display and content.

At a cost of $11,800, Roxen Platform requires a serious financial commitment even though the Challenger Web server is free. Without the costly developers' tools, Roxen Challenger offers no advantages over Apache, which is far more widely used and, as a result, better supported.

Zeus

The Zeus Web server from Zeus Technology of Cambridge, England (`www.zeus.co.uk`), is an excellent commercial Web server for Linux. Zeus consistently turns in superlative numbers in benchmark tests (like the SPECWeb99 Web server benchmarks published by the Standard Performance Evaluation Corporation, `www.spec.org/osg/web99`).

The original version of Zeus was designed for raw speed, with a minimum of overhead (features and functions). That version of Zeus is still available as version 1.0. Subsequent releases of the product include a full list of advanced functions expected in a modern e-commerce Web server. Zeus competes well with Apache in nearly every area, including speed, functionality, configurability, and scalability. The one area in which Zeus cannot best Apache is cost. Zeus Web Server version 3 currently costs $1700 (U.S.) or €1900 (Europe).

Two features of Zeus that have traditionally appealed to Web server administrators are its Apache/NCSA `httpd` compatibility (support for `.htaccess` files, for example) and the fact that it can be completely configured from a Web browser. Zeus is especially popular with Web hosting services and ISPs that host customer Web sites, and the company increasingly targets this market. Zeus is available for Unix and Linux platforms.

IBM

Most of the Web servers discovered in my survey that did not fall into one of the big three (Apache, Microsoft, Netscape) were running on some type of IBM hardware, indicated by Lotus-Domino. Most of them are really running a special version of Apache. Several years ago, IBM stunned the computing world by announcing their intention to support Apache as a Web server included with their Internet commerce solutions. They have since brought Apache to market as IBM HTTP Server, which is bundled with their e-commerce solutions such as the IBM WebSphere Application Server. IBM markets their server as being "powered by Apache." IBM HTTP Server runs only on IBM hardware.

Microsoft IIS

Microsoft's Internet Information Server (IIS) version 5 is listed here with the commercial servers, because, although it is provided free as part of the NT Option Pack 4 and Windows 2000 Server, you must purchase one of these operating systems from Microsoft in order to use it. The NT Option Pack can be downloaded from www.microsoft.com, or if you're a subscriber to the Microsoft TechNet, you'll find it on one of your subscription CDs.

The performance of IIS 5.0 will surprise you. IIS stands as an exception to the oversized, underpowered applications that often seem to hog all the resources on an NT or Windows 2000 Server system, and cry for more. Microsoft seems to be quite serious about the Web, and for shops that are heavy users of NT/2000, IIS is a very respectable platform for Web site development. IIS, however, does not run on Linux. Using IIS forces you to run Microsoft NT or Windows 2000 platform.

Covalent

The last commercial Web server that I'll discuss is actually (like Stronghold) Apache itself, but sold as a value-added product by a company called Covalent Technologies (www.covalent.net). Covalent, a small, privately held firm in Lincoln, Nebraska, once sold an Apache-based Web server with SSL security bolted on, which they called Raven SSL. In 1999, at about the time the Apache developers were completing the first beta release of Apache 2.0, Covalent received a major shot in the arm in the form of a large cash infusion from several investment capital firms. With this funding, Covalent began to assemble a team of "Apache experts" to work on the company's new Web server offerings. Since the Covalent servers were based on Apache, this meant they were also working on the open-source Apache project, but now getting paid for their contribution.

Covalent's influence on the Apache development process has been most visible with the 2.0 version of Apache. While Apache 2.0 will remain open source, it's possible that new features will appear first in the Covalent licensed servers before being fed back into the open-source version. Certainly this was true of the final beta releases of Apache 2.0.

Two things are for sure: Covalent will continue to be a major force in Apache development, and it appears to have a healthy respect for the open-source community. Partnership deals with several strong companies will also help Covalent. For example, Compaq will preconfigure its ProLiant servers with Covalent Enterprise Ready Server.

A lot of marketing spin is used to distinguish the Covalent server from standard Apache. While it is certainly true that Covalent servers have some add-on configuration and logging utilities that enhance the value of the underlying Apache engine, they are basically Apache 2.0 at heart. The real advantage of using Covalent is that, like the Red Hat Linux distribution, it comes with all the pieces tested, preconfigured, and ready-to-run. It can greatly simplify the task of setting up a new Apache server for someone who isn't familiar with the process. If you are attempting to set up a server with a fairly complex array of modules or a number of virtual hosts, Covalent may be the ticket for you. Covalent's Enterprise Ready Server, at $1495/cpu, is not terribly costly, especially when compared to full-blown Java application servers. If the cost of Covalent doesn't appear high to you, it may just be your server of choice.

Companies that use SNMP-based system management applications (like HP OpenView, IBM Tivoli, or CA's Unicenter) can purchase the Covalent Manager Server for a nominal additional charge. This server has SNMP agents that allow monitoring and configuration from a remote management console—very nice, and not a feature that can be easily added to standard Apache 2.0.

The Features of Apache

OK, I've said good things about all of the Web servers that compete with Apache for mindshare among Internet Web site developers and administrators. I even said nice things about Microsoft's IIS. Any one of these servers is capable of adequately supporting a production Web server. So why is Apache the most widely used Web server on the Internet? This section outlines the most important features.

Standards Compliance   Apache offers full compliance with the HTTP/1.1 standard (RFC 2616). Apache has strong support for all the improvements made to the HTTP protocol in version 1.1, such as support for virtual hosts, persistent connections, client file uploading, enhanced error reporting, and resource caching (in proxy or gateway servers).

Apache also supports sophisticated content negotiation by HTTP/1.1 browsers, allowing multiple formats for a single resource to be served to meet the requirements of different clients. Multiple natural language support is a good example of how this is commonly used.

Scalability   Apache provides support for large numbers of Web sites on a single machine. Virtual hosting is the subject of Chapter 6 and is of particular interest to anyone who needs to host several Web sites on a single server. Many commercial Web hosting services take full advantage of Apache's low cost and strong support for virtual hosting.

Dynamic Shared Objects   Apache also supports Dynamic Shared Objects (DSOs). This permits loading of extension modules at runtime. Features can be added or removed without recompiling the server engine. Throughout the book, when explaining how to install a module, I will demonstrate how to compile it as a DSO and enable it for use when Apache is started. There are a few modules that cannot be dynamically linked to Apache and must be compiled into the Apache runtime, but not many. The DSO mechanism will be preserved in future releases of Apache, and learning to compile and use DSO modules is a critical skill for Apache administrators.

Customizability   Apache can be fully customized by writing modules using the Apache module API. Currently, these can be written in C or Perl. The code to implement a minimal module is far smaller than one might think. Source code is completely available for examination or alteration. The Apache license permits almost any use, private or commercial.

Another important feature is customizable logging, including the ability to write to multiple logs from different virtual servers. Apache logging is the subject of Chapter 11.

Also customizable in Apache are HTTP response headers for cache control and error reporting to the client browser. See Chapter 12 on enhancing Apache performance for a discussion of mod_header.

Programmability   Apache provides support for server programming using a variety of languages and integration techniques, including PHP, Perl, Java servlets, Java Server Pages, Active Server Pages, CGI, FastCGI, and Server-Side Includes. Chapter 8 discusses the scripting/programming tools available for Apache.

Potential Use As a Caching Proxy Server   Apache is not designed for general proxy use, but by using a module called mod_proxy, you can make it a very efficient caching proxy server. In other words, Apache can cache files received from remote servers and serve them directly to clients who request these resources, without downloading them again from the origin server. Caching for multiple clients (on a local area network, for example) can greatly speed up Web retrieval for clients of the proxy server, and reduce the traffic on an Internet connection. Chapter 12 discusses the use of mod_proxy.

Security   Apache's security features are the subject of Chapters 13 and 14. They include support for user authentication and the SSL protocol:

- Support for DBM (and other databases such as Oracle or MySQL) for user authentication allows very large lists of authorized users to be searched efficiently. In Chapter 13, I'll demonstrate two methods of user authentication against databases.

- Support for SSL allows the exchange of digital certificates and the encryption of data crossing the Internet. Secure Sockets Layer is already a critical component of any Internet-based Web server used for commercial purposes. In future years, expect to see reliable server and user authentication becoming more widely used on the Internet. Apache will always support the leading security mechanisms. In Chapter 14, I show how to set up Secure Sockets Layer in Apache and configure it to use server certificates that are either self-generated or issued by a well-known certificate authority like VeriSign.

Further Benefits

None of the major features outlined for the current Apache release is unique to Apache. The feature set alone, while impressive, is not enough to justify a decision to choose Apache over other excellent alternatives. There are, however, other benefits to Apache.

Apache has been ranked (by Netcraft) the number one Web server on the Internet since April 1996, and as this book goes to press, Apache powers an estimated 60% of all Web sites reachable through the Internet. While its popularity alone doesn't indicate its superiority, it does say that a lot of successful, high-volume sites have been built using Apache. That represents a huge vote of confidence in the software. It also means Apache is thoroughly tested. Its security, reliability, and overall performance are demonstrated, documented, and unquestionable.

Apache has unparalleled support from a tremendous group of individuals. Some are programmers; most are end users and administrators. For a software system as widely used as Apache, regardless of the nature of your problem, the odds are that someone somewhere has encountered it and can offer some insight into its resolution. While it might seem logical to assume that support for no-cost software will necessarily be inferior to that provided by commercial software vendors, I haven't found that to be true at all. As a professional network administrator, the most difficult problems I've had to solve were nearly all related to commercial software (for which I usually paid dearly) and often involved licensing servers and product keys. The usual answer from Tech Support is "you need to upgrade to the next revision level." Trust me, you won't have these problems with Apache.

Apache is under intense active development at all times, and yet many Web sites continue to operate just fine with Apache engines many revisions behind the current release. I believe it is the not-for-profit motivation of its developers that is responsible for this degree of dependability in each revision. There is simply no reason for Apache developers to rush to market with incomplete, bug-ridden releases. The result is a tremendous benefit to administrators who are already stressed trying to roll out product upgrades on an almost continuous basis.

The most compelling reason to use the Apache Web server is that, by design, Apache is highly configurable and extensible by virtue of its support for add-on modules. The Apache Application Program Interface (API) gives programmers access to Apache data structures and the ability to write routines to extend the Apache core functionality. It is possible, of course, to write modifications to any server for which the source code is freely available, but only Apache makes this easy with a well-documented API that doesn't require a module programmer to understand the Apache core source code. The upshot of all of this is that there are a wide variety of third-party modules available for Apache. You'll learn about the most important of these in relevant chapters throughout this book. From these modules, you can pick and choose the ones you need and forget the rest. Most of the standard modules provided with the basic server as distributed by the Apache Software Foundation are optional and can be removed from the server core if statically linked, or simply not used if they are compiled separately as dynamically loadable modules. It's a great alternative to programs bloated with functions that are never used.

The Architecture of Apache

I'll admit, when I first saw benchmarks showing that some HTTP servers were significantly faster than Apache, I doubted the test results and then wondered why anyone would choose Apache over one of these speed-demon Web servers.

Many of these servers do, indeed, outperform Apache at serving static resources to clients, both in response time and in the number of simultaneous clients they can handle. A closer examination of what these super-fast servers are capable of, however, revealed that much of their speed is achieved by stripping them of most of the functionality that is standard in Apache.

Most of the fast, small servers handle all client connections from a single process that is written to use nonblocking synchronous I/O multiplexing. That sounds impressive, doesn't it? Essentially, it means they make use of a call to a function called `select()`, which is available in operating systems like Linux. The `select()` function allows the calling process to be notified of an incoming connection on one or more sockets. In other words, the process is not blocked waiting for connections, but can be performing other tasks rather than sitting in a listening state. Using `select()` also allows data to be written and read on multiple sockets (I/O multiplexing); it notifies the calling process of which socket has data waiting in buffers to be written or read.

Apache on Linux systems is an example of a *preforking server*. This means that the main server starts a pool of processes to handle client requests, rather than forking a new process for each incoming request. Having the pooled processes already online and waiting (idle) greatly speeds up the process of serving requests. I find this model more robust than the single-process model using multiplexed I/O, because the main Apache server process is protected (it doesn't talk to any client) and is always available to restart child processes that misbehave or die unexpectedly. In fact, the default behavior of Apache is to kill and restart each client process after it has answered an arbitrary (user-configurable) number of requests. This eliminates the possibility that a small memory leak in any process will grow into a big problem if that process is allowed to run for many days, weeks, or even months.

Apache's use of a preforked process pool rather than a single process making use of `select()` is not a bad design decision, and especially not one that leads to less than adequate performance. Perhaps a more valid criticism of Apache is that it uses a pool, or *swarm*, of multiple processes rather than *threads* to handle requests. Apache provides the administrator with some control over the Apache process swarm. However, the benefits that can be achieved from these optimization options are small even in the best cases.

Unix systems traditionally schedule CPU time by process, and Apache has definite Unix roots. Threads, however, are less demanding of resources than processes, and are generally much faster to schedule, especially on multiprocessing operating systems with multiple processors that are capable of running multiple threads simultaneously. A move to fully threaded code in Apache should result in significant performance enhancements without sacrificing functionality and versatility. Apache 1.3 for NT/Windows 2000 is multithreaded (and runs as a single process or *task*, which is an NT/Windows 2000 service that creates multiple threads to handle connections). A major new feature of Apache version 2 (previewed later in this chapter) is the use of *multiple-processing modules*.

The important thing to keep in mind about speed and Apache is just how unimportant raw speed is on most Web servers. In fact, most Web servers function with less than 10Mbps of bandwidth, and most Internet Web servers are at the end of links no faster than a T1 line, which is 1.544Mbps. Apache, on a low-end Pentium workstation running Linux with only 64MB of RAM, can easily fill these data pipes. Anything faster is simply unnecessary, and every administrator needs to balance speed against limited functionality in many of the super-fast servers. A number of criteria should be used to determine the applicability of Web server software to the needs of the business, and speed is only one of these.

New Features of Apache Version 2.0

The Apache group released Apache version 1.3.0 as a stable product in June 1998, almost one year to the day after the release of version 1.2.0 in June 1997. Since that time, various interim versions of Apache 1.3 have been issued, mainly to implement security and bug fixes, but it is the 1.3 version of Apache that has proven wildly popular with Web site developers and administrators. The stability and excellent performance of Apache 1.3 is unquestionable.

In 2000, work began on a major rewrite of Apache version 2.0. As of mid-year 2000, new development efforts for Apache were applied to a beta version of Apache 2.0. The differences between Apache 1.3 and version 2.0 are mostly internal, primarily of interest to Apache module programmers, and don't significantly change the way Apache is installed, configured, and administered. A few new modules were added to Apache 2.0, and a few old modules were given enhanced functionality, but everything in this book is accurate for version 2.0. Most of the text is also applicable to version 1.3, which many administrators may choose to continue using for some time because of its tested reliability. Development work on Apache and all third-party Apache modules will be for Apache 2.0, and it will soon replace version 1.3 on nearly all Apache Web sites.

The most significant changes to Apache in version 2.0 are designed to increase the portability of Apache, enhance the already strong support for add-on modules, and increase the performance of Apache on all platforms. The first of these changes involves moving the multiprocessing capability of Apache (currently implemented in Unix by one server process per client connection, and in Win32 as one "thread" per client) into *Multiple-Processing Modules (MPMs)*. These are responsible for mapping client requests to either a thread or a process, making it possible for one set of Apache code to work on multiple platforms. Apache version 2.0 includes MPMs for several different process-forking schemes in Unix, and MPMs for NT/2000 and OS/2. On Unix systems that support POSIX-compliant threads, there is a new mode of operation for Apache called a *hybrid mode*. This enhancement is designed to improve the scalability of Apache, not necessarily the performance or stability of the server, and will make no difference at the majority of installed Apache sites.

The second change is also intended for programmers, and is designed to increase the cross-platform portability of code written to support Apache. Apache 2.0 will be packaged with an Application Program Interface (API) implemented in an Apache Portable Run-Time (APR) layer. The APR completely masks fundamental differences in the way platforms handle things like process forking and socket connections. Programmers working on Apache 2.0 and later versions will only need to ensure that they program to the APR to ensure that their programs, or modules, run on all supported platforms. For example, using the Apache Run-Time, a programmer will not really have to know the details of how processes are forked in both Unix and NT/2000, where the system calls are quite different. The programmer will need to learn only how to spawn or fork a process in the Apache Run-Time to produce code that works identically on both platforms.

The third change to Apache in version 2.0, and the one that most affects us as system administrators, is in the way that Apache modules register *callbacks*, or functions, with the Apache server. Here again, while the details of the changes in 2.0 are germane only to the Apache programmer, the implications of this change directly affect all Apache server administrators, because modules written for Apache 1.3 will not work with 2.0 without being recoded for Apache 2.0 and recompiled. Before moving your site to Apache 2.0, carefully ensure that you have 2.0 versions of all the Apache modules you'll require. Ports of the core modules will probably be released along with version 2.0, but third-party modules may not be modified immediately.

Apache 2.0 incorporates changes that the Apache Software Foundation and the principal Apache developers consider essential to maintaining the viability of the Apache server in an increasingly commercial Internet. A move to Apache 2.0 will be essential to any Apache site that wants to remain leading edge. The question is *when would be the best time to upgrade to Apache 2.0?* As with all software in production use, the answer to that question is determined by the features that will improve your site with added capabilities or increased performance. Simply upgrading to have the very latest version is a time-consuming, frustrating, never-ending exercise. Consider all the angles before making your decision to update.

In Sum

In this chapter, we looked at what Web server software powers the Internet and saw that fully 60% of all Internet-accessible Web servers are running Apache, and most on Linux platforms. Only on the very largest Internet sites does Apache yield prominence to commercial engines, for reasons that probably have less to do with the suitability of Apache than with the fact that many large firms are still reluctant to rely on open-source software (an attitude that has rapidly eroded in the past few years, and will continue to do so as Linux grows more capable and reliable). The major Web servers that compete with Apache have some strong features, but the feature set of Apache is sufficient to sustain its dominance.

These first two chapters have served as an extended introduction to Apache and its foundations. Beginning in the next chapter, we'll (metaphorically) roll up our sleeves and start getting our fingernails dirty—that is, we'll install the server on a Linux system. Then, in succeeding chapters, we'll move on to various aspects of configuring Apache.

Part 2

Essential Configuration

Featuring

- Downloading, compiling, and installing Apache from source code
- Installing precompiled Apache binary files
- The role of Apache directives in the `httpd.conf` file
- General server directives
- Container directives
- Setting up user home directories
- How modules work
- Linking modules statically or as dynamic shared objects
- Using apxs
- IP-based virtual hosting
- Name-based virtual hosting
- Virtual hosting guidelines

3

Installing Apache

The previous two chapters presented an overview of the Web and its history, and introduced Apache as well as other Web servers commonly used on the Internet. The topics of installing, configuring, and administering Apache begin here, in this chapter.

One of the important things to realize about installing Apache is that there are two completely different ways to do it. You can choose to download the source code and compile it on your own machine, or you can take the easier route and download binary files that have already been compiled for your specific machine and operating system.

Both methods of installation have merit, and both are discussed in this chapter, with step-by-step examples of the procedures that you should use on your own Linux system. The installation of a basic Apache server is a straightforward process. Follow the instructions in this chapter, regardless of which installation method you choose, and soon you'll have a working Apache server, ready to configure.

The Decision to Compile

Before proceeding with this chapter, you should take some time to determine whether it makes sense to compile the Apache code yourself. There are a number of very good reasons to start with the source code and build your own personalized copy of Apache.

One of the reasons most often cited for the success of open-source software like Apache and Linux is that the source code is available for inspection and custom modification. That's certainly an enticement for C code hackers and for companies with the programming resources to customize the code. The vast majority of us, however, don't write customized Apache code. Instead, we benefit from the code improvements made by others.

Compiling Apache from the source code makes it possible to add user-written modifications (or *patches*) to the code. Patches are essentially files that contain changes to a source code base and are usually created by *diffing* modified source to the original—in other words, comparing the modified and original source files and saving the differences in a file distributed as a patch. Another user acquires the patch, applies it to the same source code base to reproduce the modifications, and then compiles the altered source.

Patches make it possible for nonprogrammers to make (often quite sophisticated) changes to source code and then compile it themselves. Without the ability to patch the source and compile it yourself, you need to search for precompiled binaries that already include the necessary patches. Depending on your particular platform, it might be difficult to locate binaries that include the patches you require.

Another reason to compile from source code is that it allows you to take advantage of compiler optimizations for your hardware platform and operating system. This consideration is by no means as important as it was once, because chances are you can easily find binaries for your particular system. Figure 3.1 shows the binary distributions of Apache available from the Apache Project Web site for a variety of platforms. In the unlikely circumstance that your operating system is missing from this list, you can always download and compile the Apache source yourself.

Figure 3.1   Apache binary distributions

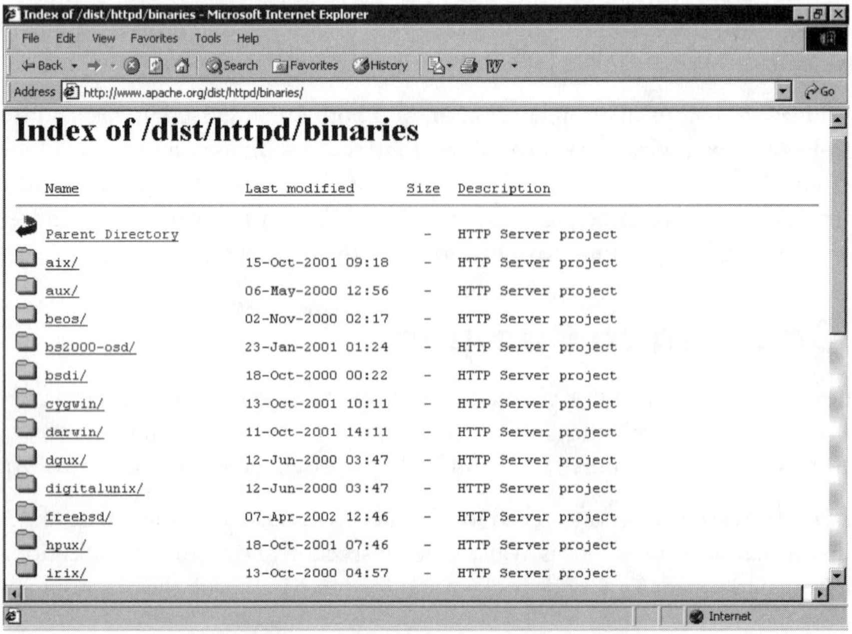

It is not necessary to compile source code on your own hardware to optimize the resulting binary. Most binaries are already optimized for a given type of hardware. For example, to run on an Intel 486 or Pentium system, download an i386 binary or an i686 binary for the Pentium II or Pentium III processor. A compiler designed to optimize code to run on an Intel processor was probably used to create the binary. It is unlikely that your compiler will produce code that performs significantly better. Some companies offer Linux distributions that are optimized for performance on Pentium-class Intel processors (Mandrake Linux is one such distribution: www.linux-mandrake.com). If the fastest possible system performance is your goal, you should consider such a Linux distribution teamed with more or faster hardware.

The Easiest Route: Precompiled Binaries

One word of warning about using binaries is in order. Often, the available binaries lag behind new releases. If you want to stay on the "bleeding edge" of changes, you must use source code distributions, which is not always the best decision for production servers.

You will need the Apache source to use Apache modules that require Apache source-code patching, or if you intend to extend Apache by writing your own Apache modules. There are very few modules that require source-code patching today and even fewer programmers who actually modify the Apache source. Chances are slim that you will need to compile Apache from source for either of these reasons.

Another reason to compile your Apache server is to take advantage of the very latest functionality of Apache modules that have rapid development cycles, and so you don't have to wait for someone to prepare a binary distribution of Apache with this new functionality. You may even be authoring your own Apache modules, in which case you absolutely *must* have access to the source code. (To be honest, there are few administrators of Apache servers that absolutely must compile Apache from source; the binary distributions, tested and true, are adequate for most production servers, and contain nearly every desirable extension module.) The real reason most Apache administrators compile from source, however, is because they simply want to, perhaps for a better understanding of the process, but more likely because that process interests and involves them. Most were drawn to Linux and open-source software for exactly that reason. So, I believe the best reason to compile Apache from source code is because you want to, and I would encourage everyone to go the compiled route at least once for the experience. Discard any notions you may have that compiling Apache is an arduous process fraught with danger (especially if you've been around long enough remember how painful the process was a decade ago, when it usually required an intimate knowledge of arcane details about your operating system). A tremendous amount of work has gone into the scripts that Apache uses to determine how best to compile itself on your platform and to optimize its performance for your hardware.

Use an Apache binary distribution whenever you need only a basic Apache server with the Apache modules included in that distribution. Say, for example, that you are a system administrator whose success relies on the security, stability, and reliability of software that has been tested and debugged (preferably by someone else) until it is good enough for your needs. You're also willing to wait on new program enhancements until these are tested and proven. If this is you, stick with a binary distribution of Apache, preferably from the vendor of your Linux distribution. Such a binary distribution will contain all standard Apache modules compiled separately from the server as DSO (dynamic shared object) modules. You can pick and choose the ones you want, using only those that you require and disabling the others to conserve the memory required to run Apache. If all the functionality you require is available in the set of standard Apache modules and your operating system is supported, you have nothing to lose by installing one of these. Even if you require a few modules not included with the binary distribution, most of these are easily compiled without requiring the Apache source; they require only minor configuration changes and a server restart to enable them.

Two major benefits of using binary distributions are standardization and speed. While compiling Apache on most of today's systems is a pretty quick process, if you have to do it for many systems, it could become a time-consuming chore. If you intend to roll out Apache to a number of servers, particularly in the case of an upgrade, using binaries will tremendously speed this process—especially if you can script it or control it remotely. And when you are done, you will have identical files stored in identical locations on all of your servers. Every major Linux distribution contains a binary copy of Apache. If that Apache version completely satisfies your requirements for a Web server, and you have no particular desire to go through the process of compiling the server from source code, the best choice for you is probably to load the binary version that comes with your Linux distribution. You'll be guaranteed that it's going to start and run, and you shouldn't worry about sacrificing either performance or functionality.

If you decide to compile Apache, continue with the next section. If, however, you decide that you can work with precompiled binaries, feel free to skip the material on compiling Apache and move ahead to the "Installing the Apache Binaries" section later in this chapter. The information on compiling Apache will always be here if you need it in the future.

Downloading Apache Source Code

Download the source code for Apache by pointing your Web browser at www.apache.org/dist or one of its mirror sites (see Figure 3.2). Download the latest Apache, which will be in Unix tar format, compressed with the GNU Zip (gzip, or simply gz) utility. The Apache 2.0 source code archive used in this chapter was named httpd-2.0.35.tar.Z, though you will probably download a more recent version.

> **NOTE**   Note that Apache versions that are earlier than 2.0 will have a file-name beginning with `apache-` rather than `httpd-`.

Figure 3.2   The Apache source code distribution site

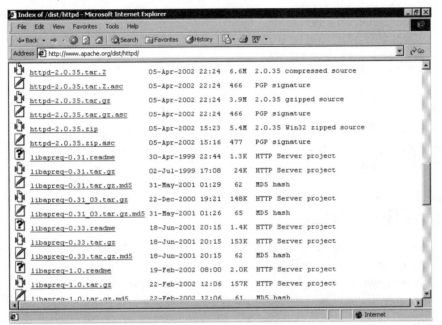

Change directory to the location where you intend to unpack the Apache source code and compile the server. A common location for source code on Linux systems is the `/usr/local/src` directory, and that's a pretty logical choice. If you want to place the Apache source in a subdirectory of `/usr/local/src`, do the following:

```
# cd /usr/local/src
```

From this directory, invoke the Linux tar utility to decompress the archive and extract the files. `tar` will automatically create the necessary directories. When the operation is finished, you will have the Apache source saved in the directory `/usr/local/src/httpd-2.0.35`.

```
# tar xvzf /downloads/httpd-2.0.35.tar.gz
httpd-2.0.35/
httpd-2.0.35/.gdbinit
httpd-2.0.35/ABOUT_APACHE
```

```
httpd-2.0.35/Apache.dsp
httpd-2.0.35/Apache.dsw
httpd-2.0.35/BuildBin.dsp
httpd-2.0.35/CHANGES
httpd-2.0.35/INSTALL
httpd-2.0.35/InstallBin.dsp
httpd-2.0.35/LICENSE
httpd-2.0.35/Makefile.in
httpd-2.0.35/Makefile.win
httpd-2.0.35/NWGNUmakefile
httpd-2.0.35/README      many files extracted
```

The top-level Apache source directory is /usr/local/src/httpd-2.0.35 and I'll refer to this as the Apache source directory frequently in the book. If you install Apache from source, you'll return frequently to this directory, to make changes to your Apache installation. This directory is distinct from the Apache installation directory, where you'll install Apache and from where you'll run it.

Compiling Apache

The very oldest (pre-1.3) versions of Apache were compiled by manually editing a Configuration.tmpl file, running the ./configure command, and then running the make utility. An editor was used to customize the compiler flags (EXTRA_CFLAGS, LIBS, LDFLAGS, INCLUDES) stored in the template as needed for a given system. To compile Apache successfully, you had to have quite a bit of knowledge about your system, or find someone who had performed the install on a similar system and would share the secret of how it was done.

One enhancement of Apache that appeared in version 1.3 was an automated configuration utility that mirrored the GNU Autoconf Project (www.gnu.org/software/autoconf/), but was not based on the GNU code. For this reason, the Apache installation script in version 1.3 was called APache AutoConf-style Interface (or, simply, APACI). All 1.3.*x* versions of Apache included the APACI configuration utility. For Apache 2.0, however, the installation scripts, which bear a strong resemblance to the Apache 1.3 APACI utility, have been rewritten to use GNU Autoconf.

The Autoconf Utility

Autoconf provides an easy way to configure the Apache source prior to compilation in order to specify certain compiler options and the inclusion (or exclusion) of Apache modules. Autoconf also performs a number of tests in order to ascertain details about your system hardware and operating system that are relevant to the Apache source compilation.

Autoconf does not compile the Apache source; its purpose is to create the files that specify how that compilation is performed. Its most important task is to create the *makefiles* that are used by the Linux make utility to direct the C compiler how to proceed, and also where to place the compiled programs when make is instructed to perform an install. Autoconf is used to generate a configure script for an application that can, in turn, be used to generate the makefiles that compile the actual C source code for the application. In compiling Apache, you'll use an Autoconf-generated configure script (which comes packaged with the Apache source) instead of using Autoconf directly.

The Need for ANSI-C

The Apache source code is written in C language that is compliant with the specifications codified by the American National Standards Institute, or ANSI-C. For that reason, you will need an ANSI-C–compliant compiler to complete the install. This is not a big deal, because your Linux distribution includes the GNU C compiler (gcc), which is the ANSI-C compiler recommended by the Apache Software Foundation. If the configure script is unable to locate a suitable compiler, you will be notified, and the configuration will abort. You can then install gcc from your Linux CD-ROM or from www.gnu.org. The Free Software Foundation makes binary distributions available for Linux and a large number of Unix platforms, or you can download and compile the source code yourself, although compiling gcc can turn into a time-consuming exercise. Binary distributions of gcc are well optimized, so it is unlikely that you can build a more efficient C compiler.

The *configure* Script

You'll find a shell script named configure in the top-level Apache source directory. This script does not compile the Apache server; its function is to examine your system to identify its capabilities and locate the supporting files it needs. The configure script may warn you that it can't build Apache, and give instructions on how to correct problems it finds. On most systems running a fairly recent version of Linux, this will not occur. Once configure determines that it can build Apache on your system, it then identifies the best possible combination of options for that system. The information it gathers and the decisions it makes about configuring Apache for your system are written into a special file that you'll find stored in config.status. In this file it stores information specific to your system (including build options you specify to configure) and information on how to create the makefiles necessary to build Apache entirely from scratch.

You will usually run `configure` with a number of options (command-line arguments) to customize your Apache configuration. In fact, if you run `configure` without command-line arguments, it will report, "Warning: Configuring Apache with default settings. This is probably not what you really want," and it probably isn't. The next few sections will show you how to specify additional options to `configure`, or override its default values. This is a procedure you'll return to many times, whenever you need to alter your Apache configuration or change its functionality by adding new modules. The following `configure` statement compiles Apache version 2.0.35. Note that this is a single Linux command with three arguments; the backslash (\) character is used to continue the command on a new line. It's a handy trick for manually entering long command lines, and can also be used to improve the readability of shell script files.

```
# ./configure \
"--with-layout=Apache" \
"--enable-mods-shared=most"
```

The `--with-layout` argument in the example above tells Apache to look for the Apache section of the `config.layout` file, which can be found in the top directory of the Apache source tree. This section of the file will be used to set default values for the directories where Apache files will be stored. The Apache layout is the most commonly used, although there are sections of the file for other layouts such as `RedHat`, which will install Apache files into the same directories as the Red Hat Linux distribution.

Any one of the default values provided by `config.layout` can be overridden, however. There are many times you may want to install into an alternate directory—for example, if you do not want to install a second Apache version alongside one that already exists. (I have five versions of Apache on my server for testing purposes.) Another reason you may want to install Apache into an alternate directory is to preserve the default locations used by a Linux distribution. For example, assume the version of Apache that comes with your Linux distribution is installed in /etc/apache instead of the default /usr/local/apache directory. Use `--prefix` to install Apache in the /etc/apache directory. (For standard file location layouts, see the discussion on the `config.layout` file below.)

To enable support for DSOs, for example, add the `--enable-shared=max` option, which causes Apache to build all modules as DSOs, with the exception of two, `http_core` and `mod_so`, both of which must be statically linked into the Apache kernel. The `http_core` module provides core directives for managing the Apache server, and `mod_so` enables the server to use DSO modules.

Why Use DSOs?

The extension of Apache Server through the use of modules has always been part of its design, but it wasn't until release 1.3 that Apache supported dynamic loadable modules. These dynamic shared objects are available in Apache on Linux and other operating systems that support the necessary system functions for a program to load a module into its address space with a system call. This is similar to the way dynamic link library (or DLL) files work in Microsoft Windows; in fact, DLLs are used to provide this functionality in the Windows version of Apache.

The use of DSO modules in Apache has several advantages. First, the server can be far more flexible, because modules can be enabled or disabled at runtime, without the need to relink the Apache kernel. Also, the exclusion of unnecessary modules reduces the size of the Apache executable, which can be a factor when many server instances are run in a limited memory space.

On Linux systems, the only significant disadvantage to using DSO modules is that the server is approximately 20 percent slower to load at startup time because of the system overhead of resolving the symbol table for the dynamic links.

In virtually all cases, Linux administrators should build their Apache server to make maximum use of DSO modules.

Most Linux users will probably want to use the --enable-mods-shared=most option to enable all the standard modules in the Apache distribution known to be usable on all platforms supported by Apache. Table 3.1 lists the modules that are installed when you specify --enable-mods-shared=most, and contains all of the most commonly used Apache modules. There are a few modules (see Table 3.2) that are not included in the Apache build using --enable-mods-shared=most. If you need one or more of these, you may decide to use, instead, --enable-mods-shared=all which compiles and installs every module in the Apache distribution.

WARNING   Red Hat Linux 7.0 users will not be able to compile Apache with mod_auth_dbm and should use the --disable-module=auth_dbm directive to disable use of that module. This problem does not occur in earlier or later versions of the Red Hat Linux distribution.

Table 3.1 Apache Modules Installed with `--enable-mods-shared=most`

Module	Purpose of the Module
mod_env	Sets environment variables for use by CGI and SSI pages
mod_setenvif	Permits the selective setting of environment variables if certain criteria are met
mod_mime	Determines the MIME type and encoding of a document based on its filename extension
mod_negotiation	Allows the server to determine the best encoding or language type sent to a client browser based on the browser's preferences and available document variations (content negotiation)
mod_alias	Permits the simple redirection of user requests and alteration of the mapping between the URL and the filesystem
mod_rewrite	Permits complex transformations of request URLs to permit complete control over redirection of requests
mod_userdir	Permits system users to set up their own Web pages under their home directories
mod_speling	Attempts to correct common spelling errors in request URLs
mod_vhost_alias	Permits virtual hosts that are dynamically configured from the request URL
mod_dir	Provides for "trailing slash" translation and for serving the directory "index" page
mod_autoindex	Provides for serving directory indexes when an index page is not provided for a directory
mod_access	Provides for the most simple form of access control based on information in the client request header (for example, the IP address)
mod_headers	Permits the use of customized HTTP request headers
mod_expires	Permits the generation of the HTTP Expires header to control browser and proxy server caching
mod_asis	Permits the sending of files that already contain their own HTTP response headers
mod_include	Permits the use of Server-Side Includes (SSI)

Table 3.1   Apache Modules Installed with `--enable-mods-shared=most` (*continued*)

Module	Purpose of the Module
mod_cgi	Permits the execution of Common Gateway Interface (CGI) scripts
mod_actions	Permits the execution of specific CGI scripts based on the document type
mod_status	Provides a page that gives information about server activity and performance
mod_info	Provides a page that gives information about the server configuration and capabilities
mod_log_config	Handles the logging of requests and responses handled by the server
mod_imap	Provides for handling of image maps (`.map` files)
mod_so	Permits the loading of DSO modules at server startup
mod_dav	Provides support for Distributed Authoring and Versioning (WebDAV)
mod_auth	Provides HTTP Basic Authentication using username/password data in plain text files
mod_auth_anon	Provides emulation of the behavior of FTP "anonymous" access
mod_auth_dbm	Provides HTTP Basic Authentication using username/password data in Unix-style DBM database
mod_auth_digest	Implements user authentication using MD5 Digest Authentication

Table 3.2 lists the very few modules that are packaged with the Apache distribution, but not enabled by use of the `--enable-mods-shared=most` option. On Linux systems, I recommend configuring Apache `--enable-mods-shared=most` and manually adding any modules from Table 3.2 that you require. For example, to manually add `mod_mime_magic` (which attempts to determine the file type from the file contents, rather than another method like the filename extension), you might use this command:

```
# ./configure "--enable-mods-shared=most mime_magic"
```

Note that the leading `mod_` is stripped from the module name, and the specified modules are separated by spaces. Whenever a single modifier contains the space character, the entire option should be enclosed in double quotes. In fact, you might get in the habit of always quoting your configure options, as it doesn't cause problems even when it isn't absolutely required.

You cannot have a single list of modules that you want to disallow from your configuration; each must be disabled with a separate option. See the example below, which is a single command, split across lines for clarity (using the "\" character at the end of the line):

```
# ./configure \
"--enable-mods-shared=most" \
"--disable-cgi" \
"--disable-include"
```

Here, mod_cgi and mod_include are disabled, essentially removed from the list of modules enabled by the --enable-mods-shared=most option.

Table 3.2   Apache Modules Omitted by --enable-mods-shared=most

Module	Purpose of the Module
mod_mime_magic	Determines a file's MIME type by examining the first few bytes of the file (the "magic" bytes). Discussed in Chapter 15.
mod_cern_meta	Emulates the "metafile" semantics of the legacy CERN HTTP server. If you don't know what this means, you definitely don't need the module.
mod_usertrack	Generates a special "clickstream" log for tracking individual user sessions and activity. Discussed in Chapter 11.
mod_unique_id	Generates a unique identifier for each client request, which can even be unique among a cluster of servers (if properly configured). These identifiers are used for arcane purposes not discussed in this book.

There are a few modules that are not installed when either "most" or "all" is passed with the --enable-modules or --enable-mods-shared switches. These modules must be manually, and individually, enabled with the configure switches shown in Table 3.3.

Table 3.3 Apache Modules That *Must* Be Manually Enabled

Module	Purpose of the Module	Switch to Enable
mod_charset_lite	An experimental module that tells Apache the source character set of resources, and a character set to which to translate the resource before serving it. mod_charset_lite does *not* perform the translation.	--disable-charset-lite
mod_cgid	Executes CGI scripts using a daemon process separate from the Apache server.	--disable-cgid
mod_ext_filter	Experimental module that allows Apache output to be passed through an external process (filter) before being sent to the client browser.	--enable-ext-filter
mod_suexec	Permits CGI scripts to run under an administrator-specified system user account.	--enable-suexec
mod_cache	Experimental module primarily used for caching either proxied data either on disk or in shared memory.	--enable-cache
mod_file_cache	Experimental module for caching frequently accessed files in memory.	--enable-file-cache
mod_deflate	Experimental module to deflate (or compress) data before sending it to the client.	--enable-deflate
mod_ssl	Provides Secure Sockets Layer (SSL) connections (covered in Chapter 14).	--enable-ssl

Essential Configuration

PART 2

Table 3.3 Apache Modules That *Must* Be Manually Enabled (*continued*)

Module	Purpose of the Module	Switch to Enable
mod_example	Provides an example to programmers of how to create an Apache module using the Apache 2.0 API.	--enable-example
mod_proxy	Implements an HTTP/1.1 proxy/gateway server, as discussed in Chapter 12.	--enable-proxy
mod_proxy_http	Required for mod_proxy to proxy HTTP requests.	--enable-proxy-http
mod_proxy_ftp	Required for mod_proxy to proxy FTP requests.	--enable-proxy-ftp
mod_proxy_connect	Required for mod_proxy to proxy CONNECT requests.	--enable-proxy-connect

Throughout the book, as I discuss adding additional modules, I'll describe how to use additional arguments to configure to alter the way Apache is built. You can tailor your configuration for any combination of modules from the Linux distribution and some that are distributed separately from other sources. In nearly every case, though, the examples given above, while simple, are as complicated as you'll need to get. For Linux systems, I consider the following command line sufficient to build an Apache 2.0 system suitable for nearly every server requirement:

```
#./configure --enable-mods-shared=most
```

The configure script essentially creates a set of instructions to the compiler for compiling the source files into a working system. It uses information you provide, along with other information about the capabilities of your system, such as what function libraries are available. The result is primarily a set of Makefiles, which instruct the Linux make utility how to compile source files, link them to required function libraries, and install them in their proper locations.

Whenever you run the configure script, it creates a file with the name config.log in the Apache source directory (or overwrites the file if it already exists). This file contains output from the Autoconf configure script and is used to debug problems that occur when configure is running. The file is generally uninteresting, but one of the first lines will contain the complete command line that was used to run configure. The first few lines of config.log typically look like the ones in Listing 3.1.

Listing 3.1: A Typical **config.status** File

```
# head config.log
[root@Lynx httpd-2.0.36]# head config.log
This file contains any messages produced by compilers while
running configure, to aid debugging if configure makes a mistake.

It was created by configure, which was
generated by GNU Autoconf 2.53.  Invocation command line was

  $ ./configure --with-layout=Apache --enable-mods-shared=all --enable-ssl
--enable-proxy --enable-proxy-http --enable-proxy-ftp --enable-cache --enable-
disk-cache --enable-mem-cache


## --------- ##
## Platform. ##
```

The *config.layout* File

The paths that Apache uses to locate files during compilation and to determine where
to move files during the installation are stored in a special configuration file named
config.layout, which you will find in the Apache source directory. This file contains
collections of directory paths to be used as defaults on different types of systems. Each
of these collections is identified by a system name, and so they are called *named layouts*. When you run configure, Apache attempts to guess the operating system using a
helper script, src/helpers/GuessOS. If its best guess matches the name of one of the
named layouts, it uses that layout to determine the correct path information. Otherwise, it uses the Apache default setup, which is defined in config.layout as layout
"Apache." The Apache layout is shown in Listing 3.2.

Listing 3.2: The Apache Path Layout in config.layout

```
#    Classical Apache path layout.
<Layout Apache>
    prefix:         /usr/local/apache2
    exec_prefix:    ${prefix}
    bindir:         ${exec_prefix}/bin
    sbindir:        ${exec_prefix}/bin
    libexecdir:     ${exec_prefix}/modules
    mandir:         ${prefix}/man
    sysconfdir:     ${prefix}/conf
    datadir:        ${prefix}
    installbuilddir: ${datadir}/build
    errordir:       ${datadir}/error
    iconsdir:       ${datadir}/icons
```

```
        htdocsdir:       ${datadir}/htdocs
        manualdir:       ${datadir}/manual
        cgidir:          ${datadir}/cgi-bin
        includedir:      ${prefix}/include
        localstatedir:   ${prefix}
        runtimedir:      ${localstatedir}/logs
        logfiledir:      ${localstatedir}/logs
        proxycachedir:   ${localstatedir}/proxy
    </Layout>
```

Each line of config.layout defines a directory pathname. Some of the paths are derived from others previously defined in the file. You might note from this layout that all the paths are derived from the one identified as prefix. Therefore, simply by running configure with the --prefix argument to change this location, you automatically change *all* of the default paths for the Apache installation.

You can specify a named layout when running configure by using the --with-layout argument. For example, if you choose to use the same file locations that Red Hat Linux uses, specify configure with the --with-layout=RedHat argument:

```
    # ./configure --with-layout=RedHat
```

It's important to realize that config.layout is a convenience and is used to provide a single location in which a number of directory paths are set. Apache will store data in these directories (or expect to find it there).

You can modify config.layout creating a custom layout, as described later, if you want to change any of these paths, or you can override and change any default with a separate configure option. Table 3.4 lists all of the configure options used to set Apache's paths.

Table 3.4   configure Options to Set Apache's Paths

Option	Specifies Location For...
--bindir=DIR	User executables
--sbindir=DIR	System executables
--libexecdir=DIR	Supporting libraries (DSO modules)
--mandir=DIR	Apache manual (man) pages
--sysconfdir=DIR	Configuration files (httpd.conf)
--datadir=DIR	Read-only data files

Table 3.4   configure Options to Set Apache's Paths (*continued*)

Option	Specifies Location For...
--iconsdir=DIR	Image files used by Apache
--htdocsdir=DIR	Read-only document files
--cgidir=DIR	Read-only CGI files
--includedir=DIR	Includes files
--localstatedir=DIR	Writeable data files
--runtimedir=DIR	Runtime data
--logfiledir=DIR	Apache log files
--proxycachedir=DIR	Proxy cache data

The following example uses path variables as configure arguments to install all of Apache's user executables in /usr/bin and all system executables in /usr/sbin, which is where the Red Hat layout puts them. All other layout options are read from the Apache layout in config.layout. The following command accomplishes the same thing as the custom layout shown later in Listing 3.3:

```
# ./configure --bindir=/usr/bin --sbindir=/usr/sbin
```

For those readers who are using the Red Hat Linux distribution, the Apache that is provided as a Red Hat Package (RPM) uses a layout that looks like this:

```
#   Red Hat Linux 7.x layout
<Layout RedHat>
    prefix:         /usr
    exec_prefix:    ${prefix}
    bindir:         ${prefix}/bin
    sbindir:        ${prefix}/sbin
    libdir:         ${prefix}/lib
    libexecdir:     ${prefix}/lib/apache
    mandir:         ${prefix}/man
    sysconfdir:     /etc/httpd/conf
    datadir:        /var/www
    installbuilddir: ${datadir}/build
    errordir:       ${datadir}/error
    iconsdir:       ${datadir}/icons
```

```
        htdocsdir:      ${datadir}/html
        manualdir:      ${datadir}/manual
        cgidir:         ${datadir}/cgi-bin
        includedir:     ${prefix}/include/apache
        localstatedir: /var
        runtimedir:     ${localstatedir}/run
        logfiledir:     ${localstatedir}/log/httpd
        proxycachedir: ${localstatedir}/cache/httpd
    </Layout>
```

Note that, since the Red Hat layout modifies the Apache prefix variable, all paths are altered, because all depend on prefix. The Red Hat layout actually tries to put files into more standard directories. Rather than storing Apache binaries in a special directory (like /usr/local/apache/bin), Red Hat places them in the Linux directories that are actually reserved for them, /usr/bin and /usr/sbin. Likewise, Red Hat prefers to keep Apache configuration files under /etc, a directory in which you'll find configuration files for a large number of other Linux utilities, such as FTP, DNS, sendmail, and others.

Creating and Using a Custom Layout

The best way to modify an Apache layout is to create a custom layout of your own. This is quite easy if you copy another layout in the config.layout file, rename it, and make your modifications to the new custom layout. You use this layout during the Apache compilation by calling it with a name of your own choosing. This is what I recommend, and Listing 3.3 shows a custom layout that I have used, named MyApache. I modified the standard Apache layout and made two changes to put the Apache executables in the same locations as the Red Hat layout shown above. I'm running a Red Hat system, and this places them where Red Hat's startup files expect to find them.

As noted, many administrators consider it inherently risky to edit the default layout directly; they prefer to leave the original layout values intact and work on a copy. Apache's use of named layouts makes it easy to follow this approach. You might add a layout to config.layout like the one shown in Listing 3.3.

WARNING Avoid leaving blank lines within a custom Apache layout; these will confuse the parser.

Listing 3.3: A Custom Path Layout

```
# Aulds' Modified Apache path layout.
<Layout MyApache>
# Use all other Apache layout options,
```

```
# but install user and system
# executables as Red Hat does
    bindir:        /usr/bin
    sbindir:       /usr/sbin
# end of changes from Apache layout
    prefix:        /usr/local/apache2
    exec_prefix:   ${prefix}
    libexecdir:    ${exec_prefix}/modules
    mandir:        ${prefix}/man
    sysconfdir:    ${prefix}/conf
    datadir:       ${prefix}
    installbuilddir: ${datadir}/build
    errordir:      ${datadir}/error
    iconsdir:      ${datadir}/icons
    htdocsdir:     ${datadir}/htdocs
    manualdir:     ${datadir}/manual
    cgidir:        ${datadir}/cgi-bin
    includedir:    ${prefix}/include
    localstatedir: ${prefix}
    runtimedir:    ${localstatedir}/logs
    logfiledir:    ${localstatedir}/logs
    proxycachedir: ${localstatedir}/proxy
</Layout>
```

To use the new custom layout, run `configure` with the `--with-layout` argument and compile:

```
# ./configure --enable-layout=MyApache
```

The Other *configure* Command Options

You can get a complete list of all `configure` options by running the command with its `--help` argument. All of the variables that are used as named layout options are available, as well as all of the configuration options discussed earlier. The options I've shown are probably the only `configure` options that you'll ever need to use, but there are several others with far more specific purposes. For example, the `--enable-rule` option is used to enable compiler rules that are needed to compile Apache on certain systems. (Linux users will never need this.) There are also a number of options that deal with suEXEC (which is discussed in Chapter 4).

Making Apache

Upon completion of the configuration phase, you have constructed a set of makefiles in various places within your Apache source tree. The `make` command is used to begin the actual compilation phase of the install:

```
# make
```

```
Making all in srclib
make[1]: Entering directory `/usr/local/src/httpd-2.0.36/srclib'
Making all in apr
make[2]: Entering directory `/usr/local/src/httpd-2.0.36/srclib/apr'
Making all in strings
make[3]: Entering directory `/usr/local/src/httpd-2.0.36/srclib/apr/strings'
make[4]: Entering directory `/usr/local/src/httpd-2.0.36/srclib/apr/strings'
/bin/sh /usr/local/src/httpd-2.0.36/srclib/apr/libtool --silent --
mode=compile gcc -g -O2 -pthread   -DHAVE_CONFIG_H -DLINUX=2 -D_REENTRANT -
D_XOPEN_SOURCE=500 -D_BSD_SOURCE -D_SVID_SOURCE   -I../include
-I../include/arch/unix  -c apr_cpystrn.c && touch apr_cpystrn.lo

-- Many lines deleted --
```

You'll find that running make creates a file, httpd, in the libs directory beneath the top-level Apache source directory. This file will vary in size, depending on the modules you have enabled, and whether or not you've chosen to compile modules as DSOs. If you chose to build Apache using DSO modules, the httpd file will be roughly half the size of a statically linked Apache executable that uses the same modules. This is because it contains only the core functionality of Apache, and primarily serves to load the DSO modules at runtime that provide the rest.

Whether you built Apache as a single executable or using DSO modules, you'll probably want to take the optional step of reducing the size of the Apache httpd file using the Linux strip command. The strip command removes symbolic information that is used only by debuggers and other developer tools. For a production version of the Apache kernel, this information should be stripped to reduce the memory required by the server. The reduction is slight, but if you are running a number of Apache processes, the savings do add up. Be aware that once you strip symbol information from a binary file, you can no longer run debugging tools if you have problems running that program.

On my server, running strip on a freshly compiled Apache 2.0.36 executable reduced httpd to about 25 percent of the original size! For a statically linked binary:

```
# ls -al /usr/local/src/httpd-2.0.36/.libs
-rwxr-xr-x   1 root     root      2552103 Jun  1 11:48 httpd
# strip httpd
# ls -al /usr/local/src/httpd-2.0.36/.libs
-rwxr-xr-x   1 root     root       682088 Jun  1 11:59 httpd
```

The size reduction (and, consequently, the memory usage of the file), is just as significant on an Apache built to use DSOs:

```
# ls -al /usr/local/src/httpd-2.0.36/.libs
-rwxr-xr-x    1 root      root     1017523 Jun  1 12:55 httpd
```

```
# strip httpd
# ls -al /usr/local/src/httpd-2.0.36/.libs
-rwxr-xr-x     1 root      root          283924 Jun  1 13:06 httpd
```

The final step of the install is to call make again, this time with the `install` argument, which moves all the compiled binaries and support files to their default locations (or locations you specified in the configuration step above). Most files are copied into directories relative to the Apache root directory that you specified with the `--prefix` argument:

```
# make install
-- lines deleted
Installing configuration files
Installing HTML documents
Installing error documents
Installing icons
Installing CGIs
Installing header files
Installing man pages
Installing build system files
make[1]: Leaving directory `/usr/local/src/httpd-2.0.36'
```

With the appearance of the message above, you have installed an Apache system that should run after making a few simple changes to its configuration file.

If you compile Apache from source code, feel free to skip down to the section "Running the Server." That's where you'll learn to start the server.

Installing the Apache Binaries

Compiling Apache from source code is so easy, especially for Linux, that it should be your choice of installation method if you plan to make any alterations to the out-of-the-box Apache configuration. If you plan to add third-party modules that are not compiled as DSO objects or if you plan to modify your server to support programming environments like mod_perl or PHP, you have no choice; you *must* work with the Apache source code and compile it yourself.

On the other hand, if you need only a simple server, and your programming needs can be satisfied with simple CGI scripts, there are much quicker ways to get up and running. If you are not concerned with implementing specialized modules that aren't among those provided with the standard Apache distribution, consider using one of two alternatives to compiling Apache. The first of these is to install Apache precompiled binaries using a Linux package manager; the second method is to download binary distributions from a trustworthy source like the Apache Software Foundation. Both methods are described below.

Which Modules Are Included?

In deciding whether to install from the RPM or source distribution, you'll probably want to know which modules each includes. Table 3.5 lists the Apache modules that are provided with the RPM and those included with the binary distribution for Linux made available on the Apache Web site (www.apache.org/dist/httpd/binaries/linux). The first column lists all the standard modules; the second and third columns indicate which of these are enabled as dynamically loadable modules by default when you install Apache. The Red Hat RPM and the Apache binary distribution vary slightly, probably because of differing ideas about what is important to Red Hat Linux users. This list is based on release 2.0.35.

Note that if you install Apache with Red Hat Linux, you'll get some freebies—the last three listed modules are installed from separate RPMs and provide PHP and Perl programming support for your Web server. PHP and Perl are discussed in detail in Chapter 8, although we'll compile and install them from source code rather than from an RPM.

Table 3.5   Apache Modules Provided with the Red Hat RPM and with the Apache Binary Distribution

Module	2.0.35 RPM	2.0.35 Binary
libproxy.so	X	
mod_access	X	X
mod_actions	X	X
mod_alias	X	X
mod_asis	X	X
mod_auth	X	X
mod_auth_anon	X	X
mod_auth_db	X	
mod_auth_dbm		X
mod_auth_digest	X	X
mod_autoindex	X	X
mod_bandwidth	X	
mod_cern_meta	X	
mod_cgi	X	X

Table 3.5   Apache Modules Provided with the Red Hat RPM and with the Apache Binary Distribution (*continued*)

Module	2.0.35 RPM	2.0.35 Binary
mod_dav		X
mod_digest	X	
mod_dir	X	X
mod_env	X	X
mod_example	X	
mod_expires	X	X
mod_headers	X	X
mod_imap	X	X
mod_include	X	X
mod_info	X	X
mod_log_agent	X	
mod_log_config	X	X
mod_log_referer	X	
mod_mime	X	X
mod_mime_magic	X	
mod_mem_cache		
mod_negotiation	X	X
mod_put	X	
mod_rewrite	X	X
mod_setenvif	X	X
mod_speling	X	X
mod_status	X	X
mod_throttle	X	
mod_unique_id	X	
mod_userdir	X	X

Essential Configuration

PART 2

Table 3.5   Apache Modules Provided with the Red Hat RPM and with the Apache Binary Distribution (*continued*)

Module	2.0.35 RPM	2.0.35 Binary
mod_usertrack	X	
mod_vhost_alias	X	X
mod_php	*	Not included
mod_php3	*	Not included
mod_perl	*	Not included

* Installed from separate RPMs by the Red Hat Linux installation program

Binary Distributions

Binary distributions of Apache, compiled for a large number of operating systems and hardware platforms, are available from the Apache Software Foundation and can be downloaded from www.apache.org/dist/httpd/binaries/linux. You may need to look elsewhere if your hardware or OS is quite old (an old Linux kernel on a 486, for example). The page listing Apache for Linux distributions is shown in Figure 3.3.

Figure 3.3   Linux binary distributions on the www.apache.org site

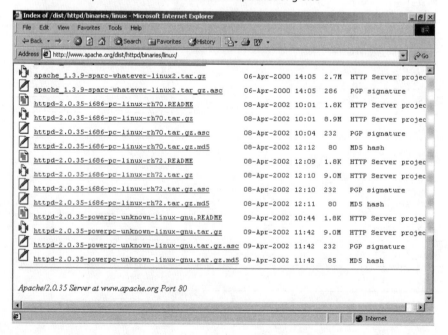

When downloading binary distributions for Intel microprocessors, you need to make sure you download a version that was compiled to run on your specific processor family. For example, the i686 family includes the Pentium II, PII Xeon, Pentium III, and PIII Xeon, as well as the Celeron processors. As of this writing, the Pentium 4 processor reports its CPU type as "if86," though this may change. If your system has a Pentium 4 processor, download code compiled for the i686 family of processors. The IA-64 (or Itanium) processor is officially in the "i786" family, but for this processor, look for a binary with -ia64- as part of the filename. The i586 family includes the Pentium and Pentium with MMX CPUs, and i386 generally indicates the 80486 family. A binary compiled for the i386 family will run on any of the processors mentioned above, including the latest Pentium CPUs, but it will not be as fast as code compiled specifically for a processor generation. If you are downloading a binary distribution for a Pentium II or Pentium III, look for an i686 distribution; if you are downloading for an 80486, you must get the i386 binaries.

There is a handy Linux utility that will query the system's processor and return its hardware family type. Enter /bin/uname -m to obtain this information (the m is for machine type). When run on my server machine, which has an old Pentium 200 MMX chip, I got this result:

```
# uname -m
i586
```

For a Pentium III running Linux, use the following steps:

1. Download the most recent binary distribution of Apache for Linux from www.apache.org/dist/httpd/binaries/linux. I downloaded httpd-2.0.35-i686-pc-linux-rh72.tar.gz, which is the binary tarball, compressed with gzip. This long filename indicates the version of Apache (2.0.35), the CPU for which it was compiled (Intel 686 family), the operating system version or Linux distribution (in this case, the binary was assembled for the Red Hat 7.2 distribution).

NOTE For every binary package on the Web site, there is a README file to accompany it. You can view or download this file for information about the binary distribution; for example, who compiled it and when, as well as what compiler options and default locations for files were built into the Apache executable.

---

2. Make sure you are in the directory where you downloaded the binary distribution (or move the downloaded file elsewhere and change to that directory). After the installation process is complete, you will probably want to delete the directory that was created to hold the installation files. All the files you need to run Apache from the binary are moved from that directory to their intended locations:

```
# cd /home/caulds
# pwd
```

```
/home/caulds
# ls httpd*
httpd-2.0.35-i686-pc-linux-rh72.tar.gz
```

3. Uncompress and extract the distribution with tar to create a new directory tree containing all the files from the distribution:

```
# tar xvzf httpd-2.0.35-i686-pc-linux-rh72.tar.gz
```

4. Change the working directory to the directory you just created:

```
# cd httpd-2.0.35
# ls bindist
bin  build  cgi-bin  conf  error  htdocs  icons  include
lib  logs  man  manual  modules
$ ls bindist/bin
ab          apr-config  apxs        dbmmanage  envvars-std
htdigest  httpd                rotatelogs apachectl  apu-config
checkgid  envvars     htdbm       htpasswd  logresolve
```

5. The binary distribution includes a shell script for installing the files in their proper locations (the locations in which the Apache daemon expects to find them). Run the shell script as follows to create the Apache folders. After it runs, you should find everything neatly installed under /usr/local/apache:

```
# ./install-bindist.sh
Installing binary distribution for platform i686-pc-linux
into directory /usr/local/apache2 ...
Ready.
    +-------------------------------------------------------+
    | You now have successfully installed the Apache 2.0.35 |
    | HTTP server. To verify that Apache actually works     |
    | correctly you should first check the (initially       |
    | created or preserved) configuration files:            |
    |                                                       |
    |    /usr/local/apache2/conf/httpd.conf                 |
    |                                                       |
    | You should then be able to immediately fire up        |
    | Apache the first time by running:                     |
    |                                                       |
    |    /usr/local/apache2/bin/apachectl start             |
    |                                                       |
    | Thanks for using Apache.        The Apache Group      |
    |                                 http://www.apache.org/ |
    +-------------------------------------------------------+
```

You can actually start the Apache server from the `httpd` file in the `bin` directory (listed in item 4 above), but it has been compiled with default values that will not allow it to operate from this location. You can verify that it is operational, though, by entering a command such as the following, which will cause `httpd` to start, display its version information, and quit:

```
# ./httpd -v
Server version: Apache/2.0.36
Server built:   May 11 2002 12:59:43
# ls -al ./bindist/bin httpd
-rwxr-xr-x    1 caulds    caulds      1056487 Apr  8 01:44 httpd
# strip httpd
# ls -al httpd
-rwxr-xr-x    1 caulds    caulds       302100 Jun  1 15:27 httpd
```

Red Hat Package Manager

For Linux users, there is probably no better way to install already-compiled programs than a package manager. The most widely used of these is the RPM. RPM is an abbreviation for Red Hat Package Manager, and it was originally developed by Red Hat (www.redhat.com) for inclusion in its Linux distribution. RPM packs a set of files into a single package, usually a file with the .rpm extension. This file can then be transferred to any other system and unpacked to reproduce the files in the exact location where they were found on the source system, creating directories where necessary. Traditionally, this is done with tar in the Unix world, and most source code is still distributed in so-called *tarballs*. But RPM is better. It can manage all the packages installed on your system, it can use newer packages to upgrade those already installed, it can cleanly uninstall packages, and it can even verify the installed files against the RPM database. Verification is useful because it detects changes that might have been made accidentally or deliberately by an intruder.

True to the spirit of open-source software, Red Hat donated RPM to the public domain, and many other Linux distributions have the ability to load RPM files. Red Hat, SuSE, Mandrake, Turbolinux, and Caldera OpenLinux are all "RPM Linux Distributions." Although other package managers exist for Linux, RPM is the most widely used, and more packages are available as RPMs than any other format.

Although you can probably find an alternate RPM that is supported by the libraries installed on your system, the safest way to install Apache using an RPM is to find one that matches your Linux distribution. You will want a Red Hat RPM, for example, if you use the Red Hat Linux distribution, preferably one that matches your distribution release. One place you're guaranteed to find one of these is on the Linux distribution CD, under the RedHat/RPMS directory. While this means that you won't always be able to add the latest and greatest version of Apache from RPMs, it also means that the one you use is guaranteed to work.

Whenever possible, I recommend installing the RPM that was packaged with your distribution release. This will ensure that the files it contains were compiled to run on a Red Hat system and that the required libraries and supporting files will be there. Hopefully, by the time you get this book in your hands, there will be a more recent version of the Red Hat Linux distribution that contains Apache 2.0. Use the RPM from that distribution, or install Apache when you install Linux (which uses the RPMs on the installation CD). When installed as an RPM, it can always be easily removed.

One other excellent source for RPMs is the RPM repository on Rpmfind.net (www.rpmfind.net/linux/RPM/). Figure 3.4 illustrates the list of Linux distributions for which RPMs are available on the site. There may be several packages from different sources for a given version of Apache, so to make a choice, we need more information about them. (My system runs Red Hat Linux 7.3, the latest version of Red Hat available at the time I wrote this.) Figure 3.5 shows the detailed display of Red Hat updates to its 7.3 distribution. This would be the latest vendor-approved version of the Apache RPM for Red Hat Linux 7.3.

Figure 3.4   The Rpmfind.net list of distributions

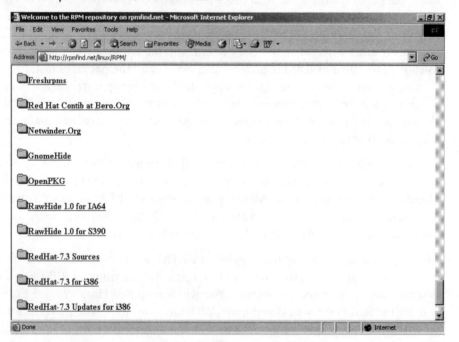

Figure 3.5   The Rpmfind.net info page for Apache 1.3.22

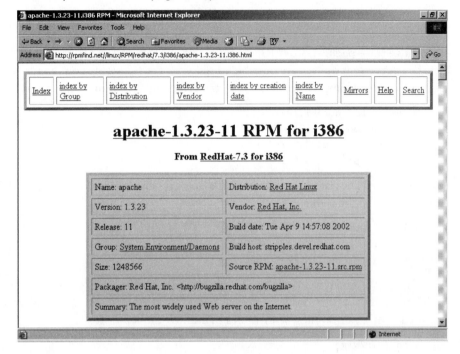

Before installing the Apache 2.0 RPM on my Linux system, I removed the existing Apache RPM that was installed when I loaded the Red Hat distribution. Then I ran rpm with the -qa argument, which says "query all installed packages," to determine which Apache RPMs were installed, and piped the output to grep to display only those lines containing the string apache:

```
# rpm -qa |grep apache
apache-1.3.6-7
apache-devel-1.3.6-7
```

This is a very old version of Apache, which was distributed with Red Hat 6.0. The -e argument to rpm erases an RPM package. It removes all files installed with the RPM package, unless those files have been modified. Uninstalling an RPM also removes all directories created when installing the RPM, unless those directories are not empty after the RPM files are removed.

In this example, removing the installed RPMs failed. The error warns that other packages were installed after, and are dependent on, the Apache RPM:

```
# rpm -e apache-1.3.6-7
error: removing these packages would break dependencies:
```

```
webserver is needed by mod_perl-1.19-2
webserver is needed by mod_php-2.0.1-9
webserver is needed by mod_php3-3.0.7-4
```

To remove the Apache-1.3.6-7 RPM, it is necessary to first remove the three RPMs listed as dependent on that RPM, which I did with the following commands (if the package removal happens without error, the rpm command returns no output):

```
# rpm -e mod_perl-1.19-2
# rpm -e mod_php-2.0.1-9
# rpm -e mod_php3-3.0.7-4
# rpm -e apache-1.3.6-7
```

Once all the RPMs are removed, install the new Apache RPM using rpm with the −i argument in the following manner:

```
# ls -al apache*
-rw-r--r-- 1 root  root  551686 Apr 11 15:54 apache-1.3.22-2.i386.rpm
# rpm -i apache-1.3.22-2.i386.rpm
```

This RPM is designed to install Apache in the /home/httpd and /etc/httpd directories, which is where you'll find it on standard Red Hat systems. The RPM installs all the required configuration files, with values that allow the server to start:

```
# cd /var/www
# ls
cgi-bin  html  icons
```

The RPM even provides a default HTML page in the default DocumentRoot directory (/var/www/html). This page allows your server to be accessed immediately after installation:

```
# ls html
index.html  manual  mrtg  poweredby.png
```

A listing of the /var/www/html directory shows two files and a subdirectory. The index.html file contains the HTML page that the newly installed server will display by default; it is a special filename used to indicate the default HTML page in a directory. The poweredby.gif file is a graphic that the server displays on the default page. The manual directory contains HTML documentation for the new Apache server. Access the manual from a Web browser using http://localhost/manual.

The Apache configuration files, logs, and loadable modules are all found elsewhere on the filesystem (in /etc/httpd). The RPM also writes the Apache executable httpd into a directory reserved for system executable binaries:

```
# ls -al /usr/sbin/httpd
-rwxr-xr-x  1 root   root   282324 Sep 21 09:46 /usr/sbin/httpd
```

Running the Server

The Apache daemon is started from a single executable file (httpd), which is usually supported by a number of modules that are loaded by the server after it reads its configuration files. The Apache server is started when httpd is invoked, either manually at the command line, or more commonly as part of a startup script. Chapter 10 discusses common ways of invoking httpd and controlling its behavior.

```
# cd /etc/httpd
# ls
conf  logs  modules
# ls modules
httpd.exp             mod_dav_fs.so        mod_negotiation.so
mod_access.so         mod_dav.so           mod_proxy_connect.so
mod_actions.so        mod_dir.so           mod_proxy_ftp.so
mod_alias.so          mod_disk_cache.so    mod_proxy_http.so
mod_asis.so           mod_env.so           mod_proxy.so
mod_auth_anon.so      mod_expires.so       mod_rewrite.so
mod_auth_dbm.so       mod_headers.so       mod_setenvif.so
mod_auth_digest.so    mod_imap.so          mod_speling.so
mod_auth_mysql.so     mod_include.so       mod_ssl.so
mod_auth.so           mod_info.so          mod_status.so
mod_autoindex.so      mod_log_config.so    mod_unique_id.so
mod_cache.so          mod_mem_cache.so     mod_userdir.so
mod_cern_meta.so      mod_mime_magic.so    mod_usertrack.so
mod_cgi.so            mod_mime.so          mod_vhost_alias.so
```

The normal behavior of httpd is to run as a system daemon, or listening server process, waiting for HTTP client connections on one or more sockets and bound to one or more of the system's network interfaces. The httpd file can also be invoked with several arguments that cause it to run, display some information, and quit immediately without going into daemon mode. A few of those arguments are demonstrated below; you can use them to test your Apache executable and display its running environment. In each case, I am invoking httpd from its standard location, although it could be placed anywhere on your filesystem without affecting its operation. On my systems, I usually choose to place the file in a protected location reserved for system binaries (/usr/sbin/).

I've already demonstrated the -v argument, which displays the version number and compile date of the httpd file.

The -V (uppercase) option provides the same information, and also displays all the default values compiled into httpd. The most useful information is the default locations in which the Apache server looks for its supporting files and writes its directories. Most of these locations can be overridden at runtime by special directives in httpd.conf, but this is rarely necessary.

```
# ./httpd -V
Server version: Apache/2.0.35
Server built:   Apr  6 2002 13:30:55
Server's Module Magic Number: 20020329:0
Architecture:   32-bit
Server compiled with....
 -D APACHE_MPM_DIR="server/mpm/prefork"
 -D APR_HAS_SENDFILE
 -D APR_HAS_MMAP
 -D APR_HAVE_IPV6
 -D APR_USE_SYSVSEM_SERIALIZE
 -D APR_USE_PTHREAD_SERIALIZE
 -D SINGLE_LISTEN_UNSERIALIZED_ACCEPT
 -D APR_HAS_OTHER_CHILD
 -D AP_HAVE_RELIABLE_PIPED_LOGS
 -D HTTPD_ROOT="/usr/local/apache2"
 -D SUEXEC_BIN="/usr/local/apache2/bin/suexec"
 -D DEFAULT_ERRORLOG="logs/error_log"
 -D SERVER_CONFIG_FILE="conf/httpd.conf"
```

The -1 argument displays the modules that are compiled into httpd (also referred to as *statically linked)*. One module, httpd_core, is always statically linked into httpd. A second module (the shared object module, mod_so) is statically linked when dynamic loading of modules is required. For this server, all other modules are available to the server only if dynamically loaded at runtime:

```
# /usr/local/apache/bin/httpd -1
Compiled-in modules:
  http_core.c
  mod_so.c
```

The –t option runs a syntax test on configuration files but does not start the server. This test can be very useful, because it indicates the line number of any directive in the httpd.conf file that is improperly specified:

```
# /usr/local/apache/bin/httpd -t
Syntax OK
```

Every configuration option for a basic Apache server is stored in a single file. On most standard Apache systems, you'll find the configuration file stored as /usr/local/apache/conf/httpd.conf. If you have Apache loaded from a Red Hat Linux distribution CD or an RPM distribution, you'll find the file in an alternate location preferred by Red Hat, /etc/apache/ conf/httpd.conf. When Apache is compiled, this location is one of the configurable values that are hard-coded into it. Unless explicitly told to load its configuration from another file or directory, Apache will attempt to load the file from its compiled-in path and filename.

This compiled-in value can be overridden by invoking the Apache executable with the -f option. This can be handy for testing alternate configuration files or for running more than one server on the system, each of which loads its own unique configuration.

Finally, you can run httpd with no arguments to start the server as a system daemon. Some simple modifications will probably have to be made to the default httpd.conf provided when you install Apache, although only very minor changes are actually required to start the server. In all likelihood, the first time you start Apache, you'll receive some error telling you the reason that Apache can't be started. The most common error new users see is this:

```
httpd: cannot determine local host name.
Use the ServerName directive to set it manually.
```

If you get an error when starting Apache the first time, don't panic; it is almost always fixed by making one or two very simple changes to Apache's configuration file. In fact, you should expect to make a few changes before running Apache. To do this, you'll modify Apache configuration *directives*, the subject of the next chapter. Chances are, the directives you need to learn about and change are those covered in the "Defining the Main Server Environment" section of Chapter 4. If your server won't start, you need to follow the instructions there.

If Apache finds an httpd.conf file that it can read for an acceptable initial configuration, you will see no response, which is good news. To find out if the server is actually running, attempt to connect to it using a Web browser. Your server should display a demo page to let you know things are working. Figure 3.6 shows the demo page from a Red Hat system.

You can also determine if the server is running the slightly more complicated way, and use the Linux process status (or ps) command to look for the process in the Linux process table, as shown below:

```
# ps -ef | grep httpd
root      8764      1  0 13:39 ?        00:00:00 ./httpd
nobody    8765   8764  0 13:39 ?        00:00:00 ./httpd
nobody    8766   8764  0 13:39 ?        00:00:00 ./httpd
nobody    8767   8764  0 13:39 ?        00:00:00 ./httpd
nobody    8768   8764  0 13:39 ?        00:00:00 ./httpd
nobody    8769   8764  0 13:39 ?        00:00:00 ./httpd
```

Figure 3.6   The demonstration Web page installed with the Apache RPM

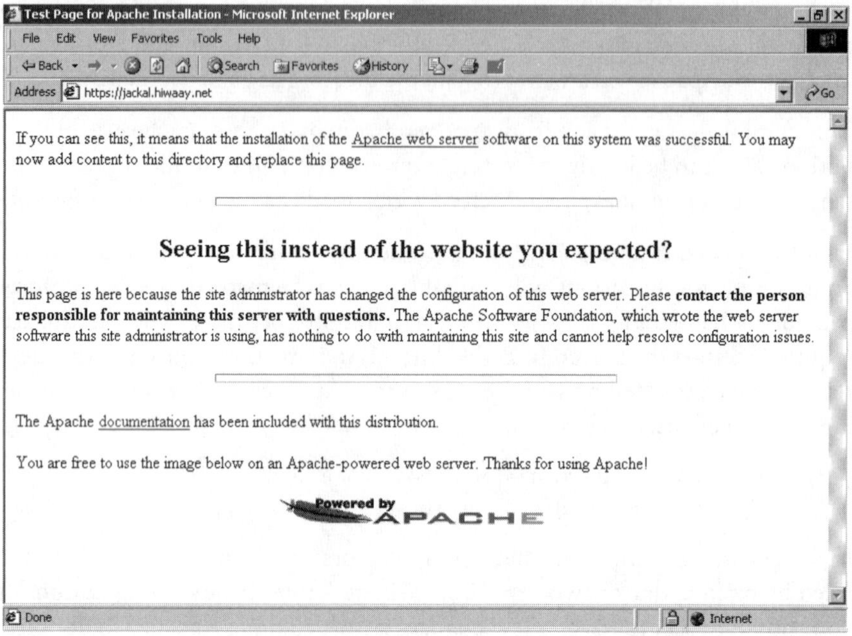

This list is more interesting than it might appear at first. I used the -e argument to ps to display all system processes, the -f argument to display the full output format, and then grep to display only those lines containing the string httpd. Note that only one of the httpd processes is owned by root (the user who started Apache); the next few httpd processes in the list are all owned by nobody. This is as it should be. The first process is the main server, which never responds to user requests. It was responsible for creating the five child processes. Note from the third column of the output that all of these have the main server process (denoted by a process ID of 8764) as their parent process. They were all spawned by the main server, which changed their owner to the nobody account. It is these processes that respond to user requests.

Stopping the Apache server with the kill command is a bit more difficult. When you start Apache, it writes the process ID (or PID) of the main server process into a text file where it can later be used to identify that process and control it using Linux signals. By default, this file is named httpd.pid, and is written in the logs directory under the server root. On my system:

```
# cat /usr/local/apache2/logs/httpd.pid
8764
```

You'll note that the number saved in the file is the PID of the main Apache server process we saw in the process status listing earlier. To shut down the server, extract the contents of the httpd.pid and pass them to the kill command. This is the line that kills Apache:

```
# kill `cat /usr/local/apache2/logs/httpd.pid`
```

Using *apachectl*

Apache comes with a utility to perform the basic operations of controlling the server. This utility, called apachectl, is actually a short shell script that resides in the bin directory under ServerRoot. It does nothing more than simplify processes you can perform by hand, and for that reason, doesn't require a lot of explanation. All of the functionality provided by apachectl is discussed in Chapter 10; for now, I'll show you how to start and stop Apache using this handy utility.

Start the server by invoking apachectl with the start argument. This is better than simply running httpd, because the script first checks to see if Apache is already running, and starts it only if it finds no running httpd process.

```
# /usr/local/apache2/bin/apachectl start
/usr/local/apache2/bin/apachectl start: httpd started
```

Stopping the server is when apachectl comes in really handy. Invoked with the stop argument, apachectl locates the httpd.pid file, extracts the PID of the main server, and then uses kill to stop the process (and all of its child processes). It is exactly what you did earlier using ps and kill, but it is much easier. That's what apachectl is, really, an easy-to-use wrapper for shell commands.

```
# /usr/local/apache2/bin/apachectl stop
/usr/local/apache2/bin/apachectl stop: httpd stopped
```

Running Multiple Apache Servers

Many administrators find that they need to run multiple Apache servers on the same physical system. They may want to run a separate server (with its own document space) to provide secure connections using Secure Sockets Layer (see Chapter 14), or run multiple versions of Apache for testing. My Linux server, for example, has Apache production versions 1.3.22, 1.3.244, 2.0.35 and 2.0.36 installed. I don't run them all simultaneously (although I could do so, by having each listen for connections on different TCP ports), but I can fire up any one of them at any time.

Apache makes it very easy to install multiple servers on the same box. All you need to do is ensure that each one starts its own unique configuration file. Generally, when you install multiple versions of Apache, you should specify different values for --prefix when running configure. When installing version 2.0.36, I instructed configure to place it in a directory other than the default /usr/local/apache:

```
# configure --prefix=/usr/local/httpd-2.0.36
```

Now, the newly installed 2.0.36 version will have its own configuration file, its own Apache daemon executable (httpd), and its own set of DSO modules.

And, if you want to run multiple copies of the same Apache server version, but with alternate configurations, you can use the -f argument to httpd. This argument lets you choose a configuration file that is read by the Apache daemon at startup and contains all the settings that define the configuration for each particular server.

```
# httpd -f /usr/local/conf/test.conf
```

Using Defines to Implement Alternate Configurations

Another way to maintain alternate configurations uses a single configuration file. If there are features that you may or may not want to implement, you can place the directives for those features in blocks that, when the configuration file is parsed, will be either read or ignored conditionally. In the configuration file, the <IfDefine var> directive is a container for directives that should be run only if var has been set. The var argument is a type of variable known as a *define*, and on the Linux command line, the -D argument to httpd sets these variables. A good example of this is provided by the Secure Sockets Layer implementation discussed in Chapter 14. When the module for SSL is installed, all of the directives it adds to the Apache configuration file are placed between <IfDefine> directives:

```
<IfDefine SSL>
    Listen 443
</IfDefine>
```

The directives in this container will be read only if the variable SSL is defined. In other words, you want the server to listen for connections on TCP port 443 (the standard port for SSL) only if you defined SSL when you started the daemon. Do this by invoking the Apache daemon, httpd, with the -D argument, like so:

```
# /usr/local/apache/bin/httpd –D SSL
```

You can do the same to store alternate configurations in a single file by setting your own defines for the different blocks that you want to be active.

In Sum

This chapter presented three methods of installing Apache:

1. By compiling the binaries yourself from the source files

2. From the downloadable binaries available from the Apache Foundation

3. From a package prepared for a Linux package manager, such as RPM

Although it's more difficult and time-consuming, compiling from source is the way I prefer to install Apache, because it permits the greatest flexibility in configuration or customization. Complete instructions were given on how to obtain, compile, and install Apache from source code. Many sites will prefer to install ready-made binaries, however, and these offer the quickest and most painless way to install Apache and upgrade it when the time comes. Full instructions on using the Apache Foundation's binary archives and third-party RPM packages were given.

In the next chapter, I'll describe the Apache configuration file (`httpd.conf`) and the most important of the core directives that can be used in that file to customize your Apache server. The core directives are always available in every Apache server; there is nothing in this chapter that does not apply to your Apache server. It is probably the most important reading you'll do in this book.

Essential
Configuration

PART 2

4

A Basic Apache Server

When properly installed on a Linux server, Apache is completely configured and ready for use. In this chapter, I'll discuss the configuration, or customization, of a very basic Apache server, suitable for serving Web pages from directories of your choosing. While most administrators will want to go further in extending the functionality of their server, the configuration changes discussed in this chapter are certainly the most common. Nearly every Apache administrator will make at least a few of the changes discussed here.

Apache's behavior and configuration options are defined by using a collection of statements called *directives*. Apache directives are rigorously defined in how and where they can be used, and they have a specific syntax, very much like the commands of a programming language. Directives are not programming commands, though, and using directives is not like programming. Directives are instructions to Apache, telling it how to behave and where to find the resources it needs, but they do not directly control the actions of Apache. Rather, they are used to customize the Apache server for the requirements of a particular Web site (or multiple Web sites hosted on a single server).

Apache directives fall into two groups: those that are always available (the so-called *core directives*) and those supplied by optional add-on *modules*. The most important of these are the core directives. These are the directives that are compiled into the Apache executable, so they are always available and require no special configuration to be used. Other configuration directives become available to the administrator only when their modules are added to the server. In fact, these directives are meaningless and unrecognized by Apache until their modules are enabled. You can enable these directives when compiling Apache by statically linking the module to the Apache kernel, or at runtime by using the LoadModule directive in httpd.conf. Chapter 5 is devoted to Apache modules and discusses the use of the LoadModule directive to load these as extensions to Apache. Many Apache add-on modules have been adopted by the Apache Software Foundation for inclusion with the Apache distribution, although their use is always optional.

Every directive is associated with a specific module; the largest module is the core module itself, which has special characteristics. This module cannot be unlinked from the Apache kernel and cannot be disabled; the directives it supplies are always available on every Apache server. Most of the directives presented in this chapter are from the core Apache module, and all of the most important directives from the core module are covered. The most important of the remaining modules and their directives are covered in relevant chapters throughout the book. (For example, mod_proxy and its directives are presented in Chapter 12's discussion of using Apache as a proxy server.) Apache's online documentation includes a comprehensive reference to all the modules and directives; Appendix D shows how to make effective use of this documentation.

The core module provides support for basic server operations, including options and commands that control the operation of other modules. The Apache server with *just* the core module isn't capable of much at all. It will serve documents to requesting clients (identifying all as having the content type defined by the DefaultType directive). While all of the other modules can be considered optional, a useful Apache server will always include at least a few of them. In fact, nearly all of the standard Apache modules are used on most production Apache servers; more than half are compiled by the default configuration and either linked into the server or made available as dynamically loadable modules.

In this chapter, we'll see how directives are usually located in a single startup file (httpd.conf). I'll show how the applicability of directives is often confined to a specific scope (by default, directives have a general server scope). Finally, I'll show how directives can be added or overridden on a directory-by-directory basis (using the .htaccess file).

Using Apache Directives

The emphasis its developers placed on a modular design has proven to be one of Apache's greatest strengths. From the start, Apache was designed with expandability and extensibility in mind. The hooks that were designed into the program allow developers to create modules to extend the functionality of Apache, and are an important reason for its rapid adoption and huge success. Apache modules add not only new functionality to the server, but also new directives.

In order to get the most out of Apache, you need to be familiar with all the standard modules. You may not need or use all of these modules, but knowing that they exist, and having a basic knowledge of what each does, is very valuable when needs or problems arise in the future.

Read this chapter in conjunction with the book's appendices. This chapter, like all of the others in this book, is a tutorial that explains when a directive should be used, what it does, and how you can use it in your server configuration. In addition, Appendix A is a tabular list of all directives enabled by the standard set of Apache modules. For each directive, the table includes the context(s) in which the directive is permitted, the Overrides statement that applies to it (if any), and the module required to implement the directive. Appendix D is a detailed guide to using the excellent Apache help system, which should be your first stop when you need to know exactly how a directive is used. In configuring Apache, you will need to make frequent reference to these appendices.

The All-Powerful *httpd.conf* File

In keeping with its NCSA httpd origin, Apache originally used three configuration files:

- The main server configuration file, httpd.conf
- The resource configuration file, srm.conf
- The access permissions configuration file, access.conf

The Apache Software Foundation decided to merge these into a single file, and in all current releases of Apache, the only configuration file required is httpd.conf. Not only does the use of a single configuration file greatly simplify creating backups and maintaining revision histories, it also makes it easy to describe your complete server configuration to a colleague—just e-mail them a copy of your httpd.conf!

> **TIP**   To follow along with the descriptions in this chapter, you might find it useful to open or print the httpd.conf on your system to use for reference. On most systems, the file is stored as /usr/local/apache2/conf/httpd.conf. If you have Apache loaded from a Red Hat Linux distribution CD or a Red Hat Package Manager (RPM) distribution, you'll find the file as /etc/apache2/conf/httpd.conf. Nearly everything you do to change the Apache configuration requires some modification of this file.

For convenience, the `httpd.conf` file is divided into three sections. Although these divisions are arbitrary, if you try to maintain these groupings, your configuration file will be much easier to read. The three sections of the `httpd.conf` are:

Section 1: The *global environment* section contains directives that control the operation of the Apache server process as a whole. This is where you place directives that control the operation of the Apache server processes, as opposed to directives that control how those processes handle user requests.

Section 2: The *main*, or default, server section contains directives that define the parameters of the "main" or "default" server, which responds to requests that aren't handled by a virtual host. These directives also provide default values for the settings of all virtual hosts.

Section 3: The *virtual hosts* section contains settings for virtual hosts, which allow Web requests to be sent to different IP addresses or hostnames and have them handled by the same Apache server process. Virtual hosts are the subject of Chapter 6.

Directive Scope and Context

One of the important things to know about any directive is the context in which it operates. The context of a directive determines not only its scope—in other words, its range of applicability—but also where the directive can be placed. There are four contexts in which Apache directives can operate:

The General Server Context   Directives that operate in the general server context apply to the entire server. Some of these directives are only valid in this context, and make no sense in any other. For example, the `StartServers` directive specifies the number of `httpd` listener processes that are spawned when Apache is first started, and it makes no sense to include this directive in any other context. Other directives (like `ServerName`, which is different for each virtual host) are equally valid in other contexts. When used in the general server context, most of these directives set default values that can be overridden when used in narrower contexts, just as a virtual host will override `ServerName` to set its own value for this directive.

The Container Context   This group includes directives that are valid when enclosed in one of the three containers: `<Directory>`, `<Files>`, or `<Location>`. These directives are applicable only within the scope defined by the enclosing container. A good example is a `Deny` directive, which prohibits access to resources.

When used within any one of the three containers mentioned, it denies access to the resource or group of resources defined by the enclosing container.

The Virtual Host Context   Although a virtual host is actually defined by the container directive <VirtualHost>, for the purpose of defining directive contexts, it is considered separately because many virtual host directives actually override general server directives or defaults. As discussed in Chapter 6, the virtual host attempts to be a second server in every respect, running on the same machine and, to a client that connects to the virtual host, appearing to be the only server running on the machine.

The .htaccess Context   The directives in an .htaccess file are treated almost identically to directives appearing inside a <Directory> container in httpd.conf. The main difference is that directives appearing inside an .htaccess file can be disabled by using the AllowOverrides directive in httpd.conf. Apache configuration directives are often included in .htaccess files in order to decentralize administration. In other words, certain users who don't have access permissions that allow them to edit Apache's httpd.conf file might be allowed to edit .htaccess files in certain directories. As the name implies, .htaccess files are most commonly used to restrict access to resources on a directory basis. The use of security directives in an .htaccess context is fully covered in Chapter 13.

NOTE   The name of the .htaccess file can be changed with the Access-FileName directive, though this is rarely done.

For each directive, Appendix A lists the context in which it can be used and the overrides that enable or disable it. For example, the information for the Action directive shows that it is valid in all four contexts, but can be overridden when used in an .htaccess file by a FileInfo override. If the FileInfo override is not specified for a directory, an Action directive in an .htaccess file in that directory has no effect. This is because the Action directive is controlled by the FileInfo override.

The Apache server is smart enough to recognize when a directive is being specified out of scope. You'll get the following error when you boot, for example, if you attempt to use the Listen directive in a <Directory> context:

```
# /usr/local/apache2/bin/httpd
Syntax error on line 925 of /usr/local/apache2/conf/httpd.conf:
Listen not allowed here
httpd could not be started
```

Essential Configuration

PART 2

Defining the Main Server Environment

General server directives are those used to configure the server itself and its listening processes. General server directives are not allowed in the other contexts we'll discuss, except for virtual hosts. As you'll see in Chapter 6, general server directives also provide default values that are inherited by all virtual hosts, unless specifically overridden.

I changed four directives, all of which were modifications of lines found in the default httpd.conf file, to get my server up and running. Once you've installed Apache, you should be able to get the server running by making only these changes, and you probably won't require all four. The default Apache configuration that you installed in Chapter 3 is complete and you can usually start the server using this configuration. However, before doing that, you should understand the purpose of the four directives in this section. These directives, while simple to understand and use, all have a server-wide scope and affect the way many other directives operate. Because of the importance of these directives, you should take care to ensure that they are set properly.

The *ServerName* Directive

Apache must always be able to determine a hostname for the server on which it is run. This hostname is used by the server to create *self-referential URLs*—that is, URLs that refer to themselves. Later, we'll see that when more than one virtual host is run on the same system, each will be identified by a unique ServerName directive. For a system that hosts only a single Web server site, the ServerName directive is usually set to the hostname and domain of that server.

When I installed Apache and ran it for the first time, I was presented with the error httpd: cannot determine local host name. To correct this, I located the ServerName directive in my httpd.conf file, and discovered that the Apache distribution had created the directive using my fully qualified hostname as the Apache ServerName, but left the directive commented out. The directive was acceptable to me, so I uncommented the line:

```
ServerName jackal.hiwaay.net
```

The *ServerRoot* Directive

The ServerRoot directive specifies the directory in which the server lives and generally matches the value of the --prefix option that was set during the installation of Apache.

```
ServerRoot /usr/local/apache2
```

Typically this directory will contain the subdirectories bin/, conf/, and logs/. In lieu of defining the server root directory using the ServerRoot configuration directive, you can also specify the location with the -d option when invoking httpd:

```
# /usr/local/apache2/bin/httpd -d /etc/httpd
```

While there's nothing wrong with using this method of starting the server, it is usually best reserved for testing alternate configurations and for cases where you will run multiple versions of Apache on the same server simultaneously, each with its own configuration file.

Paths for all other configuration files are taken as relative to this directory. For example, the following directive causes Apache to write error messages into /usr/local/apache2/ logs/error.log:

```
ErrorLog logs/error.log
```

The ErrorLog directive is covered in detail in Chapter 11.

The *DocumentRoot* Directive

The DocumentRoot directive is used to define the top-level directory from which Apache will serve files. The directory defined by DocumentRoot contains the files that Apache will serve when it receives requests with the URL /.

It's perfectly acceptable to use the Apache default, which is the directory htdocs under the Apache server root, but I usually prefer to change this to the /home filesystem, which is a much larger filesystem reserved for user home directories.

To change the value of DocumentRoot on my system, I commented out the Apache default, and added a new DocumentRoot directive of my own:

```
# DocumentRoot "/usr/local/apache2/htdocs"
DocumentRoot "/home/httpd/html"
```

Note that a full path to the directory must be used whenever the directory is outside the server root. Otherwise, a relative path can be given. (The double quotes are usually optional, but it's a good idea to always use them. If the string contains spaces, for example, it *must* be enclosed in double quotes.)

When you change the DocumentRoot, you must also alter the <Directory> container directive that groups all directives that apply to the DocumentRoot and subdirectories:

```
# <Directory "/usr/local/apache2/htdocs">
<Directory "/home/httpd/html">
```

The *ScriptAlias* Directive

The ScriptAlias directive specifies a directory that contains executable scripts; for example, CGI programs that can be invoked from a Web browser. By default, Apache creates a ScriptAlias for all URLs requesting a resource in /cgi-bin/.

I also changed the ScriptAlias directive for my server. I chose to comment out Apache's default location and add my own, which is located with the Web documents on my /home filesystem. There's nothing wrong with the Apache default location (under the

Apache server root directory) for the /cgi-bin directory, but you may want to change the location for ease of maintenance:

```
# ScriptAlias /cgi-bin/ "/usr/local/apache2/cgi-bin/"
ScriptAlias /cgi-bin/ "/home/httpd/cgi-bin/"
```

Make sure that only users specifically authorized to create executable scripts can write to the directory you name. I usually assign group ownership of my cgi-bin directory to a Web administrator's group:I usually assign user and group ownership of the cgi-bin directory (and its subdirectories, if they exist) to user and group accounts different from those under which Apache runs. Then I grant full privileges to this user and group, and grant only read and execute permissions to all other users. This ensures that Apache can read and execute the CGI scripts in this location, but the Apache processes cannot change the existing scripts or create new ones (no "write" permission). The following commands will accomplish this:

```
# chown -r www.webteam /home/httpd/cgi-bin
# chmod 775 /home/httpd/cgi-bin
```

The name of this group is arbitrary, but I use the command shown above to assign ownership of the cgi-bin directory (and all of its subdirectories and files) to a user named nobody and the group webteam. The default behavior of Apache on Linux is to run under the nobody user account. The group name is arbitrary, but it is to this group that I assign membership for those user accounts that are permitted to create or modify server scripts. The second line ensures that the file owner has full read, write, and execute permission, that members of the webteam group have read and write access, and that all other users have no access to the directory or the files it contains.

More General Server Directives

There are a number of other general server directives that you may want to modify before putting your server into operation. These directives are usually acceptable when left at their default values, but changing them rarely carries a significant risk. In all cases, if you feel that you understand the purpose of the directive well enough to add it to your httpd.conf file (or modify it if it's already there), don't be afraid to make such changes. These directives exist to make Apache as customizable as possible; they're for your use.

The *ErrorDocument* Directive

If Apache encounters an error while processing a user request, it is configured to display a standard error page, which gives the HTTP response code (see Chapter 1) and the URL that caused the problem. Use the ErrorDocument directive to define a custom error response to standard HTTP errors that are more user-friendly and understandable. Using ErrorDocument, you can configure Apache to respond to a particular HTTP error code in either of two ways:

1. By displaying custom error text. For example, the following would display a custom message for HTTP Error Code 403 (Forbidden). Note that the text begins with a double-quote that is not part of the message itself; it is not a quote-enclosed string. Do not end the message with a second quote.

   ```
   ErrorDocument 403 "You are not authorized to view this info!
   ```

2. By issuing a redirect to another URL, which may be external or internal. A fully specified URL that begins with http:// is assumed to be an external redirect. Apache will send a redirect to the client to tell it where to request the document, even if the redirect resolves to a resource on the same server. A relative URL is a local redirect, relative to the server's DocumentRoot, and Apache will serve the request directly, without sending a redirect that would require the client to request the document again. Here are examples of each of the possible redirect forms:

   ```
   #HTTP Error 401 (Unauthorized); display subscription page
   ErrorDocument 401 /subscription_info.html

   #HTTP Error 404 (Not found); redirect to error script
   ErrorDocument 404 /cgi-bin/bad_urls.pl

   #HTTP Error 500 (Internal error) Redirect to backup server
   ErrorDocument 500 http://jackal2.hiwaay.net
   ```

NOTE   If you attempt to redirect a request with an ErrorDocument 401 directive (which means that the client is unauthorized to access the requested document), the redirect must refer to a local document. Apache will not permit an external redirect for this HTTP error.

The *DefaultType* Directive

A very rarely used directive in the general server scope, DefaultType can redefine the default MIME content type for documents requested from the server. If this directive is not used, all documents not specifically typed elsewhere are assumed to be of MIME type text/html. Chapter 15 discusses MIME content types.

Apache reads its MIME-type-to-filename-extension mappings from a file named mime.types, which is found in the Apache configuration directory. This file contains a list of MIME content types, each optionally followed by one or more filename extensions. This file is used to determine the MIME content header sent to the client with each resource sent.

Essential Configuration

PART 2

The DefaultType directive is generally used in a directory scope, to redefine the default type of documents retrieved from a particular directory. In the following example, the default MIME type for all documents in the /images directory under ServerRoot is defined to be image/gif. That way, the server doesn't rely on an extension (like .gif) to determine the resource type. A file with no extension at all, when served from this directory, will be sent to the requesting user with an HTTP header identifying it as MIME type image/gif.

```
<Directory /images>
    DefaultType image/gif
</Directory>
```

Controlling Server Processes

The following directives are used to control the Linux processes when Apache is run on that platform. All remaining directives control system settings for the Apache server processes.

The *PidFile* Directive

In Chapter 2, I noted that the Linux Apache server usually runs as a pool of listening processes, all of which are under the control of a single main server process that *never* responds to client requests. The PidFile directive defines the location and filename of a text file that contains the process ID (or PID) of the main Apache server. Processes that need to know the Apache server process ID—for example, the apachectl utility, discussed in Chapter 10—read the PID from this file. It is rarely necessary to change the Apache default PID file, which is stored as httpd.pid in the logs directory under the Apache ServerRoot.

This directive changes the default to place the PID file in the location that Red Hat Linux uses:

```
PidFile "/var/run/apache.pid"
```

> **NOTE**   Note that the location of Apache's PID file is determined when Apache is installed. If you change the value of the PidFile directive in the original httpd.conf file, you will also need to change the location in the apachectl utility (discussed in Chapter 10) so that it can find the file in its new location. Open apachectl (in the bin directory of the Apache installation) with your favorite text editor, and change this file to point to the file in its new location: PIDFILE=/usr/share/apache2/httpd.pid.

The *User* Directive

This directive defines the Linux user that owns the child processes created to handle user requests. This directive is meaningful only when the Apache server is started as root. If the server is started as any other user, it cannot change ownership of child processes.

The default behavior of Apache on Linux systems is to change the ownership of all child processes to UID -1 (which corresponds to user nobody in the standard Linux /etc/password file). This is the preferred way to run Apache on Linux systems.

In the following example, I've chosen to run Apache as www, a special Web-specific user account that I create on all my Web servers. For ease of administration, Apache resources on my server are usually owned by user www and group wwwteam.

```
User www
```

The *Group* Directive

Like the User directive, this directive is used to change the ownership of the child processes created to handle user requests. Instead of changing the user ownership of these processes, however, this directive changes the group ownership.

The default behavior of Apache on Linux systems is to change the group ownership of all child process to *group ID* (GID) –1, which corresponds to the nobody group in /etc/groups. It often makes more sense to change the group ownership of the Apache server processes than it does to change the user ownership. On Linux servers where I want to give several users read/write access to my Apache configuration files and Web resources, I normally set up a special group with a name like webteam:

```
Group webteam
```

I place all the Web developers' accounts in this group and also change the Apache configuration to run server processes owned by this group.

As it must with the User directive, a stand-alone Apache server must be started as root to use the group directive. Otherwise, the server can't change the group ownership of any child processes it spawns.

The *Listen* Directive

Apache now provides just one core directive, the Listen directive, to define the IP addresses and TCP port numbers on which it listens for and accepts client connections.

The Listen directive incorporates all of the functionality of the BindAddress and Port directives that existed in Apache versions earlier than 2.0, but has several important advantages over them (in addition to eliminating the confusing overlap of functionality between the older directives). The Listen directive has a global server scope and has no meaning inside a container. Apache is smart enough to detect and warn if the Listen directive is used in the wrong context. Placing a Listen directive inside a virtual host container, for example, generates this error:

```
Syntax error on line 1264 of /usr/local/apache/conf/httpd.conf:
Listen cannot occur within <VirtualHost> section
```

If Listen specifies only a port number, the server listens to the specified port on all system network interfaces. If a single IP address and a single port number are given, the server listens only on that port and interface.

Multiple Listen directives may be used to specify more than one address and port to listen to. The server will respond to requests from any of the listed addresses and ports. For example, to make the server accept connections on both port 80 and port 8080, use these directives:

```
Listen 80
Listen 8080
```

To make the server accept connections on two specific interfaces and port numbers, identify the IP address of the interface and the port number and separate them by a colon, as in this example:

```
Listen 192.168.1.3:80
Listen 192.168.1.5:8080
```

Although Listen is very important in specifying multiple IP addresses for IP-based virtual hosting (discussed in detail in Chapter 6), the Listen directive does *not* tie an IP address to a specific virtual host. Here's an example of the Listen directive used to instruct Apache to accept connections on two interfaces, each of which uses a different TCP port.

```
Listen 192.168.1.1:80
Listen 216.180.25.168:443
```

I use this configuration to accept ordinary HTML requests on port 80 on my internal network interface; connections on my external interface (from the Internet) are accepted only on TCP port 443, the default port for SSL connections (as we'll see in Chapter 14).

The *Options* Directive

The Options directive controls which server features are available in a particular directory. The value can be set to None, in which case none of the extra features is enabled, or to one or more of the following:

ExecCGI   Permits execution of CGI scripts.

FollowSymLinks   The server will follow symbolic links (symlinks) in this directory. Following symlinks does not change the pathname used to match against <Directory> sections. This option is ignored if set inside a <Location> section.

Includes   Permits Server-Side Includes (SSI).

IncludesNOEXEC   Server-Side Includes are permitted, but the #exec and #include commands of SSI scripts are disabled.

Indexes   If a URL that maps to a directory is requested, and there is no DirectoryIndex (for example, index.html) in that directory, then the server will return a formatted listing of the directory.

MultiViews   Allows content-negotiated MultiViews. As discussed in Chapter 15, MultiViews are one means of implementing content negotiation.

All   Includes all options except for MultiViews. This is the default setting.

SymLinksIfOwnerMatch   The server will only follow symbolic links for which the target file or directory is owned by the same user ID as the link. Like FollowSymLinks, this option is ignored if set inside a <Location> section.

Normally, if multiple options apply to a directory, the most specific one is used and the other options are ignored. However, if all the options on the Options directive are preceded by a plus (+) or minus (−) character, then the options are merged. Any options preceded by a plus are added to the options currently in effect, and any options preceded by a minus are removed from the options currently in effect.

Since the default setting for the Options directive is All, the configuration file that is provided with Apache contains the following section, which enables only FollowSymLinks for every directory onunder Apache's DocumentRoot.

```
<Directory />
    Options FollowSymLinks
</Directory>
```

The following examples should clarify the rules governing the merging of options. In the first example, only the option Includes will be set for the /web/docs/spec directory:

```
<Directory /web/docs>
```

```
      Options Indexes FollowSymLinks
</Directory>
<Directory /web/docs/spec>
      Options Includes
</Directory>
```

In the example below, only the options `FollowSymLinks` and `Includes` are set for the /web/docs/spec directory:

```
<Directory /web/docs>
    Options Indexes FollowSymLinks
</Directory>
<Directory /web/docs/spec>
    Options +Includes -Indexes
</Directory>
```

Using either `-IncludesNOEXEC` or `-Includes` disables Server-Side Includes. Also, the use of a plus or minus sign to specify a directive has no effect if no options list is already in effect. No options list will be created if only these modifiers are used to specify new options.

WARNING   Be aware that the default setting for Options is All. For that reason, you should always ensure that this default is overridden for every Web-accessible directory. The default configuration for Apache includes a `<Directory>` container to do this; do not modify or remove it.

The Container Directives

The scope of an Apache directive is often restricted using special directives called *container directives*. In general, these container directives are easily identified by the enclosing <> brackets. The *conditional directives* `<IfDefine>` and `<IfModule>`, which are not container directives, are an exception. Container directives require a closing directive that has the same name and begins with a slash character (much like HTML tags).

A container directive encloses other directives and specifies a limited scope of applicability for the directives it encloses. A directive that is not enclosed in a container directive is said to have global scope and applies to the entire Apache server. A global directive is overridden locally by the same directive when it is used inside a container. The following sections examine each type of container directive.

The *<VirtualHost>* Container

The <VirtualHost> container directive encloses directives that apply only to a specific *virtual host*. As discussed further in Chapter 6, a virtual host is a Web site hosted on your server that is identified by a hostname alias. For example, assume your server is www.aulds.com and that it hosts a Web site for a local bait and tackle shop. That shop, however, does not want its customers connecting to www.aulds.com for information; it wants customers to use the Web site www.worms.com. You can solve this problem by creating a virtual host for www.worms.com on the real host www.aulds.com. The format of the <VirtualHost> container directive is

```
<VirtualHost address>
    directives
</VirtualHost>
```

The directives you enclose in the <VirtualHost> container will specify the correct hostname and document root for the virtual host. Naturally, the server name should be a value that customers of the Web site expect to see when they connect to the virtual host. Additionally, the file served to the customers needs to provide the expected information. In addition to these obvious directives, almost anything else you need to customize for the virtual host can be set in this container. For example:

```
<VirtualHost 192.168.1.4>
    ServerAdmin webmaster@host1.com
    DocumentRoot /home/httpd/wormsdocs
    ServerName www.worms.com
    ErrorLog logs/worms.log
    TransferLog logs/worms.log
</VirtualHost>
```

The example above defines a single virtual host. In Chapter 6, we'll see that this is one form of virtual host, referred to as *IP-based*. The first line defines the Internet address (IP) for the virtual host. Only connections made to the Apache server on this IP address are handled by the virtual server for this site, which might be only one of many virtual sites being hosted on the same server. Each directive defines site-specific values for configuration parameters that, outside a <VirtualHost> container directive, normally refer to the entire server. The use of each of these in the general server context was shown earlier in this chapter.

The *<Directory>* and *<DirectoryMatch>* Containers

The <Directory> container encloses directives that apply to a filesystem directory and its *subdirectories*. The directory must be expressed by its full pathname or with wildcards. The example below illustrates a <Directory> container that sets the Indexes and FollowSymLinks options for all directories under /home/httpd/ that begin with user:

```
<Directory /home/httpd/user*>
```

Essential Configuration

PART 2

```
        Options Indexes FollowSymLinks
    </Directory>
```

<Directory> containers are always evaluated so that the shortest match (widest scope) is applied first, and longer matches (narrower scope) override those that may already be in effect from a wider container. For example, the following container disables all over-rides for every directory on the system (/ and all its subdirectories):

```
    <Directory />
        AllowOverrides None
    </Directory>
```

If the httpd.conf file includes a second <Directory> container that specifies a directory lower in the filesystem hierarchy, the directives in the container take precedence over those defined for the filesystem as a whole. The following container enables FileInfo overrides for all directories under /home (which hosts all user home directories on most Linux systems):

```
    <Directory /home/*>
        AllowOverrides FileInfo
    </Directory>
```

The <Directory> container can also be matched against regular expressions by using the ~ character to force a regular expression match:

```
    <Directory ~ "^/home/user[0-9]{3}">
```

The <DirectoryMatch> directive is specifically designed for regular expressions, however, and should normally be used in place of this form. This container directive is exactly like <Directory>, except that the directories to which it applies are matched against regular expressions. The following example applies to all request URLs that specify a resource beginning with /user and followed by exactly three digits. (The ^ character denotes "beginning of string," and the {3} means to match exactly three occurrences of the previous character—in this case, any member of the character set [0–9].)

```
    <DirectoryMatch "^/user[0-9]{3}">
        order deny,allow
        deny from all
        allow from .foo.com
    </Directory>
```

This container directive would apply to a request URL like the following:

```
    http://jackal.hiwaay.net/user321
```

because the <DirectoryMatch> container directive looks for directories (relative to Docu-mentRoot) that consist of the word *user* followed by three digits.

Introduction to Regular Expressions

Many Apache configuration directives accept regular expressions for matching patterns. Regular expressions are an alternative to wildcard pattern matching and are usually an extension of a directive's wildcard pattern matching capability. Indeed, I have heard regular expressions (or *regexps*) described as "wildcards on steroids."

A brief sidebar can hardly do justice to the subject, but to pique your interest, here are a few regexp tags and what they mean:

^ and $	Two special and very useful tags that mark the beginning and end of a line. For example, ^# matches the # character whenever it occurs as the first character of a line (very useful for matching comment lines), and #$ would match # occurring as the very last character on a line. These pattern-matching operators are called *anchoring operators* and are said to "anchor the pattern" to either the beginning or the end of a line.
* and ?	The * character matches the preceding character zero or more times, and ? matches the preceding pattern zero or one time. These operators can be confusing, because they work slightly differently from the same characters when used as "wildcards." For example, the expression fo* will match the pattern *foo* or *fooo* (any number of *o* characters), but it also matches *f*, which has zero *o*'s. The expression ca? will match the *c* in *score*, which seems a bit counterintuitive because there's no a in the word, but the a? says zero or one *a* character. Matching zero or more occurrences of a pattern is usually important whenever that pattern is optional. You might use one of these operators to find files that begin with a name that is optionally followed by several digits and then an extension. Matching for ^filename\d*.gif will match *filename001.gif* and *filename2.gif*, but also simply *filename.gif*. The \d matches any digit (0–9); in other words, we are matching zero or more digits.
+	Matches the preceding character one or more times, so ca+ will not match *score*, but will match *scare*.
.	The period character matches any single character except the newline character. In effect, when you use it, you are saying you don't care what character is matched, as long as some character is matched. For example, x.y matches *xLy* but not *xy*; the period says the two must be separated by a single character. The expression x.*y says to match an *x* and a *y* separated by zero or more characters.
{n}	This operator (a number between braces) matches *n* occurrences of the preceding character. For example, so{2} matches *soot*, but not *sot*.

Introduction to Regular Expressions (continued)

If you're an experienced Linux system administrator, you're already familiar with regular expressions from using grep, sed, and awk. And if you're an experienced Perl user, you probably also have some knowledge of regular expressions. The GNU C++ Regular Expressions Library and Windows Scripting Host (WSH) even allow expressions in Microsoft's JavaScript or VBScript programs.

The only way to develop proficiency in using regexps is to study examples and experiment with them. Entire books have been written on the power of regular expressions (well, at least one) for pattern matching and replacement.

Some useful resources on regexps:

Mastering Regular Expressions Second Edition, by Jeffrey E.F. Friedl (O'Reilly, 2002)

```
http://www.delorie.com/gnu/docs/regex/regex_toc.html
http://lib.stat.cmu.edu/scgn/v52/section1_7_0_1.html
```

The *<Files>* and *<FilesMatch>* Containers

The <Files> container encloses directives that apply only to specific files, which should be specified by filename (using wildcards when necessary). The following example allows access to files with the .OurFile extension only by hosts in a specific domain:

```
<Files *.OurFile>
    order deny,allow
    deny from all
    allow from .thisdomain.com
</Files>
```

Like the <Directory> container, <Files> can also be matched against regular expressions by using the ~ character to force a regular expression match. The following line, for example, matches filenames that end in a period character (escaped with a backslash) immediately followed by the characters *xml*. The $ in regular expressions denotes the end of the string. Thus we are looking for filenames with the extension .xml.

```
<Files ~ "\.xml$">
    Directives go here
</Files>
```

The <FilesMatch> directive is specifically designed for regular expressions, however, and should normally be used in place of this form.

`<FilesMatch>` is exactly like the `<Files>` directive, except that the specified files are defined by regular expressions. All graphic images might be defined, for example, using:

```
<FilesMatch>  "\.(gif|jpe?g|png)$">
    some directives
</FilesMatch>
```

This regular expression matches filenames with the extension *gif* or *jpg* or *jpeg* or *png*. The *or* is denoted by the | (vertical bar) character. Notice the use of the ? character after the e, which indicates zero or one occurrences of the preceding character (e). In other words, a match is made to *jp*, followed by zero or one *e*, followed by *g*.

The *<Location>* and *<LocationMatch>* Containers

The `<Location>` container encloses directives that apply to specific URLs. This is similar to `<Directory>`, because most URLs contain a reference that maps to a specific directory relative to Apache's `DocumentRoot`. The difference is that `<Location>` does not access the filesystem, but considers only the URL of the request. Most directives that are valid in a `<Directory>` context also work in a `<Location>` container; directives that do not apply to a URL are simply ignored because they are meaningless in a `<Location>` context.

The `<Location>` functionality is especially useful when combined with the `SetHandler` directive. For example, to enable status requests, but only from browsers at foo.com, you might use the following (note that *status* is not a directory; it is a part of the URL, and actually invokes a server-generated status page:

```
<Location /status>
    SetHandler server-status
    order deny,allow
    deny from all
    allow from .foo.com
</Location>
```

You can also use extended regular expressions by adding the ~ character, as described for the `<Directory>` and `<Files>` container directories; but a special container directive, `<LocationMatch>`, is specifically designed for this purpose and should be used instead.

`<LocationMatch>` is exactly like the `<Location>` container directive, except that the URLs are specified by regular expressions. The following container applies to any URL that contains the substring */www/user* followed immediately by exactly three digits; for example, */www/user101*:

```
<LocationMatch "/www/user[0-9]{3}">
    order deny,allow
    deny from all
    allow from .foo.com
</Location>
```

Essential Configuration

PART 2

The *<Limit>* and *<LimitExcept>* Containers

<Limit> encloses directives that apply only to the HTTP methods specified. The <Limit> directive can be applied to any HTTP request method discussed in Chapter 1. In the following example, user authentication is required only for requests that use the HTTP methods POST, PUT, and DELETE. Any other request method (GET, for example) will not result in a prompt for username and password:

```
<Limit POST PUT DELETE>
    require valid-user
</Limit>
```

<LimitExcept> encloses directives that apply to all HTTP methods *except* those specified. The following example shows how authentication can be required for all HTTP methods other than GET:

```
<LimitExcept GET>
    require valid-user
</Limit>
```

Perl Sections

If you are using the mod_perl module, it is possible to include Perl code to automatically configure your server. Sections of the httpd.conf containing valid Perl code and enclosed in special <Perl> container directives are passed to mod_perl's built-in Perl interpreter. The output of these scripts is inserted into the httpd.conf file before it is parsed by the Apache engine. This allows parts of the httpd.conf file to be generated dynamically, possibly from external data sources like a relational database on another machine.

Since this option absolutely requires the use of mod_perl, it is discussed in far more detail with this sophisticated module in Chapter 8.

Apache's Order of Evaluation for Containers

When multiple containers apply to a single incoming request, Apache resolves them in the following order:

1. Apache will first evaluate any <Directory> container (except for those that match regular expressions) and merge any .htaccess files it finds that apply to the request. <Directory> containers are always evaluated from widest to narrowest scope, and directives found in .htaccess files override those in <Directory> containers that apply to the same directory.

2. Directives found in <DirectoryMatch> containers and <Directory> containers that match regular expressions are evaluated next. Directives that apply to

the request override those in effect from `<Directory>` or `.htaccess` files (item 1 of this list).

3. After directives that apply to the directory in which the resource resides, Apache applies directives that apply to the file itself. These come from `<Files>` and `<FilesMatch>` containers, and they override directives in effect from `<Directory>` containers. For example, if an `.htaccess` file contains a directive that denies the requester access to a directory, but a directive in a `<Files>` container specifically allows access to the file, the request will be granted, because the contents of the `<Files>` container override those of the `<Directory>` container.

4. Finally, any directives in `<Location>` or `<LocationMatch>` containers are applied. These directives are applied to the request URL and override directives in all other containers. If a directive in a `<Location>` container directly conflicts with the same directive in either a `<Directory>` or a `<Files>` container, the directive in the `<Location>` container will override the others.

Containers with narrower scopes always override those with a wider scope. For example, directives contained in `<Directory /home/httpd/html>` override those in `<Directory /home/httpd>` for the resources in its scope. If two containers specify exactly the same scope (for example, both apply to the same directory or file), the one specified last takes precedence.

The following rather contrived example illustrates how the order of evaluation works:

```
<Files index.html>
    allow from 192.168.1.2
</Files>

<Directory /home/httpd/html>
    deny from all
</Directory>
```

In this example, the `<Directory>` container specifically denies access to the /home/httpd/html directory to all clients. The `<Files>` directive (which precedes it in the `httpd.conf` file) permits access to a single file `index.html` inside that directory, but only to a client connecting from IP address 192.168.1.2. This permits the display of the HTML page by that client, but not any embedded images; these can't be accessed because the `<Files>` directive does not include them in its scope. Note also that the order of the containers within the configuration file is *not* important; it is the order in which the containers are resolved that determines which takes precedence. Any `<Files>` container directives will always take precedence over `<Directory>` containers that apply to the same resource(s).

The *.htaccess* File

Although an Apache server is usually configured completely within the `httpd.conf` file, editing this file is not always the most efficient configuration method. Most Apache administrators prefer to group directory-specific directives, particularly access-control directives, in special files located within the directories they control. This is the purpose of Apache's `.htaccess` files.

In addition to the convenience of having all the directives that apply to a specific group of files located within the directory that contains those files, `.htaccess` files offer a couple of other advantages. First, you can grant access to modify `.htaccess` files on a per-directory basis, allowing trusted users to modify access permissions to files in specific directories without granting those users unrestricted access to the entire Apache configuration. Second, you can modify directives in `.htaccess` files without having to restart the Apache server (which is the only way to read a modified `httpd.conf` file).

By default, the Apache server searches for the existence of an `.htaccess` file in every directory from which it serves resources. If the file is found, it is read and the configuration directives it contains are merged with other directives already in effect for the directory. Unless the administrator has specifically altered the default behavior (using the `AllowOverrides` directive as described below), all directives in the `.htaccess` file override directives already in effect. For example, suppose `httpd.conf` contained the following `<Directory>` section:

```
<Directory /home/httpd/html/Special>
    order deny,allow
    deny from all
</Directory>
```

All access to the directory `/home/httpd/html/Special` would be denied. This may be exactly what the administrator wants, but it is more likely that the directory exists under the Web server root so that someone can get to it with a browser. This can be accomplished by creating an `.htaccess` file in the `Special` directory with directives like the following, which overrides the directives already active for the directory:

```
allow from 192.168.1.*
```

Here, we've used a wildcard expression to specify a range of IP addresses (possibly the Web server's local subnet) that can access resources in the `Special` directory.

The *AllowOverrides* Directive

By default, whenever Apache receives a request for a resource, it searches for an `.htaccess` file in the directory where that resource resides and in every parent directory of that directory on the filesystem. Remember, this search is not limited to DocumentRoot and its subdirectories, but extends all the way up the filesystem hierarchy to the root directory ("/"). It treats each of these exactly as if it were a <Directory> container for the directory in which it is located. The directives in all .htaccess files found in the requested resource's tree are merged with any other directives already in effect for that directory. Those lower in the filesystem hierarchy override those higher in the tree; this means you can grant permission to access a directory even if that permission was denied to a higher-level directory (and, consequently, all of its subdirectories). After merging all the relevant .htaccess files with all directives from all applicable <Directory> containers, Apache applies them according to the order of evaluation described earlier.

What I've just described is the default behavior of Apache with regard to .htaccess files. You can modify this behavior through the special directive AllowOverrides, which controls how .htaccess files are handled. The AllowOverrides directive specifies which directives, when found in an .htaccess file, are allowed to override conflicting directives that are already in effect. AllowOverrides is not used to enable or disable directives, but to specify types of directives that can be overridden in .htaccess files.

The following is a list of all permissible arguments to the AllowOverrides directive. Each enables or disables a set of directives when these directives are found in .htaccess files. Consult the table in Appendix A for the applicable AllowOverrides for each directive for which an override can be specified; the AllowOverrides directive does not apply to directives shown in that table with "N/A" in the Override column.

> **All** This enables all .htaccess overrides. Therefore, all directives that are permissible in an .htaccess file can be used to override settings in the httpd.conf file.

WARNING The default behavior of Apache is to search for .htaccess files in each directory in the path of a resource as if AllowOverrides All had been specified for all directories. This makes the server hard to secure, because anyone who can write a file into any of the directories from which Apache serves files can create a bogus .htaccess file that can be used to subvert system security. It is always best to use AllowOverrides to disable .htaccess files in all directories, enabling the use of .htaccess files only for specific purposes and locations, on a case-by-case basis. Disabling the search for .htaccess files also has the added benefit of improving Apache performance (as discussed in Chapter 12).

> **None** This disables .htaccess overrides. If AllowOverrides None is specified for a directory, Apache will not read an .htaccess even if it exists in that direc-

tory. If AllowOverrides None is specified for the system root ("/") directory, no directory will ever be searched for an .htaccess file.

Authconfig   Allows the use of all user/group authorization directives (Authname, Authuserfiles, Authgroupfile, Require), which are discussed in detail in Chapter 13.

FileInfo   Allows the use of directives controlling document types.

Indexes   Allows the use of directives controlling directory indexing.

Limit   Allows the use of directives that control access based on the browser hostname or network address.

Options   Allows the use of special directives, currently limited to the directives Options and XBitHack.

Setting Up User Home Directories

In nearly every server used to support multiple users, it is useful to provide individual users with their own Web home directories. This is a very common practice among Internet Service Providers that support Web hosting for their users. Providing user home directories is similar to virtual hosting in some respects, but it is much simpler to implement. The functionality is provided by a standard Apache module (mod_userdir) that is available to the Apache server by default.

Specifying Username-to-Directory Mappings

If you intend to allow users to publish their own Web pages, the UserDir directive indicates the name of a directory that, if found in the users' home directories, contains Web pages that are accessed with a URL of the form http://*hostname*/ ~*username*/, where *username* is a Linux user account on the server (or virtual server) *hostname*. The Apache default is to name this directory public_html. There is absolutely nothing wrong with this default value, but for years, since I first administered a CERN 3.0 server, I have chosen to name this directory WWW. A simple change to the UserDir directive in httpd.conf let me reconfigure this value for all users on the server:

```
UserDir WWW
```

Now once I add this line to Apache's httpd.conf file and restart the server, each user on my system can place files in a ~/WWW subdirectory of their home directory that Apache can serve. Requests to a typical user's Web files look like:

```
http://jackal.hiwaay.net/~caulds/index.html
```

The `UserDir` directive specifies a filename or pattern that is used to map a request for a user home directory to a special repository for that user's Web files. The `UserDir` directive can take one of three forms:

A Relative Path   This is normally the name of a directory that, when found in the user's home directory, becomes the `DocumentRoot` for that user's Web resources:

```
UserDir public_html
```

This is the simplest way to implement user home directories, and the one I recommend because it gives each user a Web home underneath their system home directories. This form takes advantage of the fact that *~username* is always Linux shorthand for "user account's home directory." By specifying users' home directories as a relative path, the server actually looks up the user's system home (in the Linux `/etc/passwd` file) and then looks for the defined Web home directory beneath it).

WARNING   Be careful when using the relative path form of the `UserDir` directive. It can expose directories that shouldn't be accessible from the Web. For example, when using the form `http://hostname/~root/`, the Linux shortcut for `~root` maps to a directory in the filesystem reserved for system files on most Linux systems. If you had attempted to designate each user's system home directory as their Web home directory (using `UserDir/`), this request would map to the `/root` directory. When using the relative directory form to designate user Web home directories, you should lock out any accounts that have home directories on protected filesystems (see the section titled "Enabling/Disabling Mappings" later in this chapter). The home directory of the root account (or *superuser*) on Linux systems should be protected. If someone was able to place an executable program in one of root's startup scripts (like `.profile` or `.bashrc`), that program would be executed the next time a legitimate user or administrator logged in using the root account.

An Absolute Path   An absolute pathname is combined with the username to identify the `DocumentRoot` for that user's Web resources:

```
UserDir /home/httpd/userstuff
```

This example would give each user their own directory with the same name as their user account underneath `/home/httpd/userstuff`. This form gives each user a Web home directory that is *outside* their system home directory. Maintaining a special directory for each user, outside their system home directory, is not a good idea if there are a lot of users. They won't be able to maintain their own Web spaces as they could in their respective home directories, and the entire responsibility will fall on the administrator. Use the absolute form for defining user Web home directories only if you have a small number of users, preferably where each is knowledgeable enough to ensure that their Web home directory is protected from other users on the system.

An Absolute Path with Placeholder   An absolute pathname can contain the * character (called a *placeholder*), which is replaced by the username when determining the DocumentRoot path for that user's Web resources. Like the absolute path described above, this form can map the request to a directory outside the user's system home directory:

```
UserDir   /home/httpd/*/www
```

Apache substitutes the username taken from the request URL of the form http://*hostname*/~*username*/ to yield the path to each user's Web home directory, as in this example:

```
/home/httpd/caulds/www
```

If all users have home directories under the same directory, the placeholder in the absolute path can mimic the relative path form, by specifying

```
UserDir   /home/*/www
```

The behavior of the lookup is slightly different, though, using this form. In the relative path form, the user's home directory is looked up in /etc/passwd. In the absolute path form, this lookup is not performed, and the user's Web home directory must exist in the specified path. The advantage of using the absolute path in this manner is that it prevents URLs like http://*hostname*/~root from mapping to a location that Web clients should never access.

The disadvantage of using the "absolute path with placeholder" form is that it forces all Web home directories to reside under one directory that you can point to with the absolute path. If you needed to place user Web home directories in other locations (perhaps even on other filesystems) you will need to create symbolic links that point the users' defined Web home directories to the actual location of the files. For a small to medium-sized system, this is a task that can be done once for each user and isn't too onerous, but for many users, it's a job you might prefer to avoid.

The use of the UserDir directive is best illustrated by example. Each of the three forms of the directive described above would map a request for

```
http://jackal.hiwaay.net/~caulds/index.html
```

into the following fully qualified path/filenames, respectively:

1. `~caulds/public_html/index.html`

2. `/home/httpd/userstuff/caulds/index.html`

3. `/home/httpd/caulds/www/index.html`

Redirecting Requests for User Home Directories

Chapter 9 provides a detailed discussion of Apache's tools for redirection, but the topic is worth a quick preview here, in the context of user home directories.

A server cannot *force* a browser to retrieve a resource from an alternate location. It sends a status code showing that the server couldn't respond to the browser's requests and a `Location` directive indicating an alternate location. The browser is politely asked to redirect its request to this alternate location. In the case of `UserDir`, the server issues a redirect request to the client, which will in all likelihood request the resource again from the specified alternate location, and the user is none the wiser. The argument to `UserDir` can also take the form of a URL rather than a directory specification, in which case the mapping is sent back to the client as a redirect request. This is most useful when redirecting requests for users' home directories to other servers. The following `UserDir` directive:

```
UserDir http://server2.hiwaay.com/~*/
```

would cause a request for

```
http://jackal.hiwaay.net/~caulds/docfiles/index.html
```

to generate a URL redirect request that would send the requester to the following resource, which is on a separate server:

```
http://server2.hiwaay.net/~caulds/docfiles/index.html
```

Enabling/Disabling Mappings

Another form of the `UserDir` directive uses the keywords `enabled` or `disabled` in one of three ways.

First,

```
UserDir disabled <username1 username2 …>
```

disables username-to-directory mappings for the space-delimited list of usernames. Example:

```
UserDir disabled root webmaster
```

WARNING If you are running a 1.3 version of Apache, it is strongly recommended that your configuration include a UserDir disabled root declaration.

Next, using the disabled keyword without username:

```
UserDir disabled
```

turns off all username-to-directory mappings. This form is usually used prior to a UserDir enabled directive that explicitly lists users for which mappings are performed.

And finally,

```
UserDir enabled <username1 username2 …>
```

enables username-to-directory mappings for the space-delimited list of usernames. It usually follows a UserDir disabled directive that turns off username-to-directory mappings for all users (all are normally enabled). Example:

```
UserDir disabled
UserDir enabled caulds csewell webteam
```

Using suEXEC with User Directories

Most sites that support user directories also allow users to create and run their own CGI processes. It is easy to see how allowing users to write and run CGI programs that run with the permissions of the Web server could be disastrous. Such a script would have the same access privileges that the Web server itself uses, and this is normally not a good thing. To protect the Web server from errant or malicious user-written CGI scripts, and to protect Web users from one another, user CGI scripts are usually run from a program called a CGI wrapper. A *CGI wrapper* is used to run a CGI process under different user and group accounts than those that are invoking the process. In other words, while ordinary CGI processes are run under the user and group account of the Apache server (by default, that is user nobody and group nobody), using a CGI wrapper, it is possible to invoke CGI processes that run under different user and group ownership. In most cases, this is used to restrict access by a script to only files and directories that are accessible to the effective owner of the script, that is, the user account under which suEXEC is running the script. This is most often used to give ordinary (nonprivileged) system users the opportunity to run CGI scripts that can have access only to other files owned by that user.

There are several such CGI wrappers, but one program of this type called suEXEC is a standard part of Apache in all versions after version 1.2 (though not enabled by the default installation). SuEXEC is very easy to install, and even easier to use. There are two ways in which suEXEC is useful to Apache administrators. The most important use for suEXEC is to allow users to run CGI programs from their own directories that run under their user and group accounts, rather than that of the server.

The second way in which suEXEC is used with Apache is with virtual hosts. When used with virtual hosts, suEXEC changes the user and group accounts under which all CGI scripts defined for each virtual host are run. This is used to give virtual host administrators the ability to write and run their own CGI scripts without compromising the security of the primary Web server (or any other virtual host).

Configuring Apache to Use suEXEC

The suEXEC tool is very easy to set up using the APACI installation script. APACI's configure script is provided with a number of options that are used to configure suEXEC. The most important of these is `--enable-suexec`, which is required to enable suEXEC. All of the other options have default values that you can find by peeking into the makefile in the top Apache source directory. On my system, I chose to use all the available options when running `configure`. Even when the default values are acceptable, I include them in my `build.sh` script, borrowing the default values from the makefile and modifying them where I desire.

Listing 4.1 shows the complete `build.sh` script I used to build Apache version 2.0.36 with suEXEC support. The lines that begin with `--with-suexec-` are a little different than most configure options. Instead of defining the Apache configuration, they provide values that are compiled into the resulting `suexec` wrapper as a security measure. As "hard-coded" values, defined at compile-time, they can't be overridden with directives or command-line arguments. They are fixed until `suexec` is recompiled (or replaced by a bogus version of `suexec` by a malicious party, which is your biggest security risk using `suexec`). The default permissions on `suexec` (and the `bin` directory in which it is placed during the install) should not be changed. They ensure that only a user with administrative rights can alter or replace the wrapper.

Listing 4.1   A `build.sh` Script for Building Apache 2.0.36 with suEXEC Support

```
#!/bin/sh
##
##  config.status -- APACI auto-generated configuration restore script
##
##  Use this shell script to re-run the APACI configure script for
##  restoring your configuration. Additional parameters can be supplied.
##

##LIBS=`perl -MExtUtils::Embed -e ldopts` \
##CFLAGS=`perl -MExtUtils::Embed -e ccopts` \
./configure \
```

```
"--with-layout=Apache" \
"--enable-mods-shared=all" \
"--enable-ssl" \
"--enable-proxy" \
"--enable-proxy-http" \
"--enable-proxy-ftp" \
"--enable-cache" \
"--enable-disk-cache" \
"--enable-mem-cache" \
"--enable-suexec" \
"--with-suexec-caller=nobody" \
"--with-suexec-docroot=/home/httpd/" \
"--with-suexec-logfile=/usr/local/apache2/logs/suexec_log" \
"--with-suexec-userdir=public_html" \
"--with-suexec-uidmin=100" \
"--with-suexec-gidmin=100" \
"--with-suexec-safepath=/usr/local/bin:/usr/bin:/bin" \
"$@"
```

To build and install Apache with suEXEC, I enter three lines in the Apache source directory (build.sh is a shell script that contains the lines shown above):

```
# sh build.sh
# make
# make install
```

Apache will still start, even if suEXEC is unavailable, but suEXEC will be disabled. You have to keep an eye on this; it is unfortunate that, when suEXEC is disabled, no warning is given when Apache is started, and nothing is written into Apache's error log. The error log will only show when suEXEC is enabled. You can check inside Apache's error log (which is in logs/error.log under the Apache installation directory, unless you've overridden this default value). If all is OK, the error log will contain the following line, with a timestamp, usually just before the line indicating that Apache has been started:

```
suEXEC mechanism enabled (wrapper: /usr/local/apache2/bin/suexec)
```

If suEXEC is not enabled when Apache is started, verify that you have the suexec wrapper program, owned by root, in Apache's bin directory:

```
# ls -al /usr/local/apache2/bin/suexec
-rwsr-xr-x   1 root     root    57543 Jun  5 20:19 suexec
```

Note the s in the user permissions. This indicates that the setuid bit is set. In other words, the file, when executed, will run under the user account of the file's owner. For example, the Apache httpd process that invokes suexec will probably be running under the nobody account. The suexec process it starts, however, will run under the root account, because root is the owner of the file suexec. Only root can invoke the Linux setuid and setgid system functions to change the ownership of processes it spawns as children (the CGI scripts that run under its control). If suexec is not owned by root, and does not have its user setuid bit set, correct this by entering the following lines while logged in as root:

```
# chown root /usr/local/apache2/bin/suexec
# chmod u+s /usr/local/apache2/bin/suexec
```

If you wish to disable suEXEC, the best way is to simply remove the user setuid bit:

```
# chmod u-s /usr/local/apache2/bin/suexec
```

This not only disables suEXEC, but it also renders the suEXEC program a bit safer because it will no longer run as root (unless directly invoked by root).

Using suEXEC

While suEXEC is easy to set up, it's even easier to use. Once it is enabled in your running Apache process, any CGI script that is invoked from a user's Web directory will execute under the user and group permissions of the owner of the Web directory. In other words, if I invoke a script with a URL like http://jackal.hiwaay.net/~caulds/cgi-bin/somescript.cgi, that script will run under caulds's user and group account. Note that all CGI scripts that will run under the suEXEC wrapper must be in the user's Web directory (which defaults to public_html but can be redefined by the --with suexec-userdir configuration) or a subdirectory of that directory.

For virtual hosts, the user and group accounts under which CGI scripts are run are defined by the SuexecUserGroup directive found in the virtual host container (this single directive replaces the use of the User and Group directives in pre-2.0 versions of Apache):

```
<VirtualHost 192.168.1.1>
  ServerName vhost1.hiwaay.net
  ServerAdmin caulds@hiwaay.net
  DocumentRoot /home/httpd/NamedVH1
  SuexecUserGroup vh1admin vh1webteam
</VirtualHost>
```

Simple Request Redirection

Chapter 9 discusses the redirection of HTTP requests in detail, particularly using mod_rewrite, which permits the use of a series of rules to perform very sophisticated URL rewriting. URL rewriting is a highly flexible way to redirect requests, but it is also quite complicated. For simple redirection, the Alias core directive is very useful. As an example of how Alias permits easy access to HTML documents outside the Document-

Root directory on my server, I'll demonstrate how I redirected access to the documentation for the MySQL database on my system, which resides outside Apache's Document-Root directory.

Many applications for Linux include documentation in the form of linked HTML pages. These are ordinarily outside the hierarchy of resources that has the Apache Document-Root at its top. Apache documentation is no exception. Some provision should be made to allow access to these pages. On my system, the Apache documentation pages are installed in /usr/local/apache2/htdocs. I used the Alias directive to alias two directories outside my DocumentRoot to URLs that appear inside the DocumentRoot resource tree. The first of these is the documentation for the MySQL database, which placed its documentation in /usr/share/doc/mysql-3.23.49 when installed on my system.

```
# pwd
/usr/share/doc/mysql-3.23.49
# ls
COPYING  COPYING.LIB  INSTALL-SOURCE  manual.texi  manual.txt
mysqld_error.txt  README
```

I symbolically linked the top-level HTML file to one that Apache will read when the requested URL names only the directory and not a particular file (that is, where it matches one of the names specified in DirectoryIndex):

```
# ln -s manual_toc.html index.html
```

Using a symbolic link, rather than copying the file or renaming it, ensures that only one copy of the file exists, but can be accessed by either name. The last step was the insertion of two Alias directives into httpd.conf. Place these in a manner that seems logical to you, probably somewhere in the main server configuration section of the file, so that you can easily locate the directives at a later date.

```
Alias /MySQL/ /usr/share/doc/mysql-3.23.49
Alias /ApacheDocs/ "/usr/local/apache2/manual/"
```

Any user can now access these sets of documentation on my server using these URLs:

```
http://jackal.hiwaay.net/MySQL/
http://jackal.hiwaay.net/ApacheDocs/
```

Providing Directory Indexes

I'm ending this chapter with a discussion of a very important set of Apache directories that are not actually part of the core module, but are such an essential part of the standard distribution that they are used on every Apache server. You might notice that most Web pages are not retrieved by the specific filename. Rather than entering a URL like this:

```
http://jackal.hiwaay.net/dirname/index.html
```

you generally enter a URL like the following:

```
http://jackal.hiwaay.net/dirname
```

This URL actually maps to a directory on the server (a directory named `dirname` beneath the directory defined in the Apache configuration as `DocumentRoot`). It is only through a standard Apache module named `mod_dir` that a specific page is served to clients that send a request URL that maps to a directory. Without `mod_dir`, the second form, which does not specify a unique resource, would be invalid and would produce an HTTP 404 (Not Found) error.

The `mod_dir` module serves two important functions. First, whenever a request is received that maps to a directory but does not have a trailing slash (/) as in:

```
http://jackal.hiwaay.net/dirname
```

`mod_dir` sends a redirection request to the client indicating that the request should be made, instead, to the URL:

```
http://jackal.hiwaay.net/dirname/
```

This requires a second request on the part of the client to correct what is, technically, an error in the original request. Though the time required to make this second request is usually minimal and unnoticed by the user, whenever you express URLs that map to directories rather than files, you should include the trailing slash for correctness and efficiency.

The second function of `mod_dir` is to look for and serve a file defined as the index file for the directory specified in the request. That page, by default, is named `index.html`. This can be changed using `mod_dir`'s only directive, `DirectoryIndex`, as described below. The name of the file comes from the fact that it was originally intended to provide the requestor with an index of the files in the directory. While providing directory indexes is still useful, the file is used far more often to serve as a default HTML document, or Web page, for the root URL; this is often called the home page. Remember that this behavior is not a given; `mod_dir` must be included in the server configuration and enabled for this to work.

The *DirectoryIndex* Directive

As mentioned, the default value of the file served by `mod_dir` is `index.html`. In other words, if the Apache configuration contains no `DirectoryIndex` directive, it will look for and attempt to serve a file named index.html whenever a request URL resolves to a directory. Although this is a default behavior, the standard Apache configuration will create the following line in the httpd.conf file that it installs:

```
DirectoryIndex index.html index.html.var
```

The .var entry is a *type-map file*, which allows Apache to serve its default page in a language based on the language preference in the requesting user's browser settings. The use of type-map files is described in Chapter 15.

The last change I made was to add a second filename to the DirectoryIndex directive. I added an entry for index.htm to cause the Apache server to look for files of this name, which may have been created on a system that follows the Microsoft convention of a three-character filename extension. The files are specified in order of preference from left to right, so if it finds both index.html and index.htm in a directory, it will serve index.html.

```
# DirectoryIndex index.html index.html.var
DirectoryIndex index.html index.htm
```

Fancier Directory Indexes

I've described the behavior of Apache when a request is received that maps to a directory on the server. Through mod_dir, Apache serves a file from the directory defined in the DirectoryIndex directive (or index.html if DirectoryIndex is not specified). In cases where no such file exists, Apache uses a second module, mod_autoindex, to prepare an index or listing of the files in the directory. Figure 4.1 shows the default directory index that mod_autoindex will serve to the requesting client.

The default httpd.conf for an Apache 2.0 server will contain the following line in the main server configuration section:

```
IndexOptions FancyIndexing VersionSort
```

This directive enables the use of *fancy indexing* from mod_autoindex, which allows the administrator full control over every aspect of the listing Apache prepares for a directory that does not contain an index file. The default httpd.conf provided with the Apache distribution uses many of the directives that I'll describe in the following sections to set up the default fancy directory for use on your server.

Older versions of Apache included mod_autoindex, but disabled the fancy indexing by default. Unless manually reconfigured, an Apache server older than 2.0 displays a directory listing as shown in Figure 4.2. Removing the IndexOptions FancyIndexing directive from your server configuration will produce a listing with this generic format.

Figure 4.1 A fancy Apache directory listing

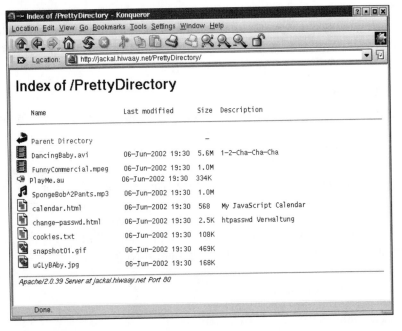

Figure 4.2 A plain Apache directory listing

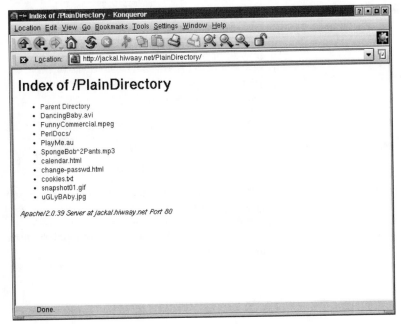

The `VersionSort` indexing option used in the default Apache 2.0 configuration file (also new in Apache versions later than 2.0) causes Apache to attempt to sort files that contain version numbers in a logical manner. This is so that, for example, a file named `httpd-2.0.9.gz` will be listed before one named `httpd-2.0.12.gz`, unlike a simple alphanumeric sort.

Index Options

`IndexOptions` can also be used to set a number of other options for configuring directory indexing. Among these are options to specify the size of the icons displayed, suppress the display of any of the columns besides the filename, and whether or not clicking the column heading sorts the listing by the values in that column. Many of these options can be utilized to disable formatting features that aren't properly displayed in older browsers. Although these indexing options allow a great amount of flexibility in determining the resulting display of directory listings, most users are perfectly content with the Apache-provided default values. Table 4.1 depicts all possible options that can be used with the `IndexOptions` directive.

Table 4.1   Index Options

Index Option	Description
DescriptionWidth=*n*	Defines the character width of the file description column.
FancyIndexing	Enables fancy indexing.
FoldersFirst	Lists subdirectories (folders) first, before all files in the displayed directory.
HTMLTable	Uses HTML tables to display the directory (may not work with some browsers).
IconsAreLinks	Makes icons part of the clickable anchor for the filename.
IconHeight=*pixels*	Sets the height (in pixels) of the icons displayed in the listing. Like the HTML tag <IMG HEIGHT=*n*...>.
IconWidth=*pixels*	Sets the width (in pixels) of the icons displayed in the listing. Like the HTML tag <IMG WIDTH=*n*...>.
IgnoreClient	Ignores all query variables from the client, including sort column and order.

Table 4.1   Index Options (*continued*)

Index Option	Description
NameWidth=*n*	Sets the width (in characters) of the filename column in the listing, truncating characters if the name exceeds this width. Specifying NameWidth=* causes the filename column to be as wide as the longest filename in the listing.
ScanHTMLTitles	Causes the file description to be extracted from the HTML <TITLE> tag, if it exists. The AddDescription directive overrides this setting for individual files.
SuppressColumnSorting	Disables the normal behavior of inserting clickable headers at the top of each column that can be used to sort the listing.
SuppressDescription	Disables the display of the Description column of the listing.
SuppressHTMLPreamble	Disables automatic HTML formatting of the header file if one is specified for the listing. No <HTML>, <HEAD>, or <BODY> tags can precede the header file, and they must be manually placed into the file contents if desired.
SuppressIcon	Disables the printing of the icon in directory listings.
SuppressLastModified	Disables the display of the Last Modified column of the listing.
SuppressRules	Disables the printing of the horizontal rules in directory listings.
SuppressSize	Disables the display of the Size column in the listing.
TrackModified	Returns the date of last modification and entity tag (or ETag) information of the current directory inside the HTTP response header. This information is useful to caching engines.
VersionSort	Attempts to sort filenames containing version numbers in a logical order.
None	Disables fancy indexing.

Options are always inherited from parent directories. This behavior is overridden by specifying options with a + or – prefix to add or subtract the options from the list of options that are already in effect for a directory. Whenever an option is read that does not contain either of these prefixes, the list of options in effect is immediately cleared. Consider this example:

```
IndexOptions +ScanHTMLTitles -IconsAreLinks SuppressSize
```

If this directive appears in an .htaccess file for a directory, regardless of the options inherited by that directory from its higher-level directories, the net effect will be the same as this directive:

```
IndexOptions SuppressSize
```

This is because as soon as the SuppressSize option was encountered without a + or – prefix, the current list of options was immediately cleared.

Specifying Icons

In addition to IndexOptions, mod_autoindex provides other directives that act to configure the directory listing. You can, for example, provide a default icon for unrecognized resources. You can change the icon or description displayed for a particular resource, either by its MIME type, filename, or encoding type (GZIP-encoded, for example). You can also specify a default field and display order for sorting, or identify a file whose content will be displayed at the top of the directory.

The *AddIcon* Directive

AddIcon specifies the icon to display for a file when fancy indexing is used to display the contents of a directory. The icon is identified by a relative URL to the icon image file. Note that the URL you specify is embedded directly in the formatted document that is sent to the client browser, which then retrieves the image file in a separate HTTP request.

The name argument can be a filename extension, a wildcard expression, a complete filename, or one of two special forms. Examples of the use of these forms follow:

```
AddIcon /icons/image.jpg *jpg*
AddIcon (IMG, /icons/image.jpg) .gif .jpg .bmp
```

The second example above illustrates an alternate form for specifying the icon. When parentheses are used to enclose the parameters of the directive, the first parameter is the alternate text to associate with the resource; the icon to be displayed is specified as a relative URL to an image file. The alternate text, IMG, will be displayed by browsers that are not capable of rendering images. A disadvantage of using this form is that the alternate text cannot contain spaces or other special characters. The following form is *not* acceptable:

```
AddIcon ("JPG Image", /icons/image.jpg) .jpg
```

There are two special expressions you can use in place of a filename in the AddIcon directive that specify which images to use as icons in the directory listing. Use ^^BLANKICON^^ to specify an icon for blank lines in the listing, and use ^^DIREC-TORY^^ to specify an icon for directories in the listing:

```
AddIcon /icons/folder.gif ^^DIRECTORY^^
AddIcon /icons/blank.gif ^^BLANKICON^^
```

There is one other special case that you should be aware of. The parent of the directory whose index is being displayed is indicated by the "`..`" filename. You can change the icon associated with the parent directory with a directive like the following:

```
AddIcon /icons/up.gif ..
```

> **NOTE**   The Apache Software Foundation recommends using AddIconBy-Type rather than AddIcon whenever possible. Although there appears to be no real difference between these (on a Linux system, the MIME type of a file is identified by its filename extension), it is considered more proper to use the MIME type that Apache uses for the file, rather than directly examining its filename. There are often cases, however, when no MIME type has been associated with a file and you must use AddIcon to set the image for the file.

The *AddIconByType* Directive

AddIconByType specifies the icon to display in the directory listing for files of certain MIME content types. This directory works like the AddIcon directive just described, but it relies on the determination that Apache has made of the MIME type of the file (as discussed in Chapter 15, Apache usually determines the MIME type of a file based on its filename).

```
AddIconByType /icons/webpage.gif text/html
AddIconByType (TXT, /icons/text.gif) text/*
```

This directive is used almost exactly like AddIcon. When parentheses are used to enclose the parameters of the directive, the first parameter is the alternate text to associate with the resource; the icon to be displayed is specified as a relative URL to an image file. The last parameter, rather than being specified as a filename extension, is a MIME content type. Look in conf/mime.types under the Apache home directory (typically /usr/local/apache2) for a list of types that Apache knows about.

The *AddIconByEncoding* Directive

AddIconByEncoding is used to specify the icon displayed next to files that use a certain MIME encoding. As discussed in Chapter 15, MIME encoding generally refers to file compression schemes and therefore determines what action is required to decode the file for use. Some typical encoding schemes and examples of the use of this directive are:

```
AddIconByEncoding /icons/gzip.gif x-gzip
AddIconByEncoding /icons/tarimage.gif x-gtar
```

Specifying a Default Icon

A special directive, `DefaultIcon`, is used to set the icon that is displayed for files with which no icon has been associated, i.e., none of the other directives mentioned above. The directive simply identifies an image file by relative URL:

```
DefaultIcon  /icons/unknown.pcx
```

Adding Alternate Text for Images

When an image is displayed in a Web page, the HTML tags used to embed the image in the page provide for an alternate text string that is displayed in browsers that cannot display graphics. This text string is also displayed as pop-up text if the user of a graphical browser right-clicks or, depending on your Web browser, when the cursor pauses or "hovers" over the image.

There are three directives that are provided by `mod_autoindex` for setting the alternate text associated with a file in the fancy directory listing. Each of these directives is analogous to one of the `AddIcon` directives shown above and uses the same syntax.

The *AddAlt* Directive

The `AddAlt` directive specifies an alternate text string to be displayed for a file, instead of an icon, in text-only browsers. Like its `AddIcon` counterpart, the directive specifies a filename, partial filename, or wildcard expression to identify files:

```
AddAlt "JPG Image" *jpg*
AddAlt "Image File" .gif .jpg .bmp
```

Note that it is possible to use a quoted string with the `AddAlt` directive, which can contain spaces and other special characters. This is not possible when specifying alternate text using the special form of `AddIcon` as shown above.

The *AddAltByType* Directive

`AddAltByType` sets the alternate text string to be displayed for a file based on the MIME content type that Apache has identified for the file. This directive works very much like its counterpart, `AddIconByType`.

```
AddAltByType "HTML Document"  text/html
```

The *AddAltByEncoding* Directive

AddAltByEncoding sets the alternate text string to be displayed for a file, based on the MIME content encoding of the file, as determined by Apache.

```
AddAltByEncoding "GZipped File" x-gzip
```

Specifying File Descriptions

The AddDescription directive is used to specify a text string to be displayed in the Description column of the listing for specific files. Files can be identified by a partial or full pathname:

```
AddDescription "My Home Page" index.html
```

Note that this example sets a description to apply to all files named index.html. To apply the description to a specific file, use its full and unique pathname:

```
AddDescription "My Home Page" /home/httpd/html/index.html
```

AddDescription can also be used with wildcard filenames to set descriptions for entire classes of files (identified by filename extension in this case):

```
AddDescription "PCX Image" *.pcx
AddDescription "TAR File" *.tgz *.tar.gz
```

When multiple descriptions apply to the same file, the first match found is the one used in the listing; so always specify the most specific match first:

```
AddDescription "Powered By Apache Logo" poweredby.gif
AddDescription "GIF Image" *.gif
```

In addition to AddDescription, there is one other way that mod_autoindex can determine values to display in the Description column of a directory listing. If IndexOptions ScanHTMLTitles is in effect for a directory, mod_autoindex will parse all HTML files in the directory, and extract descriptions for display from the <TITLE> elements of the documents. This is handy if the directory contains a relatively small number of HTML documents or is infrequently accessed. Enabling this option requires that every HTML document in the directory be opened and examined. For a large number of files, this can impose a significant workload, so the option is disabled by default.

Adding a Header and a Footer

The mod_autoindex module supplies two directives that allow you to insert the contents of a file at the top of the index listing as a page header or at the bottom of the listing as a page footer.

The HeaderName directive specifies a filename using a URI relative to the one used to access the directory. The contents of this file are placed into the listing immediately after the opening <BODY> tag of the listing. It is usually a good idea to maintain the header file in the same directory it describes, which makes it easy to reference by its filename. The default httpd.conf file that comes with Apache contains the following directive, which doesn't really need to be changed:

```
HeaderName HEADER.html
```

Files identified by the HeaderName directive must be of the major MIME content type text. If the file is identified as type text/html (generally by its extension), it is inserted verbatim; otherwise it is enclosed in <PRE> and </PRE> tags. A CGI script can be used to generate the information for the header (either as HTML or plain text), but you must first associate the CGI script with a MIME main content type (usually text), as follows:

```
AddType text/html .cgi
HeaderName HEADER.cgi
```

The ReadmeName directive works almost identically to HeaderName to specify a file (again relative to the URI used to access the directory being indexed) that is placed in the listing just before the closing </BODY> tag. I changed the default httpd.conf file that comes with Apache to better describe its function of placing a "footer" on the directory page:

```
#   Apache default
# ReadmeName README.html
#   My revised directive
ReadmeName FOOTER.html
```

Ignoring Files

The IndexIgnore directive specifies a set of filenames that are ignored by mod_autoindex when preparing the index listing of a directory. The filenames can be specified by wildcards:

```
IndexIgnore FOOTER*
```

> **NOTE**   The default httpd.conf file provided with Apache contains an IndexIgnore directive that prevents filenames beginning with README or HEADER from being displayed in the index listing by mod_autoindex. This makes these filenames obvious (but not necessary) choices for use as headers and footers for directory listings.

Ordering the Index Listing

The IndexOrderDefault directive is used to change the default order of the index listing generated by mod_autoindex, which is to sort the list in ascending order by filename.

This directive takes two arguments. The first must be either `Ascending` or `Descending` to indicate the sort direction; the second names a single field as the primary sort key and can be `Name`, `Date`, `Size`, or `Description`:

```
IndexOrderDefault Descending Size
```

The secondary sort key is always the filename in ascending order.

Example

In order to illustrate typical uses of some of the `mod_autoindex` directives discussed, I created an `.htaccess` file in the same directory that was illustrated in Figure 4.2. This file contains the following directives, all of which are used by `mod_autoindex` to customize the index listing for the directory. The result of applying these directives is shown in Figure 4.3.

```
IndexOptions FancyIndexing VersionSort +ScanHTMLTitles
AddIcon /icons/small/sound.gif .au
AddDescription "1-2-Cha-Cha-Cha" DancingBaby.avi
AddAltByType "This is a JPG Image" image/jpeg
ReadmeName FOOTER.html
```

Figure 4.3 A customized `mod_autoindex` listing

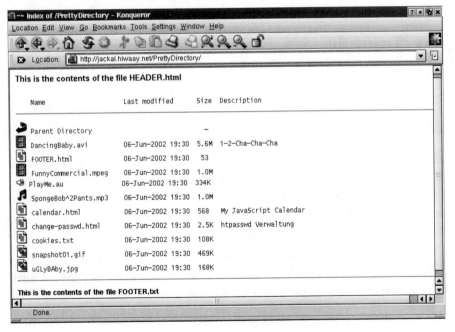

Essential Configuration

PART 2

The IndexOptions directive is used to enable the extraction of file descriptions from the <TITLE> tags of HTML formatted files (technically, files of MIME content type text/HTML). You can see this illustrated in Figure 4.3 by the files with .html extensions. If any of these files had the name index.html, the index listing would not have been generated at all; instead, index.html would have been sent (by mod_dir) to the client.

I've also provided an example of adding an icon using the AddIcon directive and a file description using AddDescription. The results of these directives can be easily seen in Figure 4.3. The alternate text for JPEG images (added with the AddAltByType directive) is not displayed in the figure, but would be seen in place of the image icon in text-only browsers. It would also appear in a graphical browser in a pop-up dialog box when the cursor is paused over the associated icon. This gives the page developer a handy way to add help text to a graphics-rich Web page, which can be particularly useful when the icon or image is part of an anchor tag (clickable link) and can invoke an action.

To demonstrate the HeaderName and ReadmeName directives, I included files with these names, the contents of which were included as, respectively, the header and footer for the directory page. Note that I overrode Apache's default value for the ReadmeName directive, which looks for a file named README.html, a name that I felt wasn't descriptive of its purpose as a page footer. Both files consisted of a single line of (boring) text. The header file contained HTML-formatting tags (<H3> </H3>) that caused it to be rendered in larger, bolder characters, and the footer used <H4> tags so it was slightly less prominent. There is no reason why either the header or footer couldn't be longer and contain far more elaborate formatting. Use your imagination.

In Sum

This chapter has covered a lot of ground, because so much of Apache's functionality is now incorporated into the configuration directives provided by its core modules, rather than through optional extension modules. We began with the essential concept of directive *context*, or the scope within which particular directives are valid. We then looked at the directives used to configure the basic server environment and how the server listens for connections. These directives are fundamental to Apache's operation, and every administrator needs to be familiar with them.

Later sections of the chapter explored the directives used to create and manage user home directories. These are not only an essential function for any ISP installation of an Apache server; they are also widely used in intranets.

The next chapter moves beyond the core modules to the use of freely downloadable third-party modules and the techniques you can use to incorporate them into your Apache server.

5

Apache Modules

I've already discussed the importance of modules to Apache's design philosophy. Without the concept of extension by module, it is unlikely that Apache would have garnered the level of third-party support that directly led to its phenomenal success in the early days of the Web. Apache owes much of that success to the fact that any reasonably proficient programmer can produce add-on modules that tap directly into the server's internal mechanisms. As administrators, we benefit greatly from the availability of these third-party modules.

At one time, it was thought that commercial Web servers, with the support that "commercial" implies, would eventually eclipse the open-source Apache server. It seemed completely logical that when a company began to get serious about the Web, it needed to look for a serious Web engine, a commercial server—not some piece of unsupported free software downloaded from the Internet. But as we've seen, Apache took the top spot from its commercial rivals and has continued to widen that lead, even while most Unix-based applications slowly gave ground to their NT competitors. Apache owes much of its success to a vibrant, innovative, and completely professional community of users and developers that you can be a part of. Apache is as fully supported as any commercial product. Virtually any feature or function you can desire in a Web server is available as an Apache module, usually offered by its author at no cost to all Apache users.

If you've used and depend on a third-party module with Apache 1.3.*x*, make very sure the module has been updated to work with Apache 2.0. Changes in the Apache programmer's interface mean that 1.3.*x* modules will *not* work with Apache 2.0 unless modified to call the new interface functions. Most modules, when ported to 2.0, should work (at least initially) the same as their 1.3.*x* counterparts.

This chapter looks at the types of modules available, how the module mechanism works, how to link modules to Apache as dynamic shared objects (DSOs), and where to find third-party modules not included in the Apache distribution. The chapter concludes with a step-by-step example of installing such a module.

Types of Apache Modules

Except for the very basic kernel code, virtually all of the capability of an Apache server is implemented in modules. Apache modules can be categorized into four groups:

The core module, which, unlike most modules, is loaded from two files, core.c and httpd_core.c, and is the only module that must always be statically linked into the Apache kernel. It is the only module that is absolutely essential to an Apache server. It cannot be removed from the server, and the functions provided by this module are available in all Apache servers. The directives furnished by the core module are always available; they are the only directives discussed so far in this book.

The standard modules are provided as part of the Apache distribution and are maintained by the Apache Software Foundation as part of the Apache server itself. Most of the standard modules are compiled by the standard installation scripts (described in Chapter 3) into the Apache code. Unlike the core module, however, any of the standard modules can be removed at the server administrator's discretion. This might be done for security reasons, but the most common reason for removing a module from Apache is to reduce the amount of memory used by each running instance of the server. (Remember that Apache maintains a pool of server processes to handle user requests. Since each process in the pool requires its own memory space, the amount of space saved by eliminating unused modules can be multiplied by the number of processes in the Apache server pool.)

Third-party modules are modules written, supported, and distributed by sources other than the Apache Group. These modules are not provided as part of the Apache distribution and must be obtained separately. Over the years, many modules that were originally distributed as third-party authored and supported have been added to the Apache distribution. This happens only if there's a wide demand for the module, and its developers have taken pains to ensure that it is reliable and performs adequately. The Apache distribution now

includes all of the most useful and most popular modules, and many site administrators will never need to install third-party modules. Two examples of modules that have recently been added to the standard Apache distribution are
mod_auth_dbm, discussed in Chapter 13, and mod_dav, which is explained in
Appendix C.

mod_perl modules are written in the Perl programming language, which has always
been a popular language for Web programmers and CGI scripters. While Apache
modules of the other three types mentioned must be written in C, mod_perl provides a second Application Programming Interface (or API) to the Apache internal
data structures and functions that allow Apache modules to be written in Perl.

How Modules Work

Apache is designed so that modules do not directly control the actions of the Apache
engine. Instead, modules remain under the control of Apache and work by registering
callbacks with Apache for the functions they provide. A *callback* is a function that is
registered with Apache so that Apache can execute the function. Callbacks are registered through *hooks* to be processed at specific points in the Apache request processing
cycle. This processing cycle begins when Apache receives a request for a resource from a
connecting client, and ends when Apache sends the client a response to the request.
Apache usually closes the network connection with the client at the conclusion of the
request processing cycle, but this is not always true. Often, multiple requests are handled over a single open network connection, although the typical behavior of Apache is
to close the network connection after each request is processed.

In Apache 2.0, there are 21 points in the request cycle (hooks) for which modules can
register callback functions to be executed. This is nearly twice the 11 phases defined in
Apache version 1.3. Most modules will register functions to be called at more than one
point in the request cycle, though few will require more than two or three hooks.

Apache's request processing cycle is categorized into four major phases. Modules can
register callback functions, or even override the standard functions in Apache, in all
four phases:

Request Parsing Phase: In this phase, the resource request is received from a
connecting client (browser), which furnishes information via the HTTP request
header as described in Chapter 1. The request itself is contained within a URL,
which is parsed in this phase, and resolved by a single resource or action, usually a file within the server's filesystem. The request could also result in a redirection, in which the request is translated and resubmitted. URL redirection is
the subject of Chapter 9.

Essential
Configuration

PART 2

Security Phase: In this phase, the server may optionally take two actions. First, the requestor might be identified (authentication), usually by requiring a username/password pair, and then some means might be used to determine if the requester is authorized to receive the requested resource (authorization). This phase is covered in Chapter 13.

Preparation Phase: The major activity performed in this phase, which occurs just prior to actually serving the request, is a determination of what resource type (language, character set, encoding) will be sent to the server. Chapter 15 discusses resource types and content negotiation, which takes place in this phase.

Handler Phase: This is the phase of the request cycle where most of the work is performed. This is when the actual resource is served to the client, which can be as simple as the unmodified contents of a static disk file, or it might be output generated by a program or script.

Incorporating Perl Scripts with *mod_perl*

Apache modules already exist for all of the common tasks that Web servers need to perform, and many administrators will never need to write their own. But if you do plan to write your own modules, or even just use modules written by other system administrators, you should know about the mod_perl module. As you'll see in Chapter 8, Perl is the scripting language most widely used by system administrators, and mod_perl is the tool that makes it available to Apache.

Before there was a mod_perl, it was not possible to write an Apache module in anything but C, and for production server applications, I'm not sure I would ever have recommended a scripting language for the task, even if it had been possible to use one. The mod_perl module changed that. With its memory-resident Perl interpreter and ability to perform one-time compilation and caching of Perl scripts, it virtually eliminates one of the most valid criticisms leveled at Perl: its lack of speed when compared with binary code compiled from source languages like C.

The mod_perl module provides a built-in handler for each of the 21 hooks in the Apache request cycle where a program can step in and interrupt Apache's processing to perform a function of its own. This makes it extremely easy to invoke a Perl function at just about any point between receipt of browser requests and the action of sending a response to the browser. For example, if you want Apache to call a Perl function that will be performed immediately following the receipt of a user request, you can register the function as a callback by placing the following lines in httpd.conf:

```
PerlModule Apache::MyModule
PerlPostReadRequestHandler Apache::MyModule::myhandler
```

The first line preloads the module into the `Apache::` namespace. The second line registers the `myhandler` function within that module as a callback during the `PostRead-Request` phase of the request cycle. When a request comes in, Apache will ensure that `myhandler`, which has already been loaded and compiled by `mod_perl`, is called. The function will have access to Apache's internal data structures and functions through the Perl Apache API calls (each of which, in turn, calls a function from the Apache API).

Although the purpose of `mod_perl` is to allow the creation of Apache extension modules in a language that many programmers find easier to use than C, most `mod_perl` users never actually create their own Apache modules. Apache administrators are most likely to install `mod_perl` to take advantage of third-party modules written to enhance the functionality and performance of Perl scripts that run on their servers. For this reason, I will discuss `mod_perl` in Chapter 8 as a Web application programming tool, rather than in this chapter, which is concerned only with modules of the other three types, always written in C.

While most Perl scripts written to run as CGI scripts will work fine when run from within `mod_perl`, there are subtle differences in how they work as opposed to the same scripts when run from the Linux shell prompt or as plain CGI scripts. The main difference is that they run in an "environment" that does not change between invocations of the script. In other words, if a script sets a variable that is scoped globally (that is, it is visible from all parts of the program), the value of that variable will linger, and the next user who runs the same script will see the same value of the variable if it is not cleared. This could be quite serious if, perhaps, the variable contained something like a password or credit card number.

Installing Third-Party Modules

There is no rigid specification to which Apache modules from third-party sources must adhere. There is no standard procedure for installing and using Apache modules. There are guidelines, however, that define a "well-behaved" Apache module, and most modules are fairly standard and therefore quite simple to install and configure.

The Two Linking Methods

Apache modules can be installed either within the Apache source tree or outside it. Those installed within the Apache source become, essentially, a part of Apache, even if their inclusion is optional. The standard Apache modules (those that are part of the Apache distribution) fall into this category. A limited number of third-party modules must also be installed in this fashion, particularly if they rely on changes made to the Apache source code. When this method is used, the module source code is usually placed in the /src/modules subdirectory with the rest of the Apache source. Special configuration directives are passed to the Apache configure script to compile the module with the rest of Apache, link it with the resulting runtime, and make the necessary changes to http.conf to enable the module. (The use of configure was demonstrated in Chapter 3.)

Most third-party modules, though, are better compiled outside the Apache source tree. In other words, they are compiled in a completely separate directory from the Apache source, as dynamic shared object (DSO) modules, and are loaded at runtime by Apache.

Although the module source can be placed inside the Apache source tree and the configure script instructed to compile it as a DSO, I strongly recommend against doing this. If you intend to use a module as a DSO, it can be compiled on its own, outside the Apache source tree, using a utility called apxs, which is provided with the Apache distribution. One advantage of compiling with apxs is that the resulting module, which will have the extension .so for *shared object*, is a stand-alone module that can be used with different versions of the server. This allows you to upgrade modules without recompiling Apache, as you must do when a module is compiled within the Apache source tree using configure. More importantly, using DSO modules compiled with apxs allows you to upgrade the Apache server without having to rerun the configuration for each module, specifying the new Apache source tree.

There are nearly as many installation procedures as there are modules. Some install inside the Apache tree; most can be compiled separately from Apache. Some simply compile a DSO and leave you to manually edit httpd.conf; some configure httpd.conf for you. Read the INSTALL file carefully before compiling any module, at least to get some idea of how the installation proceeds and what options are available. In general, though, the best way to compile and install Apache modules is to use the utility Apache has provided specifically for this purpose, apxs. Because most third-party modules are best compiled as DSOs using apxs, that is the method I describe in this chapter. The only modules I recommend installing as statically linked modules are those that come with the standard Apache distribution. These are automatically linked to Apache during the server installation unless at least one --enable-shared argument is passed to configure. Chapter 3 describes how standard modules are chosen and identified as statically linked or DSO modules.

Making the Choice

Virtually all Apache modules can be either statically linked or compiled as a DSO to be loaded at runtime, and the choice is usually yours to make. For most Apache sites, the DSO method provides the most flexibility and easiest maintainability, although you pay a small performance cost for it. Administrators should consider statically linking modules only when they rarely alter their Apache configuration. Table 5.1 summarizes the characteristics of each method of linking a module.

Table 5.1 Static vs. Dynamic Linking

Feature	Statically Linked	Linked as DSO
Installed Using:	Apache `configure`	`apxs`
Module Source Location:	Resides in the Apache source tree	Module source resides outside the Apache source tree.
Impact on Size of Apache Executable:	Increases the size of the Apache runtime executable	Keeps Apache runtime as small as possible.
Loading Speed:	Fastest loading	Increases load time of the module by about 20 percent.
Module Loaded When:	Module always loaded, even if disabled and unused	Module loaded only when specified in `httpd.conf`.
Recommended When:	The Apache configuration is simple, requiring few add-on modules and few changes and when fastest possible loading is important	Server configuration changes frequently or when modules are frequently changed, upgraded, or installed for testing.

Using Dynamically Linked Modules

DSO modules are loaded as part of the Apache server at *runtime*, that is, when the server is started. DSO modules are designed to be dynamically loaded into the running server's address space and are able to access and directly modify internal Apache data structures. Loading a DSO module is approximately 20 percent slower than if the module were statically linked into the server kernel. However, a DSO module, once loaded, is in every respect a part of Apache, and there is no performance overhead inherent in running a function in a DSO module rather than as statically linked code.

With two important exceptions, all modules distributed with Apache can be compiled as DSO modules that are loaded at runtime. The first exception is the core module, which must always be statically linked into the Apache kernel. The second module that can never be run as a DSO (for reasons I hope are obvious) is the module that provides the server with the capability of dynamically loading shared objects. No DSO module can be loaded for use by the server without mod_so, and this module must always be statically linked into the Apache kernel when Apache is compiled. When at least one –enable-shared= argument is passed to the Apache configure script (Chapter 3), mod_so automatically links into Apache when it is compiled. You can see the result of this linking by running httpd with the –l switch:

```
# /usr/local/apache2/bin/httpd -l
Compiled in modules:
  core.c
  prefork.c
  http_core.c
  mod_so.c
```

This example shows the most basic Apache 2.0 httpd daemon. It must *always* have the core modules linked into it (core.c and http_core.c), as well as one Multi-Processing Module (MPM) that determines how Apache handles multiple simultaneous clients (in the case of Linux, this will almost always be prefork.c). Optionally, it also has the mod_so module that provides support for DSO modules. All other module support is dynamically linked at runtime to the httpd process. The mod_so module supplies the server with a new directive, LoadModule, which is used in the Apache configuration file to designate a module for dynamic loading. When the server reads a LoadModule directive from the configuration during its initialization, mod_so will load the module and immediately make it available for use. Only DSO modules require the LoadModule directive.

The module name, with .c substituting for .so in the actual filename, can be used in a conditional test to determine if the module has been loaded and is available. The following test will process lines in the ssl.conf file (which contains Apache directives specific to SSL and mod_ssl) only if the module has been loaded. If the module has not been loaded, the Include directive (and any other directives that happen to be there) between the <IfModule> and </IfModule> tags is ignored.

```
<IfModule mod_ssl.c>
  Include conf/ssl.conf
</IfModule>
```

Older versions of Apache use the order in which DSO modules are loaded to determine the order in which they are called by Apache to handle URLs. This places a burden on Apache administrators to order the lines in httpd.conf that initialize the modules (using a now-defunct directive, AddModule). In Apache 2.0, however, the order in which modules are loaded and initialized is no longer relevant. Modules themselves express a preference for how much precedence they'd like to have over other modules registered for the same Apache hook. It's always up to Apache, though, to decide the order in which several modules that are registered to be called from the same hook will run. As administrators, we don't care, and the order of the LoadModule lines in httpd.conf is no longer our concern.

Using *apxs*

Since the release of Apache version 1.3, Apache has been packaged with a Perl script called apxs (for APache eXtenSion). This relatively simple utility is used to compile and install third-party modules. One important benefit of using apxs rather than placing the module in the Apache source tree and compiling it with the Apache configure script is that apxs can handle modules consisting of more than one source file; configure cannot.

A few modules have special installation requirements; these modules generally come with detailed instructions (usually in a file named INSTALL) that should be followed carefully. Generally, modules that cannot be installed using the procedures detailed in this section are those that must make modifications to the Apache source. The OpenSSL module (mod_ssl), discussed in Chapter 14, is one such module. As you'll see, during its installation this module makes extensive patches and additions to the Apache source and requires a recompilation of Apache to work.

With those exceptions, however, nearly every Apache module can be compiled with apxs. apxs is the preferred way to compile most third-party modules, and you should become quite familiar with its use.

You can invoke apxs with combinations of the following arguments to control its actions:

-g   Generates a template for module developers; when supplied with a module name (using the -n switch), this option creates a source code directory with that name and installs a makefile and sample module C source code file within it. The sample C program is a complete module that can actually be installed; however, it does nothing but print out a line indicating that it ran. Example:

```
# apxs -g -n mod_MyModule
```

-q   Queries the apxs script for the values of one or more of its defaults. When the apxs script is created during an Apache installation, default values for the following variables are hard-coded into the script: TARGET, CC, CFLAGS, CFLAGS_SHLIB, LD_SHLIB, LDFLAGS_SHLIB, LIBS_SHLIB, PREFIX, SBINDIR, INCLUDEDIR, LIBEXECDIR, SYSCONFDIR. Examples:

```
# /usr/local/apache2/bin/apxs -q TARGET
httpd
# /usr/local/apache2/bin/apxs -q CFLAGS
-DLINUX=2 -DMOD_SSL=204109 -DUSE_HSREGEX
-DEAPI -DUSE_EXPAT -I../lib/expat-lite
```

```
# /usr/local/apache2/bin/apxs -q PREFIX
/usr/local/apache2
```

TIP   The default value for any apxs hard-coded variable can be
overridden by specifying a new value with the -S switch; for example, # apxs
-S PREFIX="/usr/local/apachetest" -c -n MyModule.so

-c   Compiles and links a DSO module, given the name of one or more source
files (and, optionally, a list of supporting libraries). Using the -c argument to
apxs enables the following options:

-o *outputfile* specifies the name of the resulting module file rather than
determining it from the name of the input file.

-D *name=value* specifies compiler directives to be used when compiling the
module.

-I *directory* specifies a directory to add to the list of directories searched
by the compiler for include files.

-l *library* adds a library to the list of libraries to be linked into the module.

-L *directory* adds a directory to the list of directories to be searched for
libraries to be linked into the module.

-Wc, *flags* passes flags to the compiler. Each flag must be specified as if it
was a command-line argument, and the comma is mandatory. Example:

```
# axps -c -Wc,-O3 MyModule.c
```

-Wl,*flags* passes flags to the linker. Each flag must be specified as if it was a
command-line argument, and the comma is mandatory. Example:

```
# axps -c -Wl,-t MyModule.c
```

-i   Installs a DSO module that has already been created with apxs -c into its
correct location, which is determined by the PREFIX variable hard-coded into
apxs, if not overridden with an -S switch. Using the -i apxs argument enables
two others:

-a modifies the Apache configuration file (httpd.conf) to add LoadModule
directives to enable the newly installed module.

-A is used to add the lines, but leave them commented out so they don't take
effect when Apache is started.

-e   Works exactly like -i.

-n   Names a module that is not the same as the DSO file. Example:

```
# apxs -i -a -n mod_MyModule MyModule.so
```

The -c and -i arguments to apxs are usually combined. The following line will compile a DSO from a single source file, install it, and modify the Apache configuration to load it the next time Apache is started:

```
# apxs -c -i -a MyModule.so
```

Where to Find Modules

Third-party Apache modules are available from hundreds of sources; the official site for Apache modules, however, is the Apache Module Registry (modules.apache.org). This site does not attempt to maintain a repository of modules for download. It maintains information about all Apache modules, including a brief description of each one's function, along with information about the author and, most importantly, a link to the site where the latest version of the module is maintained for download. Figure 5.1 shows the search form for this site. Although the official registry site is still the first place I check for the availability of modules, it is not uncommon to see new versions of modules being introduced on sites like freshmeat.net or sourceforge.net, both of which support open-source development teams and projects.

> **TIP**   To request a list of all the modules available on the modules .apache.org site, simply enter an empty search string.

Example of Installing a Module

To conclude this chapter, let's work through a complete example of installing, configuring, and using a typical module. The module I chose to demonstrate is Brian Aker's mod_random (Figure 5.2), which performs three very simple tasks. The first is a URL redirector, which lets you redirect a request to a URL randomly selected from a list. You could use this feature, if you're the serious sort, to implement a simple load-balancing scheme, randomly redirecting clients to different servers. Or, you may simply use the module for fun, perhaps using it (as I have) to embed a hyperlink in a page that randomly retrieves different images or banner ads by URL. This is the only one of the three functions of mod_random that I'll demonstrate.

Figure 5.1 The Apache Module Registry

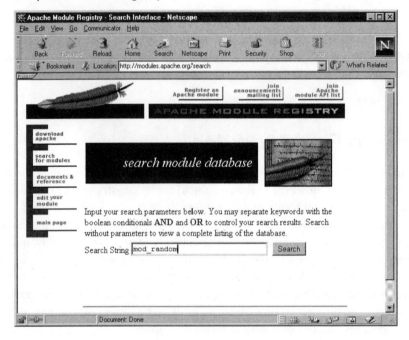

Figure 5.2 The `freshmeat.net` listing for mod_random

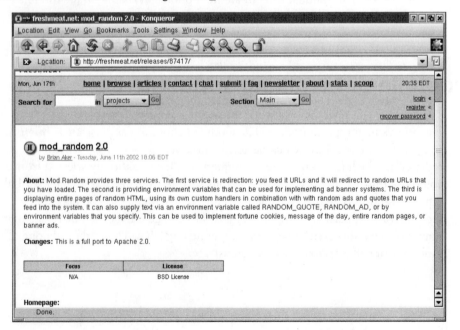

The second function this module provides is to set environment variables that can be used for ad banner systems. The third and final function is to retrieve entire pages of random HTML. These two functions are as easy to use as the random URL redirection function, and the README file that accompanies the module gives full examples of both.

1. Begin by downloading the module from the author's site, `www.tangent.org/mod_random` (or from `freshmeat.net` as I did). Download the latest archive of the module, which was `mod_random-1.4_tar.gz` when I snagged it. Unpack the archive into a location like `/usr/local/src`:

```
# pwd
/usr/local/src
# tar xvzf /downloads/mod_random-1.4.tar.gz
mod_random-2.0/
mod_random-2.0/README
mod_random-2.0/ChangeLog
mod_random-2.0/Makefile
mod_random-2.0/LICENSE
mod_random-2.0/MANIFEST
mod_random-2.0/VERSION
mod_random-2.0/mod_random.c
mod_random-2.0/modules.mk
mod_random-2.0/INSTALL
mod_random-2.0/faq.html
# cd mod_random-1.4/
```

As you can see, there's not a lot to the module; the only file you really need is the C source code (`mod_random.c`). Everything else is simply nonessential support files and documentation. This working core of the module consists of only about 100 lines of easy-to-follow C source code, and is worth a glance if you intend to write your own simple module in C. Installing and configuring the module took me about five minutes. If the authors have done their part, there's absolutely no reason for anyone to be afraid of a third-party Apache module!

2. Make sure that the directory into which you extracted the files is the working directory:

```
# cd mod_random-2.0/
# ls -al
total 60
drwxr-xr-x    2 caulds    caulds      4096 Jun  9 14:06 .
drwxr-xr-x    7 root      root        4096 Jun  9 16:12 ..
-r-r-r-      1 caulds    caulds       487 Jun  9 14:06 ChangeLog
-r-r-r-      1 caulds    caulds      5075 Jun  9 14:11 faq.html
```

```
-r-r-r-    1 caulds    caulds      189 Jun  9 14:11 INSTALL
-r-r-r-    1 caulds    caulds     1656 Jun  9 14:11 LICENSE
-r-r-r-    1 caulds    caulds     2419 Jun  9 14:11 Makefile
-r-r-r-    1 caulds    caulds       92 Jun  9 14:11 MANIFEST
-r-r-r-    1 caulds    caulds    11205 Jun  9 14:11 mod_random.c
-r-r-r-    1 caulds    caulds      156 Jun  9 14:11 modules.mk
-r-r-r-    1 caulds    caulds     1787 Jun  9 14:11 README
-r-r-r-    1 caulds    caulds        4 Jun  9 14:06 VERSION
```

3. At this point, you should read the installation instructions (INSTALL) and glance at the contents of the makefile. The makefile contains instructions for a command-line compilation and installation, and it probably even contains lines for stopping, starting, and restarting the Apache server. These lines are added by the template-generation (-g) argument to apxs, described in the last section. After demonstrating the manual use of apxs to install mod_random, I'll show how the Linux make utility can be used to simplify the already simple procedure.

4. Although you can break this up into a couple of steps, I found it convenient to compile (-c) and install (-i) the module, and configure Apache to use it (-a) all in one command:

```
# /usr/local/apache2/bin/apxs -i -a -c mod_random.c
/usr/local/apache2/build/libtool –silent
    –mode=compile gcc -prefer-pic
    -DAP_HAVE_DESIGNATED_INITIALIZER -DLINUX=2
    -D_REENTRANT -D_XOPEN_SOURCE=500
    -D_BSD_SOURCE -D_SVID_SOURCE -g -O2
    -pthread -DNO_DBM_REWRITEMAP
    -I/usr/local/apache2/include  -c -o
    mod_random.lo mod_random.c && touch
    mod_random.slo
/usr/local/apache2/build/libtool –silent
    –mode=link gcc -o mod_random.la -rpath
    /usr/local/apache2/modules -module -avoid-
    version   mod_random.lo
/usr/local/apache2/build/instdso.sh
    SH_LIBTOOL='/usr/local/apache2/build/libtoo
    l' mod_random.la /usr/local/apache2/modules
/usr/local/apache2/build/libtool
    –mode=install cp mod_random.la /usr/local/apache2/modules/
cp .libs/mod_random.so /usr/local/apache2/modules/mod_random.so
cp .libs/mod_random.lai /usr/local/apache2/modules/mod_random.la
cp .libs/mod_random.a /usr/local/apache2/modules/mod_random.a
ranlib /usr/local/apache2/modules/mod_random.a
chmod 644 /usr/local/apache2/modules/mod_random.a
```

```
PATH="$PATH:/sbin" ldconfig -n /usr/local/apache2/modules
----------------------------------------
Libraries have been installed in:
   /usr/local/apache2/modules

If you ever happen to want to link against installed libraries
in a given directory, LIBDIR, you must either use libtool, and
specify the full pathname of the library, or use the `-LLIBDIR'
flag during linking and do at least one of the following:
   - add LIBDIR to the `LD_LIBRARY_PATH' environment variable
     during execution
   - add LIBDIR to the `LD_RUN_PATH' environment variable
     during linking
   - use the `-Wl,-rpath -Wl,LIBDIR' linker flag
   - have your system administrator add LIBDIR to `/etc/ld.so.conf'

See any operating system documentation about shared libraries for
more information, such as the ld(1) and ld.so(8) manual pages.
----------------------------------------
chmod 755 /usr/local/apache2/modules/mod_random.so
[activating module `random' in /usr/local/apache2/conf/httpd.conf]
```

5. Make sure that the installation procedure modified httpd.conf to use the new module. I checked using the Linux grep utility to extract mod_random entries from httpd.conf:

```
# grep mod_random /usr/local/apache2/conf/httpd.conf
LoadModule random_module      modules/mod_random.so
```

6. Just to be absolutely sure that everything worked, I restarted the server:

```
# /usr/local/apache2/bin/apachectl restart
```

7. Then I checked the server info page to insure that mod_random is ready to rock (Figure 5.3). This interesting server status page is explored in more detail in Chapter 10.

8. One part of any module configuration is always manual. In this case, it is editing the Apache configuration to make use of the module, usually by specifying the module as a handler and by including directives supplied by the module. Our mod_random is no exception. I added the following section to my httpd.conf file to take full advantage of one of the module's features, redirection to a random site:

```
# Brian Aker's mod_random configuration
#
<Location /randomize>
```

```
        SetHandler random
        RandomURL http://www.acme.com/
        RandomURL http://www.apple.com/macosx/inside.html
        RandomURL http://www.asptoday.com/
        RandomURL http://atomz.com/
        RandomFile /usr/local/apache2/conf/random.conf
    </Location>
```

Figure 5.3   The Server Information page for mod_random

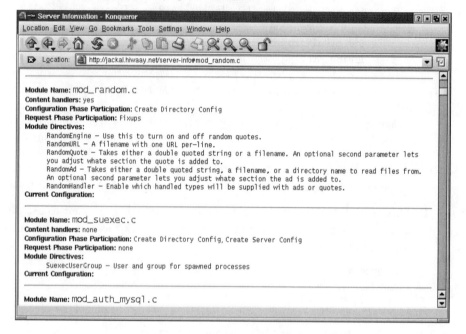

9. I first created a <Location> container, which applies to a partial URL, /randomize. This is not a directory name; it applies to a request URL. All the directives in the <Location> container apply to any arriving requests to a URL that ends in /randomize.

10. Using the RandomURL directive, I manually added a handful of URLs for random selection by the module, and then used the RandomFile directive to point to a file containing a list of URLs (one per line) that are added to mod_random's list of URLs.

11. After creating the necessary <Location> container in httpd.conf, I restarted the server to ensure that it was read, and then pointed a browser at my site, using the following URL:

    http://jackal.hiwaay.net/randomize

12. I was immediately redirected to one of the sites I'd specified for random selection in `httpd.conf`.

You may or may not eventually have a use for the `mod_random` module, but the basic procedure demonstrated in this example will be the same for any module you decide to add:

1. Download the archived file.

2. Extract it into your working directory.

3. Compile and install it (after reading the `INSTALL` file for instructions).

4. Check your `httpd.conf` file to verify that the module has been added.

5. Manually edit the configuration file to specify your new module as a handler.

6. Finally, test the configuration.

In Sum

From the very beginning, the Apache Web server was designed for easy expandability by exposing a set of functions that allowed programmers to write add-in modules easily. Support for dynamic shared objects was added with the release of Apache 1.3. DSO allows modules to be compiled separately from the Apache server and loaded by the server at runtime if desired or omitted by the administrator who wants to reduce the amount of memory required for each loaded copy of Apache.

The modular architecture of Apache is an important factor in the popularity of the server. Because of its fairly uncomplicated programmers' interface for extending the server's capabilities, a large number of modules are available (at no cost) from third-party sources.

6

Virtual Hosting

The term *virtual hosting* refers to maintaining multiple Web sites on a single server machine and differentiating those sites by hostname aliases or, less commonly, by separate IP addresses if the server is *multi-homed* and has more than one IP address. Virtual hosting is how ISPs and Web hosting services allow multiple clients to share a single Web server while permitting each to have its own Web site, accessible via its own registered domain name. This is different from the user home directories we discussed in Chapter 4, where individual Web sites are set up, but all share the same domain name and have extra path information that is provided by the browser to select a specific Web site. To a modern browser (that is, one that supports HTTP/1.1), multiple virtual hosts on a single Apache server are indistinguishable from multiple sites running on multiple servers. With the number of Web sites on the Internet constantly increasing, the ability to host many Web sites on a server efficiently is a critical feature of a first-class Web server engine. Apache provides full support for virtual hosting and is a superb choice of Web engine for hosting large numbers of Web sites on a much smaller number of physical servers.

This chapter outlines the three basic methods of configuring a single Apache engine to support multiple Web sites: IP-based virtual hosting, name-based virtual hosting, and dynamic virtual hosting. Much of the discussion focuses on the functionality provided by the standard Apache module used for virtual hosting, mod_virtual.

The mod_virtual module supports two types of virtual hosts:

IP-based virtual hosts are identified by the IP address on which client requests are received. Each IP-based virtual host has its own unique IP address and responds to all requests arriving on that IP address.

Name-based virtual hosts take advantage of a feature of HTTP/1.1 designed to eliminate the requirement for dedicating scarce IP addresses to virtual hosts. As mentioned in Chapter 1, HTTP/1.1 requests must have a Host header that identifies the name of the server that the client wants to handle the request. For servers not supporting virtual hosts, this is identical to the ServerName value set for the primary server. The Host header is also used to identify a virtual host to service the request, and virtual hosts identified by the client Host header are thus termed *name-based virtual hosts*.

Apache was one of the first servers to support virtual hosts right out of the box. Since version 1.1, Apache has supported both IP-based and name-based virtual hosts. This chapter examines both IP-based and name-based virtual hosts in detail.

The chapter also introduces the concept of *dynamic virtual hosting*, which uses another module, mod_vhost_aliases. Dynamic virtual hosts are virtual hosts whose configuration is not fixed, but is determined (using a predefined template) from the request URL. The advantage of dynamic virtual hosts is that literally thousands of these can be supported on a single server with only a few lines of template code, rather than having to write a custom configuration for each.

In general, you will want to use IP-based virtual hosts whenever you must support browsers that aren't HTTP/1.1-compliant (the number of these in use is rapidly dwindling), and when you can afford to dedicate a unique IP address for each virtual host (the number of available IP addresses is also dwindling). Most sites will prefer to use name-based virtual hosts. Remember, though, that with name-based virtual hosting, non-HTTP/1.1 browsers will have no way to specify the virtual hosts they wish to connect to and will always connect to the Apache's default Web site.

Virtual Host Directives

For both IP-based and name-based virtual addressing, the <VirtualHost> container directive encloses all directives that apply to a specific virtual host. All directives that are placed in the <VirtualHost> container are also applicable in an ordinary single-server context, although their behavior may be altered when they apply to a virtual host. When you examine the examples of virtual host configurations presented in this chapter, remember the following rules:

- Any directive inside a <VirtualHost> container applies only to that virtual host.

- All directives in the configuration file that are not part of a <Virtual Host> container define the primary server. Virtual hosts always inherit the configuration of the primary server, so, in a sense, the primary server configuration defines default values for all virtual hosts. However, directives inside a <VirtualHost> container always override the same directive if inherited from the primary server configuration. Keep virtual host directives to a minimum, overriding or augmenting the inherited primary server directives only where necessary. A Server-Name directive should be used to override the canonical name of the primary server, and a virtual host will usually have its own DocumentRoot. Use care in overriding the primary server directives beyond these two basic directives.

- Before defining virtual hosts, define the network interfaces and ports that the primary server will listen to using the Listen directive (as described in Chapter 4). These directives are not permissible in a virtual host context.

IP-Based Virtual Hosting

IP-based virtual hosts are defined by the IP address used to access them, and each IP-based virtual host must have a unique IP address. Since no server machine has more than a few physical network interfaces, it is likely that multiple IP-based virtual hosts will share the same network interface, using a technique called *network interface aliasing*. You'll see how to do this on a Linux server later in this section.

Secure Sockets Layer (SSL is the subject of Chapter 14) requires each SSL Web server on the Internet to have a unique IP address associated with its well-known hostname. Most site hosting services and ISPs that provide SSL Web sites for their customers do so by using IP-based virtual hosting, usually by aliasing multiple IP addresses to a small number of actual network interfaces on each server. This has created a demand for IP-based virtual hosts—even though its use was once declining in favor of name-based virtual hosting—and a commensurate increase in demand for IP addresses to support IP-based virtual hosting.

> **NOTE**   In September 2000, one of the world's three registrars of IP addresses, the American Registry for Internet Numbers (ARIN), announced that they would no longer accept IP-based virtual hosting as a justification for new IP number assignments (www.arin.net/policy/ipv4.html). The use of IP addresses for IP-based virtual hosting is not restricted or unauthorized, but this policy change makes it difficult for sites trying to obtain a chunk of IP addresses to be used for IP-based virtual hosting.

IP-based virtual hosts are quite easy to set up. Use the <VirtualHost IPaddr> container directive to enclose a group of directives that apply only to the virtual host specified (and identified by a unique IP address).

To create two IP-based virtual hosts on my Apache server, I placed the following section in my `httpd.conf` file, making sure that this section followed any global scope directives. In other words, any directives I wanted to apply to the Apache daemon processes or to the primary server and to provide default values for all virtual hosts are placed at the top of the file, and they are the first read when Apache is started.

For the following definitions to work, the two IP addresses (192.168.1.4 and 192.168.1.5) must be valid IP addresses for the server, either on separate interfaces or (as in my case) on the same interface using interface aliasing.

```
<VirtualHost 192.168.1.4>
    ServerName vhost1.hiwaay.net
    DocumentRoot /home/httpd/html/vhost1
</VirtualHost>

<VirtualHost 192.168.1.5>
    ServerName vhost2.hiwaay.net
    DocumentRoot /home/httpd/html/vhost2
</VirtualHost>
```

These are quite simple definitions. Appendix A lists all the directives that can be used within a virtual host scope, but here I defined only a `ServerName` for the virtual host and a path to the `DocumentRoot` for each virtual host. Connecting to the first virtual host using the following URL:

```
http://192.168.1.4/
```

causes the server to offer me the documents stored in `/home/httpd/html/vhost1`. Of course, we don't want to require users to enter an IP address. The preferred way to provide access to the virtual host is to add an address record to the network domain name server (DNS), mapping the IP address to a hostname; this makes it possible, and far more convenient, to connect to the virtual host using this URL:

```
http://vhost1.hiwaay.net/
```

Keep in mind, though, that with IP-based virtual hosts, the hostname is irrelevant (except to human users). Apache uses only the IP address to determine which virtual host will be used to serve a connection. With name-based virtual hosting, as we'll see, the hostname is the determining factor in deciding which virtual host is used to serve a connection. Figure 6.1 illustrates the complete request/resolution process for IP-based virtual hosting. Later in the chapter, you'll compare this to a similar diagram for name-based virtual hosting.

Figure 6.1   IP-based virtual hosting on a server with multiple IP addresses

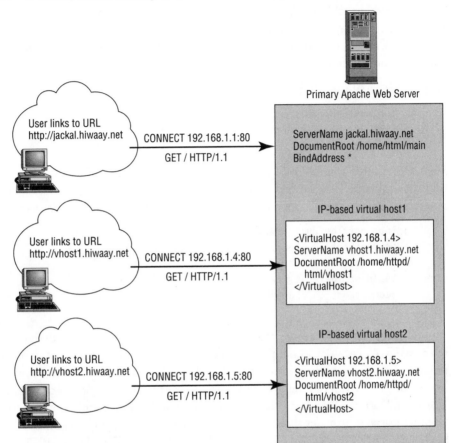

Using _default_ Virtual Hosts

For IP-based virtual hosting, if no <VirtualHost *IPAddr*> is matched—that is, if the server can be reached on one or more IP addresses for which no virtual host is defined—the primary server is always used to respond to the client's request. (Again, the primary server includes all the directives that are not part of a <VirtualHost> scope.) It is a good idea, when using IP-based virtual hosts, to provide a default server of your own instead of forcing Apache to use the primary server. Virtual hosts defined using _default_ are used for exactly this purpose. When using virtual hosting, it is best to reserve the primary server configuration as a default for directives that apply to *all* virtual hosts. Any _default_ virtual hosts (as I'll illustrate, there can be more than one) answer requests to unrecognized virtual hosts. They can be configured to return an error message to the client browser, for example, or to issue a redirect to one of the legitimate IP-based virtual hosts. A _default_ virtual host provides the flexibility and control needed to handle a variety of misdirected queries.

A special form of the <VirtualHost> directive is used to define a default virtual host:

```
<VirtualHost _default_:*>
    DocumentRoot    /home/http/html/defaultvh
</VirtualHost>
```

Here, I've defined a virtual host that will respond to all requests that are sent to any port that is not already assigned to another <VirtualHost> on any valid IP address. It is also possible to specify a single port to be used by a _default_ virtual host, for example:

```
<VirtualHost _default_:443>
    DocumentRoot    /home/httpd/html/securedefault
</VirtualHost>
<VirtualHost _default_:*>
    DocumentRoot    /home/httpd/html/defaultvh
</VirtualHost>
```

This example shows that more than one _default_ virtual host can be defined. The first <VirtualHost _default_> container defines a special default virtual host that is used for unrecognized connections on Secure Sockets Layer TCP port 443. Connections coming in on that port are served the documents found in /home/http/html/securedefault. The second <VirtualHost _default_> container handles unrecognized connections on all other ports. It provides those connections access to the documents in /home/http/ html/defaultvh. Because the specific port 443 is already assigned to another virtual host, the second <VirtualHost_default_> directive ignores port 443.

Network Interface Aliasing in Linux

Most modern operating systems have the capability of assigning multiple IP addresses to the same physical network interface, and Linux is no exception. Often referred to as *network interface aliasing*, or sometimes *IP multiplexing*, this is a way to set up multiple IP-based virtual hosts even when you have only a single network interface. It is the method I've used to configure my system to support several IP addresses on its only Ethernet interface. Below, I'll show the commands I used to create separate IP addresses that I later assigned to IP-based virtual hosts. To make this scheme work for virtual hosting, you need to create a separate DNS entry for each virtual host, each with its own IP address.

Assigning multiple IP addresses to your network interface to support additional IP-based virtual hosts has one drawback; like all IP-based virtual hosting, it consumes IP addresses that may be in short supply. However, it makes it very easy to set up virtual hosts that work with older browsers that don't support the HTTP/1.1 Host header. Although these browsers are becoming less common (many browsers that don't claim to be fully 1.1-compliant do support Host), there are still plenty of them out there. If you can spare an IP address for every virtual host you intend to configure, you may want to use the technique described in this section to give each of your virtual hosts its own IP address. One very compelling reason to do so is to run multiple SSL virtual hosts on a single server. SSL cannot be used with name-based virtual hosts for reasons that I explain in Chapter 14, which covers SSL. The best way to run multiple SSL virtual hosts on a single box is to use IP-based virtual hosts, and network interface aliasing can help you do that. Most organizations that are running non-SSL servers, however, will probably opt to use name-based virtual hosts, or because of limited IP address space, will use them out of necessity.

To add virtual IP addresses to the network interface on a Linux server, log in as root and use the ifconfig command. In the following example, I add two new virtual Ethernet interfaces for the server's one physical Ethernet interface (eth0). These IP addresses do not have to be sequential (as they are here), but they must be on the same network subnet:

```
# /sbin/ifconfig eth0:0   192.168.1.4
# /sbin/ifconfig eth0:1   192.168.1.5
```

To confirm this configuration change, I entered the ifconfig command without arguments. The output is shown in Listing 6.1. As expected, the new virtual interfaces (eth0:0 and eth0:1) appear with the same hardware address (HWaddr 00:60:08:A4:E8:82) as the physical Ethernet interface.

Listing 6.1 The Linux ifconfig Command, Showing Physical and Virtual Network Interfaces

```
# /sbin/ifconfig
eth0       Link encap:Ethernet  HWaddr 00:60:08:A4:E8:82
           inet addr:192.168.1.1  Bcast:192.168.1.255  Mask:255.255.255.0
           UP BROADCAST RUNNING MULTICAST  MTU:1500  Metric:1
           RX packets:463 errors:0 dropped:0 overruns:0 frame:0
           TX packets:497 errors:0 dropped:0 overruns:0 carrier:0
           collisions:0 txqueuelen:100
           Interrupt:11 Base address:0x6100
eth0:0     Link encap:Ethernet  HWaddr 00:60:08:A4:E8:82
           inet addr:192.168.1.4  Bcast:192.168.1.255  Mask:255.255.255.0
           UP BROADCAST RUNNING MULTICAST  MTU:1500  Metric:1
```

Essential Configuration

PART 2

```
            Interrupt:11 Base address:0x6100
eth0:1      Link encap:Ethernet  HWaddr 00:60:08:A4:E8:82
            inet addr:192.168.1.5  Bcast:192.168.1.255  Mask:255.255.255.0
            UP BROADCAST RUNNING MULTICAST  MTU:1500  Metric:1
            Interrupt:11 Base address:0x6100
lo          Link encap:Local Loopback
            inet addr:127.0.0.1  Mask:255.0.0.0
            UP LOOPBACK RUNNING  MTU:3924  Metric:1
            RX packets:58 errors:0 dropped:0 overruns:0 frame:0
            TX packets:58 errors:0 dropped:0 overruns:0 carrier:0
            collisions:0 txqueuelen:0
```

> **NOTE**   The last interface shown in Listing 6.1, lo, is that of the loopback address, which is a special virtual network interface used primarily for testing and is always available on a Linux system with networking enabled. The special IP address 127.0.0.1 is reserved on all Linux systems for this virtual interface.

I created an IP-based virtual host for each new virtual network interface I created on the server, as shown below:

```
<VirtualHost 192.168.1.4>
    ServerName vhost1.hiwaay.net
    DocumentRoot /home/httpd/html/vhost1
</VirtualHost>
<VirtualHost 192.168.1.5>
    ServerName vhost2.hiwaay.net
    DocumentRoot /home/httpd/html/vhost2
</VirtualHost>
```

The Address Resolution Protocol

Linux makes setting up network interface aliasing easy, but how do you advertise the new IP addresses to the rest of the network? For that matter, how do you ensure that Internet packets sent to the new IP addresses are now routed to the correct machine and Ethernet interface? The answer is that both the advertising and the routing are handled automatically by the *Address Resolution Protocol (ARP)*.

Your router advertises itself to other routers as a portal or gateway to your network. If you have a properly functioning Internet router, anyone on the Internet can send data to your network through that router. To make a host on your network accessible to the world, you just need to make sure that your router knows how to reach that host by its new IP address.

ARP is a "discovery protocol" used by one host to discover information about another. When you use `ifconfig` to add an IP address to a Linux interface, you instruct the system to reply to ARP broadcasts for the new IP address with the interface's physical network address. The physical network address of the interface (often called the Media Access Control, or MAC address) appears in the trace, identified earlier as `HWaddr`. The manufacturer of the *media access unit (MAU)*, in this case an Ethernet adapter, works with other manufacturers to ensure that the address is globally unique. Some Ethernet adapters allow this address to be changed, but most have an embedded address that is unalterable.

> **NOTE**   ARP is used with either Ethernet or Token Ring networks. The discussion below is based on Ethernet but applies equally to Token Ring networks, although the MAC address of a Token Ring node will differ from the Ethernet addresses shown.

Adding the IP address 192.168.1.5 to my Ethernet interface (`eth0`) instructed my Linux server to respond to ARP requests for this IP address with the Ethernet address of that interface. When my router receives an IP packet addressed to 192.168.1.5, it broadcasts an ARP packet to the 192.168.1.0 network. All hosts on that network will receive the broadcast; most ignore it. But my Linux host, now configured to reply to ARP broadcasts for 192.168.1.5, will send an ARP reply to the router instructing it to send all packets addressed to 192.168.1.5 to the Ethernet address of its `eth0` interface.

A potential for conflict exists if two network devices respond to the ARP broadcast, claiming to use the same IP address. Most operating systems are designed to prevent such a conflict by detecting the presence of other systems on the network already using their assigned IP address when they boot. (They use ARP to do this, incidentally.) The system disables the Ethernet interface with the conflicting address and notifies the administrator of the conflict. In other words, the machine that's already using the IP address gets to keep it, and new machines trying to use the interface politely defer to the incumbent.

Figure 6.2 illustrates how ARP allows other workstations (in this case an NT 4 workstation) to discover the Ethernet address of a Linux workstation that has been configured (as described above) to communicate using three IP addresses on the same Ethernet interface.

Essential Configuration

PART 2

Figure 6.2   Address discovery using ARP

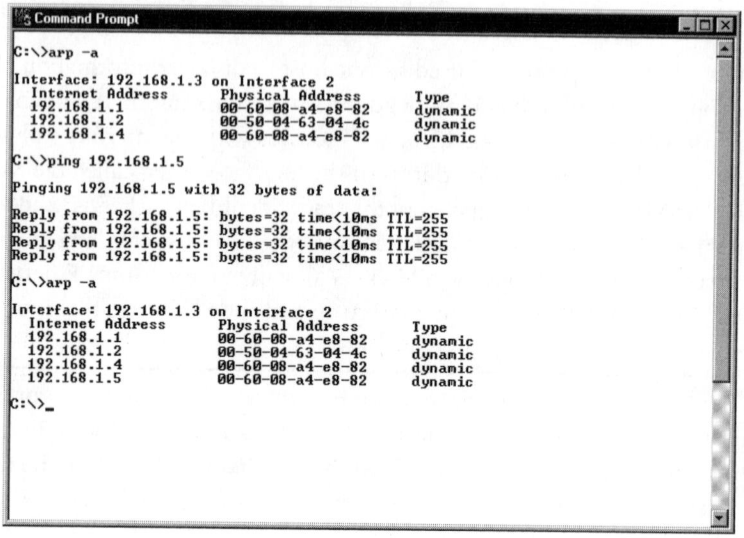

```
C:\>arp -a

Interface: 192.168.1.3 on Interface 2
  Internet Address      Physical Address        Type
  192.168.1.1           00-60-08-a4-e8-82       dynamic
  192.168.1.2           00-50-04-63-04-4c       dynamic
  192.168.1.4           00-60-08-a4-e8-82       dynamic

C:\>ping 192.168.1.5

Pinging 192.168.1.5 with 32 bytes of data:

Reply from 192.168.1.5: bytes=32 time<10ms TTL=255
Reply from 192.168.1.5: bytes=32 time<10ms TTL=255
Reply from 192.168.1.5: bytes=32 time<10ms TTL=255
Reply from 192.168.1.5: bytes=32 time<10ms TTL=255

C:\>arp -a

Interface: 192.168.1.3 on Interface 2
  Internet Address      Physical Address        Type
  192.168.1.1           00-60-08-a4-e8-82       dynamic
  192.168.1.2           00-50-04-63-04-4c       dynamic
  192.168.1.4           00-60-08-a4-e8-82       dynamic
  192.168.1.5           00-60-08-a4-e8-82       dynamic

C:\>_
```

Name-Based Virtual Hosting

Name-based virtual hosting takes advantage of a special request header introduced with HTTP/1.1. As already mentioned an HTTP/1.1 client browser sends a Host header to identify the hostname of the server that should respond to the request. A standard HTTP/1.0 request usually consists of a single line that identifies the request method, the URI (which is the trailing part of the URL, omitting the protocol and hostname), and the protocol designation:

```
GET / HTTP/1.0
```

The server that receives this request knows only the IP address of the interface on which it was received; it has no way of knowing which DNS name the client used to determine that IP address. To comply with HTTP/1.1, a second header must be present, even in a minimal request, to identify the host that should process the request. This is usually the primary Apache server, but it may be any virtual host that has been defined in the Apache configuration. An HTTP/1.1 request would look like this:

```
GET / HTTP/1.1
Host: jackal.hiwaay.net
```

The hostname (and, optionally, the TCP port) that is placed in the Host header by the client browser is determined from the URL of the request itself. In cases where the Web server is using IP-based virtual hosting or supports no virtual hosts, the Host header is usually ignored. But when name-based virtual hosts are used, the Host header can be very important. The Host header can be used to identify a specific virtual host that has a matching hostname.

> **NOTE**   Failure to specify the Host header is an error if the client identifies itself as HTTP/1.1-compliant. A client that does not want to send this header must not specify HTTP/1.1 in its request. Netscape Communicator 4.7 sends the HTTP/1.0 header, but also sends the Host field. This is not an error, but it would be an error for Netscape to send the HTTP/1.1 header and omit the Host field. I suspect that Netscape prefers to identify itself as an HTTP/1.0 client because some other behavior of the HTTP/1.1 specification is not fully implemented in Netscape and can't be relied on.

Name-based virtual hosts, which (like IP-based virtual hosts) are handled by the mod_virtual module, make use of a special directive, NameVirtualHost. This directive designates an IP address for name-based virtual hosting. When NameVirtualHost is used, the IP address it specifies becomes available only as a name-based virtual host. It is no longer accessible by non-HTTP/1.1 clients (except to connect to the Apache default Web site) and cannot be used for IP-based virtual hosting.

When Apache encounters the NameVirtualHost directive while reading httpd.conf, it sets up a virtual host table for the IP address specified. Only a single NameVirtualHost address should exist for each IP address, designating that IP address for virtual hosting. Any number of <VirtualHost> directives can identify the same IP address, however. As it parses httpd.conf, Apache adds virtual hosts to the virtual host table for each IP address whenever it encounters a <VirtualHost> directive that specifies the same IP address as one earlier designated for virtual hosting. After parsing httpd.conf, Apache has a complete list of all virtual hosts for each IP address specified in NameVirtualHost directives.

When it receives a request on any IP address specified by a NameVirtualHost directive, Apache searches the associated list of virtual hosts for that IP address. When it finds a virtual host that has a ServerName directive matching the Host header of the incoming request, Apache responds to the request using the configuration defined in that virtual host's container. This process was illustrated earlier, in Figure 6.1.

In name-based virtual hosting, illustrated in Figure 6.3, the virtual host selected to service a request is always determined from the Host header of the request. If no match is found for the virtual host requested by the client, the first virtual host defined for the IP address is served by default. This virtual host is called the *primary virtual host*. Don't confuse this with the primary server, which is defined by the directives outside all virtual host containers. Each request for a name-based virtual host must match an IP address that has been previously designated for virtual hosting with the NameVirtualHost directive. Only name-based virtual hosts will be served on an address so designated; the primary server (that is, the configuration defined outside the VirtualHost directives) will never serve any client connecting on an IP address designated for virtual hosting.

Figure 6.3   Name-based virtual hosting on a server with a single IP address

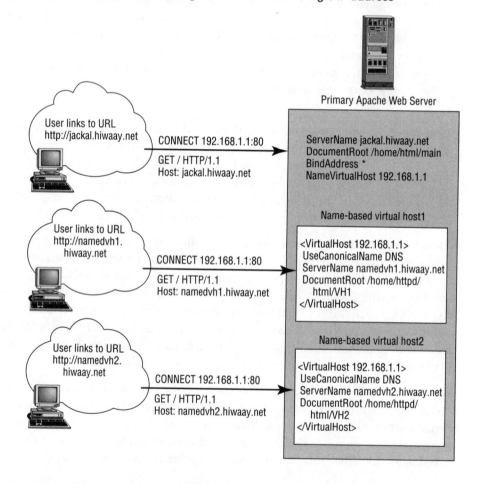

If Apache receives an HTTP/1.0 request sent to an IP address that you identified for name-based virtual hosting (using a NameVirtualHost directive), but the Host header is unrecognized (or missing), the primary virtual host always handles the request. The <VirtualHost _default_> directive can never be used as a name-based virtual host, because the <VirtualHost> directive for name-based virtual hosts must always contain a valid IP address.

With name-based virtual hosting, you should include directives for the main server that apply to *all* virtual hosts rather than trying to use the main server as a repository for directives that apply to the "default" name-based virtual host. The directives for that host should be placed in the virtual host container for the primary virtual host. Remember that the *first* virtual host you define in httpd.conf for an IP address previously designated for name-based virtual hosting is the primary virtual host for that address.

On my system, I defined two very simple name-based virtual hosts (see Listing 6.2).

Listing 6.2   Defining Two Simple Name-Based Hosts

```
NameVirtualHost 192.168.1.1

<VirtualHost 192.168.1.1>
   UseCanonicalName off
   ServerName namedvh1.hiwaay.net
   DocumentRoot /home/httpd/html/
</VirtualHost>
<VirtualHost 192.168.1.1>
   UseCanonicalName off
   ServerName namedvh2.hiwaay.net
   DocumentRoot /home/httpd/html/NamedVH2
</VirtualHost>
```

The NameVirtualHost directive is critical; it identifies the IP address 192.168.1.1 as an interface for name-based virtual hosts. All requests received on this IP address will now be handled by one of the name-based hosts associated with that address. As soon as Apache reads the NameVirtualHost 192.168.1.1 directive, the primary server can no longer be reached on this IP address. Instead, the server creates a virtual host list for this IP address and adds the names specified by the ServerName directive as it processes the virtual host configurations that follow. When this server is loaded, it will have a virtual host list for IP address 192.168.1.1 consisting of the virtual hosts namedvh1.hiwaay.net and namedvh2.hiwaay.net. As requests arrive, the name specified in the Host header of each request is compared against this list. And when a match is found, the server knows which virtual host will service that request.

Remember that (in contrast to IP-based virtual hosting) any request received on the IP address 192.168.1.1 that does not properly identify one of its name-based virtual hosts will be served by the *first named* virtual host. In Listing 6.2, this is namedvh1.hiwaay.net, which becomes sort of a default name-based host for IP address 192.168.1.1. For that

Essential Configuration

PART 2

reason, I explicitly set its `DocumentRoot` to match that of my primary server. I did this mainly to make the configuration file more readable; it is not necessary to set this value, because virtual hosts inherit the value of this directive, along with that of all other directives, from the primary server.

The second virtual host in Listing 6.2 has a separate `DocumentRoot`, and to HTTP/1.1 browsers that connect to `http://namedvh2.hiwaay.net`, it appears to be completely different from any other Web site on this server. The only hint that it's one virtual host among potentially many others is that it has the same IP address as other Web servers. This is not apparent, however, to users who know the server only by its hostname. When setting up name-based hosts that all apply to the same IP address, you should enter the hostnames as *canonical name*, or *CNAME*, records in the DNS server for the domain. This will place them in the DNS as aliases for the one true hostname that should exist (as an *Address*, or *A*) record in the DNS. To learn more about DNS resource records and DNS server configuration, see *Linux DNS Server Administration*, which is another volume in the Craig Hunt Linux Library from Sybex.

There's one more point to note about the example in Listing 6.2. The `namedvh2.hiwaay.net` virtual host can be reached only by browsers that send an HTTP/1.1 `Host` request header. It can't be reached at all by browsers that are unable to send this header. If you need to provide access to name-based hosts from browsers that don't support `Host`, read the next section.

Supporting Non-HTTP/1.1 Clients

Browsers that do not support HTTP/1.1 are rapidly vanishing from the scene, although the degree to which various browsers support it is the subject of much discussion in the newsgroups. (Some browsers that do not claim to be fully 1.1-compliant actually do support the `Host` header.) When you're virtually hosting on the Internet, you can't assume what browsers may be out there; and there are special considerations when you're trying to serve pages from name-based virtual hosts to non-HTTP/1.1 browsers. (In a corporate intranet, you as system administrator presumably have some control over the browser software being used.) As mentioned in the last section, any request arriving on an IP address designated for name-based virtual hosts will be served by the first named virtual host if that request does not carry an HTTP `Host` request header that specifically names one of the virtual hosts assigned to that IP address. Since some HTTP/1.0 browsers will not supply a `Host` header, you'll have a situation where these legacy browsers are *always* served by the first named virtual host in your list.

Apache provides the `ServerPath` directive to allow you to serve requests from name-based virtual hosts to clients running non-HTTP/1.1 browsers. This directive is a kludge that you will not want to use unless you must provide support for name-based virtual hosting to HTTP/1.0 browsers.

When the `ServerPath` directive is used to specify a URL pathname in a `<VirtualHost>` container, Apache uses that virtual host to serve all requests with URLs that match that pathname. Consider this example:

```
NameVirtualHost 192.168.1.1

    <VirtualHost 192.168.1.1>
        ServerName SomethingBogus.com
        DocumentRoot /home/httpd/
    </VirtualHost>

    <VirtualHost 192.168.1.1>
        ServerName www.innerdomain.com
        ServerPath /securedomain
        DocumentRoot /home/httpd/domain
    </VirtualHost>
```

Here, I've defined a virtual host with the `ServerName www.innerdomain.com` directive. HTTP/1.1 clients can connect directly to `www.innerdomain.com`. HTTP/1.0 clients will by default reach the `SomethingBogus.com` virtual host (even though they don't specify it) because it is the first defined, but they can access the `innerdomain.com` host using a URL that matches the `ServerPath`, like `www.innerdomain.com/securedomain`. Note, though, that they are selecting the virtual host not with a `Host` header that matches its `ServerName`, but with a URL that matches the `ServerPath`. Actually, it really doesn't matter what hostname a non-HTTP/1.1 client uses as long as it connects on 192.168.1.1 and uses the trailing `/securedomain` in its request URL.

Now, if you publish the URL `http://www.innerdomain.com`, HTTP/1.1 clients will have no trouble reaching the new virtual host; but you need some way to tell non-HTTP/1.1 clients that they need to use another URL, and that's the purpose of the first virtual host. As the first virtual host in the list, it will be the default page served to clients that don't use a `Host` header to designate a name-based virtual host. Choose a `ServerName` for this host that no client will ever connect to directly; this virtual host is a "fall-through" that will only serve requests from clients that don't provide a valid `Host` header. In the DocumentRoot directory for this virtual host, you should place a page that redirects non-HTTP/1.1 clients to `http://www.innerdomain.com/securedomain`, similar to this:

```
<HTML>
<TITLE>
Banner Page for non-HTTP/1.1 browser users.
</TITLE>
<BODY>
If you are using an older, non-HTTP/1.1 compatible browser,
```

Essential
Configuration

PART 2

```
please bookmark this page:
<BR>
<A HREF=/securedomain>http://www.innerdomain.com/securedomain
</A>
</BODY>
</HTML>
```

Also, in order to make this work, always make sure you use relative links (e.g., `file.html` or `../icons/image.gif`) in the `www.innerdomain.com` virtual host's pages. For HTTP/1.1 clients, these will be relative to `www.innerdomain.com`; for HTTP/1.0 clients, they will be relative to `www.innerdomain.com/securedomain`.

Dynamic Virtual Hosting

The techniques described above, for IP- and name-based virtual hosting, are sufficient for most applications, but they are limited in the number of virtual hosts that can be set up and administered. The number of Web sites on the Internet has grown so that it is no longer feasible to maintain each site on a single server or to dedicate an IP address to each. Many sites are now administered by Web hosting services that maintain large "server farms," with each server hosting hundreds or even thousands of Web sites. These are usually name-based hosts, each with its own unique Internet hostname and DNS entry. ISPs that provide this service to thousands of customers need a solution for hosting huge numbers of virtual hosts. Even name-based hosting is difficult to set up and maintain for so many virtual sites when an administrator has to set up each one individually, even if only a few lines in the `httpd.conf` is required for each.

Another technique, called *dynamically configured mass virtual hosting*, is used for very large numbers of Web sites. A standard module provided with the Apache distribution, `mod_vhost_aliases`, implements dynamically configured hosts by specifying templates for `DocumentRoot` and `ScriptAlias` that are used to create the actual paths to these directories after examining the incoming URL.

The entire purpose of `mod_vhost_aliases` is to create directory paths for `DocumentRoot` and `ScriptAlias` based on the request URL. It is a very simple module that is controlled by only four directives, two for name-based and two for IP-based dynamic virtual hosting.

These directives implement name-based dynamic virtual hosting:

VirtualDocumentRoot   Specifies how the module constructs a path to the DocumentRoot for a dynamic virtual host from the request URL.

VirtualScriptAlias   Works like `ScriptAlias` to construct a path to a directory containing CGI scripts from the request URL.

These implement IP-based dynamic virtual hosting:

> **VirtualDocumentRootIP**   Like VirtualDocumentRoot, but constructs the path to the dynamic virtual host's DocumentRoot from the IP address on which the request was received.

> **VirtualScriptAliasIP**   Like VirtualScriptAlias, but constructs the path to a directory of CGI scripts from the IP address on which the request was received.

Since mod_vhost_aliases constructs paths for dynamic hosts as requests arrive at the server, DocumentRoot and ScriptAlias essentially become variables that change depending on the virtual host the client is trying to reach. Thus they do not have to be explicitly specified for each virtual host in httpd.conf. In fact, no virtual host needs to be specified in httpd.conf; the administrator has only to ensure that a directory exists for each virtual host on the server. If the directory doesn't exist, the requester gets the standard Not Found message (or, if you are being user-friendly, your customized Not Found message).

Each of the directives uses a set of specifiers to extract tokens from the request URL and then embed them into one of two paths, either the path to DocumentRoot or the path to ScriptAlias for the dynamic virtual host. The specifiers that can be used are listed in Table 6.1.

Table 6.1   Specifiers for Dynamic Virtual Host Aliasing

Specifier	Meaning
%	Translates to a single % character in the path.
%p	The TCP port number of the dynamic virtual host.
%0	The entire server name, as determined by the UseCanonicalName directive (see the following section).
%N	The Nth part of the server name. If the full server name is jackal.hiwaay.net, then %1 resolves to jackal, %2 to hiwaay, and so on.
%N+	The Nth part of the server name, and all parts following. If the full server name is jackal.hiwaay.net, then %2+ resolves to hiwaay.net.
%-N	The Nth part, counting backward from the end of the string. If the full server name is jackal.hiwaay.net, then %-1 resolves to net, and %-2 resolves to hiwaay.
%-N+	The Nth part, counting backward, and all parts preceding it. If the full server name is jackal.hiwaay.net, then %-2+ resolves to jackal.hiwaay.

Essential Configuration

PART 2

Each of the parts that can be extracted from the server name can be further broken down by specifying a subpart using the specifier %*N*.*M*, where *N* is the main part, and *M* is the subpart. If the directive being evaluated refers to a hostname, for example, each part of the URL is separated by the / character; the subparts are the individual characters of each part. A URL beginning with `http://caulds.homepages.hiwaay.net` would yield the following parts:

```
%1 = caulds
%2 = homepages
%3 = hiwaay
%4 = net
```

Each of these parts can be further broken down into subparts, in this fashion:

```
%1.1 = c
%1.2 = a
%1.3 = u
```

...and so on.

A simple example should illustrate how this works on a real Web hosting server. The `mod_vhost_aliases` module translates the `VirtualDocumentRoot` directive specified below into a `DocumentRoot` path, as illustrated in Figure 6.4. The purpose of the `UseCanonicalName` directive is explained in the next section.

```
UseCanonicalName off
VirtualDocumentRoot /home/httpd/%1/%p
```

This example uses two of the specifiers that create a `VirtualDocumentRoot`. The first specifier (`%1`) returns the first portion of the server name. In this case, the server name is provided by the client in a `Host` header of the HTTP request (as described in the discussion of `UseCanonicalName` which follows this section). The second specifier (`%p`) returns the TCP port of the request for the dynamic virtual host—in this case, the Secure Sockets Layer port 443, because this Apache server has been configured to listen for connections on this port. To run CGI scripts from each dynamic virtual host, use a `VirtualScriptAlias` in exactly the same way to specify a dynamically constructed path to a directory containing these scripts.

Figure 6.4 A simple dynamic virtual host

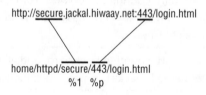

```
http://secure.jackal.hiwaay.net:443/login.html



     home/httpd/secure/443/login.html
            %1    %p
```

In the next example, an ISP has given its users their own virtual hosts and organized the user home directories into subdirectories based on the first two characters of the user ID. Figure 6.5 shows how the original request URL is mapped to a pathname using parts and subparts.

```
UseCanonicalName off
VirtualDocumentRoot /home/httpd/users/%2.1/%2.2/%2/%1
```

Figure 6.5   Dynamic virtual hosting using subparts

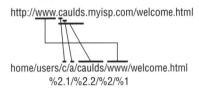

When using virtual hosts with Apache, you need to give special consideration to the hostname that Apache will use to refer to each virtual host. The next section covers the UseCanonicalName directive, which is particularly important for virtual hosting.

The *UseCanonicalName* Directive

An Apache server often has to construct a URL to refer to itself. Such a URL is called a *self-referential URL*. Part of a self-referential URL is the hostname of the server, which should be a hostname that can be resolved by DNS to an IP address for the server. This hostname is often referred to as the *canonical name* for the server.

On my local network, I connect to my Web server using its unqualified name, with a URL like http://jackal. This URL would not work for someone on the Internet, so when my server composes a self-referential URL, it always uses a fully qualified hostname and (optionally) the TCP port number. The UseCanonicalName directive controls how Apache determines the system's hostname when constructing this self-referential URL. There are three possible ways this directive can be used:

UseCanonicalName on   Apache constructs a canonical name for the server using information specified in the ServerName and Listen server configuration directives to create a self-referential URL.

UseCanonicalName off   Apache uses the hostname and port specified in the Host directive supplied by HTTP/1.1 clients to construct a self-referential URL for the server. If the client uses HTTP/1.0 and does not supply a Host header, Apache constructs a canonical name from the ServerName directives. The UseCanonical-Name off form of the directive is usually used with name-based virtual hosts.

`UseCanonicalName DNS`   Apache constructs a self-referential URL for the server using the hostname determined from a reverse-DNS lookup performed on the IP address to which the client connected. This option is designed primarily for use with IP-based virtual hosts, though it can be used in a server context. It has no effect in a name-based virtual host context. The `UseCanonicalName DNS` form of the directive should only be used with IP-based virtual hosts.

In addition to controlling how self-referential URLs are constructed, the `UseCanonical-Name` directive is also used to set two variables that are accessible by CGI scripts through their "environment," `SERVER_NAME` and `SERVER_PORT`. If you look at a CGI script that displays the environment variables, you can easily see how modifying the `UseCanonicalName` directive affects the value of these two variables. Chapter 8 includes such a script in the section on CGI programming.

IP-Based Dynamic Virtual Hosts

Dynamic virtual hosts can also be IP-based, although doing so is not common, because each host would require a unique IP address. Since dynamic virtual hosting is typically used in situations where a large number of virtual hosts must be managed on a single server, the IP-based method usually consumes too many precious IP addresses to be feasible. But if you're interested, a simple example illustrates how it works.

Two directives supplied by `mod_vhost_aliases`, `VirtualDocumentRootIP` and `VirtualScriptAliasIP`, support IP-based dynamic virtual hosting. Here's an example of the two directives in use:

```
UseCanonicalName DNS
VirtualDocumentRootIP     /home/httpd/vhost/%4
VirtualScriptAliasIP      /home/httpd/vhost/cgi-bin/%4
```

Notice that the second portion of each directive specifies a pathname constructed from the IP address on which the HTTP request was received. Therefore the %4 in both directives is filled with the fourth part of the request IP address (the fourth number in the traditional dotted quad IP address format). If a request arrives on an interface whose IP address is 127.129.71.225, the paths specified by `VirtualDocumentRootIP` and `VirtualScriptAliasIP` directories are translated, respectively, into the following directories:

```
/home/httpd/vhost/225
/home/httpd/vhost/cgi-bin/225
```

These directories need to be created on the server for the server to produce a meaningful response. Since each of the parts of an IP address can take a value from 1 to 254, this scheme permits up to 254 IP-based virtual hosts. The following directives would allow

64,516 (254×254) virtual hosts, with pathnames like /home/httpd/vhost/116/244/, but would also require an IP address for each. I show this for illustration only; you'd never find something like this being done in the real world.

```
UseCanonicalName DNS
VirtualDocumentRootIP    /home/httpd/vhost/%3/%4
VirtualScriptAliasIP     /home/httpd/vhost/cgi-bin/%3/%4
```

Also note from these examples that no ServerName directive is used to assign each virtual host its name. If the server needs to form a self-referential URL to refer to any of these virtual hosts, the UseCanonicalName DNS directive instructs it to perform a reverse DNS lookup to determine the server name from the IP address. It is *not* necessary for Apache to perform this reverse DNS lookup to serve requests from the virtual host.

Rules for Virtual Hosting

You can avoid many problems when using Apache virtual hosts by adhering to a list of simple rules:

- Always use an IP address in the <VirtualHost> directive and in every Listen directive; *never* use a hostname. Reliance on the DNS to resolve a hostname may prevent Apache from starting. Chapter 4 discusses the Listen directive.

- Be sure to specify a ServerName directive in all virtual hosts; do not rely on reverse DNS lookups to determine the server name for a virtual host.

- IP-based and name-based virtual hosts are independent and must not conflict. However, it is perfectly OK to have both IP- and name-based virtual hosts on the same server; just make sure that the IP addresses specified in each do not conflict.

- Always create a <VirtualHost _default_:*> container with no pages or with a simple error page. Otherwise, the primary server configuration will be used as the default. Avoid this by providing a default virtual host with some default behavior that you define.

- Ensure that the NameVirtualHost directive is used once, and only once, for each IP address on which you intend to host hostname-based virtual hosts.

TIP   When setting up virtual host configurations, it is often helpful to use the httpd -S command. This will not start the server, but it will dump out a description of how Apache parsed the configuration file. Careful examination of the IP addresses and server names may help uncover configuration mistakes.

Essential Configuration

PART 2

All of the examples shown so far—including those for name-based virtual hosting—have used only IP addresses in the <VirtualHost> directives. This is not an Apache requirement, but it is the best way to define virtual hosts. While it may seem more intuitive to use the hostname for name-based virtual hosts, that should *never* be done. This example shows why:

```
<VirtualHost vhost1.hiwaay.net>
    ServerAdmin caulds@hiwaay.net
    DocumentRoot /home/httpd/html/vhost1
</VirtualHost>
```

The potential problem is that Apache must know at least one IP address for the virtual host, and we haven't provided it. When Apache starts and reads these lines from its httpd.conf file, it performs a DNS lookup for the IP address of the hostname given in the <VirtualHost> directive. If, for some reason, DNS is unavailable, the lookup will fail, and Apache will disable this particular virtual host. In versions earlier than 1.2, Apache will then abort.

If we simply swap in the IP address to correct this, we introduce a second problem:

```
<VirtualHost 192.168.1.4>
    ServerAdmin caulds@hiwaay.net
    DocumentRoot /home/httpd/html/vhost1
</VirtualHost>
```

We no longer require Apache to perform a DNS lookup for the value provided by <VirtualHost>, but we haven't provided a second important piece of information required for *every* virtual host, the ServerName. Apache determines the ServerName in this case by performing a reverse-DNS lookup on 192.168.1.4 to find the associated hostname. This reliance on a DNS query when Apache is started means we haven't solved our problem yet. The addition of a ServerName directive for the virtual host eliminates the dependence on DNS to start the virtual host. The virtual host specification should read:

```
<VirtualHost 192.168.1.4>
    ServerName vhost1.hiwaay.net
    ServerAdmin caulds@hiwaay.net
    DocumentRoot /home/httpd/html/vhost1
</VirtualHost>
```

In Sum

Virtual hosting is used to maintain multiple Web sites on a single server machine. The sites are usually identified by unique hostname aliases in the DNS. Virtual hosts can be either IP-based (the IP address on which the request was received identifies the virtual host to handle the request) or name-based (the client designates the virtual host to handle the request using the HTTP/1.1 Host header).

The mod_vhost_aliases module provides a way to create dynamic virtual hosts, in which the server knows nothing about the virtual host until a request arrives. All information about a dynamic virtual host is derived from the URL of the request or the IP address on which the request arrived. Dynamic virtual hosts are usually used to support large numbers of virtual hosts on a single server with only minimal configuration changes to the Apache server. Dynamic virtual hosts can also be either IP- or name-based, although IP-based dynamic virtual hosts are rarely used because of their requirement that each host have a unique IP address.

Up until this point, I've shown how to set up a working Apache server, but now the focus of the book will be on determining how that server will respond to requests and how the content it delivers can be customized. In other words, we'll be looking at more than just the Apache engine, which is fairly simple. We'll be looking at requests and responses, and customizing the responses returned by Apache, either by configuration changes, adding additional modules, or by programming. The next chapter discusses one of the simpler, but very efficient, techniques for Web page customization, Server-Side Includes.

Essential Configuration

PART 2

Part 3

Advanced Configuration Options

Featuring

- Configuring Apache to run Server-Side Includes (SSI)

- The Common Gateway Interface (CGI) and FastCGI

- The `mod_perl` Perl accelerator

- Using PHP and ASP for Apache

- Apache/Tomcat

- Aliasing and redirection with `mod_alias`

- URL rewriting with `mod_rewrite`

- Controlling Apache manually via the command line

- GUI configuration tools

7

Server-Side Includes

Server-Side Includes (SSI) offer the simplest way to add dynamic content to a Web page. When the Web server receives a request for a page that may contain SSI commands, it parses the page looking for those commands. If it finds any, they are processed by the Apache module that implements SSI (usually `mod_include`). The results of this processing—which may be as simple as the document's last-modified date or as complex as the result of running a CGI script—replace the SSI code in the HTML document before it is sent to the requesting user. SSI commands are actually HTML comments (enclosed in `<!--` and `-->` tags) that have special meaning to the SSI processing module. A page that contains SSI commands adheres to the requirements for HTML, and the SSI commands are ignored (as comments) if they happen to reach a client browser without being parsed, processed, and replaced by the server.

Apache has included SSI for a very long time. Although it is implemented as an optional module, this module is compiled into the server by the `--enable-mods-shared=most` option, and it is available in nearly every Apache server. For simple functions, like automatically including the last date of modification of the HTML document in the document itself, using SSI is far simpler and more efficient than writing a CGI program to take care of the task. I believe every Apache server should be configured to handle server-parsed documents whenever necessary.

SSI is not powerful enough to replace a programming language for generating complete HTML pages, or for database querying, or any of the fun stuff that requires true programming (although it does allow a page to call CGI scripts that can handle those more complex tasks). SSI can't come close to replacing any of the techniques discussed in Chapter 8 for Web programming, and SSI shouldn't be considered an alternative to any of them. I prefer to think of SSI as a built-in feature of Apache that can be used to augment these techniques.

The version of SSI included with Apache is XSSI (for eXtended Server-Side Includes). XSSI has been in use for so long that it is generally considered standard SSI. Another version you may hear of is SSI+, which adds a few tags primarily of interest to Win32 programmers, the most important of which is an ODBC tag used to retrieve data from databases using the Microsoft Open Database Connectivity drivers.

Configuring Apache to Run SSI

SSI documents are an example of a technique called *server-parsed HTML*. Server-parsed documents require two things: a special handler and a way to identify documents that are to be parsed by that handler.

To use SSI on a server, you must make a few changes to the Apache server configuration. First, make sure that the mod_include module is properly installed. You can do this by linking the module to the Apache kernel at compile time, but a better way is to compile the module as a dynamically loadable module:

1. Check your Apache configuration file. If the LoadModule line shown below is commented out or missing, uncomment the line; if it does not exist, add it to the file. Also make sure that the modules directory holds a copy of mod_include.so:

   ```
   LoadModule include_module modules/mod_include.so
   ```

2. Use an Options directive to enable Includes for the directory (or directories) in which you plan to place your server-parsed pages:

   ```
   Options Includes
   ```

TIP   I first tried to set Options +Includes to say "enable the Includes option" but, much to my surprise, this did *not* work! The + operator *adds* options to an Options list that already exists. Since I had no Options list already set for my DocumentRoot directory, the statement had no effect. It was necessary for me to remove the + for the Options directive to take effect.

3. Add an Apache output filter for .shtml files:

```
AddOutputFilter INCLUDES .shtml
```

NOTE   The choice of .shtml as the extension for SSI files is conventional but not strictly necessary.

---

4. Check the Apache configuration file syntax:

```
# /usr/local/apache2/bin/apachectl configtest
Syntax OK
```

5. And then restart the server:

```
# /usr/local/apache2/bin/apachectl restart
/usr/local/apache2/bin/apachectl restart: httpd restarted
```

SSI Tags

Part of the beauty of SSI is that it is implemented with such a simple mechanism: standard HTML with embedded HTML tags that have special meaning only to the SSI parser. SSI commands are legitimate HTML comments that appear between HTML comment tags <!-- and --> and would be ignored by the client browser if they weren't parsed and removed by the Web server. SSI commands have the following general syntax:

```
<!--#command attribute=value attribute=value ... -->
```

There are two Apache directives that you can use to define the strings that mod_include uses as start and end tags for identifying SSI data embedded in a document, though there is usually no reason to do this. The default tags work well for the very reason that they are ignored by Web browsers as HTML comments, if they do manage to get past the SSI parser. If you just had the wild notion, though, you could place directives like the following in httpd.conf to specify customized SSI start and end tags:

```
SSIStartTag "<SSI-"
SSIEndTag "-SSI>"
```

Most SSI commands require at least one *attribute=value* pair. Only a few SSI commands (such as printenv) can be used without an *attribute=value* pair. To prevent confusion in interpreting the SSI line, it is a good practice to enclose the *value* in double quotes, even if that value is a nonstring data type like an integer. The comment terminator (-->) at the end of the line should be offset by white space. (This is not always required, but I had problems running SSI when I failed to separate the final SSI token from the comment terminator.)

Advanced Configuration

PART 3

SSI commands are parsed in place and do not need to be placed at the beginning of the line; you can use an SSI command to replace a single word in the middle of a sentence. In Listing 7.1 and its output (Figure 7.1) you'll see how SSI commands can be used to insert values right in the middle of a line of text.

The *<config>* Tag

The config tag specifies how certain elements of SSI are formatted or displayed. The tag has three defined attributes in standard SSI:

errmsg   The value of errmsg is displayed in the client browser if an error is returned while parsing the SSI document (see Figure 7.1, which displays an error at the bottom for any line that could not be parsed). The custom error message we create for this example is unable to tell us anything about the nature of the error (indicating the almost nonexistent error-handling capability of SSI), and is only marginally better than the default SSI error message, which is "an error occurred while processing this directive." The error in Figure 7.1 occurred because I specified a full pathname as the value of the include file attribute. This must always be expressed as a path relative to the directory in which the SSI page resides.

sizefmt   Determines how the SSI parser displays file sizes returned by the fsize tag. The value of sizefmt can be set to either bytes or abbrev (which displays the file size in either KB or MB, whichever is most appropriate for the size of the file). The sizefmt attribute affects only the use of the fsize tag and has no meaning otherwise. You'll see a demonstration later in this chapter, when we discuss fsize.

timefmt   Allows great flexibility in formatting the strings used to display date and time information. This option will be familiar to anyone who has ever worked with the Linux date utility. SSI calls the Linux strftime() routine to yield % values from Table 7.1.

Table 7.1   Format Strings Used with the <config> SSI Tag

String	Meaning
%%	Escapes a % character
%a	Day of the week abbreviated (Wed)
%A	Full name of day of the week (Wednesday)
%w	Number of day of the week (0–6; Sunday is 0)

Table 7.1   Format Strings Used with the <config> SSI Tag (*continued*)

String	Meaning
%b	Month abbreviated (Oct)
%B	Full name of month (October)
%d	The day of the month (01–31)
%e	The day of the month (1–31)
%H	Hour of the day, measured in 24-hour interval (00–23)
%I	Hour of the day, measured in 12-hour interval (01–12)
%j	Day in the year (001–366)
%M	Minute (00–59)
%p	A.M. or P.M.
%S	Second (00–59)
%y	Last two digits of the year (00–99)
%Y	The four-digit year
%Z	The time zone (CST)

Listing 7.1 is an example of a Web page, formatted in HyperText Markup Language (HTML), that uses most of the time format tags from Table 7.1. Figure 7.1 shows how that page will look when viewed in a Web browser. HTML, as you may remember from Chapter 2, is a standard method of formatting documents for display, or *rendering*. By definition, a Web browser must be able to interpret some version of HTML. Most modern browsers support HTML 4, which includes nearly every element or tag one might conceivably require (version 4 is described at www.w3.org/TR/html4/). HTML is a work in progress and variants of it have been spawned (with names like Extended HTML or Dynamic HTML), but all Web-browser software supports basic HTML.

Listing 7.1   A Test Document for the SSI config Tag

```
<HTML>
<HEAD>
<TITLE>SSI "config" Element Test Page</TITLE>
</HEAD>
<BODY>
```

```
<center>
<H1>SSI "config" Element Test Page</H1>
</center>
<!--#config errmsg="mod_include unable to parse your code!" -->
<!--#config timefmt="%A" -->
Today is <!--#echo var="DATE_LOCAL"-->.
<!--#config timefmt="%B %d, %Y" -->
The date is:  <!--#echo var="DATE_LOCAL"-->
<!--#include file="footer.html"-->
<!--#include file="/home/httpd/html/footer.html">
</BODY>
</HTML>
```

Figure 7.1   The SSI config test document displayed in a browser

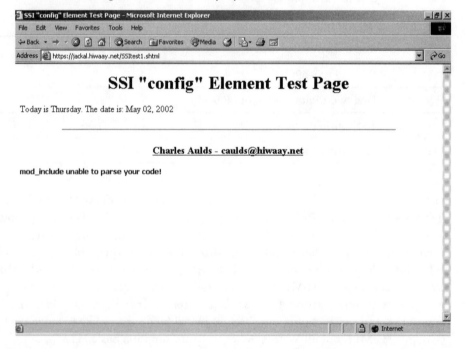

Some familiarity with HTML will be necessary to understand the SSI examples in this chapter, but the important tags, and the only ones that will be explained in detail, are the SSI tags. These can be identified in this example as those enclosed in slightly modified brackets, <!--#   -->. The first SSI tag in Listing 7.1, <!--#config, changes the

default error message to be displayed when the SSI parser encounters a problem. One of the two include file tags, which attempt to bring HTML formatted documents into this one as a page footer, is incorrect and will cause this error message to be displayed. The other footer is correct, so you can see the result in Figure 7.1. Note that HTML tags in that footer are properly rendered (as an embedded hyperlink).

This example also serves to illustrate the use of the config timefmt SSI tag to display the current system time and date. Compare the SSI tags against the output, glancing back at Table 7.1, and you can pretty easily see how these work.

A better alternative to using <config errmsg …> and <config timefmt …> within the bodies of your server-parsed documents is to set these once, for all SSI documents, in Apache's configuration. Two directives are provided for this purpose. The following examples would have the same effect when parsing the example in Listing 7.1 and Figure 7.1, except that the effect would be global and would apply to every SSI document on the server. There is no server directive for globally setting <config sizefmt …>.

```
SSIErrorMsg "mod_include unable to parse your code!"
SSITimeFormat "%B %d, %Y"
```

As you can see, at least one statement in the HTML could not be parsed. But which one? Where did the links to my e-mail come from? And why are there two separate references to a footer.html file? Not surprisingly, the answers to all those questions are related. The e-mail links are part of my standard page footer, displayed by calling my footer.html file. One of the #include statements is correct and displays the footer page, but the other has incorrect syntax and displays the error message. You'll see exactly what the error is when we look at the #include tag later in the chapter.

The *<echo>* Tag

The echo tag prints the values of SSI variables and requires at least one attribute, the name of the variable to be printed. If the variable identified in the attribute is not set, it is displayed as (none), and no error occurs. In addition to the variables available in the standard Common Gateway Interface (CGI) environment (the full list of these variables is included in the discussion of CGI in Chapter 8), SSI also sets the following SSI-specific variables:

DATE_GMT The current system date in Greenwich Mean Time.

DATE_LOCAL The current system date in local time.

DOCUMENT_NAME The filename of the SSI document requested by the user.

DOCUMENT_URI The URL path of the SSI document requested by the user.

Advanced Configuration

PART 3

LAST_MODIFIED   The last modification date of the SSI document requested by the user (when displayed by echo, the date will be formatted according to the config timefmt format).

Listing 7.2 illustrates how the echo tag is used to display the values of all four of the SSI-specific variables shown above, along with several selected variables from the CGI environment. Figure 7.2 shows the results in a browser. The three time variables (DATA_LOCAL, DATE_GMT, and LAST_MODIFIED) are displayed using the SSI default format, but could be tailored by preceding them with a config timefmt tag, as described in the last section.

Listing 7.2   A Test Document for the SSI echo Tag

```
<HTML>
<HEAD>
<TITLE>SSI "echo" Element Test Page</TITLE>
</HEAD>
<BODY>
<center>
<H1>SSI "echo" Element Test Page</H1>
</center>
<FONT SIZE=+1>
<ul>
Special mod_include Includes:
<ul>
DATE_LOCAL:<!--#echo var="DATE_LOCAL"--> <br>
DATE_GMT:<!--#echo var="DATE_GMT"--> <br>
DOCUMENT_NAME:<!--#echo var="DOCUMENT_NAME"--> <br>
DOCUMENT_URI:<!--#echo var="DOCUMENT_URI"--> <br>
LAST_MODIFIED:<!--#echo var="LAST_MODIFIED"--> <br>
<p>
</ul>
Includes from the CGI Environment:
<ul>
SERVER_NAME:<!--#echo var="SERVER_NAME"--> <br>
SERVER_SOFTWARE:<!--#echo var="SERVER_SOFTWARE"--> <br>
HTTP_USER_AGENT:<!--#echo var="HTTP_USER_AGENT"--> <br>
</ul>
</FONT>
<!--#include file="footer.html"-->
</BODY>
</HTML>
```

Figure 7.2 The SSI echo test document displayed in a browser

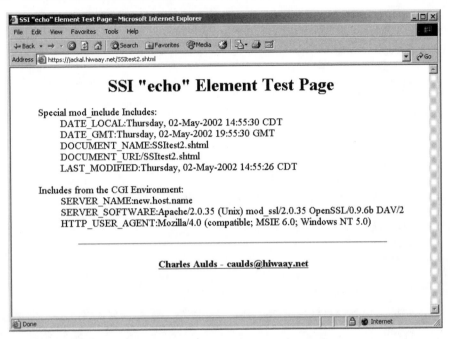

The *<exec>* Tag

The exec tag executes an external command and displays the command's standard output (stdout). The command can be either a Linux shell command in this format:

```
<!--#exec cmd="shell-command arg1 arg2 ..." -->
```

for example:

```
<!--#exec cmd="/usr/bin/parser.sh rfc2626.html" -->
```

or a CGI script:

```
<!--#exec cgi="/cgi-bin/mycgi.cgi" -->
```

If the script returns a Location: HTML header instead of output, this header is translated into an HTML anchor (an embedded hyperlink). Listing 7.3 is an example of the exec tag at work. The CGI script that it calls consists of only three lines; while it could do many other things, it simply returns a Location: string (SSI is smart enough to translate this into an anchor tag or hyperlink):

```
#!/usr/bin/perl -Tw
# This is anchor.cgi
print "Location: http://www.apache.org\n\n";
```

Advanced Configuration

PART 3

Figure 7.3 shows how a browser renders the results.

Listing 7.3: A Test Document for the SSI exec Tag

```
<HTML>
<HEAD>
<TITLE>SSI "include Tag with Location:" Test Page</TITLE>
</HEAD>
<BODY>
<center>
<H1>SSI "include Tag with Location:" Test Page</H1>
</center>
<br>
Clickable hyperlink:  <!--#exec cgi="/cgi-bin/anchor.cgi" -->
<p>
<!--#include file="footer.html"-->
</BODY>
</HTML>
```

Figure 7.3   The SSI exec tag used as anchor

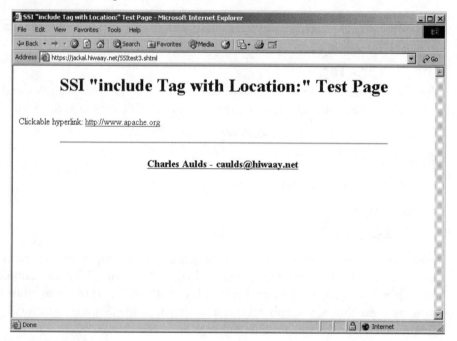

If an IncludesNOEXEC option is in effect for the directory containing the SSI file being parsed, the exec tag will be ignored. The directive Options IncludesNOEXEC should be in the .htaccess file in the directory or in the httpd.conf file.

> **WARNING**   For security reasons, you should avoid using the `<exec cgi>` SSI tag, which will execute a file anywhere in the filesystem. This violates an accepted Apache standard practice in which CGI scripts reside only in special protected directories and have specific filename extensions. Instead, use `<include virtual>`, which can execute only standard CGI scripts that are accessible only through a URL that is acceptable to Apache. This allows Apache to apply the security measures applied to ordinary CGI scripts.

The *<fsize>* Tag

The fsize tag inserts the size of a given file into a server-parsed HTML file. It has two forms, each of which is a different way of locating the file whose size is to be displayed:

> **file**   Identifies a filename and path relative to the directory containing the SSI document being parsed. The path cannot contain "../" and it cannot be an absolute path. This prevents you from including files that are outside of Apache's document root, and it cannot be above the parsed SSI document in the server filesystem. It must be in the same directory, or in a subdirectory, of the one containing the SSI document that calls it.

> **NOTE**   Use of the `<file>` tag should be avoided. Use the `<virtual>` tag instead.

> **virtual**   The virtual variable is set to the filename or path relative to Apache's DocumentRoot. Use this when you want to specify a file using a partial URL.

The fsize and flastmod tags are examples of what I like best about SSI: They both have very simple syntax and offer a very efficient way of doing what they do. Moreover, neither tries to do too many things, but each of them comes in very handy when you need it. The next section illustrates them both in the same example (Listing 7.4) because they are used in exactly the same manner. Figure 7.4 then shows how both tags are rendered by a browser.

Advanced Configuration

PART 3

TIP   Use the `config timefmt` tag, as described earlier in this chapter, to format the file size printed by the `fsize` tag.

The *<flastmod>* Tag

The `flastmod` tag inserts the date of last modification of a specified file into the SSI document being parsed at the location of the `flastmod` tag. Like `fsize`, the file is specified in one of the following two ways:

file   Identifies a filename and path relative to the directory containing the SSI document being parsed. As with the `<fsize>` element, the file named cannot be above the parsed SSI document in the server filesystem.

virtual   The virtual variable is set to the filename or path relative to Apache's DocumentRoot. Use this when you want to specify a file using a partial URL.

TIP   The format of the date printed by the `flastmod` tag is controlled using the `config timefmt` tag as described earlier.

Listing 7.4 is an example of a document that makes use of both the SSI `fsize` and `flastmod` tags. By referring to Figure 7.4, you can easily determine the use of each of these tags. Note that the first `fsize` tag uses the `file` keyword to indicate that the referenced file is relative to the directory in which the SSI document resides (in this case they must be in the same directory). The second `fsize` tag makes use of the `virtual` keyword to indicate that the file is relative to the Apache `DocumentRoot` (the file must be in the docs subdirectory of that directory).

Listing 7.4   A Test Document for the SSI `fsize` and `flastmod` Tags

```
<HTML>
<HEAD>
<TITLE>SSI "fsize" and "flastmod" Elements Test Page</TITLE>
</HEAD>
<BODY>
<center>
<H2>SSI "fsize" and "flastmod" Elements Test Page</H2>
<H3>Testing fsize and flastmod</H3>
</center>
<!--#config sizefmt="bytes" -->
<!--#config timefmt="%I:%M %P on %B %d, %Y" -->
<p>Size of this file (bytes): <!--#fsize file="SSItest4.shtml" -->
```

```
<br>Last modification of this file: <!--#flastmod virtual="/SSItest4.shtml" -->
<p>Size of suexec.html (bytes): <!--#fsize virtual="/docs/suexec.html" -->
<!--#config sizefmt="abbrev" -->
<br>Size of suexec.html (KB): <!--#fsize virtual="/docs/suexec.html" -->

<!--#config sizefmt="abbrev" -->
<!--#include file="footer.html"-->
</BODY>
</HTML>
```

Figure 7.4 The SSI fsize and flastmod test document displayed in a browser

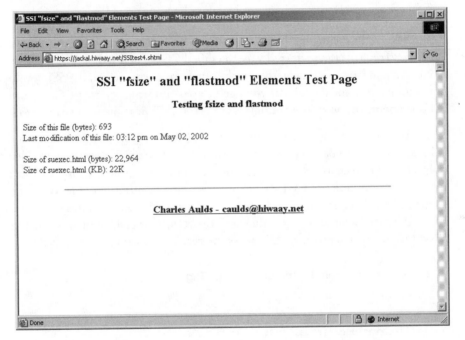

The *<include>* Tag

The include tag runs an external file, captures its output, and places that output in the document being parsed. There are two possible formats for the tag:

> **include file** The include file SSI tag is used in the examples throughout this chapter to include an HTML file as a page footer. This is the simplest possible use of the tag. When it's used in this fashion, the included file must be specified by a path relative to the directory of the calling document. (A fully qualified pathname will *not* work; that's why the second include statement back in Listing 7.1 triggered the error message you saw in Figure 7.1.) Any

access restrictions upon the directory in which the called file resides remain in effect for its inclusion in the calling document.

include virtual   The preferred way to use the include tag is to specify include virtual, which identifies the included resource by a relative URL, not by file-name or path. (This is preferred because the design of the Web is to ensure that all resources are referenced by URL, making their location as independent of sys-tem path as possible.) When used in this fashion, mod_include constructs a URL from the include virtual command, and embeds the results of this URL (what would be returned if the URL was called directly by the client) into the calling document. If the resource indicated by the URL itself includes SSI commands, these are resolved, which allows include files to be nested.

Regardless of the calling method, the included resource can also be a CGI script, and include virtual is the preferred way to embed CGI-generated output in server-parsed documents (always use this method rather than exec cgi, which the SSI developers do not recommend). Incidentally, if you need to pass information to a CGI script from an SSI document, you *must* use include virtual; it isn't possible using exec cgi.

Also, attempting to set environment variables (such as QUERY_STRING) from within an SSI page in order to pass data to a CGI script won't work. This sets a variable accessible only to mod_include and doesn't alter the environment variable with the same name. Instead, pass variables to CGI scripts by appending ?*variable=value* to the query string of the calling URL, as shown in Listing 7.5. This script demonstrates how a CGI script is called, passed a variable and value, and the results embedded in an HTML document passed to the browser. Figure 7.5 shows the resulting document displayed in a browser.

Listing 7.5   A Test Document for the SSI include Tag

```
<HTML>
<HEAD>
<TITLE>include virtual Test Page</TITLE>
</HEAD>
<BODY>
<center>
<H1>Test of include virtual SSI Tag</H1>
</center>
<!--#include virtual="/cgi-bin/test1.cgi?testvar=Testing+for+Carl" -->
<!--#include file="footer.html"-->
</BODY>
</HTML>
```

Listing 7.6 displays the contents of the CGI script that is included in Listing 7.5 above. This script must reside in a directory that has been designated in the httpd.conf file as a repository for CGI scripts (using the ScriptAlias directive). In every respect, it is a standard CGI script, and can be called independently (with a URL that references it directly) of any SSI page that might include it.

Listing 7.6   The CGI Script Used with the SSI `include` Tag Test Document

```perl
#!/usr/bin/perl -Tw
#This is test1.cgi
#
#queries a table for a value

use strict;
use CGI qw(:standard);
use CGI::Carp;

my $output=new CGI;

my $TEST=param('testvar') if (param('testvar') );

print $output->header;
print h3("Variable passed to and returned from CGI script:");
print h4("$TEST");
print $output->end_html;
```

Figure 7.5   The SSI `include` test document displayed in a browser

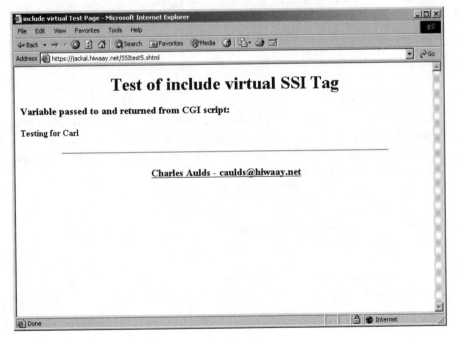

The *<printenv>* Tag

Of all the SSI tags, printenv is probably the easiest to use. It has no attributes and simply performs a single function; it returns all the system environment variables in one unformatted list. Since the list is not HTML formatted, it is usually a good idea to enclose the printenv tags in standard HTML <pre> or <code> tags that normally enclose unformatted text in an HTML page:

```
<pre>
<!--#printenv -->
</pre>
```

The *<set>* Tag

The set tag sets the value of a variable, creating the variable if it doesn't already exist. It takes two attributes: the name of a variable to be set, and a value attribute that is assigned to this variable. Both the var and value attributes need to be specified separately:

```
<!--#set var="FOO" value="someval" -->
```

Although variables set in this manner can be used for conditional tests with SSI's rudimentary flow control, as discussed in upcoming sections of the chapter, they are generally used to store data that is later displayed (with the <echo> tag) somewhere in the HTML document being parsed. If an attempt is made to echo a variable that has not been set, SSI will display the value of the variable as (none). Though not very commonly used, mod_include provides a directive, SSIUndefinedEcho, to change this default. If, for example, you wanted to display the value of unset variables in a slightly different way, you can include a directive like the following in Apache's httpd.conf file:

```
SSIUndefinedEcho "Unset Variable!"
```

Flow Control

The so-called *flow control* elements of SSI implement only the most basic execution control element, an if/else operator; they don't provide the functions of execution branching or nesting found in a real programming language. Here's the basic implementation of the if tag in SSI:

```
<!--#if expr="test_condition" -->
    HTML-formatted text
<!--#elif expr="test_condition" -->
    HTML-formatted text
<!--#else -->
    even more HTML-formatted text
<!--#endif -->
```

Note that `expr` is a keyword and must be present. The `if expr` element works like the `if` statement in a true programming language. The test condition is evaluated and, if the result is true, the text between it and the next `elif`, `else`, or `endif` tag is included in the output stream, and subsequent `endif` tests are ignored. If the result is false, the next `elif` is evaluated in the same way.

SSI test conditions are almost always simple string comparisons, and return True or False based on the result of one of the following possible operations:

Syntax	Value
`string`	True if *string* is not empty; False otherwise
`string1 = string2`	True if *string1* is equal to *string2*
`string1 != string2`	True if *string1* is not equal to *string2*
`string1 < string2`	True if *string1* is alphabetically less than *string2*
`string1 <= string2`	True if *string1* is alphabetically less than or equal to *string2*
`string1 > string2`	True if *string1* is alphabetically greater than *string2*
`string1 >= string2`	True if *string1* is alphabetically greater than or equal to *string2*
`condition1 && condition2`	True if both conditions are True (the AND operator)
`condition1 || condition2`	True if either condition is True (the OR operator)

An alternate form is to compare a string against a regular expression. If *string2* in any of the operations above is expressed as */string2/*, a regular expression comparison is made against *string1*:

```
<!---if expr=string1=/string2/ -->
```

Generally, you will be looking only for the existence of a match (using the = operator) when working with regular expressions:

```
<!--if expr=$DOCUMENT_URI=/^cgi-bin/ -->
```

However, you can also test for an expression that is not matched by negating the results of the match using the != operator:

```
<!--if expr=$DOCUMENT_URI!=/^cgi-bin/ -->
```

Use parentheses and quotation marks for clarity when expressing SSI tags with several comparisons:

```
<!--#if expr="($a = test1) && ($b = test2)" -->
```

The following example evaluates to True if the request URI begins with either /cgi-bin/ or /cgi-vep/, False otherwise:

```
<!--#if expr="($DOCUMENT_URI=/^\/cgi-bin/) ||
    ($DOCUMENT_URI=/^\/cgi-vep/)" -->
```

Listing 7.7 illustrates a very practical use of the if/else tag in SSI. If the IP address of the connecting host, which is stored in the environment variable REMOTE_ADDR, matches the regular expression in the first if expr expression, it indicates that the client is on the Apache server's subnet, and the user is presented with some information that external users will *never* see. If the REMOTE_ADDR does not match in this expression, the user is not on the local subnet, and the text in the else clause is sent to the requester. This contains a line to simply tell remote users that some aspects of the page are invisible to them. In real life, you'd probably keep them from knowing even that, instead presenting them with a document intended for their eyes. Figure 7.6 shows how the results of Listing 7.7 are displayed in a browser.

Listing 7.7   An SSI Flow Control Test Document

```
<HEAD>
<TITLE>SSI File Include Test Page</TITLE>
</HEAD>
<BODY>
<center>
<H1>SSI File Include Test Page</H1>
<!--#if expr="$REMOTE_ADDR = /^192.168.1./" -->
    <H3>You connected from the local network!</H3>
<!--#else -->
    <H3>Remote users cannot see some aspects of this page!</H3>
<!--#endif -->
<center>
<FORM METHOD = "POST" ACTION = "mailto:caulds@hiwaay.net">
<INPUT TYPE = "SUBMIT" VALUE="Click here to send me e-mail"></FORM>
</center>
<HR>
<ADDRESS>
<center>
<A HREF="mailto:caulds@hiwaay.net">Charles Aulds - caulds@hiwaay.net</A>
<BR>
</ADDRESS>
</center>
</BODY>
</HTML>
```

Figure 7.6 The SSI Flow Control test document displayed in a browser

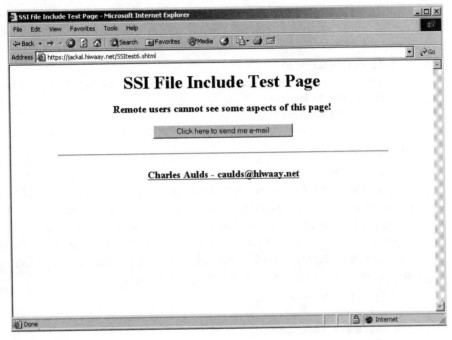

The *XBitHack* Directive

Although `mod_include` extends the Apache server to enable the parsing of a number of different tags, the module adds only one directive to Apache, and it's kind of a strange one. The `XBitHack` directive is very aptly named. It is a genuine hack, an alternative to the "proper" way of doing things. It uses the access permission attributes of a file in a completely different way than they are intended. For that reason, I don't actually recommend its use, but if you can identify a need, it works as advertised.

XBitHack allows the system administrator to identify ordinary HTML documents as candidates for server-side parsing. Whenever the `XBitHack` directive is applied to a directory from `httpd.conf` or from an `.htaccess` file, all documents in that directory that are identifiable as MIME-type text/HTML can be handled by `mod_include`, based on the Linux permissions set for the files.

The `XBitHack` directive can take three values; the behavior of each is described below:

XBitHack Off   Disables all treatment of text/HTML files as server-parsed documents.

XBitHack On   Tests every text/HTML document within the scope of the directive to see if it should be handled as server-parsed by `mod_include`. If the user-

Advanced
Configuration

PART 3

execute bit is set, the document is parsed as a SSI document. If an XBitHack On directive was applied to the directory as in the following example, index.html would not be identified as server-parsed until the chmod statement was issued to set the execute bit for the user:

```
# ls -al index.html
-rw-r--r--    1 www        www            3844 Jan 28 14:58 index.html
# chmod u+x index.html
# ls -al index.html
-rwxr--r--    1 www        www            3844 Jan 28 14:58 index.html
```

XBitHack Full Works just like XBitHack On except that, in addition to testing the user-execute bit, it also tests to see if the group-execute bit is set. If it is, then the Last-Modified date set in the response header is the last modified time of the file. If the group-execute bit is not set, no Last-Modified header is sent to the requester. This XBitHack feature is used when you want proxies to cache server-parsed documents; normally, you would *not* want to do this if the document contains data (from a CGI include, for example) that changes upon every invocation. Here's an example of setting the group-execute bit:

```
# ls -al index.html
-rw-r--r--    1 www        www            3916 Mar 10 08:25 index.html
# chmod g+x index.html
# ls -al index.html
-rw-r-xr--    1 www        www            3916 Mar 10 08:25 index.html
```

In Sum

Server-Side Includes, or SSI (often called server-parsed HTML), provides one of the simplest ways to produce dynamic Web pages without true programming. SSI is implemented through special SSI tags, but otherwise the instructions consist of standard HTML text. SSI is usually used to provide features like displaying the current time, the date, and the time of the last file modification, or including standard text from other documents. Although SSI is rarely an adequate alternative to a real programming language, it can be used for tasks like querying or updating a database, sending an e-mail message, or using conditional statements to determine whether certain actions are taken or whether or not specific text is displayed.

In the next chapter, we begin a journey through the most popular programming techniques used by Web site designers today. As an Apache administrator, you require a working familiarity with each and, in particular, knowledge of how they interface with Apache. The next chapter will tell you what you need to know to install and use the programming methodologies that power the majority of the dynamic Web sites on the Internet.

8

Scripting/Programming for Apache

In the early days of the Web, programming usually meant enhancing a Web site by adding simple user interactivity, or providing access to some basic services on the server side. Essentially, programming for the Web in those days meant interpreting input from the user and generating specific content for that user dynamically ("on-the-fly"). A simple Web program might take user input and use it to control a search engine or a database query, for example.

Web programming has evolved from those very simple programs that added user interactivity and automation to Web pages. Today, Web-based applications are often full-fledged production systems, complete electronic storefronts, or front-ends to complex, powerful databases. Such applications are often implemented using the three-tier business computing model, where the application or Web server usually makes up the middle tier, and the Web browser is often used as the bottom tier or user interface. The top tier of this model usually consists of large database server systems and has no direct interaction with the end user (or bottom tier).

Changes in the requirements for Web programming are a direct result of the changing role of the Internet Web server. The Web is no longer simply a delivery medium for static Web pages. Chances are, if you are writing programs for the Web today, they are likely to be an integral part of someone's Internet business strategy. Your ability to program an application, even a very simple application, is probably critical to the success of your Web project.

Although larger Web sites generally have both a Webmaster and a content provider, often with sharply divided responsibilities, at many sites the two roles have been increasingly merged. I don't know any sharp Apache administrator who isn't keenly interested in programming techniques for the Web. Like the topic of security (discussed in chapters 13 and 14 of this book), programming is one of those formerly peripheral topics that have become an integral part of the Apache administrator's required knowledge base.

This chapter covers a number of different approaches to programming for the Apache server. No one of them is clearly the best choice for every application. There are a number of good programming methodologies for the Web; no single language is clearly superior to all the rest, and each has its adherents and, in many cases, religious zealots. There will always be someone who will try to tell you that there's only one way to program a Web-based application, and if you aren't using that technology, you're behind the times. Don't believe it. Your choice of programming language or methodology shouldn't be based on what is most popular at the moment, but rather should fit your particular need, as well as the skills you already possess. When selecting a programming methodology, you must look at what your competencies are, and what you enjoy most; all the programming tools discussed for Web programming in this chapter are quite adequate for developing commercial-quality Web applications.

In this chapter, we'll first cover what is still the most widespread approach—using the Common Gateway Interface (CGI) or its newer variant, FastCGI, and the Perl scripting language. Later sections of the chapter will look at some of the newer tools and techniques available, including PHP, Apache/Tomcat, ASP, JSP, and Resin. Each of these tools can be used to successfully create real-world Web-based applications. They can all be used on the same server, and a single Web application might make use of more than one tool.

The goal of this chapter is not to teach you "how to program" in the languages covered; entire books are written on those topics. The focus instead is on how the tool is used with Apache. A simple programming example for each tool will serve to show the basics of how it is used. The examples I provide are simple, but not trivial. Each demonstrates how to extract data from a database using a simple Structured Query Language (SQL) query. In essence, each is a full three-tier application, providing a simple user-input form along with a mid-tier server program that takes the user input and uses it to query the third tier, a database engine, that might be on a completely separate server.

For additional information on all of the programming methodologies mentioned in this chapter, be sure to see the programming resources in Appendix B. The best of these provide numerous examples of working code. Since I believe studying program examples is undoubtedly the best way to learn programming techniques, I have provided working examples in each topic discussed in this chapter.

The Common Gateway Interface (CGI)

The Common Gateway Interface (CGI) is a very simple mechanism that permits a Web server to invoke any program, capture the output of that program, wrap it in the most basic HTTP headers, and return it to the Web browser. That's only a slight oversimplification; in fact, CGI *is* very simple. And since CGI is provided through one of the standard Apache modules (mod_cgi), it is available on every Apache server. I think of CGI as a given, a feature I can count on finding on any Web server. Among the Apache programming interfaces, it's the equivalent of the vi text editor—ubiquitous and capable enough for the most essential applications.

---

mod_cgi and *mod_cgid*

Apache 2.0 is actually distributed with two modules that provide the Web server with a CGI interface. The first, mod_cgi, is the same module provided with all pre-2.0 versions of Apache. New to Apache 2.0 is the mod_cgid module, which is intended to improve CGI performance when a "threaded" Multi-Processing Module (MPM) is used. When threading is used to provide multiple simultaneous client connections to Apache, the traditional "pre-forking" Apache child processes that handle requests can be expensive (that is, CPU-intensive). In current versions of Linux, however, a process is a single thread, and there are no advantages to using mod_cgid instead of mod_cgi; therefore the module is not discussed further in this book. Linux users should always use mod_cgi.

CGI was first implemented in the NCSA httpd Web server and quickly adopted as the de facto programming interface for the Web. Today every major Web server supports CGI. The current working specification for CGI (version 1.1) dates back to 1995. Although the 1.1 specification is still a draft IETF standard, there is now a 1.2 version of the CGI specification in the works. Progress on version 1.2 has been extraordinarily slow, and there doesn't appear to be a big demand for any of the changes under consideration for the new version. For most purposes, CGI can be considered a fairly static mechanism. Learning CGI has the advantage that you won't soon have to learn a new programming methodology or see your Web-based application suddenly become obsolete.

Any program that can be executed from the command line on the server can be used with CGI. This includes compiled programs written in C or C++, or even COBOL or Fortran. Scripting languages like Perl, Tcl, or shell scripting languages are the most popular ways to write CGI programs. Scripts are usually much quicker to write than compiled programs. Since the client browser provides the user interface for Web applications, the scripts contain only the basic code required for data I/O and are smaller and easier to maintain. Minor code changes to scripts don't require compilation and linking, which speeds up and simplifies code design, testing, and maintenance.

As a general-purpose programming interface, CGI offers some advantages over proprietary Web-programming interfaces like Netscape's NSAPI, Microsoft's ISAPI, and even the Apache programming interface. Although these interfaces offer the programmer substantially better performance and easier access to the inner workings of the Web server, CGI is far more widely used for several reasons. The first is that CGI is independent of both server architecture and programming language, allowing the programmer great freedom to choose the language best suited for a particular programming task. I regularly use a combination of C, Tcl, Perl, and even shell scripts for CGI programming tasks.

CGI also offers complete process isolation. A CGI program runs in its own process address space, independently of the Web server, and it communicates only input and output with the server. Running CGI programs outside the program space of Apache not only protects the server from errant CGI processes (even the most serious errors in a CGI program cannot affect the Web server), it can also provide protection against deliberate attempts to compromise the security or stability of the server, if the CGI scripts are properly written. If you intend to use CGI, be sure to read the section below titled "General Tips for Safe CGI Use," and also take the time to read a few online references, especially the timeless World Wide Web Security FAQ (www.w3.org/Security/Faq/).

Last, but certainly not least, CGI offers the tremendous advantage of being a simple interface to learn and use. For most programming tasks, CGI offers more than enough functionality and adequate performance, without imposing heavy demands on the programmer.

Scripting languages are so popular for CGI Web-programming tasks that many texts simply refer to CGI programs as *CGI scripts*. In fact, the Perl language owes much of its popularity to its early adoption by Web site administrators for CGI applications. In the past few years it has seen wide acceptance as a general-purpose scripting language, especially where cross-platform compatibility is a strong concern. Many programmers consider Perl to be the de facto standard for writing CGI scripts. Actually, nearly any language can be used to write CGI programs, including compiled languages like C. But Perl is the most popular, and it's the one I've chosen to best illustrate the use of CGI. Just remember that CGI is not limited to scripting languages, and Perl is not limited to Web programming.

The CGI examples provided in this section are all written in scripting languages, but there is no reason that a compiled language like C couldn't be used in exactly the same way. The main reason CGI scripts are usually written in a compiled language is to maximize their speed of execution. Server-side script accelerators (such as mod_perl, which is discussed later in this chapter) have greatly reduced the difference in execution speed between compiled and scripted languages, but if performance is of the utmost importance to you, you may want to consider using a compiled language (probably C) for your scripts.

How CGI Works

Programs that run under CGI require no special hooks into the Web server and use no CGI-specific API calls. Communication between Apache and the CGI program does not use special protocols. It is kept as simple and as generic as possible, using two mechanisms that all programs can access: the process *environment* and the standard input and output pipes.

The System Environment

In Linux, when a program is invoked, it is passed a set of data called the process environment. This is a list of *name=value* pairs. Typically, one process that is invoked by another inherits a copy of that process's environment (it is said to inherit the environment of its parent process). This provides one way for a process to pass data to a process it creates. By tailoring its own environment before starting a process, the parent process can control the environment of the process it invokes.

When Apache receives a request for a resource that it recognizes as a CGI script or program, it spawns the process by making calls to the Linux operating system. This process is completely independent of Apache, with one important exception: Its standard output pipe remains connected to the Apache server process, so that Apache receives all output from the program that is directed to standard output (or *stdout*). If the CGI program is a Linux shell script, like the example below, the echo statement is used to send text to stdout. (Later in this chapter, in the section "A Script to Return the Environment," we'll add a little formatting to this script to generate the output shown in Figure 8.1.)

```
#!/bin/sh
echo "Content-type: text/plain"
echo
echo "Environment variables defined:"
echo
env
```

Apache does not communicate directly with the CGI process it spawns. Instead, as the parent of the process, it has some degree of control over the environment in which the process runs. In order to pass data to the process it creates, Apache places its data in environment variables that can be read by the process. In our simple CGI process, the shell command env reads the environment and reports it to its standard output file handle (stdout). Apache receives this output through the pipe it maintains to the script's stdout handle and sends it to the requesting user.

To test this script, create a new file in a directory defined by a ScriptAlias directive in httpd.conf, and place in the file the statements shown above. (Chapter 4 shows how to use ScriptAlias.) An alternative method is to associate files with a specific filename extension with an Apache handler as described in the next section. For example, you could also do the following, which marks all files with the .cgi extension as executable.

```
# AddHandler cgi-script .cgi
```

Removing the leading # character that marks this line as a comment causes Apache to treat all files with a name ending in the .cgi extension as CGI scripts, and they will be executed using the CGI mechanism. Under Linux, it is not necessary to identify each type of script by a different extension; I use the .cgi extension to identify all CGI scripts on my systems, without regard to the actual content of the file. The first line of all scripts should contain the full pathname of the script processor, preceded by the hash-bang (#!) characters, as in our example:

```
#!/bin/sh
```

In general, you should use this directive within a <Directory> or <Location> container to place restrictions on which files are interpreted as scripts. ScriptAlias is the preferred method, though, and is normally used to ensure that *only* files stored in a specific location are loaded and run as CGI scripts.

Identifying CGI Resources

The important thing to remember is that the CGI resource (whether identified by its filename or extension, or its location in Apache's document space) must be associated with a *handler* provided by the mod_cgi module if it is to be executed as a CGI script. There are several ways that resources can be identified to Apache as candidates for treatment as CGI files. Each method is discussed separately in the following sections.

The Concept of the "Handler"

Apache uses the concept of a handler to determine how it should process scripts and other dynamic resources before handing the results to the requester. Each Apache handler is usually associated with a particular module that performs the handler's work. By defining a handler to process a particular resource or collection of resources, we actually specify a module that receives and processes the resource before it is passed on to the requester.

The default Apache distribution comes with a number of built-in handlers, including one for CGI programs. The CGI handler is cgi-script, which is provided by the standard module, mod_cgi. Configuring a script or program to be treated as a CGI resource is as simple as defining cgi-script as its handler. In the next sections, I'll show four ways to do this.

NOTE   Every resource served by Apache that is not associated with a specific handler is processed by a handler named (not surprisingly) default-handler, provided by the core module.

Defining Directories

The most common way to define resources for execution as CGI programs is to designate one or more directories as containers for CGI programs. Security is enhanced when CGI programs reside in a limited number of specified CGI directories. Access to these directories should be strictly controlled and careful attention paid to the ownership and permissions of files that are stored there.

Two slightly different directives provide a means of identifying a directory as a container for CGI scripts: ScriptAlias (introduced in Chapter 4) and ScriptAliasMatch. Both directives work like a simple Alias directive to map a request to a directory that may not exist under DocumentRoot, and they designate a directory as a container for CGI scripts. ScriptAlias is simpler, so we'll look at it first.

The following line, found in the standard Apache distribution, defines a directory to contain CGI scripts:

```
ScriptAlias /cgi-bin/ "/usr/local/apache2/cgi-bin/"
```

When a request comes in with a URL like http://jackal.hiwaay.net/cgi-bin/example.cgi, Apache looks for a file named example.cgi in the /usr/local/apache2/cgi-bin directory and, if it finds the file, executes the file as a CGI script. In the sample request URL, cgi-bin appears to be a subdirectory of DocumentRoot; however, the directory's actual name and location are arbitrary and it could be anywhere on the filesystem.

Pay very close attention to the permission settings for directories identified as containers for CGI scripts. Apache itself does not apply any kind of security checking to directories identified using ScriptAlias. It is up to the Apache administrator to ensure that only designated users can write to or execute files in those directories. If users need to be able to maintain their own Apache-executable scripts but not those of other users, consider using multiple ScriptAlias directives to identify several CGI directories and grant separate access permissions to different Linux groups. Also make sure that the account under which the Apache child processes run has permission to both read and execute the files in each directory, though write permission should be denied that user, which effectively prevents Apache from creating, or modifying, CGI scripts. This is a safeguard against the possibility that someone might find a way to cause Apache to write data (a malicious script) into a directory that contains CGI content. Always

Advanced
Configuration

PART 3

remember that the only security provided for CGI scripts is that of the Linux operating system, and Apache does not concern itself with protecting those resources.

When Apache is installed, you will note that it assigns ownership of the directories and files under the Apache home (usually /usr/local/apache2) to the user who installed Apache, which should ordinarily be the system "root." This user alone has write permissions to the Apache directories; the Apache child processes are unable to write into these directories. All other users are given read-only permissions to the Apache directories and files. In the case of the cgi-bin directory, it is necessary to assign read and execute permissions to the files stored there in order for them to be executed as CGI scripts. The following commands will assign read-write-execute permissions to the directory owner and read-execute permissions to members of the group owner (which is also root in most typical Apache installations on Linux servers):

```
# chmod -R 775 cgi-bin
```

Note the use of the -R (recursive) switch, which applies the commands to the directory listed on the command line as well as to all of its subdirectories.

On all Apache servers that I've administered, I've created a www group account that includes the user accounts of all the members of the Web team, but does not include the account under which Apache runs. I make this the group owner of the Apache home directory and of all its subdirectories. Now, only members of the privileged www group (and also the root user, of course) can create or modify Apache files. The following commands create a group named www (assuming it does not already exist) and then changes the group owner of all subdirectories and files of the Apache home directory to www:

```
# groupadd www
# chgrp -R www /usr/local/apache2
```

A directory listing of one of my CGI directories is shown below. You can see that the CGI scripts are all owned by the root user, and only that user, and members of the www group have full read-write-execute privileges. All other users (which includes the non-privileged account under which the Apache child processes are run) can read and execute scripts, but are denied the ability to write into this directory or any of its subdirectories, if they exist.

```
# ls -al cgi-bin/
total 80
drwxrwxr-x    2 root      www        4096 May 10 16:06 .
drwxr-xrwx   10 root      www        4096 Jul 13 17:02 ..
-rwxrwxr-x    1 root      www        2867 May 10 16:06 col66.cgi
-rwxrwxr-x    1 root      www        3522 May 10 16:06 col67.cgi
-rwxrwxr-x    1 root      www        3876 May 10 16:06 col68.cgi
```

```
-rwxrwxr-x   1 root    www       3193 May 10 16:06 CookieTest.cgi
-rwxrwxr-x   1 root    www       2467 May 10 16:06 download.cgi
-rwxrwxr-x   1 root    www        349 May 10 16:06 environ.cgi
-rwxrwxr-x   1 root    www      11914 May 10 16:06 upload.cgi
-rwxrwxr-x   1 root    www        820 May 10 16:06 gd_example.cgi
-rwxrwxr-x   1 root    www       4433 May 10 16:06 guestbook.cgi
-rwxrwxr-x   1 root    www        186 May 10 16:06 POReceipts
-rwxrwxr-x   1 root    www        274 May 10 16:06 printenv
-rwxrwxr-x   1 root    www       3854 May 10 16:06 table.cgi
-rwxrwxr-x   1 root    www         86 May 10 16:06 temp.cgi
-rwxrwxr-x   1 root    www        324 May 10 16:06 test1.cgi
-rwxrwxr-x   1 root    www        757 May 10 16:06 test-cgi
```

Defining Request URLs

The `ScriptAliasMatch` directive works just like `ScriptAlias` but uses a regular-expression match instead of a relative URL to match the request. In the following example, `ScriptAliasMatch` is used to produce the same behavior as the `ScriptAlias` example shown earlier:

```
ScriptAliasMatch ^/cgi-bin(.*) /usr/local/apache2/cgi-bin$1
```

Here, any request URL that begins with /cgi-bin (followed by any other characters) will be mapped to the filesystem using the fixed path /usr/local/apache2/cgi-bin with the content of the first back-reference to the regular expression match appended. The back-reference $1 is filled with the contents of that part of the request URL that matched the portion of the regular expression contained in parentheses. In this case, it should always match a slash followed by a valid filename containing the CGI script.

In general, use `ScriptAliasMatch` only when you find it impossible to phrase your URL match as a plain string comparison. I have never found it necessary to use `ScriptAliasMatch`, and I consider regular expressions unduly complicated for this purpose.

Defining Files

Although the simplest and most commonly used means of identifying files as CGI scripts is to place them into directories reserved for scripts, you can also identify individual files as CGI scripts. To do this, use the `AddHandler` directive, which maps an Apache handler to files that end with certain filename extensions. The following line, for example, defines the standard `cgi-script` handler to be used for processing all files ending with the extensions .pl or .cgi. Typically CGI scripts will be given the .cgi extension, but since CGI scripts can be written in more than one language, you may prefer to retain the .pl extension to more easily identify scripts written in Perl.

```
AddHandler cgi-script .cgi .pl
```

The AddHandler directive is valid only in a directory scope, either within a <Directory> container in http.conf or as part of an .htaccess file. It cannot be used as a global directive, and therefore can't be used to define all files with a certain extension as CGI scripts, regardless of where they occur.

Defining Methods

Although you are unlikely to ever need it, the Script directive, provided by the mod_actions module, invokes a CGI script whenever the requesting client uses a specified HTTP request method. The request method must be GET, POST, or DELETE.

The following Script directive calls a CGI script to handle all user DELETE requests:

```
Script DELETE /cgi-bin/deleteit.cgi
```

Defining Media Types

The mod_actions module provides one last method of defining CGI scripts. An alternative to writing a module to add a handler to Apache is to use the Action directive to define an external program (or script) as a resource handler. The Action directive provided by mod_actions invokes a CGI script whenever a resource of a particular MIME type is requested. You could use this, for example, to invoke a CGI script to process all HTML pages served. This might be a script written to search for and replace offensive words in every Web page before passing it on to particularly sensitive viewers:

```
Action text/html   /home/httpd/cgi-bin/ParseMe.cgi
```

This example defines a particular CGI script as the handler for all HTML files. When any HTML file is requested, the file will first be passed through the script ParseMe.cgi, which does a string search for dirty language and replaces it with more acceptable text.

Controlling the Environment

I've already mentioned that a CGI script receives data from Apache only through the system environment it inherits from the server when it is started. This section lists all the environment variables that are made available to a CGI script, although some of them will not always be set. In most cases, all the information the script needs is contained in this set of variables.

The following environment variables are not request-specific and are set for all requests:

SERVER_SOFTWARE   The name and version of the information server software answering the request (and running the gateway). Format: name/version.

SERVER_NAME   The server's hostname, DNS alias, or IP address, as it would appear in self-referencing URLs.

GATEWAY_INTERFACE   The revision of the CGI specification to which this server complies. Format: CGI/revision.

The following environment variables are specific to the request being fulfilled by the gateway program:

SERVER_PROTOCOL   The name and revision of the information protocol this request came in with. Format: *protocol/revision*, as in HTTP/1.1.

SERVER_PORT   The port number to which the request was sent.

REQUEST_METHOD   The method with which the request was made. For HTTP, this is GET, HEAD, POST, etc.

PATH_INFO   The extra path information, as given by the client. In other words, scripts can be accessed by their virtual pathname, followed by extra information at the end of this path. The extra information is sent as PATH_INFO. The server should decode this information if it comes from a URL before it is passed to the CGI script. Note that this environment variable will always be empty if the AcceptPathInfo directive is explicitly set to Off, something I do *not* recommend doing.

PATH_TRANSLATED   The server provides a translated version of PATH_INFO, which takes the path and does any virtual-to-physical mapping to it.

SCRIPT_NAME   A virtual path to the script being executed, used for self-referencing URLs.

QUERY_STRING   The information that follows the question mark in the URL that referenced this script. This query information should not be decoded in any fashion. This variable should always be set when there is query information, regardless of command-line decoding.

REMOTE_HOST   The hostname making the request. If the server does not have this information, it should set REMOTE_ADDR and leave this unset. Note that this environment variable will always be empty if HostnameLookups is set to Off.

REMOTE_ADDR   The IP address of the remote host making the request.

AUTH_TYPE   If the server supports user authentication, and the script is protected, this is the protocol-specific authentication method used to validate the user.

Advanced Configuration

PART 3

REMOTE_USER	Set only if the CGI script is subject to authentication. If the server supports user authentication, and the script is protected, this is the username they have used for authentication.
REMOTE_IDENT	If the HTTP server supports RFC 931 identification, then this variable will be set to the remote username retrieved from the server. Usage of this variable should be limited to logging only, and it should be set only if IdentityCheck is on.
CONTENT_TYPE	For queries with attached information, such as HTTP POST and PUT, this is the content type of the data.
CONTENT_LENGTH	The length of the content as given by the client.

The following variables are not defined by the CGI specification but are added by Apache for your convenience:

DOCUMENT_ROOT	The pathname specified in Apache's DocumentRoot directive.
PATH	Corresponds to the shell environment variable PATH that was set when Apache was started.
REMOTE_PORT	The TCP port used on the client-side of the HTTP connection.
SERVER_ADDR	The IP address on which the server received the connection.
SCRIPT_FILENAME	The absolute path to the CGI script.
SERVER_ADMIN	The e-mail address provided in Apache's ServerAdmin directive.

The following variables are not defined by the CGI specification but are added by the mod_rewrite module, if it is used:

SCRIPT_URI	The absolute URL, including the protocol, hostname, port, and request.
SCRIPT_URL	The URL path to the script that was called.
REQUEST_URI	The URL path received from the client that led to the script that was called.

In addition to the headers shown above, header lines from the client request are also placed into the environment. These are named with the prefix HTTP_ followed by the header name. Any - (hyphen) characters in the header name are changed to _ (underscore) characters. The server may choose to exclude any headers it has already processed and placed in the environment, such as Authorization or Content-type.

As a good example of how this works, consider the User-Agent request header. A CGI script will find the value of this header, extracted from the user request, in the environment variable HTTP_USER_AGENT.

Modifying the CGI Environment

Two modules, both compiled into the default configuration of the Apache server, provide a mechanism for the server to set variables in its environment that are inherited by CGI scripts. Setting environment variables is one way of passing arbitrary data to scripts. Later, I'll illustrate how an environment variable can be set to indicate to CGI scripts that the requester has been identified as a Web indexing robot. In practice, I've found this technique to be of limited use, mainly because most information available to the server about an incoming request is already available to the CGI script through existing environment variables. All HTTP headers in the request, for example, are passed to every CGI script.

You should read this section well enough to know what the directives do, and realize that they are easily available for your use through two standard Apache modules. When a real need arises that can be best fulfilled by one of these directives, you should have it in your toolkit.

The *mod_env* Module

The first of the modules that can be used to set environment variables to be passed to CGI scripts is mod_env, which contains three very simple directives: SetEnv, UnsetEnv, and PassEnv.

The *SetEnv* Directive

The SetEnv directive sets the value of an environment variable to be passed to CGI scripts, creating the variable if it doesn't already exist:

```
SetEnv PATH /usr/local/bin
```

This changes the value of the PATH variable passed to CGI scripts to include only a single path. All programs called by the CGI script must reside in this path (or be called by their full pathname) unless the author of the CGI script manually sets the value of PATH to some other value inside the script.

The *UnsetEnv* Directive

The UnsetEnv directive removes one or more environment variables from the environment before it is passed to CGI scripts:

```
UnsetEnv PATH
```

You might remove the PATH variable from the CGI environment to avoid the possibility of a malicious hacker planting a Trojan horse somewhere in the PATH where it would be executed instead of a legitimate program the script was trying to call. In general, however, the

PATH that is passed to CGI scripts (inherited from the Apache httpd process that called the script) should contain only protected directories that nonprivileged users cannot write to. Many site administrators prefer to remove the PATH and reference all external scripts or utility programs by their full pathname. This is certainly safe, but it is much better to protect the directories that are included in the PATH variable passed to CGI scripts.

The *PassEnv* Directive

The PassEnv directive specifies one or more environment variables from the server's environment to be passed to CGI scripts:

```
PassEnv USER
```

The PassEnv directive cannot be used to create a new Env variable; it can only designate a variable in the httpd process's environment that is to be included in the environment that CGI scripts inherit. In this case, we are passing the value of USER, which indicates the Linux user ID under which the Apache httpd process is running (by default, this is UID -1, corresponding to user nobody). You might wish to have a script abort with an error message if this value is not what the script expects.

The *mod_setenvif* Module

This module provides four additional directives that set environment variables based on the results of conditions that are specified in the directives themselves: SetEnvIf, SetEnvIfNoCase, BrowserMatch, and BrowserMatchNoCase. For efficiency and clarity, however, it is usually better to rely on the CGI script itself to perform these conditional tests on request header information and perform the necessary actions. Replace the BrowserMatch directive, for example, with lines in your CGI program that test the User-Agent header of the request to identify the browser used to send the request, and take action accordingly.

The *SetEnvIf* Directive

The SetEnvIf directive defines one or more environment variables based on an attribute that is associated only with the current request being processed. In most cases this attribute is one of the HTTP request headers (such as Remote_Addr, User_Agent, Referer). If not, the attribute is tested to see if it is the name of an environment variable set (by other SetEnv or SetEnvIf directives) earlier in the processing cycle for the current request (or in a wider scope, such as the server scope).

The syntax of the SetEnvIf directive is

```
SetEnvIf attribute regex envvar[=value] [...]
```

If the attribute matches *regex*, then *envvar* is set to a value defined in *=value* (if it exists) or set to 1 otherwise. If the attribute does not match *regex*, no action is performed.

The *SetEnvIfNoCase* Directive

The `SetEnvIfNoCase` directive performs its regular expression match without regard to the case of the characters but is otherwise identical to the `SetEnvIf` directive.

The *BrowserMatch* Directive

The `BrowserMatch` directive defines environment variables based solely on the `User-Agent` HTTP request header field. The first argument is a regular expression that is matched against this field. If there is a match, the rest of the arguments set environment variables and (optionally) define values to assign to them.

In this directive, the variable names can be defined in three ways:

> *varname*   Sets *varname* to 1.
>
> `!`*varname*   Unsets or removes the variable if it exists.
>
> *varname*`=`*value*   Sets the variable to the specified *value*.

If a `User-Agent` string matches more than one entry, they will be merged. Entries are processed in the order in which they appear, and later entries can override earlier ones. Example:

```
BrowserMatch ^Robot IS_ROBOT
```

CGI scripts can be written so that the presence of the environment variable IS_ROBOT, indicating that the script's output will go to a Web-indexing robot, can be tailored for indexing engines. Web-indexing robots generally ignore and don't download embedded graphics or banner ads; therefore, the page returned to robots should be text-rich and packed with key words and phrases for the indexing engine.

> **NOTE**   Keep in mind that the `BrowserMatch` and `BrowserMatchNoCase` directives are special cases of the `SetEnvIf` and `SetEnvIfNoCase` directives, and they offer no additional functionality.

The *BrowserMatchNoCase* Directive

The `BrowserMatchNoCase` directive performs its regular-expression match regardless of the case of the characters, but is otherwise identical to the `BrowserMatch` directive.

Securing Your CGI Scripts

CGI is often criticized as an insecure way to run programs on a Web server. Though security holes have been discovered in a number of commonly used CGI scripts, these are not the result of inherent security weaknesses in CGI. Problems in these ready-made

Advanced Configuration

PART 3

scripts that can be downloaded from the Internet are usually the result of inattention to the potential for misuse, and most have been modified to improve their security. When using scripts that you didn't write, make sure you have the latest available version and that the author has tried to address security concerns with CGI.

CGI has been used for dynamic Web programming for a very long time (since 1993), and for that reason, most of the vulnerabilities inherent in the use of CGI have been widely publicized. These problems are not show-stoppers, as long as you pay proper attention to detail, particularly when preparing user input to be passed to another program via the shell—for example, passing the user's address to a mail agent like sendmail. The next sections of this chapter describe how to write a safe CGI script. Remember that Unix was once criticized as inherently more insecure than Microsoft Windows NT/2000, largely because the Unix vulnerabilities had received so much exposure. Now that NT/2000 is more widely used in a server role, it is also suffering (perhaps unfairly) from the perception that its network security model is weak. When it comes to security, neither Linux nor NT/2000 has an indisputable advantage over the other; both platforms contain vulnerabilities that can be exploited by a malicious attacker. I believe that the Linux community is more open about security risks, though, and it acts more quickly to solve those that are discovered.

A properly written CGI script is no more insecure than any other Web program. A few simple guidelines can be very helpful in writing secure CGI scripts.

General Tips for Safe CGI Use

There are some general rules for safe CGI use. These rules do not absolutely guarantee secure CGI scripts, but adherence to them will protect you from the most serious, and most exploited, security vulnerabilities in CGI.

Never run your Apache server as root. The main Apache daemon, which does *not* respond to client connections, should be owned by root, but the child httpd processes it creates should be owned by a user account with limited privileges. This is covered in detail in Chapter 13.

Avoid passing user input of any kind to the shell for processing. Perl scripts pass data to the shell for processing in several ways. Perl spawns a new shell process to execute commands, which are enclosed in back-tick characters (` `` `) or included as arguments to system() or exec() function calls. This should be avoided. The following examples illustrate how user data might end up being interpreted by a shell process:

```
system("/usr/lib/sendmail -t $foo_address < $input_file");
```
or
```
$result=`/usr/lib/sendmail -t $foo_address < $input_file`;
```

In both of these lines, the shell is passed user input as an argument to the send-mail process. In both examples, the shell that processes the line can be tricked into executing part of $input_file as a separate process. If a malicious person were able to trick your system into running a line like this:

```
rm *
```

you could be in trouble. That is the main reason why the Apache processes that respond to user requests should never run as root. The code below shows a better way to pass data to a process. Note that, while the shell is used to run sendmail, the user input is passed to the sendmail process through a pipe, and the shell never sees the contents of the variable $stuff:

```
open(MAIL, "|/usr/lib/sendmail -t");
print MAIL "To: $recipient\n";
print MAIL $stuff;
```

In all CGI scripts, explicitly set the value of the PATH environment variables, rather than simply accepting the value inherited from the Apache process. I recommend setting this value to a single directory in which you place scripts or other executable programs you trust. I've already shown one way to do this using the SetEnv and UnsetEnv directives. You can also do the same thing from within CGI scripts if, for example, you don't have access privileges that allow you to modify the httpd.conf to modify the environment for all CGI scripts. The following line, when included in a Perl CGI script, clears all environment variables and resets the value of PATH to a "safe" directory:

```
delete @ENV{qw(IFS CDPATH ENV BASH_ENV)};
$ENV{"PATH"} = "/usr/local/websafe";
```

Alternatively, set PATH to a null value and call all external programs from your CGI script using their full pathname. Basically, before doing a system call, clear the PATH by issuing a statement like the following:

```
$ENV{"PATH"} = "";
```

Always enable Perl warnings and use the strict pragma. Warnings can be activated by placing the -w argument to Perl on the "shebang" line (the first line of a Perl script), as in #!/usr/bin/perl -w. The strict pragma is activated by placing a use strict; line near the beginning of your script. The use of strict is particularly advisable if you are using mod_perl, which is far more particular about proper variable scoping. Though not absolutely required, the use of strict will help you avoid many hard-to-debug "gotchas" in mod_perl, with the added benefit of making you a better Perl programmer.

Advanced Configuration

PART 3

If you are using the CGI support modules, always use the latest version. For example, for Perl, be sure to download current versions of either cgi-lib.pl or CGI.pm.

Always use Perl taint checking. The following section covers taint checking in detail.

Using Perl Taint Checking

Perl has an optional mode of operation called *taint checking*. It is designed to help prevent security problems with scripts that are run with special privileges on behalf of unknown or unprivileged users. This is exactly what happens when you use CGI; you are allowing outside users to run programs on your Web server with the privilege level assigned to the Web server.

In Perl 5, you can enable taint checking by invoking Perl with the -T command-line argument. In a CGI script, the first line of the script should look like this (the -w argument enables the output of warning messages):

```
#!/usr/bin/perl -T -w
```

> **NOTE**   If you are using mod_perl, as described later in this chapter, you can't use the -T command line switch in Perl. Instead, you need to use the PerlSwitch directive in httpd.conf to enable taint checking.

Taint checking derives its name from the fact that Perl considers any data that your script receives from an outside source, such as unmodified or unexamined user input from a Web form, to be *tainted*. Perl will not allow tainted variables to be used in any command that requires your script to fork a subshell or in the name of any file that your script attempts to access. Therefore, if taint checking is enabled and you attempt to fork a shell and pass it data that Perl regards as tainted, Perl aborts your script, reporting an error similar to the following:

```
Insecure dependency in `` while running with -T switch at temp.pl
➡  line 4, <stdin> chunk 1.
```

A Web programmer often needs to use external programs, passing data that was received as input from an unknown user. One of the most common examples of this is using a mail transport agent (on Linux, this is most likely the ubiquitous sendmail utility) to e-mail data using input received from a client. The following line is the most commonly cited example of an absolute CGI scripting no-no:

```
system("/usr/sbin/sendmail -t $useraddr < $file_requested");
```

This takes a user-entered address and filename and mails the requested file to the user. What's wrong with this? By inserting a ; character into the $file_requested command, you can easily trick the shell into believing it is being passed one command, separated from a second distinct command by this special shell *metacharacter*. The shell will often be quite happy to run the second command, which might try to do something nasty on behalf of your attacker.

If Perl is so careful not to use tainted input from the client, how is it possible to pass any input safely? There are basically two ways.

The first way is to avoid passing data directly to the shell. This works because most hackers are trying to exploit the shell itself and trick it into running unauthorized commands on their behalf. You can avoid the use of the shell by opening a system *pipe* to the program intended to accept the input. Replace the `system` command above with the following lines:

```
open(PIPE, "| /usr/sbin/sendmail -t");
print PIPE "To: $useraddr\n";
open (INFILE, "$file_requested");
while (<INFILE>) {
    print PIPE $_;
}
```

In this example, the shell never sees the user's input, which is piped directly to the `sendmail` executable. This means that attempts to exploit the shell are thwarted.

The second way is to "untaint" the data. To do this, use a regular expression pattern match to extract data from the tainted variable using ( ) groups and back-references to create new variables. Perl will always consider new variables created from data extracted from a tainted variable in this manner to be untainted. Of course, Perl has no way of knowing whether the new variables have been examined carefully to ensure that they present no security risk when passed to the shell, but it gives the programmer the benefit of the doubt. Perl assumes that any programmer who has applied a regular expression match to tainted variables has also taken enough care to remove dangerous metacharacters from the variable. It is the programmer's responsibility to make sure this assumption is a correct one.

For the e-mail example above, you could untaint the `$file_requested` variable using the following section of Perl code:

```
if ($file_requested =~ /(\w{1}[\w-\.]*)\@([\w-\.]+)/) {
    $file_requested = "$1\@$2";
} else {
    warn ("DATA SENT BY $ENV{'REMOTE_ADDR'}IS NOT A VALID E-MAIL
        ADDRESS:       $file-requested: $!");
    $file_requested = ""; # successful match did not occur
}
```

In this example, the variable is matched to ensure that it conforms to the proper format for an e-mail address. The regular expression in the first line takes a little work to interpret. First, remember the regular expression rules that { } braces enclose a number specifying how many times the previous character must be repeated to make a match, that [ ] brackets enclose sets of alternative characters to be matched, and that \w refers to a word character (defined as characters in the set [a-zA-Z0-9]). The first line can thus be read as "if the content of $file_requested matches any string containing at least one word character, followed by any number of word characters, dashes, or periods, followed by the literal character @ followed by at least one pattern consisting of word characters, dashes, or periods, then perform the following block." The parentheses are used to enclose sections of the regular expression that are later substituted into $n backreferences, where n corresponds to the number of the parenthetical match. In the next line, the first set of parentheses (which matches that portion of the variable to the left of the @ character) is later substituted into $1; the second set of parentheses (matching the portion of the variable to the right of the @ character) is substituted for $2. The result then replaces the old value of $file_requested, which, having been processed by a regular expression, is now marked as untainted for future use by Perl.

The else clause of the if statement handles those situations where the regular expression fails to match $file_requested, which means that the variable does *not* have the expected format of an e-mail message. In this case, the script will print a warning, which will be written to Apache's error log, along with the IP address of the remote host that submitted the tainted data and a copy of that data. This information might be helpful in locating a hacker trying to exploit a CGI weakness on the server. Immediately after logging the failure to match, the Perl script empties the $file_requested variable, essentially discarding the user's input.

Avoid the temptation to untaint your Perl variables without doing any real checking. This would have been easy to do in the previous example with two lines of code:

```
$file_requested =~ /(.*)/;
$file_requested = $1;
```

This fragment matches anything the user enters and simply overwrites the variable with its existing contents, but Perl assumes that a check for malicious input has been performed and untaints the variable. Absolutely nothing has actually been done, however. The programmer who does this should probably just turn off taint checking rather than resort to this kind of deception. It is likely to lull other programmers into a false assumption that since the script is taint-checked, it must be safe.

Debugging CGI Scripts

The mod_cgi module provides a special logging capability designed specifically to aid the debugging of CGI scripts. Rather than intermingling your CGI errors with Apache's error log, you can choose to capture the output and error messages generated by CGI scripts in a special file.

The ScriptLog directive identifies a file for logging CGI output. This directive serves the purpose of enabling CGI script logging and specifying a file (either by absolute path or a path relative to ServerRoot) for the log. Here's the directive for an absolute path:

```
ScriptLog /var/log/cgilog
```

And here's what it looks like for a path relative to ServerRoot:

```
ScriptLog logs/cgilog
```

The Apache httpd process owner should have write access to the log you specify. Note that the ScriptLog is valid only in a server context; in other words, you cannot place the directive within a container directive. In particular, you cannot specify different log files for different virtual hosts.

NOTE   Script logging is a debugging feature to be used when writing CGI scripts and is not meant to be activated on production servers. It is not optimized for speed or efficiency.

Since the output of *all* CGI scripts will be logged (not just error messages), your logfile will tend to grow rapidly. The ScriptLogLength directive is useful for limiting the size of the logfile. The maximum byte size set with this directive limits the size to which the log file will grow (the default value of ScriptLogLength is 1MB). The following line would set the maximum log file size to half a megabyte:

```
ScriptLogLength 524288
```

Remember that when the value of ScriptLogLength is reached, no further logging occurs; logging is simply disabled.

One other directive is used to control CGI logging. ScriptLogBuffer can be used to limit the size of entries written to the CGI log. This can be especially useful in limiting the growth of the log when the entire contents of PUT or POST requests (in which the client browser sends data to the server) are being logged. Since the contents of these two HTTP request methods are unlimited, they can quickly fill a log file. The default value of this directive is 1KB (1024 bytes). The following line will limit entries written to the CGI log to one-fourth that size:

```
ScriptLogBuffer 256
```

Using *CGI.pm*

Lincoln Stein's CGI.pm is a very large Perl module that uses Perl 5 objects to perform simple Web-related tasks, such as the HTML tagging required by many HTML elements (headers, forms, tables, etc.). The module also manages the CGI interface to the Web server by providing a mechanism for capturing user input into a Perl *hash*, or two-dimensional array. This hash contains environment variables and their values as easy-to-access data pairs. For example, in Perl, you can access (or *dereference*) the value of the environment variable QUERY_STRING using $ENV{QUERY_STRING}.

The module also provides some of the more advanced features of CGI scripting, including support for file uploads, cookies, cascading style sheets, server PUSH, and frames. The CGI.pm Perl module is designed to be used with standard CGI or Apache mod_perl (discussed in a later section) and simplifies the use of these Web-programming techniques, but does not replace either. The module is far too extensive to cover in detail here, but my CGI examples throughout this chapter make use of it and illustrate some of the basic CGI.pm methods (or functions, for those not yet thinking in object terms). Speaking of object-orientation, though, CGI.pm makes internal methods (or functions) accessible either as Perl 5 objects or as traditional functions. With CGI.pm, you can choose to use either form, or both, if you wish. CGI.pm even emulates the ReadParse function from cgi-lib.pl (a Perl/CGI library that many Web programmers cut their teeth on). This means "legacy" Perl/CGI scripts don't have to be rewritten to use CGI.pm.

You can obtain CGI.pm from the Comprehensive Perl Archive Network (or CPAN) search site at http://search.cpan.org/.

A Script to Return the Environment

In Linux, every process is started by the operating system kernel and inherits an address space referred to as the *process environment*. Prior to starting every process, Linux tailors this environment by creating variables that the process will inherit and setting the values of these variables to contain information that the process can later read. It is through the environment that information is traditionally passed to CGI scripts. When Apache starts a CGI process, it sets a number of environment variables that the CGI process can read to determine things like the request headers that were sent to Apache by the client and the request URL (which, in the case of a GET request, can contain data from a form).

Listing 8.1 depicts a Perl script that returns a neatly formatted listing of all environment variables set for the CGI script prior to its execution.

Listing 8.1   The Environ.cgi Script

```
#!/usr/bin/perl
#Environ.cgi - Show environment variables set by the server
#
print "Content-type: text/html\n\n";
print "<HTML><HEAD><TITLE>Environment Variables</TITLE></HEAD><BODY>";
```

```
print "<H2>Environment Variables:</H2>";
print "<HR>\n";
foreach $evar( keys (%ENV)){
        print "<B>$evar:</B> $ENV{$evar}<BR>";
}
print "</BODY></HTML>\n";
```

The first line of the script designates Perl as the script interpreter; in other words, this is a Perl script (the .cgi extension says nothing about the contents of the file, but it ensures that Apache spawns the file using CGI). The output of the script (the print statements) is redirected to the requester's browser in the form of an HTTP response. Note that the first response is the Content-type HTML header, which causes the browser to render the rest of the output as HTML-formatted text. This header is followed by two consecutive new-line characters (\n\n), which is an HTTP convention used to separate HTTP headers from the HTTP content or payload. Figure 8.1 shows the page as rendered by a Web browser.

If you know a little Perl, you'll realize that the script accesses a hash (or indexed two-dimensional array) named %ENV, iterating through the hash, displaying each hash entry key and value. The %ENV hash contains the environment inherited by all Perl scripts; access to the environment, therefore, requires no special function in Perl—it is provided without charge by the Perl interpreter.

Figure 8.1   Environ.cgi in a browser

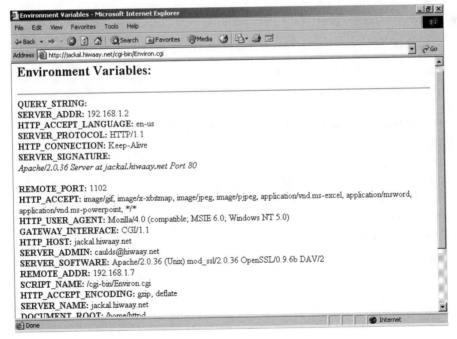

This script is extremely handy to have in your CGI directory. Take a moment now to install it and execute it from a Web browser. This will allow you to use it to view the environment provided through CGI, and that environment will change as you add certain modules or use different request methods. I can access this file on my server using

```
http://jackal.hiwaay.net/cgi-bin/Environ.cgi
```

As an experiment, you can pass a variable to any CGI script using a request URL such as:

```
http://jackal.hiwaay.net/cgi-bin/Environ.cgi?somevar=somevalue
```

When you try that on your server, you should see the additional data you passed in the environment variable QUERY_STRING: somevalue=somevar. That's how information is passed to CGI scripts when the GET request method is used. More often, however, data is sent to the Web server with the POST request method. When POST is used, Apache uses the script's standard input handle (*stdin*) to send the data to the script in a data stream. A CGI script that handles POST requests is a bit more difficult to write, but utilities like the Perl CGI.pm (discussed earlier) module make this much easier. Remember, CGI.pm is *not* required for using Perl with CGI and Apache; it is a convenience, but one well worth taking the time to learn.

A less often used method to pass data to a script is to include the data as part of the pathname to the script, separating it from the script name with a path, as though the data were actually part of the pathname. As an example, enter this URL:

```
http://jackal.hiwaay.net/cgi-bin/Environ.cgi/extra/path/info
```

This time, you should see the extra information reflected in a variable PATH_INFO, rather than in the QUERY_STRING.

A Simple Database Query Example

To demonstrate the use of the various Web-programming techniques described in this chapter, I created a simple relational database. It consists of a single table that contains slightly more than 47,000 five-digit U.S. postal delivery codes (the so-called zip codes) with the associated U.S. city and state for each. I chose this data because it is public domain information, and I was able to download the 47,000-line file in comma-separated value format.

Although any database that supports SQL queries could be used, I chose the very powerful, yet completely free, MySQL relational database management program.

MySQL, a Simple Relational Database for Linux

Many of the Web-programming examples in this book make a simple query of a relational database management system using SQL. With slight modification, these examples will work with virtually any RDBMS you can run on Linux.

I chose to use an open-source, freely obtainable database system called MySQL. You can download the very latest development releases or the latest stable production release, as well as binary distributions, or contributed RPMs, from `http://mysql.com/`. I have downloaded the source code for MySQL and found it easy to compile and install, but since I wanted only a running SQL engine and had no interest in customizing the code, I have since taken to installing MySQL from RPMs. You can get these from the `mysql.com` site, but I prefer to use the old standby, `RPMFind.net`.

MySQL's version numbers change pretty rapidly; the version I installed may be behind the current release by the time you read this. It's a database server, and performs a pretty mundane role when you get right down to it. I don't worry too much about having the latest version; I'm happy as long as I've got a stable SQL engine that is always available.

You'll need to get several pieces for a whole system. I installed the 3.23.49 version from three RPMs, straight from Red Hat 7.3 Installation Disk 3 (you'll find the RPMs located in the RedHat/RPMS directory):

`mysql-3.23.49-3.i386.rpm` The standard MySQL clients and shared libraries used by client tools. You'll need the utilities in this RPM to perform chores like creating databases and setting up security from the Linux command line. Also, you will need files in this RPM to load the others, so always load it first.

`mysql-server-3.23.49-3.i386.rpm` This RPM contains the MySQL database engine and server components as well as a few other administration utilities and supporting files.

`mysql-devel-3.23.49-3.i386.rpm` The development header files and libraries necessary to develop MySQL client applications. Though not strictly necessary, if you ever attempt to compile another application to use MySQL (like a Perl DBD driver), the linker will need these header files and libraries. Always install this RPM just to be sure (it's quite small).

Installation of MySQL is as simple as applying each of these RPMs in the following order, so that each command completes with no errors or warnings:

```
# rpm -i mysql-3.23.49-3.i386.rpm
# rpm -i mysql-server-3.23.49-3.i386.rpm
# rpm -i mysql-devel-3.23.49-3.i386.rpm
```

Advanced Configuration

PART 3

MySQL, a Simple Relational Database for Linux (*continued*)

I took one more step, however, to make the excellent documentation easily available from my server through a Web browser. Adding the following line to my `httpd.conf` allows me to read the MySQL docs using the URL `http://jackal.hiwaay.net/MySQL`:

```
Alias /MySQL "/usr/share/doc/mysql-3.23.49/ manual_toc.html"
```

The documentation provided with MySQL is the same superlative documentation available online at `mysql.com/documentation`. The local documentation is quicker to read and better formatted for printing, but the online documentation is indexed for searching. I use them both.

The first thing you should do immediately after installing MySQL is to create a password for the root user because, by default, this password is left blank. The following command invokes `mysqladmin` as user `root` and creates the new password "yourpasswd" for the root user. Make sure you remember the password you set; you'll need it!

```
mysqladmin -u root password yourpasswd
```

In MySQL, the `mysqladmin` program is used to create new databases.

```
# mysqladmin -p create zipcodes
Enter password:
Database "zipcodes" created.
```

The -p argument in the command line above (and in subsequent examples) causes MySQL to prompt for the user's password. In this case, the MySQL user's identity is that of the invoking user (and I was logged in as root when I invoked these commands). MySQL is started and the database is opened like this (in "safe" versions of MySQL, like the one packaged with Red Hat Linux, the `--local-infile=1` switch is necessary to enable reading from the local system):

```
# mysql -p zipcodes --local-infile=1
Enter password:
Reading table information for completion of table and column names
You can turn off this feature to get a quicker startup with -A

Welcome to the MySQL monitor.  Commands end with ; or \g.
Your MySQL connection id is 7 to server version: 3.23.49
```

```
Type 'help;' or '\h' for help. Type '\c' to clear the buffer.

mysql>
```

I created a single table in the database. Named `zips`, it consists of three fields: a 25-character string for the city name, a two-character string for the state abbreviation, and a five-character string for the postal zip code, which is the primary index into the table and, therefore, cannot be empty (NOT NULL).

```
mysql> create table zips (city char(25), state char(2),
    -> zip char(5) NOT NULL, primary key (zip) );

Query OK, 0 rows affected (0.00 sec)
```

The 46,796 rows of the database were retrieved from a text file using the following MySQL command line:

```
mysql> LOAD DATA LOCAL INFILE "zips.txt" INTO TABLE ZIPS
    FIELDS TERMINATED BY ',' ENCLOSED BY '"';
Query OK, 46796 rows affected (2.15 sec)
Records: 46796  Deleted: 0  Skipped: 0  Warnings: 0
```

This specifies the field delimiter as a comma and tells MySQL that the string fields in the original file are enclosed in quotes. Even on my ancient Pentium 200 MMX test server, this database was loaded (and indexed) in less than three seconds (quite impressive).

For each Web-programming language and technique in this chapter, I'll present an example that accepts a five-digit zip code entered by a user in a Web form, looks up the associated city and state from the database, and returns the result to the user. This will demonstrate not only how to program an application to accept data from a Web client, but also how to interface the application to a common database system, make a query of a database, and return the results to the requester. Although it is quite simple, the application demonstrates the basics of Web programming, particularly for database access, one of the most common tasks that must be performed by Web servers on behalf of the end user.

The input form will be the same for each Web-programming example that accesses the Zip Codes MySQL database, a very simple HTML form that takes a single input, the U.S. Postal Service Code to be looked up in a database. The Web form used to get user input is shown in Figure 8.2.

Figure 8.2 The Zip Codes database query form

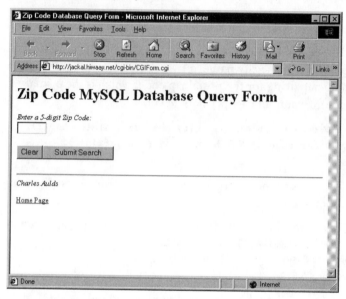

The HTML for the form is also quite simple, as you can see in Listing 8.2.

Listing 8.2 HTML Code to Produce the Zip Codes Query Form

```
<!DOCTYPE HTML PUBLIC "-//IETF//DTD HTML//EN">
<HTML><HEAD><TITLE>Zip Code Database Query Form</TITLE>
</HEAD><BODY><H1>Zip Code MySQL Database Query Form</H1>
<FORM METHOD="POST" ACTION="http://Jackal.hiwaay.net/
  cgi-bin/zipcodes.cgi" ENCTYPE="application/x-www-form-urlencoded">
<EM>Enter a 5-digit Zip Code:</EM><BR>
<INPUT TYPE="text"
NAME="zip"  SIZE=6>
<P><INPUT TYPE="reset" VALUE="Clear">
<INPUT TYPE="submit" NAME=".submit" VALUE="Submit Search">
</FORM><HR>
<HR>
<ADDRESS>Charles Aulds</ADDRESS><BR>
<A HREF="/">Home Page</A>
</BODY></HTML>
```

I didn't actually write the HTML you see above; I used CGI.pm module to do much of the work for me. Along with the features noted earlier, this module provides the ability to create most of the features of an HTML document. CGI.pm can do this using either "traditional" or object-oriented programming mechanisms. The first method uses standard Perl function calls. For those programmers who aren't completely comfortable with programming through objects, this may seem the simplest and most intuitive way to use CGI.pm. The function-oriented CGI script in Listing 8.3 generated the HTML for the simple input form shown in Listing 8.2.

Listing 8.3   Using CGI.pm to Generate the HTML for a Web Form

```perl
#!/usr/bin/perl -Tw
use CGI;

use CGI qw/:standard/;

print header;
print start_html("Zip Code Database Query Form");
print "<H1>Zip Code MySQL Database Query Form</H1>\n";
&print_prompt($query);
&print_tail;
print end_html;
sub print_prompt {
my($query) = @_;
print startform(-method=>"POST",-action=>
➥"http://Jackal.hiwaay.net/cgi-bin/zipcodes.cgi ");
print "<EM>Enter a 5-digit Zip Code:</EM><BR>";
print textfield(-name=>'zip', -size=>6);
print "<P>",reset('Clear');
print submit(-value=>'Submit Search');
print endform;
print "<HR>\n";
}
sub print_tail {
print <<END;
<ADDRESS>Charles Aulds</ADDRESS><BR>
<A HREF="/">Home Page</A>
END
}
```

To use CGI.pm in object-oriented style, you create a CGI object and then make use of methods and properties that it exposes. This is the form I recommend, for two reasons: First, it is the modern programming paradigm; second, nearly all good examples you'll find for using CGI.pm, including those in the CGI.pm documentation, use this style. Listing 8.4 is the same script, but written to use the CGI object methods rather than functions.

Listing 8.4   Using CGI.pm in Object-Oriented Fashion

```perl
#!/usr/bin/perl -Tw
use CGI;

$query = new CGI;

print $query->header;
print $query->start_html("Zip Code Database Query Form");
print "<H1>Zip Code MySQL Database Query Form</H1>\n";
&print_prompt($query);
&print_tail;
print $query->end_html;
sub print_prompt {
my($query) = @_;
print $query->startform(-method=>"POST",-action=>
➥"http://Jackal.hiwaay.net/cgi-bin/zipcodes.cgi ");
print "<EM>Enter a 5-digit Zip Code:</EM><BR>";
print $query->textfield(-name=>'zip', -size=>6);
print "<P>",$query->reset('Clear');
print $query->submit(-value=>'Submit Search');
print $query->endform;
print "<HR>\n";
}
sub print_tail {
print <<END;
<ADDRESS>Charles Aulds</ADDRESS><BR>
<A HREF="/">Home Page</A>
END
}
```

Notice several things about both examples above. First, the CGI scripts are designed only to return an HTML page to the client browser; they contain no code for data manipulation, either I/O or computation. It might seem far easier to write the HTML and save it on the server as filename.html. In this case, it probably is, but when you are required to generate your HTML dynamically or on-the-fly, CGI.pm will repay the effort you take to learn the module. Use perldoc CGI to generate the excellent documentation for the module, full of good examples.

Also note that many functions (or methods) have defaults. In the case of the header function (or method) above, I used the default, which sends the following HTML header to the client:

```
Content-Type: text/html
```

You can override the default to specify your own content type using either of these forms, which are equivalent:

```
print header('mimetype/subtype')
```

or

```
print $query->header('mimetype/subtype');
```

The third point to note is how easily an HTML form can be created with CGI.pm. With CGI.pm, it isn't necessary to know the HTML tags used by the browser to render the HTML page. Comparing the CGI scripts above with the generated HTML, you can easily see how the script generated the form. CGI.pm is best learned in exactly that fashion, comparing a script with its output. Later in this chapter, I'll demonstrate how CGI.pm is used to receive user-generated input.

Finally, note that, even if you are using CGI.pm, you can use print statements to output anything else from your script. For some of the simpler lines, I did just that, using print to output tagged HTML.

Listing 8.5 shows the actual CGI script that performs the database lookup, taking one parameter, a postal (zip) code entered by the user in the Web form. This script also loads CGI.pm, which makes it very easy to receive user form input. CGI.pm provides a Perl function (or method) called param. This function can be called with the name of a field in a Web form to retrieve the value entered by the user in that field. In this example, the value entered by the user in the zip field is obtained by calling param('zip').

Listing 8.5   The zipcodes.cgi Script for a Database Query

```
#!/usr/bin/perl -w
# queries a MySQL table for a value and returns it in
# an HTML-formatted document
#
use strict;
use DBI;
use CGI qw(:standard);
#
# Create a new CGI object
my $output=new CGI;
#
# What did the user enter in the query form?
my $zipentered=param('zip') if (param('zip') );
my($server, $sock, $db);
#
# Connect to mysql database and return a database handle ($dbh)
```

```perl
my $dbh=DBI->connect("DBI:mysql:zipcodes:jackal.hiwaay.net","root","mypass");
#
# Prepare a SQL query; return a statement handle ($sth)
my $sth=$dbh->prepare("Select * from zips where zip=$zipentered");
#
# Execute prepared statement to return
$sth->execute;
my @row;
print $output->header;
print $output->start_html("Zip Code");
print h1("ZipCODE");
#
# Return rows into a Perl array
while (@row=$sth->fetchrow_array() ) {
print "The US Postal Service Zip Code <font size=+1>
➥ <b>$row[2]</b></font> is for: <font size=+2>
➥ <b>$row[0], $row[1]</b></font>\n";
}
print "<p>\n";
print "<h3>GATEWAY_INTERFACE=$ENV{GATEWAY_INTERFACE}</h3>";
print $output->end_html;
#
# Call the disconnect() method on the database handle
# to close the connection to the MySQL database
$dbh->disconnect;
```

The database query is performed using the DBI.pm module (see the accompanying discussion). Although DBI has a number of functions, the most basic use of the module is to create a connection, compose and send a query, and close the connection. The comments in Listing 8.5 serve to explain what each line is doing. Using this example, you should be able to quickly write your own CGI script to connect to and query a relational database on your own server. You may not choose to use MySQL as I did, but by changing one line of this script (the line that calls the DBI->connect method), you can make this same script work with nearly all major relational database servers.

DBI.pm

Certainly one of the most useful of all Perl modules is the DBI module (DBI.pm). DBI stands for Database Independent, and the DBI module provides a standard set of programming functions for querying a wide variety of databases. While a full discussion of the DBI module is beyond the scope of this chapter, I have used DBI to illustrate database querying from standard CGI scripts.

DBI.pm (*continued*)

You install the DBI module once. Then you install a Database Dependent (or DBD) module for each database that you intend to access. As with most Perl modules, the latest versions of the DBD modules are available from the Comprehensive Perl Archive Network (search.cpan.net). Better yet, using the CPAN.pm module, download and install them in one easy step. To install the latest DBI.pm module and the MySQL DBD module, I entered two commands after loading CPAN.pm (as described in Chapter 1):

```
# cpan
cpan> install DBI
cpan>install DBD::mysql
```

One very interesting module that I use quite frequently is DBD::CSV, which allows you to create a flat text file consisting of rows of comma-separated values and work with it as you would a true relational database. Each line of the file is a separate data record or row, and the values on the line, separated by commas, are separate data fields. Using DBD::CSV allows you to develop database applications without having access to a true relational database. When you have things the way you want them, you simply modify your application to use a true database-dependent driver (by loading a new DBD module).

FastCGI

CGI was the first general-purpose standard mechanism for Web programming, and for a long time it remained the most used application programmer's interface to the Web server. But it has always been hampered by a performance bottleneck: Every time a CGI application is called, the Web server spawns a new subsystem or subshell to run the process. The request loads imposed on many modern servers are so large that faster mechanisms have been developed and now largely overshadow CGI. Among the first of these was FastCGI, a standard, which allows a slightly modified CGI script to load once and remain memory-resident to respond to subsequent requests.

NOTE   At the time of writing, FastCGI for Apache 2.0 was still in development. Consequently, the discussion in this section is based on Apache 1.3, and may vary somewhat from the final release for Apache 2.0. In general, because FastCGI works outside the Apache Web server, it should work almost identically under Apache 2.0.

FastCGI consists of two components. The first is an Apache module, mod_fastcgi.so, that modifies or extends the Web server so that it can properly identify and execute programs designed to run under FastCGI. The second component is a set of functions that are linked to your FastCGI programs. For compiled languages, these are provided as a shared library; for Perl, these functions are added using the FCGI.pm Perl module.

To make the functions exported from these libraries available to your program, you include a C header file or, in scripting languages like Tcl or Perl, place a line at the beginning of the script to include the code necessary to enable FastCGI support in the script. FastCGI libraries are available for C, Perl, Java, Tcl, and Python. In this section I'll demonstrate how to make the necessary modifications to the Apache server and how to modify the CGIForm.cgi Perl script to allow it to run as a FastCGI script.

How FastCGI Works

FastCGI is based on a very simple concept. Whenever a FastCGI program is loaded into memory, it remains there until it is purged as part of the cleanup process when the Web server shuts down. In other words, programs identified as FastCGI scripts are run in *persistent processes*. The overhead associated with initializing a new system process and loading the CGI script into the process's memory space becomes negligible, as these tasks are performed only once, the first time the program is requested by a client. In order for this to work, it is necessary to edit standard CGI programs to include an infinite loop. A FastCGI program actually sits idle most of the time, waiting for a signal from the mod_fastcgi module to wake up and process a request. When it receives this signal, the script processes a new iteration of the loop, which handles all of the normal functions of a CGI script. That is, it reads new information from the environment or standard input handle, processes it, and writes some kind of output to its standard output handle. Note that, with FastCGI, the process's environment may change many times during the lifetime of the process, once for each new request to be processed. This is part of the magic of FastCGI.

Installing and Compiling *mod_fastcgi*

To get started, download the latest version of mod_fastcgi from www.fastcgi.com. The module is a cinch to compile and use as a DSO.

1. Download the latest version of the module (2.2.4 when I wrote this) and then extract it into your /usr/local/src directory with this command:

   ```
   # tar xvfz /home/caulds/mod_fastcgi_2_2_4_tar.gz
   ```

2. Moving to the new source directory created, you can use a single command line to invoke the apxs utility to compile and install the module:

   ```
   # cd mod_fastcgi_2.2.4
   # /usr/local/apache/bin/apxs -i -a -o mod_fastcgi.so -c *.c
   ```

3. Then verify that the following lines have been added to `httpd.conf`:

```
LoadModule fastcgi_module     libexec/mod_fastcgi.so
AddModule mod_fastcgi.c
```

4. The last step is to restart the server, and you're in business.

Modifying CGI Scripts to Use FastCGI

FastCGI was designed to make conversions of existing CGI files as simple as possible. To illustrate, consider Listing 8.6, a simple modification of the `Environ.pl` script shown in Listing 8.1. The first thing you have to do is acquire a copy of the `FCGI.pm` module for Perl. If you are already using the `CPAN.pm` module (see the earlier sidebar titled "DBI.pm.") to maintain your installed Perl modules, this is as easy as issuing the command `install FCGI` in `CPAN.pm`'s interactive mode. Including the line `use FCGI;` at the beginning of a Perl script ensures that it will work with CGI (you would link your object code to the FCGI library to accomplish the same thing with a compiled language like C).

Now, create a loop that executes once each time a call to `FCGI::accept` returns with a value that is not negative. When this call returns with a value less than zero, the loop terminates and the program ends. Everything within the loop should look like regular CGI stuff. Incidentally, using the ab benchmark utility that comes with Apache, I evaluated the speed of this script in responding to 10,000 requests, and measured it to be 328% faster than the plain CGI script. That's a very significant increase.

Listing 8.6   The `Environ.fcgi` FastCGI Script

```perl
#!/usr/bin/perl -Tw
#Environ.cgi - Show environment variables set by the server
use FCGI; # Imports the library; this line required
while (FCGI::accept >= 0) {
  print "Content-type: text/html\n\n";
  print "<HTML><HEAD><TITLE>Environment
    Variables</TITLE></HEAD><BODY>";
  print "<H2>Environment Variables:</H2>";
  print "<HR>\n";
  foreach $evar( keys (%ENV)){
    print "<B>$evar:</B> $ENV{$evar}<BR>";
  }
  print "</BODY></HTML>\n";
}
```

You might note a new environment variable that appears when you call this script from a browser:

```
FCGI_APACHE_ROLE= RESPONDER
```

This indicates that FastCGI is operating in one of three different application *roles* it can assume. The *Responder* role provides the functionality of ordinary CGI, which cannot operate in the other two roles that FastCGI can assume. The first of these alternative roles is the *Filter* role, in which a FastCGI script is used to process a file before it is returned to the client. The other role is the *Authorizer* role, in which a FastCGI application is used to make decisions about whether or not to grant a user's request. In this role, FastCGI acts as an authorization module, like those described in Chapter 13. Both of these roles are too complex for discussion here, and neither is used often. If you're interested in exploring either of them further, your first stop to learn more should be www.fastcgi.com.

Note that other Perl modules can still be used in the same fashion as ordinary CGI scripts. Listing 8.7 illustrates this. It's a FastCGI rewrite of the zipcodes MySQL query script, rewritten to take advantage of the efficiency of FastCGI.

Listing 8.7 The zipcodes.fcgi FastCGI Script

```perl
#!/usr/bin/perl -Tw
use CGI;
use FCGI; # Imports the library; required line
$query = new CGI;
# Response loop
while (FCGI::accept >= 0) {
  print $query->header;
  print $query->start_html("Zip Code Database Query Form");
  print "<H1>Zip Code MySQL Database Query Form</H1>\n";
  &print_prompt($query);
  &print_tail;
  print $query->end_html;
  sub print_prompt {
  my($query) = @_;
  print $query->startform(-method=>"POST",
    -action=>"http://Jackal.hiwaay.net/cgi-bin/zipcodes.cgi ");
  print "<EM>Enter a 5-digit Zip Code:</EM><BR>";
  print $query->textfield(-name=>'zip', -size=>6);
  print "<P>",$query->reset('Clear');
  print $query->submit(-value=>'Submit Search');
  print $query->endform;
  print "<HR>\n";
}
sub print_tail {
print <<END;
<ADDRESS>Charles Aulds</ADDRESS><BR>
<A HREF="/">Home Page</A>
```

```
END
}
} # End FCGI loop
```

Listing 8.8 shows a simple FastCGI script written in C.

Listing 8.8   A Simple C Script in FastCGI

```
#include <fcgi_stdio.h>

void main(void)
{
    int I = 0;
    while(FCGI_Accept() >= 0) {
        printf("Content-type: text/html\r\n\r\n");
        printf("<H1>Hello World!</H1>");
        printf("<p>You've requested this FastCGI page
            %d times.\n", i++);
    }
}
```

Notice the #include statement that is necessary to use FastCGI. The program goes into a loop that is processed once every time a call to FCGI_Accept() returns with a result greater than zero. I set an integer counter outside the loop, which is incremented during the processing of the loop. Can you see how a different value of the counter is returned for each request for this FastCGI program?

mod_perl As a Perl Accelerator

Traditional Perl, as an interpreted language, has always had a reputation of being relatively slow, and this reputation is at least partially deserved. Perl certainly isn't a speed demon, but the runtime performance of Perl scripts is far less important in most situations than the fact that the Perl interpreter has to be loaded each time a script is invoked. On a Web server that may be running thousands of Perl scripts through the CGI interface every hour, launching a separate Perl interpreter in a new Linux shell process for each request can result in a substantial performance impact on the server.

In Chapter 3, I mentioned mod_perl as an alternative to using the C language for writing Apache modules, permitting Apache modules to be written completely in Perl rather than in the more arcane C language. Many Apache module developers prefer to use Perl, largely because mod_perl provides such a rich set of easy-to-use handler directives for every phases of the Apache request-processing cycle. These directives permit the specification of Perl modules to handle virtually any task, without explicitly adding the module to the Apache configuration.

A large number of such modules have emerged, adding a great variety of additional functionality to Apache (the names of these Perl modules are preceded by `ModPerl::`, which makes them easy to identify or to find at `search.cpan.org`). Many of these are stand-alone modules that require only that your Apache server is running with the `mod_perl` module. More than a few of these modules, however, function as building blocks for programmers who want to develop their own modules, leveraging the effort and expertise of other programmers in the Perl community.

To make use of these modules or, for the adventurous, to create your own Apache modules in Perl, you must first install `mod_perl`, which is, itself, an Apache module (written in C) that provides Perl equivalents of the Apache API (C functions and data structures). With `mod_perl`, you can do pretty close to anything with Apache that you can do in C, but you can code your extensions in Perl. That's exciting, at least to some of us!

Certainly one of the most interesting and useful of these third-party modules written to take advantage of `mod_perl` is `ModPerl::Registry`, a module that is distributed as an integral part of `mod_perl` and useless without it. The purpose of `ModPerl::Registry` is to emulate a CGI environment for Perl scripts (only) that enables the scripts to run without alterations that are required by other CGI accelerators like FastCGI. Unlike standard CGI, which "spawns" or "forks" a new Perl process to handle each request for every script, `ModPerl::Registry` loads and compiles each script once (actually, once per child server), and retains the compiled script in memory to greatly speed subsequent requests for the same script. This eliminates virtually all the overhead associated with Perl/CGI and puts Perl in the same league with the very fastest server-side Web-programming techniques.

Without going into great detail, `mod_perl` works its magic by linking the Perl runtime library into the Apache server, thereby giving each running copy of Apache its own Perl interpreter. This is accomplished in two ways. First, the Perl function libraries can be statically linked to the Apache `httpd` process (which requires recompiling Apache from the source code). Alternatively, the Perl libraries can be linked into the `mod_perl` DSO module that is loaded in Apache's address space at runtime. If the DSO option is chosen, you have a choice of obtaining the DSO as an RPM or compiling it yourself. (All of these methods of installing `mod_perl` are discussed in the next few sections.) This completely eliminates the need to start a new instance of the Perl interpreter in its own Linux process each time a Perl CGI script is called, which significantly improves the response time and total runtime of scripts. Consequently, this increase in server throughput results in a dramatic increase in the number of client requests that can be serviced in a given time.

The `ModPerl::Registry` module creates its own namespace and compiles Perl scripts that are called through `mod_perl` into that namespace. It associates each script with a timestamp. The next time that script is used, if the source files aren't newer than the compiled bytecodes in the `ModPerl::Registry` namespace, the module is not recompiled. Some Perl code that is called frequently from a number of different scripts (like CGI.pm) is only compiled once, the first time it is used.

The really cool thing is that mod_perl runs nearly all Perl scripts without modification. The only thing you have to do is specify mod_perl as the Apache handler for the scripts, instead of the default mod_cgi. On my server, I set up mod_cgi to handle requests to /cgi-bin and mod_perl to handle all requests to /perl.

Installing *mod_perl* from Source Code

To avoid problems with mod_perl, always install from the source code, obtained either from the CPAN repository (search.cpan.org) or directly from the mod_perl site (at perl.apache.org/dist/). Get the latest archive with a name that begins with "mod_perl-2." In the examples that follow, I am using mod_perl-1.99_04.tar.gz, one of the last prerelease ("beta") copies of mod_perl for Apache 2.0. By the time you read this, the module will certainly be in a production release, but should still install and operate in the manner I describe.

After downloading the archive, extract its contents into a working directory, one I always locate under /usr/local/src:

```
# cd /usr/local/src
# tar xzf /downloads/mod_perl-1.99_04.tar.gz
# cd mod_perl-1.99_04/
```

Again, in order to compile mod_perl as a DSO module, locate yourself in the build directory, while logged in as root. The following simple command line should compile the module and install it in the Apache modules directory:

```
# perl Makefile.PL MP_AP_PREFIX=/usr/local/apache2
# make
# make install
```

When the installation completes, you should find the DSO, compiled as mod_perl.so, in Apache's modules directory. The size of this file (over a megabyte on my machine) seems excessive, but remember that it has the entire Perl interpreter linked into it, which largely accounts for the size.

```
# ls -s /usr/local/apache2/modules/mod_perl.so
1128 /usr/local/apache2/modules/mod_perl.so
```

You can reduce the size of the file somewhat by stripping unnecessary debugging symbols (using the Linux strip command):

```
# strip /usr/local/apache2/modules/mod_perl.so
# ls -s /usr/local/apache2/modules/mod_perl.so
1048 /usr/local/apache2/modules/mod_perl.so
```

Advanced Configuration

PART 3

A reduction of only seven percent seems modest, but worth the little time it took, particularly since there will be one copy of this module loaded for every child server forked by Apache.

In the final step, you should check to make sure that Apache httpd.conf contains the necessary directive to load the module. Although the production release of the module will probably modify the file to include this line, you should check for it and add it, if necessary, with the other LoadModule directives:

```
LoadModule perl_module       modules/mod_perl.so
```

BEGIN and *END* Blocks: A Word of Caution

If you are running Perl scripts that contain BEGIN and END blocks, under mod_perl these may not behave as you intend. Because scripts are compiled and cached for later reuse by ModPerl::Registry, these blocks will not be executed each time the script is called (as usually intended). Instead, the BEGIN block will be executed once by ModPerl::Registry when it is loaded. The END block receives special treatment by mod_perl. For scripts loaded at runtime by ModPerl::Registry, the END block is called when the script finishes running; this occurs for all invocations of the script, even if it has been compiled and cached. In scripts loaded at server startup (using PerlModule or PerlRequire), the END block is executed only once, when the main server is shut down.

The behavior of BEGIN and END blocks under mod_perl does not render them unusable, but you should probably avoid their use in scripts intended to be cached by ModPerl::Registry. The BEGIN block particularly should to be avoided.

Running Perl Scripts with *mod_perl*

In general, mod_perl functions as a drop-in replacement for CGI (for Perl scripts only, of course). Using mod_perl requires no modification to ordinary CGI Perl scripts, but it runs them far faster than they run under standard CGI. This section describes how to set up mod_perl to run Perl scripts and then discusses a few modules that build on the capabilities mod_perl adds to Apache. While the most common use of mod_perl is to accelerate Perl/CGI, these extension modules are becoming quite popular for the development of extensive Web-based applications, and they put mod_perl squarely in the same field as competitors like PHP or Java servlets (both discussed later in this chapter).

Passing Data to *mod_perl* Scripts

Since mod_perl emulates the CGI interface so that traditional CGI scripts can run unaltered, the best way to pass data to mod_perl scripts is through the system environment it inherits. Two directives can be used in httpd.conf to pass information to mod_perl scripts. These are analogous to the SetEnv and PassEnv directives already discussed, but they must be used in place of those directives to modify the special environment that mod_perl sets up for scripts that run under its control. The PerlSetEnv directive creates a new environment variable and sets its value for a Perl script to retrieve from the %ENV hash:

```
PerlSetEnv logfile /var/logs/Mylog.txt
```

The second directive, PerlPassEnv, takes the name of an existing variable from the main server's environment (usually the environment of the user who started Apache, typically root). This environment variable will be included in the environment set up for the CGI script:

```
PerlPassEnv USER
```

If you are not passing data to your mod_perl scripts through the environment, you can instruct mod_perl not to set up an environment to be inherited by CGI scripts. The speed gain and memory savings are usually not substantial enough to warrant disabling this feature, but it can be done for an extra performance boost:

```
PerlSetupEnv Off
```

Another directive is PerlSetVar, provided by mod_perl to pass arbitrary data pairs to mod_perl scripts without using the environment. This directive is a tool primarily used by module programmers and generally not used by Web scripters. Retrieving this information requires a call to a special mod_perl method, dir_config(), which in turn requires a modification of standard CGI scripts. The directive looks like this:

```
PerlSetVar MyVar some_arbitrary_data
```

Supplying Perl with Command-Line Switches

The first line of a traditional Perl/CGI script specifies a path to a script interpreter (typically/usr/lib/perl), and generally looks something like #!/usr/lib/perl. Using mod_perl, however, this line is ignored because ModPerl::Registry knows about (and uses) only a single script interpreter, the one that is linked into mod_perl during its installation. Since this line will be ignored when processing scripts with mod_perl, instructions to the interpreter that are normally passed as arguments on this line are also ignored. You should avoid the use of these switches in your Perl scripts, as they will generate warnings or errors.

Of these switches, the only one that mod_perl will recognize and use is the -w switch, which turns on warnings. The other switch that is usually important to CGI programmers is the -T switch to enable taint checking. mod_perl provides a special directive that passes these switches to the Perl interpreter. I find it very useful to include the following directive in my httpd.conf file:

```
PerlWarn On
```

Advanced Configuration

PART 3

Apache Modules Packaged with *mod_perl*

For the administrator who merely wants to write dynamic or interactive Web content or access a database from Web forms, the real benefit of mod_perl comes not from its API but from a number of existing modules written to work with Apache and mod_perl. Some of these come packaged with mod_perl to extend its functionality, but there are others that perform a wide variety of different functions. Examples include modules to authenticate clients using a wide variety of databases and authentication schemes; modules that implement server-side HTML parsing using the ASP and SSI specifications; and modules that maintain shared, persistent connections to back-end databases for the quickest possible access to data stores.

All Apache modules, including older versions, are archived and available at:

    http://www.cpan.org/modules/by-module/Apache/

To find only the most recent version of each, go to the CPAN search site and search for modules matching the string *Apache*. As a shortcut, you can use the following URL:

    search.cpan.org/search?mode=module&query=Apache

The *ModPerl::Registry* Module

Of all the support modules that mod_perl relies on, ModPerl::Registry is without question the most important. The module is so important that mod_perl can't be installed or used without it. The two modules work hand in hand, and many of the functions we think of as part of mod_perl are actually performed by the ModPerl::Registry Perl module. The module performs two tasks that greatly extend mod_perl. First, it provides a full emulation of the CGI environment, allowing CGI scripts to be run under mod_perl without modification. Remember, mod_perl only provides a Perl programmer's interface to Apache and embeds a Perl interpreter into the Apache kernel. It is these functions of mod_perl that ModPerl::Registry uses to provide CGI emulation to Apache and its Perl interpreter. Although it is a separate Perl module, ModPerl::Registry is inseparable from mod_perl, and each depends on the other.

The second essential ModPerl::Registry function is called *script caching*. Perl CGI scripts are automatically loaded into a special namespace managed by ModPerl::Registry and maintained there, rather than being unloaded from memory after they are used. This means that a CGI program is loaded and compiled only the first time it is called, and subsequent calls to the same program are run in the cached code. This greatly increases the throughput of the Perl engine, as I'll show in a later section on benchmarking mod_perl.

Although ModPerl::Registry provides the functions of CGI emulation and script caching, these are usually attributed to mod_perl. Therefore, whenever I refer to mod_perl, I'm speaking of mod_perl with ModPerl::Registry and other support modules of lesser importance. Without these, mod_perl doesn't do much for the typical Apache administrator, but is merely a programmer's interface.

Configuring Apache to Use *ModPerl::Registry*

To use mod_perl to run CGI scripts, you need to declare ModPerl::Registry as the handler for those scripts. On my server, I used the following <Location> section to specify ModPerl::Registry as the handler for request URLs ending in /perl:

```
<Location /perl>
    SetHandler perl-script
    PerlHandler ModPerl::Registry
    PerlSendHeader On
    Options +ExecCGI
</Location>
```

The PerlSendHeader On line causes mod_perl to generate common HTTP headers, just as mod_cgi does when processing standard CGI. By default, mod_perl sends no headers. It is a good idea to always enable the PerlSendHeader directive, especially when using unmodified standard CGI scripts with mod_perl.

I used the following Alias directive to assign a directory outside Apache's DocumentRoot to the /perl request URL:

```
Alias /perl/ /home/httpd/perl/
```

The directory so defined does not have to be located under the Apache DocumentRoot, and in my case it is not. I used the following Linux command lines to create the new directory, copy the Environ.cgi script to it, and then change the ownership of the directory and its contents to the nobody account and the group ownership to www. On your system, ensure that the file is owned by the same user account under which the Apache httpd processes run, and that the group ownership is set to a group that includes your Web administrators.

```
# mkdir /home/httpd/perl
# cp /home/httpd/cgi-bin/Environ.cgi /home/httpd/perl
# chown -R nobody.www /home/httpd
```

After installing mod_perl, I called http://jackal.hiwaay.net/perl/Environ.pl, and the changes made to the server are in boldface type:

```
QUERY_STRING:
SERVER_ADDR: 192.168.1.2
HTTP_ACCEPT_LANGUAGE: en-us
SERVER_PROTOCOL: HTTP/1.1
HTTP_CONNECTION: Keep-Alive
SERVER_SIGNATURE:Apache/2.0.36 Server at jackal.hiwaay.net Port 80
```

Advanced Configuration

PART 3

```
REMOTE_PORT: 1193
HTTP_ACCEPT: */*
HTTP_USER_AGENT: Mozilla/4.0 (compatible; MSIE 6.0; Windows NT 5.0)
GATEWAY_INTERFACE: CGI-Perl/1.1
HTTP_HOST: jackal.hiwaay.net
SERVER_ADMIN: caulds@hiwaay.net
SERVER_SOFTWARE: Apache/2.0.36 (Unix) mod_perl/1.99_03-dev Perl/v5.6.1
DAV/2
REMOTE_ADDR: 192.168.1.7
SCRIPT_NAME: /perl/Environ.cgi
HTTP_ACCEPT_ENCODING: gzip, deflate
SERVER_NAME: jackal.hiwaay.net
DOCUMENT_ROOT: /home/httpd
REQUEST_URI: /perl/Environ.cgi
MOD_PERL: mod_perl/1.99_04-dev
UNIQUE_ID: tzpbE38AAAEAADLrW40AAAAB
REQUEST_METHOD: GET
SCRIPT_FILENAME: /home/httpd/perl/Environ.cgi
PATH:bin:/sbin:/usr/bin:/usr/sbin:/usr/local/bin:/usr/local/sbin:
➥;  /usr/bin/X11:/usr/X11R6/bin:/root/bin:/usr/java/jdk1.3.1_01/bin:.
SERVER_PORT: 80
```

ModPerl::ASP and ModPerl::DBI

Two other Apache modules for Perl, ModPerl::ASP and ModPerl::DBI, are worth mentioning but are too ambitious to cover in detail here. Both allow you to add extensive functionality to Apache. Because each of them relies on the mechanisms of mod_perl, they also offer efficiency and speed. They are available, and documented, from the perl.apache.org and search.cpan.org sites.

Apache::ASP

This Perl module provides Active Server Pages (ASP), a popular Microsoft-developed technology that originated with the Microsoft IIS server. The Microsoft Win32 version of ASP for IIS allows the embedding of Perl, VBScript, and JScript code in HTML documents. Using Apache::ASP, programmers already proficient in ASP on IIS servers can leverage this knowledge by programming ASP pages in Perl.

Apache::DBI

This module (which should not be confused with the standard DBI.pm module) enables the caching of database handles in the same way that Perl code is cached and reused by Perl scripts. The section "Persistent Database Connections" later in this chapter discusses Apache::DBI in detail.

Embedded Perl Solutions

A very popular technique used by Perl Web programmers today is embedding Perl in HTML code, in very much the same way that Active Server Pages are used. The two most popular embedded Perl techniques, however, are designed specifically for Perl, riding on top of the mod_perl Apache module for efficiency. I will briefly describe these two embedded Perl systems. Both are complete development systems in their own right, and can be used to develop complete Web-based applications.

HTML::EmbPerl

Although mod_perl and mod_include work together to allow embedded Perl in server-parsed HTML pages, this module provides another way to embed Perl in HTML documents. EmbPerl provides its own tags and commands for processing conditional statements and loops, evaluating Perl code, and building HTML structures such as tables or drop-down lists. Essentially, EmbPerl defines a new specification for server-parsed embedded HTML content. The module, although well documented (see http://perl.apache.org/embperl/), does require learning a new, nonstandard, method of using server-side includes. The module offers far more functions than are available in standard SSI provided through mod_include, and it is a rich set of development tools for programmers who prefer the embedded code approach to developing dynamic Web pages. EmbPerl enjoys active and strong support from its author as well as a large user community, an asset whose value is hard to quantify, but it is unquestionably one of the major reasons to use EmbPerl.

HTML::Mason

The newer HTML::Mason Perl module appears, on the surface, to work remarkably like its cousin, EmbPerl, but there are some critical differences between the two. While EmbPerl tends to take a grassroots approach, starting with HTML and enhancing it, Mason takes a top-down view of things. Before the HTML or Perl code ever comes into play, Mason starts with a master plan, in which Web pages are composed of the output of *components*. These components are usually mixtures of HTML, embedded Perl, and special Mason commands. The emphasis is on site design and page structure, rather than on simply embedding Perl functions in HTML documents. This approach encourages code and design component reuse. Mason is full of functions to facilitate the reuse of code, either by simple inclusion in a document or through filters (which modify the output of a component) and templates (which work somewhat like style sheets to apply a format to an entire directory of pages).

HTML::Mason is not strictly an Apache add-on. It will work in stand-alone mode or CGI mode, but the developers highly recommend that it be used with Apache supporting the mod_perl module. HTML::Mason is very well documented at the Mason Web site, www.masonhq.com/, which also hosts a small library of user-written components that can be downloaded and used or examined to learn the use of the product.

Advanced Configuration

PART 3

Improving the Performance of *mod_perl*

The techniques covered in this section are not required for using mod_perl, but they offer ways to significantly increase its performance. mod_perl relies on a memory-resident Perl interpreter for part of the magic that allows it to increase the speed of Perl/CGI scripts; it uses caching to achieve the rest. You'll see two ways of using mod_perl's caching engine more efficiently, and then the results of a few benchmark tests I ran to verify that mod_perl does, indeed, deliver on its promise of greatly increasing your Perl script performance.

Persistent Database Connections

Although our database query example was made more efficient using mod_perl because the DBI and DBD::mysql modules are cached and reused, most of the processing overhead associated with these modules occurs in establishing database connections. This is particularly true if the connections are to a remote database server, which is quite often the case on today's networks. Far greater efficiency can be realized through the use of persistent database connections, in which the database connection is opened once by Apache and shared among all clients.

The Apache::DBI module provides automatic connection caching and sharing. If this module is used instead of the regular DBI.pm module, it monitors all DBI (Database Independent module) requests issued through mod_perl. As ModPerl::Registry does for scripts, Apache::DBI caches database connections. For each running httpd process, only the first DBI->connect actually results in a new database connection. After that, whenever a script calls DBI->connect, it is given a cached database handle, rather than a new handle resulting from a fresh connection. When the script uses the disconnect call to close the handle, Apache::DBI handles this request by returning the handle to its cache rather than actually closing the database connection. The use of shared persistent database connections results in a significant improvement in the speed of Perl DBI database operations.

To use Apache::DBI, install it using CPAN.pm:

```
# cpan
cpan shell -- CPAN exploration and modules installation (v1.54)
ReadLine support enabled

cpan> install Apache::DBI
```

Then remove all use DBI lines from scripts that should use cached database handles. This will prevent calls to DBI functions from being handled by the standard DBI module. All such calls will instead be handled automatically by the Apache::DBI module.

You should *never* attempt to open a database connection during Apache's startup sequence (for example, from a mod_perl startup script). This may seem like a logical way to open database connections for later use, but the database handles created this way are shared among the httpd child server processes, rather than being opened one-per-httpd-process. This can create conflicts between httpd processes trying to use the same database handle simultaneously.

Preloading Modules

Remember that the main Apache httpd process creates child httpd processes to handle all user requests, and these child processes inherit the namespace of the main process. Each child process inherits its own copy of the Perl modules loaded by the main server to support mod_perl. As requests for CGI scripts are fulfilled, each process will also load its own copy of ModPerl::Registry and maintain its own cache of compiled Perl scripts. These child httpd processes are usually killed after answering a fixed number of requests (configured using the MaxRequestsPerChild directive). This can mitigate problems associated with potential memory leaks, but it also destroys each httpd process's ModPerl::Registry cache and requires that each be built again from scratch. This can happen thousands of times during the lifetime of the main server process.

To prevent cached Perl code from being destroyed along with the child process that loaded it, mod_perl provides two configuration directives that enable Perl scripts to be preloaded into the namespace of the main server and inherited by all the child processes it creates.

The first of these is PerlRequire, which specifies a single Perl script to load when Apache starts up:

```
PerlRequire startup.pl
```

Generally, this script contains use statements that load other Perl code. This directive is used to preload external modules that are common to a number of Perl scripts:

```
# contents of startup.pl
use ModPerl::Registry;
use CGI;
use Apache::DBI;
```

The script specified must exist in one of the directories specified in the @INC array (described in the next section).

The second directive that can be used for this purpose is PerlModule, which can specify a single module to preload when Apache starts. The startup.pl script shown can also be rewritten entirely in httpd.conf with these four directives:

```
PerlModule ModPerl::Registry
PerlModule CGI
PerlModule Apache::DBI
```

The advantage of using PerlModule is that an external startup script is not required. A limitation of PerlModule, however, is that no more than 10 modules can be preloaded using `PerlModule` directives. For most sites, this limitation is not significant, but if you need to preload more than 10 modules, you will need to use a startup script.

Handling Server Restarts

The default behavior of mod_perl is to retain all cached Perl code when the server is restarted using `apachectl restart` (as opposed to being stopped and then started). Use the `PerlFreshRestart` directive to ensure that the cached code resulting from `PerlRequire` and `PerlModule` directives in `httpd.conf` is refreshed when Apache is restarted:

```
PerlFreshRestart on
```

Benchmarking *mod_perl*

To find out just how much faster mod_perl runs than a traditional Perl script invoked through the CGI interface, I used the excellent ApacheBench benchmarking tool that comes packaged with Apache. You'll find it as ab in the `bin` directory where Apache is installed, typically `/usr/local/apache2/bin/ab`.

Listing 8.9 shows a very simple CGI script that does nothing but return the system environment.

Listing 8.9   A Test Script Used with ApacheBench

```perl
#!/usr/bin/perl
#Environ.cgi - Show environment variables set by the server

print "Content-type: text/html\n\n";
print "<HTML><HEAD><TITLE>Environment Variables</TITLE></HEAD><BODY>";
print "<H2>Environment Variables:</H2>";
print "<HR>\n";
foreach $evar( keys (%ENV)){
        print "<B>$evar:</B> $ENV{$evar}<BR>";
}
print "</BODY></HTML>\n";
```

I used ab to execute this script as ordinary CGI with the following command line:

```
# ab -n 10000 -c 20 192.168.1.1:80/cgi-bin//Environ.cgi
```

Here, -n represents the number of requests to make, and -c indicates the number of concurrent connections to my server that would be opened by ab.

I collected statistics on 10,000 requests to `/cgi-bin//Environ.cgi`, and then I executed the following command line to collect the same statistics on `/perl/environ.cgi`. These requests are handled by mod_perl and `ModPerl::Registry`.

```
# ab -n 10000 -c 20 192.168.1.1:80/perl/Environ.cgi
```

The results of my benchmark test (Table 8.1) show that the number of requests that can be answered is 350% that of unmodified Apache.

Table 8.1 Perl/CGI versus mod_perl Benchmark Results

	Apache 1.3.9/CGI	Apache 1.39/mod_perl 1.21
Server Hostname	192.168.1.1	192.168.1.1
Server Port	80	80
Document Path	/cgi-bin/Environ.cgi	/perl/Environ.cgi
Concurrency Level	20	20
Elapsed Time	355.110 seconds	96.444 seconds
Complete Requests	10000	10000
Failed Requests	0	0
Total Transferred	13001694 bytes	13590000 bytes
HTML Transferred	11480000 bytes	11110000 bytes
Requests per Second	28.16	103.69
Median Connection Times	709 ms	178 ms
Transfer Rate	35.75 Kbps received	137.60 Kbps received

Advanced Configuration

PART 3

The statistics pretty much speak for themselves. Using mod_perl, the number of requests per second increased from 28 to 104 (almost quadrupling the number of connections the server could handle in a given amount of time). User connection time dropped, too, from about seven-tenths of a second to less than two-tenths of a second (though this is less significant, and imperceptible to most users).

If the additional efficiency that could be obtained through persistent database connection sharing were introduced, these numbers would be even more impressive. That's why I ran the second set of tests shown in Table 8.2.

The results in this table show an even more remarkable improvement in speed using mod_perl. This example queries the zipcodes MySQL database 1000 times, using this command line:

```
# ab -n 1000 -c 20 192.168.1.1:80/cgi-bin/zipcodes.cgi?zip="35016"
```

I then ran the same test through mod_perl, using this command:

```
# ab -n 1000 -c 20 192.168.1.1:80/perl/zipcodes.cgi?zip="35016"
```

This test really gives mod_perl a chance to shine. It not only takes advantage of the embedded Perl interpreter, which eliminates the shell process creation overhead associated with CGI, but also allows ModPerl::Registry to open a database connection and pass the database handle to processes that ordinarily would have to open and close their own connections. With absolutely no attempt to optimize mod_perl, I saw an increase of over 400% in the number of connections served per second. I'm no benchmarking expert, and these results are from something less than a controlled scientific experiment, but they were enough to convince me that mod_perl runs circles around conventional CGI.

Table 8.2   Benchmarking Results Using Database Connection Sharing

	Apache 1.3.9/CGI	Apache 1.39/mod_perl 1.21
Server Hostname	192.168.1.1	192.168.1.1
Server Port	80	80
Document Path	/cgi-bin/zipcodes. cgi?zip="35801"	/perl/zipcodes. cgi?zip="35801"
Concurrency Level	10	10
Elapsed Time	258.722 seconds	63.691 seconds
Complete Requests	200	200
Failed Requests	0	0
Total Transferred	127000 bytes	131843 bytes
HTML Transferred	89200 bytes	90200 bytes
Requests per Second	0.77	3.20
Median Connection Times	12518 ms	424 ms
Transfer Rate	0.48Kbps received	2.05Kbps received

Programming with *mod_perl*

In addition to acting as an accelerator for Perl scripts run from Apache through CGI, mod_perl also provides two other features for programming Apache. The first allows Apache modules to be completely written in Perl (freeing Apache module developers from having to use C). The second feature, far less useful, allows the Apache `httpd.conf` file to include Perl code so that Apache directives can be dynamically created when Apache is loaded.

Using Perl Handlers

Besides linking the Perl interpreter to the Apache kernel, `mod_perl` has another important feature. It allows us to write Apache modules in Perl. We do this by using special `mod_perl` directives in `httpd.conf` to specify Perl programs as callbacks during stages of the Apache request-processing cycle and by providing the module programmer with a rich set of Perl functions that correspond to functions in the Apache API. (These were formerly accessible only to programs written in C.)

The following configuration directives are defined by `mod_perl`, each corresponding to a different phase in the Apache request-processing cycle:

```
PerlOpenLogsHandler
PerlPostConfigHandler
PerlChildInitHandler
PerlPreConnectionHandler
PerlProcessConnectionHandler
PerlPostReadRequestHandler
PerlTransHandler
PerlInitHandler
PerlHeaderParserHandler
PerlAccessHandler
PerlAuthenHandler
PerlAuthzHandler
PerlTypeHandler
PerlFixupHandler
PerlResponseHandler
PerlLogHandler
PerlCleanupHandler
PerlInputFilterHandler
PerlOutputFilterHandler
```

You may feel that you are entering real programmers' territory—but actually all of these handlers are very easy to use. They allow you to specify Perl code to perform functions at various stages during the handling of an HTTP request without having to use the specialized functions of the Apache API (although those are still available).

Listing 8.10 illustrates a very simple Perl logging program to write request information to a MySQL database. The `$r` in this example is an object that represents the HTTP request headers and is extracted from another object that is passed to the script by `mod_perl`, which contains everything Apache knows about the HTTP request being processed.

Advanced Configuration

PART 3

Listing 8.10   A Logging Program for `mod_perl`

```perl
package Apache::LogMySQL;

use Apache::compat;

use strict;

# uncomment if Apache::DBI not used
# use DBI ();

use Apache::Util qw(ht_time);

sub handler {
   my $orig = shift;
   my $r = $orig->last;
   my $date    = ht_time($orig->request_time, '%Y-%m-%d %H:%M:%S', 0);
   my $host    = $r->get_remote_host;
   my $method  = $r->method;
   my $url     = $orig->uri;
   my $user    = $r->connection->user;
   my $referer = $r->header_in('Referer');
   my $browser = $r->header_in('User-agent');
   my $status  = $orig->status;
   my $bytes   = $r->bytes_sent;

   my $dbh =
      DBI->connect("DBI:mysql:mydblog:jackal.hiwaay.net","root","password")
          || die $DBI::errstr;

   my $sth = $dbh->prepare("INSERT INTO accesslog VALUES(?,?,?,?,?,?,?,?,?)")
                | die $dbh->errstr;

     $sth->execute($date,$host,$method,$url,$user,
                   $browser,$referer,$status,$bytes) || die $dbh->errstr;
     return OK;
}

1;
__END__
```

If this file is saved as `LogMySQL.pm` under the Apache package directory (`/usr/lib/perl5/site_perl/5.6.1/i386-linux/Apache2` on my system), it can be specified as a handler for the logging phase of Apache's HTTP request cycle with the single directive

```
PerlLogHandler Apache::LogMySQL
```

Each time a request is handled, at the Log Handler phase, this program is called. Note that it creates its own namespace (`Apache::LogMySQL`). There's not a lot to know about this application, except that `$r` refers to the Apache request object, and all the information required for the log is retrieved from that object. A special function, `ht_time()` in the `Apache::Util` module is used to format the request time-stamp that is logged. Also note the commented `Use DBI()` line; that line is required only if `Use Apache::DBI` was not specified in a `startup.pl` script so that database connections will be shared. In this example, since `Apache::DBI` is used, each time this handler script calls `DBI->connect`, it is handed a database handle for a database connection already opened (by `Apache::DBI`) to use. This handle is returned when the script finishes, and it is used over and over.

This example is a bare skeleton of what is required to set up a Perl handler. Although it is a real example, it is minimal. You should evaluate DBI logging modules already written (`Apache::DBILogConfig` or `Apache::DBILogger`) before you write your own, although you may want to do it just for fun. Look for Apache logging modules at `http://search.cpan.org/`.

Using *mod_perl* to Modify *httpd.conf*

Another enhancement to Apache added by `mod_perl` is the ability to include Perl code within `<Perl>` sections in `httpd.conf`. These are interpreted when the server is started and used to dynamically generate configuration directives. I haven't found this feature very useful, and it tends to overcomplicate the server configuration. Furthermore, although using Perl code in your `httpd.conf` file may simplify and shorten that text file, the configuration that is eventually loaded by Apache and stored in memory is identical to the configuration that would be constructed using conventional configuration directives. There are no efficiency benefits to the use of Perl sections.

There are cases, however, when this feature might simplify the configuration process. You might consider using `<Perl>` sections when configuration directives can be generated programmatically (for example, by retrieving their values from a relational database). Another use is when a loop can be used to configure a number of sections (as, for example, when a list of virtual hosts is used to construct a number of `<VirtualHost>` sections).

To enable this capability, when installing `mod_perl` using the APACI or `apxs` methods, you need to specify `PERL_SECTIONS=1`:

```
perl Makefile.PL PERL_SECTIONS=1
```

To use `<Perl>` sections, you need only create variables with the same names as valid configuration directives and assign values to these, either as scalars or as Perl lists, which are interpreted later as space-delimited strings. In other words, if you wanted to create a `Listen` directive and assign it the value 80, you could use the following `<Perl>` section:

```
<Perl>
```

Advanced Configuration

PART 3

```
    $Listen=80;
</Perl>
```

When Apache is started and this configuration file is parsed, these variables are converted to regular configuration directives that are then treated as though they were read directly from httpd.conf. A couple of examples will illustrate how this works. Here, a Perl section is used to configure some general server directives:

```
<Perl>
@PerlModule = qw(Apache::Include Apache::DBI CGI);
$User="wwwroot";
$Group="wwwgroup";
$ServerAdmin="caulds@hiwaay.net";
__END__   # All text following this token ignored by preprocessor
</Perl>
```

The following example illustrates how hashes are used to store the contents of container directives. Nested containers are stored as nested Perl hashes.

```
<Perl>
$Directory{"/secure/"} = {
    @AllowOverride = (FileInfo AuthConfig Limit);
    AuthUserFile => "/usr/local/adminpwds";
    AuthGroupFile => "/usr/local/groups";
    AuthType => "Basic";
    Limit => {
        METHODS => "GET POST",
        Require => "group Webteam";
    }
}
__END__
</Perl>
```

Of course, the Perl sections in these examples offer no benefit over the use of ordinary configuration directives. The real benefit would be in cases where Perl code dynamically creates (potentially hundreds of) virtual hosts. Suppose, for example, that we had a text file that consisted of virtual host definitions, one per line, stored as sites.conf. This is a very simple example that does virtually no sanity checking, but it could be used to generate a number of IP-based virtual hosts. Whenever virtual hosts in the list need to be added, deleted, or modified, the change is made to sites.conf, and httpd.conf doesn't need to be changed.

```
<Perl>
open SITECONF, "< /usr/local/apache2/conf/sites.conf" or die "$!";
while (<SITECONF>) {
    chomp;
```

```
next if /^s*#/ || /^s*$/; # Skip comments & blank lines
my @fields = split(/:/,$_,-1);
die "Bad sites.conf file format" unless scalar(@fields)==6;
my ($sitename, $sadmin, $ip, $http_dir, $errlog, $tfrlog)= @fields;
$VirtualHost{$ip} = {
    ServerName => $sitename,
    ServerAdmin => $sadmin,
    DocumentRoot => "/home/httpd/".$http_dir,
    ErrorLog => "logs/".$errlog,
    TransferLog => "logs/".$tfrlog
};
}
close SITECONF;
__END__
</Perl>
```

If you choose to use Perl sections to configure virtual hosts dynamically, remember that you can run `httpd -S` to display the virtual host configuration.

TIP   There's a lot of excellent documentation available for mod_perl, but it is often difficult to locate. You should be able to find all the docs you need on the official mod_perl site at http://perl.apache.org/. In particular, information on mod_perl for Apache 2.0. is accessible from http://perl.apache.org/docs/2.0/. If you are serious about using mod_perl to develop full-fledged Web applications, you'll also want to read Stas Bekman's excellent *mod_perl Guide* (http://perl.apache.org/docs/1.0/guide/).

PHP

If you've been involved in Web site development during the past half-decade or so, you probably know about PHP (originally called Personal Home Page Tools). Developed in 1994 as a simple HTML-embedded (server-parsed) tool for creating dynamic content in Web pages, PHP has steadily grown into a powerful general-purpose Web development tool. It is also becoming one of the most popular. In fact, it is by far the most widely used Apache extension module. The May 2002 survey from SecuritySpace.com (www.securityspace.com) shows that twice as many Internet sites use PHP as those that use mod_perl. PHP is based on years of effort from a large number of contributors and is distributed under an open-source license from www.php.net. PHP is not a toy, and it is far more than an enhanced Server-Side Includes.

PHP built a reputation as a powerful scripting language that was simple enough to appeal to site designers who weren't necessarily professional programmers. In this regard, it has succeeded admirably. For many Web designers, embedding code in HTML pages is natural and intuitive (even though many programmers still find that approach messy and inelegant). I was surprised at how quickly I could create interesting and useful applications with PHP. There is nothing that can be done with conventional CGI that cannot be done with PHP, although mod_perl opens up a whole new world of programming.

PHP greatly enables server-parsed scripting, and it has a place in any Web programmer's toolkit. Intermixing code with HTML is great for simple requirements, but when the amount of code significantly exceeds the HMTL, the pages become difficult to read. Particularly for pages that rely on the inclusion of external documents or scripts, the benefits of server-parsed HTML can be debated.

PHP has always been great for rapid development of dynamic Web pages, but with the release of PHP 4.0 in May 2000, PHP has acquired a sorely needed performance boost and features that are required of any top-shelf Web application development environment.

PHP Documentation

One of the really nice features of PHP is the documentation provided by the developers. Not only is the documentation thorough and helpful, but there's a lot of it. You can download the entire manual as a huge PDF file (for printing and binding) in any one of 12 different languages, or you can download the HTML version of the manual and put it on your own server. The PHP manual is also available for Palm handhelds (for the PHP enthusiast on the go) in either Palm DOC or iSilo format. Oh, and I guess I should mention that you can also download the PHP docs in Windows HTML Help format.

The PHP HTML online manual is the real star of the show, though. There are hundreds of functions in the PHP language, and this well-organized and easy-to-search online manual is truly an essential resource. If that's not of tremendous value to a programmer, I don't know what is. Bookmark the PHP online documentation at php.net or at one of over 80 mirror sites around the world (Figure 8.3).

One of the really interesting and valuable features of the online HTML documentation is the user notes section at the bottom of each page. Viewers can submit notes on the page and read notes submitted by previous visitors. The comments are often informative and interesting and are a tremendous enhancement to the developer-supplied documentation. This is a feature I would like to see in the online documentation of other sites.

Figure 8.3 PHP is superbly documented.

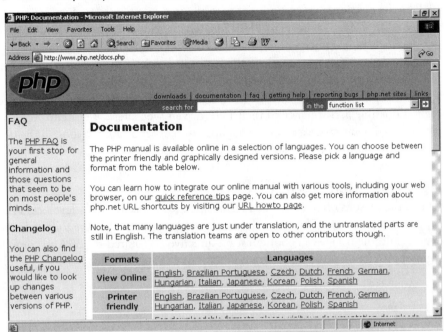

PHP 4.0

PHP 4.0 was released in May 2000, and it is the features added to that version that make PHP highly appealing. It was infinitely to the credit of the PHP development team that this release was intended to eliminate the most significant weaknesses in PHP 3.0 rather than simply stuffing in as many new eye-catching features as possible. The release of PHP 4.0 made real progress in dealing with most of the drawbacks of using PHP on a real-world server, particularly its poor speed and lack of object orientation. If you are considering PHP, you should definitely plan to download this latest version.

The most significant change in PHP 4.0 was a complete rewrite of the PHP scripting engine, incorporating a language parser called the Zend Engine, from Zend Technologies Ltd. (www.zend.com). In an odd reversal of normal reality, the Zend Engine, which is owned by Zend Technologies, was then licensed to the PHP Group (the originators of the PHP language) for free use. This truly odd partnership between the open-source PHP development team and a commercial firm has far-reaching impact. In addition to the Zend Engine, Zend Technologies also offers a freely available tool called the Zend Optimizer, which examines PHP code and performs optimizations that are claimed to double the running speed of most PHP applications.

Advanced
Configuration

PART 3

So, what's in it for Zend Technologies Ltd? While Zend promotes the acceptance of PHP by the development community with the free products already mentioned, they license add-on enhancements to PHP. For PHP developers, there is Zend Studio, a GUI-development environment, and the Zend Encoder, which functions much like a Java pseudocode compiler to compile PHP into code that is not faster at runtime, but that is unreadable (for those developers who want to distribute their product, but not in source format). One other licensed product aimed at production sites striving for the highest possible performance of their PHP-driven Web sites is the Zend Accelerator, which is claimed to increase the throughput of the Zend Engine (though the details of exactly how this is accomplished are a bit obscure).

Database Support in PHP

One of the reasons often given for PHP's wide acceptance by Web developers is its strong support for databases. The latest version of PHP supports all of the following database engines (although a special configuration directive is required for each to compile this support into the resulting module):

Adabas D

DBase

DBMaker

Empress

FilePro

FrontBase

Hyperwave

IBM DB2

Informix

Ingres

InterBase

LDAP

Linux/Unix DBM

Microsoft SQL Server

mSQL

MySQL

Oracle

Ovrimos

PostgresSQL

Solid Embedded Engine

Sybase

Velocis

One slight drawback of having native support for a wide variety of databases in PHP is that you can't add support to PHP for a new relational database system as easily as you can add a new DBD driver for Perl. You have to recompile PHP to include the standard libraries (if they have been provided) for the new database. Also, since you won't be using a database-independent layer (such as Perl's DBI or Java's JDBC), there are completely different functions for each supported database. If you work with several, this can be confusing. The performance advantages of native database support (with persistent connection supported for most), however, outweigh these minor annoyances.

Installing PHP

By far the best way to install PHP is from up-to-date source code, as a DSO module. If you'll pardon a lame pun, you should go straight to the source for your PHP source code (www.php.net). The Downloads section of that site contains source code for the latest production release versions, as well as for older versions no longer supported (at least as far back as PHP version 3.0, dated June 6, 1998).

I always recommend downloading the latest version of PHP for Apache 2.0, unless for some reason you are aware that there is an incompatibility with the version of Apache you are using. PHP works largely outside the Apache server, and therefore isn't usually too picky about the version of Apache you've chosen. One of the really nice things about Apache is that it is distributed as a single version regardless of whether you are using Apache 2.0 or legacy Apache 1.3. At compile-time, it will cleanly identify the correct version and configure the installation for it.

I extracted my source files (as I normally do) into the /usr/local/src directory on my Linux server:

```
# tar xzf /downloads/php-4.2.1.tar.gz
```

Then moved into the PHP source directory:

```
# cd php-4.2.1
```

On my system, I created a file (build.sh) that contains all the options I used to configure the source for compilation. There are a huge number of configuration options for PHP—too many to list here. To obtain a list of all valid options, run the configure script with just the --help argument. The subset below is minimal, but completely sufficient for everything I do with PHP:

```
# cat build.sh
```

Advanced Configuration

PART 3

```
./configure --with-apxs2=/usr/local/apache2/bin/apxs \
--enable-debug=no \
--enable-safe-mode \
--with-mysql=/usr \
--with-oracle=/oracle/product/9.0.1 \
--with-oci8=/oracle/product/9.0.1 \
--with-exec-dir=/usr/bin \
--with-regex=system \
--with-xml
```

In most cases, the default values provided by PHP are well thought-out and completely adequate. The only options I used that were essential were –apxs2, which enables the use of apxs to compile and install PHP as a DSO module, and --with-mysql, which will compile support for the MySQL relational database into the resulting module, as well as support for Oracle using both the Oracle7 and Oracle8 Call Interfaces. (You must have MySQL and Oracle installed on the same server for this to work. I included the Oracle lines to show how easy it is to build in the functions need to work with any of the many databases that PHP supports. If you do not have Oracle on your system, you must leave the two Oracle lines out, otherwise the PHP compilation will fail when it attempts to link to Oracle's function libraries.)

You may need to enable support for other databases or multiple databases. Without a database behind it, PHP is only half the development system.

All available options to configure are well described in the PHP documentation, but the odds are you will never need to know about or use more than a few. Keep things simple. It's probably *not* worth your time to read the many pages of documentation that cover all the options. If you ever need an additional feature of PHP, you'll be able to easily determine which configure options are used to enable that feature.

The procedure used to build and install PHP is like most others described in this book: run the configure script (either by invoking it as a shell script like the build.sh file I created or manually from the command line). PHP is an extensive system, and the configuration will run for some time, displaying hundreds of lines describing what it does. Following the configuration, run make and then make install to complete the process:

```
# ./build.sh
# make
# make install
```

The make install step places the compiled DSO into a location from which it can be loaded by Apache and then modifies httpd.conf to use the module. This should work properly for you, although my prerelease copy of PHP 4.0 failed to make the correct entries in httpd.conf.

Configuring Apache to Run PHP

Compiling source code and running make install should automatically add the necessary statements to your Apache configuration. Still, you should check to ensure that
your httpd.conf includes these two lines:

```
LoadModule php4_module         modules/libphp4.so

AddType application/x-httpd-php .php
```

By now, you should recognize the LoadModule line as the directive required to load the
PHP module and make it available to Apache. The AddType directive specifies files ending
in .php to be of type x-httpd-php, for which the server knows that PHP is the proper handler. In other words, when a file with this extension is read from disk, Apache gives it to
PHP to be parsed before sending it to the requester.

Optional PHP Configuration Directives

Optional PHP configuration directives can be placed not only in locations where normal
Apache configuration directives are allowed (anywhere in httpd.conf or in .htaccess
files), but also in a special file that must be named php.ini. This file is read only once,
when Apache starts up, and it offers no advantages over placing the PHP directives
directly in httpd.conf. It does, however, offer a convenient location to keep these directives separate from the basic Apache configuration. The path to the php.ini file (if used)
is compiled into Apache by specifying

```
--with-config-file-path=PATH
```

when the configure script is run.

An alternative is to specify this path in an environment variable, PHPRC. PHP comes
with a large file named php.ini-dist that contains all of the PHP configurable parameters, set to their default values. You can rename this file php.ini and have PHP load it
at startup, which will have no effect unless you modify some of the lines in the file. This
will make it very easy, however, to subsequently change PHP's behavior. The file is well
commented, and also serves as a great reference or learning guide to PHP runtime configuration. PHP configuration options are all fairly advanced, and they all have default
values that rarely need to be overridden. Chapter 3 of the PHP Manual discusses these
directives, and is worth a quick review, but most administrators will never need to modify the default values provided by the PHP developers.

Another very useful technique, particularly for those learning PHP, is to use the AddType
directive to define a filename extension to be associated with a new MIME content type
that PHP adds:

```
AddType application/x-httpd-php-source .phps
```

**Advanced
Configuration**

PART 3

This takes advantage of an ingenious feature for debugging HTML pages with embedded PHP commands. When a file ending in .phps is loaded, it is displayed in a Web browser with the PHP code (instead of being executed) highlighted in color to separate it from the surrounding HTML. To use this feature, you can take regular PHP source files, with the extension .php or .php4, and copy them to a file with the extension .phps. When requested from Apache with this filename, the page rendered in the browser will not execute PHP commands embedded in the documents, but will display them using colors to make them stand out. For simple HTML applications, seeing this source code is very instructional; for large applications where there's a lot of PHP in a page, it can be a tremendous debugging aid.

Some PHP Examples

To test your PHP installation to make sure that everything is working, create a simple file like the one shown in Listing 8.11. Make sure the script is accessible from the Web (in Apache's DocumentRoot, for example) and has a .php extension (or .php3 if you are using PHP 3.0). Accessing this page from a browser, you should see something like Figure 8.4.

In the most recent versions of PHP, a mode of operation called Safe Mode is enabled in the default configuration. In Safe Mode, PHP scripts can only access disk files that are owned by the same user as the script itself. This mode of operation is most useful on servers that run PHP on behalf of many script owners (as in the case of an ISP that supports PHP scripting for its clients). This level of restriction on PHP scripts is not necessary on servers that are not shared among many Web developers working separately, and most Apache administrators will want to disable Safe Mode. This can be easily done by copying the php.ini.dist file that is created with PHP when it is compiled to /usr/local/lib/php.ini, where it will be read by PHP upon startup. Within this file, look for the following line, and make sure that it sets safe_mode to Off:

```
safe_mode = Off
```

Listing 8.11 The Simplest PHP Example

```
<!-- HelloWorld.php -->
<html>
<body>
<? echo "Hello World -- PHP works!" ?>
</body>
</html>
```

The HelloWorld example is the simplest of all PHP scripts, useful for no more than testing the server. The script in Listing 8.12 is equally simple but does far more. This PHP script calls a built-in PHP function called phpinfo() and displays the output of that function. Figure 8.5 shows the resulting screen, which contains a wealth of information about PHP. Note that the exact configuration command used to build PHP is displayed. That's useful, isn't it? Take the time to review the information presented by this script. It's a good idea to save this script somewhere under a more descriptive name for future use, but make it something obscure, or better yet, restrict access to it (as described in Chapter 13) because it contains information that is better kept from public view.

Figure 8.4   The simplest PHP example viewed in a browser

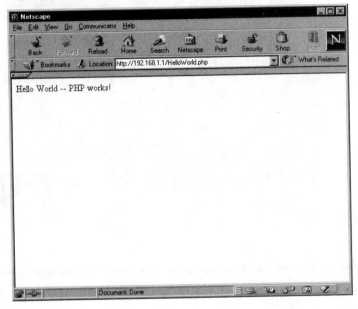

Listing 8.12   PHPinfo.php

```
<!- PHPinfo.php -->
<html>
<body>
<?php
  phpinfo();
?>
</body>
</html>
```

Note one other thing from Listing 8.12. The leading PHP tag is <?php, rather than the shorter <? form expressed in Listing 8.11. Either form can be used, but the short form is in conflict with the Extended Markup Language (XML) specification. If you are not using XML on your server it's safe to use the short form, but its use is discouraged and is best avoided completely. In fact, one of the PHP configuration options is --disable-short-tags, which disables support for this tag. Always use <?php and you should never have a problem.

Figure 8.5 The results of running PHPinfo.php

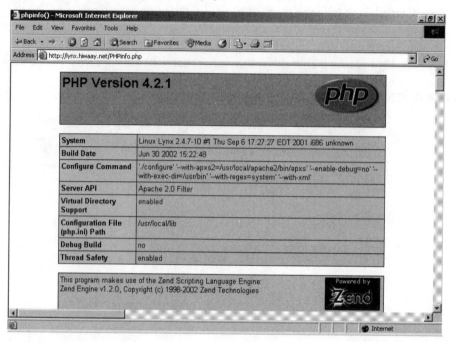

Using Alternative Tags

Besides the <? and <?php tags, there are two other ways to escape PHP from the surrounding HTML, both probably best left alone by Linux Apache programmers. The first is a generic tag for specifying embedded scripts in an HTML document:

```
<script language="php">
   echo "PHP commands go here  ";
</script>
```

The second form is familiar to anyone who has experience using Microsoft Active Server Pages:

```
<%
   echo "Parse this as PHP  ";
%>
```

This last form must be explicitly enabled by including the following configuration directive in Apache's httpd.conf, an .htaccess file, or by a line in the php.ini file:

```
asp_tags on
```

Listing 8.13 is an example of PHP that's a bit more complicated, but quite easy to understand. This example simply tests to see if the user's browser is Microsoft Internet Explorer and displays one line if it is, or reports the browser identification string in its reply if it is not IE. This is useful to the server administrator who wants to customize source documents depending on the browser that the client is using.

Listing 8.13   BrowserTest.php

```
<!-- BrowserTest.php -->
<HTML>
<HEAD>
<TITLE></TITLE>
</HEAD>
<BODY>
<H1>Browser Test PHP Script</H1>
<?php
   if(strstr($_SERVER[HTTP_USER_AGENT], "MSIE")) {
?>
You are using <b>Internet Explorer</b>
<?php
} else {
   echo "Your browser identified as: <b>$HTTP_USER_AGENT</b><p>";
}
?>
</BODY>
</HTML>
```

One of the things that makes PHP so easy to use is that it automatically makes a large number of variables available as standard variables. This includes not only the values of all the HTTP request headers but also any data passed to the server from the browser, such as data entered into Web forms. (The phpinfo() function we used earlier displays all these variables and their values.) In Listing 8.13, I've used another PHP function, strstr(), to compare the environment variable HTTP_USER_AGENT against the string "MSIE". If the string matches, the lines within the if clause (surrounded by the first set of {} braces) are processed. What may not seem completely intuitive, however, is that the line we want displayed in the browser is *not* part of the PHP. It is preceded by the ?> closing tag so that it is not processed as PHP but is rendered as HMTL-formatted text.

The else clause should be easy enough to understand. It is processed if the user's browser is not identified as Internet Explorer (that is, if the HTTP_USER_AGENT variable does not contain the "MSIE" string). Note, however, that the line to be displayed is contained within <?php   ?> tags. The echo function has to be used to output the information, which contains HTML tags and one variable value that is first interpreted.

Study this example until you understand it thoroughly. It contains the most essential elements of PHP (flow-control, use of functions, variable testing). Test it on your machine and modify it to do other things, or perform tests of other variables.

The last example I'll give introduces PHP's strongest feature: support for databases. Listing 8.14 is the HTML form introduced earlier in this chapter to grab user input in order to query the Zip Codes database. This time, however, the form does not call a CGI script, but calls a PHP file in the <FORM> tag (Listing 8.15), which happens to reside in my DocumentRoot. This means that with PHP, there is a tendency to mix static HTML documents and program code. There is nothing inherently wrong with this; in fact, PHP is intended to facilitate this mixture of coding and display formatting. This tends to fly in the face of traditional CGI programming practice, which would dictate that all pro-gramming code be placed in reserved, protected directories separate from static Web pages. I'll admit, it made me a bit uncomfortable at first, particularly when I realized how powerful PHP is. PHP is not CGI, however, and the PHP parser has been designed to avoid the well-known security vulnerabilities. PHP pages cannot really be made more secure by changing their location on the server (except perhaps from users who have local access to the server). Just try to avoid a false belief that PHP files in a special direc-tory are automatically safer to publish on the Web.

Listing 8.14 PHPForm.html

```
<!-- PHPForm.html -->
<HTML><HEAD><TITLE>Zip Code Database Query Form</TITLE>
</HEAD><BODY><H1>Zip Code MySQL Database Query Form</H1>
<FORM METHOD="POST"
    ACTION="http://Jackal.hiwaay.net/zipcodes.php"
    ENCTYPE="application/x-www-form-urlencoded">
<EM>Enter a 5-digit Zip Code:</EM><BR>
➥<INPUT TYPE="text" NAME="zip"  SIZE=6><P><
INPUT TYPE="reset" VALUE="Clear">
➥<INPUT TYPE="submit" NAME=".submit"
➥ VALUE="Submit Search"></FORM><HR>
<ADDRESS>Charles Aulds</ADDRESS><BR>
<A HREF="/">Home Page</A>
</BODY></HTML>
```

Listing 8.15 zipcodes.php Using MySQL

```
<!-- zipcodes.php -->
<HTML>
<HEAD>
<TITLE>Zip Code</TITLE>
<H1>ZipCODE</H1>
```

```
    </HEAD>
    <BODY>
    <?php
      $db=mysql_connect("localhost", "dbuser", "mypasswd");
      mysql_select_db("zipcodes", $db);
      $result = mysql_query("SELECT * FROM zips WHERE zip = '$zip'");
      if($myrow = mysql_fetch_array($result)) {
        do {
          printf("The US Postal Zip Code <font size=+1><b> $myrow[zip] </b>
            </font> is for:  <font size=+2><b> $myrow[city] , $myrow[state]");
        } while ($myrow = mysql_fetch_array($result));
      }
    ?>
    </body>
    </html>
```

This example uses four PHP directives that are specific to MySQL (mysql_connect, mysql_select_db, mysql_query, and mysql_fetch_array). Using a different relational database, you would replace these with equivalent functions that are specific to that database. This is a bit more awkward than using Perl with the database-independent (DBI) programming interface that does not require program code to be altered when the database on the back-end changes. However, using functions specific to, and optimized for, a single database leads to greater efficiency and processing speed. PHP does support at least one database-independent programmer's interface, Open Database Connectivity (ODBC), which is able to query any ODBC-compliant database. Usually this is a database on a Windows NT or Windows 2000 server that exposes the database interfaces through a data set name (or *DSN*).

PHP includes an alternate function for most PHP-supported databases (in the case of MySQL, the function is mysql_pconnect) that opens a persistent database connection (that is, it doesn't close when the PHP script ends). Instead (just as in mod_perl), subsequent connect calls to the same database that use the username and password are simply passed a handle to the open database connection.

Note that zipcodes.php contains passwords to the MySQL database. It's a good practice to place this information in a separate file that is stored somewhere other than DocumentRoot. For example, you could use the PHP include statement to insert this information when zipcodes.php is loaded, by placing this line after the <?php tag:

```
    include "/usr/local/apache2/conf/dbinfo.php";
```

The contents of the file specified in the include statement should look like this:

```
    <?php
      $username="dbuser";
      $password="mypasswd";
    ?>
```

The PHP tags instruct Apache to parse the contents of this file as PHP when it loads the file. The values of the variables are set and later used in the mysql_connect function. If you do something like this, make certain that the filename has an extension that will cause the file to be parsed by PHP. If you name the script to be included with a special extension, .inc for example, make certain that Apache is configured to process .inc files with PHP.

Listing 8.16, presented without detailed explanation, is the same PHP script modified to use the so-called Oracle8 Call Interface (OCI8) to access an Oracle database (Oracle 9i in my case).

Listing 8.16   zipcodes.php Using Oracle

```
<!-- zipcodes.php -->
<HTML>
<HEAD>
<TITLE>Zip Code</TITLE>
<H1>ZipCODE</H1>
</HEAD>
<BODY>
<?php
  $db = ociplogon("dbuser", "mypasswd");
  mysql_select_db("zipcodes", $db);
  $sql = "SELECT * FROM zips WHERE zip = '$zip'";
  $stmt = ociparse($DB_Connection, $sql);
  ociexecute($stmt);
  while (ocifetchinto($stmt, &$myrow, OCI_ASSOC))
  {
      printf("The US Postal Zip Code <font size=+1><b> $myrow[zip] </b>
        </font> is for:  <font size=+2><b> $myrow[city] , $myrow[state]")
  }
  ocifreestatement($stmt);
?>
</body>
</html>
```

ASP for Apache

Active Server Pages (ASP), or *Active Scripting*, was a Microsoft invention and for many years has been a favorite Web application development environment for Microsoft

Internet Information Server (IIS) for Windows. Currently, the only open-source ASP for Apache on Linux is the Apache::ASP Perl module, which is not too shabby and allows ASP programming (only in PerlScript, of course) on Apache systems. Experienced ASP programmers might want to keep an eye on Apache::ASP; the module author promises to have it ready for Apache 2.0 soon after the release of mod_perl 2.0. Remember that you will be able to code ASP only in Perl using this module.

Most programmers who are adept at using ASP are transitioning from a Microsoft IIS environment, and most of them will have learned to code in VBScript or perhaps JScript. Currently, there are two commercial products available that permit the use of ASP for Apache on Linux and allow coding in these two Microsoft-specific languages. InstantASP is a product from Halcyon Software that enables ASP on any Java servlet–enabled Web server.

The other commercial ASP product on Linux is from a company called Chili!Soft (www.chilisoft.com), which is now part of the Sun Open Net Environment (better known as Sun ONE). Chili!Soft produces Sun ONE Active Server Pages which, though part of the Sun ONE application server with increasingly tighter ties to the Sun ONE Web server that we used to know as iPlanet, is billed as a platform-independent version of ASP that strives to be functionally equivalent to Microsoft ASP. The target market for the product consists of firms that are trying to leverage the skills of programmers already proficient with ASP on Microsoft IIS. One feature of Sun ONE ASP for Linux is particularly interesting. The product contains ports of the Microsoft Active Data Objects (ADO) that allow use of these Microsoft-specific objects to access non-Microsoft-hosted databases. The product also supports access to objects from the Common Object Request Broker Architecture (CORBA) world, although most shops already using that heavily Unix-oriented technology are unlikely to move to a Microsoft technology like ASP.

> **NOTE**   As this is being written, Sun ONE ASP is available only for Windows Apache 2.0 versions, with a Linux version promised in the "next few months."

One last ASP solution deserves mention, particularly for use by sites that are trying to transition completely away from ASP or IIS to PHP4 on Apache. An application called asp2php, written by Michael Kohn (http://asp2php.naken.cc), converts ASP pages written in VBScript into PHP. While the FAQ for the utility admits that it won't convert everything, the program's author offers to assist in converting any VBScript the program won't handle (you don't get that kind of support everyday, even for commercial products). And they have a really nice logo and T-shirt.

Apache/Tomcat

Sun Microsystems (http://java.sun.com) introduced the Java programming language in 1995. At that time, the software that was changing the face of computing wasn't coming from the traditional big players like Sun. Java didn't even have the status of a "killer" user application; it was just a developer's tool. I can't think of less likely beginnings for something that has been as successful as Java. Nonetheless, Java put Microsoft into a frenzy of concerned activity, and there is no better indicator of a product's potential than Microsoft's knee-jerk reaction.

While it is true that Java has fallen far short of the predictions made by most of its staunchest proponents (it certainly hasn't made the Windows PC obsolete), it has managed to secure an unshakable position as a programming environment for Internet-based applications. Initially, Java was used solely to produce *applets*, programs that were downloaded to the client browser and run on the client's computer in a special Java Virtual Machine (JVM), also called a Java Runtime Environment (JRE), which is provided in most modern browser software. This model has largely given way to enterprise application development that leverages brokered objects, transaction processing, and strong database connectivity. The cornerstone of Web-based applications developed in Java is now usually a Web server capable of running *servlets*, which are nothing more than Java programs that run on the server. Sun maintains strong control over the future development of Java by releasing the base Java development tools (like the Java Development Kit, or JDK), the programmer's interface specifications to which Java products adhere, and the Java classes that implement many of the Java APIs.

Although I have no doubt that it will soon give way to "the next great programming paradigm," at the time of writing, Java is being promoted as the foundation of the Web Application Server of Tomorrow, with Sun's ONE initiative setting the standard for that future. Ignoring most of the marketing hype, you'll discover that Web application programming begins with a servlet *container*, which is simply a framework for executing Java code as a Web-based application. That is what Tomcat is and what it does.

In 1998, Sun Microsystems and the Apache Software Foundation formed the Jakarta Project (http://jakarta.apache.org) to complete a combined official reference implementation of the Java Server Pages specification running as a servlet that adhered to the latest Java Servlet API specification. Tomcat is developed in an open and participatory environment and released under the Apache Software License, which is developed and maintained by a group called Jakarta (a subproject of the Apache Software Foundation). Find out about the Jakarta Project, and Tomcat, by visiting jakarta.apache.org.

Be forewarned, though, that much of the documentation for Tomcat is for configuring it as a stand-alone server (listening for HTTP/1.1 connections), and it is perfectly feasible to use Tomcat in that manner, without a conventional Web server like Apache. The discussion of Tomcat in this chapter, however, assumes that you have decided (like most Tomcat administrators will) to use a "real" Web server as a front-end to Tomcat, which runs in the background and services requests that come *only* from the Web server. This discussion assumes that you will be using Tomcat in this manner, and that you've chosen to use the Apache Web Server.

You may well wonder why you would choose to run Tomcat as a back-end servlet container with Apache as a front-end Web server. The primary reason is that Tomcat was not designed, as Apache was, to service large numbers of simultaneous connections from multiple clients. A lot of the work that went into Apache went into making it perform robustly and quickly, under heavy client load. You simply don't want to hammer Tomcat that hard. With the configuration I describe in this chapter, Tomcat waits in the background, servicing connections from only one client, the Apache Web server, and performing only one function, that of a servlet container. Keep in mind, though, that Tomcat does contain conventional Web server capabilities, such as support for virtual hosts, SSL security, and the ability to serve static pages. The discussion that follows assumes you've chosen (I believe, wisely) to ignore these capabilities.

The Architecture of Apache/Tomcat

Although Tomcat can function independently of Apache, it really owes much of its prominence to its close association with Apache (and the affinity of the Jakarta Project developers to the Apache Foundation). You will often see Tomcat referred to as simply "Apache/Tomcat," which refers to Tomcat being used as an extension to Apache and how I describe it in this chapter.

Apache/Tomcat consists of two separate parts, as shown in Figure 8.6. The first part, an Apache module written in C, allows Apache to communicate with Tomcat. In the figure, this is shown as mod_webapp, the module I've chosen to demonstrate. The second part consists of Java code that implements the Java servlet API in a Java Virtual Machine (JVM); this part is Tomcat. The two components communicate using a special protocol understood by Tomcat, called the Warp protocol. Tomcat understands other protocols, including HTTP/1.1, but if you accept my recommendation and use the mod_webapp module, you will be using Warp.

The Apache-side component (mod_webapp) is responsible only for the exchange of information between Apache, and the Java-side component (Tomcat), which has no direct contact with the client, communicates only with mod_webapp using the Warp protocol.

> **NOTE**   To get the most out of this discussion of Tomcat, you need a working familiarity with the Java programming language. This chapter is not a tutorial on Java programming, and in order to present practical examples of the Apache/Tomcat interface, I've had to use many Java techniques and features that may be unfamiliar to newcomers.

Figure 8.6 Apache/Tomcat architecture

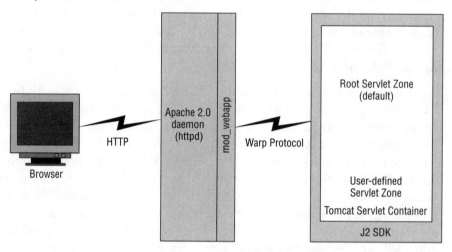

The current version of Tomcat implements Sun's Java Servlet API Specifications 2.3. To install and use Apache with the Tomcat servlet container, you need four essential components, the first of which you should already have:

1. A working Apache server

2. The Java 2 Software Development Kit or J2SDK version 1.4 (J2SDK1.4)

3. The set of Java classes that make up the Jakarta Tomcat servlet runner

4. An Apache module or *connector* (mod_webapp, which is illustrated later in this chapter) that can use one of the supported communication protocols to interface with Tomcat

Some might argue that the Java community has a tendency to overcomplicate the simple, and Java can be quite confusing when one is first exposed to it; but keep in mind that what Tomcat does is simple. It merely enables the use of Java servlets, Java programs that run on your server rather than in the client's browser (as an applet does). A servlet is really just an ordinary Java program with some wrapper classes that allow it to run within the context of a Web server (with its output usually in HTML format).

The capability to run servlets is required for using other technologies that are written as Java servlets. One of the most important of these is Java Server Pages (JSP is discussed later in this chapter). Like any Java program, all Java servlet or JSP applications are compiled into Java classes and require a Java runtime, or *virtual machine (VM)*, to run them, as well as a Java compiler to create executable classes from Java source code. The J2SDK that you'll download (from Sun Microsystems) and install contains these components, which make up the JDK. Although Sun tries to maintain a strong involvement in the development of Java (and thus some control over it), it is no longer the only source for the JDK. While the Sun JDK is probably adequate for your needs, at least initially, you should be aware that other JDKs exist, most of which are ports of the JDK released by Sun for its Solaris operating system and optimized for higher performance on non-Solaris platforms.

Installing the Java 2 SDK

Before installing Apache/Tomcat, you must make sure you have all the Java components you need, which means, essentially, a working Java Development Kit (or JDK). You can obtain this by downloading the Java 2 Software Development Kit (or J2SDK) from the Java 2 platform, Standard Edition (or J2SE). The most current version and older versions are available from Sun at `http://java.sun.com/j2se/downloads.html`. Make sure you get the version that is required by the Tomcat version you intend to install. The examples in this chapter use Tomcat 4.0.4, which works best with the 1.4 version of Sun's J2SDK. Sun supplies this as an RPM that can be used by any Linux system that can install from RPM packages. This RPM contains nothing (like startup scripts) that are specific to the Red Hat distribution.

The RPM is distributed in a somewhat unusual manner; it must be extracted (by your command shell) from a shell script before it can be passed to the `rpm` program. This shell script has the extension `.bin`. The file I downloaded to install J2SDK version 1.4.0 was named `j2sdk-1_4_0_01-linux-i586-rpm.bin`. The following steps illustrate the entire process of extracting and installing the RPM:

```
# ls -sl j2sdk-1_4_0_01-linux-i586-rpm.bin
38640 j2sdk-1_4_0_01-linux-i586-rpm.bin
# sh j2sdk-1_4_0_01-linux-i586-rpm.bin
# ls -sl j2*
38956 j2sdk-1_4_0_01-fcs-linux-i386.rpm
38640 j2sdk-1_4_0_01-linux-i586-rpm.bin
# rpm -i j2sdk-1_4_0_01-fcs-linux-i386.rpm
```

It is a good idea at this point to ensure that the system environments of users who need to run Java applications include the JDK `bin` directory in the PATH, CLASSPATH and JAVA_HOME variables. I'll show how to set these variables in Tomcat's startup script, which is unnecessary if the user starting Tomcat already has these environment variables properly set. Note that a text editor is used to set the following lines in the `.bash_profile` file in a user's home directory:

```
$ grep java /root/.bash_profile
PATH=$PATH:$HOME/bin:/usr/java/j2sdk1.4.0_01/bin
CLASSPATH=/usr/java/j2sdk1.4.0_01
JAVA_HOME=/usr/java/j2sdk1.4.0_01
export PATH CLASSPATH JAVA_HOME
```

Note the last line, which *exports* these variables to the user's environment. This line is required to ensure that the variables last for the user's entire login session; without this line, the variables will vanish as soon as the .bash_profile script completes. After modifying the user's profile, you should log in (or log in again) as that user, and type **java** to make sure that the JDK is installed and accessible:

```
$ java -version
java version "1.4.0_01"
.Java(TM) 2 Runtime Environment, Standard Edition (build 1.4.0_01-b03)
Java HotSpot(TM) Client VM (build 1.4.0_01-b03, mixed mode)
```

Installing Tomcat

For most Apache add-ons, I recommend compiling from source whenever possible, but not for Apache/Tomcat. I don't recommend this for two reasons. First, you can't simply use the standard make utility; you must use a build tool called Ant. Ant is also a product of the Jakarta Group, and is described as "a Java-based build tool. In theory it is kind of like make without make's wrinkles and with the full portability of pure Java code." To be kind, Ant has a little way to go yet before it is as widely used and understood as other installation and distribution tools.

Second, the binaries for Tomcat come complete with the following Java class packages. If you compile Tomcat from source, you will need to download each of these separately and install them. A standard installation of Tomcat 4 makes all of the following APIs available for use by Web applications (by placing their Java Archives, or jar files, in common/lib or lib):

- Java API for XML Processing, or JAXP (xalan.jar)
- Java Activation Framework (activation.jar)
- Java Secure Sockets Extension (JSSE)
- JDBC 2.0 Optional Package (jdbc2_0-stdext.jar)
- Java Naming and Directory Interface (JNDI) 1.2 base API classes (jndi.jar)
- Java Transaction APIs (jta-spec1_0_1)
- JavaMail 1.2 (mail.jar)
- Servlet 2.3 and JSP 1.2 APIs (servlet.jar)
- Tyrex XA-compatible data source from tyrex.exolab.org (tyrex-0.9.7.0.jar)
- Xerces 1.4.3 XML Parser (xerces.jar)

I recommend always installing Tomcat from a binary distribution, rather than going through the hassle of compiling it from source. Red Hat users will probably want to skip to the next section and install Tomcat from the RPM for Red Hat Linux, which contains scripts to start the server automatically (at system bootup) and to run it under a nonprivileged account for security.

Installing Tomcat from the binary file is as simple as an installation could possibly be. All you have to do is download the binary file and extract it into the directory that will become home to the Tomcat application. Release versions of Tomcat 4.0 (as binary, RPM, or source) are available at http://jakarta.apache.org/builds/jakarta-tomcat-4.0/release. To install Tomcat version 4.0.4, I downloaded the binary file, and extracted it into the /usr/local directory on my Linux server (an arbitrary location of my choosing):

```
# cd /usr/local
# tar xvf /downloads/jakarta-tomcat-4.0.4.tar.gz
# ls jakarta-tomcat-4.0.4/
bin                         RELEASE-NOTES-4.0-B3.txt
classes                     RELEASE-NOTES-4.0-B4.txt
common                      RELEASE-NOTES-4.0-B5.txt
conf                        RELEASE-NOTES-4.0-B6.txt
lib                         RELEASE-NOTES-4.0-B7.txt
LICENSE                     RELEASE-NOTES-4.0-RC1.txt
logs                        RELEASE-NOTES-4.0-RC2.txt
README.txt                  RELEASE-NOTES-4.0.txt
RELEASE-NOTES-4.0.1-B1.txt  RELEASE-PLAN-4.0.1.txt
RELEASE-NOTES-4.0.1.txt     RELEASE-PLAN-4.0.txt
RELEASE-NOTES-4.0.2-B1.txt  RUNNING.txt
RELEASE-NOTES-4.0.2-B2.txt  server
RELEASE-NOTES-4.0.2.txt     temp
RELEASE-NOTES-4.0.4.txt     webapps
RELEASE-NOTES-4.0-B1.txt    work
RELEASE-NOTES-4.0-B2.txt
```

The directory into which you extract the Tomcat files contains a subdirectory named bin, which contains a shell script to start Tomcat (startup.sh) and another to stop it (shutdown.sh). These are extremely easy to use, but some configuration is required before they can be used.

Basically, the Tomcat scripts need to be able to locate the Java files you installed with the J2SDK, and also know where to look for the Java class files that implement Tomcat (they don't make guesses about these locations). Although you can set these locations by modifying the Tomcat startup and shutdown scripts, the better way is to set variables in the environment of the user who will start Tomcat. You'll want to make sure that the profile of that user includes a path to the J2SDK bin directory in the PATH variable, and the location of the J2SDK directory should be in JAVA_HOME. Also, the value of CATALINA_HOME should point to your newly created Tomcat directory (CATALINA is the name by which Tomcat seems to know itself). The following lines are taken directly from the `.bash_profile` of the user who starts Tomcat. This should be any user who does not have root privileges on your server. Note the last line, which ensures that the value of these variables is exported to the user's environment; this line is required.

```
PATH=$PATH:$HOME/bin:/usr/java/j2sdk1.4.0_01/bin
CLASSPATH=/usr/java/j2sdk1.4.0_01
JAVA_HOME=/usr/java/j2sdk1.4.0_01
CATALINA_HOME=/usr/local/jakarta-tomcat-4.0.4
export PATH CLASSPATH JAVA_HOME CATALINA_HOME
```

If everything is properly configured, starting Tomcat is as simple as invoking the `startup.sh` script:

```
$ /usr/local/jakarta-tomcat-4.0.4/bin/startup.sh
Using CATALINA_BASE:    /usr/local/jakarta-tomcat-4.0.4
Using CATALINA_HOME:    /usr/local/jakarta-tomcat-4.0.4
Using CATALINA_TMPDIR:  /usr/local/jakarta-tomcat-4.0.4/temp
Using JAVA_HOME:        /usr/java/j2sdk1.4.0_01
```

Note that the values of the directories that the script reports are taken from the environment of the user invoking the script. If any of these is incorrect, you should fix it in the `.bash_profile` file in the user's home directory, and have the user log out and then log back in, or use the following special shell shortcut to execute the profile in the context of the current shell, typing it exactly as shown (separating the first `.` from the rest of the command line by white space):

```
# . $HOME/.bash_profile
```

Then shut down Tomcat with the `shutdown.sh` script. What could be simpler?

```
$ /usr/local/jakarta-tomcat-4.0.4/bin/shutdown.sh
Using CATALINA_BASE:    /usr/local/jakarta-tomcat-4.0.4
Using CATALINA_HOME:    /usr/local/jakarta-tomcat-4.0.4
Using CATALINA_TMPDIR:  /usr/local/jakarta-tomcat-4.0.4/temp
Using JAVA_HOME:        /usr/java/j2sdk1.4.0_01
```

Installing Tomcat from the RPM

Red Hat Linux users should get the Tomcat RPM (also available at `http://jakarta.apache.org/builds/jakarta-tomcat-4.0/release`). This not only simplifies the installation process, but it also sets up Tomcat as a Red Hat system service that starts Tomcat automatically under a specially-created account named `tomcat4`.

Note that the Tomcat RPM that contains the word "`full`" in its name now includes all the pieces you need to run Apache, and the other RPMs on which it depends should be downloaded from the same location and installed separately. This version includes support for regular expressions (jakarta-regexp), XML parsing (Xerces), JavaMail, JNDI, and full support for the Java servlet API.

Make sure you also get the Webapps RPM that contains fully working Java servlet and JSP applications you can use to test your setup. It also includes some really good working examples of using the various Java classes that provide support for things like sending e-mail, maintaining client sessions, accessing database through JDBC, and many other goodies.

```
# ls -s /downloads/tomcat*
2396 /downloads/tomcat4-4.0.4-full.2jpp.noarch.rpm
1396 /downloads/tomcat4-webapps-4.0.4-full.2jpp.noarch.rpm
```

Installing these RPMs is as simple as:

```
# rpm -i /downloads/tomcat4-4.0.4-full.2jpp.noarch.rpm
Don't forget to setup vars in /etc/tomcat4/tomcat4.conf to
adapt the RPM to your configuration.
Also edit/create /etc/java.conf to define your default JDK

For security purposes, tomcat4 service is installed
but not activated by default.
use your service installer for such purposes
ie: ntsysv
# rpm -i /downloads/tomcat4-webapps-4.0.4-full.2jpp.noarch.rpm
```

This version includes full support for JavaMail, JNDI, and Tyrex datasources. The RPM includes activation.jar, javamail.jar, JDBC2EXT, Tyrex 0.9.7.0, jndi.jar for JDK 1.2, jakarta-regexp 1.2, servlet 2.3 APIs, and Xerces 1.44.

Unlike the binary distribution, the RPM version of Tomcat uses configuration (.conf) files to store the information Tomcat needs to start. Be sure to set the value of JAVA_HOME in the file /etc/tomcat4/tomcat4.conf to point to your J2SDK; I added this line:

```
JAVA_HOME="/usr/java/j2sdk1.4.0_01"
```

Use the Red Hat chkconfig command to enable the service to start when the system enters runlevel 3 (multiuser mode), 4, or 5 (X-Windows):

```
# chkconfig --list tomcat4
tomcat4          0:off   1:off   2:off   3:off   4:off   5:off   6:off
# chkconfig --level 345 tomcat4 on
# chkconfig --list tomcat4
tomcat4          0:off   1:off   2:off   3:on    4:on    5:on    6:off
```

As with any Red Hat service, you can also start and stop Tomcat manually, using the service command:

```
# service tomcat4 start
[ OK ] tomcat4: [ OK ]
# service tomcat4 stop
Stopping tomcat4:
Using CATALINA_BASE:    /var/tomcat4
Using CATALINA_HOME:    /var/tomcat4
Using CATALINA_TMPDIR:  /var/tomcat4/temp
Using JAVA_HOME:        /usr/java/j2sdk1.4.0
```

Running Your First Web Applications in Tomcat

At this point, you should have installed Tomcat using either the binary distribution or the Red Hat RPM, and started it as described in one of the two previous sections. If Tomcat starts, you should be able to test it, and access the excellent (if simple) Java servlets and Java Server Pages that are installed with it.

If Tomcat is running, connecting to your server on port 8080 (the default TCP port used by Tomcat when running in stand-alone mode) should result in the screen shown in Figure 8.7.

Figure 8.7   Tomcat is running!

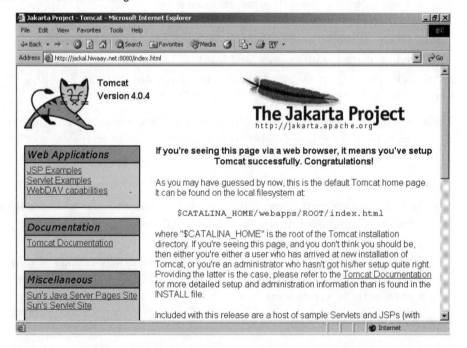

Tomcat is configured through a single file in XML format, `server.xml`, which you'll find in the `conf` directory under the Tomcat home. It is this file that you'll modify to enable new Web applications (which Tomcat knows as *Contexts*) and configure connectors on which Tomcat listens for requests.

I personally find the XML format cumbersome to use, especially in contrast to the Apache `httpd.conf` file we've been using, but, hey, I wasn't consulted by the Tomcat designers. Once you understand the pieces, it's not hard to tailor, but when you see it for the first time, it might seem confusing. The sample `server.xml` provided with Tomcat is sufficient, with no changes, to start it up, and provides support for a number of connectors. These include a stand-alone mode, which listens for HTTP/1.1 connections on TCP port 8080, just like a "real" Web server (make sure your Apache is not already listening on that port, or Tomcat won't start). We'll start Tomcat with the stand-alone mode enabled, and test Tomcat from a Web browser to make sure it's working. Then I recommend disabling this mode of operation if you intend to use Apache with Tomcat (the section titled "Configuring Apache to Use Tomcat" gives the details).

Using a Minimal Tomcat Configuration with Apache

The `server.xml` file provided with Tomcat serves as a quite excellent example of a complex Tomcat setup, with multiple connections, a stand-alone server with virtual hosts, and a number of preloaded classes all well documented by extensive commenting. For our purposes, most of the file is redundant.

More than likely, you'll want to set up your own Java servlet applications or JSP pages in a location of your choice, although you can place them under the `webapps` directory, in a directory structure parallel to Tomcat's `examples` directory. The easiest way is to simply create a new Context section in Tomcat's `server.xml` file. I recommend removing all connectors other than the Warp connector (used by `mod_webapp`), but leaving the `examples` Context for testing and fun.

My Apache/Tomcat runs just fine with the minimal setup shown (in its entirety) in Listing 8.17. Note that I've relocated all applications from the default (under Tomcat's home directory) to another location, specified by the `appbase` parameter and absolute path `/home/httpd`. I can create new Web applications simply by creating subdirectories beneath that directory. To use the servlet and JSP examples provided with Tomcat, simply copy the examples directory from the webapps directory under the Tomcat home to your new application directory, which can be accomplished with a line like this:

```
# cp -R /usr/local/jakarta-tomcat-4.0.4/webapps/examples /home/httpd
```

If you've installed Tomcat from the Red Hat RPM, the path will look a bit different:

```
# cp -R /var/tomcat4/webapps/examples /home/httpd
```

Listing 8.17   A Minimal Tomcat Configuration

```
<Server port="8005" shutdown="SHUTDOWN" debug="0">
 <Service name="Tomcat-Apache">
  <Connector
    className="org.apache.catalina.connector.warp.WarpConnector"
    port="8008" minProcessors="5" maxProcessors="75"
    enableLookups="true" appBase="/home/httpd"
    acceptCount="10" debug="0"/>
   <Engine className="org.apache.catalina.connector.warp.WarpEngine"
     name="jackal.hiwaay.net" debug="0">
    <Logger className="org.apache.catalina.logger.FileLogger"
      prefix="apache_log." suffix=".txt"
      timestamp="true"
    </Logger>
    <Realm className="org.apache.catalina.realm.MemoryRealm" />
   </Engine>
  </Service>
 </Server>
```

After restarting Tomcat with this new configuration, Tomcat will look for its applications in /home/httpd. An application referenced with a URL like http://<*servername*>/ javastuff/HelloWorld.jsp can be found as a file named /home/httpd/javastuff/ HelloWorld.jsp, providing you added the following line to your httpd.conf file:

```
WebAppDeploy javastuff conn /javastuff
```

Installing the *mod_webapp* Apache/Tomcat Module

In order for Apache to send requests to Tomcat to be processed, you must have an Apache module that can access Tomcat on one of its connectors. Over the years, a number of such connectors have been created, and proponents of each can give you many reasons why that connector should be preferred over any other. Current versions of Tomcat support five different connectors: Coyote HTTP/1.1, Coyote JK 2, HTTP/1.1, JK, and Webapp.

From my experience, the one most easily used with Apache is the Webapp connector, implemented for Apache as mod_webapp. I'll show you how to install and configure mod_webapp, and recommend that you stick with this connector unless you discover valid reasons to use any of the others.

If at all possible, you should find and use a version of mod_webapp.so (the dynamically loadable Apache module) that someone else has already compiled. I've found that increasingly difficult to do. Be careful: the mod_webapp.so binaries downloadable from jakarta.apache.org are generally compiled for the older 1.3 versions of Apache. If you can find a version of the module that is clearly meant for your versions of Apache and Tomcat, use it; if not, use the following instructions for compiling the modules.

The source code for all the Apache/Tomcat connectors are downloadable in a single file from the Jakarta Project at http://jakarta.apache.org/builds/jakarta-tomcat-connectors. Drill down to the src directory, under the release directory that matches the version of webapp, and download the archive that matches your version of Tomcat. Then extract this archive into a directory from which you'll build it:

```
# cd /usr/local/src
# tar xzf /downloads/jakarta-tomcat-connectors-4.0.4-src.tar.gz
# ls jakarta-tomcat-connectors-4.0.4-src
build.xml  common     coyote   gump.xml  http11  jk
KEYS       lib        LICENSE  scandoc   util    webapp
```

You must be in the webapp subdirectory to follow these instructions:

```
# cd jakarta-tomcat-connectors-4.0.4-src/webapp
```

Make sure that the shell scripts in the support directory are executable:

```
# chmod +x support/*.sh
```

Then invoke the buildconf.sh script in the support directory. This is the one part of the install that is likely to cause many users problems. If the version of the Autoconf automatic configuration utility on your system is not reasonably current, the script will fail with a warning. In that case, you should go to a site like rpmfind.net and look for a more recent RPM (and use the rpm -F command to "freshen" your Autoconf, because it's a good idea to have the latest version of Autoconf available anyway). If you aren't successful in locating an RPM, and you are the adventurous sort, go to http://www.gnu.org and download the source (the compilation of which I'll leave up to you).

If your version of Autoconf is current enough, you'll see lines like the following:

```
# ./support/buildconf.sh
--- Checking "autoconf" version
autoconf version 2.53 detected.

--- Creating WebApp "configure" script
Creating configure ...

--- All done
```

At this point, Autoconf will have created a configure script that you can use with the --with-apxs option to create all the makefiles necessary to accomplish the actual compile:

```
# ./configure --with-apxs=/usr/local/apache2/bin/apxs
```

Run make to create the module:

```
# make
```

At this point, most of us are used to typing `make install` to complete the installation process of most applications. The authors of this particular application, however, for reasons unknown, didn't provide that capability, so running `make install` will fail with the following error:

```
# make install
make: *** No rule to make target `install'.  Stop.
```

Not to worry. If the module was compiled okay, you can find it in one of the subdirectories and manually move it over to the Apache modules directory:

```
# find . -name mod_webapp.so
./apache-2.0/mod_webapp.so
./build/mod_webapp.so
# cp ./apache-2.0/.libs/modwebapp.so /usr/local/apache2/modules/
```

Configuring Apache to Use Tomcat

Tomcat support, using the Webapp connector, is enabled in Apache by including the following line in the Apache `httpd.conf` file (place it with the `LoadModule` lines already there):

```
LoadModule webapp_module modules/mod_webapp.so
```

Restarting Apache with this module enables three new directives for the control of `mod_webapp`; I'll explain the purpose of each, but for now, just add the following two lines to the very bottom of your `httpd.conf` file. You may later decide to get fancy and include them in virtual host containers, configure them for SSL access, or protect access to them in some manner; for now they are open to all users:

```
WebAppConnection conn warp jackal.hiwaay.net:8008
WebAppDeploy examples conn /examples
```

The `WebAppConnection` directive instructs `mod_webapp` how to connect to Apache and what communication protocol it should use to communicate with the Tomcat connnector. The first argument names the connection; in this case, the connection to port 8008 on the system `jackal.hiwaay.net` will be named "conn," and the connector on the other end understands the Warp protocol (the protocol used by the `webapp` Tomcat connector). Note that these parameters must match those used in Tomcat's `server.xml` configuration for the Context `webapp`.

It is here that you may want to configure Apache to connect to other Tomcat servers, most often because you need to support different versions of the Java servlet API or because you need to distribute your servlet processing load between more than one server.

The `WebAppDeploy` directive is used to translate a request URL into a Tomcat request. Here, requests received (by Apache) with a URL that contains `/example` are sent through the previously defined conn connection, and are interpreted in Context `examples`, which is in the webapps folder under the Jakarta Tomcat directory. The contents of this directory should exist if you installed Tomcat from the binary distribution, or if you installed the optional Webapps RPM during an RPM installation of Tomcat.

Let's test it. If you've added the LoadModule directive and the two mod_webapp directives, you should be able to restart Apache and then connect to your server with either of the following URLs (substituting your server's hostname or IP address for <servername>) to start testing:

```
http://<servername>/examples/servlets/index.html
http://<servername>/examples/jsp/index.html
```

The third and final directive that is provided by mod_webapp is WebAppInfo, which enables a useful status page displaying all of the Tomcat application contexts that are available to Apache. Include this directive, with a partial URL of your choosing that will allow you to display this page; the following line, added to my httpd.conf file, allows me to display the mod_webapp status page in Figure 8.8. Note, however, that in the Address bar I must append a / character to the URL to make it work (probably not what the author intended).

```
WebAppInfo /webapp-info
```

Figure 8.8   mod_webapp status page

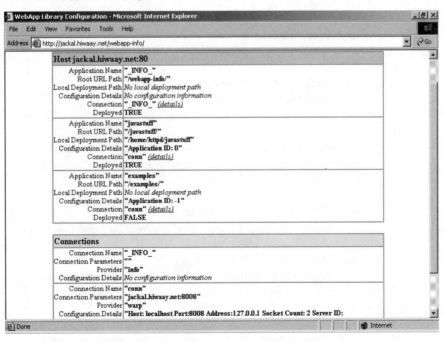

A Database Query Using Apache Tomcat

Again, I'll use my Zip Codes database to illustrate a very simple Java servlet running in the Tomcat engine. Listing 8.18 is the servlet I wrote to accept Web form input and query the MySQL database. Incidentally, to compile the file ZipCodes.java, it was necessary for me to point to the servlet classes (in a file servlet.jar), explicitly with the -classpath argument to the Java compiler:

```
javac -classpath "/usr/local/jakarta-tomcat-4.0.4
➥ /common/lib/servlet.jar" ZipCodes.java
```

Listing 8.18   A Java Servlet to Query the Zip Codes Database

```java
// /usr/local/apache/servlets/ZipCodes.java
import java.io.*;
import java.sql.*;
import javax.servlet.*;
import javax.servlet.http.*;

public class ZipCodes extends HttpServlet
{
    public void service (HttpServletRequest request,
➥      HttpServletResponse response)
        throws ServletException, IOException
    {
        super.service(request, response);
    }

    public void doGet (HttpServletRequest request,
        HttpServletResponse response)
        throws ServletException, IOException
    {
        // compose a SQL query string using the user input zip
      String query = "select * from zips where zip=\"" +
        request.getParameter("zip") +"\"";
        try {
          // Load the MySQL JDBC driver
          Class.forName("org.gjt.mm.mysql.Driver").newInstance();
        }
        catch (Exception Err) {
            System.err.println("Unable to load JDBC driver.");
            Err.printStackTrace();
        }
        try {
            // make a connection to the zipcodes MySQL database
```

```
// on localhost, using root account and password
Connection Conn = DriverManager.getConnection
  ("jdbc:mysql://localhost/
  zipcodes?user=root&password=notmypasswd");
try {
    // create a statement object which will send
    // the SQL query
    Statement Stmt = Conn.createStatement();
    // send the query, store the results in a
    // ResultSet object
    ResultSet RS = Stmt.executeQuery (query);

    String title = "Example Database Servlet";

    // set content type and other response header
    // fields first
    response.setContentType("text/html");

    // then write the data of the response
    PrintWriter out = response.getWriter();

    out.println("<HTML><HEAD><TITLE>");
    out.println(title);
    out.println("</TITLE></HEAD><BODY bgcolor=\"#FFFFFF\">");
    out.println("<H1>" + title + "</H1>");
    out.println("<H2>US ZipCode Lookup<br></h2>");

    while (RS.next()) {
    out.println("The US Postal Service Zip Code <font size=+1><b>"
    + RS.getString(3) + "</b></font> is for <font size=+2><b>" +
    RS.getString(1) + ", " + RS.getString(2) + "</b></font><br>");
    }
    out.println("</BODY></HTML>");
    out.close();
    RS.close();
    Stmt.close();
    Conn.close();
}
catch (SQLException Err) {
    System.out.println("SQLException: " +
        Err.getMessage() );
    System.out.println("SQLState:    " +
        Err.getSQLState() );
    System.out.println("VendorError:  " +
```

```
                            Err.getErrorCode() );
            }
        }
        catch (SQLException Err) {
            System.out.println("SQLException: " +
                Err.getMessage() );
            System.out.println("SQLState:     " +
                Err.getSQLState() );
            System.out.println("VendorError:  " +
                Err.getErrorCode() );
        }
    } //doGet()
} //Class
```

I installed the servlet into /usr/local/apache2/servlets, which is defined as the repository for the root servlet zone and mapped to the /servlets request URL.

Because Java can be daunting to a beginner, I tried to keep this example as simple as possible. To be honest, there's more code here than I would have liked in such a simple example. The try, throw, and catch error-trapping commands are necessary; removing them causes errors, as the Java objects appear to expect error handling. I'm sure they dramatically increase the reliability of my code, but this enforces a lot of discipline on the programmer (you can be the judge of whether that's good or bad).

The import statements make support classes available. Generally you import classes whenever you intend to use methods from those classes. The javax.servlet.* and javax.servlet.http.* classes are necessary to run Java servlets and are provided as part of the Java Servlet Development Kit (the JSDK). The java.sql.* classes implement the database calls through JDBC as explained in "Installing JDBC."

I defined a new ZipCodes class that is derived from (or *extends*) the HttpServlet class. By declaring it so, I essentially created a new class that inherited all the methods and properties of a servlet. My class, therefore, implements the standard methods of the Java servlet API. The service method is called by the servlet engine when a new user request needs to be handled. If that request is an HTTP GET request, the standard method doGet is called. Any servlet you write should implement at least one of the following methods: doGet, doPost, doPut or doDelete, each of which corresponds to a type of HTTP request.

The doGet method is passed two objects by the servlet engine: the request object and the response object. These correspond, respectively, to the HTTP client request being processed and the response to that client. Every servlet operates on these two objects. To summarize briefly, the input from the user is retrieved by calling the getParameter method of the request object, passing it the name of the field in the Web form. This value is used to construct a SQL query, which is passed through a set of methods and objects supplied in classes provided as part of the JDBC driver for MySQL (org.gjt.mm.mysql.Driver). These methods and objects are standard in the Java Database Connectivity (JDBC) database-independent programmer's interface, and will work with little or no modification for other databases. You will, of course, need to supply the proper JDBC driver classes for each database you use. See the sidebar "Installing JDBC" for instructions on downloading and installing the JDBC drivers for MySQL.

Installing JDBC

Java Database Connectivity (JDBC) is a programmer's interface for relational database management systems (RDBMS). It provides a consistent set of methods for programming database applications in Java that do not change when the database on the back-end changes. A complete change from Sybase to Oracle, for example, requires only new JDBC drivers to allow most Java database programs to work unaltered. This fits nicely into the trademarked paradigm of Java programming, which has always been to create "Write Once, Run Anywhere" programs. If you're familiar with database programming for Perl, recognize that JDBC functions a lot like the Perl DBI (database independent API) module.

The definitive site for information related to JDBC is maintained by Sun Microsystems at:

```
http://java.sun.com/products/jdbc/
```

In order to write the simple Java examples in this chapter that query the MySQL database on my Linux server, I had to download a JDBC driver for MySQL. You download a different JDBC driver for each RDBMS that you want to manipulate with Java. The Sun site maintains a database of JDBC drivers for different database engines. For my use with MySQL, I downloaded the latest release version of Mark Matthew's highly respected MM MySQL driver directly from his project site at http://mmmysql.sourceforge.net. The archive will be in Java archive format, with an unusual name like mm.mysql-2.0.14-you-must-unjar-me.jar, which contains a little hint on how to install it:

```
# cd /usr/local
# jar x < /downloads/mm.mysql-2.0.14-you-must-unjar-me.jar
# ls
analog-5.24     bin                    include
man             share                  apache2
doc             jakarta-tomcat-4.0.4   META-INF
src             apache2.036            etc
```

Advanced Configuration

Installing JDBC (*continued*)

```
lib               mm.mysql-2.0.14        var
apache2.039       games                  libexec
```

One of the really nice things about JDBC (as with most Java add-ons) is that it is available as a collection of Java classes. In other words, the only thing you have to do to install JDBC is ensure that your Java engine knows where to locate these classes. The JDBC classes come prepackaged as a Java archive (or .jar file), and I recommend using the archive as is. Although you can easily recompile the archive yourself from the .java files containing the source by using the makefile included with the MM MySQL driver, compiling the source yourself won't necessarily lead to optimizations for your hardware.

I extracted MM MySQL to my /usr/local directory, and the *only* thing I had to do to make it work was to include the JDBC classes in my system's JAVA_HOME environment variable. (Tomcat does not examine your setting for CLASSPATH, but it's a good idea to have CLASSPATH and JAVA_HOME set to the same values.) You can do this by editing the .bash_profile file in the home directory of the user starting Tomcat, or you can change the value for all system users by adding a line like the following to /etc/profile, a profile shared by all users.

```
JAVA_HOME=/usr/java/j2sdk1.4.0_01
    :/usr/local/jakarta-tomcat-4.0.4:
    /usr/local/mm.mysql-2.0.14
```

A Simple Java Server Pages Example

Listing 8.19 is a very simple Java Server Pages application that returns HelloWorld in HTML formatting, does a simple mathematical calculation, and sets a variable for later reference. It isn't meant to be useful, but merely illustrates the simplest use of JSP. Figure 8.9 shows the results in a browser.

Listing 8.19   A Very Simple JSP Example

```
<%
// Create a string variable named title and assign
// it a value
//
String title = "Hello, world!";
%>

<!DOCTYPE HTML PUBLIC "-//W3C//DTD HTML 4.0 Transitional//EN">
```

```
<head>
<meta http-equiv="Content-Type" content="text/html; charset=ISO-8859-1">

<!-- The expression tags interpolate script variables into the HTML -->

<title><%= title %></title>
</head>

<body bgcolor=white>
<h1><%= title %></h1>

<!-- JSP can be used to perform mathematical
     computations -->
<h2>2 + 2 = <%= 2 + 2 %></H2>

</body>
```

Figure 8.9 The simple JSP page in a browser

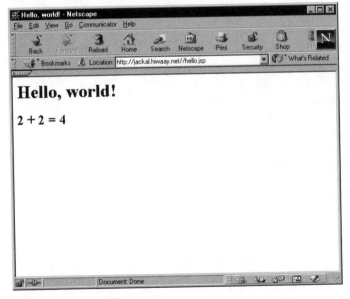

The Database Example in Java Server Pages

Coding my database query application in JSP was easier in some ways than writing it as a Java servlet. For one thing, it wasn't necessary to use the exception handling that was required in the servlet apps (the try and catch blocks). Apparently, JSP takes care of that automatically, though I couldn't find that stated in the documentation. All I know is that my application was a lot shorter in JSP. Listing 8.20 is as simple as I could make it. This JSP page, when called from a Web form and passed a postal code, performs a lookup in the MySQL database. There is no output at all from the Java code embedded in the page; it was far simpler to use HTML to format the output, inserting the values of variables where needed, using a <%= %> JSP tag.

Listing 8.20   A JSP Zip Code Database Query Example

```
<title>JSP Example Using MySQL Query</title>
</head>

<H1><center>Simple JSP Example Using MySQL Query</H1>
<body bgcolor='white'>

<%
// Use the request object to get user input
String zip=request.getParameter("zip");
%>

<h1>Zip entered was: <%= zip %> </h1>

<%
// It's really a cinch to use JDBC with JS
Class.forName("org.gjt.mm.mysql.Driver").newInstance();
Connection Conn = DriverManager.getConnection(
    "jdbc:mysql://localhost/zipcodes?user=root&password=
    notmypassword");
String query = "select * from zips where zip=\"" +
    request.getParameter("zip") + "\"";
Statement Stmt = Conn.createStatement();
ResultSet RS = Stmt.executeQuery (query);
%>

<h1><%= zip %> is the zip code for
<%= RS.getString(1) %>, <%= RS.getString(2) %>!
```

While this is much easier than writing a complete servlet for a simple application, when things get more complex, JSP can become more mangling than mingling of HTML and Java code. In complex applications, some portion of the Java code is usually separated from the HTML and imported as a Java bean. JSP supports a special <jsp:useBean tag to create an object that instantiates an external class. The properties and methods of the object are then called from the code fragments embedded in the Java server page.

An excellent guide to the advanced use of JSP can be found on Sun's Java technology site at http://java.sun.com/products/jsp/docs.html.

Resin

Make no mistake about it; installing Apache support for Java servlets or Java Server Pages can be a very confusing, often frustrating, task. In the first edition of this book, I mentioned Tomcat (an immature product at that time) only in passing, and strongly urged readers who wanted to run Java applications on their Apache servers to move to a servlet container called Resin, from Caucho Technology (www.caucho.com). Despite the tremendous amount of work that's gone into Tomcat in the ensuing 2.5 years, and the wide industry support for that "standard," I stand behind that recommendation. Resin is by far the more robust servlet container, and, hands down, the better performer.

Like the newer Tomcat product, Resin is a single solution that implements both servlets and JSP with one installation. It is freely available under an open-source license from Caucho Technology. While it may not have the large number of collaborating developers that some other Java application servers do, Resin seems to be very well supported by a very active user community, which is an invaluable asset to users of open-source software, and a very visible proponent on its development team named Scott Ferguson. Resin is billed as "the fastest servlet and JSP engine available," and independent benchmark tests seem to support the claim. Resin has far better support for "hot deployment" than Tomcat (that is, the ability to add new components, such as JavaBeans, servlets, and JSP files to a running server without having to stop and restart the server). Resin also has features like automatic servlet recompilation and load balancing support that aren't (in my opinion) fully mature in Tomcat.

Resin remains quite up-to-date with the ever-changing Java specifications from Sun Microsystems. The version I installed, while still a beta release (Resin 1.1b6) was quite current, supporting the Java Server Pages 1.2 specification and the Java Servlet 2.3 specification; these are the very latest releases of these specs that are suitable for production software. This is right on par with the Tomcat "reference implementation" from Sun and the Apache Jakarta Project.

Resin on Apache (like Apache/Tomcat) consists of two separate parts: an Apache module (written in C) and a servlet runner (written in Java, of course). Figure 8.10 depicts this configuration. A user request identified in Resin's configuration as a candidate for processing by the servlet runner is sent to that engine through a standard TCP socket connection. The servlet runner (or *srun*) is a separate program that runs Java servlets (including the servlet that parses Java Server Pages) in a standard Java virtual machine (VM) or runtime environment. Notice the similarity to the Apache/Tomcat architecture shown earlier, in Figure 8.6.

Installing Resin

While Resin is designed primarily for improving the performance of Java applications, it is also extremely simple to install, configure, understand, and upgrade.

Figure 8.10   The architecture of Resin on Apache

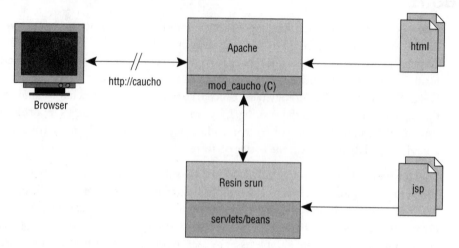

The first step is, of course, to download the latest version from www.caucho.com. I downloaded the Resin Server version 2.1 as resin-2.1.3.tar.gz and extracted the contents into /usr/local:

```
# cd /usr/local
# tar xzf /downloads/resin-2.1.3.tar.gz
# cd resin-2.1.3
```

> **NOTE**   While Resin is available under an open-source license for free downloading and use, the authors of the product reserve a copyright on their work and encourage all "funded projects" to purchase a license for the product. While a license is not required to use Resin, the developers believe that anyone making money using Resin should be fair in giving something back to ensure the future development and quality of the product. The current license still requires only a one-time fee of $500 per production server. My opinion? It's well worth it.

Make sure that JAVA_HOME is set and, if not, set it correctly. The package was a cinch to install with three commands, each issued in the Resin build directory (in my case, /usr/local/resin-2.1.3):

```
# cd /usr/local/resin-2.1.3
# echo $JAVA_HOME
/usr/java/j2sdk1.4.0
# ./configure --with-apxs=/usr/local/apache2/bin/apxs
# make
# make install
```

The Resin install is smart enough, in most cases, to make the necessary changes to your Apache server's `httpd.conf` file to load the `mod_caucho` module and point to the `resin.conf` configuration file in your Resin home directory. On my system, the following lines were added at the very bottom of my `httpd.conf` file (though I moved the `LoadModule` line so that it could be with others of its kind):

```
LoadModule caucho_module modules/mod_caucho.so
<IfModule mod_caucho.c>
  CauchoConfigFile /usr/local/resin-2.1.2/conf/resin.conf
  <Location /caucho-status>
   SetHandler caucho-status
  </Location>
</IfModule>
```

If any of these lines are missing, enter them exactly as shown, changing only the paths to the files if yours differ. This stanza of the Apache configuration file tells `mod_caucho` where to look for its configuration info, and also adds a special handler for the Resin status page (Figure 8.11). It is recommended that the `<Location /caucho-status>` section be removed on production servers, but for testing, it can be quite useful.

Before starting the servlet runner, it is necessary to modify the file `resin.conf` in the Resin home directory. For a simple JSP and Java servlet, I used the following:

```
<caucho.com>
<http-server>
  <http host='localhost' port='6802'/>
    app-dir='/home/httpd/html'>
      <servlet-mapping url-pattern='/servlets/*'
          servlet-name='invoker'/>
      <servlet-mapping url-pattern='*.jsp'
          servlet-name='com.caucho.jsp.JspServlet'/>
      <servlet-mapping url-pattern='*.xtp'
          servlet-name='com.caucho.jsp.XtpServlet'/>
  </http-server>
</caucho.com>
```

This file specifies that `mod_caucho.so` will contact the servlet runner using TCP port 6802 on the local system (`localhost`). Three servlet mappings will be used. The first mapping is for Java servlets identified by their class names. The default configuration file included with Resin looks for servlet classes in `RESIN_HOME/doc/WEB-INF/classes`. This behavior is defined by the Java Servlet 2.3 specification but can be modified with the `<classpath>` directive. The following lines could be added immediately following the `<httpd-server>` directive:

```
<classpath id='/home/httpd/html/classes'
```

Advanced Configuration

PART 3

```
                   source='/home/caulds/servletsources'>
       </classpath>
```

Figure 8.11   The Resin status page

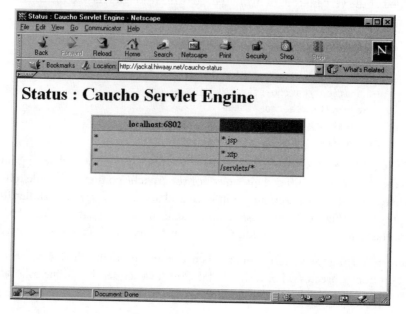

These lines redefine the location where Resin will look for supporting Java classes and servlet classes. The optional `source` keyword defines a directory where the Java source files for classes reside. If you supply `source`, Resin will automatically compile the classes for you whenever they change (or from the source if the class file doesn't already exist).

I modified my Resin configuration file to use my Apache `DocumentRoot` as the `app-dir`, and retained `/servlets/*` as the URL mapping. What this means is that if a request comes in for a resource:

```
/servlets/someclass
```

The Resin servlet runner will attempt to run:

```
/home/httpd/html/WEB-INF/classes/someclass.class
```

Resin uses either virtual hosts or Webapps to separate workspaces. Each workspace is identified by a different relative path to the `app-dir`, and each workspace contains a directory `WEB-INF` that, in turn, contains subdirectories such as `classes`. Although Caucho developers are still debating the usefulness of a hard-coded dependence on the `WEB-INF` directory, it is necessary to provide this directory in your main `app-dir` or `web-app` directories.

My second mapping defines `com.caucho.jsp.JspServlet` as the servlet that the servlet runner should use to preprocess or parse all files designated as Java Server Pages (by the `.jsp` extension). The last servlet mapping defines `com.caucho.jsp.XtpServlet` as the servlet to use for processing XML templates and can be omitted if you aren't using these. If you attempt to load a Java Server Page at this point, you will probably encounter the error indicating that the Resin servlet runner has not been started. The servlet container must be invoked manually (usually while logged on as `root`) or from Linux system startup scripts for automatic start at system boot.

When all of these changes have been made, you should be able to start the servlet runner manually (very much like starting Apache) using the following command:

```
# /usr/local/resin-2.1.2/bin/httpd.sh
Resin 2.1.3 (built Tue Jul 23 11:04:02 PDT 2002)
Copyright(c) 1998-2002 Caucho Technology.  All rights reserved.

Starting Resin on Sun, 28 Jul 2002 16:05:00 -0500 (CDT)
[2002-07-28 16:05:48.815] initializing application
➥ http://localhost:8080/
[2002-07-28 16:05:48.816] initializing application
➥ http://localhost:8080/java_tut
[2002-07-28 16:05:48.816] initializing application
➥ http://localhost:8080/examples/basic
[2002-07-28 16:05:48.817] initializing application
➥ http://localhost:8080/examples/tags
[2002-07-28 16:05:48.817] initializing application
➥ http://localhost:8080/examples/tictactoe
[2002-07-28 16:05:48.818] initializing application
➥ http://localhost:8080/examples/navigation
[2002-07-28 16:05:48.824] initializing application
➥ http://localhost:8080/examples/xsl
[2002-07-28 16:05:48.824] initializing application
➥ http://localhost:8080/examples/templates
[2002-07-28 16:05:48.825] initializing application
➥ http://localhost:8080/examples/login
http listening to *:8080
srun listening to 127.0.0.1:6802
```

If you run `httpd` (as shown in the listing) without arguments, it will run in the foreground and you'll see the status lines shown, which may be useful for debugging. In practice, though, you'll want to start the server in the background (using the `start` argument). The purpose of the following lines should be pretty clear, as they are very much like Apache's `apachectl` script:

```
# ./httpd.sh start
```

Advanced Configuration

PART 3

```
Resin httpd start at Sun Jul 28 16:09:36 CDT 2002
# ./httpd.sh restart
# ./httpd.sh stop
Stopping httpd
```

You will probably want to configure Linux to start Resin automatically when the system is started.

In Sum

Most comparisons of Web-server programming methodologies give performance considerations special emphasis, citing benchmark tests that prove one technique is unquestionably better than another. These benchmarks usually measure the ability of a Web server to generate and serve HTML pages to large numbers of concurrently connected clients. Raw performance can be a significant consideration when choosing a programming technique for a heavily-trafficked site, particularly if that Web server is furnishing data through a very large pipe (and this means more than a single T1 circuit, which has a bandwidth slightly larger than 1.5Mbps).

The truth is, though, most Web sites receive no more than a few thousand hits in a single day. Other considerations can be far more significant than raw performance in choosing a Web-programming tool.

The earliest method of interfacing external programs to the Apache Web server is the Common Gateway Interface, once the de facto standard for programming Web applications. CGI remains a viable technique for Apache programming.

The biggest drawback of traditional CGI (poor performance) has been largely eliminated, first by the use of FastCGI (implemented in the Apache module mod_fastcgi) and more recently by mod_perl. Both of these Apache add-ons eliminate the overhead of starting a new Perl interpreter process each time a CGI script is called. The mod_perl module goes a step farther and uses a caching mechanism to ensure that scripts, once compiled into Perl pseudo-code, are available for subsequent invocation without requiring recompilation.

This chapter showed how to modify Apache to use these programming techniques, and it illustrated the use of each with a simple, yet useful, application that queries a relational database using user-entered data as a search key.

When choosing a Web-programming tool or technique, don't make your decision based on a set of numbers in a table of benchmark scores. Instead, leverage capabilities and talents that you already have in-house. Always remember, too, that Web-programming languages are not mutually exclusive; you don't have to choose one technique to the exclusion of all others.

9

Aliasing and Redirection

Apache simplifies the process of locating resources by assuming that the request URL always represents a path to a resource relative to the server's Document-Root. In most cases, this assumption is correct, and a URL maps directly to a filesystem path, which provides for extremely fast resource retrieval, but this is not always the case. In some situations, the requested URL may be stored in a nonstandard location. It may be under `DocumentRoot`, but not in a location that can be deduced from the URL; it may be in a completely different location on the system; or it may be on an entirely different server! It is in these cases where an Apache administrator uses the techniques discussed in this chapter to resolve a URL to a resource when that URL does not clearly map to the path and filename of the requested resource.

Aliasing is the process of mapping a client's request URL to a nonstandard location and automatically retrieving the resource from this location. Aliasing happens on the server, invisible to the client browser and without any participation from the client browser.

Redirection is the process of responding to a browser request with a new location URL and then requesting that the browser redirect its request to the new URL. A redirection response also includes an HTTP response code indicating the reason for the redirection. An entire class of HTTP status codes is dedicated to request redirection. As you'll see later in the chapter, however, only seven codes are currently used.

Aliasing and redirection are related tasks with a fundamental difference. Aliasing is performed solely at the server; redirection requires the client browser to issue a second request for the desired resource at a new location. Aliasing is completely transparent to the requesting user. When a URL is aliased, the requester receives the requested document as usual, but does not know that its location on the server was identified by means of an alias. In redirection, however, the client (that is, the browser) receives a new URL, which will be reflected in the browser's address bar. The user can then bookmark this new URL for future use, and it is usually cached by the browser or any proxy server acting on the client's behalf.

The most common redirection is almost certainly that which occurs when a request for a directory does not include a trailing slash. In Chapter 4, I discussed how mod_dir automatically issues a redirect for such requests, which are technically incorrect. For example, on my server, if I use the URL http://jackal.hiwaay.net/Docs, where Docs is a subdirectory of my document root, I don't immediately receive a listing of that directory (or a default index page). Instead, the server sends the following redirect response:

```
HTTP/1.1 301 Moved Permanently
Date: Mon, 17 Jul 2000 17:29:45 GMT
Server: Apache/1.3.12 (Unix) mod_perl/1.24 PHP/4.0.1pl2
Location: http://jackal.hiwaay.net/Docs/
Content-Type: text/html; charset=iso-8859-1
```

Upon receiving this response, my browser automatically reissues the request to the URL specified in the Location: header, http://jackal.hiwaay.net/Docs/. The second request is automatic and performed without my knowledge, unless I happen to notice that a trailing slash is added to the URL I typed in my browser's address bar. The time required to send the second request for the resource is minimal, but it is unnecessary. Whenever possible, ensure that hyperlinks embedded in documents you serve contain properly formatted URLs for directories (which always include the trailing slash character).

The Apache distribution provides two modules to handle URL aliasing and redirection, mod_alias and mod_rewrite. Although mod_alias is probably the more important and more generally useful of the two modules, more than half of the chapter discusses mod_rewrite. The amount of space I devote to mod_rewrite is a measure of its complexity, size, and flexibility, not necessarily its usefulness. In fact, for the sake of efficiency, you should use mod_alias whenever possible, and use mod_rewrite only when you need the extra flexibility it offers.

The *mod_alias* Module

The mod_alias module handles the basic functions of both request redirection and URL aliasing. For most installations, this module (which is compiled in the basic server by default) has more than enough flexibility and power to handle all of the administrator's needs. You should strive to understand all of the directives provided by mod_alias and use them whenever they are sufficient to meet the requirement at hand. Reserve the more powerful (but complex) mod_rewrite for those situations that mod_alias can't handle.

Aliasing with *mod_alias*

The mod_alias module is probably used most often for aliasing URLs, and nearly every Apache server includes at least one directive from the module in its configuration. mod_alias provides the following directives for the purpose of aliasing URLs:

Alias

AliasMatch

ScriptAlias

ScriptAliasMatch

The *Alias* Directive

The Alias directive allows a nonstandard mapping of a URL to a destination filename. In other words, using Alias you can store documents in locations that aren't under the server's defined DocumentRoot. The directive specifies a full pathname to a directory or file for a single URL.

An excellent example is an alias to a directory containing icons or images. Here is one I use on my machine:

```
Alias /icons "/usr/local/apache2/icons"
```

I also use an Alias directive to make my Apache documentation accessible to a browser, even though I'm storing those files outside my defined DocumentRoot:

```
Alias /ApacheDocs "/usr/local/apache2/htdocs"
```

Note that if you include a trailing slash on the URL, the server will require a trailing slash in requests. If I had used trailing slashes in the above, for example, a request for //jackal.hiwaay.net/ApacheDocs would fail; the server would only respond to http://jackal.hiwaay.net/ApacheDocs/.

The *AliasMatch* Directive

The AliasMatch directive is functionally equivalent to Alias, but extends it to use standard regular expressions (including back-references, which are discussed in more detail later in this chapter) to match against the request URL. For example, I might use this directive to express both of the examples given for the Alias directive as:

```
AliasMatch ^/icons/(.*) "/usr/local/apache2/icons/$1"
AliasMatch ^/ApacheDocs(.*) "/usr/local/apache2/htdocs$1"
```

The *ScriptAlias* Directive

The ScriptAlias directive works like the Alias directive to handle nonstandard URL mapping, with one important additional feature. It also identifies the target directory as containing CGI scripts (it sets the MIME type of all files in the identified directory to application/x-httpd-cgi).

Here's an example:

```
ScriptAlias /cgi-bin/ "/usr/local/apache2/cgi-bin/"
```

With this directive in effect, a request to //jackal.hiwaay.net/cgi-bin/test.txt would attempt to run the file /usr/local/apache2/cgi-bin/test.txt as a CGI script. But if that file is (as its extension indicates) simply a text file, it is unlikely that it can be run as a shell script (though it is possible, depending on the contents of the file). If the shell is unable to parse and run the contents of this file as a script, the result will be a "Premature end of script" error in the Apache error log, and Apache will send an HTTP error code 500 (Internal Server Error) to the requester, along with a default error page indicating that the server administrator should be contacted.

The *ScriptAliasMatch* Directive

The ScriptAliasMatch directive is almost equivalent to ScriptAlias, but permits the use of a standard regular expression for the URL match. The example given for ScriptAlias can be rewritten with ScriptAliasMatch like this:

```
ScriptAliasMatch ^/cgi-bin/(.*) "/usr/local/apache2/cgi-bin/$1"
```

Redirection with *mod_alias*

mod_alias also provides basic redirection, which should be used whenever a simple one-to-one match can be defined between the request URL and a destination to which you want to redirect the requester. The mod_alias module supplies the following directives for the purpose of redirecting requests:

    Redirect

    RedirectMatch

    RedirectTemp

    RedirectPermanent

The *Redirect* Directive

Redirect is the simplest Apache directive for redirection. It has the following syntax:

```
Redirect [status] oldURLprefix newURLprefix
```

The directive performs a match against a URL prefix by checking to see if the request begins with the prefix specified by *oldURLprefix*. If the request begins with this prefix, it is mapped into a new URL that begins with a new prefix, identified in the syntax as *newURLprefix*. The URL with the new prefix is returned to the client with a redirect message indicating that the location of the resource has changed and that it can now be reached at the new URL. It is the client's responsibility to fetch the resource with a second request using the new URL. Web browsers generally do this without notice to the user, and almost invisibly. The Redirect directive can be given an optional status code, which specifies the HTTP response code sent to the client. (Table 9.1 lists the HTTP response codes for request redirection.) If no status is given, the HTTP response code sent is 302. The status code can be any valid numeric code or one of the following four values, which return the HTTP status codes shown:

permanent   Status code 301: Moved Permanently

temp   Status code 302: Found

seeother   Status code 303: See Other (indicates that the resource has been replaced rather than simply relocated)

gone   Status code 410: Gone (indicates that the resource no longer exists; used without the *newURLprefix* field)

If a numeric status code between 300 and 399 is given, the *newURLprefix* field must be given; otherwise this field must be omitted.

Table 9.1   HTTP Request Redirection Codes

Status Code	Meaning	Explanation
300	Multiple Choices	Used when there are multiple variations of the requested resource. The server provides alternate URLs for the variations available and requests that the client select one and send a separate request for it.
301	Moved Permanently	The requested resource has been permanently assigned a new URL. The client is asked to redirect the request to this URL and is informed that it should use the new URL for all future requests.

Table 9.1   HTTP Request Redirection Codes (*continued*)

Status Code	Meaning	Explanation
302	Found	The requested resource is temporarily unavailable at the request URL the client used, but that address is still valid and the client should continue to use it. The client is asked to redirect the current request but keep the old URL on file (or in cache).
303	See Other	Works like status code 307 to redirect the request temporarily. The difference between status codes 307 and 303 is subtle; code 303 should *not* be interpreted as an "alternate location for the requested resource." It is used when the usual and accepted response to the initial request is a redirection to an alternate URL (usually generated programmatically).
304	Not Modified	Used when the client has issued a conditional request (for example, using the If-Modified-Since: header) and the requested document has not been modified. In such a case, the server responds with status code 304 to inform the client to use the document it already has. Technically, the server is not responding with a redirect request.
305	Use Proxy	This code informs the client that the original request URL was good, but the resource must be obtained through a proxy server. The Location: field of the HTTP response message contains the URL of the proxy server (rather than an alternate URL for the resource).
306	(Unused)	HTTP status code 306 is obsolete and should not be used with the current version of the protocol.

Table 9.1   HTTP Request Redirection Codes (*continued*)

Status Code	Meaning	Explanation
307	Temporary Redirect	Works just like status code 303. The requested resource is temporarily unavailable at the request URL the client used, but that address is still valid and the client should continue to use it. The client is asked to redirect the current request, but keep the old URL on file (or in cache). Status code 307 is usually used with newer browsers that behave according to the HTTP/1.1 specification. Older browsers that understand only status code 303 often violate the specification, which states that the client browser is not allowed to change the method of a redirected request.

For example, with the following directive in effect:

```
Redirect permanent /download  http://dlserver.hiwaay.com/archives
```

a request for `http://jackal.hiwaay.net/download/test.zip` will be redirected to `http://dlserver.hiwaay.com/archives/test.zip`. The request URL is tested only to see if it begins with the specified prefix; whatever follows that prefix is written onto the end of the new URL prefix.

> **NOTE**   Redirect directives always take precedence over Alias or ScriptAlias directives, regardless of their relative ordering in the configuration file.

Matching Regular Expressions: *RedirectMatch*

The RedirectMatch directive is functionally equivalent to Redirect, but allows the use of standard regular expressions in matching the request URL prefix.

```
RedirectMatch (.*)\.gif$ http://2ndserver.hiwaay.com$1.jpg
```

In this example, the request URI (that portion of the URL that follows the hostname) is compared to see if it ends with the characters .gif. The $ character matches the end of the string. The backslash is necessary to *escape* the following character, a period. In other words, it tells the regular-expression engine to interpret the period literally; that is the character we are looking for here. The previous period, within the parentheses, is regular-expression shorthand meaning "any single character." The portion of the expression within parentheses is read as "any character (.) repeated any number of times (*)". This portion of the URI is used to fill in the back-reference $1 in the new URL portion of the directive. This directive would redirect a request for

```
http://jackal.hiwaay.net/images/uparrow.gif
```
to
```
http://2ndserver.hiwaay.com/images/uparrow.jpg
```

Redirecting to a Temporary Location: *RedirectTemp*

When you've had to move material on your site temporarily, use RedirectTemp, which has the following syntax:

```
RedirectTemp oldURLprefix newURLprefix
```

It sends a Redirect to the client with HTTP status code 302 (Found) and is exactly equivalent to Redirect temp.

```
RedirectTemp /mystuff /home/caulds/
```

This directive performs a very simple redirect, redirecting all requests using URLs ending in /mystuff to /home/caulds. There is no advantage to using RedirectTemp over Redirect (which has the default behavior of sending status code 302) to indicate a temporary redirect. Use RedirectTemp only to make your purpose obvious in the configuration file.

Redirecting Permanently: *RedirectPermanent*

When material on your site has moved permanently, use RedirectPermanent, which has this syntax:

```
RedirectPermanent oldURLprefix newURLprefix
```

This directive sends a Redirect to the client with HTTP status code 301 (Permanently Moved).

An alternate syntax for the RedirectPermanent directive is Redirect permanent. For example, the following two directives have identical effects:

```
RedirectPermanent /mystuff /home/caulds/
Redirect permanent /mystuff /home/caulds/
```

The *mod_rewrite* Module

The Alias directive is often quite adequate for simple URL rewriting and request redirection. For more complicated URL redirection—particularly when URL rewriting is conditional, is based on information contained outside the URL, or involves database or file lookups—there's a far more powerful module called mod_rewrite.

Its author, Ralf S. Engelschall, describes mod_rewrite as a "rule-based rewriting engine." The purpose of the module can be stated quite simply: it is responsible for rewriting incoming URLs using a set of rules and then redirecting the requester to the newly rewritten URL. The power of mod_rewrite lies in the tremendous flexibility that its rules can give Apache administrators in redirecting requests, and it has numerous uses on most Apache servers, although mod_alias is usually sufficient for most request redirection needs.

The module is complex, so I'll begin by describing how it is intended to function. Armed with this understanding of what's going on in the module (and a familiarity with basic regular expressions), you'll be able to study the examples that follow. I will start with the essential mod_rewrite directives and the simplest possible uses for mod_rewrite, and then talk about the optional directives and show examples that use the functionality these directives add. It is important to realize, though, that mod_rewrite is so complex and so flexible that it would be impossible to list all the different ways in which it can be used. The examples in this chapter illustrate only a fraction of the potential power of this module; the real limitation is your imagination.

Try to learn mod_rewrite in pieces. If you understand what's happening in each example I introduce, by the end of this section, you'll know mod_rewrite well enough to decide whether you have a need for it. Even more important than understanding how to set up URL rewriting rules with mod_rewrite is understanding what the module is capable of. Someday you'll encounter a problem or requirement for which mod_rewrite will be the perfect solution.

How *mod_rewrite* Works

As described in Chapter 5, most Apache modules can register internal functions as *callbacks* with the Apache server, so that the server calls these functions at one or more phases of the document request cycle. Mod_rewrite registers nine, but two of the callbacks do most of its work. The first one is in the URL Translation (ap_hook_translate_name) phase, in which the URL is translated to the name of a single file on the server. The other one, in the Fixup (ap_hook_fixups) phase, handles any final processing that may be required before the request is fulfilled.

When an HTTP resource request arrives at the server, the first phase of the request cycle, called the Post-Read-Request (`ap_hook_post_read_request`) is generally used to configure the server to handle the request. It is here, for example, that Apache decides which virtual host will handle the request. The very next phase is URL Translation, and it is here that `mod_rewrite` does its work.

The `mod_rewrite` module can also be used on a per-directory basis, usually by adding `mod_rewrite` directives to `.htaccess` files rather than applying rewriting rules to all incoming URLs. However, Apache processes `.htaccess` files well after the request URL has already been translated into a filename (that's how Apache was able to locate and read the proper `.htaccess` file). In order to perform a second URL translation, `mod_rewrite` performs a bit of magic. The module registers a callback with the server for the Fixup phase of the request cycle, which normally performs only perfunctory duties after all the real work of processing a request has been completed. During this late phase, `mod_rewrite` applies any per-directory rewriting rules. By this time, however, the URL has already been reduced to a single filename, so `mod_rewrite` reconstructs a URL and resubmits it to the server for processing, and the request-processing cycle begins all over again. The process is a lot more involved than that of straight per-server rewriting, and heavy use of per-directory rewriting can significantly decrease server efficiency in processing requests. There's no general rule of thumb regarding per-directory rewrites, but they should be used only when necessary and their impact always kept in mind. You should therefore attempt to reduce the number of URLs that are processed using per-directory rewriting.

Setting Up *mod_rewrite*

Mod_rewrite is a standard module provided with the Apache distribution, so it should be available without having to download and install it, as you would a third-party module. To ensure that you can use the module, make sure you specified `--enable-shared-most`, `--enable-shared-all`, or `--enable-rewrite` when running the `configure` script before compiling Apache. Then make sure your `httpd.conf` file includes the following lines (for a DSO module that has been statically linked to the Apache kernel, only the second line is needed to enable it):

```
LoadModule rewrite_module      libexec/mod_rewrite.so
```

If you've implemented virtual hosting (as described in Chapter 6), however, you may have more work to do before `mod_rewrite` is ready to use. The first time I tried to use `mod_rewrite`, I spent hours trying to figure out why it wouldn't work.

I restarted Apache with the original plain-vanilla `httpd.conf`, and `mod_rewrite` worked, writing its actions into the log file I'd defined. Obviously, some change I'd made to `httpd.conf` had broken `mod_rewrite`. I suspected a module I'd added was somehow refusing to let `mod_rewrite` do its job, and I began to take lines out of my `httpd.conf` file, one by one, hoping to find the conflicting module or directive. It wasn't until I began to remove my <VirtualHost> configurations that I realized what was going on. When setting up the virtual hosts, I had taken great pains to ensure that my main Apache server never handled requests. As you saw in Chapter 6, it's generally a good practice to configure one of your virtual hosts as a default for requests that resolve to no other virtual host, in order to prevent your main server from providing request responses. I had done exactly that, and my mod_rewrite ruleset (being applied to the main server) was never given anything to do by Apache.

The problem is that mod_rewrite directives, unlike most configuration directives, are not inherited from the primary server configuration by virtual hosts. To use rewriting rules in virtual host contexts, you must either redefine URL rewriting rules for each virtual host or use the RewriteOptions directive to enable the inheritance of rewriting rules by virtual hosts (see the discussion on this directive later in the chapter).

Whenever mod_alias and mod_rewrite are both installed in Apache and configured to handle the same user request, mod_rewrite will handle that request first, before mod_alias. This is because mod_alias translates URLs to filenames. If mod_rewrite is processed after mod_alias, the URL it expects will have already been translated to a filename that it can't process. You may be wondering why mod_rewrite (which also functions as a URL-to-filename translator) doesn't break mod_alias. Ordinarily it will, but it includes a special pass-through flag that causes mod_rewrite to change Apache's internal representation of the request from a filename to a URL when it has completed its work. This flag is discussed later along with the RewriteRule directive.

Rulesets

The URL rewriting engine of mod_rewrite works on *rulesets* that consist of rewriting rules and their optional conditions. A rewriting rule looks very much like the Redirect directives we saw in the earlier discussion of mod_alias; it consists of a pattern that is matched (using a regular expression match) against the request URL and a substitution that is applied if the URL matches the pattern.

For example, what you already know about mod_alias redirection applies to a simple rewriting rule like the following:

```
RewriteRule /mystuff /home/caulds/
```

Examining a simple rewriting rule like this one, you're probably wondering what advantage mod_rewrite provides over mod_alias. Indeed, for simple request redirection, there are no significant advantages, and that is why I recommend using the simpler mod_alias whenever possible. The advantages of using mod_rewrite only become important when multiple rules—often based on conditional tests—must be applied, and that is the purpose of rulesets.

A simple `mod_rewrite` ruleset might have a single rewriting rule preceded by a conditional test:

```
RewriteCond %{REMOTE_ADDR} ^192\.168\.1\..*
RewriteRule .* /localpages/ [R]
```

The details of how this simple (yet quite useful) example works will become apparent as you read the descriptions of the two `mod_rewrite` directives it uses. The purpose of this ruleset is to redirect all requests submitted to my server from local clients (anyone on the subnet 192.168.1.*) to a different set of Web pages. The optional flag [R] that ends the `RewriteRule` directive stands for *Redirect* and indicates that the rule performs the URL substitution and returns the results to the requester as a redirect.

Per-server rulesets are read from `httpd.conf` once when the server is started; per-directory rulesets are read from `.htaccess` files at runtime as the server follows the path to a directory corresponding to the request URL.

Although the order of the rules in a `mod_rewrite` ruleset is very important, their processing is not completely sequential. The rewriting engine starts at the beginning of the defined ruleset and works its way through the rules until it reaches the end. If the URL does not match the pattern specified in a rule, processing of that rule ends, and the rewriting engine proceeds to the next rule in the set. When it finds a rule with a pattern that matches the URL, `mod_rewrite` does not immediately process that rule, but first evaluates any rewriting conditions that apply to the rule. Like a rewriting rule, a condition contains a pattern that is matched against the URL, using regular expression matching with some enhancements added by `mod_rewrite`. The pattern resolves as either True or False, and based on this result, the substitution part of the corresponding rewriting rule is either applied or ignored.

After applying a rewriting rule, the rewriting engine continues processing additional rules in the ruleset—unless that rule has the [L] flag appended (which indicates it is the last rule to be processed). It's generally a good idea to use the [L] flag to step out of the processing loop (much like using the `last` command in a Perl loop or the `break` command in C). There are times, however, when you do wish to apply a rule and continue processing the ruleset. In complex `mod_rewrite` rulesets, often two or more rules must be applied to completely rewrite the URL.

The Essential Rewriting Directives

Only two of the `mod_rewrite` directives are required for the module to work. The first of these, `RewriteEngine`, enables the rewriting engine. The second, `RewriteRule`, is the only directive that must be present in all rewriting rulesets. I'll discuss these directives and then present a very simple but useful example of a ruleset that contains only a single rewriting rule.

Turning the Rewrite Engine On or Off: *RewriteEngine*

The RewriteEngine directive is very simple, but it is essential to mod_rewrite. It enables or disables the URL rewriting engine:

```
RewriteEngine on | off
```

The engine is off by default, and the module does absolutely nothing. To use mod_rewrite, you must have at least one RewriteEngine on directive, either in httpd.conf or in an .htaccess file.

By default, mod_rewrite rewriting configurations are not inherited (see the section on RewriteOptions later in this chapter for how to alter this behavior). This means that virtual hosts do not inherit the rewriting configuration from the primary server as they do most other general server configuration directives, so you normally need a RewriteEngine directive in each virtual host to use mod_rewrite in that context.

Defining the Ruleset: *RewriteRule*

It should come as no surprise that the RewriteRule directive is the most important part of mod_rewrite. Without a RewriteRule directive, no other mod_rewrite directive has any effect. Each RewriteRule directive expresses a single matching rule of the form

```
RewriteRule Pattern Substitution
```

Each rule consists of patterns against which the original URL is matched and actions to be taken if the match is successful. In most cases, the action is a simple replacement of the original URL with a new one that can contain fragments from the original data taken from Apache or the system environment, or the results of lookups from static text files or even databases.

The pattern is a regular expression that is matched to the current URL when the rule is applied. This current URL might not be the original request URL, which may have been altered by preceding RewriteRule directives or an Alias directive. mod_rewrite expands the regular expression matching in the following important ways:

- The regular expression can be negated by preceding it with the logical NOT character (!).

- RewriteRule back-references can be used in the regular expression. These are back-references of the form $N, where N can be an integer value 0 through 9 and is filled with the contents of the Nth set of parentheses in the *Pattern* portion of the rule. For example, in the following RewriteRule, the portion of the URL that matches the expression within the first set of parentheses replaces $1 in the substitution, and the portion matching the second set replaces $2:

```
RewriteRule ^/~(.*)/(.*) /home/$1/$2
```

- RewriteCond back-references can be used in the regular expression. These are back-references of the form %N, where N can be an integer value 0 through 9 and is filled with the contents of the Nth parentheses in the last matched RewriteCond directive. Later in the chapter, when conditional rewriting (using the RewriteCond directive) is discussed, we'll see examples of RewriteRule directives that use back-references for a value obtained from a previous RewriteCond directive.

- Environment variables: The special format %{variable} is filled with the value of variable from Apache's environment. This is particularly useful when previous RewriteRule directives have been used to set arbitrary environment variables. As we'll see in later examples, environment variables play a more important role in conditional rewriting. Occasionally, though, you may wish to use the value of an environment variable for rewriting a URL using a RewriteRule directive.

- Mapping-function calls: These are calls to mappings previously defined with RewriteMap, and take the form ${mapname:key|default}.

All the rewriting rules are applied to the substitution (in the order of definition in the configuration file). The URL is completely replaced by the substitution and the rewriting process goes on until there are no more rules, unless a RewriteRule in the set is explicitly terminated by an [L] flag.

If the substitution consists of the single character - (minus), no substitution is performed and the URL is passed unaltered to the next RewriteRule. This is useful when you want to make multiple matches (using the [C] flag to chain server RewriteRule directives) before you rewrite the URL. Another use for this is to have a RewriteRule that does not rewrite the URL, but instead has a flag that indicates a certain response to send the user, such as the [F] flag, which returns a response with an HTTP 403 (Forbidden) status.

One more note: You can even create URLs in the substitution string containing a query string part. Just use a question mark inside the substitution string to indicate that the following stuff should be reinjected into the QUERY_STRING. When you want to erase an existing query string, end the substitution string with just the question mark. Use the [QSA] flag to force the query string to be appended to QUERY_STRING. The following directive extracts a filename from the request URL and then rewrites the URL to pass this filename to a CGI script (parser.cgi), which will preprocess the file before it is served to the requester:

```
RewriteRule ^(/.*)$  /cgi-bin/parser.cgi?file=$1
```

If the rewritten URL is expressed as a relative URL, it goes back to the server engine for processing. However, if the rule precedes the rewritten URL with http:// (which makes the new URL a URI), the rewritten URL is returned to the client as an external redirect even if the [R] flag is not used.

> **NOTE**   When you begin a substitution field with the prefix http://thishost [:thisport] (in other words, if you point to the local server by server name and port), mod_rewrite automatically strips this prefix. This auto-reduction on implicit external redirect URLs is a useful and important feature when you use a RewriteMap to generate the hostname part. The result of this, though, is that an unconditional external redirect to your own server will not work with the prefix http://thishost. To achieve such a self-redirect, you must use the [R] flag (see below) to force an external redirect.

Additionally, you can set special flags for Substitution by appending [*flags*] as the third argument to the RewriteRule directive. *flags* is a comma-separated list of the following flags:

R|redirect [=*code*]   Treats the rewritten URL as a redirect. The default HTTP status code of 302 (Found) is placed on the response. You can define another response code in the range 300–400 by appending =*code* to the [R] flag, where *code* can be the number or one of the three symbolic names: temp (default), permanent, or seeother.

F|forbidden   The client is immediately sent an HTTP response with status 403 (Forbidden).

G|gone   The client is immediately sent an HTTP response with status 410 (Gone).

P|proxy   Forces the rewritten URL to be processed internally by the proxy module, mod_proxy, which must be present for this to work. (Chapter 12 discusses mod_proxy.) This flag also causes mod_rewrite processing to cease at once, and implies an [L] flag.

L|last   Indicates that mod_rewrite processing should cease with this ruleset. Note that this flag is effective only if the pattern matches the URL. If the match fails, rewriting processing proceeds immediately with the next RewriteRule directive in the current ruleset.

N|next   Starts the rewriting process over, with the first RewriteRule directive in the current ruleset. The rewriting process begins with the rewritten URL from the last RewriteRule directive.

C|chain   Chains the current rule with the next rule. If any rule in a set of chained rules fails to match, all following rules in the chain are ignored.

T|type=*MIME-type*   Forces the target file of the rewritten URL to be of a speci-
fied MIME type. This is often used to simulate the ScriptAlias directive, which
forces all files inside a target directory to have the MIME-type application/
x-httpd-cgi.

NS|nosubreq   Causes the current rule to be skipped if the current request is an
internal subrequest. Subrequests from CGI scripts sometimes cause problems,
so it is often desirable to use this flag when rewritten URLs target CGI scripts
that make requests of the server.

NC|nocase   Forces the pattern match against the URL to be case insensitive.

QSA|qsappend   If the URL being rewritten is a query string, and the rewritten
URL is also a query string (that is, begins with a question mark) this flag forces
the rewriting engine to append the rewritten query string part to the existing
URL instead of replacing it. Use this when you simply want to add more data
to the query string via a rewriting rule.

S|skip=*num*   Forces the rewriting engine to skip the next num rules if the pat-
tern matches the URL in the current rule.

E|env=*var:value*   Sets an environment variable if the pattern matches the URL
in the current rule. The value can contain both RewriteRule and RewriteCond
back-references ($N and %N, respectively). This flag is used in a similar way to the
SetEnvIf directive. It is often used to set access control conditions. You can use
the flag more than once in a single RewriteRule directive to set more than one
environment variable.

PT|passthrough   Forces the rewriting engine to set the URI field of the internal
request_rec structure to the value of the filename field. Since mod_rewrite translates URLs to filenames, the rewritten URL is known internally to the server as a
filename. This flag does not change the output of a RewriteRule directive but
internally designates it as a URI, so that it can, in turn, be processed by other
URI-to-filename translators, such as the Alias, ScriptAlias, and Redirect directives from mod_alias. Failure to use this flag will prevent these directives from
being able to process mod_rewrite output.

A Simple Redirection Example

Here's what may be the simplest (and possibly most useful) example of how a RewriteRule
might be used. This example illustrates all of the critical elements that must be understood
to use the RewriteRule directive, so be sure you understand how it works before reading
further in this chapter. It begins with an example of a URL rewriting rule that I actually use
on my server. This example is quite simple and could just as easily be implemented using the
Redirect directive in mod_alias. The purpose of the following rewriting rule is to rewrite

requests for a non-existent file environ.html to a CGI script that generates the HTML output. I did this primarily to disguise the fact that a CGI script is actually being used.

```
# mod_rewrite stuff
#
RewriteEngine on
RewriteRule    ^/environ\.html$  /environ.cgi [L]
```

Placed in the general server configuration section of my httpd.conf, this ruleset first turns on the rewriting engine (you only need to do this once in the general server context). The RewriteRule then matches against any URL that requests environ.html from my server and rewrites the URL to /environ.cgi. The [L] flag says "let this be the last rule." If this rule is processed (that is, if the match to environ.html is successful), the rewriting engine stops processing this ruleset and ignores any RewriteRule directives following this one.

TIP   One of the best ways to understand how mod_rewrite works is to practice with it. Try entering a simple rule like the one in this example in your Apache httpd.conf and restart the server. Modify the filenames used in the example, to substitute one HTML file for another, for instance. The remaining examples in this chapter will be much easier to understand if you practice with them; so I've tried to keep them simple enough that they can be implemented, with only minor changes, by the administrator of any working Apache server with mod_rewrite enabled.

Changing the rule above to include the [R], as in the following line, changes the RewriteRule to a forced redirect:

```
RewriteRule    ^/environ\.html$  /environ.cgi [L,R]
```

The effect is that the browser will now redirect its request to /environ.cgi, and that URL will display in the Location field of the browser where, before, the user only saw environ.html. Note that the request must now be submitted twice (by the client browser) before it is fulfilled; note also that you are no longer disguising the fact that a script is being accessed, instead of an HTML page, which is probably what you intend.

In addition to the forced or explicit redirect I just demonstrated, redirection can also occur implicitly, and that's what will happen if the RewriteRule is modified to this:

```
RewriteRule    ^/environ\.html$  http://192.168.1.1/environ.cgi [L]
```

Note that the [R] is missing, but the inclusion of http:// will always cause an implicit external redirect unless the server name in the rewritten URL matches the ServerName defined for the local server. That's why my rewriting rule used the IP address of the server rather than the hostname. Had I used its hostname, the redirect would have been handled as an internal redirect. The use of `http://` in the rewritten URL is also the best way to handle redirects to other servers.

There's something else that can be learned from this example. When I use a relative URL to rewrite the request URL to /environ.cgi, this URL will be processed as relative to DocumentRoot, as in this example:

```
RewriteRule    ^/environ\.html$  /cgi-bin/environ.cgi [L,PT]
```

Note that this will not, as I expected, act like a new external request ending in /cgi-bin/environ.cgi. Instead, it will be interpreted as an internal redirect, and Apache will attempt to serve a file, environ.cgi, in a cgi-bin directory beneath DocumentRoot. For this to work, you must enable CGI processing in that directory, something I do *not* recommend for production Apache servers. In fact, I generally prefer to keep my /cgi-bin directory completely separate from the entire DocumentRoot. If you need to rewrite the URL to /cgi-bin/environ.cgi (which is mapped by a ScriptAlias directive to another part of the filesystem), you must use the pass-through [PT] flag so that mod-alias will be able to process the rewritten URL.

The result of using the pass-through flag is that the rewritten request, which is normally identified by the server as a path and filename, is now marked internally as a URL for subsequent processing by modules with registered handlers for URL translation (like mod_alias). It will then be processed by any other URL translation modules in the server configuration. Thus, /cgi-bin/environ.cgi is no longer a relative path and filename but is now a URL, and mod_alias translates that URL into a path, using a ScriptAlias directive, like the one I have defined for my server:

```
ScriptAlias /cgi-bin/ "/home/httpd/cgi-bin/"
```

Conditional Rewriting: The *RewriteCond* Directive

RewriteRule directives can be preceded with one or more RewriteCond directives, each of which defines a single rule condition that evaluates to True or False to determine whether the rule will be applied. Before any RewriteRule is applied, the rewriting engine evaluates all preceding conditions. The RewriteRule is applied only if all the RewriteCond directives immediately preceding it evaluate to True. Unless multiple RewriteCond conditions are joined using an [OR] flag and evaluated as a single rule, a RewriteRule will be ignored if any condition preceding it fails. RewriteCond has the following syntax:

```
RewriteCond MatchString Pattern
```

The *MatchString* Argument

The MatchString is a plain-text string, which can also contain the following constructs that are expanded before comparing the string to the pattern:

RewriteRule back-references   These are back-references of the form $N, where N can be an integer value 0 through 9 and is filled with the contents of the Nth set of parentheses in the *Pattern* portion of the RewriteRule that follows this and all other RewriteCond directives grouped with this one.

RewriteCond back-references   These are back-references of the form %N, where N can be an integer value 0 through 9 and is filled with the contents of the Nth set of parentheses in the last matched RewriteCond directive.

Server variables   These are variables of the form %{*VARIABLE_NAME*} where *VARIABLE_NAME* is one of the following:

HTTP headers: HTTP_USER_AGENT, HTTP_REFERER, HTTP_COOKIE, HTTP_FORWARDED, HTTP_HOST, HTTP_PROXY_CONNECTION, HTTP_ACCEPT

Connection and request: REMOTE_ADDR, REMOTE_HOST, REMOTE_USER, REMOTE_IDENT, REQUEST_METHOD, SCRIPT_FILENAME, PATH_INFO, QUERY_STRING, AUTH_TYPE

Server internals: DOCUMENT_ROOT, SERVER_ADMIN, SERVER_NAME, SERVER_ADDR, SERVER_PORT, SERVER_PROTOCOL, SERVER_SOFTWARE

System values: TIME_YEAR, TIME_MON, TIME_DAY, TIME_HOUR, TIME_MIN, TIME_SEC, TIME_WDAY, TIME

Special variables: API_VERSION, SCRIPT_URI, SCRIPT_URL, REQUEST_URI, REQUEST_FILENAME, IS_SUBREQ

Environment variables   The special format %{ENV:*variable*} is filled with the value of *variable* from Apache's environment. This is particularly useful when previous RewriteRule directives have been used to set arbitrary environment variables.

HTTP headers   The special format %{HTTP:*header*} is filled with the value of *header* from the HTTP request being evaluated.

Look-aheads   The special format %{LA-U:*variable*} is filled with the value of *variable* that will normally be set later in the request cycle based on the URL. For example, if you wanted to condition your rewriting on the value of REMOTE_USER in a per-server context (that is, using directives in httpd.conf), you must use a look-ahead, because mod_rewrite does its work before the authorization phases set the variable. When the rewriting occurs in a per-directory context (from an .htaccess file), it occurs in the Fixup phase of the cycle and after the authorization phases.

Another form of the look-ahead uses the format %{LA-F:*variable*}, which is filled with the value of *variable* based on the filename, rather than the URL. This form is rarely needed.

The *Pattern* Argument

The *Pattern* in a RewriteCond directive is a regular expression that is compared to the directive's *MatchString*. If it matches, the entire RewriteCond directive evaluates to True. If it fails to match, the directive evaluates to False. This regular expression has been extended by mod_rewrite in the following ways:

- You can prefix the *Pattern* with a ! character to specify a non-matching pattern.
- Instead of a regular expression match, you can use one of the following comparisons to match the *MatchString* and *Pattern*. Each comparison evaluates to True or False.

  <*Pattern*   Treats the *Pattern* as a plain string and compares it lexically (using alphanumeric and other characters) to *MatchString*. Evaluates to True if *MatchString* is lexically less than *Pattern*.

  >*Pattern*   Treats the *Pattern* as a plain string and compares it lexically to *MatchString*. True if *MatchString* is lexically greater than *Pattern*.

  =*Pattern*   Treats the *Pattern* as a plain string and compares it lexically to *MatchString*. Evaluates to True if *MatchString* is lexically equal to *Pattern*. If the *Pattern* is just " " (two quotation marks), this compares *MatchString* to the null string. Use this to determine if a particular variable is set.

  -d   Treats *MatchString* as a pathname, and tests whether it exists and is a directory.

  -f   Treats *MatchString* as a pathname, and tests whether it exists and is a regular file.

  -s   Treats *MatchString* as a pathname, and tests whether it exists and is a file with size greater than zero.

  -l   Treats *MatchString* as a pathname, and tests whether it exists and is a symbolic link.

  -F   Treats *MatchString* as a pathname, and tests whether it exists and is accessible via all of the server's currently configured access controls for that path. This uses an internal subrequest to make the determination, so there is performance degradation with heavy use of this option.

  -U   Treats *MatchString* as a URL and tests whether it is accessible via all the currently configured access controls for that path. This option uses an internal subrequest to determine the check, so there is performance degradation with heavy use.

- Additionally, you can set special flags for *Pattern* by appending [*flags*] as the third argument to the RewriteCond directive. The flags can be either or both of the following (separated by a comma):

  ornext|OR   Combines the current condition and the next condition with a logical OR instead of the implied AND. In other words, if either statement is true, together they both evaluate as True.

  nocase|NC   Disregards character case in comparing the *MatchString* and *Pattern*.

An Example of Conditional Rewriting

To rewrite the default page of a site according to the User-Agent: header of the request, you can use the ruleset shown in Listing 9.1.

Listing 9.1   Ruleset for Conditional Rewriting Based on Client Browser Type

```
# Match strings beginning with Mozilla, followed by
# anything
RewriteCond  %{HTTP_USER_AGENT}  ^Mozilla.*
# Match strings that do NOT contain the string MSIE
RewriteCond  %{HTTP_USER_AGENT}  !^.*MSIE.*
# Rewrite the URL to /nscape.index.html
RewriteRule  ^/$                 /nscape.index.html  [R,L]


# Above rule not applied, match URLs containing MSIE
# anywhere in the string
RewriteCond  %{HTTP_USER_AGENT}  ^.*MSIE.*
# Rewrite the URL to /ie.index.html
RewriteRule  ^/$                 /ie.index.html  [R,L]


# Neither rule above applied, match URLs beginning with
# Lynx, followed by anything
RewriteCond  %{HTTP_USER_AGENT}  ^Lynx.*
# Rewrite the URL to /text.index.html
RewriteRule  ^/$                 /text.index.html  [R,L]


# None of the previous rules applied, rewrite the URL
# to the default /index.html
RewriteRule  ^/$                 /index.html  [R,L]
```

A site visitor who uses the browser Netscape Navigator (which identifies itself as *Mozilla* but does not contain the *MSIE* string) will be served the nscape.index.html page, which is optimized for the Netscape browser. Anyone using Microsoft Internet Explorer (which also identifies itself as *Mozilla*, strangely enough, but contains *MSIE*) will get ie.index.html. A visitor using Lynx, a text-only browser, will reach a text-only page, text.index.html. And finally, if none of the other conditions are met, the user will see the regular index.html. Maybe this is similar to what certain Web sites do so that they appear broken when used with a competitor's browser?

The [R,L] flag that ends each RewriteRule directive indicates that a redirect response with the rewritten URL should be returned to the requesting client and that this should be the last RewriteRule processed in the current ruleset. By default, the response sent to the client will carry a status code of 302 (Found).

An Example of Automatic Page Creation

Listing 9.2 depicts an interesting example of how a static Web page can be automatically created if it does not already exist. The !-s flag at the end of the RewriteCond directive tells mod_rewrite to interpret the match string as a path and filename to be tested to see if the file exists and has a size greater than 0 bytes. The RewriteCond directive tests to see if the requested file exists. If it does, no rewriting occurs and the document is served from the disk file. If the file does not exist (or is zero-length), the request is redirected to the CGI script shown in Listing 9.3. This script creates the requested file and then sends the lines written to this file as a response to the client. Subsequent requests for the file will not result in a redirection to this script, but will be served from the disk file.

What practical use does this have? Suppose there is a page on the server that needs to be updated on a regular basis; for example, it may contain a daily bulletin that is generated from other text files on the server. As administrator, you can schedule a process (using the Linux cron utility) to delete the file automatically at a specified time, perhaps midnight. The first request for this file after it has been deleted will cause the CGI script to run and generate a new file.

Listing 9.2 Ruleset to Create a Page Automatically When Needed

```
# Test REQUEST_FILENAME to ascertain if it exists. The
# ! operator means that this condition evaluates to TRUE
# if the file does not exist, or if it has a length of 0
# bytes
RewriteCond /home/httpd/html%{REQUEST_FILENAME}  !-s
#
# Rewrite the URL to redirect the request to the
# dynindex.cgi CGI script.
RewriteRule dynindex\.html$ /cgi-bin/dynindex.cgi [L]
```

Listing 9.3   Perl Script That Uses the Page-Creation Ruleset

```perl
#!/usr/bin/perl
#
open(OUTFILE, "> /home/httpd/html/dynindex.html");
print OUTFILE <<END;
<HTML>
<HEAD>
<TITLE>Charles Aulds's Home Page</TITLE>
</HEAD>
<body background="IMAGES/ftbckgrd.jpg">
<center>
<h1>This is my home page ...</h1>
<p>
<FORM METHOD = "POST" ACTION = "mailto:caulds\@hiwaay.net">
<INPUT TYPE = "SUBMIT" VALUE="Click here to send me e-mail"></FORM>
</center>
<HR>
<p>
</BODY>
</HTML>
END
close OUTFILE;
system("/bin/chown www.www
    /home/httpd/html/dynindex.html;/bin/chmod 755
    /home/httpd/html/dynindex.html");
print<<END;
Content-type: text/html\n\n
<HTML>
<HEAD>
<TITLE>Charles Aulds's Home Page</TITLE>
</HEAD>
<body background="IMAGES/ftbckgrd.jpg">
<center>
<h1>This is my home page ...</h1>
<p>
<FORM METHOD = "POST" ACTION = "mailto:caulds\@hiwway.net">
<INPUT TYPE = "SUBMIT" VALUE="Click here to send me e-mail"></FORM>
</center>
<HR>
<p>
</BODY>
</HTML>
END
```

An Example of Reusing Conditions

Listing 9.4 illustrates how you can reuse the result of one or more mod_rewrite directives (by setting the value of an environment variable that is referenced in later conditions). This example first uses the SetEnv directive to set the value of an environment variable trusted-host to *no*. Then it uses three RewriteCond directives to test the network address of the requesting client to see if the request came from one of three subnets. The RewriteCond directives are joined by [OR] flags to create one test that will result in a True condition if any one of the directives finds a match. The first RewriteRule directive will be evaluated only if any one of the three conditions is met. The rewriting rule is simple; it makes no actual substitution (denoted by the - character), but uses the [E] flag to set the trustedhost environment variable to *yes*, which indicates the request came from one of the trusted subnets.

The rest of the ruleset consists of two additional rewriting rules, only one of which will be applied to each request, depending on the value of the trustedhost variable. The flowchart in Figure 9.1 illustrates the logic.

Listing 9.4   Reusing the Result of a RewriteCond Directive

```
# Create a new environment variable and set its
# value to "no".  The SetEnv directive requires
# mod_env
SetEnv trustedhost=no

# Test the request URL against two IP addresses
# and one hostname
RewriteCond %{REMOTE_ADDR} ^192\.168\.1\.* [OR]
RewriteCond %{REMOTE_ADDR} ^216\.78\.169\.* [OR]
RewriteCond %{REMOTE_HOST} ^rascal\.hiwaay\.net$
# At least one of the conditions above evaluated
# to true; special RewriteRule does no rewrite
# but [E] flag resets trustedhost to yes
RewriteRule .* - [E=trustedhost=yes]

# trustedhost=no then TRUE, otherwise FALSE
RewriteCond %{ENV:trustedhost} ^no$
# not a trusted host, rewrite URL to standard
# index.html, send redirect to client
RwriteRule .* /index\.html [R]

# trustedhost=no then TRUE, otherwise FALSE
RewriteCond %{ENV:trustedhost} ^yes$
# is a trusted host, rewrite request to special
# /trusted directory, send redirect to client
RewriteRule (.*) /trusted/$1 [R]
```

Figure 9.1   Flowchart for reusing a RewriteCond directive

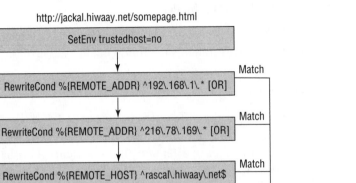

Special Considerations for Per-Directory Rewriting

Anyone planning to use mod_rewrite in a per-directory rather than a per-server context needs to be aware of a few special considerations. First, mod_rewrite uses a somewhat unusual mechanism for security. Whenever RewriteRule directives are included in a per-directory context, the FollowSymLinks option must be enabled for the intended directory. If this option is not enabled for a directory in which an .htaccess file containing mod_rewrite rules resides, the server will log the following error:

```
[Thu Mar 30 09:58:14 2000] [error] [client 192.168.1.3] Options
➥ FollowSymLinks or SymLinksIfOwnerMatch is off which implies that
➥ RewriteRule directive is forbidden: /home/httpd/html
```

In addition, the client request for a resource subject to URL rewriting is rejected with an HTTP request response code of 403 (Forbidden).

To prevent this, make sure that any .htaccess file or <Directory> container that includes mod_rewrite URL rules also contains the following lines:

```
RewriteEngine On
Options +FollowSymLinks
```

Another important consideration is the different behavior of mod_rewrite in per-directory and per-server contexts. In a per-directory context, mod_rewrite strips the per-directory prefix, which is added back after substitution occurs. For that reason, a per-server RewriteRule that contains the pattern ^/docs/.*$ will not match in a per-directory context. Since the directory prefix is stripped from the URL by mod_rewrite in a per-directory context, this pattern would be reduced to ^.*$ in a RewriteRule applied in a per-directory context to the /docs directory (probably in an .htaccess file inside that directory). In other words, whenever you include rewriting directives in an .htaccess file, make sure your MatchString does not include the directory path.

The *RewriteOptions* Directive

mod_rewrite settings are not inherited by default; this behavior must be explicitly enabled in every context where such inheritance is desired. For this purpose you can use the RewriteOptions directive. Although it was designed as a general-purpose directive to set special options for the mod_rewrite module, there is only one option that can currently be set, inherit; so there is only one form of the directive:

```
RewriteOptions inherit
```

This causes the current configuration to inherit the mod_rewrite settings of its parent. There are two completely different ways it is used, depending on the context:

Virtual host If the RewriteOptions inherit directive is set in a virtual host context, the mod_rewrite settings are inherited from the primary server. This includes rewriting conditions, rules, and maps. (We'll look at rewriting maps and the RewriteMap directive later in the chapter.)

Directory In a directory context (for example, when the RewriteOptions inherit directive is contained in an .htaccess file), the mod_rewrite settings are inherited from the parent directory's .htaccess file, if it exists.

Logging Rewriting Actions

When using mod_rewrite, it is always a good idea to enable logging for the module, especially when debugging your rewriting rules. The logging provided by the module is very complete and very useful. It can also be educational, if you take the time to follow the progress of the rewriting engine through the rulesets. I recommend that you enable logging for all servers using the module, even if you enable it only at a low level of verbosity on production servers. To use logging, you need to identify the file where the log will be maintained, and you need to set the level of information that will be logged. The mod_rewrite module provides a separate directive for each task.

Specifying the Log File Location: *RewriteLog*

The RewriteLog directive specifies the name of a file into which the server logs the rewriting actions it performs. Here's an example:

```
RewriteLog "/usr/local/apache2/logs/mod_rewrite.log"
```

Unless the name begins with a slash (/), it is assumed to be relative to the ServerRoot. The directive should occur only once per server configuration.

To disable rewrite logging, do *not* set the filename to /dev/null (although this may seem intuitive). Although no log appears to be written, this does not actually disable logging—it simply redirects logging output to the system null file handle (the so-called *bit bucket*, which essentially destroys the information). The logging activities are still performed and consume processor resources. To disable logging, either remove the RewriteLog directive or use RewriteLogLevel 0.

Setting the Logging Level: *RewriteLogLevel*

The RewriteLogLevel directive sets the verbosity level of the rewriting log file. The default level of 0 means no logging, while 9 or more means that practically all actions are logged. Example:

```
RewriteLogLevel 2
```

A RewriteLogLevel of 2 produces a log that very nicely shows the various stages of the rewriting process and can be useful in examining the effect of each RewriteCond and RewriteRule directive. Values greater than 2 will slow down your Apache server significantly and should be used only during debugging.

Listing 9.5 shows a Level 2 rewrite log for a single request handled by a RewriteRule in my httpd.conf file (that is, in a per-server context). The actual rule is the one used in my first mod_rewrite example:

```
RewriteRule    ^/environ\.html$        /environ.cgi [L]
```

In the sample log, you'll see that almost every step of the rewriting process is logged, even at this minimal level of verbosity. mod_rewrite logging can be very useful in understanding both the process of URL rewriting and the behavior of the module in processing your rewriting rules. When developing rewriting rules, always examine the log so that you understand what's going on.

Listing 9.5   A Sample from a RewriteLog

```
123456789012345678901234567890123456789012345678901234567890123456789012345678
192.168.1.3 - - [04/Apr/2000:09:33:31 -0500][jackal.hiwaay.net/sid#80bcb1c]
➡  [rid#84cb144/initial](2)init rewrite engine with requested uri /environ.html
192.168.1.3 - - [04/Apr/2000:09:33:31 -0500][jackal.hiwaay.net/sid#80bcb1c]
➡  [rid#84cb144/initial] (2) rewrite /environ.html -> /environ.cgi
192.168.1.3 - - [04/Apr/2000:09:33:31 -0500][jackal.hiwaay.net/sid#80bcb1c]
➡  [rid#84cb144/initial] (2) local path result: /environ.cgi
192.168.1.3 - - [04/Apr/2000:09:33:31 -0500][jackal.hiwaay.net/sid#80bcb1c]
➡  [rid#84cb144/initial] (2) prefixed with document_root to
➡  /home/httpd/html/environ.cgi
192.168.1.3 - - [04/Apr/2000:09:33:31 -0500][jackal.hiwaay.net/sid#80bcb1c]
➡  [rid#84cb144/initial] (1) go-ahead with /home/httpd/html/environ.cgi [OK]
192.168.1.3 - - [04/Apr/2000:09:33:31 -0500][jackal.hiwaay.net/sid#80bcb1c]
   [rid#84cb144/initial] (1) [per-dir /home/httpd/html/] pass through
➡  /home/httpd/html/environ.cgi
```

Setting a Base URL: The *RewriteBase* Directive

The RewriteBase directive explicitly sets the base URL for per-directory rewriting. The directive is applied only on a per-directory basis, possibly in a <Directory> container, but usually in an .htaccess file. It is necessary whenever the request URL does not match the local filesystem, usually because an Alias directive has been used to redirect requests to locations outside Apache's DocumentRoot.

Why is it necessary to use RewriteBase? Whenever a rewriting rule modifies a location on a per-directory basis, the actual rewriting occurs late in the request cycle, after almost all other actions have already happened. I've said that mod_alias should process the URL only after mod_rewrite has had its turn, but in a per-directory context, the rewriting rules are applied at a very late stage in the request processing cycle, after both per-server mod_rewrite rules and mod_alias have had their turns.

To make per-directory rewriting work, the URL resulting from these late-cycle rewrites is resubmitted to the server (internally), and a new request cycle begins. The URL is said to be "reinjected" into the server engine. The rewriting rule, when applied in a per-directory context, strips off RewriteBase (which, by default, is the local directory prefix), applies the rule to the remainder of the URL, and then prepends the RewriteBase. In a case where the incoming URL does not map to the local filesystem, you'll want to change the RewriteBase so that it matches the incoming URL prefix, not the local directory prefix.

For example, assume the ruleset shown in Listing 9.6 is an .htaccess file in the /usr/local/docs directory, and an Alias directive in httpd.conf has mapped this directory to the URL /docs.

Listing 9.6 A Ruleset Using the RewriteBase Directive

```
#  /usr/local/docs/.htaccess - a per-dir config file
#  The following Alias directive in the server config
#  maps this directory to /docs:
#
#          Alias /docs/ "/usr/local/docs/"
#
RewriteEngine On
#
#
RewriteBase    /docs
#
RewriteRule    ^FAQ\.html$  faqlist.html
```

Here, a request to /docs/FAQ.html is mapped (by the Alias directive) to /usr/local/docs/FAQ.html. The .htaccess file is read, and the RewriteRule strips the local directory prefix from the URL and then maps the remainder (FAQ.html) to faqlist.html. Before reinjecting the request to the server engine, mod_rewrite first prepends the value of RewriteBase, so that the reinjected URL is processed as /docs/faqlist.html. If the RewriteBase directive were removed from the .htaccess file, mod_rewrite would instead prepend the local directory prefix (which is the RewriteBase default) and submit the URL /usr/local/docs/faqlist.html for processing. The server would reject this request as invalid.

Mapped Rewriting: The *RewriteMap* Directive

The RewriteMap directive names a rewriting map for later use in a RewriteRule, and specifies the rewriting map source that can be used to look up information based on a key search and later inserted into the RewriteRule substitution string. It has the following syntax:

```
RewriteMap MapName MapType:MapSource
```

An example of such a RewriteMap, which will be used in an actual example below, is:

```
RewriteMap userfile txt:/usr/local/apache/conf/userlist.txt
```

A rewriting map is essentially a lookup table. It consists of any number of variable/value pairs and is analogous to a Perl *hash* (or *associative array*) or a *dictionary object* in VBScript or JavaScript. The closest analogy in C would be a two-dimensional array in which the name of the variable is used as a lookup for its value.

When one of the following constructs is placed inside the substitution string of a RewriteRule, it will be filled by the result of the RewriteMap lookup if the key is found in the map; otherwise the construct is replaced by the DefaultValue (if specified) or with an empty string.

```
${ MapName:LookupKey }
${ MapName:LookupKey | DefaultValue }
```

The RewriteMap directive can occur more than once. For each mapping function, use one RewriteMap directive to declare its rewriting mapfile. While you cannot *declare* a map in a per-directory context, you can *use* this map in per-directory context.

The following combinations for MapType and MapSource can be used:

Standard plain text (MapType txt)

Randomized plain text (MapType rnd)

Hash file (MapType dbm)

External function (MapType prg)

Internal function (MapType int)

> **NOTE**   For plain-text and DBM format files, the looked-up keys are cached in-core until the modification time of the mapfile changes or the server is restarted. This way, you can have map functions in rules that are used for every request. This does not slow the system significantly, because the external lookup happens only once!

Standard Plain Text

The standard rewriting map is one in which the MapSource is a plain-text file that contains key/value pairs, one per line. Blank lines are ignored. Full and partial line comments begin with the character #.

For example, you might create the following text file as /usr/local/apache2/conf/userlist.txt to serve as a rewriting map of usernames to home directories:

```
##
##  map.txt -- rewriting map
##


caulds  /            # Charles Aulds
csewell /carlstuff/ # Carl Sewell
larry   /larry/      # Larry H
```

The following RewriteMap directive would enable this file as a plain-text rewriting map that can be referred to in subsequent RewriteRule directives by the name userlist:

```
RewriteMap userlist txt:/usr/local/apache2/conf/userlist.txt
```

WARNING   If the filename specified in the RewriteMap directive does not exist, Apache will write an error message to its error log and fail to start.

A RewriteRule to access this map might look like this:

```
RewriteRule  ^.*\/userdir\/(.*)$  ${userlist:$1}
```

which uses substitution string (${userlist:$1}) of the following form:

```
${ MapName:LookupKey }
```

The pattern in this rule matches URLs that end in /userdir, followed by some string that will always be a username. The contents of the parentheses enclosing that username fill the $1 token in the substitution so that the username (for example, caulds) becomes the key in a lookup of the previously defined rewriting map named userdir. The value (a relative path to that user's Web home directory, which is in this example DocumentRoot) is used verbatim in constructing the rewritten URL. For this example to work, each user's Web home directory must be relative to the server DocumentRoot.

The example of access multiplexing presented later in this chapter gives another complete (and potentially useful) demonstration of a simple plain-text rewriting map.

Randomized Plain Text

This map type is a variation on the plain-text rewriting map just described. It looks up its value in exactly the same manner, but it performs some additional processing after the lookup. If the value retrieved contains one or more | characters, it is assumed to contain more than one alternative value, and the value substituted in the Substitution field of a RewriteRule that references this map is chosen at random from this list.

This may sound like a frivolous feature, but it was designed for load balancing in a reverse-proxy situation where the looked-up values are server names. Later in this chapter, the section titled "An Example of Randomly Generated URLs" illustrates one possible use of this feature.

Hash File

The hash file rewriting map is used exactly like a plain-text map lookup, except that the text file is first compiled into a Linux binary DBM format. DBM is implemented in Linux as a library of routines that manage datafiles containing key/value pairs and provide optimized lookups of data based on string keys. This greatly speeds the lookup process, but in most situations, a plain-text lookup will be nearly as fast as using a DBM retrieval and easier to maintain. A DBM hash file should be used only when your rewriting map grows in size until it is several hundred lines long and you are tuning for the most speed possible.

You can create a DBM hash file from a plain-text file with any DBM tool or with the script shown in Listing 9.7.

It isn't necessary to understand how the script works to use it. Use a text editor to create the file on your system (name it anything you desire, but the name txt2dbm is used in this example). Make sure the script is executable (by running chmod 755 *scriptname*) and then feed it the names of the text file you want converted to a DBM file with a command line like this:

```
# txt2dbm somefile.txt somefile.dbm
```

Listing 9.7   A Script to Convert a Text Map to a DBM File

```perl
#!/path/to/bin/perl
##
##  txt2dbm -- convert txt map to dbm format
##  Usage: txt2dbm textfile dbmfile

($txtmap, $dbmmap) = @ARGV;
open(TXT, "<$txtmap");
dbmopen(%DB, $dbmmap, 0644);
while (<TXT>) {
    next if (m|^s*#.*| or m|^s*$|);
    $DB{$1} = $2 if (m|^\s*(\S+)\s+(\S+)$|);
}
dbmclose(%DB);
close(TXT)
```

Internal Functions

There are four internal Apache functions that can be called using a rewriting map:

toupper   Converts the key to all uppercase characters.

tolower   Converts the key to all lowercase characters.

escape   Escapes special characters in the key, translating them to hex-encodings. This properly formats the key for use as a URL.

unescape   Converts escaped characters in the key (a URL with hex-encodings) back to special characters.

The first two functions are not terribly useful, but the last two can be very useful if you ever have to work with URLs containing special characters that must be hex-encoded for processing. The following RewriteRule takes a URL that may have been processed by previous RewriteRule directives and escapes it. The [R] flag then redirects the request:

```
RewriteRule  ^(.*)  ${escape:$1} [R]
```

URL escaping is often required when a URL might include characters that have special meaning. A URL that contains a ? character, for example, needs to be escaped so that the character isn't interpreted by the server as indicating parameters passed to a script. Note from this example that no RewriteMap directive is required to use these internal functions, since they already exist as built-in rewriting maps.

An External Rewriting Program

The map source can also be a user-written program. The program can be written in any language that can accept input on its *standard input* (stdin) file handle, manipulate it, and return a value on its *standard output* (stdout) file handle. Since the program will perform little more than a simple mapping of the input key into its corresponding output value, interpreted shell scripts (and particularly Perl) work well for this purpose.

This program (which must have its Linux execute bit set) is started once, when the Apache server starts up. It is designed to enter a continuous loop in which it waits indefinitely for input on its standard input. When it receives a key value from mod_rewrite, it performs some lookup and returns the associated value (always followed by a newline character) for inclusion in a RewriteRule substitution string. If the program finds no associated value for the key it is given, it should return either an empty string or the four-letter string NULL. The program should be kept as simple and as resilient as possible. If your program hangs, the Apache server will hang at the point that it processes the RewriteRule that sends data to the external program. The following example illustrates the use of an external rewriting program to authenticate users against a MySQL database.

An Example of Access Control Using *mod-rewrite*

Using an external program to do rewrite mapping offers only one clear advantage over a standard text mapping; it allows you to use any database you choose to hold the information. Listing 9.8 shows a very simple Perl external rewriting program. It illustrates one very important rule that must be remembered about external rewriting programs: You must *never* use buffered I/O. In Perl, you can specify unbuffered (or *raw*) I/O by setting the special variable $| to 1.

Advanced Configuration

PART 3

Listing 9.8 An External mod_rewrite Program

```perl
#!/usr/bin/perl
#/usr/local/bin/hosts_deny.pl
#
use strict;
use DBI;        # Use DBI for database
$| = 1;         # ALWAYS use raw I/O
#
# Create database handle
my $retval;  # create variable to hold lookup result
my $dbh=DBI->connect("DBI:mysql:hostsdb:jackal.hiwaay.net","root","password");
while (<STDIN>) {
    my $sth=$dbh->prepare("Select value from denytable where key=$_");
    $sth->execute;
    $retval=$sth->fetch();
    if ($retval) {
        print "$retval\n";
    }
    else {
        print "NULL\n";
    }
}
```

This program can be used with rewriting rules like the following:

```
RewriteMap hosts-deny prg:/usr/local/bin/hosts_deny.pl
RewriteCond ${hosts-deny:%{REMOTE_ADDR}|NOT_FOUND} !=NOT_FOUND
RewriteRule ^/.* - [F]
```

The RewriteMap directive defines the program in Listing 9.8 as a rewriting map named hosts-deny. Using the value of the HTTP header REMOTE_ADDR, the RewriteCond directive submits the remote host IP address to the external program, which attempts to find it in the MySQL database named hostsdb. If no match is found for the IP address in table denytable, the RewriteCond directive sets the value of the lookup to NOT_FOUND.

The RewriteRule shown in this example demonstrates a use for the special - (minus sign) form of a RewriteRule, which performs no rewrite at all. The [F] flag at the end of the rule indicates that the current URL is forbidden, and the request is answered with an HTTP response code of 403 (Forbidden). This rule will not be applied, though, unless the RewriteCond evaluates to True; in other words, the remote host's IP address is found in the MySQL table of denied hosts. If the host is not found in the table, the rule is not applied and the client's request is honored.

The *RewriteLock* Directive

The RewriteLock directive sets the filename for a synchronization lock file, which mod_rewrite needs to communicate with external RewriteMap programs. A lock file is used to prevent multiple attempts to access the same datafile, as might happen if multiple instances of mod_rewrite (running as part of different httpd processes) attempt to open the same file. If a RewriteLock directive is present, mod_rewrite will create this lock file whenever it accesses an external program and remove it when it is done. For simple programs that do not alter data, locking is generally not required, but if you are attempting to use a program that writes data to disk or makes modifications to a database, it is a very good idea to use this directive. This will ensure that your program does not conflict with other instances of the program that may have been spawned from other Apache processes running on the same machine. A conflict can occur when two httpd processes receive requests that cause them to run the same external program simultaneously.

Note that a lock is only required for external rewriting map programs and is *not* required for other types of rewriting maps. The lock file must always be set to a local path (never to a file on an NFS-mounted device).

For example, the following directives demonstrate the use of a lock file to prevent simultaneous attempts to access a single Perl mapping script (hosts_deny.pl):

```
RewriteLock /var/lock/rewrite_lock
RewriteMap hosts-deny  prg:/usr/local/bin/hosts_deny.pl
```

An Example of Access Multiplexing

Rewriting maps can be used to redirect requests based on information in the request header. For example, mod_rewrite can be used by a very large international organization to attempt to redirect download requests to a server that's geographically nearer the requester. (In practice, this rarely works well because of the large number of sites in top-level domains, such as .com, that give no clue as to where in the world they are located. Most organizations that host mirror sites around the world just let the user choose one near them, which usually works pretty well. But I'm not trying to solve a problem with the Internet domain-naming system here; my intention is to demonstrate the technique of reading information from a request header and processing it through a rewriting map.)

In this example, a RewriteRule examines the REMOTE_HOST header of the request, which identifies the Internet hostname of the requester's system, and attempts to choose a download site more suitable for the requester's location.

Start by creating a text file with a one-to-one mapping of top-level domains to URLs for mirror systems set up in those domains. Assume the file is stored as /usr/local/apache/conf/multi.txt, and looks like:

```
com       http://dlsite.com/download    # com domain
net       http://bigsite.net/download   # net domain
edu       http://bigsite.edu/download   # edu domain
org       http://bigsite.org/download   # org domain
au        http://bigsite.au/download    # australia
de        http://bigsite.de/download    # deutschland
uk        http://bigsite.uk/download    # united kingdom
    ... possibly many others ...
```

The following rewriting rules do the work:

```
# define a plain text rewriting map called multiplexer
# that points to the multi.txt file
RewriteMap multiplexer txt:/usr/local/apache2/conf/multi.txt
#
# Convert the request URL to one of the form:
# remotehost::<request> and chain to the next rule
RewriteRule ^/download/(.*) ${REMOTE_HOST}::$1 [C]
#
# Look up the new URL prefix in the multiplexer
# rewriting map (or apply default dlsite.com)
# and append the request
RewriteRule ^.+\.[a-zA-Z]+)::(.*)$
        ${multiplexer::$1|dlsite.com/download/}$2 [R,L]
```

The RewriteMap directive specifies the multi.txt text file as a rewriting map called multiplexer. The first RewriteRule matches all URLs of the form */download/somefile* and translates the URL to one of the form *requester.domain.tld::somefile*. The [C] is used to chain the next rule to this one. In other words, the two RewriteRule directives function as a pair; either *both* work or *neither* works, and the URL passes through the ruleset unaltered.

The last rule has been passed the rewritten URL *requester.domain.tld::somefile* from which it strips the top-level-domain (*tld*) and uses it as a back-reference ($1) to look up a corresponding URL in the multiplexer rewriting map. If no match is found, it uses the default value *dlsite.com/download/*. To this URL is appended *somefile*, which by back-reference fills $2.

The flags [R,L] indicate that the URL is returned to the requester as a redirection, and no further rewriting rules are processed.

An Example of Randomly Generated URLs

Here's a very simple example that redirects requests (at random) to one of the URLs defined in a simple text file that looks like the following:

```
URL freshmeat.net|www.acme.com/|www.asptoday.com/
```

Note that the file actually consists of a single line that begins with the index value or key of URL. The rest of the line is a list of all the URLs to be randomized, separated by the | character.

Listing 9.9 shows how a request for the URL outside.html is redirected to one of the URLs in the text file that is specified as a randomized plain-text rewriting map called servers.

Listing 9.9   Randomly Generating URLs

```
# Defines a randomized plain text rewriting map
# named servers.rnd
RewriteMap servers rnd:/usr/local/apache/conf/servers.rnd
#
# All requests to outside.html are rewritten to one of
# the servers chosen at random from the servers map
# note: the key into the file is URL
RewriteRule outside\.html$ http://${servers:URL} [R,L]
```

User Home Directories with *mod_rewrite*

One of the many potential uses for the mod_rewrite module is to provide access to user Web directories by rewriting request URLs. The RewriteCond directive must contain a set of parentheses for a back-reference to file %1, as follows:

```
RewriteCond %{HTTP_HOST} ^www\..+\.jackal\.hiwaay\.net$
RewriteRule ^(.+) /home/%1$1
```

Here's what happens. When a URL comes in of the form http://www.username.jackal. hiwaay.net, the rewriting condition evaluates to True, and the username (for example, caulds) fills the %1 back-reference. (Remember that %1 is filled with contents matched within the first set of parentheses in the last RewriteCond directive.) The RewriteRule is then used to translate the URL, taking the username from the back-reference filled by RewriteCond, and adding it, plus the request path, to /home (which fills the $1 back-reference). Thus a URL like

```
http://www.caulds.jackal.hiwaay.net/someresource.html
```

is the equivalent of:

```
http://jackal.hiwaay.net/home/caulds/someresource.html
```

Advanced Configuration

PART 3

Note a couple of things about this example, however. First, you'll need to provide each user with a DNS entry for their virtual Web site, as their username is part of the hostname used to access the site. Also note that, unlike a true virtual host, this method does not allow you to apply custom directives to your new virtual hosts (like a custom log file or server admin e-mail address). The advantage of this method is that it will support any number of user directories very efficiently with just two lines added to `httpd.conf`.

Again, this example is just to show you what kinds of things can be done. I'm sure there are a number of ways you can improve this skeletal example. You might use `RewriteMap` to define paths for each user; if these paths are not under the same directory on your system, this might be one way to avoid having too many users on a single filesystem. Use your imagination.

In Sum

Two modules (`mod_alias` and `mod_rewrite`) provide the functions of URL aliasing and URL redirection to the Apache server. Aliasing is the process of mapping a URL to a nonstandard location on the system, and occurs completely at the server. Redirection is the process of mapping a URL to a different URL and furnishing this URL to the requester, with a request to redirect the request to the new URL.

While `mod_alias` is far less complex and less extensive than `mod_rewrite`, it is generally more useful, almost essential on most servers, and should be used in all situations that do not require the additional functionality and flexibility of `mod_rewrite`.

The `mod_rewrite` module offers the additional functionality of conditional rewriting, multiple rules for a single operation, and access to environment variables for use in rewriting URLs. In addition, it can use previously defined rewriting maps to store rewriting information that is queried based on information provided in the request URL.

So far, this book has moved progressively into advanced topics for Apache server administrators, such as programming and URL rewriting; topics have centered on configuring Apache to make it do what you want it to. The remainder of the book is concerned with administering a server that is already configured. The next chapter covers the most basic administrative task of all, stopping and starting the server. There is, however, a surprising variety of ways to do this, as you'll see.

10

Controlling Apache

It's conventional to think of configuring a Web server and managing it as two separate activities: you configure the server to do what you need, and then you start it running; everything after that is "management" (until you encounter something that requires you to "reconfigure"). Microsoft IIS, for example, provides a management interface called the Microsoft Management Console that allows administrators to perform tasks like creating log files, creating new virtual hosts, or setting Web client access permissions. In Apache, that model is a less useful way of describing the administrative process. Virtually all instructions to the server take the form of directives within the httpd.conf file. Even if you are using a GUI tool, what you essentially do to make any change in the server's operation is modify httpd.conf and restart Apache. In other words, managing an Apache server almost always entails reconfiguration of the server, and almost all reconfigurations require a server restart.

This chapter serves as a transition. Earlier parts of the book focused on Apache's directive command language and the production- or user-oriented services you can set up Apache to provide, such as virtual hosting and aliasing/redirection. Later chapters will focus on maintenance issues such as performance and security. Your administrative activity will still be configuration—that is, you will still be modifying httpd.conf—but the goal will be to optimize the server's operation internally. Here, we'll take a close look at a relatively narrow topic: the different ways you can instruct the server to do routine operations like starting and stopping. In other words, the subject of this chapter is how to issue configuration commands for day-to-day administration. That may seem pretty basic, but the fact that there are several ways to accomplish these routine administrative tasks often confuses new Apache administrators.

Apache can be controlled in several ways: by invoking the httpd command with various arguments, by using a shell script provided with Apache called apachectl, by sending various Linux signals to the running Apache daemon process, and through several GUI administration tools. This chapter discusses all of these options in order to help you evaluate which one best meets your needs.

Controlling Apache Manually

Before too long, we may have really useful GUI administrative tools for Linux; certainly there is tremendous potential in that approach. It's really nice to have all the configuration settings available from a consistent interface, and GUI tools are generally easier to learn and to remember than the command line. The tools available today, however, are a long way from achieving their potential. Until I can administer my entire server from within a single graphical utility, I will continue to work from the command line. The Linux command line is the only interface that is at all consistent among all Linux versions and vendor distributions. Even if you would prefer to use a GUI tool, you should learn the basic command-line tools for administering Apache. The main reason for this is that most Apache configuration changes are made the same way: edit httpd.conf, and then restart the server. In many respects, a graphical interface that forces you to search through a settings tree for one of a hundred different property dialogs can get in the way.

httpd Command-Line Arguments

One way to control Apache is to invoke the httpd utility and provide it with one of several command-line arguments. Invoking httpd with no arguments simply starts the server *daemon*, or master process, which then starts child processes to listen for and respond to requests. The httpd daemon process should run continuously as long as the server is up. In fact, the server is properly shut down when the daemon is sent a signal telling it to shut down (the Linux -TERM signal). Before actually stopping, the daemon sends signals, in turn, to each of the child processes that it has started or *spawned*, telling them to clean up and cease their activities. To see what the httpd utility can do, enter the command with the –h option:

```
# ./httpd -h
Usage: ./httpd [-D name] [-d directory] [-f file]
               [-C "directive"] [-c "directive"]
               [-v] [-V] [-h] [-l] [-L] [-t] [-T]
Options:
  -D name           : define a name for use in
   <IfDefine name> directives
  -d directory      : specify an alternate initial ServerRoot
  -f file           : specify an alternate ServerConfigFile
```

```
-C "directive"      : process directive before reading config files
-c "directive"      : process directive after reading config files
-e level            : show startup errors of level (see LogLevel)
-E file             : log startup errors to file
-v                  : show version number
-V                  : show compile settings
-h                  : list available command line options (this page)
-l                  : list compiled in modules
-L                  : list available configuration directives
-t -D DUMP_VHOSTS : show parsed settings
 (currently only vhost settings)
-t                  : run syntax check for config
 files (with docroot check)
-T                  : run syntax check for config
 files (without docroot check)
```

Here's a closer look at the Apache httpd arguments:

-d *directory*   Specifies the initial ServerRoot directory to use instead of the compiled-in default value. Example:

```
# /usr/local/apache2/bin/httpd -d /home/alternateWeb
```

-D *name*   Sets a value for use with the <IfDefine> directive. In the following example, a variable DSS is set to indicate that httpd should be started with Secure Socket Layer enabled.

```
# /usr/local/apache2/bin/httpd -DSSL
```

-f *filename*   Specifies the server configuration file to use instead of the compiled-in default value. Example:

```
# /usr/local/apache2/bin/httpd -f
    /usr/local/apache2/conf/test.conf
```

-C *"directive"*   Processes the specified directive before reading the configuration file(s). Example:

```
# /usr/local/apache2/bin/httpd -C "ScriptAlias /usr/tmp"
```

-c *"directive"*   Processes the specified directive after reading the configuration files(s). Example:

```
# /usr/local/apache2/bin/httpd -c "DocumentHome /home/altwebhome"
```

-v   Displays the Apache version number. Example:

```
# ./httpd -v
Server version: Apache/2.0.39
Server built:   May 11 2002 12:59:43
```

-V   Displays compilation settings. Example:

```
# ./httpd -V
Server version: Apache/2.0.39
Server built:   May 11 2002 12:59:43
Server's Module Magic Number: 20020329:1
Architecture:   32-bit
Server compiled with....
 -D APACHE_MPM_DIR="server/mpm/prefork"
 -D APR_HAS_SENDFILE
 -D APR_HAS_MMAP
 -D APR_HAVE_IPV6
 -D APR_USE_SYSVSEM_SERIALIZE
 -D APR_USE_PTHREAD_SERIALIZE
 -D SINGLE_LISTEN_UNSERIALIZED_ACCEPT
 -D APR_HAS_OTHER_CHILD
 -D AP_HAVE_RELIABLE_PIPED_LOGS
 -D HTTPD_ROOT="/usr/local/apache2"
 -D SUEXEC_BIN="/usr/local/apache2/bin/suexec"
 -D DEFAULT_ERRORLOG="logs/error_log"
 -D SERVER_CONFIG_FILE="conf/httpd.conf"
```

-1   Lists modules compiled into the Apache executable. Example:

```
# ./httpd -1
Compiled in modules:
  core.c
  prefork.c
  http_core.c
  mod_so.c
```

-L   Gives a very verbose listing of all available configuration directives. Example:

```
# ./httpd -L
<Directory (core.c)
        Container for directives affecting
    resources located in the specified
    directories
        Allowed in *.conf only outside
    <Directory>, <Files> or <Location>
<Location (core.c)
        Container for directives affecting
    resources accessed through the specified URL paths
        Allowed in *.conf only outside
    <Directory>, <Files> or <Location>
<VirtualHost (core.c)
```

```
            Container to map directives to a
      particular virtual host, takes one or more host addresses
            Allowed in *.conf only outside
      <Directory>, <Files> or <Location>
<Files (core.c)
            Container for directives affecting
      files matching specified patterns
            Allowed in *.conf anywhere and in .htaccess
            when AllowOverride isn't None
<Limit (core.c)
            Container for authentication
      directives when accessed using specified HTTP methods
            Allowed in *.conf anywhere and in .htaccess
            when AllowOverride isn't None
Many lines deleted

KeepAlive (http_core.c)
            Whether persistent connections should be On or Off
            Allowed in *.conf only outside
      <Directory>, <Files> or <Location>
LoadModule (mod_so.c)
            a module name and the name of a shared
      object file to load it from
            Allowed in *.conf only outside
      <Directory>, <Files> or <Location>
LoadFile (mod_so.c)
            shared object file or library to load
      into the server at runtime
            Allowed in *.conf only outside
      <Directory>, <Files> or <Location>
```

-t   Runs a syntax test on configuration files without starting the server. This
command checks to see if all DocumentRoot entries (for the main server and all
virtual hosts) exist and are directories. Example:

```
# ./httpd -t
Syntax error on line 378 of /usr/local/apache2/conf/httpd.conf
DocumentRoot must be a directory
```

-t -D DUMP_HOSTS   Shows parsed settings for virtual hosts. Example:

```
# ./httpd -t -D DUMP_VHOSTS
VirtualHost configuration:
192.168.1.15:80        vhost1.hiwaay.com
   (/usr/local/apache2/conf/httpd.conf:1046)
Syntax OK
```

Advanced
Configuration

PART 3

-**X**   The Apache server runs as an ordinary single process. In other words, it does not fork any child processes and does not detach from the terminal and run in the background. This is used for debugging purposes and has no usefulness in a production environment.

Controlling Apache with Linux Signals

As a true Unix daemon, the Linux Apache server provides the administrator no way to communicate directly with the running server. The Apache daemon responds only to signals from the Linux operating system. Rather than communicate directly with the Apache daemon, the Apache administrator uses Linux programs to send signals from the operating system to the Apache daemon process (which must be identified by its Linux process ID, or PID). This can be done using either the Linux command line or a script. Utilities have been written to make this process more straightforward, including the apachectl shell script supplied with Apache (covered later in this section), but beneath these utilities, a fixed set of Linux signals is used to control the running server. The Linux signals that Apache responds to are –TERM, -HUP, and –USR1; and the Linux kill command is used to transmit them. In this section, I'll discuss the use of each of these signals. In order to use this technique, however, you need to understand the role of the process ID.

TIP   All kernel signals, along with their numeric values and mnemonic equivalents, are stored in a rather unusual spot on Linux systems. You'll find them in the file /usr/include/bits/signum.h, or you can enter the command kill -l for a list.

The Process ID

The process ID of the root Apache server (also known as the Apache daemon) is saved in a file named httpd.pid, which the default Apache configuration stores in /usr/local/apache2/logs. The full path to this file can be changed with the PidFile directive. If installed from Red Hat's Linux distribution RPM, the file is /var/run/httpd.pid.

NOTE   A process ID (PID) is a number that uniquely identifies a running Linux process. Process IDs are also used to maintain parent/child relationships between processes; the parent of every running process is maintained as an attribute of that process.

If this file doesn't exist for some reason, or if it doesn't contain the proper process ID for the Apache daemon process, you can determine the proper PID using the process status or ps command:

```
# ps -ef | grep httpd
root     1090    1  0 17:21 ?     00:00:00 /usr/local/apache2/bin/httpd
nobody   1092 1090  0 17:21 ?     00:00:00 /usr/local/apache2/bin/httpd
nobody   1093 1090  0 17:21 ?     00:00:00 /usr/local/apache2/bin/httpd
nobody   1094 1090  0 17:21 ?     00:00:00 /usr/local/apache2/bin/httpd
nobody   1095 1090  0 17:21 ?     00:00:00 /usr/local/apache2/bin/httpd
nobody   1096 1090  0 17:21 ?     00:00:00 /usr/local/apache2/bin/httpd
root     1299 1010  0 18:35 pts/0    00:00:00 grep httpd
```

The first process shown (owned by root, and with the lowest PID of the httpd processes, indicated in the second column of the listing) is the Apache daemon process. This is the PID you'll use to stop and start the server. The third column of the listing shows the PID of the parent process for each process. Note that all of the httpd processes (except the main httpd process) display the PID of the root process in this column. This parent/child relationship (maintained by Linux) is what enables you to control all of the httpd processes in the process group through the main httpd process. (The last process in the list, incidentally, should be ignored. It is the grep process used to extract the httpd processes from the full list of Linux processes.)

The *kill* Command and the Apache Signals

The kill command, when issued from the Linux command line and used with the process ID of the root Apache server, sends a control signal to the Apache daemon. Apache recognizes these control signals:

-TERM This signal is used to instruct any running process to shut down in an orderly manner (closing open files and device handles and, in general, doing its housekeeping work before ending). When sent to the parent process or primary server, it causes Apache to kill off all its children and then kill itself (sounds gruesome, but that's the correct terminology for what happens). Example:

```
# kill -TERM <pid>  where <pid> is the process ID of the Apache daemon.
Another way to express this is
# kill -TERM `cat /usr/local/apache2/logs/httpd.pid`
```

This is especially useful if you are writing scripts to control Apache. The portion between the single quote marks in the above command line is evaluated by the shell, and returns the contents of the httpd.pid file, which is then passed as the final argument to the kill command.

NOTE   In Linux, the default signal used by the `kill` command is TERM, so it is not necessary to explicitly specify it. If you invoke the `kill` command without specifying a signal, it will send the TERM signal to the specified process.

-HUP   Restarts the server immediately. When the daemon process receives this signal, it kills all of its children processes (the `httpd` listener processes) but does not itself die. The daemon closes all open logs, rereads the `httpd.conf` file (reinitializing itself), reopens its logs, and spawns new child processes to handle client requests. This is the signal you should use after making changes to the Apache configuration. Here's an example:

```
# kill -HUP `cat /usr/local/apache2/logs/httpd.pid`
```

-USR1   Performs a graceful restart. The daemon process signals all of its child processes to exit as soon as they've fulfilled their current requests. Processes that are not actively responding to a client request die at once. The daemon process closes all open logs, rereads the `httpd.conf` file (reinitializing itself), reopens its logs, and spawns new child processes to replace those that are dying at its request. Gracefully restarting Apache is kind to any clients that may be connected (by not forcing them to wait for an abruptly closed connection to time out). Here's an example:

```
# kill -USR1 `cat /usr/local/apache2/logs/httpd.pid`
```

While the Linux `kill` program is used to stop or kill running processes, that name is a bit misleading because the fundamental purpose of the program is to send kernel signals to running processes. It just so happens that several of the signals that can be sent using the `kill` program result in the termination of the process.

The signal names shown above are actually mnemonic equivalents for signal numbers, which can also be used. The following lines, for example, are equivalent, and send the KILL signal (which means unblockable, absolute death to any process) to the process with the PID of 931:

```
# kill -9 931
```

or

```
# kill -KILL 931
```

The default signal value (if the `kill` command is invoked with just a process ID) is to send the -TERM (15) signal to the designated process. When signal 9 (the KILL signal) is issued, Apache never actually receives the signal. Instead, Linux immediately terminates the running process, giving it no prior warning. Killing a process in this manner is a bit heavy-handed, as it doesn't give the process an opportunity to close in an orderly fashion any files or database connections it has open. Issuing the -KILL signal should be a last-resort method of shutting down Apache and used only in cases where the process refuses to shut down after receiving a -TERM signal.

The *apachectl* Utility

The Apache server is provided with a shell script named apachectl that handles many of the tasks already described. In Chapter 3, we first looked briefly at apachectl as a tool for starting Apache after installation. It is a very useful tool, but remember that it is merely a shell script that performs the tasks of invoking httpd or sending Linux signals to the Apache daemon process. It can simplify those tasks, and can even be used to control Apache programmatically (through your own shell scripts or programs). You may wish to borrow from the script or even rewrite sections of it.

You'll find apachectl in the support directory under the Apache source home. Apache's installation process will copy this file into the bin directory under the Apache home directory (the default location is /usr/local/apache2/bin/apachectl).

You can invoke apachectl with any one of the following arguments (these arguments are not meant to be used in combination):

start   Starts Apache. This is the same as entering httpd without arguments. Nothing special about this option, and yet it is the one you will use most often. Example:

```
# /usr/local/apache2/bin/apachectl start
/usr/local/apache2/bin/apachectl start: httpd started
```

startssl   Starts Apache in SSL mode. This is the same as entering httpd -DSSL. Example:

```
# /usr/local/apache2/bin/apachectl startssl
/usr/local/apache2/bin/apachectl startssl: httpd started
```

stop   Stops Apache. This is the same as entering kill –TERM <httpd PID>. This option is quite handy because it eliminates the need to look up the PID of the Apache daemon process. Example:

```
# /usr/local/apache2/bin/apachectl stop
/usr/local/apache2/bin/apachectl stop: httpd stopped
```

restart   Restarts Apache if it is already running. This is identical to kill –HUP <httpd PID>. Again, useful because the httpd PID does not have to be determined. The restart command works whether the start or the startssl command was used to start Apache. Example:

```
# /usr/local/apache2/bin/apachectl restart
/usr/local/apache2/bin/apachectl restart: httpd restarted
```

Advanced Configuration

PART 3

status   Dumps a short status screen. Using it requires the character browser lynx along with the mod_status module. It's not very useful; it is far better to use a Web browser to access the server status screen, but there may be times when you need the status information and, for some reason, have only the command-line interface at your disposal (perhaps because you're using a telnet connection). Be sure to pipe the output to more because it will scroll off the screen. Note that the mod_status module must be loaded for this to work (as discussed later in this chapter).

fullstatus   Dumps a complete status screen. It also requires the character browser lynx, along with mod_status. Its display looks like the regular status screen, but with more information. Later in the chapter, I'll show how to access this same information using a graphical Web browser. You'll almost certainly prefer that method, as the information is much easier to read, but be aware that the text status screens are available if you ever find yourself without Web access to the server—for example, if you are dialed in on a standard serial modem connection. Also requires mod_status.

graceful   Performs a graceful Apache restart. Causes Apache to wait for all open requests to be serviced. This is identical to kill -USR1 <*http PID*>. Example:

```
# /usr/local/apache2/bin/apachectl graceful
/usr/local/apache2/bin/apachectl graceful:
   httpd gracefully restarted
```

configtest   Performs a syntax test on Apache configuration files. I rely heavily on this option for discovering problems that prevent Apache from starting, particularly with virtual hosts. It's a good idea to run this before restarting Apache after making extensive edits to httpd.conf. Example:

```
# /usr/local/apache2/bin/apachectl configtest
Syntax error on line 641 of /usr/local/apache2/conf/httpd.conf
ScriptAlias not allowed here
```

help   Prints a screen describing apachectl usage. This command is redundant, because it yields the same result as running apachectl with no argument at all.

Starting Apache Automatically

The techniques you've just seen for starting and stopping Apache are useful whenever manual intervention is needed. Most of the time, of course, you can simply let Apache start automatically, launching it along with Linux.

Apache 2.0 was redesigned to allow a choice of Multiple-Processing Modules (MPMs), which is usually determined by the operating system of the server on which Apache runs. As discussed in Chapter 2, current versions of the Linux operating system tend to favor the use of process forking (using the prefork MPM) to create a pool of Apache listener (or daemon) processes. In this preforking mode of operation, Apache operates as a process swarm, in which a single daemon process (usually an httpd process owned by root) starts a number of child httpd processes that run under a nonprivileged system account and respond to client requests. The daemon process is responsible for keeping an eye on all its child processes, starting new ones whenever necessary to meet increases in server load, and periodically killing excess processes. This mode of operation maintains a pool of processes that are waiting to respond to client HTTP requests, and since Linux works well at sharing CPU time between processes, is generally very efficient while eliminating the overhead associated with creating new processes.

GUI Configuration Tools

When I began to write this chapter, I had no experience with any of the Apache/Linux configuration tools that use a graphical user interface (GUI), but I had high hopes of finding one that would simplify routine administration chores and save time. It simply didn't happen. I tried them all and found something to like about all of them, and someday I'll do virtually all of my Linux administration with utilities that use a graphical interface. But the tool I'll use will be a single configuration utility that will provide a consistent interface to managing all of the system software services and applications, hardware configurations, network settings, and user accounts. For that reason, I tend to shy away from Apache-only configuration utilities. I would use any of the tools discussed below if it meant I had to know nothing about the httpd.conf file and how to configure it. But for now, you cannot be a strong Apache administrator unless you learn to use its configuration directives.

Another problem with many of the tools here is their dependencies. Nothing hurts a good Linux utility like dependence on supporting software that may or may not be on the system you're administering. If a utility requires that I be at an X Window console to use it, I'm not interested. The utilities that show the most promise are those that offer the simplest interfaces: either a character-based interface that can be used via a telnet session or, better yet, HTML support for browser management.

Admittedly, the tools with the nicest interfaces are those that require specialized support from the system. It comes at a price, though. Not only do these often present difficulties in managing the system across the network, but X Window and function libraries built on it (like Tk) impose serious performance demands on even the most powerful server. On a real-world Web server with many connecting clients, if you devote half your CPU cycles to the X sessions running on the console, you definitely won't need to worry about increasing the speed of your Web programs. While I'm at it, I might mention that running CPU-intensive screensavers on your system console is a very bad idea if you are hosting services supporting other users.

The conclusion I can draw from practicing with each of the GUI configuration utilities I discuss is that the best compromise between a pure command-line tool and a full GUI interface is a browser-based tool. Offering complete portability across platforms and acceptable performance across a network, browser tools are ideal for this purpose, even if they are always just a little less than what you *really* want.

Comanche

Comanche (a freely available product supported by Covalent Technologies, `www.covalent.net/projects/comanche`) is an ambitious attempt to develop a cross-platform GUI administrative interface for Apache. Not only is Comanche (the name derives from COnfiguration MANager for ApaCHE) intended to run on all platforms that support Apache (Unix flavors, Linux, and NT), it is also designed to be extended modularly and to provide multi-language support. Figure 10.1 gives some idea of the interface Comanche provides in an X Window session.

Figure 10.1   Using Comanche in an X Window environment

The Comanche for Unix source package requires functions from the Tcl and Tk libraries (as well as the `wish` Tk interpreter), which is usually not a problem since these are installed by most standard Linux distributions. Comanche has the easiest installation of all the GUI configuration utilities I'll discuss, because the standard package contains a single (enormous) binary that includes all the parts needed to run it. Needless to say, it also requires X Window and does not function without it (from the command line or from a Web browser). Just make sure to download the distribution earmarked for Linux (`noarch`), uncompress it, and execute the largest file you'll find in the directory that is created. If you're in a graphical shell, Comanche will load and run. If you don't intend to run a graphical user interface on your Apache/Linux server, don't bother installing Comanche. It won't work.

Developed primarily as an Apache configuration tool, Comanche is quite good at what it does. However, Comanche suffers most, I believe, from being limited in the number of ways it can be used. Comanche doesn't provide text-based or HTTP access. That is, it cannot be used from a character terminal session (`telnet` or `ssh`) or from a Web browser. These are fairly serious drawbacks if you are attempting to administer multiple Apache servers on more than a single piece of server hardware. Even Covalent, which still supports the Comanche project, supplies its own Web-based Covalent Management Portal with its high-end Enterprise Ready Server (discussed in Chapter 2).

Webmin

Of all the GUI configuration and administration tools for Linux, Webmin (www.webmin.com/webmin/) is my hands-down favorite (Figure 10.2). Originally developed by an independent group, the Webmin project received a tremendous shot in the arm when it was acquired by Caldera, a major Linux distributor. Although Webmin is still packaged as the standard administration tool with Caldera OpenLinux eServer bundle, support for Webmin now comes from MSC.Software (www.msclinux.com), vendors of a Linux distribution intended primarily for high-performance clustered servers. Webmin can be freely downloaded and used with any other Linux distribution, and is extremely simple to install and configure. Upon entering the following single command line, Webmin was installed and Web access enabled, with no further configuration required. Note that, while "root" access must be used to access Webmin the first time, administration privileges can be granted to other users from the Webmin interface.

```
# rpm -U webmin-0.970-1.noarch.rpm
Operating system is Redhat Linux 7.2
Webmin install complete. You can now login to http://Lynx:10000/
```

Figure 10.2   The Webmin Apache administration module

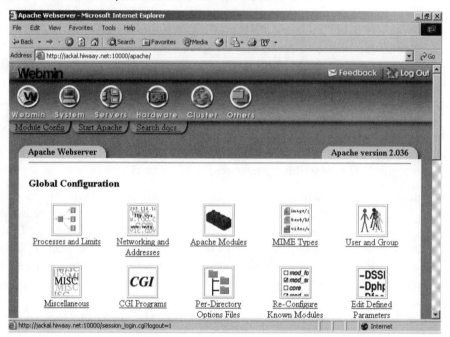

Webmin is a modular product, and Apache is one of many servers administered through Webmin using an add-on module. You can easily add additional modules (downloadable as single files with the .wbm extension) to upgrade an existing Webmin. If you're adventurous, you can even write your own add-on modules for Webmin. This is actually a pretty neat feature, because the BSD license under which Webmin has been released permits anyone to modify and distribute the product and new modules for either commercial or noncommercial reasons. That's a pretty broad license.

Another strong feature of Webmin is its support for SSL connections. Using the OpenSSL library (we'll install it for SSL support in Chapter 14) and the Apache Net::SSLeay module (easily retrieved and installed using the Apache CPAN module), Webmin communicates with your browser over an SSL connection.

While its Apache administration module could be a bit stronger, Webmin is a good, sound tool, well documented, efficient, secure, and extendable. As a general-purpose utility for Linux administrators, it holds great promise. Web-based administration tools aren't the easiest and most enjoyable to use, but they sure are liberating—using a Web browser and Webmin, you can handle most Linux admin chores. You won't be able to completely administer an Apache server with just this GUI product (or any other), but with its strong corporate support, Webmin shows tremendous promise.

Linuxconf

Linuxconf is a general-purpose administration tool for Linux, downloadable from www.solucorp.qc.ca/linuxconf. Some version of Linuxconf has always been distributed with the most popular Linux distribution (Red Hat), and it has always been closely associated with that distribution, but Linuxconf can be used with any Linux distribution. Make sure you download the latest Red Hat RPM for Linuxconf, and install it like any other RPM.

Invoke Linuxconf by typing **linuxconf** at the command prompt while logged in as "root." If you get a "segmentation fault" error, it is almost certainly because one of its modules is unable to parse a customized configuration file for a particular service. One common problem, I've found, is with the DNS service (named). If loading Linuxconf fails with a segmentation fault, unload the named module with the following command and then try to start Linuxconf:

```
# linuxconf --unsetmod dnsconf
```

If this doesn't work, you may need to unload other Linuxconf modules, perhaps even the Apache module, if you've manually edited the Apache httpd.conf file:

```
# linuxconf --unsetmod apache
```

The Linuxconf configuration file bundled with RPM contains a list of all modules that are available (and very little else). You can look in this file, /etc/conf.linuxconf, to see what modules can be disabled if you are having trouble loading Linuxconf. Look for modules that correspond with system services you've manually configured (by editing text files, in most cases).

By far the nicest feature of Linuxconf is that it provides full support for three different user interfaces. Use them interchangeably; they all modify the same files and have the same functionality (although the HTML version has some limitations for security reasons). In fact, they are all run from the same executable file (/bin/linuxconf):

Character   The character interface to Linuxconf appears when you invoke Linuxconf from the command line while operating in a character shell (like you would from a telnet or ssh session). Figure 10.3 depicts Linuxconf operating in character mode. Although everything is in character mode, very good use is made of the *ncurses* library, which allows a carefully written character application to support features like scrolling windows, and here we see a tree structure with nodes that can be expanded. Standard DEC VT100 terminal emulation on a telnet client is all that is required to make this work.

Advanced Configuration

PART 3

Figure 10.3 The Linuxconf character interface

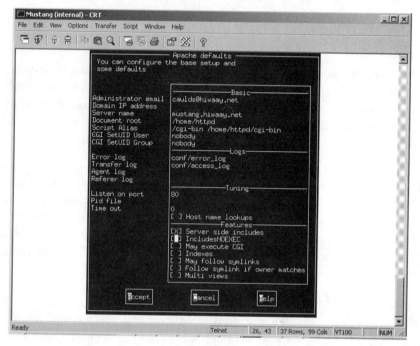

Graphical Figure 10.4 shows Linuxconf in a graphical environment (in this case the Gnome desktop). You invoke the same executable for graphical Linuxconf as you do for the character-based interface. Linuxconf is intelligent enough to recognize when it has been invoked from the command line in a windowed shell and will run itself in graphical mode.

Web The Web or HTML version of Linuxconf is what I like best about it. It's not the fanciest way to go, but it sure is convenient (Figure 10.5). Note that I access Linuxconf by connecting to TCP port 98 on my Apache server. Linuxconf is set up so that the very same executable that is used for the character and graphical interfaces is spawned (with a special switch) to handle the request.

Linuxconf is written in C. It requires no special libraries and no special configuration to operate. You won't, of course, be able to use the graphic version unless you are running some graphical Linux shell. I have found that the HTML version is quite adequate for the tasks I needed it to perform.

Figure 10.4   The Linuxconf graphical (Gnome) interface

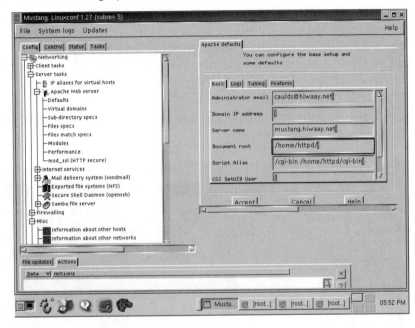

Figure 10.5   The Linuxconf HTML interface

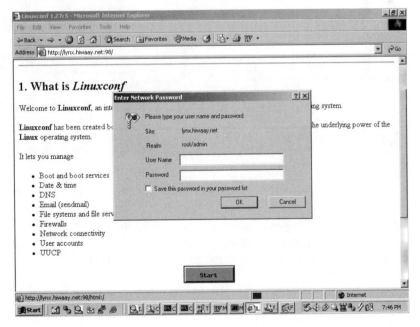

A drawback of using Linuxconf with a Web browser is that it doesn't (yet) support SSL connections; instead, it uses two forms of security. You first have to explicitly list every IP address from which you are willing to accept connections to the Linuxconf management socket (port 98). Figure 10.6 shows how this is done using the graphical interface running in Gnome. Figure 10.7 illustrates how easily you can view and modify basic Apache server parameters using the HTML interface. Notice the line of links at the top of the page, which makes it easy to determine your place in the hierarchy of HTML pages and to ascend the tree. There is no tree view of all the pages in the HTML interface, although it is rarely necessary.

Figure 10.6   Configuring Linuxconf for HTML clients from the graphical interface

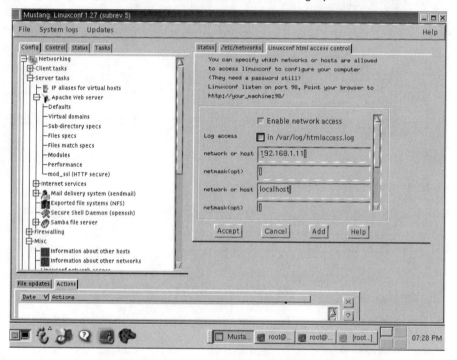

To access the Linuxconf HTML interface from a Web browser, you must enable the Linuxconf Web service which, for security, is disabled by default. To enable the Linux-conf Web service to start when you start Linux, open the file /etc/xinetd.d/linux-conf-web in a text editor and, making no other changes, make sure that the setting for the disable parameter is set to the value no, as in Listing 10.1.

Figure 10.7   Basic server parameters in the Linuxconf HTML interface

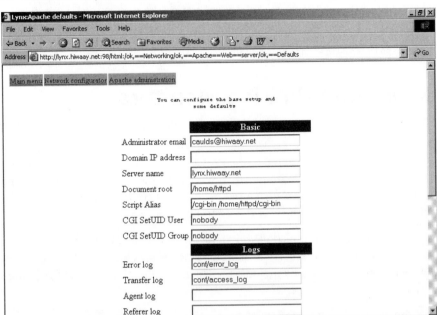

Listing 10.1   xinetd configuration file for Linuxconf

```
# default: off
# description: The Linuxconf system can also be accessed via a web \
#              browser.  Enabling this service will allow connections to \
#              Linuxconf running in web UI mode.
service linuxconf
{
        socket_type    = stream
        wait           = yes
        user           = root
        server         = /sbin/linuxconf
        server_args    = --http
        flags          = NOLIBWRAP
        disable        = no
}
```

After making this modification, the Linuxconf Web service will start automatically when Linux is booted, or you can manually start the service with the following command, issued while logged in as "root":

```
# /sbin/service xinetd reload
```

Apache's Built-In Web Monitors

This chapter has been devoted to the tools available for stopping and starting the server, but it hasn't said anything so far about how you determine the need to intervene and take those steps. Here's a quick look at the two Apache modules, mod_status and mod_info, that provide the capability to serve status and information pages. For monitoring Apache and getting a formatted listing of its configuration, the status pages provided by mod_status are the best things going.

When mod_status is compiled into Apache (or linked as a DSO module), it installs a new handler, server-status. This handler must be specified as a handler for requests to the URL /server-status by including a <Location> section like the following in httpd.conf:

```
<Location /server-status>
    SetHandler server-status
    Order deny,allow
    Deny from all
    Allow from 192.168.1.*
</Location>
```

You'll find such a section in the default httpd.conf after installation, but it will be commented out. Uncomment the lines, and be sure to specify your network subnet number (or a list of individual IP addresses) for those hosts that are allowed to access the status screen (shown in Figure 10.8). This status page is accessible from a browser on any computer attached to the subnet 192.168.1.*. An attempt from any other site will be rejected.

You can display additional status information, including information on the most recent requests answered by each child httpd process, by enabling mod_status's only directive, ExtendedStatus. Set the value of this directive to On to enable extended status information (shown in Figure 10.9).

```
ExtendedStatus On
```

This directive is also provided for you in the default httpd.conf file, but it is commented out. Uncomment the line to have mod_status always display extended status information.

Figure 10.8   The basic status screen displayed by mod_status

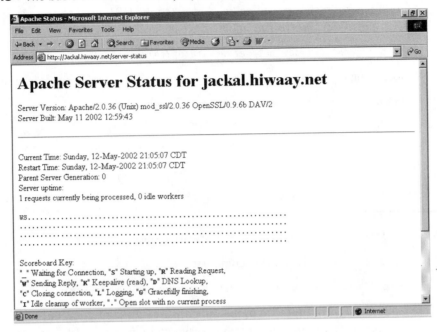

Figure 10.9   You can display greater detail by using the ExtendedStatus On directive.

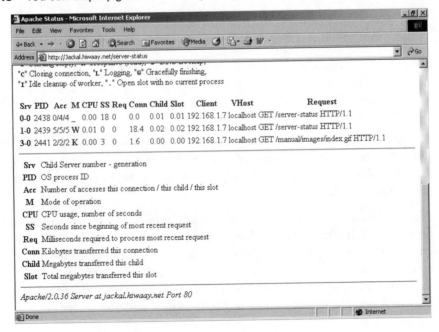

Advanced Configuration

PART 3

There are several options you can specify when retrieving mod_status pages. One of the most useful is refresh. Appending ?refresh=N to the URL used to retrieve the status page will cause your browser to update the page every N seconds, as in

```
http://jackal.hiwaay.net/server-status?refresh=5
```

Not specifying the number of seconds causes the page to refresh every second:

```
http://jackal.hiwaay.net/server-status?refresh
```

By default, the page that is returned uses HTML tables. To view a page with a browser that does not support tables (very rare these days), you can specify the notable option:

```
http://jackal.hiwaay.net/server-status?notable
```

Finally, the auto option returns a page of raw data, intended for parsing by a script or program:

```
http://jackal.hiwaay.net/server-status?auto
```

These options can be also used in combination:

```
http://jackal.hiwaay.net/server-status?notable?refresh=5
```

The module mod_info (installed in the standard Apache configuration) provides additional server configuration information, as shown in Figure 10.10. This information is available through another <Location> directive, again provided in the default httpd.conf file but commented out.

```
<Location /server-info>
    SetHandler server-info
    Order deny,allow
    Deny from all
    Allow from 192.168.1.1
    Allow from 192.168.1.3
</Location>
```

The information provided by mod_info is static; it will not change between invocations unless the configuration files are edited. The information is read from the Apache configuration files and may not necessarily reflect the contents of those files when the server was started.

Nonetheless, the information provided by mod_info can be very useful. It shows not only the default settings for the Apache daemon, but also which modules are enabled and a little about what each of those modules does. Scrolling further in the page (which should be quite long), you can see in Figure 10.11 that for each module, mod_info shows any handlers provided by the module, which phases of the HTTP request cycle are handled by the module, and any directives provided by the module.

Figure 10.10   The Apache Server Information page

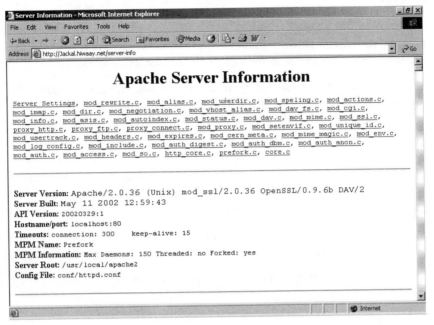

Figure 10.11   Module information displayed by mod_info

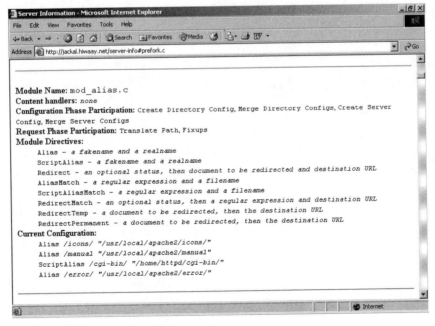

In Sum

This chapter has focused on the various ways of controlling Apache—starting and stopping the server, and performing other routine administrative tasks. The variety of methods available often seems daunting to new Apache administrators.

We looked first at the tools for starting and stopping Apache manually: the command-line arguments you can use with httpd, the Linux signals transmitted to Apache via the kill command, and the shell script utility apachectl. The chapter then surveyed some graphical utilities currently available for Apache administration. I found something to like about each of them, but abandoned them all to go back to using the traditional and "standard" means of administering Apache. In the hands of an experienced Linux administrator, Apache's configuration text files offer a flexibility that is unmatched by any graphical utility currently available.

The last section showed how to use the mod_info and mod_status monitoring tools, so you'll be aware of conditions that might require you to stop and restart the server manually.

The next chapter continues the topic of monitoring by exploring Apache's logging tools.

Part 4

Maintaining a Healthy Server

Featuring

- Error and access logging
- Tracking user sessions
- Using log analyzers
- Controlling listener processes
- Using Apache as a proxy server
- Apache's basic security tools
- Implementing Secure Sockets Layer in Apache
- Using metainformation for content negotiation

11

Apache Logging

The previous chapter showed how you can display the current status and configuration of an Apache server. This information, while important, cannot inform the administrator of a working server about unusual conditions, problems, or client usage. This kind of information is written (or *logged*) continuously to files that provide a historical record of the activity of the server and any unusual conditions it encounters. There are two main types of logfiles that are important to the Apache administrator. Request logs (also called *transfer logs*) record the network activity of the server, and they include all logfiles that record information about client requests and information that can be gathered about the clients making the requests. The most important request log is the access log, which contains a single line entry for each HTTP request the server receives. The second type of log provided by Apache is the error log, in which the server records errors, warnings, and unusual conditions it encounters while running.

Apache has a very complete, highly configurable logging capability. Error logging, intimately associated with the inner workings of the Apache server engine, is provided by the core module. The standard request logging, provided by the mod_log_config module, is designed to capture information about all client requests and also to store errors generated by the server or other processes (like CGI scripts) that it spawns. Additional modules designed to track an individual user's chain of requests (a *session*) provide information that you can later use to determine user preferences or predict user behavior. This chapter covers both the standard logging capabilities and the use of add-on modules to support session logging. It includes a look at two third-party log analyzers I've used, Analog and Webalizer, and a brief look at one log analyzer that is available commercially, Enterprise Reporting Server by WebTrends.

Error Logging

Two basic logs are a part of every standard Apache installation: an error log and a request log. Most of the chapter is devoted to request logging, simply because that is a more complex topic and Apache's capabilities for it are more extensive. Error logging is pretty straightforward.

On a properly functioning server, error logs should be fairly small, and they can be examined directly by the administrator to determine problems that need to be corrected. The majority of these will be malformed HTTP requests, usually requiring modification of Web pages that contain "broken" links. Though less frequent, errors are also written by the server if it encounters problems performing its function. These usually require the attention of the administrator, particularly those that are written immediately after the server is started. Typical log entries indicate problems in loading modules, implementing configuration directives, or setting up virtual hosts.

Apache's error logging is provided by the core module (mod_core) and is an error log that Apache uses to contain error messages that it or one of its modules generates or that Apache captures from a process it spawns (like a CGI script). You don't need to do anything to enable the Apache error log. By default, Apache will write its errors into logs/error_log under the directory defined as ServerRoot. The ErrorLog directive, however, allows you to control the location of the error log (or even turn it off). This directive takes several forms, each of which is illustrated below by example.

This line uses ErrorLog to redefine the log location by giving the full path to a new logfile:

```
ErrorLog /var/logs/apache2/error_log
```

This line redefines the name of the error log but doesn't specify a full path to the file:

```
ErrorLog logs/newname_log
```

If the file pathname does not begin with a slash (/), it is assumed to be relative to the directory defined as ServerRoot.

The following directive uses the special keyword syslog to indicate that logging should be performed by the system-logging daemon (or syslogd):

```
ErrorLog syslog
```

The syslogd utility is a part of every Linux system and provides not only system kernel logging, but also a means for applications to use it for logging, via a set of syslog *facilities* that are defined in /etc/syslog.conf. By default, Apache will use the facility designated as local7 in /etc/syslog.conf. If you look in that file, you'll find a line like the following:

```
local7.*              /var/log/boot.log
```

If you use the ErrorLog syslog directive without specifying a syslog facility, your Apache errors will be logged with all the other stuff in the system boot log (/var/log/boot.log). If you use syslogd for Apache error logging, you should set up a special facility for Apache logging. Do this by creating a new line in /etc/syslog.conf like the following:

```
local5.*              /var/log/apache2/httpd_error.log
```

Here I'm using one of the predefined facilities that syslogd provides for application use (local0–local7). For this change to take effect, you need to restart the syslogd service. On Red Hat systems, this is as simple as issuing this command:

```
# service syslog restart
Shutting down kernel logger: [  OK  ]
Shutting down system logger: [  OK  ]
Starting system logger: [  OK  ]
Starting kernel logger: [  OK  ]
```

An alternative method that can be used on all Linuxes, is to send the -HUP signal to the running syslogd process. Use the ps command to determine its process ID (302 in the following example) and the kill command to send the -HUP signal to the process:

```
# ps -aux | grep syslogd
root   302  0.0  0.8  1156   528 ?      S   ·07:34   0:16 syslogd -m 0
root   580  0.0  0.7  1168   456 pts/1  S    16:24   0:00 grep syslogd
# kill -HUP 302
```

Once you've configured syslogd to use the new httpd facility, you must use the following directive in your Apache httpd.conf file to ensure that Apache pipes its log output to the syslog daemon:

```
ErrorLog syslog:local5
```

TIP　　　　Logging to the syslog daemon is a trick I've found especially useful on systems where I've installed syslog-ng (www.balabit.hu/en/downloads/syslog-ng/). This drop-in replacement for standard syslogd permits you to filter messages using regular expression searches for specific strings in the message.

The last form of the ErrorLog directive opens a system pipe to a program or script that processes errors written to the log. The process starts when Apache is invoked, and the pipe stays open until Apache is shut down. *System pipes* are an efficient mechanism for interprocess communication, and can be a pretty efficient way to handle logging information, particularly if you want it parsed in a stream:

```
ErrorLog |/usr/local/apache2/bin/logfilter.pl
```

In this case, `logfilter.pl` is a Perl script that is designed to accept error-logging information from Apache. The pipe connects Apache's error-logging output to the standard input handle of the `logfilter.pl` process, which will simply read data line-by-line from its standard input handle. Such a process could be used to check each error message and filter out uninteresting data before writing messages to a logfile. A script could easily be written in Perl to notify the administrator immediately when specific messages are written to the log. Notification could be via e-mail, pager, console message, or a combination of all three.

> **WARNING** If error logging is defined by `ErrorLog` as a pipe to a program, that program will run under the user who started `httpd`. This is normally `root`, so precautions should be taken to ensure that the program is secure (that is, an ordinary user cannot write to it).

The `LogLevel` directive specifies which of eight verbosity levels Apache should use in logging errors. Table 11.1 lists these levels, which correspond to the same error levels used by the Linux system log. To set the `LogLevel` to `error` (a lower level of verbosity is *not* recommended), use this directive:

```
LogLevel error
```

Error logging is automatically enabled for all levels in Table 11.1 above the one specified. That is, if you have used `LogLevel` to set the error-logging level to `warn`, Apache will also write all errors that are defined for levels `emerg`, `alert`, `crit`, and `error`. The `LogLevel` directive is an Apache core directive; it is always available, and applicable to all modules that use logging. The default value is the same as specifying `LogLevel error`, which on production servers is generally verbose enough to diagnose most errors. I recommend setting the verbosity level at least one step higher (`warn`), and I usually use `LogLevel info` on my servers. Many of the additional log entries that will be written at this level are useful and informative, but not so numerous that they fill the logfile too quickly. `LogLevel debug` is usually useful only to programmers—particularly when they have written modules specifically to write debugging messages—and should never be enabled on a production server. You should never reduce the logging verbosity level below `LogLevel crit` (in other words, never use the `emerg` or `alert` levels); this will cause you to miss important warnings and error conditions that can notify you of problems either present or impending.

Table 11.1   Error-Logging Levels

Level	Description	Example
emerg	Emergency conditions that render the system unusable	"No active child processes: shutting down."

Table 11.1   Error-Logging Levels (*continued*)

Level	Description	Example
alert	Conditions that require immediate action	"Child 1234 returned a Fatal error. Apache is exiting!"
crit	Critical conditions	"Parent: Path to Apache process too long."
error	Error conditions	"master_main: create child process failed. Exiting."
warn	Warning conditions	"Child process 1234 did not exit; sending another SIGHUP."
notice	Advisory conditions that do not indicate abnormal activity	"httpd: SIGUSR1 received. Doing graceful restart."
info	Informational only	"Shutdown event signaled. Shutting the server down."
debug	Messages displayed only when running in debug mode	"Loaded module mod_vhost.c."

Request Logging

In addition to logging errors, the standard Apache configuration also allows administrators to log all access to the server. Access logging is also known as *request logging*.

The most basic request-logging capability is provided in Apache by the standard module mod_log_config, which is either compiled in the server or compiled as a DSO and loaded at runtime. This standard module does the work that was formerly performed by three modules, mod_log_common, mod_log_agent, and mod_log_referer. Those modules were used for logging all user accesses, user-agent (browser) used, and any referring URLs, respectively. They were made obsolete by mod_log_config and should not be used in Apache with a version number higher than 1.3. Check your httpd.conf file to see if they are enabled. If they are, ensure that mod_log_config is either compiled into Apache or loaded at runtime as a DSO, and remove the other modules.

The mod_log_config module provides a number of directives to enable standard logging, using what is called the *Common Log Format (CLF)*, which is discussed in the next section. The simplest of these access-logging directives is TransferLog, which can be used to enable access logging into a file it defines:

```
TransferLog /usr/local/apache2/logs/access_log
```

Maintaining a Healthy Server

PART 4

When enabled with TransferLog, Apache logging uses the format defined by the most recent LogFormat directive or, if no format has been defined, it uses the CLF. Like the ErrorLog directive, TransferLog can also pipe its output to a filter program that receives the logging information via its standard input.

The TransferLog directive is provided in mod_log_config for backward compatibility with the original, but now obsolete, Apache logging module, mod_log_common. That module was very basic, supporting CLF logging to a single file only. The mod_log_config module is capable of defining multiple logs, each with its own custom log format. The standard Apache configuration no longer includes the mod_log_common module. It has been replaced by mod_log_config, which replaces TransferLog with the LogFormat and CustomLog directives. These are used, as described below, to implement all logging, even traditional CLF logging. While you can still use TransferLog, I recommend that you learn and begin using the newer directives instead.

Unlike error logging, which is written to a default location even if no ErrorLog directive is specified, access is not logged unless either a TransferLog or CustomLog directive is used to specify a location for an access log.

WARNING As with error logging, if access logging is defined by TransferLog as a pipe to a program, that program will run under the user who started httpd. This is normally root, so the same precautions should be taken to ensure that the program is secure.

The Common Log Format

Most Apache servers use the Common Log Format (or some close variant of that format) for access logging. The Common Log Format was loosely defined way back in the beginning by the World Wide Web Consortium (W3C) and is documented at www.w3.org/Daemon/User/Config/Logging.html. The format is not complex or rigidly defined, but it has become the default format for logging in most Unix-based Web servers, and it has always been the default access log format for Apache.

Each request received by the server makes up one line of the access log, and each line in CLF is defined as follows:

```
remotehost identd authuser [date] "request URL" status bytes
```

The fields mean the following:

> **remotehost** The IP address of the client that sent the request or the client's fully qualified hostname if hostname lookup is enabled. (Performing hostname

lookups for each request can significantly slow an Apache server; see the discussion of `logresolve` later in the chapter.)

identd   If the `identd` protocol is used to verify a client's identity, this is the identity information resulting from an `identd` response from the client. `identd` is a user identification protocol (defined by RFC 1413) in which a machine is queried for the identity of the user who owns a process that initiated a TCP/IP connection. The protocol is not widely implemented and imposes a burden on the server, which must wait for `identd` responses from each client, most of which probably do not even support `identd`. Consequently, `identd` checking is disabled by default, and this field is normally filled by a hyphen character as a placeholder.

authuser   If the request was for a protected document and requires user ID and password information, the user ID furnished by the client fills this field. If no credentials were required to access the requested resource, this field normally contains a hyphen in the log.

[date]   A date-and-time stamp for the request, which is filled in by the server and enclosed in brackets [].

"request URL"   The URL received from the client, enclosed in quotes, and omitting the leading `http://servername` portion.

status   The three-digit status code returned to the client.

bytes   The number of bytes returned in the body of the response to the client (does not include any of the response headers).

Each field of the CLF line is delimited (set apart from surrounding text) by the space character. The two fields that commonly contain spaces are enclosed in special delimiter characters: braces ([]) enclose the request date, and quotes ("") enclose the request URL. Any CLF log analyzer or filter program needs to be able to deal with these characters.

Here are three lines I pulled from my `access.log` to give you an idea of what CLF format looks like when written to the Apache log:

```
192.168.1.2 - - [20/May/2002:13:33:27 -0500] "GET / HTTP/1.1" 200 3918
192.168.1.2 - - [20/May/2002:13:37:41 -0500] "GET / HTTP/1.1" 304 -
192.168.1.2 - caulds [20/May/2002:13:38:41 -0500]
    "GET /AuthTest/secret.html HTTP/1.1" 200 221
```

The first line shows a request for my home page (the URL is simply /), which was answered with an OK response (code 200) and a 3918-byte response body (my `index.html` page). The second line is for the same resource, but it's a bit more interesting. The browser I used this time was HTTP/1.1-compliant, and sent with its request a special header, `If-Modified-Since`, with the timestamp of the resource it had previously requested and cached. Because the resource hasn't changed since last requested, the server doesn't send a new copy of the resource; it simply provides a 304 (Not Modified) header in the response. Neat, huh? For large files (like images) this can greatly reduce the response time for the client and ease the burden on your server.

The last line shows a request for a resource in a protected area. I was required to furnish a username and password to retrieve the resource, and my username was logged in the third field.

That's Common Log Format, and it is (as the name implies) the most commonly used Web log format. Although several other "standard" log formats have been developed, none of them has seen such widespread use, and most sites that don't use CLF use a custom log format that is usually a slightly modified version of CLF.

One attempt to standardize a modified CLF log is the Extended Common Logfile Format, also known as the Combined Log Format. First introduced in NCSA HTTPd 1.4, this is the standard CLF with two additional fields, referer and agent, which appear at the end of the line enclosed in quotation marks. While there is no official standard for this format, it is the most commonly used alternative to CLF and is supported by most Web servers and logfile analyzers. The referer field logs the value of the Referer HTTP header (if it exists). The presence of this field in a request indicates that the request was generated by clicking a link in a page from another site, and the content of this header indicates the URL of this page. The content of the agent field indicates the browser type used by the client that sent the request. The Extended Common Logfile Format is specified by the W3C organization as Working Draft *WD-logfile-960323* (www.w3.org/TR/WD-logfile.html).

Defining What to Log: Using *LogFormat*

The most important directive provided by mod_log_config is LogFormat. This directive allows a great deal of customizability in defining the format of each line written to the access log (which is defined in a CustomLog directive as discussed in the next section). The LogFormat directive consists of two parts: a format string and a nickname used to refer to the defined format. In the default httpd.conf, you will find the following line, which defines the Common Log Format with the tokens enclosed in quotes and assigns the format to the nickname common.

```
LogFormat "%h %l %u %t \"%r\" %>s %b" common
```

The default value of LogFormat is the CLF, but without a nickname. Any CustomLog directive that does not reference a named format uses the CLF. A % character always precedes the tokens in the format specification. The flexibility of LogFormat lies in the wide variety of log parameters that can be specified using these tokens, including all

HTTP request headers and the contents of any environment variable. The possible tokens are:

%a   The remote host IP address.

%A   The local host IP address.

%B   The number of bytes sent, excluding HTTP headers.

%b   The number of bytes sent, excluding HTTP headers. Sends a dash (-) character rather than a zero when no characters are sent to comply with the CLF specification.

%{ENV VAR}e   The contents of the environment variable specified by ENV VAR.

%f   The filename of the logfile.

%h   The remote hostname (requires the HostnameLookups directive to enable reverse hostname lookups). If HostnameLookups has not been enabled, or if a reverse hostname lookup cannot resolve a client IP address to the hostname, the IP address of the requestor is logged.

%H   The request protocol and version (for example, HTTP/1.1).

%{header_line}i   The contents of one or more header_line entries, each specified within braces, taken from the request sent to the server.

%l   The remote logname (from identd, if IdentityCheck is enabled) supplied by the client machine, if it is running identd.

%m   The request method (typically GET).

%{note}n   The contents of one or more note entries specified within braces, taken from another module.

%{header_line}o   The contents of one or more header_line entries, specified within braces, taken from the reply to the client.

%p   The canonical TCP port of the server serving the request (set by the Port configuration directive).

%P   The process ID of the child httpd process that serviced the request.

%q   The query string (prefixed with a ? character if a query string exists; otherwise an empty string).

%r   The first line of the request.

%s   For requests that were redirected internally, this is the status of the original request. Using **%>s** returns the status of the last request.

%t   The time, in CLF time format (standard English format).

%{format}t The time, in the form specified by the **format** template within the braces, which must follow the Linux **strftime** rules).

%T The time taken to serve the request, in seconds.

%u The remote user. A 401 response (Unauthorized) could mean that the user ID supplied by the user (and logged) was bogus; or the user ID could be OK, but the password is missing or incorrect. It may be unreliable if the return status (**%s**) is 401.

%U The URL path requested.

%v The canonical **ServerName** of the server that is serving the request.

%V The server name according to the **UseCanonicalName** setting.

Custom Logging Options

The default httpd.conf file provided with Apache contains the following line that defines the Extended Common Log Format discussed earlier, which Apache refers to by the nickname combined:

```
LogFormat "%h %l %u %t \"%r\" %>s %b \"%{Referer}i\"
    \"%{User-Agent}i\"" combined
```

The format remains unused, however, until a CustomLog directive names the combined format.

In addition, it is possible to insert any number of HTTP response codes behind the % character to apply the token conditionally. The following token, for example, will log referring URLs only in cases where the response is 404 (Not Found); in other words, it will log Web pages that contain a link to a resource that's not on the current site.

```
LogFormat "%h %l %u %t \"%r\" %s %b %404{Referer}i"
```

You can also use the ! (negation) character to precede the list of HTTP response codes, so that the format specification will be used only when the response code is not in the list:

```
LogFormat "%h %l %u %t \"%r\" %s %b %!200,304,302{Referer}i"
```

In this case, the referring URL is appended to the log line only if the response code is not 200 (OK), 302 (Found), or 304 (Not Modified). Note that the negation refers to the entire list of codes, not just to the single code it precedes.

Here are two sample LogFormat directives, with examples of lines that will be written to the logs using these formats:

```
LogFormat "%h %l %u %t \"%r\" %>s %b" common
192.168.1.2 - - [23/Mar/2000:12:44:20 -0600] "GET / HTTP/1.0" 304 -

LogFormat "%h %l %u %t \"%r\" %>s %b %{User-agent}i" common
```

```
192.168.1.2 - - [23/Mar/2000:12:44:48 -0600] "GET /
    HTTP/1.0" 304 - Mozilla/4.7[en] (WinNT; I)
```

In both cases, the first field shown (corresponding to the %h specifier) is the IP address of the requestor. The second two fields, shown here as dashes, are filled in only if the request was for a resource that requires authentication of the requestor (as described in Chapter 13). The second field, corresponding to the %l specifier, is the remote user's login name, as determined by identd authentication; this field is rarely used. The third field, also represented by a hyphen in these examples, is filled in with the requesting user's name if authentication is enabled and a username and password are supplied with the request.

Creating the Logfile: Using *CustomLog*

Whether you specify a custom access-logging format with the LogFormat directive or decide to use the default CLF, you need to use the CustomLog directive to instruct Apache to use the format. This directive actually creates and enables a logfile. It specifies the location and name of the logfile and, optionally, the name of a previously defined log format to use for that logfile. If no named format is specified, CustomLog uses either the last LogFormat directive that did not assign a name or CLF if no previous LogFormat has been specified.

The default Apache configuration file configures CLF logging into the access_log file using this pair of directives:

```
LogFormat "%h %l %u %t \"%r\" %>s %b" common
CustomLog /usr/local/apache/logs/access_log common
```

An alternate way, perhaps simpler, is to define a LogFormat without a name and follow it with a CustomLog directive, also without a name:

```
LogFormat "%h %l %u %t \"%r\" %>s %b"
CustomLog /usr/local/apache/logs/access_log
```

Actually, since the default value of LogFormat is the CLF, that directive is redundant, even in the simplified example above.

The standard Apache file also defines three other formats:

```
LogFormat "%h %l %u %t \"%r\" %>s %b \"%{Referer}i\"
    \"%{User-Agent}i\"" combined
LogFormat "%{Referer}i -> %U" referer
LogFormat "%{User-agent}i" agent
```

CustomLog directives that use these formats are also included in the httpd.conf file but commented out.

```
#CustomLog logs/access_log combined
```

```
#CustomLog logs/referer_log referer
#CustomLog logs/agent_log agent
```

The last two define logs that are separate from, and written in addition to, the regular `access_log` file. The combined log format, intended to replace the CLF log, should be uncommented only if you comment out the common log format. Otherwise, you will have two `CustomLog` directives defining the same file. This is permissible, but you will have two lines with slightly different formats written to that file for every server request.

Conditional Logging

The `CustomLog` directive has a special conditional format that determines whether a particular request is logged based on the existence or absence of a particular environment variable. This is usually used in conjunction with a `SetEnvIf` directive, as the following example illustrates:

```
SetEnvIf Request_URI \.gif$ image
SetEnvIf Request_URI \.jpg$ image
SetEnvIf Request_URI \.png$ image
CustomLog logs/images_log common env=image
CustomLog logs/access_log common env=!image
```

Here we simply want to log requests for images separately from other access. The `SetEnvIf` directives define an environment variable, `image`, for URLs that indicate a request for images. Log entries will be written to one of two logs, based on whether this variable is set (`env=image`) or not set (`env=!image`).

Here's an example where we log all requests from a particular network into a special directory for later review, possibly because we suspect malicious behavior originating from there. Note that, in this case, those requests will be written twice, once to the `intruder_log` and once to the normal `access_log`:

```
CustomLog logs/access_log common
SetEnvIf Remote_Addr ^208\.229\.24 intruder
CustomLog logs/intruder_log common env=intruder
```

Logging for Virtual Hosts

If you're implementing virtual hosts on your server, as described in Chapter 6, it is often useful to log those hosts separately. To do that, you can create separate logging directives within each `<VirtualHost>` container so that all requests handled by that virtual host are written to a log separate from the primary server and all other virtual hosts. Otherwise, if a `<VirtualHost>` section contains no `TransferLog` or `CustomLog` directives, the logs defined for the main server are inherited and used by that virtual host.

Each logfile opened by Apache consumes a new system file handle, a resource for which there are hard limits imposed by the Apache kernel. Although in recent versions of Apache these limits are usually so large they aren't a concern, Apache could run out of file handles if you use a large number of virtual hosts, and each opens two logs (an access log and an error log). An alternative to using separate logfiles for each virtual host is to log the server name with each log entry in the main server log. The %v format specification is used to log the name of the server that handles each request. For example, the following directives accomplish this by making a slight modification to the Common Log Format. Note that I renamed the format revised to distinguish it as a custom format:

```
LogFormat "%h %l %u %t \"%r\" %>s %b Serving Host: %v" revised
CustomLog /usr/local/apache/logs/access_log revised
```

A request for http://namedvh2.hiwaay.net/ is now logged as:

```
192.168.1.2 - - [23/Mar/2000:15:35:55 -0600]
   "GET /oracle-b.gif HTTP/1.0" 404
   281 Serving Host: namedvh2.hiwaay.net
```

Logfile Security

There are two reasons that adequate measures must be taken to ensure that nonprivileged users cannot access Apache logfiles. First, the data in the Apache logs should be considered sensitive, and could reveal information about your server configuration that could aid hackers in infiltrating your system. Second, since the root user can write to Apache logs, you must ensure that no one else has write access. A malicious hacker who has write access to these files could create a symbolic link from an Apache log to a critical system file; the next time Apache tries to open the logfile for writing, the symbolic link will open that file instead and the system file will be corrupted.

While in the Apache logs directory, under ServerRoot, issue the following commands to correctly set the ownership and permissions of that directory and the files it contains. Note that the group account www is one that will have to be set up separately, and can be any account name you choose; I recommend establishing such a group account and assigning membership to trusted Apache administrators.

```
# pwd
/usr/local/apache/logs
# chown root.www . *
# chmod 750 .
# chmod 650 *
# chmod 640 *
total 799
```

```
drwxr-x---   2 root     www       1024 Jul 29 14:43 .
drwxr-x---  12 root     www       1024 Jul 29 12:24 ..
-rw-r-----   1 root     www    1107233 Jul 29 15:41 access_log
-rw-r-----   1 root     www      31705 Jul 29 12:55 error_log
-rw-r-----   1 root     www          5 Jul 29 12:55 httpd.pid
```

The first command, pwd, was issued to ensure that we are in the proper directory; the chown command sets both the user and group ownership of the directory, and all of its files, to root. The results of the chmod command (the first of which sets permissions on the logs directory and the second for its files) are shown in the ls listing produced by the last command, essentially granting read and write access to the root user, read-only access to members of the www group, and no access at all to all other users. Users in the www group will be able to examine the logfiles and run logfile analyzers on them.

Tracking User Sessions

User tracking, or the logging of a user-specific piece of information for each Web request, permits a later analysis of the logs to compile information on user habits or preferences: Which of our pages did a particular user access? What link was followed to reach our page (derived from the Referer header)? How long did the user stay at our site? This analysis is usually designed to reveal the behavior of the typical user. When combined with demographic data (hopefully volunteered by the user), user-tracking data maintained in logfiles can be used to determine the buying habits and Web viewing habits of different population groups. The proliferation of Web-based commerce has made session logging more important than in the past, as companies use their Web access logs to develop Web usage profiles of their clientele.

The standard logging of error messages and HTTP requests in Apache that we've discussed so far, however, cannot provide this information about individual user sessions. While it might seem that the IP address would uniquely identify each connecting user in the logs, in practice this doesn't work. Business users are increasingly hidden behind firewalls and HTTP proxy servers that effectively mask their IP addresses, so that they appear to be using the IP address of the proxy server. Also, most ISPs dynamically assign IP addresses to their users, which is not helpful in identifying particular users.

To meet this need, Apache provides two modules, mod_usertrack and mod_session, that attempt to track users by assigning a unique piece of information to a connecting user and including this information with the log entry of each HTTP request received from that user. Both of these modules that implement user tracking will be discussed later in this chapter.

Cookies

When Netscape introduced *cookies*, they were quickly and widely adopted as an efficient way to track user information. Cookies are pieces of information generated by the Web server and stored by the client browser. When the same browser makes subsequent requests to the server that issued the cookie, it attaches the cookie to the request. This enables the Web server to identify the user and perhaps load a customized page or return to a stored state in a transaction session.

Cookies are very simple to use. To set a cookie on a client's workstation, the server sends a Set-Cookie header with its HTTP response. That header looks like the following and passes five fields (only one of which is mandatory) in no specific order:

```
Set-Cookie: name=value; expires=date; path=path; domain=domain_name; secure
```

Unless the user's browser is incapable of storing cookie data (highly unlikely these days) or the user has specifically disabled the browser from accepting and storing cookies, the cookie data is written somewhere on the client's hard disk by the browser. The following data fields are passed to the browser in a cookie:

name   The name of the cookie. This is the only required attribute of a cookie. This field can be set by the CookieName directive in mod_usertrack but defaults to Apache.

expires   A date string that specifies a time and date after which the cookie is considered expired and is no longer used or stored on the client's machine. The CookieExpires directive in mod_usertrack sets this field. If this optional field is not specified, the cookie expires when the current session ends (usually when the browser is closed).

path   The URLs on the server for which the cookie is valid. If this optional field is not specified, it is assumed to be the same path as returned in the header that contains the cookie.

domain   Used as a key to look up the cookie in the stored cookies file, this is usually set to the server host or domain name. If this optional field is not specified, it is assumed to be the hostname of the server that generated the cookie.

secure   This is a keyword that, if present, will mark the cookie to be transmitted only over an encrypted communication channel (essentially meaning SSL). If not included, the cookie will be sent as regular, unencrypted traffic.

Netscape cookies were first implemented in Apache by a now-obsolete module called mod_cookies. That module has since been replaced with one called mod_usertrack, which implements user tracking (primarily using the standard Apache log) with cookies. This module is enabled with the --enable-shared option to Apache's configure script.

Maintaining a
Healthy Server

PART 4

The nice thing about cookies is their simplicity, and mod_usertrack is a simple module to use. It is enabled in the default Apache configuration, and its facilities should be available in the standard Apache server. All you need to do to use cookies for user tracking is enable this feature with the CookieTracking directive:

```
CookieTracking on
```

When thus enabled, mod_usertrack will start generating and sending cookies for all new user requests for resources within the scope of the directive. The CookieTracking directive can be used to enable user tracking in virtual hosts, directory contexts, and .htaccess files, but it is not permitted in <Files> containers. This means that we can't elect to disable the use of cookies for tracking requests of a specific file type (like .GIF files), although we can disable cookies for a specific directory that might be reserved to contain files of type GIF:

```
CookieTracking on

<Directory /images>
  CookieTracking off
</Directory>
```

The CookieName directive is used to set the name of generated cookies for tracking purposes. If the directive is not used, the name of all cookies issued by mod_usertrack is Apache. The CookieExpires directive is expressed as a duration for which the cookie is valid, and it takes a single argument that can be expressed either as a number of seconds or as a time period expressed in combinations of years, months, weeks, hours, minutes, and seconds. The following example illustrates the use of all three mod_usertrack directives:

```
CookieTracking on
CookieName MyApacheCookie
CookieExpires "2 days 1 hour"
```

Placing these directives in my httpd.conf file caused the response header I received for a simple HTTP query to look like the following:

```
HTTP/1.1 200 OK
Date: Wed, 26 Jun 2002 23:07:20 GMT
Server: Apache/2.0.39 (Unix) DAV/2 mod_webapp/1.2.0-dev
Content-Location: index.html.en
Vary: negotiate,accept,accept-language,accept-charset
TCN: choice
Set-Cookie: MyApacheCookie=192.168.1.7.1025132840572593; path=/;
➥      expires=Sat, 29-Jun-02 00:07:20 GMT
Last-Modified: Sat, 01 Jun 2002 01:48:14 GMT
```

```
ETag: "7c700-5b0-8e533380;7c719-94f-8e533380"
Accept-Ranges: bytes
Content-Length: 1456
Keep-Alive: timeout=15, max=100
Connection: Keep-Alive
Content-Type: text/html; charset=ISO-8859-1
Content-Language: en
```

The Set-Cookie line includes the new name of my server-issued cookies and a value that is unique to this server/browser session. Note that it sends an expiration time relative to the server's clock time, rather than sending the cookie's valid duration and letting the browser compute the expiration time.

```
GET / HTTP/1.1
Accept: */*
Accept-Language: en-us
Accept-Encoding: gzip, deflate
User-Agent: Mozilla/4.0 (compatible; MSIE 6.0; Windows NT 5.0)
Host: jackal.hiwaay.net:80
Connection: Keep-Alive
Cookie: MyApacheCookie=192.168.1.7.1025132840572593
```

The format of the Cookie response header in the example shown, which is the mod_usertrack default, is the same format developed by Netscape back in the beginning of Web time, and is usually referred to as the *Netscape style* of cookie. This style of header and the cookie it issues are still recognized by every major browser, though its use is discouraged in favor of the new "standard" for browser cookies, defined by Request for Comments (RFC) 2965 ("HTTP State Management Mechanism"). It is recommended that you include the following directive in your httpd.conf file to enable the use of this modern style of cookie response header:

```
CookieStyle RFC2965
```

With this directive in effect, mod_usertrack returns a Set-Cookie2 header, which indicates the use of the RFC 2965–style cookie (all response headers are shown, but the only relevant line is shown in boldface):

```
HTTP/1.1 200 OK
Date: Wed, 26 Jun 2002 23:58:41 GMT
Server: Apache/2.0.39 (Unix) DAV/2 mod_webapp/1.2.0-dev
Content-Location: index.html.en
Vary: negotiate,accept,accept-language,accept-charset
```

```
TCN: choice
Set-Cookie2: MyApacheCookie=192.168.1.7.1025135921548778; path=/;
➥      max-age=176400
Last-Modified: Sat, 01 Jun 2002 01:48:14 GMT
ETag: "7c700-5b0-8e533380;7c719-94f-8e533380"
Accept-Ranges: bytes
Content-Length: 1456
Keep-Alive: timeout=15, max=100
Connection: Keep-Alive
Content-Type: text/html; charset=ISO-8859-1
Content-Language: en
```

One additional directive provided by mod_usertrack that you should be aware of, but will probably never use, is CookieDomain. This directive allows you to specify a domain name that is added to the cookie, and is used in cases where multiple Web servers are set up as a "server farm," so that any one of them might receive requests from the same browser using the same URL. Setting the CookieName directive as follows

```
CookieDomain .hiwaay.net
```

will produce a response header from the Apache server that adds the specified domain to the cookie, as shown below (the portion added as a result of the CookieDomain directive is in boldface):

```
Set-Cookie2: MyApacheCookie=192.168.1.7.1025136323057554; path=/;
➥    max-age=176400; domain=.hiwaay.net; version=1
```

The browser will recognize all cookies issued by .hiwaay.net servers (for request URLs that are affected by this directive) as applying to the same server. Note that the use of the "." character preceding the domain name is mandatory; leaving it off will cause Apache to fail to start and will generate a configuration file syntax error.

Analyzing Logs

On any server with a significant amount of client traffic, Apache access logs rapidly grow until they become so large that you'll need a good program to analyze the data they contain. Simple Perl scripts are one good way to extract specific information from Apache's access logs, for those who have the time and inclination to write them. Most site administrators, however, are better served by one of the many good log analyzers available for download on the Internet.

What makes a good log analyzer? The most important criterion is efficiency or speed in processing the logfile. I have used analyzers that produced useful statistics or charts, but ran so slowly that it literally took hours to get the results. A good analyzer should also be configurable for a wide variety of log formats. Ideally, you should be able to configure your analyzer to read any format you can express using the LogFormat directive described earlier in the chapter. The other criterion of major importance for a log analyzer is that the information it returns is useful and presented in a fashion that makes it easy to understand. Basically, you want to know which of your pages are most popular, where the majority of your clients are from, which of your pages generated errors, and what other sites on the Internet (referrers) are referring people to your site.

Of the many analyzers available, Analog and Webalizer are two I'm familiar with.

Analog

For years I have relied on only one log analyzer, Dr. Stephen Turner's Analog (www.analog.cx), or its predecessor, getstats (written by Kevin Hughes). These two have long held the distinction of being the most popular Web access log analyzers available, and for good reason. Analog meets all the important criteria for a log analyzer: it is fast, extensively configurable, and produces a fully-customizable output that includes practically everything that can possibly be extracted from the access log.

Analog is an easy program to compile and install. Download the latest source archive (a file named analog-5.24.tar.gz when I wrote this), and create a directory to hold it. Unlike most programs, Analog isn't packaged to install into a working directory from a separate source directory. Unpack the distribution archive into the parent directory of Analog's intended home and then go to that directory:

```
# pwd
/usr/local
# tar xzf /downloads/analog-5.24.tar.gz
# cd analog-5.24
```

Analog has a configuration file, analog.cfg, in which you can set a large number of values to control it. Each of these values (C program variables) is also initialized in several include files (header files with a .h extension). Prior to compiling the program, you can modify these header files to change the compiled program's default values, but I don't recommend this. Instead, make all your configuration edits to analog.cfg. There are a huge number of configuration values, most of which will never concern you. They are well documented both in the included HTML files and on the Analog Web site and its mirrors.

Compiling Analog is as simple as typing:

```
# make
```

The installation is complete when the program is compiled. You'll find a single executable file (named `analog`) in the directory where you installed the program. Invoke that executable to generate a report:

```
# ls -al analog
-rwxr-xr-x   1 root      root         343036 Jun 26 19:56 analog
# ./analog
```

I won't attempt to show even a small percentage of the many configuration variables that can be used in Analog. Instead, I'll explain the configuration values you will probably want to consider changing from their defaults, and I'll show you the values I used for each. In the file `analog.cfg`, I changed or added the following seven values before running Analog the first time:

HOSTNAME   This is simply the name that will appear at the top of the Analog report; it does not have to be a hostname. Enclose it in quotes if the value contains spaces:

```
HOSTNAME "My Apache Server"
```

HOSTURL   The name entered in the configuration file as HOSTNAME is a hyperlink on the display report. When the link is clicked, this is the URL to which the browser is redirected:

```
HOSTURL "http://jackal.hiwaay.net"
```

ANALOGDIR   The directory where Analog will look for its support files and configuration when loaded:

```
ANALOGDIR "/usr/local/analog-4.1/"
```

LOGFILE   The location of your Apache access file:

```
LOGFILE "/usr/local/apache2/logs/access_log"
```

OUTFILE   By default, this is set to `stdin` (the Linux standard output file handle). You may want to change this to the name of a file, as I did, or you may want to run Analog from a script that automatically redirects the output to a specially generated filename (that might, for instance, contain a datestamp):

```
OUTFILE "/home/httpd/html/analog.html"
```

IMAGEDIR   The directory in which Analog will look for the support images it displays. (Note that the value of IMAGEDIR is used to form URLs to reference the images, and should be expressed as a URI that can be reached on your server.) I placed the images that came with Analog in my Apache image file and set this variable to that directory:

```
IMAGEDIR "icons/"
```

LOGFORMAT The same as the `LogFormat` directive used in Apache to create your log. In fact, the Analog documentation for the use of this configuration variable refers to the Apache documentation:

```
LOGFORMAT "%h %l %u %t \"%r\" %>s %b
    \"%{Referer}i\" \"%{User-Agent}i\""
```

Properly configured, Analog will know where to find the Apache logs and where you write them. The default value is to send the output to the Linux `stdout` handle, which means your screen. You'll need to redirect the output into an HTML file that you can retrieve using a Web browser:

```
# /usr/local/analog-5.24/analog > /home/httpd/May24Log.html
```

With the configuration changes I made to `analog.cfg`, all I had to do to generate a report for my Apache logs was enter this command:

```
# /usr/local/analog-5.24/analog
```

The results were instantly available on my server, and are shown in Figure 11.1.

Figure 11.1 A report generated by Analog 4.1

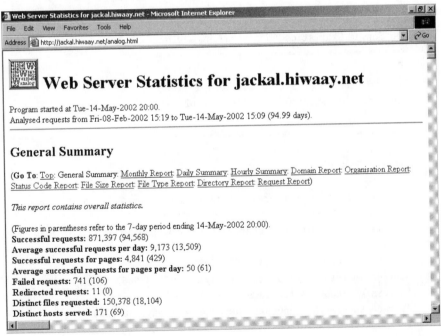

Another strong feature of Analog is its multilanguage support. As of this writing, Analog can provide output in any of 31 different languages (with more promised) using a variable called LANGUAGE. Refer to the documentation for a list of the supported languages. The default is:

```
LANGUAGE ENGLISH
```

Analog also supports another way of adding language support, from a special language file that you can download either from the Analog site or from another user:

```
LANGFILE lang/hindi.lng
```

Analog offers plain text as an optional alternative to HTML-formatted output, which is nice for reports that will later be cut and pasted into other documents or for e-mail that doesn't support HTML-formatted message bodies. Use the following configuration line to produce plain-text output:

```
OUTPUT ASCII
```

Listing 11.1 is a sample of the plain-text output from Analog, showing only a few of the 13 output reports it can generate.

Listing 11.1 Plain-Text Output from Analog

```
Web Server Statistics for jackal.hiwaay.net
============================================


Program started at Sat-18-May-2002 16:17.
Analysed requests from Fri-08-Feb-2002 15:19 to Tue-14-May-2002 15:09 (94.99
  days).
----------------------------------------------------------------------


General Summary
---------------
This report contains overall statistics.

(Figures in parentheses refer to the 7-day period ending 18-May-2002 16:17).

Successful requests: 871,397 (35,608)
Average successful requests per day: 9,173 (5,086)
Successful requests for pages: 4,841 (179)
Average successful requests for pages per day: 50 (25)
Failed requests: 741 (94)
Redirected requests: 11 (0)
Distinct files requested: 150,378 (7,246)
```

Distinct hosts served: 171 (54)
Data transferred: 8.843 gigabytes (328.436 megabytes)
Average data transferred per day: 95.328 megabytes (46.919 megabytes)

Monthly Report

This report lists the activity in each month.

Each unit (+) represents 30 requests for pages or part thereof.

```
   month:   reqs: pages:
--------: ------: -----:
Feb 2002: 152786:  1353: ++++++++++++++++++++++++++++++++++++++++++++++
Mar 2002: 221847:  1216: +++++++++++++++++++++++++++++++++++++++++++
Apr 2002: 331947:  1524: ++++++++++++++++++++++++++++++++++++++++++++++++++++
May 2002: 164817:   748: +++++++++++++++++++++++++
```

Busiest month: Apr 2002 (1,524 requests for pages).

Daily Summary

This report lists the total activity for each day of the week, summed over
  all the weeks in the report.

Each unit (+) represents 25 requests for pages or part thereof.

```
day:   reqs: pages:
---: ------: -----:
Sun:   5498:    46: ++
Mon: 180235:   788: +++++++++++++++++++++++++++++++++
Tue: 194718:   876: ++++++++++++++++++++++++++++++++++++
Wed: 169543:  1319: +++++++++++++++++++++++++++++++++++++++++++++++++++++
Thu: 162101:  1094: ++++++++++++++++++++++++++++++++++++++++++++
Fri: 139611:   599: ++++++++++++++++++++++++
Sat:  19691:   119: +++++
```

Hourly Summary

This report lists the total activity for each hour of the day, summed over
  all the days in the report.

Each unit (+) represents 15 requests for pages or part thereof.

```
hour:  reqs: pages:
----: -----: -----:
   0:  1426:   13: +
   1:   726:   12: +
   2:   294:    3: +
   3:    24:    3: +
   4:  1736:    3: +
   5:  7080:    7: +
   6: 13271:   48: ++++
   7: 37484:  233: +++++++++++++++
   8: 76573:  490: +++++++++++++++++++++++++++++++++
   9: 97388:  473: +++++++++++++++++++++++++++++++++
  10: 97755:  397: ++++++++++++++++++++++++++++
  11: 94105:  408: +++++++++++++++++++++++++++++
  12: 82582:  386: ++++++++++++++++++++++++++++
  13: 78084:  457: ++++++++++++++++++++++++++++++++
  14: 79728:  433: +++++++++++++++++++++++++++++++
  15: 79873:  504: +++++++++++++++++++++++++++++++++++
  16: 71265:  605: ++++++++++++++++++++++++++++++++++++++++++
  17: 28676:  167: +++++++++++
  18: 10261:   52: ++++
  19:  4757:   53: ++++
  20:  3177:   34: +++
  21:  2301:   32: +++
  22:  1565:   18: ++
  23:  1266:   10: +
```

Status Code Report

This report lists the HTTP status codes of all requests.

Listing status codes, sorted numerically.

```
  reqs: status code
------: -----------
625204: 200 OK
    42: 206 Partial content
    11: 301 Document moved permanently
246151: 304 Not modified since last retrieval
   741: 404 Document not found
```

```
File Type Report
----------------
This report lists the extensions of requested files.

Listing extensions with at least 0.1% of the traffic, sorted by the amount
    of traffic.

   reqs: %bytes: extension
------: ------: ---------
506078: 95.26%: .php  [PHP]
 92409:  2.84%: .htc
155840:  1.29%: .css  [Cascading Style Sheets]
 51979:  0.29%: .js   [JavaScript code]
 60182:  0.18%: .gif  [GIF graphics]
  1107:  0.12%: .html [Hypertext Markup Language]
  3802:  0.02%: [not listed: 5 extensions]
-------------------------------------------------------------------------


Directory Report
----------------
This report lists the directories from which files were requested. (The
    figures for each directory include all of its subdirectories.)

Listing directories with at least 0.01% of the traffic, sorted by the amount
    of traffic.

   reqs: %bytes: directory
------: ------: ---------
749032: 95.24%: [root directory]
 47943:  2.05%: /tdc_forms/
 28351:  1.46%: /tdc_data_access/
  3997:  1.13%: /test/
 41840:  0.12%: /imgs/
   234:        : [not listed: 4 directories]
-------------------------------------------------------------------------


This analysis was produced by analog 5.24.
Running time: 17 seconds.
```

The best way to find out what Analog can do is to compile a copy and run it on your server logs. Even if you're running another log analyzer, it is quite likely that some features of Analog will be useful in augmenting the other analyzer.

Webalizer

The only other Web log analyzer I have used regularly is Brad Barrett's Webalizer (www.mrunix.net/webalizer/), mostly for its excellent use of graphics. While Analog excels at in-depth statistics about your Web server's activity, Webalizer does an excellent job of providing high-level summaries of the data, presented in bar charts, pie charts, and tables that highlight trends and time-period comparisons (Figure 11.2). Webalizer compiles hourly, daily, monthly, and yearly summaries in a variety of graphic formats, including tabular.

Figure 11.2 Webalizer can provide graphical summaries of Web access statistics.

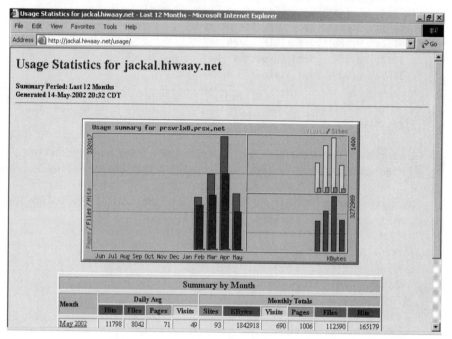

Webalizer is a good tool to use in conjunction with other log analyzers. One of its limitations is that it doesn't support fully customized logs. Currently it only supports CLF, combined, and two less-used formats, squid and wu-ftp logs. In the next release, it is expected to include support for native IIS and W3C extended logs.

> **NOTE** The W3C format (www.w3.org/TR/WD-logfile) is an extensible format in which the format specification is included within the log itself (something like XML).

Webalizer makes use of the GD libraries to render its graphics. Quite honestly, I thought that I didn't have them on my Linux system, having never linked to them or used them before. These were part of my Red Hat installation, however, and I was able to compile and install Webalizer with the following simple commands:

```
# ./configure
# make
# make install
```

Webalizer installs its executable (by default) into `/usr/local/bin/webalizer`. It also creates a sample configuration file, `/etc/webalizer.conf.sample`. This file should be renamed `webalizer.conf`, and modified as necessary. I made two modifications to it, pointing Webalizer to the proper Apache access log and also specifying a location for Webalizer's output files. Webalizer will write HTML files and supporting GIF images (all of which will automatically be assigned a name that includes the current date) into this output directory:

```
LogFile       /usr/local/apache2/logs/access_log
OutputDir     /home/httpd/html/webalizer
```

Webalizer allows incremental processing, so you can process small pieces of a log rather than trying to accumulate weeks or months of data into one huge log. With incremental logging, you can rotate your logs, for example, on a weekly basis and process each weekly log separately, combining the results. Monthly summaries, too, are saved, eliminating the need to have previous logfiles available for generating long-term historical charts.

Webalizer is very fast and quite easy to use. While it might not answer all of everyone's log analysis needs, it is one program I highly recommend to all Apache administrators, even those already happily using another log analyzer.

Advanced Log Analyzers

In today's electronic commerce world, Web site traffic analysis is often far more sophisticated than the methods I've described in this chapter. Newer tools for analyzing Web access patterns (a process usually termed *Web analytics*) usually work pretty much the same as the standard logging methods I've described that analyze standard logfiles. In addition, however, most attempt to draw conclusions from that data about client usage patterns. The high-end variety often correlate log data in some way with demographic data supplied by the site's customers and stored in databases. This type of customer profiling is usually aimed at determining not just what visitors to your site access while there, but how they got there in the first place and the paths they followed once they arrived.

Most of these commercial log analyzers are able to work with a large number of log formats, although the Extended Common Log Format is the format most often used on

Apache servers. These advanced analyzers should be considered separate products, not as Apache add-ons. For that reason, I will only mention one, as an example of the best of breed. Although the number of commercial Web site tracking tools is constantly increasing and the field is in constant fluctuation, the current stand-out favorite for Apache on Linux Web servers is the Analysis Suite from WebTrends (www.webtrends.com). At WebTrends' Web site, you can view a sample of every report and graph that the Analysis Suite can produce, and even download a trial demo copy if you'd like. WebTrends also produces a simple Log Analyzer that is available for a moderate license fee of $500 per Web server. Though not an expensive utility, for most administrators this tool offers no compelling advantage over the open-source products shown earlier in this chapter.

The real value of high-end commercial Web site log analyzers lies in the efficiency with which they can summarize extremely large logfiles (WebTrends claims to be able to analyze daily logfiles of over 160 million requests) and the quality of the summary reports they generate from standard log data. WebTrends will output its reports in both Microsoft Word and HTML for viewing and in Microsoft Excel format for analysis.

An even newer approach to Web customer profiling is behavioral analysis. This involves embedding metadata within HTML-formatted documents (actually JavaScript code that runs within the client browser). When the document is retrieved, this special code is "fired" to record information about the retrieving client, often temporary data that is accumulated from the user during the current session and will not be written to logfiles for later retrieval. Again, WebTrends stands as a current best-of-breed example of such a product with its high-end Intelligence Suite (formerly CommerceTrends) product.

Rotating Apache Logs

On heavily trafficked Apache servers, logfiles often grow quite large (quite rapidly). Most sites use some scheme to *rotate* logfiles. In other words, at specific time intervals (usually daily, during a period of low traffic volume), they quit writing to the current log, close it, rename it, and begin logging to a fresh, empty logfile. At first glance, it might seem impossible (or at least a *very* bad idea) to close and rename a file that Apache is actively using for its logfile. The Apache developers have made this easy, however, and you can change the active log without having to shut down the server completely. It's actually quite simple and completely safe, though there is a small trick involved.

Apache knows the logfile by its initial *inode*, rather than its filename. The inode is a numerical entry into a table that shows how disk clusters are allocated to files. When you rename a file, the file itself remains unchanged on the hard disk. Since Apache is writing to the file by inode, changing its name has no effect; and when the logfile is renamed,

Apache continues to write to the file by its new name. This allows you to issue a command like the following to change the name of the Apache request logfile on the fly:

```
# mv /usr/local/apache2/logs/access_log
     /usr/local/apache2/logs/access.0730
```

You can do this through a script (usually scheduled to run automatically under Linux's cron utility). After renaming the file, the Apache server is restarted by sending it the -USR signal. This signal causes Apache to perform a graceful restart, ensuring that all current connections are closed only after their requests are fulfilled and there will be no interruption of service. The restart will cause Apache to read its configuration file, and it will create a new logfile using the name specified in the TransferLog of the configuration file and begin writing its logging information there. Use either the Linux kill command or the apachectl utility to perform a graceful restart (as described in Chapter 10):

```
# kill -USR1 'cat /usr/local/apache2/logs/httpd.pid'
# /usr/local/apache2/bin/apachectl graceful
```

Although this process is quite simple and easy to script, it is essentially a manual process. Apache, however, provides an alternative method. In Apache's bin directory you will find another utility called rotatelogs. This utility is designed to be used with the log-to-pipe functionality described earlier in this chapter. The utility must be used with a TransferLog directive that indicates that logging should be piped to this utility, as in this example:

```
TransferLog "|rotatelogs /usr/local/apache/logs/access_log 86400"
ErrorLog "|rotatelogs /usr/local/apache/logs/error_log 86400"
```

In this example, rotatelogs will automatically rotate your logs, appending the system time to the filename specified, so that a filename like error_log.0964828800 is created. The number at the end is the number of seconds that has elapsed since a fixed point in time, called the *epoch*; every second, that large integer is incremented by one. Without doing the math, I will accept the Linux designers' word that the epoch is 00:00:00 on January 1, 1970, Coordinated Universal Time (UTC).

The numeric argument to rotatelogs is the number of seconds between each log rotation. In the example, rotatelogs will rotate access_log to access_log.*nnnn* every 86,400 seconds (24 hours), and open up a new access_log file.

One disadvantage of rotatelogs is that it does not permit a lot of control over the names assigned to the rotated logfiles. Also, the extension that it assigns to rotated files can be inconvenient. Your log analyzers won't care about the long numeric extension (they will use only the internal dates in preparing their summary statistics), but it will make it difficult for human administrators to find the log entries for a particular day, for example. For that reason, you may wish to consider an open-source alternative to `rotatelogs` called `cronolog` (available from www.cronolog.org). This program works quite similarly to Apache's `rotatelogs`, except that it determines the frequency of log rotation and directory paths to the rotated logs according to a template that uses the same format specifiers as the Linux date command. For example, if you wanted to rotate your logs on a daily basis, you would use a template like the following:

```
CustomLog "|bin/cronolog /usr/local/apache/logs/%Y/%m/%d/access.log common"
ErrorLog "|/bin/cronolog /usr/local/apache/logs/%Y/%m/%d/errors.log"
```

This template would maintain logfiles in separate directories for each year, month, and day, as follows:

```
/usr/local/apache2/logs/2000/07/27/access.log
/usr/local/apache2/logs/2000/07/27/errors.log
```

Using *logresolve*

Although Apache logging can be configured to look up and log hostnames for every request, this is never desirable on heavily loaded servers. Reverse DNS lookups (in which the DNS is queried to find the hostname corresponding to an IP address) require time and put Apache processes into a wait state while the results are being fetched. Eliminating the requirement for the hostname lookup eliminates these expensive wait states. You should enable `HostnameLookups` only on a lightly used server.

If you desire hostnames instead of IP addresses in your log analyses, you can use an Apache utility named `logresolve` to perform the reverse-DNS lookups on entire logfiles prior to analysis. You'll find this utility in the `bin` subdirectory under the Apache installation directory (usually `/usr/local/apache2`).

You cannot use `logresolve` with an open logfile, but after you rotate your logfile (as described in the previous section), you can run `logresolve` on the file to convert IP addresses into hostnames (assuming the IP address can be resolved into a hostname). The utility is very simple, reading from its standard input handle and writing to its standard output handle. You use I/O redirection to specify the input and output, as follows:

```
logresolve < access.log > access.log.resolved
```

The `logresolve` utility can take two optional arguments. Provide the `-s` argument to have `logresolve` write statistics it gathers to a separate file, as in

```
logresolve -s logstats.txt < access.log > access.log.resolved
```

The `-c` option instructs `logresolve` to use double-reverse DNS lookups. This checks for bogus (*spoofed*) hostnames by checking that a hostname associated with an IP actually maps to that IP address. After resolving an IP address to a hostname (with a reverse DNS lookup), `logresolve` will then do a DNS lookup for the IP address of that hostname (it may receive several). Before `logresolve` will accept a hostname it has determined from a reverse DNS lookup, one of the IP addresses it receives when supplying this hostname in an address lookup query must match the original IP address. I do not recommend using this feature, for two reasons: it will greatly increase the time required to process a log, and the benefits are minimal. When used with `logresolve`, double-reverse DNS lookup does nothing to enhance the security of your site, and the bogus entries it catches are far more likely to be the result of misconfigured DNS servers than the result of deliberate attempts to spoof a hostname.

In Sum

Logging is an essential function of any Web server. This chapter discussed how Apache provides logging, both as part of the core module for error logging and through the `mod_log_config` module for request logging. It showed how to configure an Apache server for logging, how to specify the location for logfiles, how to determine the severity of errors that will be logged, and how to customize request logs.

Although request logs are often examined in detail, usually to determine the action logged for a specific request, these logs are so extensive that they are viewed in summary to determine client patterns, trends, and preferences. Scripting languages like Perl or Python are very useful for summarizing Apache request logs. For most administrators, however, a far more convenient solution is to use one of the many log analyzers written for just this purpose. Some of the best are freely available as open source. I offered two as examples of the best of these. One produces graphical, or presentation-oriented, output; the other produces tabular, textual data. I have found both quite useful. There is also a new breed of log analyzer, tailored to electronic commerce solutions and generally targeted at creating a profile of customer preferences, usually correlated with demographic data from another data source.

The next chapter continues the discussion of administering a working server; it discusses a number of ways to increase the performance of an Apache server, particularly the use of proxying and caching.

Maintaining a Healthy Server

PART 4

12

Proxying and Performance Tuning

Once you have a working Apache Web server, you will want to tune the server to optimize its performance. This would mean minimizing the delay experienced by users in retrieving resources from your server and maximizing the number of requests you can adequately respond to in a given time.

Well, if you're the type who likes to tweak software, the bad news is that there's not a lot you can do to improve the performance of Apache. The good news is that it usually isn't necessary; Apache is already well tuned for the highest performance, and most of the development work being done on the current Apache release is geared more toward higher performance than feature enhancement.

In this chapter, I'll first discuss the few performance directives you have at your disposal as an administrator, and then explore one of the most important tools you can use to minimize document retrieval times on a local area network: Web caching using Apache as a proxy server.

Performance Directives

One way to optimize Apache's performance is by increasing the number of process threads available to handle requests. Recall from Chapter 2 that Apache's default *stand-alone* mode of operation starts the main Apache process at boot time. The main Apache process starts the process pool (or *swarm*), which consists of up to 256 Apache server processes that handle incoming requests. Apache's pool of waiting processes is under the control of the main Apache server process (which does not, itself, respond to client requests). The number of processes in the pool is not static; it changes as requirements dictate. The server administrator sets three parameters in `httpd.conf` to control the number of processes started when Apache is invoked. The following general server directives (which have server-wide scope) are used for that purpose:

MinSpareServers   Specifies the minimum number of spare servers (idle servers waiting for incoming connections) that reside in the process pool. The main Apache process ensures that at least this many idle servers are always available to handle client requests. Usually, the default value of five spare servers is changed only on servers with very heavy or light loads. With a heavily loaded server, you'll increase this value to ensure more standby servers so that clients never experience a delay while a new process is created. On very lightly loaded servers, you may choose to reduce the number of servers waiting idle but consuming system memory.

MaxSpareServers   Specifies the maximum number of spare servers in the process pool. If the number of idle servers exceeds this number, the main Apache server kills excess servers until there are fewer idle Apache processes than specified in this directive. Usually, the default value of 10 is changed only on very heavily or very lightly loaded servers.

StartServers   Specifies the number of spare server processes that are created when Apache is started. The default value of 5 rarely needs to be changed, although it may be increased on heavily loaded servers to ensure an adequate pool of Apache processes is available to handle a large number of client connections. I usually set this value on my servers to match `MinSpareServers`.

Here's an example. My personal Apache/Linux server, which is used mainly for testing and to host resources that are shared with colleagues, is very lightly used. The number of connections is measured in hundreds per day. Listing 12.1 is an `httpd.conf` file that starts 10 listener processes when Apache starts (twice the Apache default), always keeps 10 in reserve, and ensures that the number of active listener processes is always 10 or greater.

Listing 12.1   Allocating Listener Processes

```
#MinSpareServers 5  Apache default
MinSpareServers 10

#MaxSpareServer 10  Apache default
MaxSpareServers 20
```

```
#
# Number of servers to start initially --- should be
# a reasonable ballpark figure.
#StartServers 5     Apache default
StartServers 10
```

A benchmarking utility like ApacheBench (demonstrated in Chapter 8) or the excellent WebStone utility (open-source software available from MindCraft, `www.mindcraft.com/webstone`) can be used to determine when these values need to be increased. If you can run these benchmarking tools on a nonproduction server, you should do so with a large variety of test URLs, varying the number of server processes and concurrent client processes. Strive to get a baseline estimate of the number of requests your server is capable of processing; look for the breakpoint where increasing the number of server processes no longer results in a performance increase. WebStone can be configured to automatically increment the number of concurrent client processes at each of several iterations of a benchmark test. The results can then be used to predict performance decreases that will occur as request loads increase.

There is no hard-and-fast rule for determining the optimum number of `httpd` processes, but in general, you should increase the number of running listener processes whenever measured connection times start to increase (indicating that client connections are being queued to be handled by the next available listener process). Collecting benchmark data regularly is the best way to discern trends in server usage and keep an eye on server response. You will need to experiment with different values of the Apache performance directives to optimize them for your server, but most sites will probably find that the Apache defaults are perfectly adequate.

Controlling Client Connections

In addition to the directives available for controlling server processes, Apache also provides a set of directives you can use to control the number and size of client connections:

MaxClients   This directive sets a limit to the number of `httpd` listener processes that can run simultaneously (one per connected client). The default is 256, which is the maximum that can be set without modifying the value of HARD_SERVER_LIMIT in *Apache_source*/include/httpd.h and recompiling the server. This parameter rarely needs to be increased. If you do increase the value, make sure your system can handle the load (it needs a fast CPU and fast disk I/O, but especially lots of system RAM). This limit is a fail-safe value to keep your server from crashing under extreme load, and the value you set should exceed the number of clients you are actually serving by about 25 percent.

If your server load is so heavy that you find 256 processes insufficient, consider adding another physical server on your network. You may wish, however, to limit the total number of Apache server processes that can run if you have a system with limited resources (particularly if you have only 32 or 64MB of RAM). There is no hard-and-fast way to determine the maximum number of processes your system can support, so you might need to experiment a little. If your system is crashing because of an excessive number of Apache processes, however, you should immediately reduce the maximum number specified in this directive.

ListenBacklog Apache does not immediately refuse new client connections once the maximum number of httpd processes has reached MaxClients. Instead, it holds them in a queue to be handled by the httpd processes that complete the servicing of a request and are free to accept a new one. This queue can grow up to the number of requests specified in ListenBacklog. When the queue reaches this limit, all arriving connections are rejected with a 503 (Service Unavailable) HTTP response code. By default, this value is set to 511, and it rarely needs to be changed. If your number of backlogged connections consistently grows to this size, you should try to reduce the backlog rather than increase the allowable number of backlogged connections.

Timeout Apache uses a single value to determine when to time out and close a connection while waiting for a response from a client. When any of the following three wait intervals exceeds the value set by the Timeout directive, the client connection is closed:

- The time it takes to receive a GET request from a client after that client connects
- The time between receipt of individual TCP packets on a HTTP POST or PUT request, in which the server is accepting a stream of data from the client
- The time Apache will wait for acknowledgments (ACKs) to individual TCP packets it sends

  The default value for Timeout is 300 seconds, or 5 minutes. That's an extraordinarily long time to wait for any one of the three responses for which this timeout is valid. For most servers, this value can safely be reduced to something like 60 with this directive:

```
Timeout 60
```

Clients on very slow links may be disconnected prematurely, but a value of a full minute is not unreasonably small in today's Internet.

```
SendBufferSize
```

This value (expressed in bytes) will set the size of the TCP output buffer size. The default value of this buffer is set in the Linux kernel, but you can override it, particularly if you need to queue data for high-latency links (where the time required to receive an acknowledgment to a sent packet is in the range of 100ms or more). This directive should be used with caution, because every TCP/IP buffer created by

Apache will be sized to this value, and a large value can have a significant effect on memory consumption, especially for sites with many child Apache processes.

KeepAlive   This simple directive can be set to either On or Off to enable or disable HTTP/1.1 persistent connections. HTTP/1.1-compliant browsers use persistent connections to submit multiple requests over a single TCP connection to a Web server. Enabling this feature usually offers a tremendous speed advantage over traditional connectionless HTTP, in which the client has to establish a new connection to the server for each request. A Web page that has a number of inline images can request all of these over the same TCP connection, rather than opening a new request for each.

The default value of `KeepAlive` is On, which means Apache will allow persistent connections requested by browsers that support them (as nearly all up-to-date browsers now do). It should never be necessary to disable this feature, except for browsers that do not properly support persistent connections but request them anyway. The default Apache configuration identifies two such browsers and disables persistent connections for them by setting the `nokeepalive` environment variable using a `BrowserMatch` directive. You can also set this environment variable to disable persistent connections selectively, but you are safe in leaving the directive set to `KeepAlive on`.

KeepAliveTimeout   Specifies the length of time Apache will wait for a subsequent request after receiving a client request with an HTTP `Keep-Alive` header requesting a persistent connection. The default value is 15 seconds, which you will find defined in your default Apache configuration by this directive:

```
KeepAliveTimeout 15
```

If no subsequent request is received in this length of time, Apache completes the processing of the current request for that client and closes the connection.

MaxKeepAliveRequests   Limits the number of requests allowed per persistent connection. By default, the value is set to 100, which should be a sufficient value for all sites:

```
MaxKeepAliveRequests 100
```

If the number is set to 0, unlimited requests will be accepted over a single request. This is something you should never do, however. It opens your Apache server to a form of denial-of-service attack in which a malicious client opens, but doesn't close, a large number of persistent HTTP connections.

LimitRequestBody   Sets a limit, in bytes, to the size of an HTTP request body. You can set the value to any number from 0 (the default, which means "unlimited") up to 2,147,483,647 bytes (2GB). Use this directive to set a limit on the size of data sent by a client in a POST or PUT HTTP request. This directive is valid in a directory context. To set the value to 10KB for CGI scripts that receive client uploads, use this:

```
<Location /cgi-bin/*>
LimitRequestBody 10240
</Location>
```

NOTE   In Linux kernel version 2.4, which is now available and shipping as the default kernel for many distributions, the 2GB limit for an HTTP request body has been eliminated.

LimitRequestFields   Allows the Apache administrator to limit the number of HTTP headers that can appear in a single client request. The default value is 100, which well exceeds the typical number of headers in a request (rarely over 20). This directive is rarely needed, but many administrators choose to set a lower limit than the default value to provide some measure of protection against malformed requests using a directive like this:

```
LimitRequestFields 40
```

LimitRequestFieldSize   Limits the size (in bytes) of all HTTP request headers. Here again, the value rarely needs to be changed from its compiled-in default of 8190 bytes. If you wish to reduce or increase this limit, however, you can do so with a directive like this:

```
LimitRequestFieldSize 1000
```

To increase the value beyond 8190 bytes, it is necessary to modify the value of DEFAULT_LIMIT_REQUEST_FIELDSIZE in Apache_source/include/httpd.h, and recompile the Apache kernel.

LimitRequestLine   Limits the allowable size (in bytes) of all HTTP request lines. The request line consists of the HTTP method, the URI, and optionally the protocol version. This value rarely needs to be changed from its compiled-in default of 8190 bytes. To decrease it, use a directive like this:

```
LimitRequestLine 500
```

To increase the value beyond 8190 bytes, you'll need to modify the value of DEFAULT_LIMIT_REQUEST_LINE in Apache_source/include/httpd.h, and recompile the Apache kernel.

Listing 12.2 is a portion of an `httpd.conf` file for controlling the number and size of client connections.

Listing 12.2   Controlling Client Connections

```
MaxClients 512
ListenBacklog 1000
Timeout 45
SendBufferSize
KeepAlive on
KeepAliveTimeout 30
MaxKeepAliveRequests 50
LimitRequestBody 10000
LimitRequestFields 40
LimitRequestFieldSize
LimitRequestLine 1000
```

First, the MaxClients 512 directive increases the maximum number of simultaneous httpd processes from the default of 256. Next, the ListenBacklog 1000 directive increases the number of TCP connections that will be waiting for an available httpd process from its default of 511, again to prevent connections from being rejected on our heavily loaded server.

We also decrease the length of time that our server will wait for a response from each client before closing the connection from the default of 300 seconds (5 minutes) to 45 seconds.

The SendBufferSize directive is usually changed only when the Apache server will be communicating over high-latency links (like intercontinental transmission lines), and it isn't changed in this example.

The KeepAlive on directive enables HTTP/1.1 persistent connections, and the KeepAliveTimeout 30 directive doubles the default value of 15 seconds for the maximum time that Apache will wait for a second request from a client with an open persistent connection. MaxKeepAliveRequests 50 sets a limit on the number of requests that will be permitted from a client on a single persistent connection, reduced by half from its default value of 100.

On this server we are not accepting uploads from clients (in the form of PUT requests), so the LimitRequestBody 10000 directive limits the byte size of HTTP requests. The LimitRequestsFields 40 directive then greatly reduces the number of headers that can be received in a single HTTP request; the default setting of 8190 is far too many for a legitimate request. Again, we do this to reduce the potential for abuse of the server. With the LimitRequestFieldSize directive, we accept the (quite sane) default limit of 8190 bytes on the size of a single HTTP request header. Finally, the LimitRequestLine 1000 directive reduces the default limit of 8190 characters on the length of a single request line. The default is probably larger than will ever be necessary, but not unreasonably so; this line is included mainly for the purpose of illustration.

**Maintaining a
Healthy Server**

PART 4

Using Apache as a Proxy Server

So far in this chapter you've seen how to tune Apache's performance by adjusting the values of various parameters related to server processes and client connections; and you've seen that the benefits of that approach are limited, because Apache's default values for these parameters are already well optimized for performance.

Thanks to its mod_proxy module, Apache can also be used as a proxy server, a strategy that can provide significant performance benefits on intranet or LAN installations and enhance security on all Apache servers. The remainder of this chapter examines the different approaches to proxying and the tools that Apache's mod_proxy module provides.

How Proxies Work

The most common form of proxy server is a *forwarding proxy server,* illustrated in Figure 12.1. Notice that the server designated as the proxy server sits outside the requesting network's firewall and responds to requests from internal hosts for resources on the Internet. The proxy server forwards these requests to the remote Internet host, often because (for security reasons) the originator of the request does not have direct access to the Internet. The request is not literally forwarded; the proxy server reissues it with a new IP header. The remote server responds directly to the proxy server and is unaware that the request originated on another system. When the proxy server receives the response, it replaces the IP header with a new header, which has the address of the internal host that originated the proxy request.

Most proxy servers are capable of performing this task for a variety of application protocols. The protocols that are most often proxied are HTTP (Web connections), Secure HTTP (HTTPS), and the File Transfer Protocol (FTP). While the original purpose of using proxy servers was to provide Internet access through a network firewall, that role has changed significantly. Today, as more Web servers are used in intranets, the importance of a proxy server is increasingly related to *caching* HTTP requests. A proxy server configured for HTTP caching saves a copy of each Web object (pages, images, files) that it retrieves on behalf of clients. These saved copies of Web objects are written to disk storage on the proxy server. If a subsequent request for a cached Web object is received (and the object's expiration time has not passed), the proxy server sends the cached object, rather than making a new request of the remote host from which it was originally obtained. From the requester's point of view, this greatly speeds the retrieval of the resource.

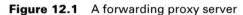

Figure 12.1   A forwarding proxy server

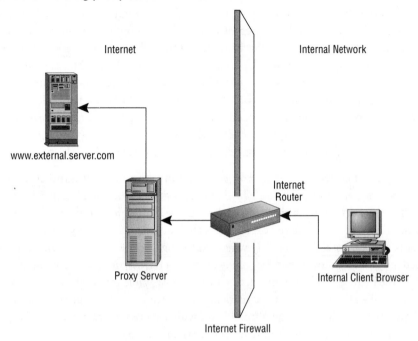

HTTP caching results in two forms of performance improvement for intranets. First, whenever a Web object is served from cache rather than by making an HTTP request of a remote host, there is a significant reduction in the *latency* of the request. In other words, the requester gets the object much faster when it comes from cached data. This has the effect of making the network appear much faster than it actually is. The second improvement that is realized from HTTP caching is reduced bandwidth usage. Every request that can be served from cached data means less traffic on the Internet connection. Of course, both benefits depend on the assumption that in a given network, a high percentage of Web traffic will go to a relatively small number of sites whose content does not expire too frequently.

Most Web browser software is capable of caching copies of retrieved documents. For resources that rarely change and are frequently reused (like inline images and icons), retrieval from cache storage rather than from the remote server can significantly reduce the amount of time required to load a Web page. A browser-based cache is often referred to as a *private cache*. When the cache resides on a proxy server that is capable of serving locally stored copies of documents to a number of client browsers, it is called a *shared cache*.

**Maintaining a
Healthy Server**

PART 4

In earlier versions of Apache, caching was an integral part of mod_proxy, but in Apache 2.0, the two functions of proxying and caching, though usually closely related, are separated and implemented in different modules. The content-caching functions are provided in mod_cache, which must be installed to cache content retrieved by mod_proxy. Not only that, but you must also load one other module in order to use it. This module will most likely be mod_disk_cache, which provides traditional caching of content in disk files, although a later section of this chapter will discuss the mod_mem_cache module, which provides memory-based caching. Most Apache administrators will choose to use a combination of mod_disk_cache with mod_proxy, thus providing the best compromise of speed with a caching space limited only by available disk space.

On my local network, I set up mod_proxy on my Apache server, and configured all my browsers to retrieve HTTP and FTP documents through it. Then I added caching capabilities to the server with mod_cache and mod_disk_cache. Since I have only a few client workstations, I did not expect shared caching to significantly affect the way my browsers performed. I was very surprised, particularly when requesting documents with a large number of embedded images, to discover that mod_proxy caching on my Apache server is significantly faster than the browser cache on my client workstations. While this seems implausible, and I can't guarantee you'll have the same experience, I do recommend mod_proxy and mod_cache for shared Web caching, even on a small LAN with a shared Internet connection. It seems to work nearly as well on a small scale as it does on a large one.

Reverse Proxying

As illustrated in Figure 12.2, proxy servers can also be configured to work in the opposite direction. A *reverse proxy* server sits outside the serving network's firewall, and is configured to respond to requests from HTTP clients on the Internet for resources that reside on internal Web servers. The proxy server in this scheme takes these external requests and forwards them to the correct internal server. The reverse proxy server here primarily plays a security role, providing access to internal data providers that are not directly accessible from the outside world. Caching of these resources is generally a secondary concern when a reverse proxy is used.

In the following sections I'll show how to set up mod_proxy as a forward and reverse proxy. Keep in mind that a single proxy server can simultaneously serve in both roles. You do not have to select one role to the exclusion of the other.

The *mod_proxy* Module

Apache's tool for implementing a proxy/cache is the mod_proxy module. It implements proxying capability for HTTP/0.9, HTTP/1.0, and FTP. Using the CONNECT protocol, which supports TCP port 443 for SSL and TCP port 563 for Snews by default, the module can also be configured to connect to other proxy modules for these and other protocols.

Figure 12.2   A reverse proxy server

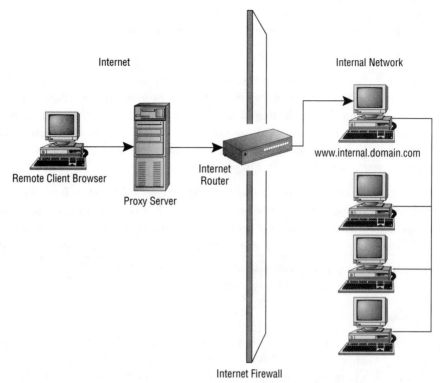

Internet

Internal Network

Remote Client Browser

Proxy Server

Internet Router

www.internal.domain.com

Internet Firewall

Setting Up a Forward Proxy

To use mod_proxy as a forward proxy, you just need to ensure that the module is either statically linked into the Apache kernel or compiled as a DSO module and dynamically loaded at runtime. You can verify the availability of this or any other module by running httpd -l, or via the URL /server-info if you have that capability (as described in Chapter 10).

If you used the --enable-shared=most switch when running the Apache configure script, you'll find that the module is compiled as mod_proxy.so. Ensure that your httpd.conf file contains the directives necessary to load and enable the module:

```
LoadModule proxy_module modules/mod_proxy.so
LoadModule proxy_ftp_module modules/mod_proxy_ftp.so
LoadModule proxy_http_module modules/mod_proxy_http.so
```

A properly installed mod_proxy will add a number of directives to your httpd.conf file, in a section clearly labeled *Proxy server directives*. Like all optional directives, they are initially commented out, so you'll need to uncomment them. While you will probably

Maintaining a
Healthy Server

PART 4

not need to change any of these directives to use Apache as a proxy server, this chapter describes all of them, and you should understand what each one does. The most important directive you'll need to enable in `httpd.conf` is this:

```
ProxyRequests on
```

Once this forward proxying is enabled, the Apache server will respond to requests for resources on the server by sending them directly, as usual. But it will proxy requests for all other resources by attempting to retrieve the resource from the server named in the URL and returning the results to the requesting client. In networks where a firewall blocks internal hosts from direct access to the Internet, this is the only way that these hosts can retrieve Web resources from the Internet.

While it is perfectly okay to let your main Apache server proxy request documents that it cannot serve directly from its own local stores, I usually prefer to set up a virtual host, listening on a TCP port other than the main server's default of port 80, to handle proxy requests. My Apache `httpd.conf` file contains this `<VirtualHost>` container:

```
<VirtualHost 192.168.1.1:8080>
   ServerName jackal.hiwaay.net
   ProxyRequests on
</VirtualHost>
```

This container ensures that only requests received on TCP port 8080 are proxied. It's only a convention, but that is the TCP port proxy servers commonly use, and you'll often see that port used in documentation on configuring proxy clients. Note that my `httpd.conf` must also contain a `Listen 8080` directive (outside the virtual host container) to ensure that Apache accepts connections on that port.

The `ProxyRequests` directive is used to halt proxy services as follows (this is the default setting for the directive):

```
ProxyRequests off
```

I doubt you'll ever have an occasion to specify this directive.

Mirroring Remote Sites

One common use of a proxy server is to mirror remote Web sites, making them appear to be local. The `ProxyPass` directive is used to map remote Web URLs to a URL that would ordinarily point to a resource on the local server.

For example, the following directive can be used to make documentation from the Linux Documentation Project's main site appear to be local to my server (and once a resource has been retrieved by the proxy and held in cache, it will be served as a local resource):

```
ProxyPass /LinuxDocs/ http://www.tldp.org/
```

Here, whenever my proxy server receives a request from a client trying to connect to `http://jackal.hiwaay.net/LinuxDocs/`, the request is automatically and invisibly referred to The Linux Documentation Project `http://www.tldp.org/`.

Setting Up a Reverse Proxy

You can also use `mod_proxy` to configure your Apache server as a reverse proxy, which gives remote clients access to resources on your internal servers without exposing those servers to direct connections from the outside. Indeed, in most situations where a proxy server is used in this manner, an Internet firewall renders servers totally invisible and completely inaccessible from the outside world.

As with forward proxying, the first step to setting up a reverse proxy server is to ensure that `mod_proxy` is either compiled into Apache or loaded as a DSO module. And just as you do for a forward proxy server, enable proxy services with this directive:

```
ProxyRequests On
```

Some special considerations are necessary to ensure reverse proxy operation, however. First, the goal is to provide outside clients with transparent access to resources on your internal servers, without connecting to those servers directly. These remote clients will see only one server, your proxy server, and will connect only to that system. This server only appears to serve all the resources the client requests. To perform this feat of magic, some means is necessary to map each requested URL received from remote clients by the proxy server to a URL on an internal server. This is provided by the `ProxyPass` directive, and you will need one to map each request into a URL that can be used to request the resource from an internal server. Here's an example that maps requests to `/CPAN` on the proxy server to a server named `archive.fubar.com`, and all embedded images are retrieved from a second server, `rascal.fubar.com`:

```
ProxyPass /CPAN/ http://archive.fubar.com/CPAN/
ProxyPass /images/ http://rascal.fubar.com/images/
```

The second configuration that's necessary for reverse proxy use is to include a `ProxyPassReverse` directive. Because the internal server that eventually answers a request from a remote host will place its own hostname in the `Location` header of redirect requests sent to the client, the Apache reverse proxy server needs to replace this hostname with its own; that's what the `ProxyPassReverse` directive does. This ensures that redirected requests from an internal Web server are adjusted so that the proxy server receives them.

To make things really convenient, the `ProxyPassReverse` directive takes exactly the same arguments as the `ProxyPass` directive, and you can easily create a matching `ProxyPassReverse` directive for each `ProxyPass` directive.

```
ProxyPassReverse /CPAN/ http://archive.fubar.com/CPAN/
ProxyPassReverse /images/ http://rascal.fubar.com/images/
```

Configuring a Browser for a Forward Proxy

Once you have an Apache server configured with mod_proxy to act as a (forward) proxy server for HTTP (and FTP) requests, you need only to configure your client browsers to make requests of this server, rather than trying to connect to the desired resource directly.

When a browser is configured to use a proxy server, it will connect to that server, and make a request for that server to act as a proxy in retrieving the desired resource from the remote server. Every browser has its own procedure for configuring it to use one or more proxy servers. The procedure I describe is for Netscape Communicator/Navigator and serves only to illustrate the basic steps required.

In Communicator, select Preferences from the Edit menu and, in the Preferences window, expand the Advanced node in the command tree and click Proxies. The window will now look like Figure 12.3.

Figure 12.3   Begin configuring a Netscape Communicator/Navigator browser by opening the Preferences window.

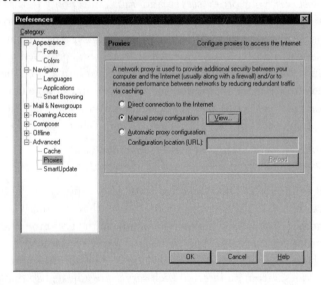

Make sure Manual Proxy Configuration is enabled, and click the View button. In the dialog box that appears (Figure 12.4), enter the IP address (or hostname) of your proxy server for each protocol you intend to proxy (the Security option means SSL). In Figure 12.4, I've configured my browser to connect to TCP port 8080 on my Apache server for HTTP and FTP requests. That TCP port number is commonly used by proxy servers, but it is arbitrary. In fact, I usually configure my Apache server to proxy requests received on the standard HTTP port (80). The module will proxy only those requests that it cannot satisfy directly (in other words, only remote resources).

Figure 12.4   Manual proxy configuration in Netscape

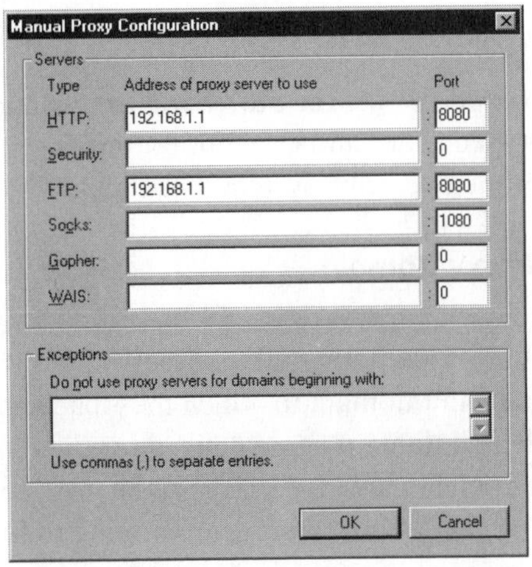

Now that Netscape is configured to use a proxy to retrieve resources, when you request a document with a URL like this:

```
http://www.apache.org
```

the browser will connect to TCP port 8080 on the proxy server, and issue a request that looks like this:

```
proxy://www.apache.org
```

This tells the server to fulfill the request by proxy.

If you have many client browsers behind a firewall that need to be set up to use a proxy server, consider distributing these instructions to your users. Setting up Web browsers to use a proxy server is a straightforward process that administrators shouldn't be burdened with performing for every client workstation.

Controlling the Proxy Engine

The mod_proxy module contains a number of directives that basically fit into either of two categories: those that control the module's proxy engine in receiving resources on behalf of clients, and those that control the caching of resources already retrieved and stored by the proxy engine. This section discusses the first group; I've already shown two of these, ProxyPass and ProxyPassReverse. The next section, "Setting Up a Disk-Caching Proxy," covers this second category of directives.

Maintaining a
Healthy Server

PART 4

Increasing Throughput of Proxied Requests

Although mod_proxy rarely requires performance tuning, there is one directive that is specifically designed to increase request throughput. The ProxyReceiveBufferSize directive allows the administrator to set a buffer size for HTTP and FTP requests. This directive takes one argument, the desired buffer size in bytes, which must be greater than 512:

```
ProxyReceiveBufferSize 4096
```

In Linux, I prefer to explicitly set the buffer size to 0, which indicates that the system's default buffer size is used. The Linux default buffer size of 64KB is already set to the maximum value that the operating system will allow.

Setting a Default Proxy Domain

In an intranet, you may want users to be able to omit your domain name from the URL when requesting resources from internal servers. To do this, you can use the ProxyDomain directive to specify a default domain to which the Apache proxy server belongs. This works just like the default domain name defined for the Linux server itself. If a request that omits the host's domain name is received to be proxied, the proxy server appends the domain defined by ProxyDomain before attempting to fulfill the request.

To illustrate, if the following ProxyDomain directive was in effect:

```
ProxyDomain .intranet.corporate.com
```

the proxy server would attempt to proxy a request for:

```
http://somehost/docs/index.html
```

by retrieving a resource from:

```
http://somehost.intranet.corporate.com/docs/index.html
```

Forwarding Proxy Requests

Often, it is desirable to configure a proxy server to redirect a part of its workload to other proxy servers. This is one way to distribute the tasks of resource retrieval and caching among several proxy servers. Use the ProxyRemote directive to define proxies to which the server will send certain requests instead of trying to retrieve the resource directly. Here's an example of how this might be used:

```
ProxyRemote http://www.thissite.org/
    http://proxy.corporate.com
```

Here, whenever my local Apache server, acting as a proxy, receives a request destined for www.thissite.org, it will automatically refer the request to a corporate proxy server. The corporate proxy not only caches responses from Internet Web sites, it is also the only way to retrieve Web resources through the corporate firewall, so it accomplishes two goals: enhanced security for the corporate intranet and more efficient Web retrieval.

Because mod_proxy can only communicate using HTTP, this directive will not support any other protocol for communication with the remote server. You can, however, refer requests received with other protocols if you specify only HTTP in the remote URL, as in:

```
ProxyRemote ftp http://ftpproxy.mydomain.com:8080
```

Here, any attempt to proxy an FTP request is referred to an FTP proxy server (which is probably a dedicated proxy server, although it could be another Apache 2.0 server proxying FTP requests). Note that HTTP is used to communicate with this remote proxy server. The original FTP request is encapsulated in HTTP for this request, which is probably not the most efficient technique. In these cases, it is usually better if the client browsers are configured with separate proxies for the HTTP and FTP protocols.

The special asterisk character (*) means "all requests," as in the following example, where all requests to this server are sent through a remote proxy:

```
ProxyRemote * http://proxy.mydomain.com
```

The NoProxy directive, which has a misleading name, is used to turn off ProxyRemote behavior for specific hostnames, domains, subnets, and individual IP addresses. For example:

```
ProxyRemote * http://proxy.mydomain.com
NoProxy 192.168.1.0/24 www.corporate.com
```

In this case, we've used ProxyRemote to specify that all requests received should be forwarded to a remote proxy. Then the NoProxy directive is used to identify all sites on the local subnet and one specific Web site as exclusions from this rule. The proxy server directly handles requests received for these sites, and all others are forwarded to the remote proxy to be served.

Blocking Proxy Requests

It is sometimes necessary to block certain remote sites from being accessed by a proxy server or, alternatively, to block certain clients from using the proxy server. The Proxy-Block directive accomplishes the first task. Provided with a list of words, hostnames, or domain names, this directive blocks all proxy requests for URLs containing these keywords and site names:

```
ProxyBlock blockeddomain.com gambling
```

In the above example, our proxy would refuse to honor requests for anything from the site blockeddomain.com or any URL that contains the string *gambling*. This is not really the best way to block a large number of sites, but it can come in handy if your proxy server is your LAN's only HTTP access to the Internet, and you need to block access to a few sites.

Interestingly, if a hostname is specified that can be resolved to an IP address when Apache starts, this IP address is cached, so that users can't bypass your ProxyBlock by using the blocked site's IP address instead of its hostname.

While ProxyBlock is useful in blocking specific remote sites from your proxy clients, it cannot be used to prevent specific clients from using the proxy server. To do that, you can take advantage of the fact that when a proxy client is configured to request HTTP resources through a proxy server, the URL it submits begins with the word proxy://, rather than with http://. Therefore, you can use a <Directory> section like the following to prohibit or allow use of the proxy by specific clients:

```
<Directory proxy:*>
  Order deny,allow
  Deny from all
  Allow from 192.168.1
</Directory>
```

In this case, I am permitting the use of my proxy server only from hosts connected to my local subnet (192.168.1).

Setting Up a Disk-Caching Proxy

In addition to the general proxy directives provided by mod_proxy, you'll almost certainly want to enable the disk caching of resources retrieved by the proxy engine. Two modules, mod_cache and mod_disk_cache, provide the directives discussed in this section. In order to set up a disk-caching proxy server, you will need to enable both modules. If you are compiling Apache from source, these modules will be created by including both of the following command-line arguments when running configure:

```
--enable-cache --enable-disk-cache
```

The modules, if compiled as DSO modules, must be loaded by the server when it is started by including these directives in httpd.conf:

```
LoadModule cache_module modules/mod_cache.so
LoadModule disk_cache_module modules/mod_disk_cache.so
```

Since directives from both modules are used to implement disk caching, it is useful to keep these directives together in your httpd.conf file, much as I've shown in Listing 12.3, which displays the section of my Apache httpd.conf that sets up proxying and caching for a small private network. You should be able to copy this, verbatim, into your httpd.conf file to enable Apache to act as a caching proxy server, or use it as a complete example of configuring a proxy server with disk-caching capabilities.

Listing 12.3   A Working Disk-Caching Proxy

```
#
# Proxy Server directives. Uncomment the following lines to
# enable the proxy server:
#
<IfModule mod_proxy.c>
ProxyRequests On
<Proxy *>
    Order deny,allow
    Deny from all
    Allow from 192.168.1
</Proxy>

#
# Enable/disable the handling of HTTP/1.1 "Via:" headers.
# ("Full" adds the server version; "Block" removes all outgoing Via: headers)
# Set to one of: Off | On | Full | Block
#
ProxyVia On

#
# To enable the cache as well, edit and uncomment the following lines:
# (no caching without CacheRoot)
#
<IfModule mod_cache.c>
CacheOn On
CacheGcInterval 1.5
CacheDefaultExpire 259200
CacheMaxExpire 604800
CacheLastModifiedFactor 0.1

<IfModule mod_disk_cache.c>
CacheEnable disk /
CacheRoot "/tmp/proxy"
CacheSize 40960
CacheDirLevels 3
CacheDirLength 2
CacheForceCompletion 75
</IfModule>

</IfModule>
# End of proxy directives.
```

Maintaining a
Healthy Server

PART 4

The mod_cache and mod_disk_cache modules provide the following directives:

CacheOn   The default value of this directive is off, so it is necessary to include this directive to enable caching. Omit the directive, or comment it out, to disable caching.

CacheGcInterval   Sets the interval (in hours) between cache size checks and garbage collection. During the garbage collection phase, the cache is purged of its oldest entries until it occupies less disk space than specified in the CacheSize directive. Beware: if you do not specify this directive, the garbage collection task will never run, and your cache will grow indefinitely. My server is set to perform this cleanup every 90 minutes:

```
CacheGcInterval 1.5
```

CacheDefaultExpire   If a resource is retrieved that does not have an expiry time, this value (in seconds) is used. This directive has no affect on resources that are retrieved with an expiry time in their HTTP header; however, those resources will still be subject to the caching limit set with CacheMaxExpire. The default is 24 hours, which I extended on my server to three days (or 72 hours):

```
CacheDefaultExpire 259200
```

CacheMaxExpire   Sets a maximum time for which cached resources are served without being validated by the origin server. This directive specifies the absolute maximum time that a cached document will be considered valid. This restriction applies even if the origin server specified a later expiry date for the resource or if CacheDefaultExpire is set to an even larger time interval. The default value is 86,400 seconds, or one day. On my server, I increased this to seven days:

```
CacheMaxExpire 604800
```

CacheLastModifiedFactor   Specifies a factor used to estimate an expiry date for a document that was delivered without one. The following formula is used to estimate the expiry period, which is always relative to the time of the last modification of the document:

```
expiry-period = time since last modification x factor
```

If the factor is set to 0.1 (the default value, and the one I use on my server), it essentially resolves to an expiry period equal to one-tenth the time elapsed since the document was last modified. In other words, if a received document was last modified 10 days ago, compute an expiry date based on one-tenth of this time interval (or one day from the date of receipt).

CacheEnable   This directive tells mod_cache what URLs to cache and what type of content cache to set up. It specifies a partial root URL, and all URLs that fall below this root are cached. For disk caching on a typical proxy server, the directive will take the following form, which specifies that a disk cache (implemented in mod_disk_cache) will be used to cache all URLs beginning with a "/" character, or in other words, all URLs requested. Note that this includes all local URLs and all remote URLs that are being retrieved by the proxy server.

```
CacheEnable disk /
```

There is also a CacheDisable directive that works similarly to CacheEnable, but disables the caching for certain URLs. This directive is not recommended for use with a proxy server, because it is usually not possible to determine what resources retrieved by proxy should not be cached. CacheDisable is better suited for local resource memory caching as provided by mod_mem_cache and discussed briefly below, where the administrator can identify resources that should not be cached in memory (large image files, for example).

CacheRoot   Sets the name of the directory to contain cached files. This directive is mandatory for caching, but if it does not exist, Apache won't generate an error; it simply won't do any caching.

The CacheRoot directive must be writeable by the user account under which the Apache child processes are running. It can be located anywhere on your system, but make sure that it is writeable by the user account specified by the User directive in httpd.conf. In the default configuration, this will be user "nobody" and it is perfectly suitable to retain this default. I don't want to include my Apache disk cache with my nightly backups, and prefer to consider it temporary storage, so I find it logical to place mine in an area reserved as a temporary workspace:

```
CacheRoot /tmp/proxy
```

CacheSize   Sets the maximum size of the cache (expressed in kilobytes). The cache can exceed this value but will be cut back to this size during a regular cleanup phase. You will probably want to reduce this quite a bit from its huge default value of roughly 1GB. On my home office server, I set my cache size to only 40MB:

```
CacheSize 40960
```

CacheDirLevels   Sets the number of subdirectory levels that can be used to store the cache. For extremely large caches, a larger number of directories can be used to speed searching the cache. It is rarely necessary to change this directive, however, from its default value of 3.

CacheDirLength   Sets the number of characters in proxy cache subdirectory names. This leads to subdirectories of the cache (taken from letters in the URL used to retrieve resources) that look like:

```
/usr/local/apache/proxy/A/n/w
```

I have never found it necessary to change this from its default value of 2.

`CacheForceCompletion`   Sets a percentage value that is used to determine if a document being retrieved to cache should be completely downloaded and cached if the HTTP transfer is aborted. For example, if this value is set to 60 (the default) and the user aborts the retrieval while the document is still only 50% transferred, the portion already received will be discarded and the document will not be cached. But if the transfer is 65% complete when aborted, the document will be completely retrieved and cached. I set the value of this directive to 75% on my server, slightly greater than the default value of 60%:

```
CacheForceCompletion 75
```

There are other types of caching besides disk caching, but these are primarily of interest in caching resources on a heavily accessed server, and are not really relevant to proxy servers. Memory-based caching (using the mod_mem_cache module) is discussed separately, later in this chapter.

Controlling Resource Expiration

A crucial element of caching is the concept of document or resource expiration. Web users don't just want their requests served immediately; they want to be sure they have retrieved the most current version of the resource. A proxy server that implements a cache needs some way to determine whether it can safely return the copy of a given resource it has already cached or whether it needs to retrieve a newer one. That is the role of the HTTP Expires header, the most important tool for controlling caching server behavior. This is the basic header sent by a server with each HTTP response to control how that document should be treated by all caching mechanisms (not only shared proxy server caches, but browser-based private caches as well). This header declares a date and time, expressed in Greenwich mean time (GMT), after which the document can no longer be considered valid and should not be served from cache without first *validating* the document with the server from which it was originally retrieved.

To validate a document, the proxy server checks with the origin server to see if the document has changed in any respect since it was last retrieved and stored to cache. The proxy server does not retrieve a new copy of the document unless the origin server indicates that the modification time of the original document is later than the timestamp on the copy in cache. If the document has been modified since it was cached, a new copy is requested, and the old cached copy is deleted.

The mod_expires module gives the Apache administrator control over the Expires header, and you should make certain this module is enabled on your Apache server. It is probably a part of your standard Apache build, especially if you ran Apache's configure script with the –enable-shared=most option. The module is simple to use, supplying only three directives for controlling Expires headers: ExpiresActive, ExpiresDefault, and ExpiresByType.

The *Cache-Control* Header

In the HTTP/1.1 protocol, the functionality of the Expires header has been superseded by the Cache-Control header (which is discussed in "HTTP/1.1 Support for Caching" later in this chapter). This directive, however, has not been fully incorporated in all Web-caching engines (proxy servers and browsers). Apache's mod_proxy, for example, is not even aware of the Cache-Control header. Until the use of this directive becomes more widespread, the Expires directive remains the predominant mechanism for controlling Web resource caching. Apache administrators can use both headers to increase the odds that caching proxies will properly handle expiration dates associated with resources.

Enabling the *Expires* Header

The ExpiresActive directive, which can take only the values on and off, enables the generation of Expires headers for the documents that are in its scope. For example, if you place this directive in an .htaccess file, Expires header generation is enabled only for the directory that contains that file.

```
ExpiresActive on
```

Setting a Default *Expires* Value

The ExpiresDefault directive specifies a time offset for generating the default value of the Expires header for all documents affected by the directive. You can apply the ExpiresDefault directive in several different <Directory> containers or .htaccess files to specify different values for different scopes. The time value that will be generated for a document can be relative either to the last modification time of the file or to the time of the client's last access to it.

The time intervals can be expressed in two different formats. One format is more economical but more cryptic, and the other is a little more verbose but more easily understood. In the first format, the time is always expressed in seconds, and prefixed with an A if it's relative to the last access or with an M if relative to modification. In this example, we set the default expiration to one week (604,800 seconds) after the browser's last access:

```
ExpiresActive on
ExpiresDefault A604800
```

In the easier-to-use alternate form, we express the time in terms of years, months, weeks, days, hours, minutes, and seconds, relative to either last access or last modification times. The module documentation fully describes this "alternate syntax." Note that the ExpiresDefault directive is expecting a single argument, so you must enclose multiword strings in quotation marks so that they are considered as a single argument. Rewriting the example in this syntax gives us the following equivalent set of directives:

```
ExpiresActive on
ExpiresDefault "access plus 1 week"
```

After enabling the Expires header with the previous directives, I got the following headers placed on the response from my server:

```
HTTP/1.1 200 OK
Date: Tue, 30 May 2000 16:20:00 GMT
Server: Apache/1.3.12 (Unix)
Cache-Control: max-age=604800
Expires: Tue, 06 Jun 2000 16:20:00 GMT
Last-Modified: Wed, 24 May 2000 13:45:21 GMT
ETag: "34062-f66-392bdcf1"
Accept-Ranges: bytes
Content-Length: 3942
Connection: close
Content-Type: text/html
```

Note that the time given in the Expires header is exactly one week after the date of access. Notice also that mod_expires has created a Cache-Control header, stating that under no circumstances should this document be served from any cache when it has been there for more than 604,800 seconds (one week). All HTTP/1.1-compliant browsers and proxy servers are required to honor this directive from the server.

While mod_expires appears to be somewhat compliant with HTTP/1.1, I looked at the source code and found that it supports only the max-age directive (one of 19 directives that HTTP/1.1 defines for the Cache-Control header). Generating this header is a nice "extra" from mod_expires, but you will not be able to make further use of the Cache-Control header with this module (or with mod_proxy, which does not yet support the Cache-Control header). Until HTTP/1.1 becomes more widely used, the Expires header is the tool you will manipulate and use to control the caching of documents served from Apache.

Expires Headers for a Specific MIME Type

The ExpiresByType directive specifies the value of the Expires header for a specific MIME type (e.g., text/html). Again, the time value that will be generated can be relative either to the last modification time of the disk file or to the time of the client's last access.

Here's an example in which the Expires header generated for documents of type text/html will be relative to the last modification time of HTML pages (type text/html), but computed as relative to the client's access time for GIF-formatted inline images (type image/gif):

```
ExpiresActive on
ExpiresByType text/html M604800
ExpiresByType image/gif A2592000
```

Rewriting the example in the alternate (but equivalent) syntax yields:

```
ExpiresActive on
ExpiresByType text/html "modification plus 1 week"
ExpiresByType "image/gif access plus 1 month"
```

This distinction based on type would make sense for sites in which graphic images are part of the site's design or decoration (such as a corporate logo) and presumably change much less frequently than the site's text. Of course, for art that's closely related to the site's text content, you would not do this.

Proxying Other Protocols

The CONNECT method is not really defined by the HTTP specification, but is reserved in that specification as an alternate method to be implemented by proxy servers. It is an HTTP request method (like GET or PUT) that allows connections via other protocols to be tunneled for security through a proxy server to a remote server. The AllowConnect directive specifies a list of port numbers through which clients using the proxy CONNECT method can connect to your Apache server. A CONNECT request is issued by a client that wishes to connect to a remote server via some protocol other than HTTP or FTP. CONNECT requests are commonly issued by SSL browsers, which connect to the proxy server using a URL that begins with https:// in order to connect using HTTP proxy tunneling to some remote server—for example, when the user of an e-commerce site clicks a link that initiates a secure transaction. The proxy server establishes the connection to the remote server, and it maintains this connection (using the client's desired CONNECT protocol) throughout the entire session. All traffic received by the proxy server from the remote is tunneled to the client, which also maintains a connection to the proxy server for the entire session.

Two of the most common protocols tunneled in this fashion are provided in the default configuration: TCP port 443, which is SSL, and TCP port 563, which is Snews. To override this default and specify telnet (TCP port 23) as an additional CONNECT protocol instead of Snews, use the directive as follows:

```
AllowConnect 443 23
```

A Web browser that is configured to use a proxy server for protocols other than HTTP or FTP (for example, the `telnet` protocol) will connect to that proxy server and issue a `CONNECT` request. For example, a client can establish an ordinary HTTP connection to the proxy server and issue a `CONNECT` command that looks like the following:

```
CONNECT remotehost.com:23 HTTP/1.0
```

The proxy server will establish a connection to `remotehost.com` on its TCP port 23 (a `telnet` daemon or server will accept the connection), and this connection will be tunneled to the requesting client using HTTP.

HTTP/1.1 Support for Caching

The HTTP/1.1 protocol significantly extends support for proxy caching through the addition of two new headers (HTTP/1.1 is documented in RFC 2616). Of these, the only new header that is implemented in Apache `mod_proxy` (which is still considered an HTTP/1.0-compliant proxy server) is the `Via` header, discussed in the next section. Most of the enhanced support for caching in HTTP/1.1, however, is in the new `Cache-Control` header, which is not implemented in the current version of `mod_proxy`. This new HTTP response header is actually a container for 19 directives to caching servers in the response chain (which may be proxy servers or even a caching Web browser). According to the HTTP/1.1 specification, these directives must be obeyed by all caching mechanisms that call themselves HTTP/1.1-compliant, and they must be passed through to all caching mechanisms further downstream (closer to the requesting client).

The directives that can be specified in the `Cache-Control` header fall into four categories, all defining in different ways what can be cached. There are directives that determine which HTTP responses can be cached, directives that specify what types of resources can be cached, directives to control the expiration of resources (which do the work of HTTP/1.0's `Expires` header), and directives that control revalidation and reloading of cached resources. A typical `Cache-Control` header, using two of the directives defined in RFC 2616, might be this:

```
Cache-Control: max-age=3600
```

This header instructs all proxy servers that cache copies of this document to consider the cached copy stale after 6 hours (3600 seconds). After that, whenever the server receives a new request for a resource, the proxy server must check the server for a fresh copy of the document, and if it finds one, download it to replace the one in cache.

Another common use of the `Cache-Control` header is shown below:

```
Cache-Control: must-revalidate
```

This header instructs cache servers to always connect to the server and check for a fresh copy of the cached document before serving it to the requesting client. The proxy server still saves time by not downloading the document from the server if validation determines that the cached copy is still fresh.

Since mod_proxy, in its current state, does not support the HTTP/1.1 Cache-Control header, I will simply mention several of the most interesting of the directives it implements. These will, eventually, become the directives used to control HTTP caching server behavior:

public Marks the HTTP response message as cacheable, even if it normally would not be. For instance, normal cache server behavior is to never cache responses that require username/password authentication. This directive marks those responses as cacheable.

private Indicates that the response message is intended for a single user (hence, the name of the directive) and must never be cached by a shared cache (one used by more than one user), though it can be cached by a browser.

no-cache Forces cache engines (both proxy server and browser) to always validate the request with the origin server before releasing a cached copy. Note that the requester may still receive a cached copy of the requested resource, but that copy will have been validated by the origin server (to ensure either proper authentication or freshness of the cached date).

max-age=[n] Specifies the maximum amount of time (in seconds) that an object will be considered fresh.

s-maxage=[n] Like max-age, but applies only to shared (proxy server) caches, not to browser caches.

max-stale This directive can be placed in a Cache-Control header by a client browser, and it indicates to cache engines that the client is willing to accept responses that have exceeded their expiration times. An origin server can override this directive with the must-revalidate directive.

must-revalidate Tells cache engines that they must validate all subsequent requests for this requested object with the origin server. This is to prevent a caching server from being configured to ignore the server's instructions on expiration intervals. This directive relies on all HTTP/1.1-compliant caching servers adhering to the rule that they must obey all Cache-Control directives.

proxy-revalidate Like must-revalidate, but applies only to proxy caches (not browser caches).

Using HTTP/1.1 Caching with Apache

I've mentioned eight of the directives that can be used with the HTTP/1.1 Cache-Control header. These are the most useful, and should serve to give you some idea of the usefulness of this method of caching control when it does become widely available.

Until mod_proxy (or a replacement module) fully implements HTTP/1.1 caching control, you can still manually add the header to your Apache responses, using the Header directive. This directive is provided by a standard module, mod_header, which is compiled into Apache by default. The Header directive is the only directive supplied by mod_header, and it implements the only function of the module, which is to allow the Apache administrator to customize the HTTP response headers by adding an arbitrary header or removing standard headers.

The Header directive is valid in nearly every possible context, so it can apply to a specific directory, to all files of a specific MIME type, or to specific files by name. The following directive, for example, appends the specified Client-Control header to all response messages to which the directive applies:

```
Header append Client-Control: "max-age=3600, must-revalidate"
```

The *Via* Header

Although mod_proxy is described as implementing an HTTP/1.0-compliant caching proxy server, it does include support for one new header from the HTTP/1.1 specification. The Via HTTP header is used to track the flow of a response through a chain of proxy servers and gateways, providing a record of all parties in the request chain. Its purpose is to identify the flow of a request, avoiding possible loops, and the supported protocol of all proxies in the chain. According to the HTTP/1.1 specification, all HTTP/1.1-compliant proxy servers must attach a Via header that indicates the server's identity (and optionally a comment indicating that server's software revision levels).

I'm sure you've seen e-mail messages in which the message headers indicate all the mail servers that have handled the message (using the Simple Mail Transport Protocol Received header). The HTTP Via header is designed to work similarly to that, providing some record of all the servers that have had a hand in delivering an HTTP resource.

Apache's mod_proxy support for the Via header is minimal, with one directive, ProxyVia, taking one of the following four values:

off The default setting for ProxyVia, this indicates that no Via header will be added to any HTTP response handled by mod_proxy. Since mod_proxy doesn't aspire to be an HTTP/1.1 proxy, it does not have to adhere to that specification's requirement that all proxy servers append a Via header.

on   Adds a Via header that identifies the current server to every request handled by mod_proxy.

full   Generates a Via header that includes an optional comment field displaying the Apache server version.

block   Removes all Via headers from requests passed through mod_proxy. Actually, this is something of a no-no, as it violates a requirement of the HTTP/1.1 specification that these headers be passed through all proxy servers unaltered. It's not illegal yet, but it is probably bad behavior. Don't use ProxyVia block.

Using *mod_mem_cache*

As an alternative to mod_disk_cache, another experimental module, mod_mem_cache, is provided for caching objects in memory or, alternatively, caching open file descriptors. Because this module is still a work in progress, I won't say much about it, except to describe how it works and provide a short, but useful, set of configuration directives for making it work with Apache.

In order to use the cache, you must include --enable-mem-cache in the configure script prior to compiling Apache. The following directives in httpd.conf will enable memory caching for all files requested with a URL that begins with the string /. This should resolve to the directory defined by Apache's DocumentRoot. Because this is an in-memory cache, you use the CacheDisable directive to disable caching for image files to save memory. This URL probably resolves to an images directory beneath DocumentRoot, but this is not a requirement. Through redirections, it could refer to any directory of the filesystem, and very often will.

```
<IfModule mod_mem_cache.c>
  CacheEnable mem /
  CacheDisable /images
  MCacheSize 4096
  MCacheMaxObjectCount 100
  MacheMinObjectSize 1
  MCacheMaxObjectSize 2048
</IfModule>
```

An alternative to caching entire objects in memory is to open the file that contains the resource, and then cache only the Linux file descriptor that points to this open file. Significant performance gains can be achieved when caching file descriptors for frequently accessed files in this manner. While the contents of the open files still need to be read and served to the client, leaving these files open after the first request and using cached file descriptors to access them eliminates the overhead of opening each file. File descriptor caching works almost exactly like memory caching, but the keyword fd is used instead of mem to denote that only file descriptors, rather than entire objects, are to be cached in memory. In the example above, the CacheEnable directive for file descriptor caching would be changed to

```
CacheEnable fd /
```

WARNING   The number of open file descriptors that are allowed for a single process limits the number of file descriptors that can be cached. In most recent versions of Linux, this value is 1024. You can enter **ulimit -a** to determine this value for your system. Make sure you run it as a nonprivileged user (some user other than root) as this is how the Apache listener processes will run.

Squid: A Proxy Server for Linux

Apache, with the mod_proxy module, is quite adequate for most site administrators. Its caching engine is quite efficient and robust. In spite of its ability to tunnel other protocols, mod_proxy is primarily an HTTP proxy server. Sites that find it necessary to proxy other protocols should consider the use of a dedicated proxy server specifically designed to handle simultaneous requests from multiple clients and high loads. Although many commercial proxy servers are available, there is an open-source alternative that has an excellent reputation among its users on Linux platforms.

If a full-featured, dedicated proxy server is what you need, be sure to evaluate Squid, an open-source solution, freely available from www.squid-cache.org. Squid proxies not only HTTP, but also FTP, WAIS, Gopher, and SSL.

TUX: An HTTP Accelerator

Beginning with version 7.1, the Red Hat Linux distribution contains a kernel-based HTTP server, which it now calls the Red Hat Content Accelerator. Most of the Linux community, though, knows it better as "TUX." The basic purpose of TUX is to act as a Web server for static file resources (including embedded image files), serving them as fast as physically possible from a Red Hat Linux server. It does this by running within the Linux kernel; at its core, TUX is a set of modifications to Linux. TUX is designed solely to respond to requests for static resources, and that is just about all it does. With a very limited feature set, TUX does not support any of the Apache features discussed in this book (virtual hosts, customizable logging, user authentication, programming, and so on), and most administrators would never consider TUX as a replacement for

Apache. TUX is most commonly used as a front-end to a "normal" Web server (most often, Apache), passing all requests that it can't fulfill to this Web server.

For most sites, TUX greatly reduces the load on an Apache server by directly handling requests for static resources (particularly images), alleviating the need for Apache to handle these requests. TUX can be thought of as an accelerator for an Apache server, not as a separate Web server. Apache is unaware of TUX and receives the TCP connection (from TUX) without knowing that the connection has already been handled by TUX. Apache sees requests that it has and that TUX cannot process as new incoming connections, requiring absolutely no configuration changes in Apache.

One of the nice things about TUX (if you are using Red Hat Linux) is that it's a cinch to install and use. If you're using Red Hat, there's a strong possibility that TUX is already installed on your server, and simply needs to be configured for use. TUX is implemented in two parts: The first is a kernel module that is usually installed with Red Hat Linux, and the second is a set of utilities and configuration files that are installed from a Red Hat RPM. Note that TUX is installed as a part of any Red Hat Linux Package Groups. In order to install TUX during the installation of Red Hat, you must check the Select Individual Packages check box on the Package Group Selection screen, and then find and select the TUX package.

You can verify if these are on your system by querying the RPM database for the TUX package:

```
# rpm -q tux
tux-2.1.0-2
```

If the TUX RPM has not been installed, mount and load Red Hat Installation Disk 1 (this example uses a Red Hat 7.1 CD):

```
# mount /mnt/cdrom
# cd /mnt/cdrom/RedHat/RPMS/
# ls tux*
tux-2.1.0-2.i386.rpm
# rpm -iv tux-2.1.0-2.i386.rpm
Preparing packages for installation...
tux-2.1.0-2
```

The most commonly modified TUX parameters are configurable through a configuration file (/etc/sysconfig/tux) that can be edited prior to starting the TUX service. Listing 12.4 shows the contents of this file, which contains comments to explain the handful of parameters that can be changed there. Use an editor to change any desired settings and start (or restart) TUX as shown below. The one setting you'll most likely want to change is DOCROOT, which serves the same purpose as Apache's DocumentRoot directive (defining the directory where TUX will look for documents and other files, such as images).

Listing 12.4   TUX Init Configuration File

```
# /etc/sysconfig/tux

# TUXTHREADS sets the number of kernel threads (and associated daemon
# threads) that will be used.  $TUXTHREADS defaults to the number of
# CPUs on the system.
# TUXTHREADS=1

# DOCROOT is the document root; it works the same way as other web
# servers such as apache.  /var/www/html/ is the default.
DOCROOT=/var/www/html/

# CGI_UID and CGI_GID are the user and group as which to run CGIs.
# They default to "nobody"
# CGI_UID=nobody
# CGI_GID=nobody

# DAEMON_UID and DAEMON_GID are the user and group as which the daemon runs
# They default to "nobody"
# This does not mean that you should execute untrusted modules -- they
# are opened as user/group root, which means that the _init() function,
# if it exists, is run as root.  This feature is only designed to help
# protect from programming mistakes; it is NOT really a security mechanism.
# DAEMON_UID=nobody
# DAEMON_GID=nobody

# CGIs can be started in a chroot environment by default.
# Defaults to $DOCROOT; set CGIROOT=/ if you want CGI programs
# to have access to the whole system.
# CGIROOT=/var/www/html

# each HTTP connection has an individual timer that makes sure
# no connection hangs forever. (due to browser bugs or DoS attacks.)
# MAX_KEEPALIVE_TIMEOUT=30

# TUXMODULES is a list of user-space TUX modules.  User-space TUX
# modules are used to serve dynamically-generated data via tux.
# "man 2 tux" for more information
# TUXMODULES="demo.tux demo2.tux demo3.tux demo4.tux"

# MODULEPATH is the path to user-space TUXapi modules
# MODULEPATH="/"

LOGGING=1
```

TUX is installed as a Red Hat service, and is intended to be started when the system is first booted. In general, you will want to start the service this way. Use the Linux `chkconfig` utility to enable the service to start when the operating system goes into multi-user mode (runlevel 3):

```
# chkconfig --list tux
tux             0:off   1:off   2:off   3:off   4:off   5:off   6:off
# chkconfig --level 3 tux on
# chkconfig --list tux
tux             0:off   1:off   2:off   3:on    4:off   5:off   6:off
```

As with any Linux service, you can also start and stop TUX manually, using the `service` command that is provided for that purpose. This command also provides a convenient way to reload TUX if you make modifications to its configuration file. Here are some examples of how the `service` command can be used:

```
# service tux status
tux is stopped
[# service tux start
Starting tux: [  OK  ]
# service tux status
tux (pid 8757 8756 8755 8754 8753 8752 8751 8750 8749
➡  8748 8746  is running...
# service tux reload
Stopping tux:
Starting tux: [  OK  ]
```

The parameters in Listing 12.4 are only a few of the configuration parameters that can be used with TUX, and are the only ones that can be set permanently through a configuration file. Most TUX parameters can only be set through changing in-memory data structures used by the Linux kernel. (Remember, part of TUX is installed as a kernel module and, as such, is part of the Linux operating system.) These configuration parameters are changed by writing data to the /proc *pseudo filesystem*. You can list the current values of these parameters by viewing the contents of files in the /proc/sys/net/ tux directory. This is not really a directory, and what appear to be files within it are not really files at all; everything you find beneath the /proc directory is really a special interface to kernel data structures. Data written to these "files" actually modifies data structures in memory used by the Linux kernel.

While most of the parameters in /proc/sys/net/tux will never need to be changed, there are a few that you might want to modify to better suit your environment. Listing 12.5 shows a few of these, and gives an example of how to go about changing them. A complete list of configuration changes that can be made through /proc can be found at http://www.redhat.com/docs/manuals/tux/TUX-2.2-Manual/parameters.html. Change these only when you fully understand what they do. Remember that parameters set in this fashion are not retained when the memory in which they reside is cleared as it will be in a server reboot. You must be prepared to set these parameters each time you start TUX, and the best place to do this is in /etc/init.d/tux, the TUX startup script. Place lines similar to the "echo" lines in Listing 12.5 in the startup section of that script, after the line that starts TUX (that line will probably begin with the special script keyword "daemon").

Listing 12.5 Setting Common TUX Parameters

```
# cat /proc/sys/net/tux/logging
0
# echo "1" > /proc/sys/net/tux/logging
# cat /proc/sys/net/tux/logging
1
# echo "8008" > /proc/sys/net/tux/clientport
# echo "/home/httpd/cgi-bin" > /proc/sys/net/tux/cgiroot
```

Compressing Content with *mod_deflate*

An easy way to increase the throughput of an Apache Web server, particularly one for which the bottleneck would appear to be a limitation of network bandwidth, is to compress content before sending it to the requesting client browser. Two documents (IETF RFC 1351 and RFC 1352) specify how compression of HTTP content is performed in a manner that will work with any browser that adheres to the same specifications. These documents describe two methods. The first uses the DEFLATE compressed data format, and the second uses a common Unix/Linux compression scheme, GZIP. Virtually all Web browsers in use today support either scheme. mod_deflate (contrary to what its name would lead one to expect) implements the GZIP compression scheme and is a standard part of the Apache 2.0 distribution, though currently not enabled by default and available only if manually enabled. This module has been around for quite some time, but having been documented only in the Russian language, its acceptance by the Apache community has been slow and, for a long time, mainly limited to very technical types who were in an "experimental" frame of mind. mod_deflate should, however, be considered mature and reliable.

The module itself is very easy to use, and completely transparent in its operation. Compression is usually enabled for a specific resource type on the server (generally HTML documents) and decompression is automatically performed by the user's browser. Like most Apache modules, the module is compiled and made available for use by the inclusion of the --enable-deflate parameter on the command line when running the `configure` script. Make sure that the script writes the correct `LoadModule` line into your `httpd.conf` file (adding it manually, if necessary) and restart Apache:

```
LoadModule deflate_module modules/mod_deflate.so
```

As an example of enabling `mod_deflate` for a single directory (and resource type), here's my entire `Directory` container for the Apache documentation that is installed with Apache:

```
Directory "/usr/local/apache2/manual">
    Options Indexes FollowSymLinks MultiViews
    AllowOverride None
    Order allow,deny
    Allow from all
    SetEnv gzip-only-text/html 1
    SetOutputFilter DEFLATE
</Directory>
```

The last two lines within the container shown above are the relevant ones. Note that a `SetEnv` directive (rather than a `mod_deflate`-specific directory, as might be expected) is used to enable compression for documents of MIME type `text/html` only. This is a practice recommended by the module authors, who say that some (unspecified) browsers do not adequately handle compressed resources of other content types. The `SetOutputFilter` simply specifies a content filter (DEFLATE) for the resources that fall within the control of this container—in this case, everything served from the `/usr/local/apache2/manual` directory. The module itself determines if the resource type is one that is specified for compression.

There are several directives that allow you to change the behavior of `mod_deflate`. For example, you can change the size of the buffer used by the DEFLATE compression algorithm (which compresses data in blocks of a fixed size) and limit the amount of memory that is used by the module. These directives are not yet documented fully (at least not in the English language), and shouldn't be changed without full knowledge of their effects; the default values are perfectly adequate for most sites.

Controlling Web Robots (Spiders)

To find information on the World Wide Web, nearly everyone, at one time or another, has used one of the major Internet search engines and will recognize names like Yahoo!, Excite, AltaVista, or Google. Each of these builds its indexed databases of Web sites using *robots*. Also known as *Web crawlers* or *spiders*, these are programs designed to traverse the Internet, parsing Web pages for embedded hyperlinks that are followed to discover new sites, storing what they find in huge databases that the public can then search by topic or keyword.

Most public Web sites welcome and try to attract the attention of the major search engines that serve as indexes for the Internet. In fact, there have been books written on how to attract visitors to Web sites, and inclusion by these search engines in their indexes of Web sites is an important part of publicizing a Web site. There are times, however, when it is desirable to limit the activities of these robots. The most important reason for controlling robots is to prevent the wide publication of Web sites that are not intended for the general public, although they may be generally accessible. Another reason, less important today than in earlier years, is that Web robots can reduce the performance of a Web site by crawling it too rapidly, degrading the response time for real users.

In 1994, the major Web robot developers of the time agreed on a scheme that Web site administrators could use to identify their preferences to visiting Web robots. This scheme is informally known as the *robot exclusion standard*. Adherence is completely voluntary, but it has always been the accepted way to limit the activities of Internet Web robots. When I first heard about this standard, I was skeptical—it would only control well-behaved robots, not the ones I wanted to keep off my site. The truth is, though, that most search engines that crawl the Web are well behaved and will abide by the conditions you specify.

Using the robot exclusion standard is very simple. It specifies the URL /robots.txt as the location where search engines will look for your instructions about what to exclude. First of all, your Web site must be able to respond to a request for a resource at that URL. The simplest way to do this is to create a file named robots.txt under your server's DocumentRoot, although you could also serve this file from other locations or even scripts (using techniques like URL rewriting). Well-behaved Web robots will ask for this file before taking any other action, and they will comply with the instructions you place in it.

The syntax to use in the robots.txt file is fairly simple. The file should contain one or more sections (separated by blank lines) that apply to different Web robots or groups of robots. Each section begins with one or more User-Agent: lines. These identify robots that should comply with the rules in that section. Remember that the robots themselves read robots.txt, and if one finds the section that applies to itself, it is responsible for reading the rules of that section and abiding by them. One and only one default section can exist; it contains rules that apply to all robots not matching one of the other sections. The default section begins with the line:

```
User-agent: *
```

Each section then contains a Disallow: rule, which identifies portions of the site that are not to be crawled and indexed by any of the robots identified in the section's User-Agent: lines. These portions are identified by partial URL. To specify that no robot should access any portion of your Web site, for example, you could have a robots.txt file that contains only the following two lines:

```
User-agent: *
Disallow: /
```

This asks all robots not to request any URL beginning with a / character, which will, of course, include all possible request URLs.

Listing 12.6 is a robots.txt file that first requests all robots to refrain from requesting resources using URLs that begin with the string /private/. The next section removes this restriction for a single robot, InfoSeek. One spider, NastySpider, is asked not to index any resource on the site.

Listing 12.6   A Sample robots.txt File

```
#robots.txt
User-agent: *
Disallow: /private/

User-agent: InfoSeek
Disallow:

User-agent: NastySpider
Disallow: /
```

Unfortunately, now that robot technology is being used in all sorts of end-user products, the robots.txt file is becoming less useful. Many spiders that crawl the Web today don't use the file, which formerly would have been considered extremely antisocial behavior. Still, it is a good idea to create the file if you want to control the behavior of robots that are indexing your public Web site, even if your file includes only a single default rule section.

Besides following the rules in all robots.txt files it encounters, a socially responsible robot should be registered with the Web Robots Database at www.robotstxt.org/wc/active.html. The same site (www.robotstxt.org/) also provides a FAQ page that describes the complete syntax and is very useful in determining User-agent: strings to use in your robots.txt file for various robots.

In Sum

The default configuration provided with Apache is highly optimized for performance on Linux servers. As a result, there is very little that the administrator needs to do to tweak more performance out of the server. There are several server performance directives that the administrator should understand and be able to modify. This chapter discussed these directives and gave examples of their use.

Generally, however, when additional performance is required from an Apache server, it is obtained through the use of a module designed to improve the performance of the Apache engine. In Chapter 8, I mentioned mod_perl and mod_fastcgi, both of which are common methods of squeezing extra performance out of Apache running scripts through the CGI interface. In this chapter, I mentioned two more mechanisms, mod_proxy and Red Hat's TUX kernel-level server, both of which are designed to optimize the performance of Apache when serving static HTML pages.

The chapter closed with a discussion of the robot exclusion standard, which is used to prevent server performance degradation caused by Web spiders attempting to index all the resources on the site. This is primarily of importance to the administrators of sites that have a very large number of Web pages publicly accessible through the Internet.

The next two chapters discuss securing an Apache server. Chapter 13 covers basic user authentication; Chapter 14 discusses one of the most widely used Apache modules, mod_ssl, which provides Secure Sockets Layer, the underpinning of most secure Web e-commerce sites on the Internet today.

Basic Security for Your Web Server

Security is an essential topic for administrators of both Internet-connected and internal (intranet) servers. Web servers are particularly attractive targets, it seems, for purveyors of mayhem on the Internet or (even more seriously) those who have the goal of compromising system security and stealing information such as credit card numbers. Security is a very broad topic, about which many books have been written. This chapter and the next focus on the security precautions you can easily take to protect Apache.

Most organizations that maintain Web servers usually divide them into two groups, separated by a firewall router. Internal Web servers (inside the firewall) are those intended for access only by the organization's internal hosts, and external servers are those outside the firewall, exposed to access from the Internet. The most certain way to protect a Web server completely from unwanted access is to ensure that it can't be accessed from the Internet. This is perfectly fine for intranet Web servers, but it defeats the very purpose of most Web servers, which are public information systems or Internet commerce servers (supporting marketing, sales, ordering/shipping, product support, and customer relations).

The best thing we can do to protect a Web server from malicious intrusion is to protect private resources using some mechanism that forces users to enter a set of credentials to identify themselves. In this chapter I discuss those security measures that you can take to protect a Web server by ensuring that you know who is connecting to the server (*authentication*) and establishing rules that govern what these users are permitted to access (*authorization*).

Chapter 14 covers Secure Sockets Layer (or SSL), which goes a bit further than basic authentication and creates an encrypted connection with Web browsers to permit the secure exchange of sensitive information (the most common example being credit card numbers). By providing users with a sense of confidence and trust in the privacy and security of Web servers, SSL has been a vital component in making electronic commerce a reality.

Apache's Basic Security Tools

The modules that are responsible for controlling access to Apache resources are implemented fairly simply. Regardless of the complexity of an access control module, its task is to make a judgement about a single HTTP request and return one of two values to Apache: OK if the request should be honored, FORBIDDEN if the request should be denied.

Modules that are responsible for safeguarding protected resources in Apache are applied during three phases of the request-processing phase:

Access Control   During this standard phase of Apache request processing, a module can deny access to the requested resource based on information provided by the HTTP request or encapsulating IP packet. The only module discussed in this chapter that operates in this request phase is mod_access, which is responsible for allowing or denying client access based on the network address from which the request originates.

Authentication   Any module that is called during the authentication phase must verify the identity of the requester, based on credentials presented by the user. These credentials can be as elaborate as a digital certificate, perhaps signed by a trusted third-party certificate authority. By far the most common user credential is a simple username/password pair provided by the user through a standard dialog box provided by a Web browser, or perhaps furnished from cached data.

Authorization   When a module is called during the authorization phase, the user's identity is assumed to be already known, and the module checks access control information (such as access control lists) to determine if the user has permission to access the requested resources. Again, the response of the module must be either OK or FORBIDDEN.

Most modules that restrict access based on user identification provide handlers for both of the latter two phases, first identifying the user (authentication) and then determining if that user, once identified, will be permitted access to the requested resource (authorization). Most of this chapter is devoted to these modules, but first I'll discuss mod_access, a module that functions during the access control phase of the request phase to restrict access to clients based on the IP address from which the request originates.

Restrictions Based on Client Origin

The very simplest means of restricting access is provided by the standard mod_access module, which operates at the access control stage of the Apache request phase (very early in the request cycle, before almost anything else has been done). At this point, Apache knows nothing about the user request; indeed, it has not even examined any of the HTTP headers. During the access control phase, mod_access is used to determine if the request will be honored, based solely on the requesting client's hostname or IP address.

Although it is quite simple, the functionality this module provides is very useful. The directives supplied by the module operate in a directory context (either in a <Directory> container or an .htaccess file). Access restrictions imposed by these directives apply to all resources in the applicable directory and cannot be used to restrict access to specific files.

In most cases, mod_access is used to deny access to clients connecting from locations (IP addresses) that are either specifically prohibited or absent from a list of addresses that are specifically approved. Two basic directives are used to specify hosts that are either permitted or prohibited access to resources in a directory:

> **allow**   Specifies hosts that can access resources in the associated directory.
>
> **deny**   Specifies hosts that are denied access to resources in the associated directory.

Hosts can be specified in these directives using any of the following forms:

- The special all keyword, meaning all hosts:

  ```
  deny from all
  ```

- Partial or full IP addresses:

  ```
  allow from 192.168.1.1 192.168.1.2
  ```

- Partial domain names:

  ```
  deny from .some.domain.com
  ```

- A network-number/subnet-mask pair. All of the following are equivalent:

  ```
  allow from 192.168.1
  allow from 192.168.1.0/255.255.255.0
  allow from 192.168.1.0/24
  ```

Another directive, order, determines the order in which the allow and deny directives are applied. The order directive can take one of three possible forms:

> **order deny,allow**   Applies all deny directives before the allow directives. This is generally used to prohibit most hosts from accessing a directory but specifically allows access from a select few. This works much like tight firewall (least

Maintaining a
Healthy Server

PART 4

permissive) rules; generally access is first denied to all and then opened for a limited number of users. Typically this order is used with a `Deny All` directive, which will be applied before all `Allow` directives.

order allow,deny Applies all `allow` directives before the deny directives. This is generally used to allow most accesses, but specifically designating a few hosts or Internet subnets as prohibited. Typically this order is used with an `Allow All` directive, which will be applied before all `Deny` directives.

mutual-failure Allows access to any hosts that appear on the `allow` list but not on the deny list.

TIP Make sure that you enter these directives exactly as shown. The order directive takes only a single argument. A common mistake administrators make is adding a space character within the argument. The directive order deny, allow will generate an Apache error; it needs to be entered as order deny,allow.

To better understand the use of the `order` directive, consider an example. Suppose the following directives appeared in a `<Directory>` container or an `.htaccess` file:

```
order deny,allow    # this is the default value
allow 192.168.1
deny from all
```

They would deny all access to the relevant directory except from the 192.168.1 subnet, because the order directive causes the `deny from all` directive to be applied first, even though it follows the deny directive in the configuration. Now suppose the `order` directive were changed to this:

```
order allow,deny
```

This time, the `allow` directive, being applied first, would grant access to the 192.168.1 subnet, but that access would be immediately overridden by the `deny from all` directive that is applied last. The order of the directives in the configuration file is irrelevant, so pay close attention to the order directive, which defaults to `order deny,allow` if not specified.

An alternate form of the `allow` and deny directives can be used to control access to a directory based on the existence of an environment variable:

```
allow from env=<env var>
deny from env=<env var>
```

Usually this variable is *set* or created by a preceding `BrowserMatch` or `SetEnvIf` directive that has performed some test on one or more of the HTTP request headers. Here's an example:

```
BrowserMatch MSIE ie_user
```

```
<Directory /Explorer>
    order deny,allow
    deny from all
    allow from env=ie_user
</Directory>
```

Here, if the requester is using the Microsoft Internet Explorer browser (determined by the User-Agent HTTP request header of the request), an environment variable ie_user is set and later used to allow access to the /Explorer directory. Users of other browser types will receive a 403 (Forbidden) response. Consider another example, where SetEnvIf is used to set a variable based on an arbitrarily chosen header:

```
SetEnvIf Referer "someremotehost\.com"    deny_this
<Directory /audio>
    order allow,deny
    allow from all
    deny from env=deny_this
</Directory>
```

In this example, requests for audio files are denied if those requests are the result of a link in a page on a host that is known to provide links to audio files on our server, effectively stealing our bandwidth. All other requests for the same files are honored.

Restrictions Based on User Identification

You've seen that it's easy to configure access restrictions based on the origin of the request (that is, the IP address), a technique that's useful when you want to grant only a few hosts or network subnets access to certain resources (like server status pages). This approach, however, is not very flexible. For one thing, you are basing access on the network address of the client, something that you do not always control and that is subject to change. In most cases, this is fine if you want to restrict access only to subnets or hosts under your control, but a good general access control method involves both the identification of a user (authentication) and some means of controlling what resources that user can access (authorization).

The HTTP protocol describes two types of authentication that should be supported by all Web servers and clients (browsers). The first of these, which is by far the most commonly used, is basic HTTP authentication, which involves the unencrypted exchange of user authentication information, consisting of a username and password combination. The HTTP standard also describes a second form of user authentication, called digest authentication, that works similarly but uses a mechanism to encrypt user credentials before transmission, essentially eliminating the threat of passwords being intercepted in transit. You'll learn about digest authentication later in the chapter.

Apache's standard method for basic HTTP authentication stores user credentials in text files, and I'll discuss that method first. The use of text files for storing user information imposes performance penalties that become significant when those text files grow large (roughly 1000 users or more). Most sites that use basic HTTP authentication use some type of database to store user information. This chapter discusses two common methods. DBM is a common key/value database method that is included in all Linux distributions; I'll also discuss authentication against a relational database. My example uses MySQL, a relational database that is widely used by Linux administrators, but the configuration described will be almost identical for any authentication module that uses another relational database, and modules are available for virtually every database system in use on Linux.

Basic HTTP Authentication

RFC 2617 ("HTTP Authentication: Basic and Digest Access Authentication") defines the requirements of basic and digest authentication that are implemented in all HTTP-compliant Web servers and browsers. When the server receives a request for a resource that has been identified as protected using basic authentication, it returns a 401 (Unauthorized) response. The response also includes an HTTP WWW-Authenticate header, which contains a *challenge* to the user and identifies the authentication *realm*. The authentication realm is defined in the HTTP protocol standard as a "protection space." This means, essentially, that it is a set of resources that are logically related but may not be in the same directory. All resources in a realm are usually protected with the same authentication scheme and authorization datasource. This means that a user who has been validated for a specific realm should not have to enter a new username and password for other resources in the same realm during the same browser session. After the first authentication, subsequent requests for resources in the same realm result in credentials being supplied from the browser cache.

If no credentials are held in cache for an authentication realm, the browser will attempt to get this information from the user by presenting a dialog box like that shown in Figure 13.1. The username and password are forwarded to the server in the Authorization header in a new request.

If the browser has cached user credentials for the identified realm, it will automatically (and transparently to the user) repeat the initial HTTP request that returned a 401 error, adding an Authorization header containing the cached credentials without requesting them again from the user.

Figure 13.1 The Konqueror browser's username/password dialog box

When the server receives a resource request with an `Authorization` header, it first attempts to verify the validity of the information provided and then, if the user is identified, checks to see if the user has been granted access to the resource. If the username is not valid, if the password can't be matched, or if the user is denied access to the resource, the server returns a second 401 (Unauthorized) response. The browser will interpret this second response as an authorization failure and will usually generate a dialog box like that shown in Figure 13.2.

Figure 13.2 The Konqueror browser's "Authorization Failed" dialog box

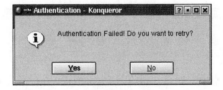

Clicking Yes to retry the request will bring up the authentication dialog (Figure 13.1) a second time; clicking No should bring up a page like that shown in Figure 13.3.

Incidentally, this is a standard error page for HTTP response code 401 that can be overridden using the `ErrorDocument` directive:

```
ErrorDocument 401 /401.html
```

You can place this directive in `httpd.conf` to designate a new error page for response code 401 wherever authorization errors occur. You can also use this directive in narrower contexts (in an `.htaccess` file, for example, to designate a special page that applies only to a specific directory). My revised version of the 401 error page (named `401.html` and stored in my `DocumentRoot`) is shown in Figure 13.4.

Figure 13.3 The Konqueror browser's authorization error message

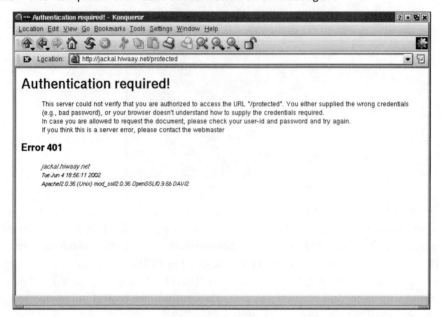

Figure 13.4 A customized error page displayed using the ErrorDocument directive

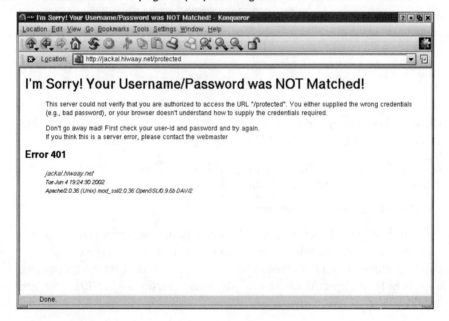

> **TIP**   To simplify creating a customized error page, start by deliberately generating the standard error page. Then use your browser's View Source option and copy the HTML source code for the page to a document you can edit.

Apache Modules for Authentication and Authorization

By now, you should understand that authentication (who is the user?) and authorization (what is the user allowed to access?) are separate functions. In fact, Apache request processing includes separate phases for each of these functions. Most Apache authorization modules (and there are many), however, perform both authentication and authorization by providing callback functions for both phases of request processing. In general, when you apply an authorization module (to authenticate a user against a text file, database, or authentication server), that module both identifies the user with an acceptable degree of accuracy and determines whether the user's request should be honored, based on an access rights list of some kind.

Just like the simpler mod_access described in the last section, the more sophisticated modules that restrict access based on a user's identity and an access rights list also return a simple OK or FORBIDDEN response. In addition, however, most can also be set to be *authoritative*; in other words, the access they grant or deny cannot be superseded by a lower-level module.

The task of authenticating user requests can be passed from one module to the next, based on the order in which the modules are called to handle a given request. In versions of Apache prior to 2.0, the order in which modules were called was based on the reverse of the sequence in which the (now obsolete) AddModule statements were added to the Apache module list. That is, the priority order of the modules was determined by the order of the AddModule statements in httpd.conf. In Apache 2.0, the order in which modules are called during any specific phase of the request cycle can be influenced by the module author, but is no longer under control of the Apache administrator and cannot be determined by the ordering of directives in httpd.conf.

If any authentication module is specified as authoritative (the default behavior for most modules), authentication will not be passed to lower-priority modules, and acceptance or rejection of user connections by that module will be absolute. In order to allow authentication to be passed to lower-level modules, you can specify nonauthoritative behavior explicitly by using a module directive specifically for that purpose, as in the following example. Since the order in which directives are invoked cannot be predicted in Apache 2.0, it is recommended that these directives not be used with that server. Remember, this means that when any authentication module specifically grants or denies access to a user, no other module will have an opportunity to override that determination. In most cases, this will work fine, as long as you don't make any assumptions about the order in which the modules are called.

Authentication by mod_auth is performed against a text file that is created by htpasswd, a utility that is packaged as a standard "accessory" with Apache. You should find this script in the /bin directory under the Apache installation directory. This utility is used to create a user file that contains usernames and associated passwords. While the file is an ordinary text file, it does not store passwords as readable text. Instead, it will encrypt the password for each user using one of several schemes. The default encryption scheme uses the standard Unix crypt function to encrypt the password.

You can enter htpasswd, with no command-line arguments, to get a listing of all the options for the function. Usually, though, you will create a new user file with htpasswd, using a line like this:

```
htpasswd -c /usr/local/apache2/auth/userfile caulds
```

The -c (create) argument is used here to create a new file (userfile in the auth directory under the Apache home). The htpasswd always requires a username argument. In this case, the new file will be created with one user, caulds, and htpasswd will prompt for that user's password and then prompt again for confirmation. The password is encrypted (using the Unix crypt system function by default), and the contents of the file will look like this:

```
caulds:cnVPtfAz2xw6o
```

Additional users are added to this file by simply omitting the creation (-c) argument:

```
htpasswd  /usr/local/apache2/auth/userfile csewell
```

Adding the -b (batch) switch instructs Apache to read the password from the command line, with no prompts, and is useful for scripting user account creation:

```
htpasswd -b /usr/local/apache2/auth/userfile csewell fubar
```

The other arguments, −m, -s, and −p, are used to specify alternate forms of password encryption: respectively, MD5, SHA, and plain text (no encryption). Regardless of the encryption chosen, mod_auth will usually be able to authenticate users, although some configurations do not allow plain-text passwords (which aren't a good idea anyway). Here's a user file that contains one example of each encryption type (crypt, MD5, SHA, and plain text). I used this file without problems, proving that it is safe to mix and match encryption types:

```
caulds:Xsfs6UqwWLZJY
csewell:$apr1$44SVx...$YMk.PPHr7HvBHf3hCIAdMO
linda:{SHA}lituavWnx6/8ZLKNZVc4F2rbpSU=
donkey:mypasswd
```

To enable authorization for an HTTP authentication realm (in practice, usually a directory), you create an .htaccess file in the directory to be protected. This file must contain, as a minimum, the following lines:

```
AuthName        "mod_auth Test Realm"
```

```
AuthType Basic
AuthUserFile /usr/local/apache2/auth/userfile
require user caulds csewell linda donkey
```

The first line defines the authorization realm, and the second specifies the authorization type (currently only basic and digest are supported). The next line specifies that a user file is created using htpasswd, and finally a require user line specifies a list of users who are permitted access. Note that even if the user provides a username and password that are valid in the AuthUserFile, if that valid account is not specified in the require user line, the request is rejected. In that case, the user passed the test of authentication, but failed the authorization test. Remember, most authentication modules perform both functions.

You can avoid specifying all valid users by creating a group file that contains a list of groups and members of each of those groups. This file is a plain-text file and is generally created and edited with your favorite text editor. An example of such a file would be:

```
admins: caulds csewell
friends: linda csewell
associates: donkey
```

Here, I've broken my user file into three groups: admins, friends, and associates. Note that a user can be a member of more than one group.

The group file is specified in .htaccess as follows:

```
AuthName        "mod_auth Test Realm"
AuthType Basic
AuthUserFile  /usr/local/apache2/auth/userfile
AuthGroupFile /usr/local/apache2/auth/groupfile
require group admins friends
```

In this example, authorization is being granted to members of the admins and friends groups. One of my users (donkey) is not a member of either group and will be denied access to the resources in this directory.

Group files are used to provide authorization information. That is why the AuthUser-File line is still required. That line identifies a file used to verify users; the require group line is used to determine whether the user is authorized to access the protected resources, not to verify the validity of the credentials that user presents.

All user authentication schemes use similar configuration directives. Each will provide:

- An AuthName directive identifying an authentication realm.
- An AuthType directive specifying either basic or digest authentication.
- A directive indicating the source file or database for the user/password information pairs. Each module will have a different form of this directive, as in these examples:

Maintaining a Healthy Server

PART 4

```
AuthUserFile /usr/local/apache2/auth/userfile
AuthDBMUserFile /usr/local/apache2/auth/password.dbm
```

- A directive indicating a file to contain group names and members. Again, different modules will express different forms of this directive. This directive is optional and used only when access is being granted to groups rather than individual users. Later in this chapter, I'll show how Apache provides a special form of this directive (require valid-user) to grant access to any valid user without having to specify individual users or groups for even greater simplicity.

- A directive indicating which users or groups are granted access; typically, this is the require directive.

- A directive to indicate whether the module is authoritative in its decision to accept or reject a user's request. If the module is not authoritative, any existing lower-level authentication modules are then used to process the request, any one of which may be able to authenticate the user. This directive is optional, and the default value is On, but it is a good idea to explicitly specify whether or not each module is authoritative.

I mentioned earlier that the HTTP standard provides for two types of user authentication. Basic user authentication, just described, is by far the most common of these. The next section discusses the other method, message digest authentication.

Message Digest Authentication

Regardless of the authentication method used on the server, basic authentication uses the procedure already described, in which the server returns a 401 (Not Authorized) response and the client sends user credentials in plain text. HTTP also provides a second authentication type, called digest access authentication. Like basic authentication, this scheme proceeds as a challenge-response dialog. The difference is that the password is never sent across the wire; it is used only by the browser to compute a checksum that must match the same checksum created on the server in order for user authentication to succeed. Various checksum schemes can be used but, by default, digest authentication uses Message Digest 5 (MD5).

Although digest authentication is more secure than basic authentication, it is limited in significant ways. For one thing, the only part of the communication between browser and server that is protected is the password. All other communication is completely in the clear. Also, digest authentication is not consistently implemented in most browser software. If your site requires greater security than that offered by the basic authentication schemes described here, you should consider using SSL, as described in the next chapter, rather than using digest authentication.

If you do attempt to use MD5 authentication, be aware that not all browsers support it fully.

Implementing Digest Authentication in Apache

Digest authentication is provided by two standard Apache modules, mod_digest and the newer mod_auth_digest. Both are included in the standard Apache distribution, but neither is compiled into the server in the default configuration.

> **NOTE**   In March 2002, eWEEK Magazine announced that eWEEK Labs had discovered a "security incompatibility" between Microsoft Internet Explorer's implementation of MD5 digest authentication and that in Apache's mod_digest. The announcement stated that digest authentication is a "relatively new technology," which it certainly is not. Digest authentication based on MD5 is not new.

Once you've made these modules available, use the htdigest file command to create a user database for MD5 authentication:

```
# htdigest -c /usr/local/apache2/auth/password.md5 "Simple MD5 Digest Auth"
➥caulds
Adding password for caulds in realm Simple MD4 Digest Auth.
New password:
Re-type new password:
```

This produces the following file:

```
# cat /usr/local/apache2/auth/password.md5
caulds:Simple MD5 Digest Auth:49afdef1311ec591ed02559e2a19ef45
```

Notice that the authentication realm is stored with each user's information. Since the same username cannot be stored twice in the same file, it is usually necessary to have separate files for each authentication realm. Group files are in the same format as ordinary mod_auth group files; in fact, the same group files can be used and specified by the AuthDigestGroupFile directive. The following example of a Location directive specifies a location (URL) to protect with digest authentication:

```
<Location /MD5Protected/>
  AuthName "Digest Authentication"
  AuthType Digest
  AuthDigestFile /usr/local/apache2/auth/password.md5
  AuthDigestGroupFile /usr/local/apache2/auth/groups
  AuthDigestDomain /MD5Protected/ /private/
  Require group WebAdmins
</Location>
```

In this example, notice first that the AuthDigestDomain directive lists URLs that are part of this authentication realm. The directive should always be specified and should contain at least the root URL. Also note that there is no directive to specify whether digest authentication is authoritative. When digest authentication is used, it is always authoritative, and other authentication schemes cannot be used to grant access to an MD5-protected realm.

Database Authentication (Unix DBM)

Basic authentication is perfectly adequate for many systems, particularly if no more than about 1000 users must be authenticated. The level of confidence that can be placed in the identity of users authenticated by mod_auth is as good as other schemes that use the basic HTTP authentication. However, a significant drawback of mod_auth is that it does use unindexed text files to store user and group information. To match user-provided credentials against these text files, the file must be opened and a string comparison made of each username against each line of the text file until a match is made or the end of file is reached.

When the number of users for whom credentials are maintained on the server grows to 1000 or greater, it's time to move to some type of database to store the information. There are many options, and modules are available to provide basic HTTP authentication against all major commercial relational databases as well as some lightweight, but highly efficient, open-source alternatives (like my favorite, the MySQL database). Table 13.1 lists most of the available database authentication modules; check modules.apache.org if your database isn't listed.

Table 13.1   Some Database Authentication Modules

Module	Database Used With
mod_auth_db	Berkeley DB
mod_auth_dbm	Unix DBM
mod_auth_mysql	MySQL
mod_auth_ora7	Oracle version 7
mod_auth_ora8	Oracle version 8
mod_auth_pgsql	PostgreSQL
mod_auth_tds	Microsoft SQL Server and Sybase
mod_auth_solid	Solid

Using the DBM Database for Authentication

All distributions of Linux (like virtually all Unix systems) come with at least one variation of a database system called DBM, usually implemented as a system object code library that can be linked into other programs. Not only are these databases built-in system functions, they also use highly optimized single key/value indexing schemes for super-fast lookups (which usually makes them faster for simple queries than a full-featured relational database like Oracle). There are two major databases used, either Berkeley DB (sometimes called BSD DB) or one of several schemes called DBM that go by names like NDBM, SDBM, and Gnu DBM (GDBM).

Since all use a common set of functions, changing from one package to another usually doesn't require rewriting applications but can be accomplished by recompiling with a new header file and linking to the new database library. In the case of an interpreted language like Perl, changing database packages usually means simply reading the new module into the script's namespace. The functions that are called within the Perl program remain the same. The major difference between the different DB and DBM variants is the file format, which is incompatible between them. That means, simply, that if you create a file for DB or one of the DBM libraries, you can read that file only with applications designed to read files of the same type.

> **NOTE**   mod_auth_db, which was part of earlier versions of the Apache distribution, was removed and replaced with mod_auth_dbm in Apache 2.0. Work is being done to update mod_auth_db to work with Apache 2.0, but if you prefer to use Berkeley DB instead of one of the Unix/Linux DBM flavors, you might have a little trouble obtaining it. In this chapter, I discuss only the module for authentication based on DBM.

All DB and DBM implementations are designed to provide quick retrieval of data based on a key value, and all systems are implemented as key/value pairs, in much the same way that Perl uses hashes. In fact, a common way to use DB or DBM with Perl is to *tie* the DB/DBM database to a standard Perl hash and then manipulate the hash, without regard to the underlying database or filesystem. Perl simply thinks it's working with an in-memory hash. I mention Perl because a Perl script is provided with Apache to create and maintain a DB or DBM database that contains user authentication information. In fact, you should read the Perl documentation for more information on the different system databases supported by Perl. Enter the following to see that formatted page:

```
# perldoc AnyDBM_File
```

User authentication against DBM databases is provided by a standard module called mod_auth_dbm. This module is compiled for the server explicitly using the --enable-auth-dbm or if either the most or all keywords is passed to the --enable-modules or --enable-mods-shared directives, as in these examples:

```
--enable-modules=most
--enable-mods-shared=all
```

Managing a DBM User Database

In order to create a DBM user file, you use a special script named /usr/bin/dbmmanage. This Perl script is similar to the htpasswd script used for mod_auth authentication. The file it creates is a set of username/password pairs. The main difference is that this file will be in DB format, not viewable or editable with a text editor, but far more efficient for looking up a specific user's information.

If you open the dbmmanage script with a text editor, you'll find the following line:

```
BEGIN { @AnyDBM_File::ISA = qw(DB_File NDBM_File GDBM_File)}
```

This line expresses the script author's preferences for Berkeley DB, because the string DB_File (actually the name of a Perl module) appears first in the @ISA array. When dbmmanage is invoked with this line, it will use the Berkeley DB libraries if they are available; failing that, the script will choose NDBM. If the NDBM libraries do not exist, the script uses GDBM. You *must* change the order of entries in this line if you intend to use mod_auth_dbm. For Berkeley DB, no change is required (and that suits us just fine).

Invoking dbmmanage with no argument lists all the available command-line options. Each of these will be explained by example:

```
# dbmmanage
Usage: dbmmanage [enc] dbname command [username
➥   [pw [group[,group] [comment]]]]

    where enc is  -d for crypt encryption (default except on
➥     Win32, Netware)
                  -m for MD5 encryption (default on Win32, Netware)
                  -s for SHA1 encryption
                  -p for plaintext

    command is one of: add|adduser|check|delete|import|update|view

    pw of . for update command retains the old password
    pw of - (or blank) for update command prompts for the password

    groups or comment of . (or blank) for update command retains
➥       old values
    groups or comment of - for update command clears the
➥       existing value
```

    groups or comment of - for add and adduser commands is
➡   the empty value

Use the adduser command to add a new user to the database or to create a new database:

```
# dbmmanage /usr/local/apache2/auth/dbmpasswds adduser caulds
New password:
Re-type new password:
User caulds added with password encrypted to FcYdV5OgbOaEQ using crypt
```

Note that the user's password isn't displayed when typed, so that a person looking over your shoulder has to read your fingers instead. No dbmmanage command will ever display a user-readable password. The view command can be used to display the database entry for a specific user:

```
# dbmmanage /usr/local/apache2/auth/dbmpasswds view caulds
caulds:.1iWwtF3v4Qkw
```

The dbmmanage script encrypts passwords using the standard Linux crypt system function. The crypt function is based on the Data Encryption Standard (DES). You can also choose to use MD5 encryption, though you will first need to install the Crypt::PasswdMD5 Perl module. The -m switch will cause htpasswd to encrypt the password with MD5:

```
# ./bin/dbmmanage -m /usr/local/apache2/auth/dbmpasswds adduser caulds
New password:
Re-type new password:
User caulds added with password encrypted to
➡ $apr1$4w6ElbhO$Ozt2jp8JkM9SWPnDlKPMX/ using md5
```

Unless you have very good reasons for using another encryption scheme, crypt is good enough and should be used. If a hacker has unrestricted access to your DB database, given enough time and the right cracking tools, that person will break any standard encryption method.

The import command is used to import data from a username/password list. The most common use of this command is importing a standard mod_auth authorization file. (Note that the passwords in this file are already encrypted; import does not permit the encryption of plain-text passwords being imported.) I converted my AuthUserFile with this command line:

```
# dbmmanage /usr/local/apache2/auth/dbpasswds import < userfile
User caulds added with password encrypted to I7G7qC9E9DgPc
➡ using crypt
User csewell added with password encrypted to FoebWZ210Tef.
➡ using crypt
User linda added with password encrypted to cj7OMmHuU6xsk
➡ using crypt
```

```
User larry added with password encrypted to NFrrBvMvmOO56
➥ using crypt
```

The entire contents of the database can be viewed with the view command without expressing a user name:

```
# dbmmanage /usr/local/apache2/auth/dbpasswds view
caulds:I7G7qC9E9DgPc
linda:cj70MmHuU6xsk
larry:NFrrBvMvmOO56
csewell:FoebWZ210Tef.
```

The add command adds one user whose username and encrypted password are both passed on the command line (some method of encrypting the password has to be used first; perhaps the password was copied from a user file on another Linux system):

```
# dbmmanage /usr/local/apache2/auth/dbpasswds add AdminGuy I7G7qC9E9DgPc
User AdminGuy added with password encrypted to I7G7qC9E9DgPc
➥ using crypt
```

Use the update command to change a user's password in the database:

```
# dbmmanage /usr/local/apache2/auth/dbpasswds update larry
New password:
Re-type new password:
User larry updated with password encrypted to 1tLbQexG8jRXc
➥ using crypt
```

The check command checks the password in the database for a user. It will tell you if the password you are attempting to use, when encrypted, matches the one in the database:

```
# dbmmanage /usr/local/apache2/auth/dbpasswds check linda
Enter password:
password ok
```

Finally, the delete command removes the database entry for a single user:

```
# dbmmanage /usr/local/apache2/auth/dbpasswds delete linda
'linda' deleted
```

Configuring Apache for DBM Authentication

If you've compiled mod_auth_dbm support into your server, at least one of the following lines will be in your httpd.conf file:

```
# grep dbm /usr/local/apache2/conf/httpd.conf
LoadModule auth_dbm_module modules/mod_auth_dbm.so
```

The LoadModule line is required only if you've compiled mod_auth_dbm as a DSO; otherwise the module is linked into the Apache server, and always available.

DBM authorization is easy to set up, and it works very much like standard `mod_auth` authorization. The following `.htaccess` file protects resources on my server by authenticating users against a DBM database:

```
AuthName          "DBM Authentication Realm"
AuthType          basic
AuthDBMUserFile /usr/local/apache2/auth/dbmpasswds
require valid-user
AuthDBMAuthoritative Off
```

The `AuthName` directive, which is required, names a new authentication realm. Remember that users, once authenticated against the realm, are automatically granted access to other areas that specify the same realm. `AuthType` is, again, basic, which is really the only value you will ever use for this directive. The `AuthDBUserFile` points to a DBM database of usernames and passwords, as described in the next section. The `require` directive, again, grants access to any user presenting credentials that can be validated against this DBM database. Finally, the `AuthDBAuthoritative Off` directive specifies that the acceptance or rejection of a user by this module is not authoritative and the user credentials should be passed to any lower-level authentication module in the Apache module list. (Remember that the order in which modules are called cannot be determined in versions of Apache later 2.0, as in previous version of Apache).

A group file can also be used; again, this is a list of groups and members and is identical in format to the group file used for `mod_auth` authorization in the last section. In fact, you can use the same file:

```
AuthName          "DBM Authentication Realm"
AuthType          basic
AuthDBUserFile    /usr/local/apache2/auth/dbpasswds
AuthDBGroupFile   /usr/local/apache2/auth/groups.dbm
require group WebAdmins
AuthDBAuthoritative On
```

Using the MySQL Database for Authentication

If you are using Apache 2.0 on a Linux platform, and wish to authenticate users against a MySQL database, an excellent choice of module for this purpose is the `mod_auth_mysql` module, which is downloadable from `www.heuer.org/mod_auth_mysql`. This section describes the installation and use of this module to create a user database in a MySQL database and authenticate Apache users against that database.

The `mod_auth_mysql` module allows you to authenticate users against a MySQL database (running on either the same server or another). For heavily loaded servers, it is considered far more efficient than flat file–based searches, and probably more secure. For extra security, the user passwords are stored in encrypted form in the MySQL database. Really nice.

As in all authentication schemes, mod_auth_mysql is responsible for accepting credentials presented by a user (usually by entering username and password information into a dialog presented by a Web browser), and then comparing this information against a collection of username/password pairs in a data repository of some kind (in this case, a MySQL database and table). The module returns a status of OK or FORBIDDEN to state whether or not the user will be granted access to the requested resource.

Download the source archive (mod_auth_mysql.tgz) from the site listed above. This archive will expand into several files that explain the installation and use of the module and the only file you really need to make it work, the C source file mod_auth_mysql.c. Expand the archive from *within* the directory in which you wish to build the module (you'll need to create this directory):

```
# cd /usr/local/src
# mkdir mod_auth_mysql
# cd mod_auth_mysql
# tar xvzf /downloads/mod_auth_mysql.tgz
INSTALL
htpasswd.sql
mod_auth_mysql.c
changes
example_data.html
```

Using the apxs utility, you can compile and install the module and modify the httpd.conf file in one easy step. The apxs command line seems a bit complex at first glance, but it's quite straightforward. The first three arguments to apxs can be in another order, but the command line shown below has them in their proper order of execution. The -c argument indicates that the last argument on the line (the filename) is to be compiled; -i tells apxs to "install" the resulting module, by copying it to Apache's module directory; and -a instructs apxs to "activate" the modules, by adding a LoadModule line to the httpd.conf file. Two other arguments specific to this module are actually instructions passed to the Linux linker. They tell it to link a library (mysqlclient is expanded to libmysqlclient.a) to the object it is creating and where it can find that module (in the /usr/lib/mysql directory):

```
# /usr/local/apache2/bin/apxs -c -i -a -L/usr/lib/mysql
➥    -lmysqlclient mod_auth_mysql.c
/usr/local/apache2/build/libtool --silent --mode=compile gcc
➥    -prefer-pic  -DAP_HAVE_DESIGNATED_INITIALIZER -DLINUX=2
➥    -D_REENTRANT -D_XOPEN_SOURCE=500 -D_BSD_SOURCE -D_SVID_SOURCE
➥    -g -O2 -pthread -DNO_DBM_REWRITEMAP -I/usr/local/apache2/include
➥    -c -o mod_auth_mysql.lo mod_auth_mysql.c && touch
➥      mod_auth_mysql.slo
```

```
/usr/local/apache2/build/libtool --silent --mode=link gcc
➥   -o mod_auth_mysql.la -rpath /usr/local/apache2/modules -module
➥   -avoid-version  -L/usr/lib/mysql -lmysqlclient
➥   mod_auth_mysql.lo
/usr/local/apache2/build/instdso.sh
➥   SH_LIBTOOL='/usr/local/apache2/build/libtool' mod_auth_mysql.la
➥   /usr/local/apache2/modules
/usr/local/apache2/build/libtool --mode=install
➥   cp mod_auth_mysql.la /usr/local/apache2/modules/
➥   cp .libs/mod_auth_mysql.so
➥   usr/local/apache2/modules/mod_auth_mysql.so
➥cp .libs/mod_auth_mysql.lai
➥/usr/local/apache2/modules/mod_auth_mysql.la
➥   cp .libs/mod_auth_mysql.a
➥   /usr/local/apache2/modules/mod_auth_mysql.a
ranlib /usr/local/apache2/modules/mod_auth_mysql.a
chmod 644 /usr/local/apache2/modules/mod_auth_mysql.a
PATH="$PATH:/sbin" ldconfig -n /usr/local/apache2/modules
----------------------------------------------------
--------------Libraries have been installed in:
/usr/local/apache2/modules

If you ever happen to want to link against installed libraries
in a given directory, LIBDIR, you must either use libtool, and
specify the full pathname of the library, or use the `-LLIBDIR'
flag during linking and do at least one of the following:
    - add LIBDIR to the `LD_LIBRARY_PATH' environment variable
      during execution
    - add LIBDIR to the `LD_RUN_PATH' environment variable
      during linking
    - use the `-Wl,--rpath -Wl,LIBDIR' linker flag
    - have your system administrator add LIBDIR to `/etc/ld.so.conf'

See any operating system documentation about shared libraries for
more information, such as the ld(1) and ld.so(8) manual pages.
----------------------------------------------------------------
chmod 755 /usr/local/apache2/modules/mod_auth_mysql.so
[activating module `auth_mysql' in /usr/local/apache2/conf/httpd.conf]
```

Using a relational database for authenticating users is really no more difficult than using a flat file. You only have to create the database and fill it with user data; the module itself knows how to look up user information. The following instructions apply to

MySQL, but you will follow very similar steps in creating a database for another relational database application like Oracle or PostgreSQL.

Although there are Apache directives that allow you to change the name of the database and tables that mod_auth_mysqlwill use to query user data, there is no real reason to change these. Save yourself some trouble, and create a MySQL user named htpasswd and a MySQL database also named htpasswd that contains three tables named host_info, user_info, and group_info. Create the database as follows (while logged into Linux with a user account that has been granted database creation rights):

```
# mysqladmin -p create htpasswd
Enter password:
```

After creating the database, invoke MySQL, logged in as a user who can set privileges on the htpasswd database, and issue a single "grant" command that will create a new user htpasswd, assign that user a password, and grant that user select privileges to the htpasswd database. Note that the username and password can be anything you choose, but they will need to match those used in the Apache directives, as mod_auth_mysql will log in as this user account to query the htpasswd tables to authenticate the user requesting protected resources. For security purposes, this user should have privileges no greater than select.

If the database you are creating is on a separate system from your Apache server, make sure that localhost is changed in the example to the hostname of the host server (from which the login to MySQL from mod_auth_mysql will be made). The host can be identified by hostname or IP address, and wildcards can be used; to grant access from anywhere on my local area network, I could use 192.168.1.%, for example. Remember, though, that there is a default grant for localhost that must be overridden. You should always grant permissions to access the database from localhost if you intend to log in to MySQL from the same box, even if another grant (perhaps for an address range) would appear to include the system:

```
# mysql -p
Enter password:
Welcome to the MySQL monitor.  Commands end with ; or \g.
Your MySQL connection id is 5 to server version: 3.23.49

Type 'help;' or '\h' for help. Type '\c' to clear the buffer.

mysql> use htpasswd
mysql> grant select on htpasswd.*
➥ to htpasswd@localhost identified by 'secret';
Query OK, 0 rows affected (0.14 sec)
```

> **WARNING** MySQL will allow you to grant access from any and all addresses, in a sense disregarding the origin of the connection, with a line like the following:
>
> ```
> grant select on htpasswd.* to caulds@"%";
> ```
>
> This is, however, a questionable practice, and whenever possible, you should try to grant access to the database only from hosts you know and trust.

Though you could continue to use the same account that created htpasswd to administer the tables (add/delete records), you may wish to create a special user account for this purpose, granting all privileges on the database to that user. While logged into MySQL, invoke the mysql process and use the following grant command to create the user, assign the user a password, and give that user full privileges to the htpasswd database and all its tables:

```
mysql> grant all privileges on htpasswd.*
➥ to htadmin@localhost identified by 'adminpass';
Query OK, 0 rows affected (0.14 sec)
mysql> flush privileges;
Query OK, 0 rows affected (0.00 sec)
mysql> quit
```

Note the flush privileges command that is issued after grant. This special command (which works the same as the associated flush-privileges command in mysqladmin) causes MySQL to immediately flush its grant tables and reload them from the administrative database where the information is stored. The grant command shown would not take effect until after this was done (or MySQL was stopped and started afresh).

Listing 13.1 shows the table structures required by the module. You can add fields to those shown, to store information for your own use, but the fields shown are the minimum required. You can enter the commands (omitting those that are marked by a leading "#" character as comment lines) manually while logged into MySQL as the new owner of the database, or you can use a text editor to store the commands in a file. If Listing 13.1 was stored in a text file named htpasswd.sql, you could set up these three tables with the following command line, which logs into MySQL as the newly created owner of the database and creates the tables from the file:

```
# mysql -u htadmin -p htpasswd < htpasswd.sql
```

Listing 13.1   Database Creation Script htpasswd.sql

```
#
# Table structure for table `host_info`
#
```

```
# the fields created, updated, and isadmin are not needed by the module!
# they may help you creating a php-htpasswd frontend
#

CREATE TABLE host_info (
   id int(14) NOT NULL auto_increment,
   host char(255) NOT NULL default '',
   host_group int(14) NOT NULL default '0',
   PRIMARY KEY  (id),
   KEY host (host)
) TYPE=MyISAM PACK_KEYS=1;
# --------------------------------------------------------


#
# Table structure for table `user_group`
#

CREATE TABLE user_group (
   id int(14) NOT NULL auto_increment,
   user_name char(50) NOT NULL default '',
   user_group char(20) NOT NULL default '',
   host_group int(14) default NULL,
   PRIMARY KEY  (id),
   KEY host_group (host_group),
   KEY user_group (user_group)
) TYPE=MyISAM PACK_KEYS=1;
# --------------------------------------------------------


#
# Table structure for table `user_info`
#

CREATE TABLE user_info (
   id int(14) NOT NULL auto_increment,
   user_name char(30) NOT NULL default '',
   user_passwd char(20) NOT NULL default '',
   host_group int(14) NOT NULL default '0',
   PRIMARY KEY  (id),
   UNIQUE KEY user_name (user_name,host_group)
) TYPE=MyISAM PACK_KEYS=1;
```

Probably the most time-consuming part of the mod_auth_mysql setup is the creation of the database tables, and most sites that use database authentication will choose to automate this process with scripts or Web front-ends to the database. However, the process I demonstrate is manual and uses the MySQL client while logged in as the owner of the mod_auth_mysql database (user htpasswd in the examples).

The host_info table is used to store the hostname or virtual hostname of all servers that will have Web pages protected by mod_auth_mysql. It must contain at least one record, that of the main Web server, and the names of virtual hosts, if those are used. The simplest example is a server without virtual hosts. The following example loads MySQL and enters the hostname of the server:

```
# mysql -u htadmin -p htpasswd
Enter password:
Reading table information for completion of table and column names
You can turn off this feature to get a quicker startup with -A

Welcome to the MySQL monitor.  Commands end with ; or \g.
Your MySQL connection id is 21 to server version: 3.23.49

Type 'help;' or '\h' for help. Type '\c' to clear the buffer.

mysql> insert into host_info(id,host,host_group) values
➥ (null,"jackal.hiwaay.net",1);
Query OK, 1 row affected (0.00 sec)

mysql> select * from host_info;
+----+-------------------+------------+
| id | host              | host_group |
+----+-------------------+------------+
|  1 | jackal.hiwaay.net |          1 |
+----+-------------------+------------+
1 row in set (0.01 sec)
```

In this example, note that the id column is automatically assigned a unique number if the value you enter is null. This column is used to ensure that there is always at least one field that has a unique value that can be used to identify each individual row. The host field contains the hostname of the Apache server (or virtual server if those are used). It should always match the value of a ServerName directive, either in the main server portion of httpd.conf or within a <VirtualHost> section. The last column, host_group, is used to store a number that refers to a group of hosts that you wish to treat as a group when assigning access permissions. If you aren't going to assign permissions by server group, assign the same value to this field for all rows in the host_group table. The choice is arbitrary, as long as the value you enter is a valid integer.

The user_info table is the most important of the three tables. It contains a row for each user who will be given permission to access pages protected by mod_auth_mysql, so the

Maintaining a
Healthy Server

PART 4

table can be quite large. (That's the reason a relational database, rather than a flat file, is being used to store the data.) Create entries in this table with an insert statement like the following:

```
# mysql -u htadmin -p htpasswd
Enter password:
Reading table information for completion of table and column names
You can turn off this feature to get a quicker startup with -A

Welcome to the MySQL monitor.  Commands end with ; or \g.
Your MySQL connection id is 23 to server version: 3.23.49

Type 'help;' or '\h' for help. Type '\c' to clear the buffer.

mysql> insert into user_info(id,user_name,user_passwd,host_group) values
  (null,"caulds",encrypt("mysecret"),1);
Query OK, 1 row affected (0.01 sec)
```

The id column has the same purpose as it did in the host_info table—uniquely identifying the new row in the table—and is automatically assigned a value if you pass null as its value in the insert statement. The user_name column stores the username that will be looked up when the user attempts to gain access to mod_auth_mysql-protected resources.

The user_password column is interesting. A built-in MySQL command is used to encrypt the password (Unix crypt encryption is used) before it is stored in the database, just in case someone is able to view or read the table. Always make sure you store passwords in encrypted form, not only for this reason, but because mod_auth_mysql expects them to be encrypted, and will not like it if you store passwords in plain text.

```
mysql> select * from user_info where user_name='caulds';
+----+-----------+---------------+------------+
| id | user_name | user_passwd   | host_group |
+----+-----------+---------------+------------+
|  1 | caulds    | IoRONGXjgOnK. |          1 |
+----+-----------+---------------+------------+
1 row in set (0.00 sec)
```

You can have multiple records for the same user, if that user is to be granted access to more than one host group, in which case you will also have multiple rows in the host_info table. When a user attempts to access a server, mod_auth_mysql will check to see if there is a row in user_info table with a value of host_group that matches any entry in the host_info table to determine if that user has access to resources on that server. Most users will probably not opt to use host groups with mod_auth_mysql, but be aware that the capability is there. The .htaccess example in Listing 13.2 shows how to configure authentication by user.

The last table, group_info, is the only table of the three that is not required to use mod_auth_mysql. This table is used only if you wish to grant access based on groups, by determining if a user, once logged in, is a member of a group authorized to access the requested resource. I won't explain the use of the id and host_group columns of the table, as these have the same function as they do for user_info. Although the author of mod_auth_mysql plans to simplify the table and reduce the number of rows that must be stored, the current version requires that the table contain a row for each user/group combination. In other words, if there are three groups, each with 10 members, the table will contain 30 rows. The following example adds a single user (caulds) to a single group (Admins). A row will be required for each group in which this user has membership, and the number of rows required can be quite large. The .htaccess example in Listing 13.2 also shows how to configure authentication by group.

```
mysql> insert into user_group(id,user_name,user_group,host_group) values
       (null,"caulds",'Admins',1);
Query OK, 1 row affected (0.01 sec)

mysql> select * from user_group;
+----+-----------+------------+------------+
| id | user_name | user_group | host_group |
+----+-----------+------------+------------+
|  1 | caulds    | Admins     |          1 |
+----+-----------+------------+------------+
1 row in set (0.01 sec)
```

Listing 13.2   An .htaccess File That Uses mod_auth_mysql

```
# The following directives are identical to those
# used for Basic authorization and define the authentication
# type as "Basic" and the authentication realm that is used
# by the browser to determine which username/password pair
# to send

AuthType Basic
AuthName TopSecret

# The following lines are required to make a connection to
# the MySQL database, identifying the database by name,
# the MySQL server name (localhost), userid and password required
# to access the table.

AuthMySQLHost localhost
AuthMySQLUser htpasswd
```

Maintaining a
Healthy Server

PART 4

```
AuthMySQLPassword secret
AuthMySQLDB htpasswd

# Make MySQL authentication authoritative. In other words,
# if this module accepts or denies access to a user, that
# decision is final; no other auth module can override

AuthSQLAuthoritative On

# Keep the connection to MySQL (from Apache) open between
# authentication attempts (for efficiency)

AuthSQLKeepAlive on
#
# standard "require" to specify authorized users
# or use "require valid-user" to specify that any user in
# the user_info table has access

require user caulds csewell

#
# or, alternatively, use groups to control access

# require group Admins
```

Although using .htaccess files is the best way to protect resources in protected directories, the same thing can be accomplished using <Location> tags in the Apache httpd.conf file. The following would accomplish the same thing as placing the directives beginning with Auth in an .htaccess file in the directory protected. You might note that the <IfModule> tags cause the directives to have no effect if the required module is not accessible.

```
<IfModule mod_auth_mysql.c>
  <Location /protected>
  AuthType Basic
  AuthName TopSecret
  AuthMySQLHost localhost
  AuthMySQLUser htpasswd
  AuthMySQLPassword secret
  AuthMySQLDB htpasswd
  AuthSQLAuthoritative On
  AuthSQLKeepAlive off
  </Location>
</IfModule>
```

In addition to modules that provide true user authentication, there is one module you should be aware of, although it isn't widely used. The next section discusses mod_auth_anon, which provides "anonymous" Web access in the same fashion that many FTP servers provide anonymous or guest accounts.

"Anonymous" Authentication: The *mod_auth_anon* Module

The mod_auth_anon module (part of the standard Apache distribution, though not compiled into the default configuration) provides an interesting form of authentication. This module allows "anonymous" user access to specified areas in the same way that anonymous access is provided on many FTP servers. The user who enters one or more "magic" usernames is allowed access without having to provide a password. A long-standing convention with anonymous FTP servers is to request that users enter their complete e-mail addresses for logging purposes, though this is usually not required. To use this module, make sure that the following lines are in your httpd.conf file:

```
LoadModule anon_auth_module   libexec/mod_auth_anon.so
AddModule mod_auth_anon.c
```

The .htaccess file in Listing 13.3 provides examples of all possible mod_auth_anon directives. The comments in the listing provide all the information you need to make this simple module work.

Listing 13.3 An .htaccess File That Uses mod_auth_anon

```
# .htaccess file for anonymous HTTP access
# The AuthType directive is required
AuthType basic
#
# Provides the prompt in user's login dialog box
AuthName "Use 'anonymous' & Email address for guest entry"
#
# Specify logins 'anonymous' and 'guest' for anonymous
# access; this directive required
Anonymous anonymous guest
#
# Do not permit blank username field, set to on to
# allow null usernames
#
Anonymous_NoUserId off
#
# User must specify an e-mail address as a password; set
# to off to allow null passwords.
Anonymous_MustGiveEmail on
#
```

```
# Set to on to check for at least one '@' character and
# one '.' character in password provided; does NOT guarantee
# that the e-mail address is valid
Anonymous_VerifyEmail on
#
# When set to on, this directive causes the user e-mail
# address (password) to be written in error.log
Anonymous_LogEmail on
#
# Set to On to disable fall-through to other authorization
# methods.  Access is by use of anonymous usernames only
Anonymous_Authoritative On
#
# Mandatory, even though no user file is used or specified
require valid-user
```

Authentication Servers

In addition to modules that authenticate users against databases, there are a large number of third-party Apache modules to provide authentication against directory services and specialized authentication servers. For a complete and up-to-date list of these, enter **authentication** as the search term at modules.apache.org. Table 13.2 lists modules for the most widely used user authentication schemes.

> **WARNING** Before attempting to use modules from modules.apache.org, make sure the module has been updated to support Apache 2.0. If you can't tell from reading the module description on the Web site, write the author. Most of the Apache modules available from this Web site should be available for Apache 2.0 by the time you read this, or a 2.0 version should be in the works.

Table 13.2 Authentication Server Apache Modules

Module	Authentication Scheme
mod_auth_kerb	Kerberos
mod_auth_ldap	LDAP
mod_auth_nds	NDS (Novell)
mod_auth_notes	Lotus Notes
mod_auth_nt_lm	NT domain controller

Table 13.2   Authentication Server Apache Modules (*continued*)

Module	Authentication Scheme
mod_auth_radius	RADIUS server
mod_auth_samba	Samba
mod_auth_smb	SMB (LAN Manager)
mod_auth_sys	Authentication against system files
mod_auth_tacacs	TACACS+
mod_auth_yp	NIS (Yellow Pages)
mod_securid	SecurID token authentication

In most cases, these authentication modules work just like authentication modules for database authentication. The actual querying of the authentication server takes place behind the scenes. From the client standpoint, there is no difference; users are presented with the standard dialog for their browser and prompted for a username and password, exactly as in any other scheme.

The Remote Authentication Dial-In User Server (RADIUS) is one of the most common authentication servers in use today, providing authentication of dial-in users for most large Internet Service Providers (ISPs). To provide Web services for client users only, ISPs might choose to authenticate Web client access against their existing RADIUS database. The mod_auth_radius module (https://www.gnarst.net/authradius/mod_auth_radius.html) makes this a fairly straightforward task. While the details aren't important, the process is as simple as compiling mod_auth_radius as a DSO module (using the apxs utility, as described in Chapter 5), configuring Apache to load the module, and ensuring that the module can locate and communicate with a RADIUS server by adding a line like the following to the httpd.conf file:

```
AddRadiusAuth radius01.hiwaay.net:1645 tanstaafl
```

The line shown above identifies the hostname of the RADIUS authentication server (and connection port number) and a shared secret used to establish encrypted communication with this server. Listing 13.4 shows an .htaccess file that can be created in a directory to grant access to that directory only to valid RADIUS account holders. This example is very simple, requiring only that the RADIUS server is able to authenticate the connecting user. In most cases, this is completely adequate, but if you intend to make full use of mod_auth_radius, you may wish to take advantage of more advanced features such as group authentication and the use of temporary cookies to eliminate the need for frequent queries of the RADIUS server.

Listing 13.4   An `.htaccess` File That Uses `mod_auth_radius`

```
# Use basic password authentication.
AuthType Basic
#
AuthName "RADIUS authentication for jackal.hiwaay.net"
#
# Use mod_auth_radius for authentication
AuthRadiusAuthoritative on
#
# mod_auth_radius grants access to all valid RADIUS users
#
require valid-user
```

In Sum

Securing an Apache Web server is probably one of the most important topics covered in this book, especially to administrators of Internet-accessible servers (as most are today). This chapter and the next both discuss mechanisms that are used with Apache to provide three types of security:

- Access control based solely on the details of the incoming request packet, which essentially means controlling access based on the network address of the originator. A single module, `mod_access`, provides this functionality in Apache.

- User authentication is any mechanism used to verify the identity of the user. This chapter has discussed authentication modules that match unencrypted usernames and passwords against stored data on the server; the next chapter discusses the use of digital *certificates* to facilitate a public key exchange that permits encryption of all data (including user passwords) between a Web server and client browser.

- Authorization is the determination of what resources a user is permitted to access. Although the functions of user authentication and authorization are completely separate, most Apache modules for controlling access to server resources perform both roles.

Because of the additional security required to implement real business applications on the public Internet, the simple user authentication and authorization discussed in this chapter are rapidly being replaced by Secure Sockets Layer, which encrypts the data passing between server and client browser. Apache is easily modified to support SSL. Because of the importance of this technology, the next chapter is devoted to SSL.

14

Secure Sockets Layer

The previous chapter discussed common methods that can be used by all Web servers to authenticate users based on an unencrypted username and password sent "in the clear." In Apache, these schemes are implemented as modules that combine the functions of user authentication and access authorization. There are two weaknesses in this traditional Web security model. First, the data transmitted between Web server and client browser is not secure from eavesdropping, and there is a possibility (if slight) that someone with malicious intent and the ability to snoop on network packets can view sensitive information (the prime targets are passwords). The second weakness of conventional security is that, while the Web server has a reasonable degree of assurance that the client user is legitimate (based on the provided user ID and password), the client has no way of determining if the Web server is actually the one that it is attempting to access. Thieves have been known to spoof servers on the Internet, attempting to appear, in every respect, like the legitimate host in order to capture information that the unwitting user believes is being sent to a completely different server. Although they are rare and require a good deal of knowledge and planning to execute, these "man in the middle" schemes are likely to become more common as the stakes in the Internet commerce game increase with the proliferation of such things as online shopping and Internet banking.

In the mid-1990s, Netscape Communications developed a scheme to close both of the security vulnerabilities in the traditional Web security model. The Secure Sockets Layer (SSL) protocol provides a private channel of communication between Web server and browser, and also assures clients that the Web server to which they are connected is the proper one. This is done by comparing the URL encoded in the certificate and presented by the remote Web server to the URL that the browser used to locate the server. These URLs must match. SSL also provides a reasonable degree of confidence that the server's certificate was not forged. In this chapter, I'll explain how an SSL Web server uses digitally signed certificates of authenticity to allow a client browser to verify its authenticity, and how a temporary (or "session") encryption key is shared by the SSL server and client to encrypt all data that is passed between them. I'll also give a full demonstration of how to create, distribute, and use a server certificate.

In Apache 2.0, SSL was incorporated as a standard, or core, module named mod_ssl, which was previously distributed independently by Ralf S. Engelschall (www.openssl.org). Consequently, the process of setting up an Apache server to use SSL became much easier than the old way, which required patching the Apache source code with code from one of two providers of an SSL module for Apache. SSL is based on cryptography, specifically on what is referred to as public key cryptography (an asymmetric encryption scheme in which the key used to encode data is different from, but mathematically related to, the key used to decrypt the same data). The next section is a very basic primer on cryptography. Cryptography is math, but you don't need to be a mathematician to understand how it is used. You should read the following section as an introduction to using digitally signed certificates, the basis of SSL.

Microsoft .NET Passport

The need for reliable online client identification has long been recognized as critical to the success of online business and commerce, but surprisingly little has actually been done about it. While the mechanisms are in place to provide such client certificates, signed by established certificate authorities like VeriSign, the use of client certificates is almost nonexistent, and the proliferation of online business has continued without this critical piece of the puzzle. With the release of its XP operating system in late 2001, Microsoft made a bold move to do something about it, and capitalized on the failure of the rest of the computing industry to do what all admit is necessary. As part of Microsoft's .NET initiative, the Passport identity storage system uses *tickets* in the same fashion as the venerable Kerberos technology on which it is based. Passport is marketed as a *single sign-on* system, in which you are presented with a sign-on dialog the first time you attempt to access a Passport-secured site. A simple username/password pair is used to sign onto Passport, but once signed on, you can proceed to access any of thousands of Passport-secured Web sites around the world, without having to know or provide any other password. With all the complexities removed, Passport essentially boils down to this: once you log onto Passport, you'll receive a ticket from the Passport

> **Microsoft .NET Passport (*continued*)**
>
> server that your browser automatically presents to Passport-secured Web sites (via an SSL encrypted session) to authenticate you. In Microsoft's visionary .NET world of the future, this is the only password you'll ever need. Unlike X.509 client certificates described elsewhere in this chapter, Passport is a true escrow server, and personal information about you is stored in your Passport profile on a Microsoft server. Microsoft becomes the holder of everyone's keys, and absolute trust in the Microsoft Corporation is essential to the success of .NET Passport. Enough has been said about this Microsoft-proprietary technology in Linux books, but if you are at all interested, you can find out more about Microsoft .NET Passport at www.passport.com.

Symmetric and Asymmetric Encryption Schemes

There are two major types of encryption schemes, symmetric and asymmetric. In symmetric key encryptions, a single key is used to encrypt and decrypt a message or a communication stream. Symmetric key encryption schemes have the advantage of being very fast and are normally used when large amounts of data must be encrypted before being sent and rapidly decrypted on the opposite end (like data passing between sites in a communication session). The disadvantage of symmetric key systems is that both participants must know the single key used.

Asymmetric encryption is so called because two keys are used. One encryption key is used to encode a message or transmission, and a completely different decryption key is used to decode it. How is it possible to encode a message with one key and decode it with a different key? For this to work, the two keys are generated at the same time, and they are related to one another mathematically. Although there are several accepted ways to generate asymmetric encryption keys, they all work pretty much the same. It is only necessary to understand that a block of data that has been encrypted with either of the two keys of the pair can be decrypted only by using the other key of the pair.

While the mathematical operations used to compute two such keys are quite complex, the use of asymmetric key schemes is actually pretty easy to understand. It's based on the concept of a *public key encryption system*, in which one of the two key halves in the key pair is considered the *public key*, and the other, the *private key*. As its name implies, the

Maintaining a Healthy Server

PART 4

public key is usually distributed in some fashion (by download from a Web or FTP site, for example), while the owner of the key pair keeps the private key a closely guarded secret. The simplest exchange of information using a public key encryption system works like this: A user wishing to send confidential information to the owner of a public key encrypts that information with the other user's public key (remember, the public key is not a secret). Now only the holder of the private key that matches this public key can decrypt and view the message. Unless that private key has been compromised, only the intended recipient of the message can view it.

Public key encryption systems are not commonly used for encrypting data, however; they are more often used to authenticate individuals, and it is in authentication that public key encryption plays a strong role in SSL, as I'll show. Authentication using public key encryption works like this: If you encrypt a block of data (any data) with your private key, only the matching public key can be used to decrypt that data. If the public key correctly decrypts the data, it is known with a high degree of certainty that the private key holder encrypted the data. That is, the recipient of the data is assured of the identity of the sender, because the sender's identity has been authenticated.

The mathematical operations (or algorithms) used to implement public key encryption are complex, comparatively slow, and CPU-intensive (*expensive* might be a better term). For that reason, in practice, public key encryption is used to securely pass a symmetric encryption key between the SSL server and client. This symmetric key is then used to encrypt and decrypt the data being transmitted between the two. Symmetric key schemes are far more efficient, remember.

That brings us to SSL. Secure Sockets Layer uses both symmetric and asymmetric encryption. When an SSL connection is established between a Web server and a browser, the communication session between the two is encrypted and decrypted using an efficient symmetric key algorithm, agreed on by the two sides, and using a single shared key. The real genius in SSL is a secure method of exchanging this symmetric *session key*. That's where public key encryption plays a part. For SSL to work, all SSL servers hold digital authentication *certificates* to identify themselves.

The certificates used by SSL are basically digital packages that contain the public half of a key pair belonging to an SSL Web server. The certificate is used as a trusted means of putting this public key in your hands. Once you have the public key of an SSL Web site, you can encrypt a message to that site that can be decrypted only by the holder of the unique private half of the key pair. This allows you to transmit the aforementioned session key, which is used to set up a secure tunnel through the Internet for communication between you and the SSL site.

These SSL certificates are issued by organizations known as root *certification authorities* (CAs), which are trusted to certify that the certificate owner is exactly what it claims to be. Web browsers come prepackaged with a long list of CAs from which they'll accept certificates of authenticity. You might be surprised at how many CAs your browser trusts. If you doubt this, take a look. In Internet Explorer 5.5, for example, there are over 30 certificate signers listed as trusted! Uncover this information in IE by selecting Tools ➢ Internet Options ➢ Content ➢ Certificates, and then select the Trusted Root Certification Authorities tab. Figure 14.1 shows part of the list.

Figure 14.1   Internet Explorer trusted certificate signers

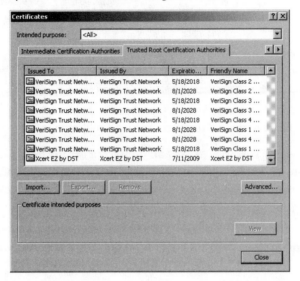

Several formats have been proposed for digital certificates, but only one of these is in widespread use. Originally proposed in 1988 as part of the X.500 directory services by the organization now known as the International Telecommunication Union (ITU), the X.509 certificate specification was adopted for use with SSL. The X.509 standard is now a joint international standard of the ITU and the International Organization for Standardization (ISO), and it is the only type of digital certificate you will probably ever need to be concerned about, especially for SSL.

In addition to the certificate holder's public key, an X.509 certificate also contains such information as the expiration date of the certificate, details about the certificate's issuing authority, and the certificate holder. Figure 14.2 shows the certificate for my Web site. The most important element of the certificate, though, is the wrapper, or envelope, that you don't see. The wrapper that encloses the certificate information contains the signature of the certificate's issuing authority. This signature indicates that the contents of the certificate have been verified and can be trusted (as long as you trust the issuing certificate authority).

Maintaining a
Healthy Server

PART 4

Figure 14.2 Viewing the contents of an X.509 certificate

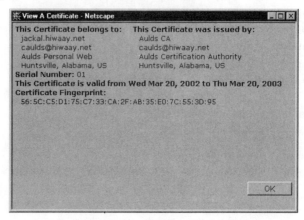

The SSL certificate authentication scheme works like this:

1. A Web site that wishes to use SSL presents a *certificate request* to one of the well-known certificate authorities. This request contains the public key of that Web site, along with other information about the company who owns the site.

2. The certificate authority, after verifying that the certificate request is valid and came from the source it claims to represent, uses the information in the certificate request to create an X.509 certificate that it encrypts with its private key. The certificate is returned to the site that requested it.

3. The Web site for which the certificate has been created and signed by the certificate authority installs the certificate in its Web server(s). The process is described for Apache 2.0 later in this chapter.

4. Now whenever an SSL-capable client connects to the site's SSL Web server, this certificate is sent to the client.

5. The client, trusting the CA that issued the certificate, validates the certificate with the trusted CA's public key, which ensures that the certificate was signed by that CA with its closely guarded private key. A certificate is considered completely valid for the server that presents it if it meets three criteria:

   - A CA trusted by the browser must issue the certificates.

   - The certificate must not be expired (its expiration date and time must be later than the current system date and time).

   - The certificate must be for the server that the browser believes it is connected to; in other words, the certificate offered by the server *must* match the URL used to make the request.

6. Having validated the certificate, the client now opens it and extracts the Web server's public key.

7. The client then generates a symmetric session key and encrypts that key with the Web site's public key. Remember, *only* the site holding the correct private key can decrypt the session key, so when it is properly decrypted, only the browser that generated the key and the Web server know it.

8. For the rest of the SSL session, the client and the server use this shared symmetric key to encrypt all traffic. The slower public key encryption scheme is used only to authenticate the server to the browser and to ensure a safe transmission of the session key between the two.

This whole process is actually more complex than I've described. Although you don't need to understand all the details in order to set up SSL for an Apache server and use it, it is important to understand enough of what's going on to follow the many setup steps required.

A Matter of Trust

Recent developments in the field of encryption technology tend to gloss over the fact that all such security is built on systems of trust. This is particularly true where the encryption software is sold as a complete solution or product add-on to companies that have very little knowledge of the underlying mathematics; and this is especially ironic in a business world where suspicion of one's competitors and even business partners is often the rule.

Most authentication and data encryption schemes rely on the use of public key encryption. This is true even of SSL, which uses certificates that have been signed with the private key of a known and trusted root certificate authority. The public keys of these root CAs are public knowledge, embedded in browser software, and the ability to open and read a certificate with one of these public keys ensures that the CA did, indeed, sign the certificate using one of its highly secret, closely guarded private keys.

Originally, the plan for public key distribution was to have public keys registered with trusted "escrow" holders, third parties trusted by both partners in a public key exchange. We would all go to these escrow servers to get public keys that we would then trust because we had complete trust in the escrow holder. The early designs for these systems would require that every time I need to validate a certificate from a Web server, I'd retrieve that Web server's public key from an escrow server.

A Matter of Trust (*continued*)

The problem was that no one wanted to trust any of the entities that offered their services as pubic key escrow holders. The United States government drew the loudest protestations when the National Security Agency proposed that it be the key escrow holder for everyone who wanted to engage in Internet commerce (this was back when the U.S. government thought it owned the Internet because it built the initial infrastructure). The resistance was especially strong after it was revealed that, upon orders of a U.S. federal court judge, anyone's *private* key could be delivered to law enforcement agencies. Private corporations didn't receive too much support either, in their bid to act as key escrows, primarily because of their profit motivations.

When I started learning about SSL and certificate authorities, I was very curious to know how they planned to implement it without the use of an escrow server, or a trusted third party, for every transaction. Certificate authorities do not hold public keys in escrow; instead, they enclose the public key half of the pair in a so-called digital certificate that is signed with the CA's private key. Since the public keys of the CAs are available to everyone who has a browser, these certificates can be opened and the contents examined by virtually anyone. If a particular CA's public key successfully opens a certificate, this is considered absolute proof that the CA's private key was used to create/encrypt the certificate. This is how a certificate is known to be trustworthy and valid. The public key it contains for the Web server it represents is considered absolutely reliable. The world's certificate authorities, while they don't possess the private keys of the companies they certify, are like escrow servers in one important sense: everyone has to trust them implicitly for this whole scheme to work.

There is absolutely no reason that large corporations can't act as their own certificate authorities, and many do, setting up complex hierarchies of trust between certificate servers that ensure the privacy of their internal communications and even with their trading partners in some cases. The U.S. automobile industry set up one of the most elaborate and successful of these systems.

Largely because the technologies underlying public key authentication and encryption are not well understood, and because of the difficulty of setting up hierarchies of trusted certificate servers, companies like VeriSign and Thawte have assumed the role of trusted authorities, and they do it strictly for money. When the two companies merged to form a single group, they furnished fully 90 percent of all certificates in use on the Internet, although this figure has been dropping steadily since, to about 65 percent today (as measured by the Internet site survey group SecuritySpace at www.securityspace.com). Who monitors the activities and motivations of these certificate authorities to ensure that they always act in the

A Matter of Trust (*continued*)

best interest of the global Internet community? No one, actually, but we trust them anyway—perhaps only because they've never betrayed that trust.

Is there a fundamental flaw in the system of universal trust that makes Internet commerce possible? Is it wise to place complete trust in a single profit-motivated entity simply because "everyone else does"? Perhaps this is yet another example of commerce and industry failing to understand the full implications of a technology that marketers have said we must all implement. On the other hand, it does seem to work, and for the simple reason that may also make it dangerous—because "everyone does it."

Implementing SSL in Apache

Apache's implementation of SSL is based on an impressive open-source package called OpenSSL (www.openssl.org). OpenSSL is basically installed on a Linux system as two system libraries:

- libcrypto.a
- libssl.a

These two libraries are linked into a large number of Linux programs. On most systems, you'll also find the dynamically loadable equivalents of these libraries:

- libcrypto.so
- libssl.so

The OpenSSL SSL/TLS library (libssl.a/libssl.so) contains functions that implement the Secure Sockets Layer and Transport Layer Security protocols, and the crypto library (libcrypto.a/libcrypto.so) contains a huge number of functions that implement a wide array of cryptographic (mathematical) algorithms.

In addition to these libraries, you'll get an extensive command-line utility (/usr/bin/openssl) that is used to access functions provided by these libraries for the creation of keys and certificates. OpenSSL also provides functions that allow you to create a certificate authority for signing your own certificates. The last section of this chapter will show how that functionality is used, if you choose to sign your own certificates (as you probably will if you are administering secure servers on a controlled intranet).

OpenSSL contains a number of different mathematical libraries to perform the nitty-gritty functions of encryption required to implement SSL, and it allows you to use the implementations of these complex algorithms without having to understand them. Later, when you install mod_ssl, you will generate a public key pair for your server. mod_ssl will use the OpenSSL libraries to do this, and will offer you a choice of two public key encryption schemes. The most widely used digital public key encryption system for SSL is the RSA public key cryptosystem. The mathematical algorithm for RSA was protected by a U.S. patent issued to RSA Security (www.rsasecurity.com) until that patent expired on September 20, 2000. Although OpenSSL provides the Digital Signature Algorithm (DSA) as an alternative to RSA to comply with this patent, there is no longer any reason to use DSA instead of RSA encryption, nor is there any need to buy a commercial OpenSSL package simply to acquire the RSA license. Therefore, the examples in this chapter illustrate the use of RSA encryption.

OpenSSL is described as a "toolkit" that implements SSL and a large number of cryptography schemes. Make no mistake about it; OpenSSL is a massive application and a very impressive piece of work, especially considering its ease of installation, complete reliability, and price (essentially free). Most current distributions of Linux include OpenSSL and, at least in the Red Hat distribution, form an integral part of the distribution's security model. Apache's mod_ssl requires that the OpenSSL be installed on your Linux system. Every major Linux distribution will install some version of OpenSSL, but you should verify that it is available on your system before attempting to install Apache's mod_ssl.

The following command line will show the version of OpenSSL installed on your system; this one is from a Red Hat 7.3 system:

```
# openssl version
OpenSSL 0.9.6b [engine] 9 Jul 2001
```

On a Red Hat Linux system, check to see if OpenSSL was installed from an RPM (as it will be if yours is a standard Red Hat Linux system):

```
# rpm -q openssl
openssl-0.9.6b-18
```

If you find that OpenSSL was installed by an RPM, you must have the associated developer's RPM (which supplies header files that are needed to compile new programs to use the installed OpenSSL libraries). You must ensure that the associated developer's RPM is also installed; the version number should exactly match that of the OpenSSL RPM:

```
# rpm -q openssl-devel
openssl-devel-0.9.6b-18
```

If it is necessary to install the developer's RPM, you can either find it on the second CD in your Red Hat set under RedHat/RPMS or download it from rpmfind.net. Again, make sure it matches the installed OpenSSL RPM.

The next section describes how to install OpenSSL from source code, which is something you should do *only* if your system does not already have an installed version of OpenSSL (increasingly unlikely) or if you cannot find the associated developer's RPM. Otherwise, you should ignore this section.

> **WARNING** A complete install of Red Hat 7.3 systems will show about 40 packages that list a dependency on either `libssl` or `libcrypto` and require `openssl` as an RPM. Removing the `openssl` RPM will break these packages. It is best to consider OpenSSL as part of the Linux system on those distributions (like Red Hat) that rely heavily on it. Don't remove it; and don't attempt to install upgrade RPMs without a definite reason to do so.

Installing OpenSSL from Source

If your system has no OpenSSL installed, you should install it from source code, which is a straightforward process for Linux. Follow these instructions only for systems that have no OpenSSL installation:

1. Download the latest version of OpenSSL from `www.openssl.org` and uncompress it into a convenient location like `/usr/local/src`:

   ```
   # cd /usr/local/src
   # tar xzf /downloads/openssl-0.9.6c.tar.gz
   # cd openssl-0.9.6c
   ```

2. Run the `config` utility, using the following command line (the `shared` option is necessary to ensure that the shared libraries are created for modules that rely on these):

   ```
   # ./config shared
   ```

3. The following commands complete the process. They will take quite some time, and generate *lots* of output:

   ```
   # make
   # make test
   # make install
   ```

   The make `install` command creates the `libcrypto.a` and `libssl.a` libraries under a special directory, `/usr/local/ssl/lib`. It also creates the `openssl` utility in `/usr/local/ssl/bin`.

4. To see if things are working, try entering a couple of `openssl` commands. For example, the `version` command reports the `openssl` version—not much of a test, but at least it will show you that the command-line tool

and libraries are in place (note that the `openssl` executable is placed in a `bin` directory of its own):

```
# /usr/local/ssl/bin/openssl version
OpenSSL 0.9.6c 21 dec 2001
```

Installing and Using *mod_ssl*

The process of configuring Apache to use SSL consists of five steps:

1. Compile `mod_ssl` into Apache.

2. Create a server key.

3. Use your server key to create a *certificate signing request* (or *CSR*).

4. Submit your CSR to a commercial certificate authority for signing, or, as an alternative, create your own CA for certificate signing.

5. Configure Apache to use your signed SSL certificate(s).

Each of these steps is covered in detail in this section, and each step should be completed before moving on to the next.

Step 1: Installing *mod_ssl*

In Apache 2.0, `mod_ssl` has the status of a standard Apache module, though it is not enabled by default. In other words, it's packaged with the Apache 2.0 source code, but will not be compiled into the Apache server unless you enable it explicitly with the `--enable-ssl` switch (see Chapter 3).

When running the `configure` script, Apache will be built with SSL support when you supply the `--enable-ssl` switch. The following command lines will build and install Apache 2.0, and include all of the most common standard modules plus SSL support:

```
# ./configure --enable-mods-shared=all --enable-ssl
# make
# make install
```

Step 2: Creating a Server Key

For each Apache Web site you will host, you must create a separate, unique server key. This key becomes part of that SSL site's certificate, which, when signed by a CA, becomes the certificate of authentication that is sent to each Web browser that connects to the SSL site.

Create your server key with a command line like the following. Note that the key name is arbitrary, but should give some indication of the associated server's identity, and the `.key` filename extension is customarily used to denote a digital key. For my server, which has the fully qualified name jackal.hiwaay.net, I created a server key with the name Jackal.key, which I'll use in all of the following examples.

```
# openssl genrsa -des3 -out Jackal.key 1024
Generating RSA private key, 1024 bit long modulus
......++++++
..........++++++
e is 65537 (0x10001)
Enter PEM pass phrase:
Verifying password - Enter PEM pass phrase:
```

Prior to creating the key, OpenSSL will prompt you for a *passphrase*, which is used to encrypt the key. Although this password protection can be removed for convenience (as for an unattended startup of Apache/SSL), it is usually best to use a passphrase.

Without knowledge of the passphrase, the key is useless, so make sure you remember the phrase. A passphrase longer than a single word is recommended, and it can be a sentence. The basic rule is "easy to remember, but hard to guess." Another technique is to use a seemingly random sequence of characters that you remember as a phrase; for example, you might remember the password *mmdlmtts* as "my mother doesn't let me talk to strangers." In general, the more tightly you want to protect the encrypted key, the more characters you should use. An Internet search for "good passphrases" turned up several sites that give pointers on how to choose an effective passphrase. One that is particularly succinct is www.stack.nl/~galactus/remailers/passphrase-faq.html.

Though you won't learn much from it, you can view the contents of the key, which is composed of alphanumeric characters:

```
# cat Jackal.key
-----BEGIN RSA PRIVATE KEY-----
Proc-Type: 4,ENCRYPTED
DEK-Info: DES-EDE3-CBC,9BF3F716B45F02E7

RofntDKIHNjJl1xChjWYIEMtZhPr7Wr6i5NCvSlvvrNpvpUwqMMMz1QJKXfESMbm
PmHRmftgTnI2Lf57xKYOVC56xzQIJIWmTG7pdxkFscWZcIZvpl42HE+Sg8Ctpp3Q
s2OAp33FrP6lJ3BrmkeIUrf6aUlx4OgG9HXEmgqel68utoRgK35omqig2zHwz7vc
JgQ4PELF8M3r98KOOKDU9w3rUyGEPknIIRCHEFcAKZZqdCRaeHNRjO63G42THjF+
c46ckIOJzmQLaL/8FhYNqFwTEqcmiKdDk7wnPARVOV6ds4oCFHsiJS5dddRHUHDq
SUtcGyY1krM1ZK6Ja7LFVEoXu6loOvqisXE7M6WbBhGLyp3p84qtkJ+zEWaoAxvx
QCOVBOkxTjgllguZoVdPgh1+K/rH/8kAtRjkdfkVTdONPNeEGN/YtW4tfegfkvAD
44U/ff2rwmgZe1X1X9JdFYxmlkzY67N2FQpPEHBXwCy8Sjo6XgaHj1yRZDfYfioh
PtO26h2Jrzx9QzNbGr+Pt5a2WOgKi+NQMV+tKtt5yMaaPTDKT+O9Xd7fwrGfc27d
vZUVUKyOUrexI2eB70+w8zNhWDNiYzs9GyfEQ+8UPKXOhediVt2NUymsVdvwBmZ6
Ow0YMYgYggZPR4t/3hlgdYTxsIZ3e8Hb9bkAXkC7s/5iPp4v6IWEOqv32DsXhi7N
```

```
Ov8fwzedtP3v83JYGG/AoOa3Uqs3QJ+nj2V117YAcmDFqdHoqGGQTc2cCy1VA3qG
8fUKaceaduwTG7qFJpm57a4nVuNLNLrNeWEXwk1OtjzfHayO/1FWuw==
-----END RSA PRIVATE KEY-----
```

Step 3: Creating a Certificate Signing Request (CSR)

Next you'll create an X.509 digital certificate signing request (CSR) for your site, using its private key, with the following command lines:

```
# openssl req -new -key Jackal.key -out Jackal.csr
Using configuration from /usr/share/ssl/openssl.cnf
Enter PEM pass phrase:
You are about to be asked to enter information that will be
➡  incorporated
into your certificate request.
What you are about to enter is what is called a Distinguished
➡  Name or a DN.
There are quite a few fields but you can leave some blank
For some fields there will be a default value,
If you enter '.', the field will be left blank.
-----
Country Name (2 letter code) [AU]:US
State or Province Name (full name) [Some-State]:Alabama
Locality Name (eg, city) []:Huntsville
Organization Name (eg, company) [Internet Widgits Pty Ltd]:Aulds
➡  Personal Web
Organizational Unit Name (eg, section) []:
Common Name (eg, your name or your server's hostname)
➡  []:jackal.hiwaay.net
Email Address []:caulds@hiwaay.net

Please enter the following 'extra' attributes
to be sent with your certificate request
A challenge password []:
An optional company name []:
```

Note that the passphrase you enter here is the password or phrase you entered earlier in Step 2. In this case, you need it to decrypt the server key in order to extract information needed to create the CSR. The X.509 certificate signing request you create should look similar to this:

```
# cat Jackal.csr
-----BEGIN CERTIFICATE REQUEST-----
MIIBODCCATkCAQAwgY8xCzAJBgNVBAYTA1VTMRAwDgYDVQQIEwdBbGFiYW1hMRMw
EQYDVQQHEwpIdW50c3ZpbGxlMRswGQYDVQQKExJBdWxkcyBQZXJzb25hbCBXZWIx
```

```
GjAYBgNVBAMTEWphY2thbC5oaXdhYXkubmVOMSAwHgYJKoZIhvcNAQkBFhFjYXVs
ZHNAaGl3YWF5Lm5l1dDCBnzANBgkqhkiG9w0BAQEFAAOBjQAwgYkCgYEAq/A2/1+y
19ZSEtQFd2AmfQcI9XE+PCdCMUfg/41e3lH4LKIukOtuGH4ublmVZUWXZF2r81EO
XlxVzw7Ni6pinmD26jNNvLAxErhKpOdIqBcpxSPWvnzySwhLOxqn8fcstYV1fHth
IC1b+7TEjt+SDAMU7Risfx8VRkQpThxpeuUCAwEAAaAAMA0GCSqGSIb3DQEBBAUA
A4GBADl1P1cXR+nPM4gujZf8zHuwQlYE5quqhZL9x2kO/3PfMT+1cWAbtIrYNRCh
TtW9rN2lhpYZp7P1Nu/2HEORdu7DIUN8xNcX/I3WuTkOE6I3Dq4lVegPDFoqp3vw
sgF2BZ1Pv8OK+Kg88CBvpvlyGY+umjyobG1z+JeGavU13rgb
-----END CERTIFICATE REQUEST-----
```

Step 4: Obtaining Your Server Certificate

The X.509 certificate signing request you created in Step 3 is then sent to a certificate authority. The CA uses it to generate your server certificate, authenticated with their digital signature, and then returns it to you by e-mail. When you have that certificate in hand, you'll go on to Step 5. If you choose to set up your own CA for signing your own security certificates, you should skip this section and go directly to the section titled "Acting As Your Own CA," and return to Step 5 when you have your own self-signed certificate in hand.

This step is only for those who are setting up an Internet Apache server and want to take advantage of a certificate issued by one of the widely recognized certificate authorities. There are a number of these, but, as I mentioned in the sidebar earlier in the chapter ("A Matter of Trust"), the VeriSign/Thawte merger resulted in approximately 65 percent of all digital certificates traversing the Web being issued by this one body.

Choose a CA whose certificates are recognized by all common browser software. To make things as easy as possible for the users of your Web site (especially for nontechnical users), you will probably go with one of the big certificate authorities, which is why they are big. While the procedure for obtaining a digital certificate varies between issuing CAs, the procedure is basically as follows:

1. You submit a CSR. This is often as simple as pasting a PEM-formatted (i.e., unencrypted) CSR into a Web form on the CA's site. On my server, I used the contents of the file `Jackal.csr`. See Figure 14.3, which illustrates a screen from www.verisign.com.

2. Much of the information required by the CA is read from the CSR. You will be asked to verify this information, possibly explain or correct any inconsistencies, and provide some additional information they will use to identify your organization.

3. You will need to submit some documentation of your organization's identity. VeriSign requires, for example, your Dun & Bradstreet number to more accurately

identify your organization (Figure 14.4). This assumes Dun & Bradstreet (a major provider of credit information for business-to-business commerce) has already performed some verification of your information, which was not the case in my test application. Higher levels (or *classes*) of authentication are also available, though not widely used. These involve much more stringent procedures for identifying yourself to the CA.

4. Once you've completed all the required information in the certificate application and arranged to pay for the digital certificate, the certificate will be mailed to you. It will arrive in clear text (not encrypted), but encoded in PEM format along with instructions for using it. For Apache with mod_ssl, all you have to do is paste the certificate text into the proper CRT file. (For my Apache 2 configuration, this is /usr/local/apache2/conf/ssl.crt/Jackal.crt).

Figure 14.3 Entering your site's CSR

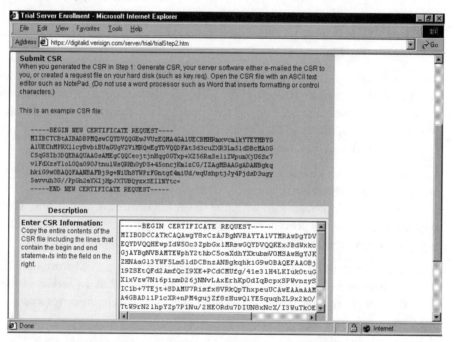

When you receive an X.509 certificate from a commercial certificate authority, incidentally, it will be in a format called PEM (Privacy Enhanced Mail). This format is an encoding that renders the certificate difficult to read, but don't make the mistake of thinking it is encrypted. It is not encrypted and can be easily converted into its human-readable form, which is shown in Listing 14.1.

Figure 14.4   Documentation of identity

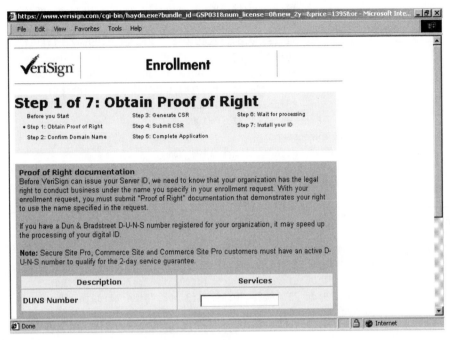

Listing 14.1   A Test Certificate in Readable Form

```
# openssl x509 -noout -text -in server.crt
Certificate:
    Data:
        Version: 3 (0x2)
        Serial Number: 5 (0x5)
        Signature Algorithm: md5WithRSAEncryption
        Issuer: C=XY, ST=Snake Desert, L=Snake Town, O=Snake Oil, Ltd,
            OU=Certificate Authority, CN=Snake Oil CA/Email=ca@snakeoil.dom
        Validity
            Not Before: Jan  5 21:05:41 2000 GMT
            Not After : Jan  4 21:05:41 2001 GMT
        Subject: C=US, ST=Alabama, L=Huntsville, O=Sybex, OU=Author,
            CN=jackal.hiwaay.net/Email=caulds@hiwaay.net
        Subject Public Key Info:
            Public Key Algorithm: rsaEncryption
            RSA Public Key: (1024 bit)
                Modulus (1024 bit):
                    00:bb:80:16:1c:31:25:40:68:58:d3:85:c5:6d:a9:
```

```
                    54:34:9f:b5:ea:23:89:d9:00:50:e0:2c:01:ed:d1:
                    f7:32:9d:f4:59:03:44:ee:18:4c:b9:2b:2a:ba:d9:
                    52:cb:9f:74:e8:6e:ba:83:88:66:8a:05:1a:05:5f:
                    51:23:8d:d4:d2:65:94:52:7f:de:cc:09:47:21:a5:
                    ab:4d:6e:b2:5c:8d:af:36:0f:f7:b4:be:be:16:23:
                    f5:2e:a6:28:9a:df:b3:e6:d9:14:d7:f1:05:a8:04:
                    85:cb:44:7b:0f:6a:a5:66:af:77:b1:ba:8c:b9:35:
                    85:ae:e2:d8:f5:bb:18:bd:2b
                Exponent: 65537 (0x10001)
        X509v3 extensions:
            X509v3 Subject Alternative Name:
                email:caulds@hiwaay.net
            Netscape Comment:
                mod_ssl generated test server certificate
            Netscape Cert Type:
                SSL Server
    Signature Algorithm: md5WithRSAEncryption
        3b:39:a6:ac:2d:fe:91:fb:f0:cb:1e:2f:9b:a6:58:fc:56:4f:
        da:7f:f1:b6:e1:79:de:90:c5:3c:20:3f:67:d7:34:11:f0:9e:
        ee:13:39:dc:23:06:29:5b:89:94:3a:06:f8:34:23:3a:d5:db:
        1c:7c:87:26:31:ed:df:e7:54:67:74:78:cd:5c:38:36:04:ed:
        2d:75:93:51:f8:46:8d:74:6f:81:09:9e:46:82:53:2b:36:72:
        0a:c4:6b:e4:5f:7d:27:da:03:a0:5b:d2:04:f8:c9:e3:03:8e:
        f5:ee:20:57:b9:0d:db:60:59:03:e4:7f:f5:fd:ca:32:44:41:
        db:be
```

You'll note that the certificate contains a lot of information. The essential elements of all X.509 digital certificates include the following:

- The certificate owner's common name (usually the hostname of the Web server)

- Additional information for a contact at the site, such as an e-mail address

- The site's public key (the matching private key is on the server, closely guarded, but must be accessible by the SSL code)

- The expiration date of the public key

- The identity of the CA that issued the certificate

- A unique serial number for the certificate

- The digital signature of the issuing CA

Step 5: Configuring Apache to Use SSL

You'll find that the installation procedure (Step 1) adds the commands to load and enable the SSL module to the Apache `httpd.conf` file wrapped in `<IfDefine SSL>`

commands, which attempts to load the module only if Apache was started with the SSL option:

```
<IfDefine SSL>
LoadModule ssl_module modules/mod_ssl.so
</IfDefine>
```

The installation also places a file named `ssl-conf` in the conf directory of your Apache home (the same directory that contains the `httpd.conf` file we've been working with from the start). This file contains the directives necessary to configure Apache for SSL, and also sets up a virtual host to listen for connections on the default SSL port (TCP port 443). These configuration directives are read during the Apache configuration process when the server is started by the following set of directives, conveniently added to your Apache `httpd.conf` during the Apache installation:

```
#
# Bring in additional module-specific configurations
#
<IfModule mod_ssl.c>
    Include conf/ssl.conf
</IfModule>
```

Note that the `IfModule` test ensures that the directives in `ssl.conf` are never read and applied if the `mod_ssl` module isn't loaded. If you've created and installed a server certificate as described earlier, you should be able to start the server in SSL mode by using the following command line:

```
# /usr/local/apache2/bin/httpd –DSSL
```

or its equivalent:

```
# /usr/local/apache2/bin/apachectl startssl
```

Either way, if you encrypted your server key, you will be prompted for your passphrase. The server cannot be started in SSL mode unless the key can be decrypted and read, which requires the manual entry of a secret passphrase.

The installation will also create a new virtual host to respond to connections on the default SSL TCP port 443:

```
<VirtualHost _default_:443>
DocumentRoot "/usr/local/apache2/htdocs"
ServerName jackal.hiwaay.net:443
ServerAdmin caulds@hiwaay.net
ErrorLog logs/error_log
TransferLog logs/access_log
SSLEngine on
```

```
SSLCipherSuite
  ALL:!ADH:!EXPORT56:RC4+RSA:+HIGH:+MEDIUM:+LOW:+SSLv2:+EXP:+eNULL
SSLCertificateFile /usr/local/apache2/conf/ssl.crt/server.crt
SSLCertificateKeyFile /usr/local/apache2/conf/ssl.key/server.key

-- many other SSL configuration lines deleted --

</VirtualHost>
```

> **TIP**   SSL can be used only with IP-based virtual hosts and never with
> name-based virtual hosts (Chapter 6), because Apache cannot read the `Host:`
> HTTP header from the client prior to setting up the SSL connection. An SSL
> connection is always established before the exchange of HTTP headers.

I've deleted most of the lines that mod_ssl places in the virtual host container. These lines control default settings for mod_ssl and are better left alone. Each of these directives is thoroughly documented in a comment statement that precedes it in the file.

You can change the locations where mod_ssl will look for its certificate and key files, for example (using the SSLCertificateFile and SSLCertificateKeyFile directives, respectively), or the names of the certificate and key files that Apache looks for. In the example above, I used Jackal.crt and Jackal.key, the certificate and server key, respectively, that I created earlier in the chapter. The default values are as good as any other and most administrators will decide to use them. The important thing to realize is that SSL is implemented in Apache as a virtual host that can have its own DocumentRoot and ServerAdmin settings, among others. For all purposes, you should consider the SSL server a separate server, granting access only to resources that require the protection of SSL. For a corporate intranet server, you may even want to disable connections on port 80 (the standard HTTP port) and use only SSL.

Start the server in SSL mode, and attempt to connect to it using a URL beginning with https, rather than http:

```
https://jackal.hiwaay.net
```

This will initiate a connection to the default SSL TCP port 443. If an alternate TCP port was chosen, you can use a command like the following instead (this one assumes that SSL is configured to accept connections on port 8001):

```
http://jackal.hiwaay.net:8001
```

As a test, try connecting to the SSL-protected site. The first time you connect, your browser should present a dialog box similar to the one shown in Figure 14.5.

Figure 14.5   Internet Explorer's unrecognized certificate dialog

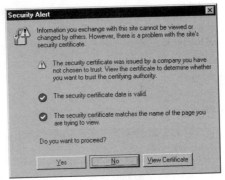

Internet Explorer may receive a security certificate that it cannot automatically accept, because 1) the root CA is unrecognized, 2) the expiration date of the certificate has been reached, or 3) the URL encoded in the certificate does not match the URL entered in IE's address bar (a possible indication of a spoofed or bogus server). When this happens, it asks only if you wish to proceed. Clicking Yes instructs IE to accept the certificate for the current session only. You can also click the View Certificate tab to view the contents of the certificate, but in practice, you should avoid accepting certificates that prompt this dialog. This is especially true if you are attempting to establish an SSL session with an Internet server for the purpose of exchanging privileged information (for example, if you are attempting to check out during an online purchase). In this case, I believe Internet Explorer is a bit remiss in ensuring that its users understand (perhaps through a confirmation dialog) that accepting a certificate that doesn't meet proper acceptance criteria is potentially risky.

If the certificate presented by the secure Web site to which you connect is acceptable to your browser, or if you manually instruct your browser to use the certificate, an SSL connection will be established between the browser and the server. All Web browsers display some indication on the screen that a secure (encrypted) session has been established with the remote server. Figure 14.6 shows the tiny padlock that will be displayed in the lower-right corner of the Internet Explorer window to indicate that the current page being displayed was received via an SSL connection to the remote Web site.

Figure 14.6   Internet Explorer's Secure Connection icon

To see details about the current SSL session, click the padlock icon to bring up IE's Certificate dialog (Figure 14.7), with tabs that allow you to view the contents of the current certificate that was used to establish the current SSL session. You might want to do this, for example, to double-check that the certificate applies to the Web site you believe you are accessing, especially if you manually accepted the site's security certificate without viewing its contents first.

Figure 14.7 Viewing certificate details in Internet Explorer

I copied my `environ.cgi` script to the directory defined by `ScriptAlias` as a CGI directory for my SSL server. Running the script, I saw a lot of new information that was added by the SSL module, as shown in Listing 14.2. Note the large number of environment variables that have been added by SSL. The information provided by these variables is available to your CGI scripts; it indicates exactly the type of encryption used, and provides details about the X.509 certificate used to authenticate the connection. For the most part, this is not information that you will need to pass to back-end scripts; it's actually more interesting to review than it is useful.

Listing 14.2 Running the `environ.cgi` Script

```
SSL_SESSION_ID =
➥8FDD7AD978C891A290AF79E7B422407102DBB7B0D0635B2866E32C6BD4AAC027
SSL_SERVER_I_DN = /C=XY/ST=Snake Desert/L=Snake Town/O=Snake Oil,
   ➥ Ltd/   OU=Certificate Authority/CN=Snake Oil~CCA/Email=ca@snakeoil.dom
SERVER_SOFTWARE = Apache/1.3.12 (Unix) mod_ssl/2.6.4
   ➥ OpenSSL/0.9.5a GATEWAY_   INTERFACE = CGI/1.1
```

```
DOCUMENT_ROOT = /home/httpd/html
SSL_SERVER_I_DN_C = XY
SSL_PROTOCOL = SSLv3
SSL_CIPHER_ALGKEYSIZE = 128
SSL_SERVER_I_DN_OU = Certificate Authority
REMOTE_ADDR = 192.168.1.2
SSL_SERVER_I_DN_ST = Snake Desert
REQUEST_METHOD = GET
SSL_SERVER_A_SIG = md5WithRSAEncryption
SSL_VERSION_LIBRARY = OpenSSL/0.9.4
SSL_SERVER_S_DN = /C=US/ST=Alabama/L=Huntsville/O=Sybex/OU=Author/
➥     CN=jackal.hiwaay.net/Email=caulds@hiwaay.net
QUERY_STRING =
SSL_SERVER_I_DN_L = Snake Town
SSL_SERVER_S_DN_C = US
SSL_CIPHER_EXPORT = true
SSL_SERVER_S_DN_OU = Author
SSL_SERVER_I_DN_O = Snake Oil, Ltd
HTTP_ACCEPT = image/gif, image/x-xbitmap, image/jpeg,
➥ image/pjpeg, image/png, */*
SSL_SERVER_A_KEY = rsaEncryption
REMOTE_PORT = 1158
SSL_SERVER_S_DN_ST = Alabama
SERVER_ADDR = 192.168.1.1
HTTP_ACCEPT_LANGUAGE = en
HTTPS = on
HTTP_ACCEPT_ENCODING = gzip
SCRIPT_FILENAME = /home/httpd/cgi-bin/environ.pl
SSL_SERVER_S_DN_L = Huntsville
SERVER_NAME = jackal.hiwaay.net
SSL_SERVER_S_DN_O = Sybex
SSL_SERVER_M_VERSION = 3
SERVER_PORT = 443
SSL_CIPHER_USEKEYSIZE = 40
SERVER_ADMIN = root@jackal.hiwaay.net
UNIQUE_ID = OHS3Tn8AAAEAABmkEkI
SSL_CLIENT_VERIFY = NONE
SSL_VERSION_INTERFACE = mod_ssl/2.4.9
SERVER_PROTOCOL = HTTP/1.0
SERVER_SIGNATURE =
Apache/1.3.9 Server at jackal.hiwaay.net Port 443
SSL_SERVER_I_DN_Email = ca@snakeoil.dom
SSL_SERVER_V_START = Jan 5 21:05:41 2000 GMT
HTTP_USER_AGENT = Mozilla/4.7 [en] (WinNT; I)
```

```
SSL_CIPHER = EXP-RC4-MD5
PATH = /usr/bin:/bin:/sbin:/usr/bin:/usr/sbin:/usr/local/bin:
➥ /usr/local/sbin:/usr/bin/X11:/usr/X11R6/bin:/root/bin
HTTP_CONNECTION = Keep-Alive
SSL_SERVER_I_DN_CN = Snake Oil CA
SSL_SERVER_S_DN_Email = caulds@hiwaay.net
SSL_SERVER_V_END = Jan 4 21:05:41 2001 GMT
SSL_SERVER_M_SERIAL = 05
SCRIPT_NAME = /cgi-bin/environ.pl
REQUEST_URI = /cgi-bin/environ.pl
HTTP_ACCEPT_CHARSET = iso-8859-1,*,utf-8
SSL_SERVER_S_DN_CN = jackal.hiwaay.net
HTTP_HOST = Jackal
```

Locate the server certificate on your server; more than likely it resides in the /usr/local/ apache2/conf/ssl.crt directory as a file named server.crt. Use the openssl utility to view the contents of the server certificate.

Acting As Your Own Root CA

Certificates obtained from one of the well-known root certificate authorities are the easiest to use, because they will be recognized and accepted as valid by all major Web browsers. You will need such a certificate if you intend to operate an SSL Web server on the Internet, perhaps for an application that requires a high degree of security, such as online credit card validation.

These certificates must be purchased, however, and they must be renewed as they expire. You can avoid the expense of purchasing your SSL certificates by acting as your own root certificate authority. This section shows you how to create your own root CA, which can then be used to sign the SSL certificates for your Web sites. These are often called *self-signed certificates*.

If you intend to use self-signed certificates, you will need to configure each Web browser that will access your SSL servers to recognize these certificates. For that reason, self-signed certificates are best used on corporate intranets where all the Web browsers can be configured to accept all certificates signed by the corporate CA. This section demonstrates the process of setting up a root CA, how to distribute the certificate of your root CA, and how to use your root CA to sign certificates for your Web sites.

A private company that signs its own certificates and configures all of its internal browsers to accept those certificates is, in effect, acting as a *private CA*, a term you may hear. That approach requires the certificate issuer to have some measure of control over all the client browsers in order to configure them to accept the certificates so issued.

Creating Your CA

Creating a self-signed certificate is often all that is required, if, for example, all of your clients are willing to accept a certificate signed by your server acting as its own certificate authority. In a corporate intranet, this might be a perfectly reasonable expectation. On the World Wide Web, however, you will probably send your server.csr (certificate signing request) to a third-party certificate authority for signing.

You actually create a certificate authority when you create its unique private key with OpenSSL. This private key contains information about the signing authority, certificate details, and two large numbers that are the prime factors of a larger prime number. (This method of public key encryption relies on the difficulty of discovering the factors of a very large prime number.) The private key of the certificate authority should be protected, perhaps placed on a machine that is not connected to a network. It will be used to "sign" all digital certificates used on all corporate intranet Web sites. The name of the key is arbitrary, but should indicate its purpose:

```
# openssl genrsa -des3 -out AuldsCA.key 1024
Generating RSA private key, 1024 bit long modulus
..................................................++++++
v...............................++++++
e is 65537 (0x10001)
Enter PEM pass phrase:
Verifying password - Enter PEM pass phrase:


# ls -al AuldsCA.key
-rw-r--r--    1 root     root          963 Mar 19 13:35 AuldsCA.key
```

This private key will be used to sign SSL certificates that your new CA certifies as valid, and you must have access to this key when signing certificates. Keep this key absolutely secure; it's a good idea to place it on removable media (like a CD-RW disc). You can bet that VeriSign doesn't keep its private keys on an Internet-accessible computer.

Just like a server key, the private key of your CA is in printable text characters, but yields little information upon inspection:

```
# cat AuldsCA.key
-----BEGIN RSA PRIVATE KEY-----
Proc-Type: 4,ENCRYPTED
DEK-Info: DES-EDE3-CBC,BE673A0C014EDAB1

RjVytdHEhA2c2OdvTpG4+mpLGKrAK79v2WdCGEJVM1pmF+1FriKCHfpJ8nrLXrFK
8YYX8kArylj4fMZabwqzHqmPf6Jq6rWZ9QLQLeBI3C0kb6sOjgNxzT/Bd3Liackl
YDmPA/4BZHAbmHno7K5+YNClVVvPosS3xNggS9bx/xr2jDTwo+FAZTtaz7LUkniT
Op6dKvVjfWVXBhNm/kiZYKVONppM7iqC4HnNxEHxlv+k7Dk2LCLaJxO2/XfZ+f9o
```

```
7rSAalg7eabm9gKscgFWW7UQddf03xV4i1t5atnBY1HOtS/WZEwzjKnL/A18gnvs
zfv4vOmyqdjh7wGmMaM2kCwg5vGtC3JDp9ATfT9xXfKnHYAd2hyL72ZHTQlZG9yy
eQOndojU1E/Oeh1OsGixG67dyVi2y33Tah6/U4i5ruEICF3KKg9M4dCgbrEznz5z
VfCIawHOLFiuLvMJOdVOcL18r44MZg4ZDbrrmsYkEUW3OKku/J/EEHDZNSMdkM3n
9mo29Q04ZSKPW7GkEuPN6+YMrny7YrkUi9/t6jcGL24RJbqc5WQV21HRf3w7qs3V
gCfECTQabKxDoxalSlyg++Tz9Y+OR3ZNEOn39Omt7jgEONZd6EOR4XfuNVchFfc/
hFlzqD3FEWI8exzVnIs3Y0lo3KOxX6/AJoqRxo9bwQtUr3jnaNLyuCmF2O7/GcvX
k2OrUFr8OopJd5F95nALBNKEoFntHex87EmZM7Ob86Q0ZO6feG3dzkV9xrx4vTJy
ZtUiP71gGW3OehG9eWBDxURi2YZI99FZP7U8iusKZUEKL8Vme6YEqA==
-----END RSA PRIVATE KEY-----
```

Though perhaps no more educational, you can also display the contents of the key with OpenSSL. One thing that this will make quite obvious is the mathematical nature of the key. Note that you'll need to specify the key type (RSA) and provide your encryption passphrase to decrypt and display the key contents:

```
# openssl rsa -noout -text -in AuldsCA.key
read RSA key
Enter PEM pass phrase:
Private-Key: (1024 bit)
modulus:
    00:ac:65:c3:aa:2f:6c:1b:65:12:60:cc:25:ff:45:
    40:45:47:a4:ae:ff:ea:cf:68:30:5d:77:9c:1f:8a:
    ac:10:87:9d:1f:8b:8e:aa:46:57:b6:2c:49:0a:44:
    21:9e:21:82:fb:26:b6:a1:c9:58:89:68:63:18:95:
    bf:a2:6f:5c:48:54:d1:dd:f9:ae:00:82:39:1c:60:
    51:3d:c7:26:ec:b9:d4:49:d2:66:25:ec:c3:68:10:
    eb:61:6b:56:cb:8d:dc:f5:e7:75:30:af:de:96:10:
    6b:e8:e6:96:e1:a1:86:06:24:77:f3:45:99:03:e2:
    ea:1d:bd:9e:16:60:66:dd:f1
publicExponent: 65537 (0x10001)
privateExponent:
    00:88:9d:f0:6b:ca:3e:d2:8a:cb:00:98:67:38:1e:
    c9:ea:dc:f6:7d:93:e2:a1:50:40:9b:a1:30:c0:b2:
    24:de:c8:89:54:39:44:ea:5c:ea:1f:3c:82:f9:36:
    ba:a9:54:87:36:be:1c:16:a3:b7:9c:d4:73:4b:45:
    48:62:d1:fa:ff:2d:53:c2:37:f1:64:06:04:a3:04:
    ca:80:c7:bf:69:0c:2c:9c:4a:ea:ec:e2:3d:74:8d:
    64:23:41:00:9d:a9:89:c3:38:6f:43:dd:76:8b:5f:
    36:8a:9f:8f:a1:3e:f0:51:62:e3:9e:58:31:15:b5:
    22:c6:41:44:f8:07:48:25:9d
prime1:
    00:df:9c:33:43:4a:76:e3:e7:6f:23:2b:47:fb:ed:
    d3:9e:24:0b:3a:b6:2d:55:3d:31:a6:f9:f7:1f:93:
```

```
        28:51:a0:92:89:7f:25:92:7f:af:71:17:20:75:4b:
        a5:8d:a6:d0:7c:6b:32:3a:7a:1e:56:52:6b:24:06:
        2b:ba:1b:b0:af
prime2:
        00:c5:5e:85:c9:fc:06:13:23:84:e6:9a:62:cc:3b:
        8b:42:f2:54:18:a0:15:c9:75:f1:31:7c:2c:ce:d5:
        53:4d:50:48:a3:c5:82:37:61:59:fc:cb:7e:a0:6f:
        95:76:2d:88:99:87:3c:11:7c:b5:df:5c:a9:c5:80:
        81:94:e5:c3:5f
exponent1:
        00:b8:87:8b:9a:55:62:25:93:40:98:d2:47:d6:34:
        1e:75:9b:a3:14:b1:70:59:ae:65:42:39:77:e1:3b:
        ac:83:28:32:a5:7b:22:c3:71:d1:93:4f:15:7f:16:
        8d:29:87:66:f7:b5:f2:be:65:36:91:df:f4:00:c7:
        82:e0:53:a7:8b
exponent2:
        74:69:87:22:16:bb:82:88:5d:b8:22:71:89:a2:c9:
        46:28:66:7f:cb:d4:6d:ea:59:e3:e5:29:0c:a9:f8:
        a3:4e:6a:39:e6:a2:22:86:12:2c:af:de:35:44:fb:
        74:23:f1:41:14:e9:d2:2a:ab:9f:5e:29:68:ab:9e:
        42:b3:ae:a3
coefficient:
        00:ac:1d:6e:fb:eb:a8:9d:6f:ee:9b:b1:61:62:01:
        ab:90:a1:c0:ad:b8:3a:57:9c:f9:ce:ab:20:35:05:
        04:da:95:5c:8d:72:ba:95:28:75:2c:c6:9a:ba:44:
        9f:ee:38:c3:2b:93:2a:26:c2:37:7d:e5:61:fd:28:
        23:6e:92:87:4b
```

Starting Apache/SSL Automatically

An encrypted server key means that someone will have to manually start the Apache server and enter the passphrase when prompted. This is a good security measure, as the server key is unusable without the passphrase, but having to start Apache manually can be very inconvenient. If you absolutely must be able to start Apache with SSL support automatically during system bootup, you can unencrypt your server key by entering a command line like this:

```
# mv Jackal.key Jackal.key.ORIG
# openssl rsa -in Jackal.key.ORIG -out Jackal.key
read RSA key
Enter PEM pass phrase:
writing RSA key
```

Starting Apache/SSL Automatically

If you choose not to encrypt the private server key, take extra precautions to protect the key. It is the identity of your server; don't let someone steal it! Run this command line to make sure that the file can be read only by root:

```
# chmod 400 Jackal.key
```

As alternative approach to removing the encryption on your server key is to use the SSLPassPhraseDialog facility. This directive, when used, provides the path to a program that is called when Apache/SSL starts to obtain the password necessary to decrypt the server key. The program can be as simple as a script that does nothing more than write the password to its standard output, in which case it would provide no real advantages over the use of an unencrypted server key. The real intent of this facility is to provide the administrator with an opportunity to build security checks into the program to ensure that an attacker is not running it. Do not use SSLPassPhraseDialog unless you intend to provide some internal logic to ensure that it is being run only in the proper context of an Apache/SSL startup. A program that doesn't have adequate built-in security checks for improper use provides a false sense of security. You should use this mechanism only if you are quite confident that you can provide adequate security checks in your program and if the program is accessible only by root.

Now use the private key you just created for the new CA to create an X.509 digital certificate for the certificate authority. This certificate is distributed to browsers that are configured to trust certificates signed by the certificate authority. The certificate that is distributed contains the public component of the CA's private key, which allows the browser to determine (with a *very* high degree of confidence) that a certificate was signed using the CA's private key.

The following command instructs OpenSSL to create a new X.509 digital certificate with an expiration date that is 365 days in the future. (The default life of a certificate is 30 days.) The new certificate is to be created from the AuldsCA private key, and should be named AuldsCA.crt. Some descriptive fields are used to provide human-readable information to attach to the certificate.

```
# openssl req -new -x509 -days 365 -key AuldsCA.key -out AuldsCA.crt
Using configuration from /usr/share/ssl/openssl.cnf
Enter PEM pass phrase:
You are about to be asked to enter information that will be
➥ incorporated
```

```
into your certificate request.
What you are about to enter is what is called a Distinguished
➡ Name or a DN.
There are quite a few fields but you can leave some blank
For some fields there will be a default value,
If you enter '.', the field will be left blank.
-----
Country Name (2 letter code) [AU]:US
State or Province Name (full name) [Some-State]:Alabama
Locality Name (eg, city) []:Huntsville
Organization Name (eg, company) [Internet Widgits Pty Ltd]:Aulds
➡ Certification Authority        .
Organizational Unit Name (eg, section) []:
Common Name (eg, your name or your server's hostname) []:Aulds CA
Email Address []:caulds@hiwaay.net
```

Just for fun, you might want to view the contents of your new root CA certificate and the information it contains. Use this command line to list the contents of any X.509 certificate:

```
# openssl x509 -noout -text -in AuldsCA.crt
Certificate:
    Data:
        Version: 3 (0x2)
        Serial Number: 0 (0x0)
        Signature Algorithm: md5WithRSAEncryption
        Issuer: C=US, ST=Alabama, L=Huntsville, O=Aulds Certification Authority,
➡ CN=Aulds CA/Email=caulds@hiwaay.net
        Validity
            Not Before: Mar 19 19:50:03 2002 GMT
            Not After : Mar 19 19:50:03 2003 GMT
        Subject: C=US, ST=Alabama, L=Huntsville, O=Aulds Certification Authority,
➡ CN=Aulds CA/Email=caulds@hiwaay.net
        Subject Public Key Info:
            Public Key Algorithm: rsaEncryption
            RSA Public Key: (1024 bit)
                Modulus (1024 bit):
                    00:c4:e6:5b:6f:a4:4f:ee:75:f3:9e:92:16:df:34:
                    47:c4:76:be:8c:8e:4c:a5:89:b2:d9:04:fe:2c:ee:
                    7f:a7:dc:72:2f:94:07:61:7e:b2:4c:c0:77:69:28:
                    f5:78:df:18:f2:5c:72:ad:f5:e3:98:29:0a:a7:87:
                    22:df:cd:bf:1f:24:b0:43:fa:0d:63:0a:bd:86:38:
                    68:26:f4:2e:70:08:ce:0b:57:c7:48:5b:a5:57:14:
                    74:66:23:94:8e:6f:f0:3d:84:f8:16:fe:76:f2:7d:
                    8d:82:11:65:f6:cf:2b:9c:53:99:e1:0f:6a:29:69:
```

```
                20:db:6b:c7:1c:92:3e:d6:23
              Exponent: 65537 (0x10001)
       X509v3 extensions:
           X509v3 Subject Key Identifier:
           3A:76:77:2B:5C:5D:7C:80:5C:B8:E6:02:D1:54:BA:73:A5:F3:E2:7F
           X509v3 Authority Key Identifier:
        keyid:3A:76:77:2B:5C:5D:7C:80:5C:B8:E6:02:D1:54:BA:73:A5:F3:E2:7F
               DirName:/C=US/ST=Alabama/L=Huntsville/O=Aulds
    Certification Authority/CN=Aulds CA/Email=caulds@hiwaay.net
               serial:00

           X509v3 Basic Constraints:
               CA:TRUE
      Signature Algorithm: md5WithRSAEncryption
          be:45:13:05:3e:01:ae:78:a0:c2:2d:4b:10:8a:f8:52:40:0e:
          0e:8a:32:a5:13:96:e8:1f:68:2f:9d:2e:88:d3:ab:98:76:28:
          cf:78:fc:53:d8:38:73:3b:60:9f:3a:06:c4:4b:9d:db:07:7c:
          69:7b:31:47:9b:38:c5:19:82:5d:6c:70:94:47:0f:9f:09:81:
          de:00:a0:f2:b1:ab:72:4d:71:1e:1e:cf:64:42:88:15:ea:e5:
          09:59:52:c3:8a:6d:84:2e:65:d0:7c:8a:e1:38:d0:37:78:46:
          d1:d3:d6:ab:52:04:b1:1e:a4:63:7e:78:a7:4f:ed:7b:a9:e3:
          9a:f0
```

Signing X.509 Certificates

To create a self-signed certificate, use the following command line:

```
# openssl req -x509 -key ./ssl.key/server.key \
> -in ./ssl.csr/server.csr -out ./ssl.crt/server.crt
```

Here, openssl creates an X.509 certificate from the server's certificate signing request (server.csr) and signs it with the server's private RSA key (server.key). The result is a signed certificate, output as a file named server.crt.

After creating your self-signed certificate, install it in the location defined by the SSLCertificateFile directive in httpd.conf, overwriting the test certificate there; the location is probably:

```
/usr/local/apache2/conf/ssl.crt/server.crt
```

After restarting Apache in SSL mode, I reconnected to my server and ran environ.cgi a second time to make sure that my server was using the new certificate. This time in the output, note the change in the following environment variable:

```
SSL_SERVER_I_DN: /C=US/ST=Alabama/L=Huntsville/O=Sybex/OU=Author/
➥    CN=jackal.hiwaay.net/Email=caulds@hiwaay.net
```

This is the *distinguished name* of the issuing certificate authority, in this case derived from my server's private RSA key.

Distributing Your Root Certificate

In order to act as your own private CA, you need some relatively secure means of distributing your key to all of the clients who will access your server. A corporate IT department that intends to set up its own private CA for signing security certificates for its secure internal sites has any number of ways to distribute the private CA certificates while offering the recipient a reasonable degree of assurance that the certificate came from a corporate IT. One simple solution would be to place the certificate on a file-sharing system that can be accessed only by authenticated network accounts.

In any event, the goal is to make available to every potential user of your secure Web sites the private CA certificate they need to install into their browsers as a trusted root certificate authority. The next section describes how the user would install the certificate into their browser, a process that needs to be done only once. Thereafter, the browser will accept certificates signed by the private CA, now a trusted root CA, as long as the certificate hasn't expired.

Adding Your CA to Internet Explorer

Although I'll illustrate the process of adding a private CA to your client browser with Internet Explorer, the procedure for doing this in Netscape Navigator is similar.

In Internet Explorer, select Tools ➤ Internet Options, and click the Content tab to bring up the dialog shown in Figure 14.8.

Figure 14.8 Internet Options dialog in IE

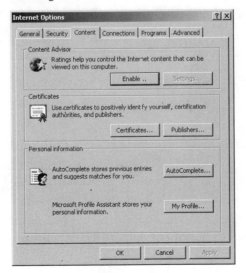

Next, click the Certificates button and then the Trusted Root Certification Authorities tab to bring up the dialog shown in Figure 14.9.

Figure 14.9 The Trusted Root Certificate Authorities tab in the Certificates dialog

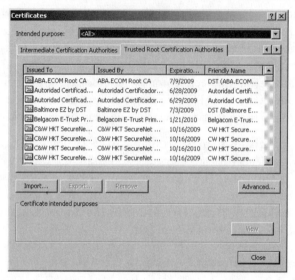

Click the Import button, and use the file dialog (Figure 14.10) to locate the certificate of your private CA. Note that the certificate is of type X.509 and should have a default file extension of .crt.

Figure 14.10 Locating the certificate of your private CA

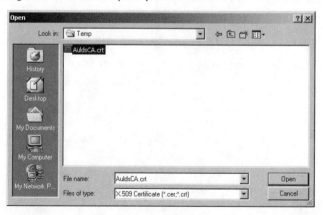

Figure 14.11 shows the Certificate Import Wizard just before it loads the certificate.

Figure 14.11   IE's Certificate Import Wizard

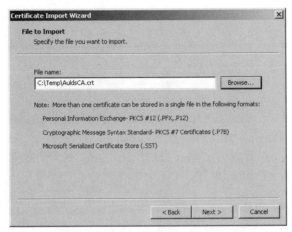

When prompted to choose an import location (Figure 14.12), click Next to accept the default value ("Automatically select the certificate store based on the type of certificate"). IE will place the X.509 certificate in the trusted root certification authorities certificate store.

Figure 14.12   Selecting a certificate store in IE

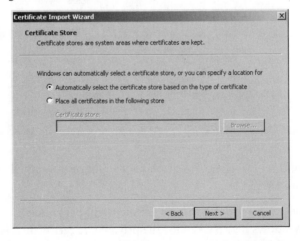

If you agree with the information presented in the confirmation dialog (an example is shown in Figure 14.13), press Yes to confirm. Continue to confirm any other dialog boxes until IE tells you that the certificate import was successful.

Figure 14.13 An example of a Root Certificate Store confirmation dialog

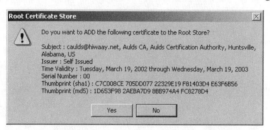

You should now find your private CA listed among IE's trusted root certification authorities, as in Figure 14.14.

Figure 14.14 Verifying that your CA is installed

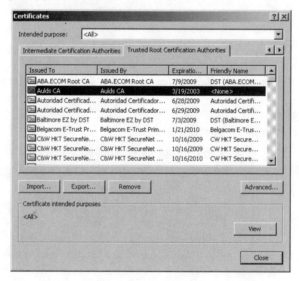

You can click the View option to display information contained in the private CA certificate (Figure 14.15).

An alternative to this procedure, and the method I personally recommend and use, is to export the Windows registry key for the private CA certificate (as a Windows .reg file) from a system on which the certificate has already been installed. This .reg file (and the associated CA certificate) can then be imported on any other Windows system by simply double-clicking the .reg file in Windows Explorer, or it can be mailed as an Outlook attachment.

Figure 14.15   Viewing the contents of your private CA

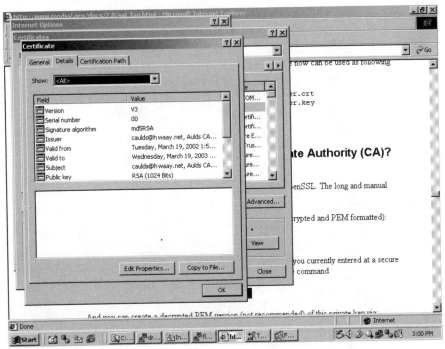

Some familiarity with the Windows `regedit.exe` program will be necessary to do this. On a Windows system, the one on which you've already installed your private CA certificate, invoke `regedit.exe` (or `regedt32.exe` for Windows NT systems), and locate the `My Computer\HKEY_CURRENT_USER\Software\Microsoft\SystemCertificates\Root\Certificates` key. There should be only a couple of subkeys beneath this, one of which will be the key for your private CA. View the Blob values of each key until you see information that identifies your key. The information shown in Figure 14.16 sufficiently identifies my private CA key.

Make sure you select the proper certificate, then on the menu bar select Registry ➤ Registry Export File and enter a filename for the exported key. If you are running Windows 2000, be sure to select Win9x/NT in the Save As Type drop-down list if you intend to import this key into the registries of Windows 95/98 or NT machines. See Figure 14.17.

Distribute the `.reg` file, either from a network file share, a Web server, or through e-mail. Importing the key is simple; the user need only click the file in Explorer (or Outlook) in most cases. Users will be presented with the dialogs shown in Figure 14.18, to which they'll respond with Yes and then OK to confirm the import.

Figure 14.16   Viewing the root certificate value in regedit

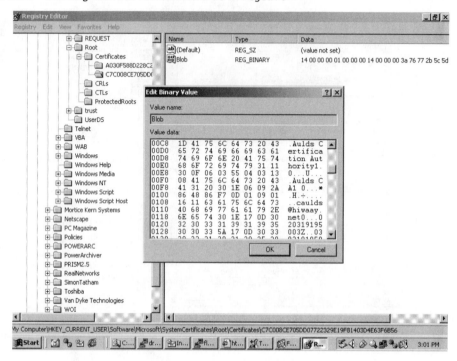

Figure 14.17   Exporting a root CA as a registry key

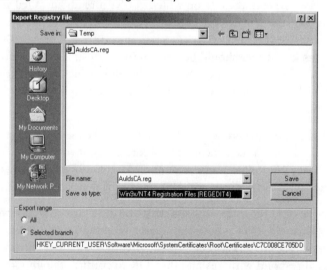

Figure 14.18   Registry key import prompts

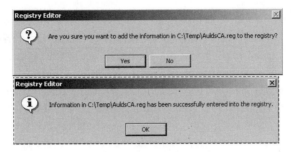

Client Certificates

So far, I've talked only about server certification, in which a client receives a digital certificate from an SSL server, and if a trusted CA has signed the certificate, the server is also trusted and an SSL connection established. SSL also permits *client* certification, where the server maintains its own list of trusted CAs and will establish SSL connections only with clients who can furnish a certificate signed by one of those CAs. By default, mod_ssl accepts certificates signed with its own private key, so you can set up SSL to accept only certificates signed by itself. This can be useful for corporate intranets, for example, to gain some measure of control over who connects to the server. Currently, this is the most common use for client certification, but in the future, it is conceivable that many commercial Web sites might require client authentication using digital certification, perhaps in lieu of credit card numbers and other forms of identification that are more open to fraudulent use.

The current state of client authentication on the Internet is woefully inadequate (a fact that is largely and conveniently ignored) and consists primarily of simple user/ID password pairs. Although SSL is usually used to insure that your password (along with other sensitive data like credit card numbers) is encrypted during transmission across the Internet, the Web server really has no assurance that you are who you claim to be. You aren't presenting a digital certificate, signed by a recognized certificate authority, to authenticate yourself.

While reliable client authentication remains a *major* requirement for an Internet economy and new identity-verification schemes continue to be proposed (some quite sophisticated, like retinal or fingerprint recognition), the fact is that client authentication almost never consists of more than a shared password. It's sad, but it's true; and I devote almost no space in this chapter to a topic that really deserves more.

Though there appears to be little progress being made toward the respectable goal of more rigid client authentication, I'll describe how the scheme would work in SSL. An SSL server would maintain a list of acceptable well-known certificate authorities (just as your browser does), and only certificates signed by any one of these recognized CAs are accepted.

There are two ways that such certificates can be maintained. First, each individual certificate can be placed in the location identified by the `SSLCACertificatePath` directive in `httpd.conf`. This is the directory that, by default, contains the server certificate (it is usually `/usr/local/apache2/conf/ssl.crt`), meaning that the server accepts a certificate signed by itself. You can obtain individual server certificates, and place them in this directory. To be accessed, symbolic links to certificates must be created with hash filenames. The directory contains a makefile that creates these symlinks, and from within that directory you simply run `make update` to create these files:

```
# pwd
/usr/local/apache2/conf/ssl.crt
# make update
ca-bundle.crt    ... Skipped
Jackal.crt       ... 90fa7563.0
JackalVeriSign.crt ... eab160c5.0
server.crt       ... 72d31154.0
snakeoil-ca-dsa.crt ... 0cf14d7d.0
snakeoil-ca-rsa.crt ... e52d41d0.0
snakeoil-dsa.crt ... 5d8360e1.0
snakeoil-rsa.crt ... 82ab5372.0
```

> **TIP**   As of this writing (late July 2002), the makefile required to create the hash files for the `SSLCACertificatePath` and `SSLCACertificateFile` directives was not included and installed with Apache 2.0, but this omission is expected to be corrected soon. In the meantime, you can obtain this file from a source distribution of mod_ssl intended for use with Apache 1.3.*x* versions (`www.modssl.org`). As a wrapper for OpenSSL commands, it works exactly the same. In the source archive, you'll find the files as `Makefile.crt` for certificate files and `Makefile.crl` for certificate revocation lists (discussed later in this chapter). Rename both of these as `Makefile` in their respective directories before running the make utility.

You must run `make update` after placing new certificates in this directory to make them available for use. For a small number of certificates, or if you intend to sign all client certificates yourself, this is not a terribly inconvenient way to deal with certificates.

A second way to maintain your certificates is to concatenate all of your server certificates into a single file named `ca-bundle.crt`. Take a look at the one provided with mod_ssl; it includes a very large number of well-known certificate authorities. Bear in mind, though, that all of these certificates have an expiration date, and eventually you'll need an updated list of certificates, which you can download from a variety of sites across the Internet. There is no need to create hash values for this file. To use the list, simply include a reference to it in `httpd.conf` with the `SSLCACertificateFile` directive, like this:

```
SSLCACertificateFile conf/ssl.crt/ca.crt
```

Certificate Revocation Lists (CRLs)

Perhaps one of the reasons that client certificates are not more widely used is that there is a lot of overhead in maintaining what are known as *certificate revocation lists* (CRLs). A CRL is a group of certificates that have been revoked before their scheduled expiration dates. An SSL Web server consults its CRL before accepting a client certificate. The maintenance of these CRLs, which on an Internet scale must contain revoked certificates from all major commercial CA's, is a major administrative task. Imagine if every person who wanted to do online buying had to apply for a client digital certificate (a good idea, it would seem at first glance). The number of revoked certificates would soon number in the millions, and the task of keeping the CRLs on all Internet shopping sites up-to-date would be overwhelming.

For that reason, client certificates are, in practice, useful only on tightly-controlled corporate intranets. The creation, issuance, and installation of client certificates is outside the scope of this chapter, but all major Web browsers provide the capability of using client certificates. (In IE, your personal certificates are stored in Tools ➤ Internet ➤ Options ➤ Content ➤ Certificates ➤ Personal.) In a corporate intranet, client certificates need to be revoked when employees leave. So when using client certification, it is usually necessary to maintain certificate revocation lists (CRLs). If your client certificates were issued by one of the commercial CAs, the CRL is also obtained from the issuing CA. You can download these from the CA, and once you've downloaded a CRL file, you can place current certificates into the directory defined in `ssl.conf` with the `SSLCARevocationPath` directive:

```
SSLCARevocationPath /usr/local/apache2/conf/ssl.crl/
```

Copy the CRL files here and then run `make update` to ensure that a hash is created for each.

Alternatively, most CAs issue their revocation lists as single files containing concatenated certificates. These are much easier to use. You need to acquire current CRLs for the CAs you support, concatenate them into one large file, and then point to this file in `http.conf` using the `SSLCARevocationFile` directive:

```
SSLCARevocationFile /usr/local/apache2/conf/ssl.crl/ca-bundle-client.crl
```

You can use this method in place of or in addition to maintaining individual CRL files.

Commercial SSL Servers

No discussion of SSL on Apache would be complete without a quick look at the commercial versions of Apache already patched for SSL that eliminate all of the effort of compiling and installing the various packages required to make it work. The most widely used of these is Stronghold, formerly from C2Net but now sold by Red Hat, Inc. (`www.redhat.com/software/apache/stronghold/`); Stronghold replaces Red Hat's Secure Web Server (SWS), which was based on Apache/SSL rather than `mod_ssl`. The April 2000 surveys of SSL from SecuritySpace.com showed that Stronghold SSL servers generated 30 percent of all SSL traffic on the Internet. By April 2002, this market share had dropped dramatically to about 5 percent. Most SSL servers on the Internet (approximately 55 percent) are Apache/`mod_ssl` servers, with Microsoft's Internet Information Server coming in at a distant second place (28 percent).

One other Apache/`mod_ssl` server sold commercially is the Enterprise Ready Server from Covalent Technologies (`www.covalent.net/products/enterprise_ready/`), formerly marketed as Raven. This server is essentially Apache/`mod_ssl` with some value-added features.

I don't personally recommend using a commercial Apache/SSL server unless you find the procedures discussed in this chapter too time-consuming. The ones I mentioned are based on `mod_ssl` and OpenSSL and offer no features you can't put together for free (not counting your investment in perspiration and time). Prior to the expiration of the patent restricting the commercial use of RSA Data Security's encryption algorithms, the included license was a major benefit to most sites that chose commercial SSL applications. This benefit is no longer relevant.

You might consider commercial vendor support a major benefit of these commercial `mod_ssl` offerings. It might be; the fact is, though, that all the software is open source and is best supported by the open-source community. When you run into problems, chances are you'll turn to a stranger on the Internet for help, and the one thing that might prevent you from getting that help is some obscure difference between the commercial version you are using and the "real" open-source version. So although I don't advise you *not* to choose a commercial Apache/SSL product, I do advise you to consider the open-source alternative first. After all, this is Linux we're talking about, right?

In Sum

The Secure Sockets Layer (SSL) protocol enables a greater degree of security than the standard user authentication methods described in the preceding chapter. SSL uses a certification scheme based on public key data encryption to securely pass information between SSL Web servers and SSL client browsers. The SSL server provides a *certificate* to the SSL browser that is examined for authenticity. The browser, already configured with the public keys of a number of *certificate authorities* (CAs), is able to decode this certificate, authenticating the Web server and extracting its public key. This public key is used to encrypt a session key that only the legitimate Web server can decode. This session key is used to establish an encrypted data tunnel with the server. During the entire SSL session, all information passing between Web server and client browser is encrypted to protect against eavesdropping. The benefits of certificate authentication of SSL servers (by widely trusted certificate authorities) and secure data communications have made SSL the de facto standard for today's electronic commerce applications; and it has been deemed secure enough for applications that range from online credit card sales to electronic banking.

In Apache 2.0, SSL was incorporated as a standard, or core, module named mod_ssl, which was previously distributed independently. The SSL implementation described in this chapter (mod_ssl) requires five steps: installing mod_ssl, creating a server key, creating a CSR, obtaining your server certificate, and configuring Apache to use SSL.

The next and final chapter of this book discusses HTTP/1.1 content negotiation, something that not every site administrator will need to know a lot about. If you are running a server that has multilingual content and serves a variety of different pages to clients with different needs, however, you will want to know how Apache can be configured to support this feature.

Maintaining a Healthy Server

PART 4

15

Metainformation and Content Negotiation

In most cases, the resources a Web server delivers to a client are documents formatted in HyperText Markup Language. This is, essentially, a default resource type, but the HTTP protocol is capable of delivering virtually any type of information. We have all used Web browsers to retrieve many different types of data, including embedded images, streaming multimedia, binary data files, Java applets... there is no limit to the variety of data types that can be delivered by a Web server.

In order to do its job and deliver the optimum content acceptable to each client, Apache needs to know as much as possible about each resource that it serves. Information about other information, often called *metainformation*, not only tells the server how to process the data, it also instructs the client browser on how to handle the data, determining which application to pass the data to if the browser is incapable of dealing with it directly. There are four items of metainformation that the server and the browser need for any resource:

- The content type
- The language used for text
- The character set used for text
- The encoding, usually a compression scheme

NOTE   You may also hear the term metainformation used to describe information within HTML-formatted documents in the form of META tags embedded inside the document. The HTML META tag is reserved for use with information types that do not correspond to standard HTTP headers, and may describe the document's authors, revision history, and that sort of thing. Apache is not concerned with this type of metainformation, so it is not discussed in this chapter.

The subject of this chapter is this metainformation—how Apache determines it for the files it serves, and the three ways in which it is used. Each of the uses for metainformation is discussed in a separate section of the chapter. The uses are

- To instruct the browser how to handle the document. Special HTTP headers that precede data sent from Apache convey information to the receiving browser. Information that Apache can send the browser includes the type of the resource, its language, and the character set required to display it.

- To determine an appropriate Apache handler for the document before it is delivered to the requesting client browser. A content handler is usually an Apache module that performs certain functions with Web-delivered data before it is sent to the client. The most common example is that of server-parsed HTML, in which an Apache module scans the document looking for "tags" that it replaces with program-generated text before forwarding the document to the client. Chapter 7 introduces Server-Side Includes, which do just that.

- To negotiate a suitable version of a document with an HTTP/1.1-compliant browser. When multiple versions of a document exist, Apache uses content negotiation to send a version of the document that best meets the preferences expressed by the client.

The standard Apache module that is responsible for associating metainformation with resources that reside on the server is mod_mime. In this chapter, we'll examine several directives that are supplied by this module. The first, AddType, maps a MIME content type to one or more file extensions. The module provides similar directives to map the other three types of metainformation to additional filename extensions: AddLanguage, AddCharset, and AddEncoding. You'll see that two other Apache modules can also play a role: mod_mime_magic implements the traditional Unix technique of determining a file's type by looking at its first few bytes for a "magic number," and mod_negotiation implements the process of content negotiation.

First, we'll look at the four types of metainformation Apache works with.

Passing Metainformation to the Apache Server

Before Apache can use the metainformation about a file in any of the ways outlined above, the file's creator first needs to inform Apache about the four basic characteristics. As you'll see, the most common method is via the filename extension. For the content type, a second method, using Unix "magic numbers," is also available but less efficient.

The MIME Content Type

Without a doubt, the most critical piece of metainformation that Apache needs to know about a file is its content type, usually referred to as the MIME type of the file. Originally, MIME (which stands for Multipurpose Internet Mail Extensions) was introduced as a standard method of encoding nontext files for attachment to Internet electronic mail messages. MIME is documented in RFC 1521 and RFC 1522 ("Multipurpose Internet Mail Extensions, Parts 1 and 2"). This specification describes a method for encoding a binary file as standard ASCII text characters for transmission (called MIME Base-64 encoding), and also a standard means for the sender to describe the encoded attachment.

The adoption of MIME as a standard for encoding e-mail attachments is what permits the exchange of binary (or nontext) files between e-mail applications from different vendors. Today, virtually all e-mail attachments that cross the Internet use MIME (a.k.a. Base-64) encoding, preceded by MIME *headers*, which include information about the attachment (or each of the attachments, if multiple attachments are used). Typical MIME headers for an e-mail message look like this:

```
Content-Type: image/gif; name="cancun.gif"
Content-Transfer-Encoding: base64
```

Here you see the two main parts of MIME: the type description in the Content-Type header, and the identification of the standard MIME Base-64 encoding format in the Content-Transfer-Encoding header. These headers will instruct the e-mail application that receives the message how to decode the attachment and then how to interpret the results. Even if the decoded file did not carry the .gif extension, the Content-Type header instructs the receiving application how to interpret the file, in some cases by invoking a separate application that knows how to handle files of that type.

The best method of telling Apache the content type of a document is by associating the document's filename extension with one of the standard MIME types. The list of all MIME types that Apache knows about and supports is stored in the default location conf/mime-types, under the Apache directory. This file contains a list of MIME types and subtypes, along with the filename extensions that Apache associates with each. For example, the entry in this file for JPEG-encoded images looks like this:

```
image/jpeg                        jpeg jpg jpe
```

When Apache receives a request for a file that has the extension jpg, jpeg, or jpe, this line in the mime-types file instructs it to use a Content-Type HTTP header to identify the file as MIME type image, subtype jpeg.

You can edit this file directly to add new content types, which may or may not be officially recognized by the Internet Assigned Numbers Authority (IANA). In the early days of the Web, when new multimedia applications and "plug-ins" were constantly being introduced, I had to edit this file several times a year to accommodate new applications. Adding new MIME types isn't required nearly so often today. In fact, direct editing of the mime-types file is no longer even recommended. To add a new type (or a new filename extension) to the list of types that Apache recognizes, use the AddType directive instead. This directive has basically the same format as a line in mime-types. To illustrate, suppose we want Apache to recognize files with the extension .giff as GIF images. You would use the following AddType directive in httpd.conf:

```
AddType image/gif    gif giff
```

The AddType directive overrides (or replaces) the same MIME type in the mime-types file, so when you are trying to replace an existing mapping, make sure you specify all filename extensions you want to map, not just the new ones you want to add.

If you also wanted to add support for an application you've written that writes files ending in the extension .myapp, you could add the following line:

```
AddType application/myapp .myapp
```

Incidentally, you can change the location of the mime-types file using the TypesConfig directory, specifying a new relative or absolute path to the file:

```
TypesConfig /usr/local/apache2/conf/mime-types
```

Using Magic MIME Types

Reading a filename extension is an efficient means of determining the MIME type of the file's contents. With this method it isn't necessary to open the file or read metainformation about the file from some other source. It is essentially the same method used by most PC operating systems, which maintain an *association* between the extension of a file's name and the application required to read it. Traditionally, however, Unix systems haven't used this mechanism. Linux (and most versions of Unix) come with a utility named file that is used to guess the nature of a file by opening it and reading the first few bytes, in this way:

```
# file *.EXE *.gif *.gz
PLAYER.EXE:                    MS-DOS executable (EXE)
sound1.gif:                    GIF image data, version 89a
apache_1_3_12.gz:             gzip compressed data
```

The `file` utility takes a peek into a file and attempts to determine the file type from the bytecodes it finds there. Programmers often include a few bytes (commonly called *magic numbers*) somewhere near the beginning of a datafile that uniquely identify that file to be of a specific type.

Here are a couple of examples to illustrate how the contents of a file can be used to identify the MIME type of its contents. I'm using a standard Linux utility, od (octal dump), to view the contents of a GIF file, piping the output to the head command so that only the first four lines are displayed.

```
# od -a leftarrow.gif | head -4
0000000   G   I   F   8   9   a dc4 nul syn nul   B nul nul del del del
0000020 del   3   3   L del del   L   L   L  em  em  em   f nul nul   3
0000040   3   3 nul nul nul   !   ~   N   T   h   i   s  sp   a   r   t
0000060  sp   i   s  sp   i   n  sp   t   h   e  sp   p   u   b   l   i
```

As defined in the Graphics Interchange Format specification, the first three characters of any GIF file are G, I, and F. In a moment, I'll show how we can use this fact to identify a GIF file by these magic characters. First, though, let's look at a JPEG representation of the same image:

```
# od -h leftarrow.jpg | head -4
0000000 d8ff e0ff 1000 464a 4649 0100 0001 0100
0000020 0100 0000 dbff 4300 0800 0606 0607 0805
0000040 0707 0907 0809 0c0a 0d14 0b0c 0c0b 1219
0000060 0f13 1d14 1f1a 1d1e 1c1a 201c 2e24 2027
```

In this case, it isn't as obvious, but all JPEG files can be identified by the first 16 bits of the file. On an Intel machine (which is often referred to as "little-endian" because the bytes at lower addresses have lower significance), these 16 bits are shown as the two hex bytes d8 and ff. The same file stored on a "big-endian" machine (such as a machine built around one of the Motorola family of chips) might be stored with the bytes that make up this 16-bit value reversed. For that reason, when looking for byte values in a file, you must specify the order. In this case, to identify a JPEG image, we would look for the file to begin with 0xd8ff in little-endian order, or 0xffd8 in big-endian order.

The standard Apache module `mod_mime_magic` can determine a file's type by opening the file and searching for magic numbers it recognizes. The module supplies a single directive, `MimeMagicFile`, which specifies the location of a text file that maps recognized magic numbers and other data patterns to associated MIME types. Note that there is no default value provided for this directive. As a result, `mod_mime_magic` is activated only when `httpd.conf` contains a line like the following:

```
MimeMagicFile conf/magic
```

The active lines in this file contain four mandatory fields and an optional (rarely used) fifth field, in this format:

```
byte_offset data_type_to_match match_data MIME_type [MIME_encoding]
```

The fields are as follows:

byte_offset   The byte number to begin checking from; > indicates continuation from the preceding line

data_type_to_match   The type of data to match, whether a string or some type of integer

match_data   The specific contents to match, such as the string "GIF"

MIME_type   The MIME type Apache should assign to the file

MIME_encoding   The MIME encoding Apache should assign to the file (optional)

To determine the content type of a file, mod_mime_magic compares the file against each line of the magic file. If a successful match is found, the associated MIME type is returned (along with the optional encoding if specified).

As an example, consider this line from the standard magic file that comes with the module:

```
0       string          GIF             image/gif
```

Here, mod_mime_magic is being instructed to begin matching with the first byte of the file (offset 0) and look for a string matching the pattern "GIF." If that's found, the MIME type returned for the file is image/gif. That's simple enough to understand. To identify a file containing a graphic image in JPEG format, this line is used:

```
0       beshort         0xffd8          image/jpeg
```

Here, the magic number we are looking for is a two-octet or 16-bit (short) integer value, but we aren't sure exactly how these two bytes will be stored—in other words, our match needs to be independent of the machine we run it on, so we have specified big-endian notation for the match. That way, regardless of whether the file contains the bytes stored big-end first or little-end first, the two octets are converted to big-endian notation before matching against 0xffd8. In big-endian format, where the most significant byte is expressed first, this will always equal 0xffd8, regardless of the actual ordering of the octets.

The following data types are defined for the magic file:

Data Type	Explanation	Example
Byte	single byte	64
Short	machine-order 16-bit integer	0xffd8

Long	machine-order 32-bit integer	0x4e54524b
String	text string	HTML
Leshort	little-endian 16-bit integer	0xffd8
Beshort	big-endian 16-bit integer	0xd8ff
Lelong	little-endian 32-bit integer	0x4e54524b
Belong	big-endian 32-bit integer	0x4b52544e

Provided with mod_mime_magic is an example file that includes most standard file formats. It is unlikely that you will need to edit this file to add other formats. You will need specific knowledge of file formats, though, if you intend to describe them so that mod_mime_magic can identify them. If you wrote the file format, that shouldn't be too big an order to fill. The example file provided with the module serves as an excellent example for creating your own magic file entries. The documentation for the module is not terribly instructive, and the source code not especially easy to follow. The best way to learn to write patterns for your magic file is to study the examples already there to determine what patterns they are looking for in existing file formats.

In the magic file that comes with the module, you'll see some lines preceded with the greater-than (>) character. This identifies the line as a continuation of the preceding line. Think of this line as a conditional line; it will only be used if the preceding line matched. The example for a compiled Java file demonstrates how this works:

```
0       short       0xcafe
>2      short       0xbabe            application/java
```

Here, the second line will be used to test the file only if the first 16-bit short value equals 0xcafe. (Since the Java file is compiled to a specific machine, the byte order is not significant here, because it will always be the same for files compiled to run on this machine's specific architecture, and no other notation needs to be considered.) We need to do this because identifying a compiled Java file requires matching the first two octets, ignoring the second two, but requiring a match of the third pair of octets. Kind of tricky. If the first 16 bits of the file (offset 0) match 0xcafe, then (and only then) compare the third 16 bits (offset 2), and if they match 0xbabe, consider this a file containing content of type application/java.

Additional levels of indentation can be used to further nest conditional statements, but you will probably never need to do this.

mod_mime_magic is almost never used as the primary means of identifying a file's content type, mainly because it is inefficient to open the file and compare its contents against stored data, looking for comparison clues. It is far more efficient to use a mechanism like the filename extension (or file location) for this purpose.

MIME Language

There are no international boundaries to the Internet, and an increasing number of Web sites are offering their Web pages in more than one language. Later in the chapter, I'll show how the new HTTP/1.1 standard supports content negotiation, a methodology that can be used to provide content according to the requester's language preference.

In addition to content type, the language used in a Web-based document can be identified. Again, a filename extension is usually used to inform Apache of what language to associate with a resource. mod_mime supplies the AddLanguage directive to make the association between content languages and filename extensions. An AddLanguage directive should be used for each supported language type, although a single AddLanguage directive can associate a single language with multiple filename extensions.

The default httpd.conf provides a number of these directives for the most widely used languages of the world, and these serve as good examples of the use of the AddLanguage directive:

```
AddLanguage en .en
AddLanguage fr .fr
AddLanguage de .de
AddLanguage da .da
AddLanguage el .el
AddLanguage it .it
```

The two-letter language extensions are usually used in addition to any other extensions used to identify the content type of the same file. For example, a valid filename for an HTML document in Italian might be:

```
index.html.it
```

The two-letter language tags used are those defined by the International Organization for Standardization in ISO 639, "Names of Languages." If you need a reference to these, refer to this site:

```
www.unicode.org/unicode/onlinedat/languages.html
```

MIME Character Set

In addition to different languages, documents can also use different character sets. Client browsers also need to support these character sets, and Apache needs to pass along the information about them.

The AddCharset directive maps a character set to one or more filename extensions. The following lines were included in my default httpd.conf file; the first includes several character sets used for rendering Japanese text, and the second supplies glyphs needed for some Central European languages:

```
AddCharset ISO-2022-JP .jis
AddCharset ISO-8859-2 .iso-pl
```

The character encoding specified provides a mapping between each character in the set and the numeric representation of that character. In order to use an alternate character set, you first create documents using that character set, which usually requires a special (non-English) version of your software application. You would assign the file you create an extension that relates it to the character set used, and then, using `AddCharset`, ensure that Apache is able to determine the character set for purposes of informing client browsers and in content negotiation as discussed later in this chapter.

The character set names are registered with the IANA and can be found at:

```
http://www.iana.org/assignments/character-sets
```

Note that the IANA does not act as a standards body, and the various encoding schemes registered with the IANA conform to a number of different specifications published by a wide number of different standards organizations.

MIME Encoding

In addition to a MIME content type, language, and character set, a Web-delivered document can also have an encoding. Fortunately, this one's easy to deal with. As far as Apache is concerned, the encoding of a file is generally a compression scheme.

The `AddEncoding` directive maps an encoding type to one or more filename extensions. The default `httpd.conf` file comes preconfigured for two:

```
AddEncoding x-compress Z
AddEncoding x-gzip gz zip
```

You may want to add directives for the more common compression schemes, such as this:

```
AddEncoding mac-binhex40 hqx
```

Some browsers have been written that allow on-the-fly decompression of data compressed with one of these schemes. Most browsers, however, use information about the compression scheme to spawn an external application to decompress the data.

MIME encoding is not used in content negotiation, and it is important only in informing the client browser how data is compressed so that it can properly deal with the data.

How Apache Uses Metainformation

Once Apache has learned a document's content type, language, character set, and encoding, how does it carry out the essential tasks of conveying the metainformation to the browser, assigning a handler for any server-side processing the content type may require, and performing content negotiation with HTTP/1.1 browsers? That's what we'll explore in the rest of this chapter.

Instructing the Browser

HTTP has always been a binary transfer protocol. In other words, no special encoding of data is required to deliver it to the recipient. However, all HTTP transmissions begin with a set of headers that describe the data to follow. One of the most important of these is borrowed directly from MIME, the Content-Type header, which is a mandatory header on all HTTP responses from a Web server and is the last header in the sequence. A typical HTTP response header, this one for an image to be used as an embedded icon in a Web page, looks like this:

```
HTTP/1.1 200 OK
Date: Sun, 21 Jul 2002 17:14:54 GMT
Server: Apache/2.0.39 (Unix) DAV/2
Last-Modified: Fri, 10 May 2002 20:58:37 GMT
ETag: "18c2c2-916-fe85940"
Accept-Ranges: bytes
Content-Length: 2326
Keep-Alive: timeout=15, max=99
Connection: Keep-Alive
Content-Type: image/gif
```

The Content-Type header always identifies a content media type, which can be anything the browser recognizes as a valid media type. In nearly every case, however, the header will contain one of the many commonly recognized Internet media types. The IANA maintains a list of Internet media types, which constitutes the de facto standard for the Content-Type MIME (and HTTP) header. You can find this list at

```
www.isi.edu/in-notes/iana/assignments/media-types/media-types
```

Just as Apache comes preconfigured to recognize most common MIME types, most browsers also recognize many common document types. Figure 15.1 shows the Netscape configuration for documents received of type image/gif. Notice that Netscape is defined as the handler for documents of this type. In other words, Netscape uses its internal image viewer to display GIF images. A user who prefers a different image viewer could configure Netscape to invoke that application to display GIF images. Use the Edit button to edit the configuration for known types.

Figure 15.1   The Netscape browser's default configuration for the GIF_Image MIME type

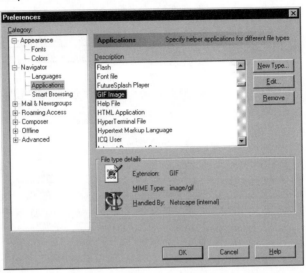

Generally, the only MIME types you will serve from Apache are the standard types that most browsers already recognize and support. If it's necessary to define new MIME types in Apache, however, you will also need to configure the browser to recognize those types. In that case, you can use the Add button in the Preferences window to add new MIME types to Netscape. For example, if you have configured Apache to serve files with the extension .myapp, adding a Content-Type header identifying these as type application/ myapp, you must also configure your browser to handle these. Figure 15.2 shows how Netscape is configured to add support for files of this type.

Since every browser has to be individually configured to support nonstandard MIME types, you would normally do this only in an environment where you have some control over the client browser, such as a corporate intranet. In a manufacturing facility, for example, I have had to configure client browsers to automatically recognize CAD/CAM formats and invoke the appropriate application to view these. This gave line workers the ability to use a standard Web browser to view manufacturing specifications and engineering drawings on the shop floor, without having a CAD/CAM workstation.

The content media type of a Web-delivered document is by far the most important piece of information furnished to the client browser. However, when relevant, Apache also furnishes other information about the document, also in the Content-Type header. The possible options that can be set are the language, character set, and encoding. Oddly enough, the character set is specified with the media type in the Content-Type header:

```
Content-Type: text/html; charset=windows-1251
```

Figure 15.2   Adding a MIME type (Netscape)

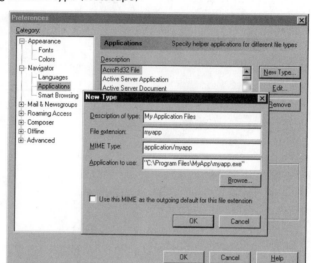

The language encoding and compression (if used) are specified with two HTTP headers used specifically for that purpose:

```
Content-Language: it
Content-Encoding: gzip
```

Setting a Handler or Filter

We've just seen how identifying a file's content type is required in order to generate the headers that tell the browser what type of data is being received. The second purpose for identifying a file's content type is so that Apache can invoke the correct content handler or filter specific to that type of data, so that Apache knows what to do with the data that is read from a disk file. This section discusses directives that are used to associate handlers and filters with specific content types. Additional directives are also shown that associate a handler or filter with the directory in which a document resides or that associate with a partial URL, which is especially useful for those cases when a resource is generated by a module and no disk file is associated with the request.

The use of the directives introduced in this section is generally documented with the modules that provide the handlers or filters. For example, to set up a handler for CGI scripts, you would refer to the documentation for mod_cgi (or Chapter 8) for instructions, rather than the documentation for mod_mime, which supplies the AddHandler directive to Apache.

The difference between a handler and a filter is generally not important, and in many cases a module designer can choose to use either method to generate output. A handler is usually thought of as a set of actions (a program) that is run when a certain type of file is loaded, as in the case of the `cgi-script` handler provided by `mod_cgi`, which is called when a file identified as a CGI script is loaded. Most documents (such as HTML-formatted documents and image files) pass through a handler called `default-handler`, which is implemented in the Apache core. Apache's `default-handler` performs the task of serving every document to the browser, and every resource served will pass through this handler.

Filters (a new feature in Apache 2.0) are used to make on-the-fly changes to data received by the server from the browser (in the case of an input filter) or data being sent to the browser by the server (an output filter). Filters accept data from Apache, manipulate it, and return it to Apache for further processing, and are especially suited for use with data streams that need to be altered slightly as they pass through the filters. This is the case with Server-Side Includes (as discussed in Chapter 7), which is HTML with special embedded tags that are replaced as they pass through the `INCLUDES` filter, which is supplied by `mod_include`. One way to see all available content handlers and filters for the currently running Apache server is to invoke the Server Info screen, as described in Chapter 10.

Although support for both handlers and filters is provided by `mod_mime`, and is usually associated with a specific MIME type, it is often best to associate a filename extension directly with a handler or filter by name, rather than associating a filename extension with a MIME type (using the `AddType` directive) and then specifying a handler or filter for that MIME type. `mod_mime` supplies the `AddHandler` and `AddFilter` directives that are used to create this association between filename extension and, respectively, handlers and filters. One such handler that you will probably find in your default `httpd.conf` is the one that defines files with the extension `.var` as having the `type-map` MIME type:

```
AddHandler type-map var
```

This directive specifies that the `type-map` handler (supplied by `mod_negotiation`) will be called when files with names ending in the `.var` extension are requested.

Filters are enabled in much the same way as handlers, using the `AddInputFilter` or `AddOutputFilter` directives, which specify whether the filter will be applied to input data (received from the browser) or output data (sent to the browser). Here's an example in which the `INCLUDES` filter is defined as an output filter, which will receive all data that Apache is preparing to send to a requesting browser. The `INCLUDES` filters (supplied by `mod_include`) parses this HTML data, replacing the SSI tags that are found with its own values. This happens at the very end of the request cycle, immediately before the data is put on the network, in route to the requester.

```
AddOutputFilter INCLUDES .shtml
```

The following directives undo the effects of their `Add` counterparts just discussed, removing handler or filter associations with filename extensions. You would be most likely to do this from a .htaccess file in a directory to disable the special filename associations for that directory alone. In general, though, you will probably never need to do this, but you should be aware that the capability is always there.

```
RemoveHandler .htm .html
RemoveInputFilter .someext
RemoveOutputFilter .shtml
```

The SetHandler, SetInputFilter, and SetOutputFilter directives are similar to their Add counterparts, but are used to associate named handlers or filters with specific directories or request URLs, rather than with filename extensions. Note that there is no Remove counterpart to these directives to nullify a handler or filter for a directory or URL.

```
<Location /status/jserv>
  SetHandler jserv-status
  order deny,allow
  deny from all
  allow from localhost, 192.168.1.2, 192.168.1.3
</Location>
```

In this example, the SetHandler directive is applied to the URL identified in the <Location> container directive. Note that this SetHandler directive is applied to all request URLs that begin with /status/jserv, which may not map to a specific directory (and probably doesn't). All requests the server receives that begin with this pattern, however, are passed to the jserv-status handler for processing.

Content Negotiation

So far in this chapter, we've discussed the four elements of metainformation that Apache can maintain about any resource: MIME content type, language, character set, and the encoding (compression scheme), if any. We've also looked at two of the ways Apache can use that information: simply passing the information to the browser via headers, and selecting a handler for any server-side processing that needs to be done. Now it's time to examine the most complex and powerful use of metainformation: *content negotiation*.

Content negotiation is a process that occurs between Apache (or other servers) and HTTP/1.1-compliant browsers when the server has multiple variants of a given resource available for serving. It is the process by which the server attempts to match the needs of the client user as closely as possible.

What is a variant of a resource? A *resource*, as the term is used in Internet documentation (and as I've used it throughout this book), is any entity that can be identified by a URL. It may be a single file or a directory. A given resource may exist in more than one *representation*, or version, varying by the categories of metainformation discussed at the beginning of this chapter. Each of these versions is known as a *variant*.

Three elements are necessary for the server to begin the negotiation process when it receives a request for a resource:

Identifying Variant Types   The server first needs to identify the content type and other metainformation variables for all resources, using the methods discussed earlier.

Determining the Client Preference   The server also needs to know what content types, etc., the client browser can accept.

Determining the Available Variants   The server finally needs to know what variants it has available for a requested resource.

Client Preference

Probably the most important part of the content negotiation process is the client's preference. In most cases, the client's stated document preference is honored, if the server has a matching version of the requested document. Why serve the client English text, if the client's browser has stated a preference for Italian and the server has an Italian version ready for delivery? Content negotiation is a process that attempts to find a suitable compromise between server and client document preferences, but usually the only relevant preference is that of the client. I'll discuss first how client preferences are communicated to Apache.

HTTP/1.1 defines four headers that clients can use in their request to a Web server: `Accept`, `Accept-Language`, `Accept-Charset`, and `Accept-Encoding`.

The *Accept* Header

The `Accept` header lists the MIME content types that the client is willing to accept. These types are the same as those that Apache uses in its `mime-types` file. Here's an example:

```
Accept: text/html, text/plain
```

This client is expressing a willingness to accept either an HTML-formatted document or one that is in plain ASCII text. The browser has not expressed a preference, however, and the server is completely at liberty to serve either. In such a case, the server will use its own preference settings to determine which variant (among those that are stored on it) it will serve, and we'll cover this later in the chapter.

The browser can also send `Accept` headers that contain an optional quality value for each media type. This quality factor (expressed as a q value) can take a value of 0.000 (completely unacceptable) to 1.000 (the highest preference). Here, the media types that are acceptable to the client are given quality values:

```
Accept: text/html, application/pdf;q=0.8, text/plain;q=0.4
```

Since the default quality value is 1.0, HTML-formatted text is requested with the strongest preference value. A PDF document is acceptable with a slightly lower preference, and the user will accept plain text if that's all that the server has to offer.

The `Accept` header can also contain wildcard characters for the media types. If the client browser sent the following `Accept` header, it would be expressing a willingness to accept any document that has a text MIME type, regardless of the subtype:

```
Accept: text/html, text/*
```

The PDF version would *not* be acceptable in this case.

Many browsers send a wildcard (`*.*`) with each request, as a way of saying "if you don't have the explicit types I asked for, send whatever you have":

```
Accept: image/gif, image/jpeg, *.*
```

Since no quality values are assigned to any of the preferences expressed in this example, you might assume that all have an equal preference (the default quality value of 1.0). But Apache doesn't assign default preference to wildcards. Instead, it assigns a quality value of 0.01 to `*.*` and 0.02 to a wildcard subtype, like our example of `text/*`.

The *Accept-Language* Header

The `Accept-Language` header identifies all languages that the client will accept, with an optional quality value (defaults to 1.0 if not specified).

```
Accept-Language: en;q=0.8, de;q=0.4, it;q=0.2
```

Here, the client has expressed a preference for English, but is willing to accept German or Italian (a very multilingual reader here) with successively lower degrees of enthusiasm.

Figure 15.3 shows how language preferences are configured in a client browser (in this case, Netscape Navigator). This information will be conveyed to the server in an `Accept-Language` HTTP header.

The *Accept-Charset* Header

`Accept-Charset` identifies all character sets the client is willing to accept. Again, quality values can be used; if they are not used, ISO-8859-1 (the Latin-1 set for West European languages, the standard U.S. encoding) is deemed to be acceptable to every client. Note, too, that if the media type of a document on the server is `text/html`, and no other character set is associated with the document (either by a filename extension or type-map file), the document is assumed to be in ISO-8859-1.

```
Accept-Charset: ISO-2022-JP;q=1.0, ISO-8859-2;0.5
```

Figure 15.3   Client browser language preference

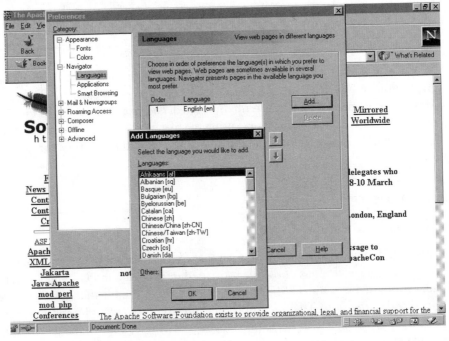

The line above expresses a preference for a Japanese character set, with a lesser preference for ISO-8859-2 (Latin-2, which covers most Central European languages). If neither of these is available, the server will send the document in ISO-8859-1, which is always deemed acceptable to any client.

The *Accept-Encoding* Header

The Accept-Encoding header identifies all encodings that the client will accept. Quality values can be assigned by the client. Unencoded versions of files are always preferred and will be served, if they exist.

```
Accept-Encoding: gzip;q=0.8, zip;q=0.5
```

Determining Source Variants

The final requirement for content negotiation is the determination of what variants of each document are available to be served by Apache. When Apache receives a request for a resource, it uses one of two different methods—MultiViews or a type map—to build a list of all servable variants of that document. The number of variants potentially includes all combinations of the four ways in which a document can be classified.

MultiViews

MultiViews is an Apache option that can be set on a per-directory basis. MultiViews is enabled by including the following line in the directory's .htaccess file:

```
Options +Multiviews
```

MultiViews works by using filename extensions to create a list of all source variants for a given resource. When a request is received for a resource—for example, /somedoc—and MultiViews is enabled for the directory indicated, mod_negotiation looks for all resources in the directory that match the name, using the filename extensions to build a list of variants for that document. It may find the following files in the directory, for example:

```
somedoc.html
somedoc.html.en
somedoc.html.de
somedoc.pdf.en
somedoc.pdf.de
```

This would indicate to mod_negotiation that five variants of the same resource exist: English language versions of the file formatted in HTML and PDF, and German versions formatted in both HTML and PDF. What about the file that has no two-letter language code extension? That file can be interpreted in two ways by mod_negotiation. Usually it is interpreted as having no language attribute, and will be served only if the client expresses no language preference, but you can modify this behavior using the DefaultLanguage directive. When this directive is used in a per-directory context (in either a <Directory> container or an .htaccess file), it specifies a language to be assigned to all files in that directory that do not have a language attribute assigned:

```
DefaultLanguage en
```

The DefaultLanguage directive can only specify a single language.

When MultiViews is used to create a list of variants for a resource, the LanguagePriority directive can also be used to set a precedence for language selection that is used whenever a client does not express a language preference:

```
LanguagePriority en de
```

If the above directive is in effect and a client requests /somedoc.html, then the English version, formatted as HTML, is always served. The German version is served only to clients that specifically express a preference for it, by sending a header like the following:

```
Accept-Language: de;q=1.0, en;q=0.6; fr;q=0.2
```

MultiViews is used by Apache to store multiple language versions of the default page that is served when your server is first installed and started. If you'll look in the initial directory defined by the DocumentRoot directive in the httpd.conf file provided with the distribution, you'll see a separate file for each language supported. (In some cases, you'll see variants of character sets for languages that don't use the Latin alphabet, which is generally used for written English.) These files offer excellent examples of how to use MultiViews to serve files in multiple languages or that use different character sets.

Be sure to examine `httpd.conf` for examples of how meanings are given to the filename extensions, using the `AddLanguage` and `AddCharSet` directives described earlier.

The Type-Map File

An alternative to MultiViews is the use of a type-map file, a document used to itemize a list of document variants that Apache can serve. This file contains a section for each document that can be served from the directory containing the type-map file, and uses a set of headers to define the available variants for each document.

`type-map` is actually the name of an Apache handler, supplied by `mod_negotiation`, and the use of type maps is enabled by using the `AddHandler` directive to associate this handler with a filename extension. By convention, `.var` (for *variant*) is usually appended to the name of the type-map file:

```
AddHandler type-map .var
```

Apache uses type maps to store the standard error response pages with all the different language variants supported. You can find this in the error directory under the Apache install directory (the typical location is `/usr/local/apache2/error`). These provide excellent examples if you are interested in using type maps to serve multiple language variants. No configuration is required; Apache is fully set up to use type maps stored with the `.var` extension.

Since `type-map` is defined as a handler for documents saved as files ending in `.var`, type maps are invoked when the client requests a resource that ends with `.var`. Of course, you've never actually submitted a request like `http://jackal.hiwaay.net/somedoc.var`, though that would be a valid way to call a type map. Most servers use some form of URL rewriting (discussed in Chapter 9) to redirect a request to a type map. Using `mod_rewrite`, for instance, you could redirect all requests for files ending with `.html` in the `DocumentRoot` directory to an associated type-map file using these directives:

```
<Location />
RewriteRule ^(.*)\.html$ $1.var [NS]
</Location>
```

The advantage of using type maps instead of MultiViews is that they allow you to set a server precedence for variants of a document. For each variant of a document, type maps can instruct `mod_negotiation` to use a *quality source factor* (or qs value). Remember that the quality value included in a client's `Accept` request header is distinctly different from the quality source factors assigned to resources on the Apache server. Content negotiation is basically a process in which the server objectively arrives at a compromise between the client's expressed preference and the server's. The server uses a fixed algorithm to perform this arbitration, as described in the next section. Fortunately, it is rarely necessary to understand this process, although you might find it helpful to know how it is done. Generally, your work is complete when you assign quality source factors (qs values) to create a precedence for different variants of the same document.

The contents of a type-map file are a set of records, one for each variant of the document (each of which is stored under a different filename, of course). The attributes of each variant are expressed on a separate line within each variant record, and each must begin with one of the following headers:

URL   The URI of the file that contains the variant (even though the header is URL, the resource is identified by a URI). This URI is always relative to the type-map file; a URI that consists of only a filename is assumed to be in the same directory as the type-map file. Note that variants defined by the type-map file do not have to be in the same directory as that type-map file, and a single type-map file can contain variants from any number of directories.

Content-Type   The MIME content media type of the variant and, optionally, the quality source factor, or qs. The qs level has the same meaning as that expressed by the client in Accept headers. The qs factor for a variant must be expressed only in the Content-Type header for that variant and cannot be placed after any other header.

Content-Language   The language in which the variant was written, using one of the two-character codes defined in ISO 639.

Content-Encoding   If the file is compressed or otherwise encoded, rather than simply raw data, this describes the encoding used, typically x-gzip or x-compress.

Content-Length   The byte size of the file.

Description   A human-readable description of the variant. If Apache cannot find an appropriate variant to return, it will return an error message that lists all available variants, with these descriptions. The client can then request one of these directly.

Consider a sample .var file:

```
Content-Type: text/html; qs=1.0
Content-Language: en
<html>
<head></head>
<body>
<h3>This is the English Version</h3>
</body></html>
```

```
Content-type: text/html; qs=0.8
Content-Language: fr
<html>
<head></head>
<body>
<h3>Ca c'est la version française.</h3>
</body></html>
```

This is a very simple example, in which our server maintains separate English and French versions of the same HTML-formatted document. The English version is preferred.

Like the client-preference q value, the qs factor can take values of 0.000 to 1.000. A value of 1.000 is assigned to any variant in the file for which a qs factor is not expressed. A variant with a value of 0.000 will never be served. The quality source factor expressed in the type map is combined with the quality value expressed by the client browser to negotiate the variant actually sent to the client. In this case, if the client sent a header such as:

```
Accept-Language: de; q=1.0, en; q=0.6; fr; q=0.2
```

mod_negotiation will multiply the quality source factors for the server and the quality value provided by the browser to derive a joint factor:

en: $1.0 \times 0.6 = 0.6$

de: $0.8 \times 1.0 = 0.8$

In this case, even though English is preferred on the server side, the German version wins out and is the one that will be returned to the client. And although the client expressed a willingness to accept French, there is no matching variant on the server, so this doesn't enter into the content negotiation process.

The Apache Negotiation Process

Whenever there are multiple variants of the same document, trying to determine which is the optimum variant to send to the client can be very confusing. Fortunately, we don't get involved in that process; mod_negotiation takes care of it for us. There may be times, however, especially when using type maps, that we want to influence mod_negotiation's selection process. For that reason, I'll describe the content negotiation process the module follows whenever a request is received for a document that has multiple variants to select and returns a single variant to the client (or an error if the request can't be resolved to a single variant):

1. Build a list of all available variants of the requested file, either from a type map or using MultiViews. If a type map is used, prioritize these according to quality (qs) values in the type map, assigning default values where no qs value is specified. If MultiViews is used, all variants have equal priority.

2. Extract the Accept headers from the client request, and build a list of the variants the client can accept. Prioritize these according to quality values, if provided; otherwise assign default values. Compare this list against the list of available variants compiled in step 1, eliminating any server variants the client hasn't specified as acceptable. When this step is complete, you should have a list of all variants available on the server that are acceptable to the client. From this list, one will be chosen as optimum and served to the client.

3. If no variant on the server is acceptable to the client, a 406 (No acceptable representation) HTTP error is returned to the client. The error message will also contain a list of all available variants, using the Description header from the type map (if available), allowing the client to resubmit a request for one of these variants.

4. For each variant in our list, multiply the quality factor from the client Accept header with the server's qs factor (which is taken from the type map, if used, or always 1.0 for MultiView). If one variant has a higher score than the rest, it is chosen and sent to the client. If the high score is tied between two or more variants, eliminate all other variants and continue.

5. The list has now been reduced to variants that have matching scores. Of these, consider only the client's language quality value, as specified in the Accept-Language header. If the Accept-Language header wasn't provided by the client, use the server's language preference in the LanguagePriority directive if one exists. If one variant has a higher language quality value than all the rest, it is chosen and sent to the client. If two or more variants tie, eliminate all other variants and continue.

6. Of the remaining variants, select the one that has the highest value for the content type. This value is available only if type maps are used; otherwise, the text/html content type is given a level of 2; all other media types are assigned a level of 0. If one variant has a higher value than all others, send it to the client. If two or more variants tie for the highest-level value, eliminate all other variants and continue.

7. From the variants remaining in our list (which should by now be growing quite short), select the variant with the highest character set priority, as determined from the Accept-Charset HTTP header provided by the client. If this header was not provided by the client, eliminate all variants that do not use the ISO-8859-1 character set (remembering that all text/html documents that are not specifically identified as using another character set are assumed to be in ISO-8859-1). If the list has now been reduced to a single variant, send it to the client. If the list still contains two or more variants, continue.

8. If the remaining list contains any variants that are *not* ISO-8859-1, we know that the client must have specified some other character set in its `Accept-Charset` header. So remove all ISO-8859-1 variants from the list and continue. If the list has only ISO-8859-1 variants, keep the list intact and continue.

9. Select the variants from the list that are specified in the client's `Accept-Encoding` HTTP header. If the client did not provide an `Accept-Encoding` header and our list contains only variants that are encoded, or only variants that are *not* encoded, continue. If the list has a mixture of encoded and unencoded variants, discard all the encoded variants to reduce the list to unencoded variants only.

10. Of the variants remaining in the list, select the one that has the smallest content length and serve it to the client. If two or more tie for the distinction of being smallest, continue.

11. If you reach this point and still have a list of at least two variants (seems unlikely, doesn't it?), select the first in the list (that is, the first defined in the type map if it is used, or the first alphabetically if using MultiView). Serve this file to the client.

In Sum

In closing this last chapter, it seems almost ironic to me that so little has been said about the information that Apache has the role of delivering to its clients. After all, the Web exists for the purpose of exchanging information. However, Web servers (like Apache) are only one component of the Web, and those servers are not responsible for the interpretation or rendering (display) of information. For that reason, there has been almost no discussion in this book of document-formatting standards like HTML. For the most part, the Apache server and its administrator require little knowledge of document content. The role of determining the content type of a document, deciding how to display it, or which external application to load to process the document could be left entirely up to the browser. Browsers could, for example, be instructed to interpret all files they receive with a filename extension .html as HTML-formatted text. That's a safe enough assumption. That's not how things work, however. Part of the role of the Web server is to provide its client with several important pieces of information about the document it is sending to that client.

Metainformation is information describing other information resources. Apache always sends several pieces of metainformation with the resources that it serves to clients. The metainformation is obtained from different sources and is often inferred from a disk file attribute (for example, the filename extension, or even the folder in which the file is located).

**Maintaining a
Healthy Server**

PART 4

Apache deals with four basic pieces of information about files: content type, natural (human-readable) language, character set, and encoding. In its simplest configuration, Apache determines these information attributes about a resource and simply informs the client (with the pertinent HTTP headers) of this information about the file it is serving. That's the purpose of the module mod_mime, discussed first in this chapter.

HTTP/1.1 provides additional headers (both client-request and server-response headers) to support *content negotiation*, in which the client (generally from a browser configuration) identifies required or desired attributes for the files it requests, and the server, in turn, offers information about the different resource versions it offers. Content negotiation is used whenever multiple versions of resources are available. The most common application for this capability is when a server supports multiple language versions of resources it hosts (often in alternate character sets).

Appendices

Apache Directives

Table A.1 lists all the directives included in the standard Apache distribution as of version 2.0.39. This is, of course, subject to change with each Apache revision. The columns represent the following information:

Directive   The name of the Apache directive.

Module   The name of the module that must be loaded and enabled in Apache for the directive to be available for use.

Context   Where in the server's configuration the directive may appear, which may be one or more of the following:

Server   The directive (indicated in the table by the letter S) can occur only in one of Apache's configuration files (usually `httpd.conf`, but also `srm.conf` and `access.conf`, if either of these now-obsolete files is used).

Virtual Host   The directive (indicated in the table by the letter V) can appear only inside a `<VirtualHost>` container directive, and it applies only to the relevant virtual host.

Container   The directive (indicated in the table by the letter D) can appear only inside `<Directory>`, `<File>`, or `<Location>` containers, which restrict its applicability.

.htaccess   The directive (indicated in the table by the letter H) can appear only inside a per-directory `.htaccess` file, and applies only to files that reside in that directory (if no override is in effect for the directive).

Override   For directives that can appear in an .htaccess context, this column lists the value that will enable the associated directive. This value must appear in an AllowOverride directive (unless the default value AllowOverride All is in effect). For example, the override value is FileInfo for the Action directive. Thus, the Action directive is enabled in an .htaccess file only if an AllowOverride FileInfo directive is already in effect. See "The AllowOverrides Directive" in Chapter 4.

Default   The default value for the directive, if any.

NOTE   A few of the modules in this table were not discussed in the book, as they are relevant only to Web page designers (content providers) and aren't related to Apache server administration.

Table A.1   Apache Directives

Directive	Module	Context	Overrides	Default
<Proxy>	mod_proxy	S,V	None	N/A
<ProxyMatch>	mod_proxy	S,V	None	N/A
AcceptPathInfo	Core	S,V,D,H	None	Default
AccessFileName	Core	S,V	None	.htaccess
Action	mod_actions	S,V,D,H	FileInfo	N/A
AddAlt	mod_autoindex	S,V,D,H	Indexes	N/A
AddAltByEncoding	mod_autoindex	S,V,D,H	Indexes	N/A
AddAltByType	mod_autoindex	S,V,D,H	Indexes	N/A
AddCharset	mod_mime	S,V,D,H	FileInfo	N/A
AddDefaultCharset	Core	S,V,D,H	None	Off
AddDescription	mod_autoindex	S,V,D,H	Indexes	N/A
AddEncoding	mod_mime	S,V,D,H	FileInfo	N/A
AddHandler	mod_mime	S,V,D,H	FileInfo	N/A
AddIcon	mod_autoindex	S,V,D,H	Indexes	N/A
AddIconByEncoding	mod_autoindex	S,V,D,H	Indexes	N/A
AddIconByType	mod_autoindex	S,V,D,H	Indexes	N/A

Table A.1 Apache Directives (*continued*)

Directive	Module	Context	Overrides	Default
AddInputFilter	mod_mime	S,V,D,H	FileInfo	N/A
AddLanguage	mod_mime	S,V,D,H	FileInfo	N/A
AddModuleInfo	mod_info	S,V,D,H	None	None
AddOutputFilter	mod_mime	S,V,D,H	FileInfo	N/A
AddType	mod_mime	S,V,D,H	FileInfo	N/A
Alias	mod_alias	S,V	None	N/A
AliasMatch	mod_alias	S,V	None	N/A
Allow	mod_access	D,H	Limit	N/A
AllowCONNECT	mod_proxy	S,V	None	443 (https) 563 (snews)
AllowOverride	Core	D	None	All
Anonymous	mod_auth_anon	D,H	AuthConfig	N/A
Anonymous_Authoritative	mod_auth_anon	D,H	AuthConfig	N/A
Anonymous_LogEmail	mod_auth_anon	D,H	AuthConfig	On
Anonymous_MustGiveEmail	mod_auth_anon	D,H	AuthConfig	On
Anonymous_NoUserID	mod_auth_anon	D,H	AuthConfig	Off
Anonymous_VerifyEmail	mod_auth_anon	D,H	AuthConfig	Off
AuthAuthoritative	mod_auth	D,H	AuthConfig	On
AuthDBMAuthoritative	mod_auth_dbm	D,H	AuthConfig	N/A
AuthDBMGroupFile	mod_auth_dbm	D,H	AuthConfig	N/A
AuthDBMType	mod_auth_dbm	D,H	AuthConfig	Default
AuthDBMUserFile	mod_auth_dbm	D,H	AuthConfig	N/A
AuthDigestAlgorithm	mod_auth_digest	D,H	AuthConfig	MD5
AuthDigestDomain	mod_auth_digest	D,H	AuthConfig	N/A
AuthDigestFile	mod_auth_digest	D,H	AuthConfig	N/A
AuthDigestGroupFile	mod_auth_digest	D,H	AuthConfig	N/A

Table A.1   Apache Directives (*continued*)

Directive	Module	Context	Overrides	Default
AuthDigestNcCheck	mod_auth_digest	S	None	Off
AuthDigestNonceFormat	mod_auth_digest	D,H	AuthConfig	N/A
AuthDigestNonceLifetime	mod_auth_digest	D,H	AuthConfig	300 (seconds)
AuthDigestQop	mod_auth_digest	D,H	AuthConfig	Auth
AuthGroupFile	mod_auth	D,H	AuthConfig	N/A
AuthName	Core	D,H	None	N/A
AuthType	Core	D,H	None	N/A
AuthUserFile	mod_auth	D,H	AuthConfig	N/A
BrowserMatch	mod_setenvif	S,V,D,H	FileInfo	N/A
BrowserMatchNoCase	mod_setenvif	S,V,D,H	FileInfo	N/A
CacheDefaultExpire	mod_cache	S	None	N/A
CacheDisable	mod_cache	S	None	N/A
CacheEnable	mod_cache	S	None	N/A
CacheFile	mod_file_cache	S	Indexes	N/A
CacheIgnoreCacheControl	mod_cache	S	None	N/A
CacheIgnoreNoLastMod	mod_cache	S	None	N/A
CacheLastModifiedFactor	mod_cache	S	None	N/A
CacheMaxExpire	mod_cache	S	None	N/A
CacheNegotiatedDocs	mod_negotiation	S	None	Off
CacheOn	mod_cache	S	None	Off
CharsetDefault	mod_charset_lite	S,V,D,H	FileInfo	N/A
CharsetOptions	mod_charset_lite	S,V,D,H	FileInfo	DebugLevel=0 NoImplicitAdd
CharsetSourceEnc	mod_charset_lite	S,V,D,H	FileInfo	N/A
CheckSpelling	mod_speling	S,V,D,H	Options	Off
ContentDigest	Core	S,V,D,H	None	Off

Table A.1   Apache Directives (*continued*)

Directive	Module	Context	Overrides	Default
CookieDomain	mod_usertrack	S,V,D,H	FileInfo	N/A
CookieExpires	mod_usertrack	S,V,D,H	FileInfo	N/A
CookieLog	mod_log_config	S,V	None	N/A
CookieName	mod_usertrack	S,V,D,H	FileInfo	Apache
CookieStyle	mod_usertrack	S,V,D,H	FileInfo	Netscape
CookieTracking	mod_usertrack	S,V,D,H	FileInfo	Off
coreDumpDirectory	Core	S	None	ServerRoot
CustomLog	mod_log_config	S,V	None	N/A
Dav	mod_dav	D	None	Off
DavDepthInfinity	mod_dav	D	None	Off
DavLockDB	mod_dav	S,V	None	N/A
DavMinTimeout	mod_dav	D	None	0
DefaultIcon	mod_autoindex	S,V,D,H	Indexes	N/A
DefaultLanguage	mod_mime	S,V,D,H	FileInfo	N/A
DefaultType	Core	S,V,D,H	None	text/html
DeflateBufferSize	mod_deflate	S	None	8096
DeflateFilterNote	mod_deflate	S	None	N/A
DeflateMemLevel	mod_deflate	S	None	9
DeflateWindowSize	mod_deflate	S	None	15
Deny	mod_access	D,H	Limit	N/A
Directory	Core	S,V	None	N/A
DirectoryIndex	mod_dir	S,V,D,H	Indexes	index.html
DirectoryMatch	Core	S,V	None	N/A
DocumentRoot	Core	S,V	None	N/A
ErrorDocument	Core	S,V,D,H	FileInfo	N/A

Table A.1 Apache Directives (*continued*)

Directive	Module	Context	Overrides	Default
ErrorLog	Core	S,V	None	logs/ error_log
Example	mod_example	S,V,D,H	None	N/A
ExpiresActive	mod_expires	S,V,D,H	Indexes	N/A
ExpiresByType	mod_expires	S,V,D,H	Indexes	N/A
ExpiresDefault	mod_expires	S,V,D,H	Indexes	N/A
ExtendedStatus	mod_status	S	None	Off
ExtFilterDefine	mod_exp_filter	S	None	N/A
ExtFilterOptions	mod_exp_filter	D	None	N/A
FileETag	Core	S,V,D,H	FileInfo	N/A
Files	Core	S,V,D,H	None	N/A
FilesMatch	Core	S,V,D,H	None	N/A
ForceLangaugePriority	mod_negotiation	S,V,D,H	FileInfo	Prefer
ForceType	Core	D,H	None	N/A
Group	prefork	S,V	None	-1 (group number)
Header	mod_headers	S,V,D,H	FileInfo	N/A
HeaderName	mod_autoindex	S,V,D,H	Indexes	N/A
HostnameLookups	Core	S,V,D	None	Off
IdentityCheck	Core	S	None	Off
IfDefine	Core	S,V,D,H	None	N/A
IfModule	Core	S,V,D,H	None	N/A
ImapBase	mod_imap	S,V,D,H	Indexes	http:// <servername>
ImapDefault	mod_imap	S,V,D,H	Indexes	nocontent
ImapMenu	mod_imap	S,V,D,H	Indexes	N/A

Table A.1   Apache Directives (*continued*)

Directive	Module	Context	Overrides	Default
Include	Core	S	None	N/A
IndexIgnore	mod_autoindex	S,V,D,H	Indexes	N/A
IndexOptions	mod_autoindex	S,V,D,H	Indexes	N/A
IndexOrderDefault	mod_autoindex	S,V,D,H	Indexes	N/A
ISAPIAppendLogToErrors	mod_isapi	N/A	N/A	N/A
ISAPIAppendLogToQuery	mod_isapi	N/A	N/A	N/A
ISAPIFileChache	mod_isapi	N/A	N/A	N/A
ISAPILogNotSupported	mod_isapi	N/A	N/A	N/A
ISAPIReadAheadBuffer	mod_isapi	N/A	N/A	N/A
KeepAlive	Core	S	None	Off
KeepAliveTimeout	Core	S	None	15 (seconds)
LanguagePriority	mod_negotiation	S,V,D,H	FileInfo	N/A
Limit	Core	S,V,D,H	None	N/A
LimitExcept	Core	S,V,D,H	None	N/A
LimitRequestBody	Core	S,V,D,H	None	0 (bytes)
LimitRequestFields	Core	S	None	100
LimitRequestFieldSize	Core	S	None	8190 (bytes)
LimitRequestLine	Core	S	None	8190 (bytes)
LimitXMLRequestBody	Core	S	None	1000000 (bytes)
Listen	prefork	S	None	N/A
ListenBackLog	prefork	S	None	511 (connections)
LoadFile	mod_so	S	None	N/A
LoadModule	mod_so	S	None	N/A
Location	Core	S,V	None	N/A

Table A.1 Apache Directives (*continued*)

Directive	Module	Context	Overrides	Default
LocationMatch	Core	S,V	None	N/A
LockFile	Core	S	None	logs/ accept.lock
LogFormat	mod_log_config	S,V	None	N/A
LogLevel	Core	S,V	None	warn
MaxClients	prefork	S	None	256
MaxKeepAliveRequests	Core	S	None	100
MaxRequestsPerChild	prefork	S	None	10000
MaxSpareServers	prefork	S	None	N/A
MaxThreadsPerChild	N/A	N/A	N/A	N/A
McacheMaxObjectCount	mod_mem_cache	S	None	1000
McacheMaxObjectSize	mod_mem_cache	S	None	10000 (bytes)
McacheMinObjectSize	mod_mem_cache	S	None	0 (bytes)
MCacheSize	mod_mem_cache	S	None	102400 (bytes)
MetaDir	mod_cern_meta	D	None	.web
MetaFiles	mod_cern_meta	D	None	Off
MetaSuffix	mod_cern_meta	D	None	.meta
MimeMagicFile	mod_mime_magic	S,V	None	N/A
MinSpareServers	prefork	S	None	5
MMapFile	mod_file_cache	S	Indexes	N/A
MultiviewsMatch	mod_mime	S,V,D,H	FileInfo	N/A
NameVirtualHost	Core	S	None	N/A
NoProxy	mod_proxy	S,V	None	N/A
NumServers	not in prefork MPM	N/A	N/A	N/A
Options	Core	S,V,D,H	None	All

Table A.1 Apache Directives (*continued*)

Directive	Module	Context	Overrides	Default
Order	mod_access	D,H	Limit	N/A
PassEnv	mod_env	S,V,D,H	FileInfo	N/A
PidFile	prefork	S	None	All
ProxyBlock	mod_proxy	S,V	None	N/A
ProxyDomain	mod_proxy	S,V	None	N/A
ProxyErrorOverride	mod_proxy	S,V	None	Off
ProxyIOBufferSize	mod_proxy	S,V	None	N/A
ProxyMaxForwards	mod_proxy	S,V	None	10
ProxyPass	mod_proxy	S,V	None	N/A
ProxyPassReverse	mod_proxy	S,V	None	N/A
ProxyPreserveHost	mod_proxy	S,V	None	Off
ProxyReceiveBufferSize	mod_proxy	S,V	None	N/A
ProxyRemote	mod_proxy	S,V	None	N/A
ProxyRemoteMatch	mod_proxy	S,V	None	N/A
ProxyRequests	mod_proxy	S,V	None	N/A
ProxyTimeout	mod_proxy	S,V	None	300 (seconds)
ProxyVia	mod_proxy	S,V	None	Off
ReadmeName	mod_autoindex	S,V,D,H	Indexes	N/A
Redirect	mod_alias	S,V,D,H	FileInfo	N/A
RedirectMatch	mod_alias	S,V,D,H	FileInfo	N/A
RedirectPermanent	mod_alias	S,V,D,H	FileInfo	N/A
RedirectTemp	mod_alias	S,V,D,H	FileInfo	N/A
RemoveCharset	mod_mime	D,H	None	N/A
RemoveEncoding	mod_mime	D,H	None	N/A
RemoveHandler	mod_mime	D,H	None	N/A

Table A.1 Apache Directives (*continued*)

Directive	Module	Context	Overrides	Default
RemoveInputFilter	mod_mime	D,H	None	N/A
RemoveLanguage	mod_mime	D,H	None	N/A
RemoveOutputFilter	mod_mime	D,H	None	N/A
RemoveType	mod_mime	D,H	None	N/A
RequestHeader	mod_headers	S,V,D,H	FileInfo	N/A
Require	Core	D,H	AuthConfig	N/A
RewriteBase	mod_rewrite	D,H	FileInfo	N/A
RewriteCond	mod_rewrite	S,V,D,H	FileInfo	N/A
RewriteEngine	mod_rewrite	S,V,D,H	FileInfo	Off
RewriteLock	mod_rewrite	S	None	N/A
RewriteLog	mod_rewrite	S,V	None	N/A
RewriteLogLevel	mod_rewrite	S,V	None	0
RewriteMap	mod_rewrite	S,V	None	N/A
RewriteOptions	mod_rewrite	S,V,D,H	None	N/A
RewriteRule	mod_rewrite	S,V,D,H	None	N/A
RLimitCPU	Core	S,V	None	Unset
RLimitMEM	Core	S,V	None	Unset
RLimitNPROC	Core	S,V	None	Unset
Satisfy	Core	D,H	None	Any/All
ScoreBoardFile	prefork	S	None	logs/ apache_status
Script	mod_actions	S,V,D	None	N/A
ScriptAlias	mod_alias	S,V	None	N/A
ScriptAliasMatch	mod_alias	S,V	None	N/A
ScriptInterpreterSource	Core	D,H	None	script
ScriptLog	mod_cgi	S	None	N/A

Table A.1 Apache Directives (*continued*)

Directive	Module	Context	Overrides	Default
ScriptLogBuffer	mod_cgi	S	None	1024 (bytes)
ScriptLogLength	mod_cgi	S	None	10385760 (bytes)
ScriptSock	mod_cgid	S	None	logs/cgisock
SendBufferSize	prefork	S	None	N/A
ServerAdmin	Core	S,V	None	N/A
ServerAlias	Core	V	None	N/A
ServerLimit	prefork	S	None	256
ServerName	Core	S,V	None	N/A
ServerPath	Core	V	None	N/A
ServerRoot	Core	S	None	/usr/local/ apache
ServerSignature	Core	S,V,D,H	None	Off
ServerTokens	Core	S	None	Full
SetEnv	mod_env	S,V,D,H	FileInfo	N/A
SetEnvIf	mod_setenvif	S,V,D,H	FileInfo	N/A
SetEnvIfNoCase	mod_setenvif	S,V,D,H	FileInfo	N/A
SetHandler	Core	S,V,D,H	None	N/A
SetInputFilter	Core	S,V,D,H	None	N/A
SetOutputFilter	Core	S,V,D,H	None	N/A
SSIEndTag	mod_include	S,V	None	-->
SSIErrorMsg	mod_include	S,V,D,H	All	an error occurred while pro- cessing this directive
SSIStartTag	mod_include	S,V	None	<!--

Table A.1 Apache Directives (*continued*)

Directive	Module	Context	Overrides	Default
SSITimeFormat	mod_include	S,V,D,H	All	%A, %d-%b-%Y %H:%M:%S %Z
SSIUndefinedEcho	mod_include	S,V	None	<!-- undef -->
SSLCACertificateFile	mod_ssl	S,V	None	N/A
SSLCACertificatePath	mod_ssl	S,V	None	N/A
SSLCARevocationFile	mod_ssl	S,V	None	N/A
SSLCARevocationPath	mod_ssl	S,V	None	N/A
SSLCertificateChainFile	mod_ssl	S,V	None	N/A
SSLCertificateFile	mod_ssl	S,V	None	N/A
SSLCertificateKeyFile	mod_ssl	S,V	None	N/A
SSLCipherSuite	mod_ssl	S,V	AuthConfig	N/A
SSLEngine	mod_ssl	S,V	None	Off
SSLMutex	mod_ssl	S	None	N/A
SSLOptions	mod_ssl	S,V,D,H	Options	N/A
SSLPassPhraseDialog	mod_ssl	S	None	builtin
SSLProtocol	mod_ssl	S,V	Options	All
SSLRandomSeed	mod_ssl	S	None	N/A
SSLRequire	mod_ssl	D,H	AuthConfig	N/A
SSLRequireSSL	mod_ssl	D,H	AuthConfig	N/A
SSLSessionCache	mod_ssl	S	None	none
SSLSessionCacheTimeout	mod_ssl	S,V	None	300 (seconds)
SSLVerifyClient	mod_ssl	S,V,D,H	AuthConfig	none
SSLVerifyDepth	mod_ssl	S,V,D,H	AuthConfig	1
StartServers	not in prefork MPM	N/A	N/A	N/A
StartThreads	not in prefork MPM	N/A	N/A	N/A

Table A.1   Apache Directives (*continued*)

Directive	Module	Context	Overrides	Default
SuexecUserGroup	mod_suexec	S,V	None	N/A
ThreadLimit	not in prefork MPM	N/A	N/A	N/A
ThreadsPerChild	not in prefork MPM	N/A	N/A	N/A
TimeOut	Core	S	None	300 msec
TransferLog	mod_log_config	S,V	None	N/A
TypesConfig	mod_mime	S	None	conf/ mime.types
UnsetEnv	mod_env	S,V,D,H	FileInfo	N/A
UseCanonicalName	Core	S,V,D,H	None	On
User	prefork	S	None	uid -1
UserDir	mod_userdir	S,V	None	public_html
VirtualDocumentRoot	mod_vhost_alias	S,V	None	N/A
VirtualDocumentRootIP	mod_vhost_alias	S,V	None	N/A
VirtualHost	Core	S	None	N/A
VirtualScriptAlias	mod_vhost_alias	S,V	None	N/A
VirtualScriptAliasIP	mod_vhost_alias	S,V	None	N/A
XBitHack	mod_include	S,V,D,H	Options	Off

Online References

This appendix lists the online sources of information (and in some cases, software) that I have found most useful as an Apache administrator. Along with many Web sites, you'll find some mailing lists and Usenet newsgroups. Entries are grouped into the following categories:

- Information about the Web and HTTP
- General Apache resources
- Information about Apache modules
- Information about Apache security
- General programming resources
- Information about PHP programming
- Information about Perl/CGI programming
- Information about Java programming

The URLs and addresses listed here were verified shortly before this book went to press, but all are subject to change.

WWW and HTTP Resources

Not surprisingly, the Web and its underlying protocol, HTTP, are among the most thoroughly documented subjects on the Internet.

HTTP: HyperText Transfer Protocol

`http://www.w3.org/Protocols`

Everything you could possibly ever want to know about the HyperText Transfer Protocol (HTTP) is at the World Wide Web Consortium's (W3C) site devoted to HTTP.

HTTP Made Really Easy

`http://www.jmarshall.com/easy/http`

Subtitled "A Practical Guide to Writing Clients and Servers," this is James Marshall's excellent simplification of the HTTP specification—what it is and how it works.

W3C: The World Wide Web Consortium

`http://www.w3.org`

Created in 1994, the World Wide Web Consortium works to promote and standardize the Web and to provide information to its community of developers. Great source for specifications for the official standards of many Web technologies (like HTTP, HTML, CSS, XML, XSL, XLST, URI/URL, and many more).

HyperText Transfer Protocol: HTTP/1.1

`http://www.w3.org/Protocols/rfc2616/rfc2616.html`

Request for Comments (RFC) 2616 is the specification that describes the latest version of the HyperText Transfer Protocol, version 1.1.

mnot: Web Caching

`http://www.mnot.net`

Mark Nottingham's Web-caching site contains a lot of information on Web caching, caching engines, and proxy servers, and how to control Web caching from the server.

Chart of MIME Types

`http://www.bc.edu/bc_org/tvp/email/helpers.shtml`

A handy reference list of MIME types and associations with their applications, provided by Boston College.

Persistent Client State HTTP Cookies (Netscape Cookies Specification)

`http://www.netscape.com/newsref/std/cookie_spec.html`

Netscape "invented" the Web cookie. This is where they specify how the technology should work.

The Virtual Library of WWW Development

```
http://wdvl.internet.com/Vlib
```

One of the oldest bookmarks I have, the WWW Virtual Library is a source of links on a lot of topics. You are sure to find a few links of interest.

History of the Web

Learning about the Web's history may or may not make you a better Apache administrator, but it's interesting and fun. Whenever you want to know about where the Web came from, start with these sources.

Chapter 2: A History of HTML

```
http://www.w3.org/People/Raggett/book4/ch02.html
```

This chapter from *Raggett on HTML 4* (Dave Raggett et al. Addison-Wesley Longman, 1998) provides a good historical look at the World Wide Web. It's got pictures, too!

Connected: An Internet Encyclopedia

```
http://www.FreeSoft.org/CIE/index.htm
```

A good searchable source for history and information of all kinds related to the Web.

Hobbes' Internet Timeline

```
http://www.isoc.org/guest/zakon/Internet/History/HIT.html
```

Considered the definitive Internet history, Hobbes' Timeline of the Internet has been around forever and continues to be updated with new developments.

General Apache Resources

These sites and mailing lists provide information about various aspects of Apache.

Apache HTTP Server Project

```
http://www.apache.org
```

The home page of the Apache Software Foundation, this is the definitive site for all things Apache, and it is the most important URL in this appendix.

Mailing List

To receive announcements of new Apache product releases and news, send a message with anything in the body of the message (or leave the body blank) to:

```
announce-subscribe@apache.org
```

Apache Directives

http://www.apache.org/docs/mod/directives.html

A list of the directives in all the standard Apache modules.

Apache Today

http://apachetoday.com

Excellent online publication filled with articles and links to all manner of Apache-related topics and news. Be sure to sign up for a free user account and their mailing list.

A User's Guide to URL Rewriting with the Apache Web Server

http://www.engelschall.com/pw/apache/rewriteguide

The best single piece of documentation available for mod_rewrite, by Ralf S. Engelschall, the module's author.

Apache Week

http://www.apacheweek.com

Another great publication, *Apache Week* is issued weekly. It's very newsy, with good feature articles, and it's a great way to keep up with Apache "happenings." Don't fail to be on their once-a-week mailing.

Mailing List

To receive *Apache Week* via e-mail, send a message to:

majordomo@apacheweek.com

The body of the message should contain

subscribe apacheweek

for a text-formatted mailing or

subscribe apacheweek-html

for HTML format.

Apache Toolbox

http://www.apachetoolbox.com/

Apache Toolbox is a shortcut to compiling Perl from source code. With a simple character-based menu, it allows the user to specify modules to be compiled and enabled, including all modules in the standard Apache distribution and many third-party modules (like mod_perl, mod_frontpage, and others). Not available for Apache 2.0, as of the publication of this book.

Microsoft FrontPage 2002 Server Extensions Resource Kit

http://officeupdate.microsoft.com/frontpage/wpp/serk

The FrontPage 2002 Server Extensions for Unix/Linux are part of this resource kit, and this is the site for all things related to the FP Server Extensions.

Newsgroup

Microsoft maintains this Usenet newsgroup for discussion of the FrontPage Extensions for Unix (note, this is *not* a Web site):

news://microsoft.public.frontpage.extensions.unix

O'Reilly's OnLamp.com Apache Site

http://www.onlamp.com/

This Web site includes technical information dedicated to Web developers and Apache administrators. As part of the O'Reilly Network, it devotes considerable space to books published and conferences organized by O'Reilly.

Ready-to-Run Software (FrontPage Extensions)

http://www.rtr.com/Ready-to-Run_Software/

The FrontPage 2002 Server Extensions for Unix/Linux were written by Ready-to-Run Software, Inc. This is an alternate site for the FP Extensions, and contains a FAQ and discussion group not available at the Microsoft site.

RPM Repository

http://rpmfind.net/

The best site for Linux RPM packages; it is mentioned as a source throughout this book.

The Web Robots Pages

http://www.robotstxt.org/wc/robots.html

The best site for information on Web robots: how they work, how to attract them to your site, and how to control the darned things when they do find you.

Web Server Comparisons

http://www.acme.com/software/thttpd/benchmarks.html

Although the information is quite dated, these are excellent comparisons of Web server performance in benchmark tests on various platforms. There's also good (still valid) information here on how the different Web servers differ technically.

Web Techniques

http://www.webtechniques.com

Although it was terribly unfortunate that *Web Techniques* magazine had to reinvent itself with a less technical focus, as *NewArchitect* (what a name, huh?), the entire archives of the old printed publication *Web Techniques* appear here. They go all the way back to 1996, with excellent examples and source code. Very programmer- and developer-oriented.

WebReference.com: The Webmaster's Reference Library

http://www.webreference.com

Covering all aspects of Web development, this site is a free service of internet.com Corporation.

Mailing List

Sign up at www.Webreference.com for weekday HTML mailings and/or a weekly text summary of articles on all manner of Web development topics. I recommend the weekly summary, as the daily mailings are large and repetitive.

Apache GUIs

http://gui.apache.org

A focus point to make sure that all Apache GUI projects are publicized.

Covalent Technologies

http://www.covalent.net/projects/comanche

Covalent Technology's site for the open-source Comanche Apache GUI configuration utility.

Apache on Linux Newsgroup

comp.infosystems.www.servers.unix

A newsgroup for all things related to Web servers for Unix/Linux platforms. Most of the discussion is directly relevant to Apache.

Resources for Apache Modules

These sites provide information about Apache's standard modules, discussed in Chapter 5, or about specific third-party modules.

Apache Standard Modules

http://httpd.apache.org/docs-2.0/mod/

Official documentation for all of the modules that are part of the Apache distribution.

Apache Module Registry

http://modules.apache.org

A registry service provided by the Apache Software Foundation for third-party modules, with a searchable database of links to sites where the modules can be obtained.

Apache::ASP Perl Module

http://www.nodeworks.com/asp

The official site for the commercially supported Apache::ASP module, which permits the use of Perl in Active Server Pages with Apache.

mod_perl FAQ

http://perl.apache.org/docs/2.0/

The source site for all Apache/mod_perl documentation.

Take23: *mod_perl* News and Resources

http://www.take23.org/

Great site for keeping up with changes in the mod_perl world. Great articles and pointers to mod_perl development sites.

Apache Security Resources

These sites provide information about Apache tools for implementing security (discussed in Chapters 13 and 14) or about specific security issues.

Apache-SSL

http://www.apache-ssl.org

Everything you could ever want to know about Apache-SSL, as discussed in Chapter 14.

CERT/CC: Understanding Malicious Content Mitigation

http://www.cert.org/tech_tips/malicious_code_mitigation.html

This page, published by the Computer Emergency Response Team (CERT) Coordination Center, describes a problem with malicious tags embedded in client HTTP requests.

mod_ssl: The Apache Interface to OpenSSL

    http://www.modssl.org

The official page for the mod_ssl implementation of SSL for Apache.

Mailing Lists

You can join the following mailing lists at http://www.modssl.org/support/:

    modssl-announce
    modssl-users

OpenSSL: The Open Source Toolkit for SSL/TLS

    http://www.openssl.org

Official page for the OpenSSL toolkit, which is used to provide a cryptography library
for other applications (like SSL).

SSLeay and SSLapps FAQ

    http://www2.psy.uq.edu.au/~ftp/Crypto

This FAQ, although it has not been updated in quite a few years, provides a lot of good
information on the SSLeay cryptographic library on which OpenSSL is based. Much of
the information here is still very useful.

General Programming Resources

These sites provide information about various programming topics that may be of
interest to Apache administrators, as discussed in Chapter 8.

ASP Today

    http://www.asptoday.com

Full of articles of interest to Active Server Page programmers.

Developer Shed: The Open-Source Web-Development Site

    http://www.devshed.com

Covers all aspects of Web programming.

Web Application Benchmarks

    http://www.chamas.com/bench/

Though sadly in need of an update, Joshua Chamas' site is oriented toward comparisons of programming methodologies, rather than hardware platforms.

EmbPerl: Embed Perl in Your HTML Documents

```
http://perl.apache.org/embperl
```

This is the site for `EmbPerl`, a set of Perl modules that implement embedded Perl code in HTML documents.

Mason HQ

```
http://www.masonhq.com/
```

This is the site for `Mason`, a set of Perl modules that implement embedded Perl code in HTML documents.

MySQL

```
http://mysql.com/
```

The source for all things related to the MySQL open-source relational database.

Mailing List

To subscribe to the main MySQL mailing list, send a message to this e-mail address:

```
mysql-subscribe@lists.mysql.com
```

libcurl

```
http://curl.haxx.se/libcurl/
```

A very interesting library of functions, implemented as a dynamically linkable library that implements a number of network based protocols (essentially, any protocol you can express as a URL, such as FTP, HTTP, and `telnet`) and can be used from within applications you write in any of a number of languages (e.g., C, Java, Perl, PHP, Python, Ruby, and many others). Many code examples provided.

Purple Servlet FAQ and Resources by Alex Chaffee

```
http://www.jguru.com/faq/Servlets
```

Hosted by JGuru (Alex Chaffee), this is a very valuable list of Frequently Asked Questions (and answers) on Java servlets.

The Server-Side Includes Tutorial

```
http://www.carleton.ca/~dmcfet/html/ssi.html
```

An excellent beginner's tutorial on implementing Server-Side Includes (SSI). The tutorial hasn't changed since 1995, but then neither has SSI (at least not substantially).

BigNoseBird.Com's Server-Side Includes Page

```
http://bignosebird.com/ssi.shtml
```

Another good guide to SSI. You might want to check out some of the other resources on the BigNoseBird site, although most are oriented toward site design rather than programming or Apache.

Webmonkey

```
http://hotwired.lycos.com/webmonkey
```

HotWired's "Web Developer's Resource," this is probably one of the hottest Web developer's sites on the Internet.

PHP Programming Resources

These sites provide information about the PHP hypertext preprocessor, discussed in Chapter 8.

PHP HyperText Preprocessor

```
http://www.php.net
```

The official PHP page, this is where to get PHP and where to learn about it. The online documentation is some of the best I've ever seen.

PHP: Links to Code Samples and Tutorials

```
http://www.php.net/links.php3
```

A page on the PHP site that contains links to a number of other sites offering instruction and useful sample code for PHP applications.

PHP: MySQL Tutorial

```
http://hotwired.lycos.com/webmonkey/databases/tutorials/tutorial4.html
```

This is a really super tutorial that shows how to use PHP as a front-end to a MySQL relational database.

PHPBuilder.com

```
http://phpbuilder.com/
```

A good resource site for PHP developers, with loads of programming examples.

Alternative PHP Cache

`http://apc.communityconnect.com/`

APC is the Alternative PHP Cache, which compiles and caches PHP scripts.

Perl/CGI Programming Resources

These sites and newsgroups provide information about Perl/CGI programming, as discussed in Chapter 8.

The Perl Language Home Page

`http://www.perl.com/`

Though commercially hosted, this site proclaims itself the official page of the Perl language and, hey, I'll buy that. I'd rather acknowledge their claim than that of the Microsoft/Activestate alliance, which would seem to also want to "own" the Perl language. If it has to do with Perl, you can find it here.

Apache/Perl Integration Project

`http://perl.apache.org`

Naturally very oriented toward the mod_perl module, this is the official site for Perl and Apache integration.

Mailing List

To subscribe to a mailing list for mod_perl, send an e-mail message to:

`modperl-request@apache.org`

CGI.pm: A Perl5 CGI Library

`http://stein.cshl.org/WWW/software/CGI/cgi_docs.html`

Author Lincoln Stein's official site for the CGI.pm Perl module.

FastCGI Home

`http://www.fastcgi.com`

The official page for FastCGI, as discussed in Chapter 8.

MM MySQL JDBC Drivers

http://www.worldserver.com/mm.mysql

The MM JDBC drivers are widely considered the best Java Database Connectivity drivers for MySQL, and the ones I use.

mod_perl Guide

http://perl.apache.org/docs/1.0/guide/

Actually far more than a "Guide," this is a very complete and indispensable set of documentation to the mod_perl module, and definitely required reading for anyone programming for mod_perl.

Getting Help and Further Learning

http://perl.apache.org/guide/help.html

Actually part of the mod_perl Guide, this page lists a number of good links to other sites for information on mod_perl.

The CGI Resource Index

http://cgi-resources.com

This is quite an old site, but with a new look, and it hosts a tremendous number of CGI samples. Most are in Perl, of course, but there are examples in C, Unix shell, and others.

The CPAN Search Site

http://search.cpan.org

The official repository of registered, supported Perl modules, with mirror sites around the world, this is the site to search for Perl modules. The modules found here are retrievable by the CPAN.pm module on Linux systems.

Perl Newsgroups

These are three of the most valuable newsgroups for discussing Perl:

comp.lang.perl.misc

The newsgroup for all things related to Perl. I've read this one faithfully for years.

comp.lang.perl.announce

Stay up-to-date on the new product announcements for Perl.

```
comp.lang.perl.module
```

A newsgroup for questions and discussions relating to Perl modules, not directly related to the Perl language itself.

Java Programming Resources

These sites provide information about programming with Java and related tools, as discussed in Chapter 8.

Blackdown JDK for Linux

```
http://www.blackdown.org
```

The most respected (for high performance) port of Sun Microsystem's Java Development Kit to Linux. Get your JDK for Linux and learn how to set it up here.

Java Server Pages Developer's Guide

```
http://java.sun.com/products/jsp/docs.html
```
A super tutorial on Java Server Pages by the writer of the JSP specification,
Sun Microsystems.

Java Server Pages Technology

```
http://java.sun.com/products/jsp
```

The official JSP page from Sun Microsystems. Links here to JSP information of all kinds.

Java Server Pages Technology: White Paper

```
http://java.sun.com/products/jsp/whitepaper.html
```

Good executive overview, or "white paper," on Java Server Pages.

JDBC Basics

```
http://java.sun.com/docs/books/tutorial/jdbc/basics/index.html
```

Learn the very basic skills necessary to use Java Database Connectivity (JDBC) with Java programs.

JDBC Guide: Getting Started

```
http://java.sun.com/products/jdk/1.1/docs/guide/jdbc/getstart/introTOC.doc.html
```

A good document from Sun that provides a very comprehensive look at JDBC programming.

Servlets

```
http://java.sun.com/docs/books/tutorial/servlets/TOC.html
```

Sun Microsystem's tutorial on Java servlets. A very good learning tutorial.

java.sun.com: The Source for Java Technology

```
http://www.javasoft.com
```

This is the pinnacle for all Java programming–related pages on Sun Microsystems' site. From here, you should be able to find just about any Java specification or implementation.

The Java Tutorial

```
http://java.sun.com/docs/books/tutorial
```

Nearly all of these online tutorials are worth working through. Most are online reprints of material available as the printed book *The Java Tutorial*, by Mary Campione and Kathy Walrath (Addison-Wesley, 1998).

Writing Java Programs

```
http://java.sun.com/tutorial/java/index.html
```

A good tutorial for those just starting out with Java programming, this site also provides a good introduction to object-oriented programming, classes, and namespaces.

Resin

```
http://www.caucho.com/
```

Caucho Technology provides this site for information about Resin. To subscribe to the Resin mailing list, send mail to:

```
resin-interest-request@caucho.com
```

with a body containing the one word:

```
subscribe
```

Usenet Newsgroup Archives

```
http://groups.google.com/
```

Following its acquisition of the Deja.com newsgroup archives, Google.com now maintains what was once known as Deja News, the most extensive archive of Usenet discussion groups available. Google Groups is a valuable resource for questions that have been asked and answered on Usenet newsgroups, and an invaluable historical archive (in my humble opinion).

Transferring Files to Apache

This book is devoted to the Apache Web server on Linux. For that reason, very little has been said about the client side of any Web connection, the browser component. Although the use of Web browsers running in Linux desktop environments is rapidly increasing, the majority of Web browsers in use on the Internet run on Windows-based PCs. The same is true of most Web application development and HTML editing systems; most are Windows products, and there are a surprising variety of them. I still use a couple of the older and more established HTML editing systems (HotDog from Sausage Software, and SoftQuad's HoTMetaL Pro).

The traditional Webmaster's role usually included a healthy amount of time spent creating Web pages. As the Internet becomes increasingly important in supporting business processes (especially in the areas of marketing, sales, and customer support), however, the tasks of site administration and page authoring are often separated. As an Apache administrator, you may have little need to know how to use HTML. For that reason, I've devoted little space to issues involving Web site authoring.

As an Apache administrator, even if you are only hosting pages composed by others, you need to provide some means by which the documents Apache delivers can be uploaded or moved to your Apache server. This is most commonly done using the ubiquitous File Transfer Protocol (FTP), and many Web-authoring tools have strong built-in support for FTP. Most readers will already be aware of FTP, but I will mention a strong FTP client utility that I've used for years and recommend to anyone who needs such a tool. Most of this appendix is devoted to two Apache "add-ons" that support client file uploading (or *publishing*, if you prefer the term), mod_put and the FrontPage Extensions for Linux.

Using Samba

On a local area network, the easiest way to transfer files from a Windows-based Web-authoring tool is to export directories using Samba, a suite of programs that is installed as an integral part of all major Linux distributions. Samba enables a Linux server to communicate with Windows systems (which must be running TCP/IP) using the Microsoft Server Message Block (SMB) networking protocol. In other words, Samba allows Linux to participate in a Windows network, as a file/print server or client. It even allows you to use the Microsoft user authentication schemes (MS-CHAP and NT domain authentication).

A complete description of Samba configuration is beyond the scope of this appendix. For more information on Samba, I recommend reading David Wood's *SMB HOWTO*, available from the Linux Documentation Project (www.linuxdoc.org) or the book *Linux Samba Server Administration* by Roderick W. Smith (Sybex, 2001).

> **WARNING** Samba should never be enabled on an Internet-connected server that is not protected by a firewall.

I will demonstrate how I shared my Apache DocumentRoot using Samba on my Linux server for access by Windows 98 and NT workstations on my local area network.

The first step is to create a password file for Samba. While it is possible to use Unix authentication with Windows 95/98 workstations, this will generally not work with Windows NT, 2000, or XP systems that have recent service packs installed. These do *not* attempt to authenticate users across a network with a plain-text password (the older LAN Manager style of user authentication used by Windows 95). I included the following statements in the smb.conf file:

```
encrypt passwords = yes
smb passwd file = /etc/smbpasswd
```

To create the initial smbpasswd file, it is easiest (particularly if you have a large number of accounts to manage) to use the mksmbpasswd.sh utility provided with Samba. In the following command line, mksmbpasswd.sh takes the Linux /etc/passwd file as input, and the output is redirected into a new file, /etc/smbpasswd:

```
# /usr/bin/mksmbpasswd.sh < /etc/passwd > /etc/smbpasswd
```

Then, after creating the password file, I assigned a new password to each authorized user, beginning with myself:

```
# smbpasswd caulds newpass
Password changed for user caulds.
```

I added the following section to the `httpd.conf` file to export my Apache `DocumentRoot` directory (which will be seen by Windows systems on the network as a share named `WebStuff`). Access is limited by setting `public` to `no`, which indicates that access to the file share will be granted only to the users on the `valid users` line. Both of these users must have a valid entry in the `/etc/smbpasswd` file. They both have write access to the share (`writeable = yes`).

```
[WebStuff]
comment = Apache DocumentRoot
path = /home/httpd/html
valid users = caulds csewell
public = no
writable = yes
```

Once I had Samba configured, the `WebStuff` folder on my Linux server was fully accessible from my NT workstation, as you can see in the view from Explorer illustrated in Figure C.1.

Figure C.1   Using Explorer to Access a Samba Share

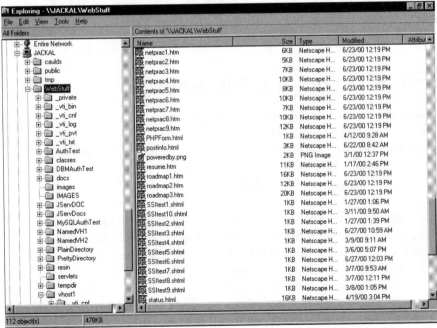

Using FTP

The best way to upload files to a Linux server from a remote host is using the File Transfer Protocol (FTP). FTP is supported by nearly every Linux server, and many client application options exist, from simple command-line tools to sophisticated GUI tools that allow easy drag-and-drop or mark-and-copy capability. The ability to copy an entire directory tree with one operation makes publishing Web resources via FTP far easier than you may realize (especially if you have only used the command-line version).

While tools like Netscape Composer and FrontPage 2002 seek to simplify Web publishing directly from the authoring tool itself, they alleviate only a small part of the work required to develop and publish Web pages. These are fine tools, but a good FTP client is something every Web developer and administrator should possess.

Several years ago, it seemed that the trend in file-transfer utilities on PCs was to merge them with the Windows Explorer so that files could be moved to remote servers with Explorer drag-and-drop operations. While I applaud the developers' efforts to present the user with a single unified interface to file management, trying to deal with a number of files in different physical locations through a single hierarchical tree structure is inefficient and often confusing. I've often dropped files into the wrong location because it had the same folder and filenames as another drive. Fortunately, most FTP clients still support the two-pane window, where local and remote files are clearly differentiated. I highly recommend a shareware utility called WS_FTP (available from www.ipswitch.com), which I've used since I first began administering a Web server in 1994. Figure C.2 shows a typical WS_FTP session in which I'm about to transfer a whole tree of files from my local hard disk to my Apache server.

Using the *mod_put* Module

Another tool for file transfer takes advantage of the HTTP request method PUT, which was specified as optional in HTTP/1.0 but is standardized in HTTP/1.1. Clients use PUT to send a resource (usually a local disk file) to the server, by specifying a URL that identifies a location where the server should place the resource. In other words, PUT allows client uploading of files. While the POST method in HTTP/1.0 permitted clients to send resources, these were sent in a stream to the server. A server application (usually a CGI file that received the stream on its stdin file handle) had to parse this stream into its components, whether it consisted of form input or entire files. PUT is designed specifically for file uploads. It allows the HTTP client to say to the server, "Here's a file; store it in /home/caulds/stuff/MyLogo.jpg."

Figure C.2   Using WS_FTP to upload Web files

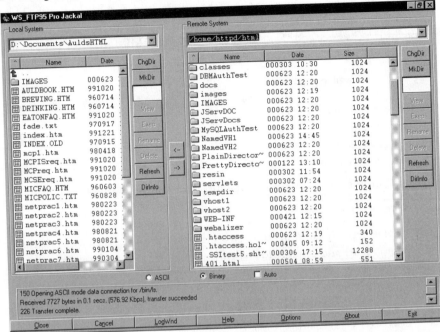

> **NOTE**   As this book goes to press, an Apache 2.0 version of mod_put is not available. The examples and information given here are from the Apache 1.3 version of mod_put, but should apply to the 2.0 version upon its release.

A small third-party module called mod_put implements both the HTTP/1.1 PUT and DELETE methods in Apache. Standard Apache, without this module, does not support those HTTP/1.1 methods. Although mod_put isn't a new module, it has never been one of the modules accepted as part of the standard Apache distribution. I believe this is because allowing Web clients to upload files to your server can be very risky, unless the administrator has given special attention to system security by allowing uploads only into directories designated for that purpose.

The mod_put module has been included with Red Hat's Apache distribution (it's installed by the Apache RPM on the Red Hat Linux distribution CD) and is loaded as a DSO module by Apache on Red Hat Linux systems.

If you're using a different Linux distribution, you can download mod_put from its author's site at http://hpwww.ec-lyon.fr/~vincent/apache/mod_put.html or find a link to a source at modules.apache.org. The module is packaged as a .gz archive (mod_put.tar.gz), which contains the C source code for the module and an HTML-formatted page of documentation. Download the file into any directory and extract its contents:

```
# ls -al mod_put_tar.gz
-rw-r--r--   1 caulds    caulds        5021 Jun 22 10:02 mod_put_tar.gz
# tar xvzf mod_put_tar.gz
mod_put-1.3/
mod_put-1.3/mod_put.html
mod_put-1.3/mod_put.c
```

Change into the newly created source directory for the module:

```
# cd mod_put-1.3
```

The archive actually contains only two files, the .c source file (which is the only necessary component) and a single HTML-formatted page of documentation:

```
# ls -al
total 18
drwx------   2 20       gopher   1024 May 11  1999 .
drwxr-xr-x  37 caulds   root     4096 Jun 22 10:03 ..
-rw-------   1 20       gopher   6892 May 11  1999 mod_put.c
-rw-------   1 20       gopher   5455 May 11  1999 mod_put.html
```

Installation of mod_put, including the necessary modifications to the httpd.conf file, is a simple single-step operation using the apxs utility. The following command line will compile the module as a DSO, place it into the libexec directory under the Apache installation, and make the necessary modifications to Apache's httpd.conf file to load and enable the module when the server is started:

```
# /usr/local/apache2/bin/apxs -c -i -a mod_put.c
gcc -DLINUX=2 -DMOD_SSL=206104 -DUSE_HSREGEX -DEAPI -DUSE_EXPAT
➥   -I../lib/expat-1
ite -DUSE_RANDOM_SSI -DUSE_PARSE_FORM -fpic -DSHARED_MODULE
➥   -I/usr/local/apache1
_3_12/include  -c mod_put.c
gcc -shared -o mod_put.so mod_put.o
cp mod_put.so /usr/local/apache1_3_12/libexec/mod_put.so
chmod 755 /usr/local/apache1_3_12/libexec/mod_put.so
[activating module `put' in
/usr/local/apache2/conf/httpd.conf]
# grep mod_put /usr/local/apache2/conf/httpd.conf
LoadModule put_module            libexec/mod_put.so
```

The most important mod_put directives, EnablePut and EnableDelete, enable or disable the HTTP/1.1 PUT and DELETE request methods for a single directory or for all resources accessed with a specific request URL. While mod_put directives are valid in <Directory> and <Location> containers, I find that it is always best to combine these directives with a user authentication and authorization scheme in .htaccess files. This ensures that only authorized users can use these methods to upload files into the affected directory or delete files from it.

WARNING Always ensure that write access to files using mod_put is limited to trusted users and that the module is enabled only for specific directories that you keep a close eye on.

For example, the following .htaccess file uses basic file-based authentication to permit only two users (caulds and csewell) to upload files into my personal home directory (as described in Chapter 4), and also to prohibit both users from using the HTTP/1.1 DELETE method to remove files from it:

```
# /home/caulds/public_html/.htaccess
#
EnablePut On
EnableDelete Off
AuthType Basic
AuthName "CAulds personal Web"
AuthUserFile /usr/local/apache2/auth/userfile
require user caulds csewell
```

mod_put provides one additional directive, umask. This directive is used like its Linux counterpart to set the new-file creation bitmask (expressed in octal). This bitmask is used to determine the file access permissions assigned to all new files created by mod_put. The default value of 0007 sets the permissions on newly created files to 770, which means that the file owner and group have read, write, and execute or full access and all others have no access. If I change the default bitmask, I usually include the following directive in my .htaccess file:

```
umask 0037
```

A file created with this umask in effect will have permissions set to 740 (or read/write/execute access for the file owner, read-only access for group members, and no access for all others). If you don't want to do the octal math yourself, Table C.1 is provided as a helpful aid in determining the bitmask value for each possible combination of access permissions. For example, the octal value of the bitmask used to grant read-only privileges is 3 (in octal). Your umask command would contain a 3 in the second position to grant read-only access to the file owner, in the third position for the group, and in the last position for all users. A umask command that will cause new files to be created with full access assigned to the owner, read and execute for the group owner, and read-only access to all other users would look like this:

    umask 0023

Table C.1   Numeric umask File Modes

	0	1	2	3	4	5	6	7
Read Access	X	X	X	X				
Write Access	X	X			X	X		
Execute Access	X		X		X		X	

While mod_put can be used to upload files from any client application that can submit an HTTP/1.1 PUT command (usually a Web page in a browser), one of the most common uses of this module is to support the Composer component of Netscape Communicator. Although Netscape Composer is not the most full-featured Web-authoring system available, I've been impressed with its ease of use and convenience. It's great for those with relatively light demands for HTML composition. Figure C.3 shows a typical use of Netscape Composer. Here I've opened an HTML page from my server in Composer (which also downloads all supporting files like embedded images). I used the Composer editor to modify the page and then used the Publish option to place it back on the server.

FrontPage 2002 Extensions

Included in the FrontPage CD is a suite of programs called the FrontPage Extensions for Unix, which makes it easy for users of Microsoft's FrontPage Web-authoring application to publish Web pages to an Apache server and manage the pages already there. Users of FrontPage access FrontPage webs (a "web" in FrontPage is essentially a collection of pages that functions as a single Web site and is equivalent to a virtual host or user directory on an Apache server) by URL. To access and manage the root FrontPage web on my server (which corresponds to my Apache DocumentRoot), you would enter the URL http://jackal.hiwaay.net/ as the "location" of the published web. FrontPage webs, therefore, are already valid directories, virtual hosts, or user directories on the Apache server.

FrontPage 2002 is, of course, Microsoft's HTML-authoring application, once the most widely used software of its kind. Because of the popularity of FrontPage, nearly every major Web-hosting service once provided FrontPage webs for its clients. Although the provision of FrontPage Extensions by Web-hosting services is no longer the absolute given it once was, FrontPage is still in use by a large number of these Web-hosting services. FrontPage support is still provided by a healthy percentage of the sites surveyed each month by SecuritySpace.com, and it is one of the most popular Apache add-ons.

Figure C.3   Netscape Composer using the functionality provided by `mod_put`

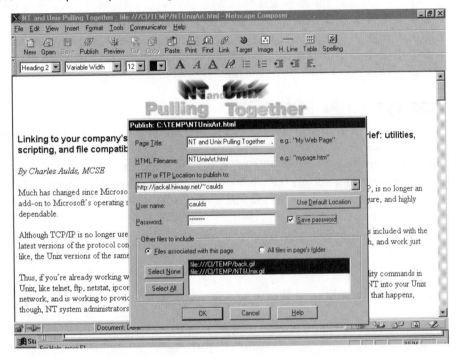

Obtaining the FrontPage Extensions

FrontPage Extensions for Unix is available from Microsoft or from a company called Ready-to-Run Software (`www.rtr.com/Ready-to-Run_Software/`). You can get it from either place, though Ready-to-Run seems to release new versions and patches before they appear on the Microsoft site. In either case, make sure you download two files. The first is the installation script (`fp_install.sh`), which is used to install the second file, the FrontPage Extensions themselves. The version of this file for Linux is named fp50.linux.tar.Z if you download it from Microsoft, or `fp50.linux.tar.gz` if you get it from `www.rtr.com`. The files are identical when uncompressed.

The installation is fairly straightforward. You run the `fp_install.sh` shell script, and answer the questions by pointing it to the FrontPage archive (the `.Z` or `.gz` file, as the case may be), to your Apache executable, and to a utility (`zcat` on Linux) that can extract the contents of the archive.

I won't go through the process of installing FrontPage Extensions for Linux, because, as of this writing, no Apache 2.0 version exists. Indeed, the Extensions may never be released for Apache 2.0 since the more standard WebDAV is poised to replace the proprietary FrontPage Extensions. However, for those who have chosen to use and install the Front-Page Extensions for Apache/Linux, I'll demonstrate the process of setting up FrontPage webs, which is something usually done for individuals (as in the case of an ISP) or for groups of developers working on the same project or Web site.

Adding FrontPage Webs

When you have installed FrontPage Extensions, it will support only the root FrontPage web of our server (which maps to the location defined by Apache's `DocumentRoot` directive). In many cases, this is wholly sufficient. There are also two types of FrontPage webs that serve files outside the scope of the root FrontPage web: any virtual hosts we have defined (either name- or IP-based), and user directories (accessed using a URL ending in `~username`). These were discussed in Chapter 6, and they should be created on your server as outlined in that chapter before you attempt to create a FrontPage web for each of them. The creation of a FrontPage web only allows a FrontPage user to manage a virtual host or user directory that Apache already knows about.

A command-line utility called `fpsrvadm.exe` is provided with the FrontPage Extensions to create additional FrontPage webs. I'll demonstrate how it is used to create both virtual and subwebs in this section. The documentation for the utility is a bit difficult to locate, but you'll find it on the FrontPage 2002 Server Extensions Resource Kit Web site at `officeupdate.microsoft.com/frontpage/wpp/serk/adfpsr.htm`.

FrontPage Extensions for Unix/Linux also comes with an optional patch for the Apache server that makes it is possible for users to create their own subwebs using the FrontPage client application. Most administrators who maintain FrontPage Extensions for multiple developers (for example, a Web hosting service that supports FrontPage clients) will want to apply this source patch and recompile Apache.

Virtual Webs

For each virtual FrontPage web on your server for which you intend to support web publishing from FrontPage, you need to run `fpsvradm.exe` using the following syntax:

```
# fpsrvadm.exe -o install -p 80 -m virtualWeb -u AdminName
    -pw AdminPassword -t server_type -s httpd.conf  -xu UNIXUserName
    -xg UNIXGroupName
```

Where:

-o is the operation to be performed; use -o install to install a new FrontPage web for a virtual server.

-p gives the port number of the web.

-m is the domain name of the new virtual server.

-u is the username of the FrontPage web's administrator. This administrator can add authors using the FrontPage client.

-pw is the password of the FrontPage web's administrator.

-t is the server type. Use apache-fp if you've patched your Apache server to support FrontPage Extensions, or apache for an unpatched server.

-s specifies the full path to the server's configuration file.

-xu is the Linux user account that the FrontPage Server Extensions will use; files published by FrontPage will be given this account owner.

-xg is the Linux group account that the FrontPage Server Extensions will use; files published by FrontPage will be given this group account owner.

Here's the command I used to install FrontPage Extensions for a name-based virtual host on my system:

```
# fpsrvadm.exe -o install -t apache-fp -m vhost1.hiwaay.net
➡   -u caulds -pw mysecret -s "/usr/local/apache2/conf/httpd.conf"
➡   -xu nobody -xg nobody
Starting install, port: vhost1.hiwaay.net:80, web: "root web"


Creating web http://vhost1.hiwaay.net
Chowning Content in service root web
Chmoding Extensions in service root web
Install completed.
```

Adding Subwebs or User Webs

You use fpsvradm.exe to create a subweb or user web at a specified directory within an existing FrontPage web. Note that, instead of specifying the –o install command, this form of the command uses –o create. The syntax is:

```
# fpsrvadm.exe -o create -p 80 -Web subwebname -xu unixuser
➡   -xg unixgroup -u username -pw password
```

Where:

-o is the operation to be performed by fpsvradm.exe; use create to create a new subweb or user web.

-p is the port number of the new subweb.

-xu is your Linux user account (which must exist in /etc/passwd).

-xg is your Linux group account (which must exist in /etc/groups).

-u is the FrontPage user ID (which does not need to match a Linux account).

-pw is the FrontPage user password.

-t is the type of Apache server (apache or apache-fp).

-s is the path to your httpd.conf file.

Here's an example of the command line I used to install a FrontPage subweb matching my user account:

```
# fpsrvadm.exe -o install -p 80 -w "~caulds" -xu "caulds"
➥  -xg "mypass" -u "CharlesA" -p w "FPpasswd"
Starting create, port: 80, web: "~caulds"

Creating web http://jackal.hiwaay.net/~caulds
Chowning Content in service ~caulds
Chmoding Extensions in service /~caulds
Install completed.
```

Information about FrontPage Extensions

As mentioned earlier, the FrontPage Extensions for Unix are developed for Microsoft by Ready-to-Run Software (www.rtr.com) and are available from RtR's Web site or directly from Microsoft (http://msdn.microsoft.com/library/en-us/dnservext/html/fpse02unix.asp).

Both sites contain a lot of good documentation. Most of the documentation I used to install and set up FrontPage on my Apache server was linked from Microsoft's FrontPage Server Extensions Resource Kit page (officeupdate.microsoft.com/frontpage/wpp/serk), but RtR's Web site features a "must-see" FAQ and a discussion group that has answers and solutions to a large number of questions and problems. See www.rtr.com/fpsupport/documentation.htm for both of these online resources. Another source for information on the FrontPage Extensions is the Usenet newsgroup, microsoft.public.frontpage.extensions.unix.

While FrontPage Extensions is still important to many Apache administrators, it is on WebDAV and the mod_dav Apache module that I suggest you focus your attention, and it is to that module that I now turn my own.

Apache *mod_dav*

While Microsoft was pushing its proprietary FrontPage Extensions for Web servers, the Internet standards bodies weren't sitting idly by. The result of their efforts was the creation of a specification for Web-based document authoring and versioning known as the Distributed Authoring and Versioning system, which is far more popularly known simply as WebDAV. WebDAV is a very simple system that consists of a set of extensions to the HTTP protocol to allow client access to resources on a Web server. Proposed as an "official" extension to the HTTP protocol and specified in RFC 2418 (http://asg.web.cmu.edu/rfc/rfc2518.html) and the much more recent RFC 3253, which adds document versioning extensions, WebDAV took a little while to catch on, but its use is rapidly increasing. WebDAV is now supported in every major Web server and is a "feature" in most applications used to author Web pages.

WebDAV operations are quite simple, allowing a WebDAV client application to create new resources on a Web server, delete resources, or open existing Web-based resources (with locking to prevent two clients from opening the same resource). WebDAV seems likely to replace the far more popular Microsoft FrontPage Extensions for working with Web server–based resources, except, perhaps, at sites that use FrontPage extensively for Web site development. Microsoft seems committed to supporting WebDAV in its products, perhaps as a replacement for their proprietary FrontPage Extensions.

The list of WebDAV client applications is always growing, so I won't try to list them or describe any single one of them, because each supports WebDAV in a different fashion. Some of the applications that now support WebDAV will already be familiar to most readers. These include most Adobe applications (GoLive, Acrobat, FrameMaker, Illustrator), applications in office suites like OpenOffice and Microsoft Office XP/2000 (using Web folders), HTML editors like Macromedia Dreamweaver and SoftQuad's HoTMetaL and XMetaL, and version management utilities like PVCS from MERANT. A more current list is maintained at the official site of the IETF WebDAV Working Group (http://ftp.ics.uci.edu/pub/ietf/webdav/). Web developers and administrators of WebDAV-enabled servers will find much useful news and information about WebDAV at http://www.webdav.org/, an informal site maintained to support the WebDAV community.

In most cases, WebDAV client applications adapt the WebDAV HTTP extensions to existing methods of working with resources. A WebDAV client application with a GUI interface (like a Microsoft Office application) uses traditional File menu options (like File➤ Open, File➤ Save, and File➤ Close) to manipulate Web resources in exactly the same manner as local disk files or files stored on a network-shared drive. Another application (that Linux users may find quite useful) is Cadaver (URL), a command-line WebDAV client utility. Cadaver uses FTP-like commands that are already familiar to most Linux users (get, put, mget, mput, and pwd). Cadaver can be installed in seconds using an RPM and used immediately without configuration.

In Apache 2.0, WebDAV support (through mod_dav) is built into the server when the --enable-most option is used to configure Apache for compilation. WebDAV support can also be "turned on" by the --enable-dav option (though, oddly, no --disable-dav switch was provided). Once mod_dav is made available to the Apache server, the only thing that then needs to be done to use it is to turn it on, usually within a container for specific directories, for example:

```
<Location /protectedDAVdocs>
   Dav On
</Location>
```

Note that the example shown will allow WebDAV access to all resources in /protectedDAVdocs, without discrimination, which is a very poor practice. You might well wonder how WebDAV protects resources from being accessed by "undesirable" clients. Well, it doesn't; user authorization is not a part of the WebDAV specification. As an extension to HTTP, WebDAV does not reproduce functionality already in the HTTP protocol. Since security and user authentication are not part of WebDAV, resources are protected from unwanted access by using exactly the same methods discussed in Chapter 13, which includes information on securing WebDAV-accessible resources. In short, to protect WebDAV resources, make sure that DAV is enabled only in containers (or using .htaccess files in WebDAV-accessible directories) that are already protected by conventional user authentication/authorization methods, much like this:

```
<Location /protectedDAVdocs>
   Dav On
   AuthType Basic
   AuthName DAV
   AuthUserFile conf/user.pass
   Require user
</Location>
```

It probably goes without saying that the resources protected by the container shown above might also be subject to SSL encryption and server authentication, as described in Chapter 14. While resource security and access restriction is the most important consideration in setting up mod_dav, you should bear in mind that security and user authorization are not WebDAV functions.

Support for WebDAV is provided at the filesystem level by Microsoft operating systems, as long as the Web Folders extension to Microsoft Internet Explorer (first introduced way back with IE 5) has been installed. This is a really neat feature that will escape the notice of most users; chances are, your PC has built-in WebDAV client capability you didn't even know about (mine did). You can find out by opening My Network Places, either from the Desktop or from Windows Explorer. If you have installed the Web Folders component of IE, you'll see an Add Network Place option. Clicking this option will bring up a Wizard dialog like the one shown in Figure C.4. To access a WebDAV server, you must enter a URL for the WebDAV resource "collection" on the server. Figure C.4 shows the URL I would use to access the /protectedDAVdocs resources I specified in the Apache examples shown earlier.

Figure C.4   Microsoft Add Network Place Wizard

If the WebDAV collection is protected in some fashion (as it should be), you'll be presented by the familiar login dialog (shown in Figure C.5) before the Web folder can be mounted like any other shared folder.

Figure C.5   Logging into a WebDAV collection

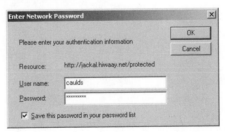

The final phase of the Wizard will allow you to assign a name to the new Web folder (Figure C.6); this name is arbitrary and should be chosen as a meaningful reference to the WebDAV resource collection.

Figure C.6 Naming the Web folder

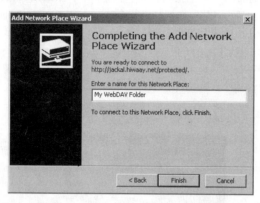

Upon completion of this simple, intuitive process, you'll be able to see a new shared folder in Explorer (Figure C.7), into which you can save new Web pages. In other resources, such as images, you can edit existing files, which will be locked by WebDAV on the server side. It's very cool when you think about it, and Microsoft's support for the WebDAV standard, without attempts to control or own it, is a very welcome boost for WebDAV.

Figure C.7 WebDAV Web Folder in Explorer

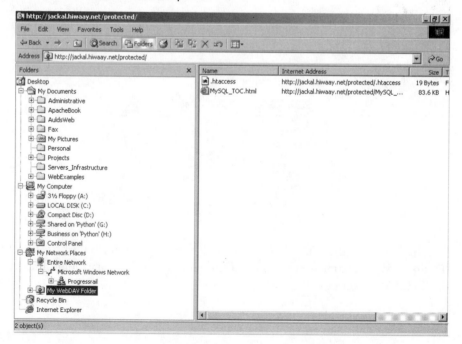

Using Apache
Documentation Effectively

Because of the decentralized, modular approach by which it has been developed and extended, Apache is the work of a large number of developers, scattered all over the globe. It should come as no surprise, then, that the documentation for Apache is not all located in any one place, but is also scattered across the Internet. In fact, many of the core developers of the Apache Software Foundation have provided valuable documentation on the use of their respective parts of Apache as articles you can find on the excellent Webzines like *Apache Today* and *Apache Week* (see Appendix B).

Many of the third-party add-on modules to Apache are documented by README files and HTML pages provided with the source files. Look for these whenever you download and install a new module that is not one of the Apache standard modules. The Web sites for these modules usually include good documentation, often supplemented with tutorials, FAQ lists, and online discussion forums. Always visit these sites when you install a new module and familiarize yourself with what's available there, especially if the module is extensive (like mod_ssl, for example).

Apache is documented very well (if not extensively), according to the loosely standardized documentation format used by the Apache Software Foundation. The Apache documentation is always available online at www.apache.org/docs. This same set of documentation (without the search features) is also provided with the source distribution of Apache.

Figure D.1 shows the main documentation page for Apache 2.0.

Figure D.1 Apache 2.0 documentation

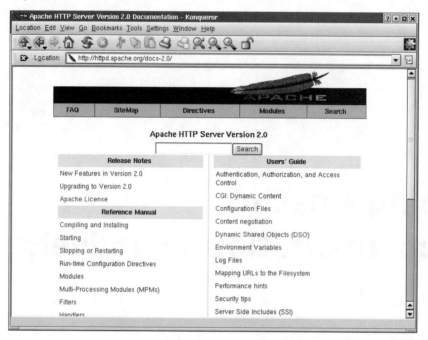

Figure D.2 Documentation for Apache directives

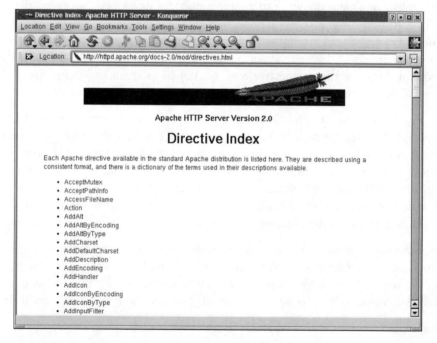

Figure D.3   Documentation for Apache standard modules

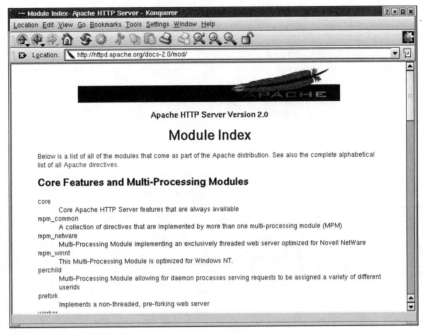

From this page, you can directly access the two most important pages used to document the Apache server and the standard Apache modules distributed with it. These are accessed through the Directives link (Figure D.2) and the Modules link (Figure D.3). These pages are actually different indexes into the documentation pages for the Apache modules. Each Apache module is documented through a single Web page that provides examples and syntax for each directive supplied to Apache by the module.

Since either of these links leads directly to the documentation page for selected modules (or to the directive within that page, if you choose), the documentation pages are the same for both the modules and the Apache runtime directives used to control them. I'll describe a typical documentation page to help you understand the documentation for both Apache modules and directives.

Figure D.4 shows the documentation for the `UseCanonicalName` directive, part of the core module and an integral part of the Apache server.

As Figure D.4 illustrates, each page includes the following information:

Syntax   Shows the format of the directive, as it should appear in the Apache configuration file. In the `UseCanonicalName` directive, you can see that the directive is used with one of three keywords (`on`, `off`, or `DNS`) appearing immediately behind it.

Figure D.4 Documentation for UseCanonicalName

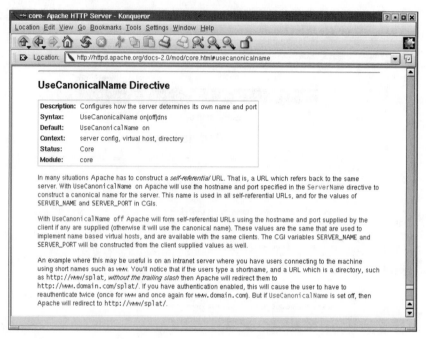

Default Indicates default values for directives. If no default value for a directive has been defined, the value should be indicated as None. Otherwise, the default value is usually shown as a complete and valid use of the entire directive in an httpd.conf file. You will find that some of these defaults are actually placed in Apache's default httpd.conf file, even though their inclusion is unnecessary. This is done for clarity, so that the default behavior is made obvious and explicit. Default values are very important—possibly the most important thing to know about most directives—because they determine the behavior of Apache if the directive is omitted from the server configuration. In that sense, the behavior of an unmodified Apache server is almost completely defined by the default values of its core directives and of the directives supplied by all its active modules.

Context Indicates the scope in which a directory is valid. The value can be any one (or more) of the following:

server config The directive applies to the entire server configuration, but it may not appear in narrower scopes (such as a <VirtualHost> or <Directory> container). Most directives that are valid in the server config context are also valid in these containers, but this must be explicitly stated. A directive that operates only in the server config context (a good example is the Listen directive) must not appear in any other context.

virtual host   The directive may appear inside a `<VirtualHost>` container.

directory   The directive may appear inside `<Directory>`, `<Files>`, and `<Location>` containers.

.htaccess   The directive is valid when it appears inside an `.htaccess` file and has a per-directory scope.

Override (not shown in the image)   Indicates which configuration overrides must be in effect for the directive to be processed if it is found inside an `.htaccess` file. Unless the controlling override for a directive has been explicitly activated for a directory (by an `AllowOverride` directive set for that directory or one of its parent directories), the directive is ignored if found in an `.htaccess` file in that directory. For example, the controlling override for all directives supplied by authentication modules is `AuthConfig`. Unless the `AuthConfig` override has been activated for a directory, directives used to implement authentication schemes (for example, `Require`, `AuthName`, and `AuthGroupFile`) are ignored if found in an `.htaccess` file for that directory. The Overrides column in Appendix A indicates which overrides must be in effect before a directive can be used in an `.htaccess` context.

Status   Specifies one of the following four values to indicate the degree to which the directive is integrated into the Apache server:

Core   Means that the directive is a part of the Apache core and cannot be removed or disabled; it is always available for use.

Base   Indicates that the directive is supplied by one of the standard Apache modules and is part of the base distribution. The module that supplies the directive is compiled into the standard Apache product; however, its use is optional and it can be removed.

Extension   Means that the directive is supplied by one of the standard Apache modules and is part of the base distribution. The module that supplies the directive is not compiled into the standard Apache product, however, and it must be explicitly compiled and enabled before the directive can be used.

Experimental   Indicates that the directive is being supplied as part of a module that is not necessarily supported by the Apache development team. In other words, this is a directive to use at your own risk.

Module   Names the module that supplies the directive.

When Apache is installed, as part of the installation, it places a copy of the complete documentation for the installed Apache version under the directory defined by the `DocumentRoot` directive in the default `httpd.conf` file. This documentation is available from the default home page for the new server (Figure D.5).

Figure D.5 The default home page for a newly installed Apache server includes a link to the documentation.

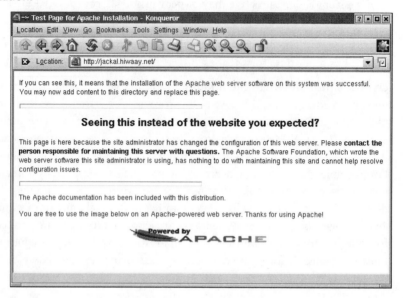

The documentation pages are most quickly and conveniently accessed when they are maintained on your own server. If you modify the location of your Apache DocumentRoot directory (as I recommended in Chapter 3), this documentation will probably no longer be readable from a Web browser. To make the Apache documentation accessible from the new Web server, you can copy it to your new DocumentRoot directory (or create a symbolic link to it), but I find it more convenient to simply provide an alias to the documentation file. The following Alias directive will accomplish that:

```
Alias /ApacheDocs "/usr/local/apache2/htdocs/manual"
```

Now, the docs can be accessed with the following URL:

```
http://jackal.hiwaay.net/ApacheDocs
```

While the documentation pages provided with Apache are complete, viewing them from your own server (while convenient) is limited in two ways. First, the documentation will not be updated until you install a newer version of Apache, and second, you will not have the search capability of the Apache Web site (although you will have a link to the main Apache site for searches). For quick lookups of directive usage, though, you'll save time by referencing the documentation on your server. Consider creating a hyperlink to it on your home page.

Index

Note to Reader: In this index, **boldfaced** page numbers refer to primary discussions of the topic; *italics* page numbers refer to figures.

Index

V

W

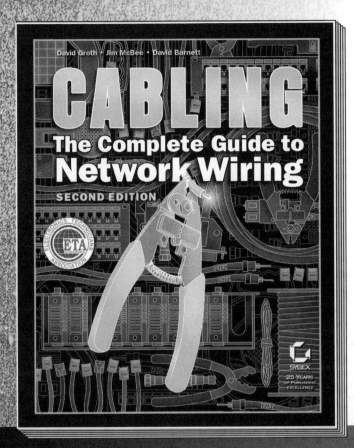

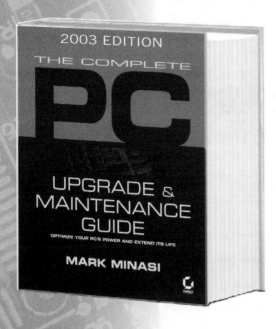

TELL US WHAT YOU THINK!

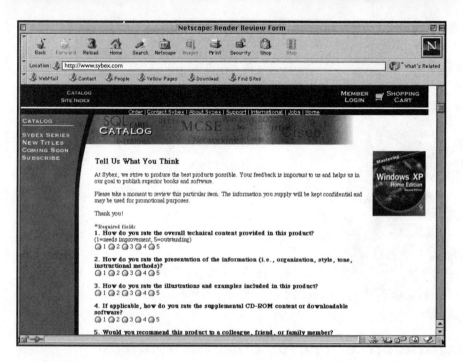

Your feedback is critical to our efforts to provide you with the best books and software on the market. Tell us what you think about the products you've purchased. It's simple:

1. Go to the Sybex website.
2. Find your book by typing the ISBN number or title into the Search field.
3. Click on the book title when it appears.
4. Click **Submit a Review.**
5. Fill out the questionnaire and comments.
6. Click **Submit.**

With your feedback, we can continue to publish the highest quality computer books and software products that today's busy IT professionals deserve.

www.sybex.com

SYBEX Inc. • 1151 Marina Village Parkway, Alameda, CA 94501 • 510-523-8233

SYBEX®